# THE OXFORD HANDBOOK OF

# PHILOSOPHY OF EMOTION

This volume contains thirty-one state-of-the-art contributions from leading figures in the study of emotion today. The volume addresses all the central philosophical issues in current emotion research, including: the nature of emotion and of emotional life; the history of emotion from Plato to Sartre; emotion and practical reason; emotion and the self; emotion, value, and morality; and emotion, art, and aesthetics.

Anyone interested in the philosophy of emotion, and its wide-ranging implications in other related fields such as morality and aesthetics, will want to consult this book. It will be a vital resource not only for scholars and graduate students but also for undergraduates who are finding their way into this fascinating topic.

**Peter Goldie** was the Samuel Hall Chair of Philosophy at the University of Manchester.

D1546949

# THE OXFORD HANDBOOK OF

# PHILOSOPHY OF EMOTION

*Edited by*

PETER GOLDIE

OXFORD
UNIVERSITY PRESS

# OXFORD

UNIVERSITY PRESS

Great Clarendon Street, Oxford OX2 6DP
United Kingdom

Oxford University Press is a department of the University of Oxford.
It furthers the University's objective of excellence in research, scholarship,
and education by publishing worldwide. Oxford is a registered trade mark of
Oxford University Press in the UK and in certain other countries

First published 2010
First published in paperback 2012
Reprinted 2013

British Library Cataloguing in Publication Data
Data available

Library of Congress Cataloging in Publication Data
Data available

ISBN 978-0-19-965437-6

# CONTENTS

## PART III  EMOTIONS AND PRACTICAL REASON

## PART IV  EMOTIONS AND THE SELF

## PART V EMOTION, VALUE, AND MORALITY

## PART VI EMOTION, ART, AND AESTHETICS

# About the Authors

........................................................................................

**Kate Abramson** is Assistant Professor of Philosophy at Indiana University. She specializes in early modern philosophy and contemporary ethics, with a particular focus on Hume's ethics. Her publications have appeared in *Philosophical Studies, Pacific Philosophical Quarterly, Archiv für Geschichte der Philosophie*, as well as other journals and numerous collections. At the time of going to press, she was in the final stages of completing a monograph on the evolution of Hume's ethics over the course of his lifetime entitled *The Artifice of Nature in Hume's Moral Philosophy: From Philosopher to Reflective Man.*

**Aaron Ben-Ze'ev**, Professor of Philosophy, is the President of the University of Haifa. He received his B.A. in Philosophy and Economics (1975) and his M.A. in Philosophy (1977) from the University of Haifa, and received his Ph.D. from the University of Chicago (1981). Professor Ben-Ze'ev's research focuses on the philosophy of psychology, and especially the study of emotions. Most recently, his research has centred on love. His major books are: *In The Name of Love: Romantic Ideology and its Victims* (Oxford University Press 2008); *Love Online: Emotions on the Internet* (Cambridge University Press 2004); *The Subtlety of Emotions* (MIT Press 2000); and *The Perceptual System* (Peter Lang 1993).

**Louis C. Charland** is Associate Professor in the Departments of Philosophy and Psychiatry, and the Faculty of Health Sciences, at the University of Western Ontario in London, Ontario, Canada. He specializes in the philosophy of emotion and the philosophy and history of psychiatry, and is the co-editor of *Fact and Value in Emotion* (John Benjamin Press 2008) with Peter Zachar.

**Roddy Cowie** is Professor of Psychology at Queen's University, Belfast. He studied Philosophy and Psychology as an undergraduate, and received his Ph.D. from Sussex on relationships between human and machine vision. His enduring interest is the relationship between subjective experience and models of human cognition based on 'rational reconstruction', particularly computational models. He has pursued it in diverse areas, including 'impossible objects'; picture perception; the subjective experience of deafness; and the information that speech conveys about the speaker. Recently he has focused on emotion-oriented computing through a series of projects funded by the European Union. He has authored or edited several landmark publications in the area, including special issues on emotion-related research in *Speech Communication* (2003) and *Neural Networks* (2005).

**Justin D'Arms** is Professor of Philosophy at Ohio State University. His research areas include metaethics, moral theory, value theory, moral psychology, and related areas of philosophy of mind, action, and biology, including the philosophy of emotion. He has published articles on these topics in various journals and collected volumes. He is presently working on empathy, on evolutionary ethics, and, with Daniel Jacobson, on a collaborative book articulating and defending a sentimentalist theory of value.

**John Deigh** is Professor of Law and Philosophy at the University of Texas at Austin. He works in ethics, political, and legal philosophy and is chiefly interested in topics in moral psychology. He is the author of two collections of philosophical essays, *The Sources of Moral Agency* (Cambridge University Press 1996) and *Emotions, Values, and the Law* (Oxford University Press 2008). He is former editor of *Ethics*.

**Ronald de Sousa** is Professor Emeritus of Philosophy at the University of Toronto and Fellow of the Royal Society of Canada. He is the author of *The Rationality of Emotion* (MIT Press 1987) and *Why Think? Evolution and the Rational Mind* (Oxford University Press 2007). His current research interests focus on emotions, evolutionary theory, cognitive science, sex, and the puzzle of religious belief. His next book, also from Oxford University Press, will be *Emotional Truth*.

**Sabine A. Döring** is Professor of Philosophy at Eberhard-Karls-Universität Tübingen. Her main research areas are (meta-)ethics and the theory of practical reason, with an emphasis on emotion and the question of what role the emotions have to play in the theory of value and the theory of agency. She is also interested in aesthetics and the theory of art. She is the author of various articles on emotion, and of *Gründe und Gefühle: Zur Lösung "des" Problems der Moral* (de Gruyter 2009), *Ästhetische Erfahrung als Erkenntnis des Ethischen: Die Kunsttheorie Robert Musils und die analytische Philosophie* (mentis 1999), editor of *Philosophie der Gefühle* (Suhrkamp 2009), and co-editor with Rainer Reisenzein of *Emotion Review* 1.3 (2009), Special Issue on *Emotional Experience*, and co-editor of *Die Moralität der Gefühle* 4 (2002), Special Issue of *Deutsche Zeitschrift für Philosophie*.

**Jon Elster** holds the Chair of Rationalité et Sciences Sociales at the Collège de France. His main research interests are the theory of individual and collective decision-making, the empirical study of distributive and retributive justice, and the history of social thought. His recent writings include *Alexis de Tocqueville: The First Social Scientist* (Cambridge University Press 2009), *Le désintéressement* (Seuil 2009), *Agir contre soi* (Odile Jacob 2006), *Closing the Books: Transitional Justice in Historical Perspective* (Cambridge University Press 2004), and *Alchemies of the Mind: Rationality and the Emotions* (Cambridge University Press 1999).

**Susan L. Feagin** is Visiting Research Professor of Philosophy at Temple University and editor of *The Journal of Aesthetics and Art Criticism*. Her research interests include philosophy of literature, especially tragedy, philosophy of the visual arts, and topics at the intersection of mind and art, such as emotion, empathy, intentions, appreciation, and the relation between narrative and agency. She is the author of *Reading with Feeling: The Aesthetics of Appreciation* (Cornell University Press 1996), co-editor of *Aesthetics* (Oxford University Press 1997), and editor of *Global Theories of the Arts and Aesthetics* (Blackwell Publishing 2007).

**Christopher Gill** is Professor of Ancient Thought at the University of Exeter. His work is centred on psychology and ethics in Greek and Roman thought, especially ideas about personality and self. A current focus is on Stoic philosophy and its significance in the contemporary philosophical context. He is the author of *Personality in Greek Epic, Tragedy, and Philosophy: The Self in Dialogue* (1996), *The Structured Self in Hellenistic and Roman Thought* (2006), and *Naturalistic Psychology in Galen and Stoicism* (forthcoming). He has edited a number of volumes of essays, including *The Person and the Human Mind: Issues in Ancient and Modern Philosophy* (1990) and *Virtue, Norms, and Objectivity: Issues in Ancient and Modern Ethics* (2005) (all these books published by Oxford University Press).

**Peter Goldie** is The Samuel Hall Chair of Philosophy at The University of Manchester. His main philosophical interests are in the philosophy of mind, ethics, and aesthetics, and particularly in questions concerning value and how the mind engages with value. He is continuing his research on emotion and character, and is also working on narrative and empathy, and their connections with his other areas of interest. He is the author of *The Emotions: A Philosophical Exploration* (Clarendon Press 2000), *On Personality* (Routledge 2004), co-author with Elisabeth Schellekens of *Who's Afraid of Conceptual Art?* (Routledge 2009), editor of *Understanding Emotions: Mind and Morals* (Ashgate Publishing 2002), and co-editor of *Philosophy and Conceptual Art* (Oxford University Press 2007).

**Patricia Greenspan** is Professor of Philosophy at the University of Maryland at College Park. Her research interests centre on moral philosophy and the philosophy of action, with current work on practical rationality and free will. She has published two books on emotion, *Emotions and Reasons: An Inquiry into Emotional Justification* (Routledge 1988), and *Practical Guilt: Moral Dilemmas, Emotions, and Social Norms* (Oxford University Press 1995), along with numerous articles on emotion and other topics relevant to metaethics and moral psychology.

**Anthony Hatzimoysis** is Assistant Professor at the HPS Department of the University of Athens. His main philosophical interests are in the theory of value, and the nature of self-consciousness in both the analytical and phenomenological schools of thought. He is the editor of *Philosophy and the Emotions* (Cambridge University

Press 2003); he is currently completing a monograph on *The Philosophy of Sartre* (Acumen), and is editing a volume on *Self-Knowledge* (Oxford University Press).

**Bennett W. Helm** is Professor of Philosophy at Franklin and Marshall College. His central interests lie at the intersection of philosophy of mind and ethics, centring around the role of emotions in the evaluative attitudes, like caring, valuing, and loving. He is author of *Emotional Reason: Deliberation, Motivation, and the Nature of Value* (Cambridge University Press 2001) and of *Love, Friendship, and the Self: Intimacy, Identity, and the Nature of Persons* (Oxford University Press forthcoming).

**R. Peter Hobson** is Professor of Developmental Psychopathology in the University of London, based at the Tavistock Clinic and the Institute of Child Health, University College. He trained as a psychiatrist and psychoanalyst, and has a Ph.D. in experimental child psychology from the University of Cambridge. His principal areas of research are early childhood autism and mother–infant interaction. The unifying theme in his work is the centrality of early interpersonal relations for children's understanding of the mind, and for the development of their imaginative capacities and language. He has written two books, *Autism and the Development of Mind* (Erlbaum 1993), and *The Cradle of Thought* (Macmillan 2002/Oxford University Press 2004).

**Daniel Jacobson** is Professor of Philosophy at the University of Michigan. He works in moral philosophy, mostly broadly construed, including normative theory and metaethics, the relation between moral and aesthetic value in art, freedom of speech, the role of the emotions in evaluative thought and judgment, and the history of ethics. He is currently working on two book projects: one on John Stuart Mill, and a collaborative work, with Justin D'Arms, developing a sentimentalist ethical theory.

**Matthew Kieran** is Professor of Philosophy and the Arts at the University of Leeds. His main philosophical interests concern inter-relations between aesthetics, ethics, epistemology, and psychology, particularly in questions concerning character and value. He is the author of *Revealing Art* (Routledge 2005), editor of *Contemporary Debates in Aesthetics and the Philosophy of Art* (Blackwell 2006), and co-editor with Dominic Lopes of *Knowing Art* (Springer 2006) and *Imagination, Philosophy and the Arts* (Routledge 2003).

**Peter King** is Professor of Philosophy and of Medieval Studies at the University of Toronto. His main philosophical research interests are in medieval philosophy of psychology, both cognitive and affective. He has published many articles in all areas of medieval philosophy as well as several translations. His non-historical interests include philosophy of film, rational choice theory, and personal identity.

**Derek Matravers** lectures in philosophy at The Open University. His current interests lie in aesthetics, particularly with our engagement with various forms of art. To this end he is working on a book on value, and also researching mental states, such as empathy, and what role (if any) they play in our engagement with narratives. He is the author of *Art and Emotion* (Clarendon Press 1998), as well as numerous articles in aesthetics, ethics, and the philosophy of mind.

**Adam Morton** has a Canada Research Chair in Epistemology and Decision Theory at the University of Alberta. He is currently working on intellectual virtues of adaptation to one's own and human limitations, while writing on imagination and morality in a scattered way that he hopes eventually to bring together. He is the author of seven books, most recently *On Evil* (Routledge 2004) and *The Importance of Being Understood* (Routledge 2002).

**Kevin Mulligan** is Professor of Analytic Philosophy at the University of Geneva and Deputy-Director of the Swiss National Centre of Competence in Research (NCCR) in the affective sciences. His main philosophical interests are in analytic metaphysics, the philosophy of mind and the history of Austrian philosophy from Bolzano to Musil and Wittgenstein. He has written about many aspects of the relations between emotions and values and recently co-edited *Robert Musil—Ironie, Satire, falsche Gefühle* (mentis Verlag 2009).

**Jerome Neu** is Professor of Humanities at the University of California, Santa Cruz, where he has at various times been Chair of the programs in Philosophy, History of Consciousness, and Legal Studies. He is the author of *Emotion, Thought, and Therapy* (Routledge and University of California Press 1977), *A Tear Is an Intellectual Thing: The Meanings of Emotion* (Oxford University Press 2000), *Sticks and Stones: The Philosophy of Insults* (Oxford University Press 2008), and editor of the *Cambridge Companion to Freud* (Cambridge University Press 1991).

**A. W. Price** is Reader in Philosophy at Birkbeck College, London. He has touched on the emotions in two books, *Love and Friendship in Plato and Aristotle* (Clarendon Press 1989/97), *Mental Conflict* (Routledge 1995), and in a number of articles. He enjoyed a Leverhulme Research Fellowship in 2006–2008, out of which should emerge a monograph on practical reason in Plato and Aristotle. He is also the author of *Contextuality in Practical Reason* (Clarendon Press 2008).

**Jesse J. Prinz** is Distinguished Professor of Philosophy at the City University of New York, Graduate Center. His research focuses on the perceptual, emotional, and cultural foundations of human psychology. He is author of *Furnishing the Mind: Concepts and Their Perception Basis* (MIT Press 2002), *Gut Reactions: A Perceptual Theory of Emotion* (Oxford University Press 2004), and *The Emotional Construction of Morals* (Oxford University Press 2009). He also has two forthcoming books: *The Conscious Brain* (Oxford University Press) and *Beyond Human Nature* (Penguin/ Norton). All of these books bring research in the cognitive sciences to bear on traditional philosophical questions, and, in particular, all defend and extend core tenets of classical empiricism.

**David Pugmire** is a Visiting Research Fellow at the University of Southampton. His interests lie in the philosophy of mind (especially the philosophy of emotion) and aesthetics. He is the author of *Rediscovering Emotion* (Edinburgh University Press 1998) and *Sound Sentiments* (Oxford University Press 2005).

**Matthew Ratcliffe** is Professor of Philosophy at Durham University. His recent work addresses issues in phenomenology, philosophy of psychology, and philosophy of psychiatry. Most of it is focused around the interrelated topics of intersubjectivity, feeling, and anomalous experience in psychiatric illness. He is currently working on a detailed phenomenological study of emotional changes in depression, and also on the phenomenology of touch. He is author of *Rethinking Commonsense Psychology: A Critique of Folk Psychology, Theory of Mind and Simulation* (Palgrave 2007) *and Feelings of Being: Phenomenology, Psychiatry and the Sense of Reality* (Oxford University Press 2008).

**Robert C. Roberts** is Distinguished Professor of Ethics at Baylor University. His main interest is the moral psychology of the virtues. He also works on ancient moral psychology and epistemology, and the writings of Søren Kierkegaard. He is at work on a sequel of *Emotions: An Essay in Aid of Moral Psychology* (Cambridge University Press 2003) entitled *Emotions and Virtues: An Essay in Moral Psychology.* He is the author, with W. Jay Wood, of *Intellectual Virtues: An Essay in Regulative Epistemology* (Clarendon Press 2007) and *Spiritual Emotions* (Wm. B. Eerdmans Publishing Company 2007). He has published articles in *The Philosophical Review, Philosophical Studies, American Philosophical Quarterly,* and other journals.

**Jenefer Robinson** is Professor of Philosophy at the University of Cincinnati. Her work in emotion theory and in aesthetics has been published in *Journal of Philosophy, Philosophical Review, Erkenntnis, Philosophy, Australasian Journal of Philosophy, Journal of Aesthetics and Art Criticism, British Journal of Aesthetics,* and elsewhere. She is author of *Deeper than Reason: Emotion and its Role in Literature, Music, and Art* (Oxford University Press 2005) and editor of *Music and Meaning* (Cornell University Press 1997).

**Amelie Rorty** is a Visiting Professor of Philosophy at Boston University and a Lecturer in the Department of Social Medicine, Harvard Medical School. She is the author of *Mind in Action* (Beacon 1976) and numerous articles on moral psychology and the history of ethics. She has also edited *Explaining Emotions* (University of California Press 1980), *The Identities of Persons* (University of California Press 1976), *Perspectives on Self-Deception* (University of California Press 1988), *The Many Faces of Evil* (Routledge 2001), *The Many Faces of Philosophy*

(Oxford University Press 2003), *Philosophers on Education* (Routledge 1998), and four anthologies on Aristotle.

**Michael Stocker** is Guttag Professor of Ethics and Political Philosophy at Syracuse University. His main interests are ethics and moral psychology, particularly emotions, and their interconnections. Many of his works, including the one in this volume, are focused on descriptions of our evaluative and moral psychological practices and lives. He has written *Plural and Conflicting Values* (Oxford University Press 1990) and, with Elizabeth Hegeman, a practising psychoanalyst, *Valuing Emotions* (Cambridge University Press 1990).

**Christine Tappolet** is Canada Research Chair in Ethics and Meta-ethics and Full Professor in the Philosophy Department at the Université de Montréal. Her research interests lie mainly in meta-ethics, normative ethics, moral psychology, and emotion theory. She has edited a number of volumes, including, with Sarah Stroud, *Weakness of Will and Practical Irrationality* (Oxford University Press 2003), and, with Luc Faucher, *The Modularity of Emotions* (*Canadian Journal of Philosophy*, supp. vol. 32, 2008). She is the author of *Émotions et valeurs* (Presses Universitaires de France 2000), and co-author with Ruwen Ogien of *Les Concepts de l'éthique. Faut-il être conséquentialiste?* (Hermann Éditeurs 2008).

# INTRODUCTION

## PETER GOLDIE

PHILOSOPHICAL research in the emotions is now extremely active and productive, and it is a testament to this fact that Oxford University Press commissioned this Handbook, containing thirty chapters of original research from top scholars working in this field.

It is now a familiar point that only a relatively short while ago philosophical interest in the emotions was really quite sparse; a browse through a typical handbook of philosophy of mind in the 1960s might well reveal little or nothing in the index under 'emotion', let alone anything so grand as an entry on its own. Philosophy of mind in the Anglo-Saxon tradition was for a long time (and in some ways still is) preoccupied with the mind–body problem, involving such questions as how mental properties and events can have a place in a material world, and had little truck with the work of the phenomenologists, much of which included insightful discussions of the emotions. If one is concerned with the mind–body problem, it is perfectly natural to focus on what are, so to speak, paradigmatic mental properties and events, such as being in pain, or coming to believe that it is raining. The emotions are messier, seeming somehow to be represented on both sides of the mind–body divide—both paradigmatically mental, and paradigmatically bodily. So it would be odd to choose, as an entry-point into the mind–body debate, the emotion of fear or disgust for example, instead of pain or belief. Furthermore, there was a tendency in Anglo-Saxon philosophy of mind—a tendency exemplified in decision theory and functionalism—to assimilate emotion into other more familiar (and supposedly better understood) kinds of mental state such as belief and desire, leaving the 'feeling' side of emotion to the psychologists.

Why has this dramatic change in philosophical interest in the emotions taken place? There are, perhaps, a number of reasons, and thinking about what they are might help to throw some light on the rationale for this Handbook and for the individual chapters that it includes.

To begin with, philosophers of mind have become increasingly interested in empirical work in other disciplines, exemplified by the growth of cognitive science, which is the interdisciplinary study of mind, including philosophy, developmental psychology, evolutionary psychology, social psychology, artificial intelligence, neuroscience, linguistics, and anthropology. These other disciplines have for a long time taken a close interest in the emotions. For example, evolutionary psychology and anthropology have been engaged in the question of which emotions, and which facial expressions of emotion, are 'basic', pan-cultural amongst humans, and shared with non-human animals (Darwin, 1889/1998; Ekman, 1972); developmental psychologists have engaged with the emotions in young children (Harris, 1989), and with the emotions in our sense of self and in various kinds of psychopathologies (Blair et al., 2005); neuroscientists have engaged with the neural correlates of emotion in humans and other animals (LeDoux, 1998); and emotion-oriented computing has been concerned with how to emulate emotionality in robots (Trappl et al., 2002).

Secondly, and bound up with this, there has been an increasing awareness on the part of philosophy of the importance of emotion in practical reason, combined with an acceptance that this is not simply an issue for empirical psychology (Rorty, 1980). To begin with (as was accepted by Plato and Aristotle), emotions can help to explain the phenomenon which has proved the bane of decision theory: weakness of the will (*akrasia*), which involves acting against one's own judgement about what it is best to do, or acting impetuously and without due deliberation. For example, one might decide that it is best not to make that retort at the meeting to the infuriating remark of one's colleague, and yet, in spite of this, one speaks up, regretting it later as 'an angry outburst'. In contrast, and equally in need of explanation, emotion can sometimes lead to the right kind of action. Many thinkers now claim that the deliverances of our emotions can give rise to fast responses to the environment, involving little or no conscious deliberation, and that having these 'fast and frugal' responses can be adaptive for the individual, and even can be rational—although it is much disputed what norms of rationality this kind of thinking conforms to, and precisely how it relates to the cooler, more considered kind of reasoning in what has been called the 'two-track mind' (Gigerenzer, 2000; Gigerenzer & Selten, 2002; Samuels et al., 2002).

A third factor that has generated such an increase in philosophical interest in the emotions is a change in the landscape of philosophical ethics. Once dominated by Kantian and utilitarian ethics, there seemed to be little place for the emotions, but with the arrival of virtue-theoretical approaches (Anscombe, 1958), and recalling the work of Aristotle and the sentimentalists such as David Hume, the importance of emotion in ethics began to be properly appreciated. Combined with this has been an enormous increase in well-informed empirical research into how people come to make moral judgements—what has been called the 'cognitive science of morality' (Sinnott-Armstrong, 2008). For a long time, it has been known that 'intuition' has an important role in ethics (Stratton-Lake, 2002), and it is now increasingly accepted, in the light of research on the two-track mind, that the emotions are somehow implicated in intuitive thinking. For example, Paul Slovic (2007) has considered our responses to genocide and mass suffering, which tend to involve less motivation to help than our responses to salient individual suffering. What is missing when we deliberate about large numbers of people, Slovic argues, is emotion. Of course it remains an open question whether our intuitive reponses deliver up good, justifying reasons, or merely explanatory reasons as to why we make the judgements that we do (Singer, 2005).

Fourthly, work in philosophical aesthetics now shows a real appreciation of the role of emotion in our responses to works of art: to music and literature (Robinson, 2005; Budd, 1985; Kivy, 1989); to film and theatre (Carroll, 2001); and, more controversially, to the plastic arts—pictures and sculptures in particular. Again, this work is often informed by empirical research in psychology and neuroscience. Also, much recent philosophical research is being done at the intersection of ethics and aesthetics (Levinson, 1998; Hagberg, 2008; Goldie, 2007), so it is increasingly important to consider how the aesthetic emotions bear on morality and on moral thought and talk, and vice versa—how the moral emotions bear on the aesthetic (Gaut 2007).

So, for these and other reasons, what we now have is a philosophical environment which is very receptive to emotion research, involving a highly stimulating synthesis of empirical and conceptual work. It is with this intellectual background in mind that the particular contributions to this Handbook were invited and have been written. The Handbook presents the best, state-of-the-art, views on the emotions from the top scholars in the field. But it does not purport to give the final word on all the topics surveyed; rather, it hopes to enhance future research in this increasingly important philosophical area.

# Part I:  What Emotions Are

Part I of the Handbook is concerned with the very lively debate about just what emotions are—a debate that, in many respects, revisits the debate in psychology in the late nineteenth and early twentieth centuries (Reisenzein & Döring, 2009).

There are, on the one hand, those theories that owe their ancestry to the work of William James (1884; 1890/1981), arguing that emotions are bodily feelings or perceptions of bodily feelings; and, on the other hand, those theories that owe their ancestry to Aristotle and the Stoics, arguing that emotions are cognitive, world-directed intentional states. Other philosophers have argued that, whilst there are analogies to be drawn between emotion and other kinds of mental state, emotions are, at bottom, *sui generis* (de Sousa, 1987; Goldie, 2000).

**John Deigh**, in 'Concepts of Emotions in Modern Philosophy and Psychology', begins Part I with a survey of these two main theories of emotion, and a recent variant of the intentionalist view, the theory that emotions are specifically *perceptual* world-directed states. Arguing that feeling theories are unable to accommodate the obvious world-directed intentionality of emotion, and that cognitivist theories are unable to accommodate the simple fact of emotion in beasts and babies, Deigh suggests that any concept of emotions that is adequate for understanding the emotions of beasts, babies, and adult human beings must incorporate some account of how the emotions that are distinctive of adult human beings are the product of moral education.

**Aaron Ben-Ze'ev**, in 'The Thing Called Emotion', puts forward his own theory of what an emotion is. The category of emotion, he says, is prototypical, without necessary and sufficient conditions for membership. Accordingly, he argues, the right approach to the question of what emotions are is through a description of a typical emotion: its causes, characteristics, and components. In the light of their complexity and variety, Ben-Ze'ev argues that emotions are best understood as a unique kind of mental mode.

**Roddy Cowie**, in 'Describing the Forms of Emotional Colouring that Pervade Everyday Life', takes a different approach. He considers the enormous difficulties in getting a fix on how emotions feature in our everyday lives—in what Cowie calls our 'emotional life'. This is important not only for developing effective and ethically sound human–machine emotion interaction, which is Cowie's direct concern, but also for drawing comparisons (often quite surprising) between the broad emotional colouring of our everyday lives, and the artificial and isolated conditions of the controlled experiment.

**Ronald de Sousa**, in 'The Mind's Bermuda Triangle: Philosophy of Emotions and Empirical Science', expresses doubt about whether philosophy alone, in the form of introspective phenomenology, can give reliable access to the meaning of our mental states, and of our emotions in particular. What is needed is proper interaction with the sciences, and de Sousa goes on to argue that a scientifically informed understanding of the two-track mind can throw light on a number of puzzles involving emotion.

# PART II: THE HISTORY OF EMOTION

The six contributions to Part II show clearly how much there is still to be learned from a careful study of the history of philosophical work in the emotions: without this kind of study, the history of philosophy, like history, is bound to repeat itself, often with little or no gain on what has gone before.

**A. W. Price** considers the intricate and subtly shifting conceptions of emotions that we find in Plato and Aristotle, each of whom came to see emotions as involving both body and soul, and as resisting reduction either to mere feelings accompanying bodily states, or to pure mental cognition. Price denies that the 'spirited' part of Plato's tripartite soul in the *Republic* incorporates all emotion, but notes that Plato later loosens his conceptions both of the spirited part and of tripartition. He shows how Plato increasingly emphasizes the phenomenology of emotional experience in addition to its cognitive aspect. In this he paves the way for Aristotle, who may or may not have thought that belief is necessary for emotion, but held that, when beliefs are involved, they may well be creatures of appearance (or *phantasia*).

The traditional reading of the view of emotions in Stoicism (and to some extent Epicureanism) is that it is firmly cognitive, with, for example, the Stoics defining emotion in terms that would exclude beasts and babies from emotionality. But **Christopher Gill**, in his chapter, makes it clear that this cognitivism by no means excludes human emotions from having a role beyond cognition, particularly in human physiology, in value and natural functioning, and in interpersonal and social relations. Gill discusses a key difference between the Stoic and the Epicurean positions, in that the latter held that our natural constitution leads us to pursue pleasure, although this does not exclude the possibility of our caring about interpersonal relationships.

**Peter King** surveys some of the competing theories of the emotions prevailing in the Middle Ages. Beginning with Augustine's response to Stoic theories of the emotions and his formulation of an eclectic mix of ancient theories, King traces the ways in which Augustine's views influenced the rest of the Middle Ages. In the twelfth century, Anselm and Abelard explored the idea that emotions are closely linked to volition. In the thirteenth century, Aquinas and others tried to offer a systematic theory of emotions along the lines of an Aristotelian science. Other thinkers, such as Scotus and Ockham, offered an alternative theory at the end of the thirteenth and start of the fourteenth centuries. Later scholastic thought developed the debates in such a way as to prepare the ground for the wholesale rejection of medieval theories in Renaissance and early modern philosophy.

**Kate Abramson**, in her chapter, sets out to defend Hume and his sentimentalist contemporaries against a familiar charge, Kantian in spirit, directed towards their emphasis on the sentiments of disdain, shame, and contempt. Taking contempt, for example, the intimately related charges at issue are that this sentiment denies the wrongdoer all moral worth, that it necessarily involves a 'globalizing' attitude (attributed to the person as a whole), that its typical forms of expression effectively exclude a person from the community of moral agents rather than hold her accountable, and that contempt—like other attitudes in this family—is not even felt from a standpoint which *could* be responsibility-conferring. In reply, Abramson argues that contempt need not involve any of these objectionable features. And she also argues that the sentimentalists did not think of contempt in these objectionable ways.

In 'Emotions in Heidegger and Sartre', **Anthony Hatzimoysis** argues that the essential insight of the phenomenologists is to place emphasis on the role of emotion in our engagement with the world—their world-directedness, attaching less importance to the subjective experience of emotion. For Heidegger, our affective states are bound up with our cognition and perception; unless we approach the world in an appropriate affective state—with the right 'attunement'—we will not grasp the world as it really is. And, as Sartre emphasizes, there is not only our immediate affective engagement with the world but our reflective engagement with our experiences, where our emotions themselves become an object of consciousness.

**Louis Charland** notes first that the passions have now been more or less marginalized: we now live in the 'age of emotion'. Drawing on the history of psychopathology, Charland argues for a reinstatement of the passions, understood as complex, long-lasting affective states, as contrasted with the shorter-lived emotions; 'passion', Charland says, is a 'necessary theoretical posit and category in affective science'.

# PART III: EMOTIONS AND PRACTICAL REASON

We have already noted the increasing awareness of the importance of the role of emotions in practical reason, but precisely what this role is remains a subject of contention. Once it is seen that emotions are not simply non-rational impulses, no more part of an explanation of, or motivation for, an action than a shove in the back, questions arise about precisely what the role of emotions is here. Emotions somehow have to have a *rational* role, but nevertheless a role that can somehow *conflict* with reason, notably in cases of weakness of will. Another contentious question here is the motivating role of emotions, and whether emotions motivate in virtue of a disposition to act in some way, or from the presence of desire as a constituent part of the emotion, or in some other way.

**Jon Elster**, in 'Emotional Choice and Rational Choice', argues that the standard model of action explanation needs to be modified to account for the role of emotion. The components of the standard model can each be influenced by emotion: action can be influenced directly in cases of weakness of will; desire can be influenced in cases of temporary preference reversal; belief can be influenced directly in cases such as wishful thinking; and belief can be influenced indirectly in cases where the urgency of emotion unduly influences the processes of information-gathering.

**Sabine Döring** is also concerned with the role of emotion in agency. This role, she argues, is not in terms of rational guidance, so as to allow for rational or even moral *akrasia*. On Döring's view, the emotions instead fulfil an indispensable epistemic function and can help us to question our existing reasons, and to formulate new and better ones. Therefore she claims, first, that agents should take their emotions into account when reflecting on what they have reason to do, even though this may temporarily lead to conflicts between emotions and 'better' judgements: in the end, these conflicts may be productive. Secondly, Döring thus concludes that agency does not exhaust itself in the rational guidance of isolated actions at singular moments but also manifests itself in the ongoing cultivation and improvement of reasons for action over time.

The next two chapters are concerned with the rational role of emotion in motivation. **Bennett W. Helm** distinguishes between mere goal-directedness and intentional actions, arguing that the latter normally are 'rational responses to what we care about', to what has 'import' to us, where this import is seen as a reason for action. Emotions, Helm argues, play an essential role in motivating action insofar as they are commitments to import—a role that neo-Jamesian accounts of emotions cannot accommodate.

**Christine Tappolet**, in 'Emotion, Motivation, and Action: The Case of Fear', is also concerned with the motivational component of emotion. She argues against two familiar theses, using fear as her leading example, largely because fear is a type of emotion where these theses might seem to have greatest appeal. The first is the thesis of motivational modularity: the thesis that emotions involve rigid and innate behavioural dispositions, often described as 'action-tendencies'. Even if plausible for certain non-human animals, Tappolet argues that it is implausible for humans. The second is the thesis of motivational egoism: the thesis that motivation aims only at the interests of the organism. Tappolet argues, against this, that fear, when it is fear for others, involves altruistic motivations.

# PART IV: EMOTIONS AND THE SELF

Apart from their role in practical reason, in ethics, and in aesthetics, emotions and feelings are often taken to be—and surely rightly so—important to each of us as the sort of person we are, and, moreover, important epistemically in guiding us towards knowledge in our engagement with the world.

**Matthew Ratcliffe** examines the special importance of mood. He argues that mood differs from emotion in its phenomenology and in its nature much more than many scholars suggest. He focuses on the phenomenology of those moods that are responsible for the 'meaning of life'—that constitute the experienced meaningfulness of the world. These kinds of mood, Ratcliffe argues, are not intentional states but are instead 'part of the background structure of intentionality and are presupposed by the possibility of intentionally directed emotions'; moods are that through which we experience the world. He then goes on to argue that 'deep' moods, unlike emotions in this respect too, are pre-intentional, non-conceptual bodily feelings which provide 'spaces of significant possibility'.

Unlike other animals, we can think and talk about our emotions. In 'Saying It', **David Pugmire** examines the vexed question of whether our emotions can change by our giving 'verbal form' to them, and, furthermore, he asks whether some of our emotions resist verbal expression—whether they are ineffable. He argues in favour of 'reticence': what we say can be inadequate to the feeling, or distorting, or distancing. And yet, as he goes on to discuss, there is also something to be said in the opposite direction, in favour of what he calls 'affirmation'—giving verbal expression to one's emotions.

**Adam Morton** argues for a vital role for epistemic emotions—for emotions such as curiosity and intellectual interest that guide us in the acquisition of true beliefs. He begins by contrasting these emotions and their related epistemic virtues, and shows that on certain occasions virtue alone is not enough: for example, in exploring a range of possibilities in some intellectual enquiry, experiencing the epistemic emotions themselves can make a difference to the acquisition of knowledge, and enquiry without these emotions would be shallower.

**Michael Stocker** is also concerned with the role of emotion in the domain of intellectual enquiry—what he calls intellectual emotions, such as pleasure, delight, love of truth, and interest. He begins by showing that there are such emotions, many of which (anger, jealousy, and courage, for example) also occur outside the intellectual domain, and that their presence has been noticed by many of our philosophical predecessors. Then he addresses a concern that is shared with Morton's chapter—a concern to show that intellectual emotions are essential to successful intellectual activity. Again, being 'an intellectual', and yet without intellectual emotion, is not enough; and, in this respect, as Stocker notes, this need for having the right feelings is in accord with Aristotle's account of virtue.

It is often argued that ambivalence—lack of clarity or purity of mind—is at all times to be avoided. In 'A Plea for Ambivalence', **Amelie Rorty** argues against what she calls the 'purists', showing that sometimes ambivalence is appropriate, constructive, and worth preserving. She argues that there are norms of epistemic responsibility concerning when and in what way ambivalence is an appropriate and constructive state to be in, and that being able to deploy ambivalence appropriately in the public sphere is a civic virtue.

The final chapter in Part IV, by **Peter Hobson**, addresses different concerns about emotion and the self. As we have already seen, philosophical debate about the emotions has for several millennia been haunted by distinctions among feeling, thought or cognition, and motivation. Hobson argues that the fact that we are able to make these distinctions, using distinct concepts, by no means shows that they are in reality distinct components of our mental economy. Taking a developmental perspective on our 'social emotions' of interpersonal engagement, and drawing on his studies of autism, Hobson argues that in infants, feeling, cognition, and motivation are 'inextricably linked', and that this continues into adulthood: 'we are *drawn to* and *moved by* our affective engagement with others'. Hobson's more radical claim is that the acquisition of propositional attitudes depends on this being so.

# PART V: EMOTION, VALUE, AND MORALITY

As we have seen, the traditional Kantian and utilitarian picture, particularly when it concerns morality, is that our practical reasoning ought to be free of emotion: our emotional responses represent the 'animal' side of our nature rather than the rational side (Kant, 1785/1964); and these responses are part of our evolutionary heritage which we would be better off without in deciding what to do (Singer, 2005). This is not the position of any of the contributors to this Handbook: they all consider emotion to be a valuable, or even essential, aspect of our ability to grasp values and to respond as we should, with thought, feeling, and action. But there remain many pressing questions about the details of the relation between emotion and value, answers to which will of course depend on one's preferred account of these two things.

In 'Emotions and Values', **Kevin Mulligan** addresses three central issues. First, he evaluates the view that emotions, understood as world-directed states, play an epistemic role in furnishing knowledge of value, including in particular the very interesting question of whether emotions are responses to *felt* value. Secondly, he considers whether value can be understood, or analysed, or explicated, in terms of appropriate emotion. And thirdly, he considers the question of whether emotions might exemplify value, and even whether some emotions might be intrinsically valuable.

Jerome Neu also raises questions concerning the relation between emotion and value, asking whether there are emotions that we morally ought and ought not to feel—whether, for example, we ought not to hate our enemies but to love them, as the Bible commands. If so, this raises questions about emotion and the will: can we control our feelings, and, if not, how can the injunction to have certain feelings have any force? Here Neu distinguishes between the possibility of directly willing to change our emotions, and the more feasible possibility of indirectly changing our emotions through, for example, controlling the kinds of situation that we are in.

Jesse Prinz, in 'The Moral Emotions', begins by asking what contribution emotions make to morality, distinguishing between their role in moral motivation and their role in moral epistemology. Secondly, he considers what particular kinds of emotion are involved, distinguishing such emotions as blame, anger, disgust, contempt, guilt, and praise, each of which, he says, has a different functional role, sometimes epistemic, sometimes motivational, and sometimes both. And finally, he asks whether there are distinctively moral emotions, much as Stocker asked about intellectual emotions.

In 'Learning Emotions and Ethics', Patricia Greenspan discusses the importance of emotions in early moral learning, arguing that innate, 'basic' emotions of the kind postulated in evolutionary psychology do not involve fixed, invariable patterns of responses but rather that they have a degree of plasticity which allows for cultural influences to shape our responses from a very early age. In adults, cognition and language can be vehicles of cultural influence on our moral emotions, and these emotions can in turn play a role in epistemically registering objective values, and in individual motivation to comply with moral norms.

Continuing the discussion of emotion and value, Robert Roberts, in 'Emotions and the Canons of Evaluation', begins with the familiar dispute between Aristotelians and Humeans: can our emotions *track* evaluative truth, or is evaluative truth properly a *product* of our emotions? Roberts presents his view that emotions are perceptions of value with propositional structure, and shows why the best prospect for sentimentalism lies with a view like his. However, he argues, the sentimentalist needs to base his explanatory project on emotion types that are rich enough in content to yield norms, yet have not themselves been shaped by cultural norms, and Roberts holds that emotions simultaneously satisfying these two conditions are not likely to be found.

Roberts' chapter engages directly with the work of Justin D'Arms and Daniel Jacobson, whose chapter we come to next in this collection. In this chapter, D'Arms and Jacobson consider the sphere of sentimental values, such as the funny, the shameful, and what is worthy of pride. What they call rational sentimentalism holds that these values should be explained in terms of the fittingness of a particular sentiment: for example, what is funny is what it is fitting to be amused by. The particular challenge for sentimentalism that D'Arms and Jacobson address is the 'instability of affect': our sentimental responses are 'notoriously fickle', a fact which is in tension with the fact that we take values to be stable properties of objects. They argue that what matters in assessing someone's evaluative stance is their underlying, more stable, sensibilities, not the vicissitudes of their actual responses or judgements.

# Part VI: Emotion, Art, and Aesthetics

There are manifold connections between emotion and the arts. On what might be called the side of production, the artist might well experience emotions in the making of the artwork, and these emotions might, in one way or another, come to be manifest in, or expressed in, the artwork. On the side of appreciation, there are the feelings and emotions that we experience on engagement with an artwork. There is, then, the question of how these two are related, and in particular whether our emotional engagement with artworks should somehow 'pick up on' the emotions expressed by the artist, and, if so, how. And furthermore, in appreciation there is the question of how our emotional engagement with artworks, including in particular narrative artworks, is revelatory of, or expressive of, aspects of our own character. The chapters in this section deal with all of these issues.

**Derek Matravers**, in 'Expression in the Arts', addresses the way in which emotions are manifest in artworks, and in particular in music and painting. Surveying the work of the main philosophers working on expression, the central problem which he considers is how to clarify just what expression is, in order to throw light onto our understanding of art. This is a problem which has proved to be extremely intractable, and Matravers concludes that the reason for this is that, on close examination, the problem fragments: 'there was no single problem to be solved in the first place'.

**Susan Feagin** and **Jenefer Robinson** are both concerned with our affective responses to art: Feagin to literature, and Robinson to music. In 'Affects in Appreciation', Feagin focuses on feelings, as contrasted with emotions—for example, a feeling of anxiety or of alienation. She argues that these feelings do not, as some claim, get in the way of appreciation of a literary work but rather are a way of appreciating it, revealing its intricacy, complexity, and depth.

**Jenefer Robinson** starts with the commonplace that music can give rise to emotions in the listener, very much as other things in the world can do: we are saddened by the music, just as we are saddened by the loss of something we value.

And yet this immediately reveals a puzzle, which is how this can be so, given that we do not make any sort of 'appraisal' of the music in the way that we do elsewhere: there is nothing in the music for the listener to be sad about. Robinson considers the possibility that some of these responses are moods rather than emotions, and goes on to discuss how both emotion and mood can be a means towards aesthetic understanding and appreciation.

In 'Emotion, Art, and Immorality', **Matthew Kieran** addresses certain asymmetries in our emotional responses to artworks, as compared with our emotional responses in real life. In real life we tend to spurn evil people and morally terrible situations, and yet we are strangely drawn to them in art, and even seem to find value in the imaginative experience, suspending or withholding our normal moral responses. Kieran argues that our empathizing with evil characters in fiction, and otherwise responding with interest and enjoyment in what they do, presents an epistemic and moral challenge that has to be met in working out exactly when, where, and why what we imagine may be morally praiseworthy or condemnable.

Finally, as editor of this volume, I would like to express my thanks to all those involved at Oxford University Press for their support throughout the editorial and production process, and especially to Peter Momtchiloff for suggesting the Handbook to me, and to Michael Janes for doing such a superb job as copy-editor. Most of all, of course, my thanks go to the individual contributors: each chapter really does make a significant advance in emotion research, and I am sure that readers of this Handbook will find them as fascinating and enjoyable to engage with as I have done.

# REFERENCES

ANSCOMBE, G. E. M. (1958). Modern Moral Philosophy. *Philosophy* 33, 1–19.

BLAIR, R. J., Mitchell, D., & Blair, K. (2005). *The Psychopath: Emotion and the Brain.* Malden, Mass.: Blackwell.

BUDD, M. (1985). *Music and the Emotions.* London: Routledge and Kegan Paul.

CARROLL, N. (2001). *Beyond Aesthetics: Philosophical Essays.* Cambridge: Cambridge University Press.

DARWIN, C. (1889/1998). *The Expression of Emotion in Man and Animals.* London: HarperCollins.

DE SOUSA, R. (1987). *The Rationality of Emotion,* Cambridge, Mass.: MIT Press.

EKMAN, P. (1972). Universals and Cultural Differences in Facial Expressions of Emotion. In J. Cole, ed. *Nebraska Symposium on Motivation* (pp. 207–83). Lincoln: University of Nebraska Press.

GAUT, B. (2007). *Art, Emotion and Ethics.* Oxford: Oxford University Press.

GIGERENZER, G. (2000). *Adaptive Thinking: Rationality in the Real World.* New York: Oxford University Press.

—— & SELTEN, R., eds. (2002). *Bounded Rationality: The Adaptive Toolbox.* Harvard, Mass.: MIT Press.

GOLDIE, P. (2000). *The Emotions: A Philosophical Exploration.* Oxford: Clarendon Press.

—— (2007). Towards a Virtue Theory of Art. *British Journal of Aesthetics* 47, 372–87.

GRIFTHS, P. (1997). *What Emotions Really Are: The Problem of Psychological Categories.* Chicago: University of Chicago Press.

HAGBERG, G., ed. (2008). *Art and Ethical Criticism.* Oxford: Blackwell.

HARRIS, P. (1989). *Children and Emotion: The Development of Psychological Understanding.* Oxford: Blackwell.

JAMES, W. (1884). What is an Emotion? *Mind* 9, 188–205.

—— (1890/1981). *The Principles of Psychology.* Cambridge, Mass.: Harvard University Press.

KANT, I. (1785/1964). *Groundwork of the Metaphysics of Morals.* (H. J. Paton, Trans.) New York: Harper & Row.

KIVY, P. (1989). *Sound Sentiment: An Essay on the Musical Emotions.* Philadelphia: Temple University Press.

LEDOUX, J. (1998). *The Emotional Brain.* London: Orion Books.

LEVINSON, J., ed. (1998). *Aesthetics and Ethics: Essays at the Intersection.* Cambridge: ambridge University Press.

REISENZEIN, R. & DÖRING, S. (2009). Ten Perspectives on Emotional Experience: Introduction to the Special Issue. *Emotion Review,* 1, 195–205.

ROBINSON, J. (2005). *Deeper than Reason: Emotion and its Role in Literature, Music, and Art.* Oxford: Clarendon Press.

RORTY, A. O., ed. (1980). *Explaining Emotions.* Berkeley: University of California Press.

SAMUELS, R., STICH, S., & BISHOP, M. (2002). Ending the Rationality Wars: How To Make Disputes About Human Rationality Disappear. In R. Elio, ed., *Common Sense, Reasoning, and Rationality* (pp. 236–68). New York: Oxford University Press.

SINGER, P. (2005). Ethics and Intuitions. *The Journal of Ethics* 9, 331–52.

SINNOTT-ARMSTRONG, W., ed. (2008). *Moral Psychology.* Volume 2: *The Cognitive Science of Morality.* Cambridge, Mass.: MIT Press.

SLOVIC, P. (2007). 'If I Look at the Mass I Will Never Act': Psychic Numbing and Genocide. *Judgment and Decision Making* 2, 79–95.

STRATTON-LAKE, P., ed. (2002). *Ethical Intuitionism.* Oxford: Clarendon Press.

TRAPPL, R., PETTA, P., & PAYR, S., eds. (2002). *Emotions in Humans and Artefacts.* Cambridge, Mass.: MIT Press.

# PART I

## WHAT EMOTIONS ARE

# CHAPTER 1

......................................................................

# CONCEPTS OF EMOTIONS IN MODERN PHILOSOPHY AND PSYCHOLOGY

......................................................................

## JOHN DEIGH

Two major themes characterize the study of emotions in modern philosophy and psychology. One is the identification of emotions with feelings. The other is the treatment of emotions as intentional states of mind, that is, states of mind that are directed at or toward some object. Each theme corresponds to a different concept of emotions. Accordingly, the study has divided, for the most part, into two main lines of investigation. On one, emotions are conceived of as principally affective states. The concept on which this line proceeds is feeling-centered. On the other, emotions are conceived of as principally cognitive states. The concept on which this line proceeds is thought-centered. Both concepts reflect revolutionary changes in the theoretical study of emotions that began to take place at the end of the nineteenth century and continued for several decades into the twentieth. The two main lines of investigation come out of objections to the concept of emotion that dominated philosophy and psychology in the eighteenth and nineteenth

I am grateful to Owen Flanagan and Peter Goldie for comments on an earlier draft of this chapter.

centuries. The revolution in our thinking about emotions begins with the abandonment of this older concept.

# I

The older concept is a fixture of empiricist psychology in the modern tradition. Empiricists of the eighteenth and nineteenth centuries saw the mind as a single field of thought and feeling, fully conscious and transparent to itself. Its chief inhabitants are distinct ideas and impressions. The latter include visual, auditory, and tactile impressions as well as other sensations of external things. The former are products of these impressions. They are either simple or complex, and, if complex, then one can always understand them as combinations of simples. In Hume's wonderful simile, impressions and ideas are "like players in a theater who successively make their appearance, pass, repass, glide away, and mingle in an infinite variety of postures and situations" (1978, p. 253). The class of impressions includes more, though, than sensations of external things. It also includes both localized and unlocalized feelings of pleasure and pain. The latter are the emotions. They are in Locke's words "internal sensations" (1975, pp. 229–30) and in Hume's "secondary" or "reflective" impressions (1978, p. 275). The basic ones are simple impressions of pleasure or pain whose connection to ideas, physiological activity, and conduct is either that of cause to effect or conversely. Specifically, on Locke's view, these internal sensations result from ideas of good and evil; on Hume's, their immediate causes are impressions of pleasure and pain along with, in some cases, ideas of external things. At the same time, on the empiricist's view, we can conceive of these basic emotions in abstraction from their typical causes and effects, just as we can conceive of simple sensations of color or sound. Abstracted from their causes and effects, according to classical empiricism, emotions are discrete, episodic, and purely affective states of consciousness.

The traditional empiricist concept of emotions came under a withering attack by William James. The attack was part of James's broadside, in the famous ninth chapter of *The Principles of Psychology*, against traditional empiricism's general understanding of mental states as either wholly simple states or complex states composed of these simples. Hume's simile nicely presents James's target. The empiricist understanding of mental states, James observed, presupposed that "sensations came to us pure and single" (1950, vol. 1, p. 233), that they recurred at different times in our experiences of the world, and that the great mass and constantly changing flow of thought in our minds was due entirely to the combination and recombination of these simple sensations and their corresponding simple ideas. None of these three suppositions, James argued, can be sustained. Sensory experience is no more made up of individual units of sensation than rivers are made up of individual drops of water. Our thought, James argued, naturally appears to us as "sensibly continuous", like a stream (1950, vol. 1, p. 237). It can no more be broken down into mental atoms whirling in a void than its correlative brain activity can be broken down into discrete, concatenated events. Secondly, this stream of thought is Heraclitan. One never, James insisted, had the same sensation twice. Indeed, sensations, according to James are unrepeatable items of experience. Because each sensation corresponds to some modification of the brain, there could be no recurrence of the exact same sensation. For that to happen, the second occurrence would have to occur "in an unmodified brain", which is "a physiological impossibility" (1950, vol. 1, pp. 232–3). Thirdly, if, contrary to Locke's supposition, there are no simple, recurrent sensations, then there are no corresponding simple, recurrent ideas either. Consequently, human thought does not break down into elementary units of feeling and thought. The continuous change in what we feel and think does not consist in the combining and recombining of the same set of simple, immutable sensations and ideas.

We are led to think otherwise, James observed, by our habit of identifying sensations of sight, sound, taste, and so forth by their objects. We speak of the same sounds when we hear the same thing on different occasions, a musical note, say, or a bird's chirp. Inattentive to variations in our sensory experience, we say that the sensations are the same when, in fact, there is no individual sensation on any of these occasions and therefore no relation of identity holding between sensations on different occasions. What is the same is the object of sensation. When we listen to the performance of a sonata, for example, we hear the same notes repeated at different intervals and in different arrangements, yet it would be wrong to think that, each time we heard some note during the performance, we had a distinct auditory sensation that was separate from and a successor of an equally distinct auditory sensation we had in hearing the previous note and that was identical to an auditory sensation we had when we last heard this note. The experience of hearing the sonata does not consist of separate, individual sensations of sound experienced sequentially and repeated at different intervals. It is only the tendency to confuse these sensations with their objects that leads us carelessly to think of the experience in this way and to speak of having the same sensation when we hear the same note.

We are not, of course, liable to confuse emotions with their objects, for we do not identify them by their objects. Fear, after all, is fear whether it is fear of spiders or fear of earthquakes. Nonetheless, emotions too are misconceived on the traditional empiricist understanding of them as either simple, recurrent states of mind or compounds of such states. "Pride and humility", Hume tells us, at the very beginning of his discussion of these passions, are "simple and uniform impressions" (1978, p. 277). So too, he says, are the other passions (though later, in book II of the *Treatise*, he identifies several passions, respect, contempt, and amorous love, as mixtures of two other passions (1978, pp. 389–96)). The traditional empiricist misconception, in this case, is due, not to their mistaking emotions for their objects, but rather to their modeling emotions on external sensations. Thus, Locke, having begun his study with simple, external sensations, then introduces pleasures, pains, and passions, which arise with external sensations, either through impact on the body of some external object or with our thoughts of good and bad. The latter are emotions, and we experience them, Locke says, as internal sensations. Similarly, though more elegantly, Hume identifies external sensations as primary impressions, the simple ones being the starting points of his investigations, and then, when he takes up emotions, identifies them as secondary impressions. The understanding of emotions, in either case, therefore inherits the mistakes James criticized in the traditional empiricist treatment of external sensations. And James then went on in chapter twenty-five of *The Principles* to level the same criticisms of the traditional empiricist understanding of emotions. "The trouble with the emotions in psychology", he wrote, "is that they are regarded too much as absolutely individual things. So long as they are set down as so many eternal and sacred psychic entities, like the old immutable species in natural history, so long all that can be done with them is reverently to catalogue their separate characters, points, and effects" (1950, vol. 2, p. 449).

James's objection to the traditional empiricist concept of emotions was thus continuous with his objection to the traditional empiricist understanding of mental states generally. To identify each type of emotion as a distinctive, recurrent inner sensation or feeling, James argued, is to misunderstand the nature of emotional states of mind. At the same time, James accepted the traditional empiricist characterization of emotions as feelings. The feelings that he identified with emotions, however, were feelings produced by changes in the body. Emotions, according to James, were those feelings that arose as the result of the physiological and neurological changes that typically occurred as the result of the perception of some exciting fact. As James put it, "My theory . . . is that *the bodily changes follow directly the perception of the exciting fact, and that our feeling of the same changes as they occur* is *the emotion*" (1950, vol. 2, p. 449). By so identifying the emotion with these feelings, James reversed the common sense order of events in an episode of emotion. For common sense has it that what excites the emotion is the perception of a fact, and the emotion then causes the bodily changes that express it. According to common sense, a person perceives a charging bear, for example, feels fear, blanches, and runs, whereas, on James's account, the perception of the charging bear causes the person to blanch and run, and the feeling of these bodily movements is the fear. In effect, then, on James's account, the emotion does not cause the behavior that expresses it or the behavior it is commonly said to motivate. Rather such behavior is the direct effect of the perception of some fact, and feeling the bodily changes the behavior consists in is the emotion. Emotions, on James's account, are therefore epiphenomenal. They are the products of bodily changes, but they do not themselves cause any action.[1]

# II

James's identification of emotions with bodily feelings is one of two major innovations behind the abandonment of the traditional empiricist concept of emotion. The other emerged in treatments of emotion that oppose the epiphenomenalism in James's account. James, to be sure, regarded his reversing the commonsense account of the relation of emotions to their behavioral expressions as an advance in the study of emotions. But not every contributor to the study did. Some stuck with common sense. On the commonsense account, emotions are springs of action. They have motivational force. In reversing common sense, James implicitly denied that they had such force, and this consequence of his program is the rub. For it is not easy to give up citing emotions to explain actions.[2]

The traditional empiricist concept of emotions supported such explanations. On traditional empiricism, emotions are motives of actions. Specifically, they arise from thoughts or perceptions and immediately move their subjects to action. A good example is Hume's account of the emotions he called "the direct passions". The direct passions, on Hume's account, include desire and aversion, joy and grief, hope and fear, anger and benevolence, among others. Like all secondary impressions in Hume's psychology, they are inner feelings, each being qualitatively distinct from the others. At the same time, instances of each vary according as the feeling they consist in is more or less turbulent and as it is more or less forceful. Hume, that is, distinguished between the phenomenal character of an emotion and its motivational strength. Emotions are either violent or calm depending on how

---

[1] In taking James's rejection of the common sense order of events in an episode of emotion as affirmation of the view of emotions as epiphenomenal, I do not mean to suggest that James held that all mental states were epiphenomenal. In *The Principles of Psychology*, chapter 5, James appears to reject the latter view on grounds of common sense. Hence, his express challenge to common sense in his theory of emotions implies that he is making an exception in this case to the rule of common sense that he invokes in rejecting epiphenomenalism as a general theory of the mind. See James, 1950, vol. 1, pp. 128–44, esp. p. 144.

[2] Indeed, while James's considered view was to deny that emotions had motivational force (lest they precede rather than succeed the bodily movements that express them), he too sometimes fell back to the commonsense understanding of emotions as springs of action. Thus, in the chapter on instincts, chapter 24, he wrote, "*Sympathy* is an emotion . . . Some of [whose] forms, that of mother with child, for example, are surely primitive, and not intelligent forecasts of board and lodging and other support to be reaped in old age. Danger to the child blindly and instantaneously stimulates the mother to actions of alarm and defense" (1950, vol. 2, p. 410).

much agitation in the mind they entail. They are either strong or weak depending on the amount of force with which they motivate action. Further, on Hume's account, the degree to which an emotion is calm or violent is independent of the degree to which it is weak or strong (1978, p. 419). Consequently, a passion may be calm; it may produce little agitation in the mind; yet it may be stronger than some violent, co-occurring passion and so move its subject to actions that are contrary to the actions the more violent passion is prompting. As Hume put it, "'Tis evident passions influence not the will in proportion to their violence, or the disorder they occasion in the temper; but on the contrary, that when a passion has once become a settled principle of action, and is the predominant inclination of the soul, it commonly produces no longer any sensible agitation" (1978, pp. 418–19)

Indeed, any passion, Hume observed, "may decay into so soft an emotion, as to become, in a manner, imperceptible" (1978, p. 276). Certain calm ones, in particular, "are more known by their effects than by the immediate feeling or sensation" (1978, p. 417). What I shall call "Hume's doctrine of the calm passions" implies both that we can know of an emotion independently of its phenomenal character and that we can conceive of it as present and operative even though it lacks a phenomenal presence. The doctrine, consequently, suggests a different concept of emotion from that employed in traditional empiricism. It suggests a concept focused on the motivational rather than the affective character of emotions. Hume of course did not make this concept explicit. He could hardly have done so and kept quiet, as he did, about the seeming incoherence he introduced into his system in referring to an imperceptible impression. An unfelt feeling, after all, is a contradiction in terms. Hume, in other words, could not have maintained the doctrine of calm passions unqualified without having to abandon his notion of an emotion as a secondary impression. More generally, he could not have maintained the doctrine without abandoning the framework of traditional empiricist psychology within which he worked. On that framework the mind is a field of consciousness, and its states, therefore, are essentially conscious. The doctrine of the calm passions, to the contrary, implies the possibility of some emotions, though states of mind, occurring outside of this field. Some emotions may be, in a word, unconscious.

The idea that emotions need not always be conscious states is the second major innovation behind the abandonment of the traditional empiricist understanding of emotion. While Hume's doctrine of the calm passions suggests this innovation, it was not until Freud developed his theory of the unconscious, a hundred and fifty years later, that it was fully realized. Freud was not the first thinker to propose that there were unconscious mental states. He readily acknowledged predecessors. But those precedent proposals did not present much of a challenge to the traditional empiricist framework. Typically, what was proposed was that some thoughts and ideas existed just beyond the periphery of the mind, in a subconscious part, and if not easily retrievable, could become conscious nonetheless without effort. Examples were ideas corresponding to words that are "just on the tip of our tongues", as we say, that we struggle to recall only to have them suddenly appear clearly in consciousness, and ideas that must occur to us during sleep since it is not uncommon for someone, upon waking up in the morning, to see immediately the solution to a problem that had vexed him the night before. Freud, by contrast, held that some ideas and thoughts were deeply buried in an unconscious part of the mind and were blocked from being retrieved by repression. One's mind, as it were, generated force to keep them from becoming conscious. Such repression was necessary because the repressed thoughts and ideas were themselves charged and energetic and would immediately rise to consciousness if there were no counter-force to keep them in check. Examples of such repressed ideas and thoughts were beliefs about being personally responsible for some traumatic event that occurred when one was very young. Such beliefs, while they may never become conscious, reveal themselves in dreams, self-defeating behavior, even illness. That they mani-fest themselves in this way is Freud's reason for understanding them as charged. Unconscious thoughts and ideas could not have the influence on people Freud saw in their dreams, irrational behavior, and illnesses that lack organic causes unless they were forceful in their own right. Freud called the tension between their force and that of repression "the dynamic unconscious". The great originality of his theory of mind was due to this way of conceiving of unconscious thoughts and ideas.

Freud took emotions too as capable of being repressed (Freud, 1915, 1923, 1924) They too could be unconscious. Consequently, he could not conceive of emotions as feelings. Nonetheless, he is commonly interpreted as having so con-ceived of them, notwithstanding the evident incoherence his taking emotions as feelings would, as in Hume's case, introduce into his theory (see, e.g., Lear, 1990, pp. 88–90). The passages that are commonly cited to support this interpretation are not decisive, however, and, I would argue, are better read as supporting an interpretation on which Freud gives meaning to the term "unconscious emotion" while acknowledging that the term "unconscious feeling" is self-contradictory (Freud, 1915; Deigh, 2001). Emotions may be unconscious, but feelings are neces-sarily conscious. Hence, Freud did not identify emotions with feelings. He identi-fied them instead with states whose expression included feelings or that had the potential for such expression, a potential that was blocked from being realized by repression. Be this as it may, ideas of unconscious love, fear, hate, anger, and the unconscious sense of guilt are fixed points in Freud's theory, and because of the theory's great influence on twentieth-century thinking about human psychology and culture, reference to them has become commonplace in our everyday thought and talk about the human mind. Freud's theory, therefore, whatever Freud's express opinion of the possibility of unconscious emotions was, offers a concept of them, a concept that is a major alternative to James's. It remains then to define this concept.

To begin with, Freud took emotions to be states of mind we are conscious of through the feelings that manifest them. As such, they are distinct from those feelings, and they may exist and operate in us even when we are unconscious of them. In addition, Freud sought, in the operations of unconscious emotions, explanations of a great range of phenomena of human life including odd behavior like parapraxes, unconventional sexual conduct such as fetishism and bestiality, inappropriate feeling or lack thereof, excessive fear, for example, or flat affect, and somatic illnesses that had no obvious organic cause. Such explanations were among the most distinctive explanations of psychoanalytic theory. They required not only identification of an emotion that was either not manifest in what, if anything, the subject was feeling or, though manifest in the subject's feeling, concerned with something other than the ostensible object of those feelings but also identification of the person, thing, event, or state of affairs toward which the emotion was actually directed. The latter requirement indicates Freud's special concern with the true objects of people's emotions. While these were often people, things, events, etc. that produced the emotion, they were sometimes merely the products of the subject's fantasies. As Freud put it, when he came to explain certain hysterical symptoms in his patients as the products of repressed pseudo-memories of sexual trauma in early childhood, whether incidents of sexual abuse really occurred or were fantasized made no difference from the patient's viewpoint. Because the fantasized events seemed to the patient as real as if they had actually occurred, the repressed pseudo-memories and the terror they instilled in the latter case had the same effect on him as genuine memories of real abuse. In effect, then, Freud, in giving these explanations, fixed on emotions as intentional states of mind. He saw, with each, how it was related to its object so as to give meaning or import to the feelings, behavior, and conditions that manifested it. For Freud, such intentionality was the core element of the concept of emotions he invented in introducing unconscious emotions into the theory of the mind.

At the same time, Freud did not expressly consider what an emotion's intentionality consisted in or what constituted an emotion's distinctive relation to its object. To introduce a concept of emotion that was a genuine alternative to the one James defined, it was sufficient for Freud to have made the intentionality of emotions and the import it gave to them the focus of his conception. Accordingly, on the concept he introduced, emotions are not, as distinct from the one James defined, epiphenomena. Rather they can be causes, and what they cause are actions. Secondly, being sometimes unconscious states, emotions are not, contrary to James, identical with feelings. Rather they are expressed by feelings. Thirdly, the feelings that express emotions are meaningful phenomena, whereas for James they are merely indices of bodily processes. Feelings of grief, shame, fear, or the like, on Freud's view, have the same meaning or import as the emotions they express, and indeed that import is transmitted from the emotion to them. Grief, for example, has the import of loss, and in feeling grief one feels the loss over which one is grieving. Shame has the import of one's appearing unworthy before others whose esteem one values, and in feeling shame one feels unworthy of them. On the concept James defined, by contrast, the feelings an emotion consists in, being nothing over and above the feelings of bodily changes, are not meaningful in this way. Their being feelings of grief, say, or shame is, rather, mere happenstance, a consequence of the concept that ultimately yielded telling empirical criticism.[3]

# III

The concept of emotion that Freud introduced thus stood in need of an account of the meaning that he located in an emotion's intentionality. In the last third of the twentieth century, many philosophers and psychologists, often without recognizing their debt to Freud, converged on such an account.[4] While the theories of emotion they advanced differed from each other in specifics, they agreed in taking some form of evaluative judgment as an essential element of an emotion and in citing the thought content of such a judgment to explain the intentionality of emotions. On these theories, for instance, judgments about good fortune are essential to joy, and judgments about undeserved misfortune are essential to pity. Accordingly, the import of the feelings expressing joy or pity derives from these judgments. Feelings of joy, therefore, concern something good that has happened to one, and feelings of pity concern undeserved misfortune that has befallen someone. The feelings that express emotions are, then, importantly different from feelings and sensations that merely register some physiological disturbance. The latter, being symptoms of bodily changes, do not concern anything. They have no import. When, after sudden exertion, say, one is short of breath and feels weak or wobbly, the feeling is symptomatic of respiratory difficulty and nothing more. If, by contrast, upon a sudden attack of panic one is short of breath and feeling wobbly, the feeling is not just a symptom of respiratory difficulty. It concerns, rather, something of which one is intensely afraid and what determines the object of one's fear is the judgment that one is in danger. The object of one's fear, in other words, is what one thinks is endangering one. And the same pattern of analysis, so these theories hold, applies to emotions generally. Every emotion, that is, is necessarily about something, however vague or indeterminate, and what it is about

---

[3] Experimental work by Stanley Schacter and Jerome Singer (1962) is generally thought to have established that the bodily processes a person who is feeling some emotion undergoes are not by themselves sufficient to determine the type of emotion the person is feeling.

[4] Some, however, clearly recognized this debt. See Solomon, 1976, pp. 180–2.

is determined by the evaluative judgment it contains. Consequently, such a judgment is an essential element of the emotion.

To take such a judgment as an essential element of an emotion, and not merely a common concomitant, is therefore to understand an emotion as essentially a cognitive state. This understanding, which now prevails among philosophers and psychologists who study emotions, represents a recovery of ideas about emotions that were prominent in the thought of the ancients. Indeed, Aristotle is often cited in the expositions of contemporary cognitivist theories of emotion as a source of their central thesis. And the boldest of them go so far as to endorse the ancient Stoic theory on which emotions are taken to be identical to evaluative judgments of a certain kind (Solomon, 1976; Nussbaum, 2001; see also Nussbaum, 1994, chs. 9–13). Most of these theories, however, are less bold and give accounts of emotions that include, as essential elements, other things besides evaluative thought and articulate some complex relation among these elements. Agitation of the mind, autonomic behavior, and impulses to action are the usual additions. But even in these theories evaluative judgment is the primary element in the mix, for it is the element by which each emotion is principally identified. It is the element the theories principally use to define different types of emotion (Deigh, 1994, pp. 835–42).

A theme that is common to these theories is that emotions, like other cognitive states, belong to intelligent thought and action. They are in this respect on a par with beliefs and other judgments, decisions, and resolutions. They are, that is, states that one can regard as having propositional content, which their subjects accept or affirm. Accordingly, one can treat them as warranted or unwarranted, justified or unjustified, by the circumstances in which they occur or the beliefs on which they are based. Thus, fear would be warranted if its object evidently posed some threat to one and unwarranted if it evidently posed no threat. Likewise, anger would be justified if it were a response to a genuinely demeaning insult and unjustified if based on one's mistaking an innocent remark for such an insult. In either case, the emotion is warranted or unwarranted, justified or unjustified, because the evaluative judgment in which the emotion consists, either in whole or in part, is warranted or unwarranted, justified or unjustified. In general, then, on these theories, an evaluative judgment is an essential component of an emotion. It is, moreover, the component by which one type of emotion differs from another. If you want to understand the difference between contempt and anger, say, then according to these theories the difference lies in the type of evaluative judgment that is essential to each emotion. When you have contempt for someone because he has behaved badly, you judge the person to be low or unworthy of your esteem in view of that behavior. When you are angry at someone because he has behaved badly, you judge the person to have injured or insulted you or someone close to you by so behaving. I will call this model of cognitivist theory "the standard model".

The standard model is subject to two powerful and related objections. First, sometimes one can experience an emotion toward something that one knows lacks the properties it must have for the emotion to be warranted. Consider, for example, the fear people typically experience when looking down from a precipice. They may know that they are perfectly safe and in no danger of falling, yet fear falling nevertheless. Similarly, common phobias such as snake and spider phobias supply examples of fear of an object the subject knows is harmless. Again, people sometimes feel disgust at foods they know are nutritious, benign, and perhaps even tasty.[5] Defenders of cognitivist theories that fit the standard model must, to account for these examples, describe the subjects of these emotions as making contradictory judgments or holding contradictory beliefs. Yet familiarity with such experiences tells us that when, for example, one feels fear on looking down from a precipice, knowing that one is perfectly safe, one doesn't judge or believe that one is in any danger of falling. To react with fear, it is sufficient that one look down and see the steep drop below. The reaction is automatic, as it were. It does not depend on one's making a judgment or forming a belief about one's circumstances' being dangerous. Cognitivist theories that fit the standard model cannot, then, satisfactorily account for such fear.

The second objection to the standard model is that it cannot satisfactorily account for the emotions of nonhuman animals and human infants—beasts and babies. Like the first objection, this second objection identifies a class of emotions that resist being understood as consisting either wholly or in part in evaluative judgments of the kind that the standard model identifies as the essential cognitive element in emotions. The reason for this resistance is plain. Such judgments, like beliefs, are states of mind that imply acceptance or affirmation of propositions. Consequently, to have emotions requires being capable of grasping and affirming propositions. That is to say, one must have acquired a language. Since beasts never acquire a language and babies have yet to acquire one, the standard model cannot account for their emotions. The result is not entirely surprising. The most important antecedent of the standard model, the cognitivist theory of emotions that the ancient Greek and Roman Stoics advanced, denied that beasts and babies ever experienced emotions. Because beasts and babies lacked language, the Stoics argued, they were incapable of making evaluative judgments of the kind with which the Stoics identified emotions. But their view, like Descartes's cognate view that only human beings have minds, has long since been reduced to an historical curiosity. Consequently, any theory of emotions must acknowledge that beasts and babies are capable of having emotions, and it must account for these as well as the emotions of mature human beings. Cognitivist theories that fit the standard model fail in this respect.

---

[5] See Rozin and Fallon, 1987.

# IV

In view of these objections, recent defenders of cognitivist theories have dropped the standard model in favor of a broader account of the evaluative cognition that is essential to emotions (see Nussbaum, 2001; and Roberts, 2003). Such cognition, they argue, need not be an evaluative judgment of the kind that implies grasping and affirming a proposition. It may, instead, be a perception. Indeed, some defenders of cognitivist theories now argue that emotions are primarily forms of perception. The theories they defend fit what I'll call "the perceptual model". Since perceiving something does not imply that you make any judgment or form any belief about it, the first objection does not threaten cognitivist theories that fit this model. When you look down from a precipice, knowing you are in no danger of falling, the fear you experience need not consist in or involve a belief or judgment that you are in danger of falling. You perceive danger in falling, but you do not believe or judge that you are in danger of falling. Hence, in feeling fear of falling you do not make contradictory judgments or hold contradictory beliefs. And the same goes for other examples that generate the first objection to the standard model.

Does the perceptual model also escape the second objection? Can it account for the emotions of beasts and babies? Defenders of this model maintain that it can. Because perception is sometimes a more primitive form of cognition than the kind of evaluative judgment that the standard model identifies as essential to emotions, they argue, it is possible on the perceptual model for beasts and babies to have evaluative cognitions of the kind that is essential to emotions. Specifically, because not all perception requires propositional thought, attributing perceptions to beasts and babies does not presuppose that either has any linguistic capabilities. The fear a dog feels, say, when a man threatens him with a stick consists at least in part in the dog's seeing the threatening motions his would-be attacker makes with the stick as dangerous. The dog's perception, so defenders of the perceptual model would argue, is like the perception we have when we look at a straight stick partially submerged in a deep pool of water. We see it as bent. Our so seeing the stick does not require any propositional thought on our part, and by the same token the dog's seeing the man with the stick as dangerous does not require any propositional thought on the dog's part.

This argument for recognizing that the perceptual model is beyond the reach of the second objection would succeed if the point of that objection, when pressed against the standard model, were a point about the mode of cognition that on this standard model characterizes the evaluative judgments the model represents as essential to emotions. It would succeed, that is, if the reason the standard model fails to account for the emotions of beasts and babies is that the model takes such evaluative judgments to be states or acts of mind in which some proposition is affirmed or denied. Some perceptions, after all, are cognitive states in which the mind neither affirms nor denies a proposition. They are of a different mode of cognition. Hence, the second objection would have no force against the perceptual model since this alternative mode may characterize some of the perceptions the model represents as essential to emotions. But one could be making a different point in advancing the second objection. One could be making a point about the cognitive content of the evaluative judgments that the standard model represents as essential to emotions. In that case, the argument has not succeeded in showing that the perceptual model is beyond the reach of this objection. For the cognitive content of a perception of someone, the man with the stick, say, as dangerous is the same as the cognitive content of a judgment that this man is dangerous. In either case, the concept of danger is deployed in a cognitive representation of the situation, and to have and deploy a concept of danger is to be capable of propositional thought. Hence, the perceptual model too runs afoul of the second objection.

Defenders of the perceptual model will of course balk at this result. They will argue, in response, either that one does not need to have a concept of danger to see something as dangerous or that it is possible to have concepts even if one has no language or has yet to acquire one. Neither response, however, rescues the model from defeat by the second objection. Let us consider the second response first. By a concept, I understand, following the standard view in Anglo-American philosophy, what words, particularly substantival words, express when they are used in sentences that express propositions. They are, that is, what such words mean when they occur in meaningful sentences.[6] Thus, the meaning of a word, its sense, as we sometimes say, is the concept it expresses. To have concepts independently of one's having a language implies either of two possibilities. On the one hand, it may imply that one's concepts are innate and part of what takes place, when one learns language, is one's matching words to them and constructing sentences that match the combinations of them one has created. On the other, it may imply that one first acquires concepts through sensory and affective experiences and later learns how they are encoded in language. The first possibility captures a view of language acquisition according to which it follows and results from the emergence and development of rational thought in children. Since animals other than human beings are not rational and never acquire language, the first possibility is not available to defenders of the perceptual model. The second possibility treats concepts as ideas in the mind that derive from one's sensory and affective experience. On this possibility, the acquisition of such ideas is not exclusive to human

---

[6] On this understanding of what concepts are, having the concept of x entails more than having the power to discriminate between x's and other things. The point is as old as Plato's early dialogues, but it sometimes needs to be brought forward because of the tendency among writers on topics in psychology to use the words "concept" and "idea" interchangeably.

beings. At the same time, this possibility entails a semantics for natural language according to which the meanings of our words are these ideas in our minds. While such a semantics was once widely held by classical empiricist philosophers and the positivist philosophers whose theories of meaning dominated Anglo-American philosophy in the first half of the twentieth century, powerful objections to these views that critics of positivism developed in the latter half of the twentieth century have shown this semantics to be untenable.[7] Consequently, the second possibility is also a nonstarter. Defenders of the perceptual must avoid attributing concepts to beasts and babies if they are to save the model from defeat by the second objection.

We are left, then, with the alternative response, that one does not need to a have a concept of danger to see something as dangerous. With regard to this response, the first thing to ask is what seeing something as dangerous amounts to. Specifically, is it like seeing a straight stick as bent when it is partially submerged in a pool of water? Or is it more like seeing an extended hand as an offer of friendship when you first make someone's acquaintance? In the latter case, the perception entails an interpretation that consists in applying a concept, the concept of an offer of friendship, to a gesture. So if seeing something as dangerous is like this latter case, then the alternative response fails to save the perceptual model. In the former case, the perception, by contrast, arguably need not involve any application of a concept. In describing our perception as one of seeing a straight stick as bent, we describe how the stick appears to us in circumstances in which we know it would appear differently if we looked at it through a uniform medium. The expression 'seeing as' is apt in this case, not because we are interpreting how the object appears to us but because we are perceiving the object through one of our sense modalities, vision, and the circumstances are ones in which we know that the way it appears to us visually is not the only way in which it can visually appear to someone. We are thus remarking a sensory property an object appears to have but may not in fact have. It is a property of a kind of which we are directly aware through one or more of our sense modalities. The question, then, is whether being dangerous is similarly a sensory property of objects, whether it is a property of a kind of which we are directly aware through one of our sense modalities.

If it were, then we would teach children what the word 'dangerous' meant in the same way that we teach them the meaning of words for sensory properties like 'yellow' and 'sweet'. When one teaches a child words for such properties one assumes prior acquaintance with the properties. That is, one assumes that the child's sense modalities have developed, worked well, and been exercised. When one teaches a child color words, for instance, one finds objects that display the colors vividly, presents those objects to the child, and has it apply the different words to them. Other objects that are similar in color are also presented to the

---

[7] See Putnam, 1975.

child, and it is taught to group them according to color. On the assumption, then, that the child can recognize the objects in each group as similar to each other, it is taught to apply the word to what each member in the group has in common with every other.

Plainly, a different method is used to teach children what the word 'dangerous' means. Children are not presented with a collection of objects such as pencils with sharp points, rubber balls, plastic bags, matches, and billfolds and invited to group them according as they are dangerous or benign. One does not assume prior acquaintance with the property. That is, one does not assume that children can recognize, prior to their learning the meaning of the word 'dangerous', similarity among objects all of which are dangerous. Otherwise one would naturally teach them what the word means by teaching them to apply the word to what they already recognize as the property the objects have in common. Rather children are taught the meaning of the word by being told which things are dangerous and which are not. Teaching them the meaning and teaching them how to recognize the property are therefore one and the same. One assumes, that is, that the child is ignorant of which things have the property and which do not, that it cannot, without instruction, recognize a thing's being or not being dangerous. Whether it's strangers or matches or busy streets, a child is taught about the danger each poses, and the teaching typically includes some explanation of the harm that each can cause. Likewise, one teaches a child not to be afraid of things that initially frighten it when they are not dangerous. In so doing, one is not correcting a child's misperception of danger. Rather, one is teaching the child that not everything scary is dangerous, and this teaching too may include a demonstration that these scary things do not cause harm. If being dangerous were a sensory property, such teaching would be unnecessary for getting children to recognize danger. A method of teaching like that of teaching children the meaning of color words would be sufficient. As it is not, we may conclude that being dangerous is not a sensory property. It is not a property of which we are directly aware through one of our sense modalities.

What then should we say about the dog that is afraid of the man threatening him with a stick? It is tempting, of course, to say that the dog sees the man as dangerous. After all, if a man threatened you with a stick, you would certainly see him as dangerous. But we need not suppose that the dog can perceive the property of being dangerous to understand the dog's fear. We need only suppose that the dog sees the man as an imminent source of pain in that the dog anticipates pain from this man owing, say, to the man's threatening behavior and the dog's having previously experienced being violently struck with a stick. The previous experience and the perception of the man are jointly sufficient to explain the dog's fear. For having once been traumatized by pain, the dog will anticipate again feeling pain when he is in a similar situation, and consequently the occurrence of a similar situation is bound to trigger fear of the objects in that situation from which he anticipates pain. The mechanism is familiar. Think, for example, of the apprehension you experience when a nurse is about to draw blood or administer an anesthetic and you see in her hand a syringe with a long needle. We need not suppose any evaluative cognition to understand the inward shudder you feel as the nurse approaches. And the same is true of the dog.

Cognitivist theories of the emotions on which evaluative cognition is essential to emotions have been the predominant theories for the past forty or so years. The attraction of these theories is the account of the intentionality of emotions they give. The account promises both a way of understanding the relation of an emotion to its object and the orientation toward the object that the emotion affords its subject. Yet they fall short of giving a satisfactory account of the intentionality of the emotions to which beasts and babies are liable. And since these are the first emotions that men and women who become capable of experiencing emotions whose intentionality does consist in evaluative cognition experience, it would seem that the soundest theory of emotions that proceeds from a concept of emotion on which intentionality is its core element should begin with an account of the intentionality of these primitive emotions and build on it an account of how they are transformed through moral development and education into emotions whose intentionality consists in evaluative cognitions (see Deigh, 2008).

# V

Recently, under the influence of work on emotions in neuroscience, there has been a return to conceiving of emotions as essentially feelings. Indeed, those in the forefront of this development have invoked James's account as the source of their program.[8] Accordingly, let us call them "neo-Jamesians". The neo-Jamesians, like James, take the feelings in which emotions consist to be the feelings of the bodily changes that occur during an episode of emotion. Unlike James, however, the neo-Jamesians hold that these feelings do not merely register those bodily changes. Rather they are also meaningful. The neo-Jamesians, in other words, accept the fundamental idea on which the concept of an emotion that Freud introduced into psychology is constructed, the idea that emotions are intentional states. One can therefore characterize their account of emotions as a hybrid produced by grafting this idea onto James's account of emotions. This hybrid's distinctive thesis, then, is that the feelings of bodily changes in which an emotion consists are intentional phenomena. Plainly, if the neo-Jamesians can sustain this thesis, they will have

---

[8]  See Damasio, 1995; Prinz, 2004.

made a significant advance on cognitivist theories. For they will have given a uniform account of the intentionality of emotions, an account that fits equally well the emotions of beasts and babies, on the one hand, and the emotions of men and women, on the other. They will have done so, that is, given that on this hybrid, emotions, whether of beasts and babies or of men and women, consist in feelings of bodily changes and given that their intentionality has the same character in either case.[9] They will have therefore given an account that eludes the problem that, as we saw, puts the cogency of cognitivist theories in doubt.

At the same time, there is reason to wonder about the coherence of a hybrid that results from grafting the fundamental idea of the concept of emotion Freud introduced onto James's account. To begin with, Freud introduced his concept out of an interest in citing unconscious emotions to explain a broad range of human behavior, feelings, and bodily conditions. His point was that an emotion need not be a conscious state to have influence in human lives, and, by identifying intentionality as the core element in our understanding of the nature of emotions, he secured that point. The point is obviously lost, however, when one takes the feelings of bodily changes to be the vehicle of an emotion's intentionality. Indeed, neo-Jamesians would appear to have to reject the possibility of unconscious emotions. Feelings of bodily changes cannot be unconscious. So one may wonder what the point is of their taking intentionality as an essential feature of emotions. Is their doing so just a case of amalgamating two otherwise independent features into a single conception?

In addition, Freud's use of a concept of emotion on which intentionality is the core element served to maintain the commonsense view of emotions as springs of action. To grasp an emotion's intentionality is to understand how the emotion orients its subject toward the world or toward certain persons or things in it and what sorts of action to expect in response to that orientation. James's account is meant to oppose common sense on this point, for, on his account, the actions common sense takes as springing directly from an emotion are among the bodily movements the feeling of which the emotion consists in and therefore cannot be explained by the emotion. So again one may wonder what the point is of the neo-Jamesians' taking intentionality to be an essential feature of an emotion if they mean to be faithful to James's account and, particularly, to its treating emotions as epiphenomena. Taking emotions, instead, as states of motivation that are distinct from and can give rise to feelings would appear, in view, say, of Hume's doctrine of the calm passions, to make better sense if one did not conceive of emotions as epiphenomena.

---

[9] NB: We can assume that their intentionality is the same in either case since it depends on the nature of these feelings and not on the nature of any cognitions and since in the lives of beasts and babies the feelings of bodily changes do not differ in kind from those in the lives of men and women.

Be this as it may, we need to examine the neo-Jamesian program as expounded by its adherents to see whether it makes sense and so progress within the philosophical study of emotions. A useful starting place is Antonio Damasio's theory of emotions in his influential book *Descartes' Error*. Damasio draws his theory from his research in neuroscience on the brain. Damasio's research yields a description of the neurological activity that occurs as we confront and respond to new and different situations. His main observation is of neurological activity that signals a need for adjustment or action that will promote one's survival, correct for deviation in one's functioning that threatens one's health, say, or that will restore one to a condition of functioning well. The signals, in other words, enable us to monitor what is happening in and to our bodies and to make adjustments and take actions as necessary. We are the recipients of these signals, and we use them to regulate our welfare. In setting out his views on the nature of emotions, Damasio expressly claims James's account as their principal antecedent. The feelings of bodily changes that James took emotions to consist in are, according to Damasio, a means by which we monitor what is happening in and to our bodies during an episode of emotion. They signal the need for us to make adjustments and to take action. Accordingly, Damasio characterizes them as perceptions of the body. In doing so, he renders them intentional phenomena. He therefore offers a way of understanding the intentionality of emotions on James's account. And because of his thesis that these feelings are perceptions of the body, it is natural to take him as an adherent to the neo-Jamesian program.

Damasio, however, despite regarding himself as following James in giving his account of the emotions, does not. Specifically, he does not deploy James's concept of emotion in his theory. Rather he deploys a concept on which emotions are distinct from the feelings to which they give rise. He deploys a different concept because he misreads James as identifying emotions with a bodily process, as "stripping emotion down to a process that involved the body" (1995, p. 129). Thus, having identified emotions with a bodily process, he takes the feelings of the corresponding bodily changes as the internal perceptions of this bodily process. "If an emotion is a collection of changes in body state connected to particular mental images that have activated a specific brain system, *the essence of feeling an emotion is the experience of such changes in juxtaposition to the mental images that initiated the cycle*" (1995, p. 145). On his theory, then, feelings are distinct from emotions. His proclaimed descent, as a theorist of emotion, from James notwithstanding, Damasio bases his theory on a concept of emotion that is much closer to Freud's than to James's. And while the theory includes a thesis attributing intentionality to the feelings of emotion, the intentionality of these feelings, as Damasio understands it, does not correspond to the intentionality of the emotion that gives rise to them.

This last point should be obvious. The intentionality of an emotion consists in the emotion's being directed at or toward something. Typically, the object at which an emotion is directed is an object in the world, either real or imagined. When you fear an assailant who is threatening you with a knife, for instance, the object of your fear is the assailant. In experiencing such fear, your heart may race and your breathing may be labored. As a result, the experience may include your feeling your heart racing and your being short of breath. But these feelings, though part of your experience of fear, don't change what the object of your fear is. It is still the assailant, in this case, and not your racing heart or your shortness of breath. If it were either of the latter, then we would expect the fear to move you to look for some heart medicine or an inhaler rather than to move you to flee or hide from the assailant. That it does not, that it moves you to flee or hide from the assailant, is sufficient to show that, whether or not we regard the feelings to which the emotion gives rise as perceptions of the body, they do not exhibit the intentionality of the emotion.

Philosophers who are firmly in the neo-Jamesian camp have recognized that Damasio's thesis that the feelings of an emotion are internal perceptions of bodily changes fails on its own to yield a satisfactory account of the intentionality of emotions. Remaining faithful to James in taking emotions to consist in feelings of bodily changes, they have offered different accounts of the intentionality of these feelings. Here is an example due to Jesse Prinz (2004, pp. 52–78; see also Robinson, 2006). The feelings of bodily changes that emotions, on James's account, consist in, besides being perceptions of those changes, are also representations of properties related to their subjects' vital interests. Feelings of grief, for instance, represent loss; feelings of shame represent unworthiness of others' esteem; feelings of pity represent undeserved suffering; and so forth. That the feelings emotions consist in represent these properties is what explains their intentionality. The explanation requires some spelling out, however, to be grasped.

Accordingly, emotions are said to be mental representations of these properties in a special sense of the term "representation". On this sense, a mental state S represents something O (an object, a property, a state of affairs, etc.) just in case two conditions hold. First, O must be the sort of thing that reliably causes mental states of the type to which S belongs. That is, in the jargon of the theory of perception in psychology, S must carry information about O. Examples of one thing's carrying information about another are drooping leaves on a plant, which because they are a sign of dehydration, carry information about the plant's lack of water, and wet pavement on city streets, which, because it is a sign of rain, carry information about its having rained. Consequently, using this piece of jargon, we can restate the first condition as follows: S must carry information about O. Second, it must be possible for S to be misleading. Specifically, it must be possible for S to carry information about O that is erroneous because the cause of S is not O or anything similar to O. For this second condition to be met it is necessary that S be a mental state of a type instances of which regularly further some vital interest of their subject in virtue of their being caused by things like O, for in that case we can understand S as serving a function in the life of its subject and of its subject's being misled by S if it is not caused by O or anything like O. Thus, sour smells carry information about their source. In the case of eggs, for instance, the information the smell carries would be that the eggs are rotten. Yet because sulfur has the same smell, it would in circumstances in which one could easily attribute it to rotten eggs carry erroneous information.

It is clear that emotions, on James's account of them, satisfy these two conditions. First, the feelings an emotion consists in carry information about the object whose perception excites the bodily changes that, on James's account, produce those feelings. The feelings carry information about this object since objects of this type reliably cause such feelings when they are perceived by their subject. For example, because acting wrongly reliably causes feelings of guilt in someone with a conscience, the feelings carry information about his action. Second, it is possible for the feelings an emotion consists in to carry erroneous information, for they may have other causes than those on whose reliability their carrying information depends. A person brought up in a strict household, for example, may feel guilt over leaving food on his dinner plate because his parents, out of misplaced concern for waste, enforced a rule about eating every last morsel of food served one at dinner. In this case his guilt feelings are misleading because the information they carry is that his action is wrong, and there is nothing wrong with leaving some food on one's plate if one has eaten enough to satisfy one's hunger. Feelings of guilt, then, as illustrated by this example are mental representations. They represent wrongful action and sometimes misrepresent such action. And, more generally, emotions are mental representations. They represent properties related to their subjects' vital interests that are detectable through the feelings the emotions consist in. In this way, we can identify emotions with feelings of bodily changes and at the same time understand their intentionality. Indeed, the feelings count as non-cognitive evaluations. Or so the neo-Jamesians argue.

Yet this account of the intentionality of emotions, like Damasio's, misidentifies what it aims to explain. Emotions, to repeat, are intentional states in virtue of being directed at or toward something in the world, real or imagined. Take again the example of fear of an assailant who is threatening you with a knife. The assailant is the object of your fear, and the intentionality of the emotion consists in its orienting you toward him. On the alternative neo-Jamesian account we are considering, by contrast, the fear consists in feelings that represent danger. Nothing in this relation of representation, however, implies that these feelings are directed at or toward any object in the world, real or imagined. Nothing in the relation implies that they orient you toward the threat you are facing. In particular, even though the assailant is the object about which the feelings carry information in the sense of "information" borrowed from the theory of perception, nothing in the relation implies that the feelings are directed toward him. For their carrying information about him just means that he, being dangerous, is a reliable cause of such feelings, and his being a reliable cause of the feelings implies nothing about the feelings being directed at or toward him. Obviously nothing changes if the information they carry about the object is erroneous, if for instance you mistook a deliveryman with a cell phone for an assailant wielding a knife. We have no more reason to regard the feelings in this case to be directed at or toward their cause than we had in the case of correct information. The feelings, in either case, represent danger exactly as the sound made by an alarm that is part of a home security system represents a home invasion. Just as the alarm's sound is not directed at or toward whoever sets off the alarm, so the feelings are not directed at or toward the assailant or anyone, like the deliveryman, mistaken for one.

The upshot is that the feelings do not explain whatever action you take in response to the threat you face. Since they merely represent danger and are not directed at the threat, they do not guide you in your dealings with it. In particular, they are not an evaluation you make in reaction to it. To identify them as such is to mischaracterize them. They no more count as an evaluation of something than the sound of a home security alarm counts as an evaluation of something. They are the effects of bodily changes and have no direct role in explaining further actions that follow upon those changes. Like James's account, then, emotions on this neo-Jamesian alternative are epiphenomenal. The alternative's failure to explain the intentionality of emotions simply draws attention to this fact. It draws attention, that is, to the fact that what it does explain is entirely consistent with James's view and adds nothing significant to it.

# VI

A rather different proposal for using feelings to understand the intentionality of emotions is due to Peter Goldie, 2000. Like the neo-Jamesians, Goldie takes feelings to be an essential element of the experience of emotion. At the same time, he does not identify these feelings with feelings of bodily changes. Hence, his proposal lies outside of James's theory. Goldie's thesis is that an experience of emotion is an intentional state that consists in part in feelings toward the emotion's object. These feelings are themselves intentional, and for that reason they are not identical with the feelings produced by the bodily changes that occur during an experience of emotion. Further, being intentional, these feelings are integral to the intentionality of the emotion that they partly constitute. One cannot, Goldie holds, treat them in abstraction from the latter as if they were a separable part. Attempts to separate the two by, say, distinguishing between the phenomenal or subjective character of the emotion's object and its cognitive or objective character are misguided. While it is easy to suppose "first" that one can understand the intentionality of an emotion by specifying the emotion's object and those features of it by virtue of which the emotion is an appropriate response and to suppose "second" that the features are conceivable independently of any feelings, Goldie denies this supposition. He holds, instead, that the intentionality includes as well how these features, as features of the object, appear to the subject. Such an appearance, Goldie maintains, is colored by the feelings toward the object that are an essential element of the experience.

Clearly, Goldie's proposal represents a different challenge from that of the neo-Jamesians to the concept of emotion that Freud introduced. On Freud's concept, the emotion's intentionality is distinct from any of the emotion's associated feelings. It thus makes it possible to include unconscious emotions in a theory of the mind, for it allows one to deny that emotions are identical with or consist partly in feelings. But if the intentionality of emotions is itself determined by feelings the subject has toward the object, then Freud's concept must be abandoned. On Goldie's proposal, Freud's concept gives at best an incomplete account of an emotion's intentionality.

The challenge, it should be evident, is not that Freud's concept excludes the possibility of there being feelings toward an object, though of course to maintain the concept one must understand such feelings as manifestations of an emotion rather than as constituents of it. The concept no more excludes the possibility of such feelings than it excludes the possibility of behavior toward an object. And nothing in Freud's concept brings the latter into doubt. Nothing in it, that is, raises any doubts about our common description of behavior that expresses an emotion as behavior toward the emotion's object. Thus, when someone laughs at a joke, his laughter expresses his amusement at the joke. Similarly, when he shakes his fist at some antagonist, his behavior expresses his anger toward that antagonist. So too, when feelings express an emotion, they may be felt toward the object of the emotion. They too may be intentional on Freud's concept.

The challenge is to the implicit separation, on Freud's concept, of the intentionality of the emotion from the feelings that go into an experience of emotion. Yet the thesis that the features of an emotion's object by virtue of which one can understand the emotion as an appropriate response to the object must include their phenomenal character appears to be too strong even if one sets aside the possibility of unconscious emotions. To be sure, some emotions are such that one cannot understand them as appropriate responses to their object without including among the features of the objects in virtue of which they are appropriate responses features that are phenomenal or subjective. Horror, for example, is an emotion the object of which is typically something grisly or gruesome, and there is no understanding of what is grisly or gruesome apart from how grisly or gruesome things make one feel. Similarly, disgust at something that is foul or offensive to the senses, disgust at scum one suddenly finds oneself swimming in, is an emotion whose object would not be well understood if how scum feels when one comes into contact with it were omitted from the features that make it an appropriate object of disgust. But the intentionality of emotions whose objects are more abstract, disappointment, say, at not being hired for a job one had applied for and was keen on getting or embarrassment at confusing one's guest with his brother seems fully understandable without bringing in any phenomenal features. Indeed, it is unclear how either event could be better understood as the object of disappointment or embarrassment in these cases. What this observation suggests, then, is that Goldie's proposal does not so much challenge Freud's concept as remind us that some and perhaps many emotions, while distinct from the feelings that express them, cannot be understood apart from those feelings.

## References

DAMASIO, A. (1995). *Descartes' Error*. New York: Avon Books.

DEIGH, J. (1994). "Cognitivism in the Theory of Emotions", *Ethics* 104: 824–54, reprinted in *Emotions, Values, and the Law*.

—— (2001). "Emotions: The Legacy of James and Freud", *International Journal of Psychoanalysis* 82: 1247–56, reprinted in *Emotions, Values, and the Law*.

—— (2008). *Emotions, Values, and the Law*. New York: Oxford University Press.

FREUD, S. (1915). *The Unconscious. The Standard Edition of the Complete Psychological Works of Sigmund Freud (S.E.)*, vol. 14, ed. and tr. by J. Strachey, London: Hogarth Press, 1981.

—— (1923). *The Ego and the Id. S.E.*, vol. 19.

—— (1924). *The Economic Problem of Masochism. S.E.*, vol. 19.

GOLDIE, P. (2000). *The Emotions: A Philosophical Exploration*. Oxford: Oxford University Press.

HUME, D. (1978). *A Treatise of Human Nature*, ed. L. A. Selby-Bigge. Oxford: Clarendon.

JAMES, W. (1950). *The Principles of Psychology*, vols. 1 & 2. New York: Dover.

LEAR, J. (1990). *Love and its Place in Nature: A Philosophical Interpretation of Freudian Psychoanalysis*. New York: Farrar, Strauss, and Giroux.

LOCKE, J. (1975). *An Essay Concerning Human Understanding*, ed. P. H. Nidditch. Oxford: Clarendon.

NUSSBAUM, M. (1994). *The Therapy of Desire: Theory and Practice in Hellenistic Ethics*. Princeton, NJ: Princeton University Press.

—— (2001). *Upheavals of Thought: The Intelligence of Emotions*. Cambridge: Cambridge University Press.

PRINZ, J. (2004). *Gut Reactions: A Perceptual Theory of Emotion*. Oxford: Oxford University Press.

PUTNAM, H. (1975). "The Meaning of Meaning", in *Mind, Language and Reality: Philosophical Papers*, vol. 2. Cambridge: Cambridge University Press.

ROBERTS, R. (2003). *Emotions: An Aid in Moral Psychology*. Cambridge: Cambridge University Press.

Robinson, J. (2006). *Deeper than Reason: Emotion and its Role in Literature, Music and Art.* Oxford: Oxford University Press.

Rozin, P. and Fallon, A. (1987). "A Perspective on Disgust", *Psychological Review* 94: 23–41.

Schacter, S. and Singer, J. (1962). "Cognition, Social, and Physiological Determinants of Emotional State", *Psychological Review* 69: 379–99.

Solomon, R. (1976). *The Passions.* New York: Doubleday.

CHAPTER 2

...................................................................

# THE THING
# CALLED EMOTION

...................................................................

## AARON BEN-ZE'EV

THE question "What is an emotion?" has haunted philosophers and psychologists for many years. The typical replies proposed to this question reduce emotions to one of their components, such as state, capacity, feeling, or action readiness, or to something else, such as brain state. The perplexity surrounding this issue indicates that simple answers will be of little value.

In order to capture the complexities and subtleties of emotions, I use two major methods: (a) describing a typical emotion, and (b) defining emotions as a mental mode. In different ways, both approaches answer the question "What is an emotion?" By combining the two approaches, we might arrive at a more comprehensive understanding of the nature of emotions.[1]

## 2.1 DESCRIBING TYPICAL EMOTIONS

...................................................................

Emotions are probably the most complex mental phenomena, as they involve all types of mental entities and states that belong to various ontological levels. In light of their complexity, the description of emotions requires the use of conceptual

---

[1] The first approach is used in Ben-Ze'ev, 2000, and the second in Ben-Ze'ev, 2004b.

tools that are sensitive to diversity and complexity. One such tool is the use of multidisciplinary perspectives and multi-levels descriptions of the various characteristics and components of emotions.

Another conceptual tool for coping with the complexity of emotions is that of using prototype categories. Unlike a binary category, which provides a clear criterion that constitutes the sufficient and necessary conditions for membership, a membership in a prototypical category is determined by an item's degree of similarity to the best example in the category: the greater the similarity, the higher the degree of membership. Contrary to a binary category, a prototypical one has neither clear-cut boundaries nor an equal degree of membership.[2] Emotions in general, as well as each particular emotion separately, constitute prototypical categories. Inclusion is determined by the degree of similarity to the most typical case. Membership in the general category of emotions, as well as membership in the general category of a particular emotion, is a matter of degree rather than an all-or-nothing affair. The typical aspects of emotional experiences are fully manifest in prototypical examples; in less typical examples, these characteristics occur in a less developed form and some may even be absent. Hence, there is no single essence which is a necessary and sufficient condition for all emotions, and no simple definition of emotions or even whether one type of emotion exists.[3]

Once we have acknowledged that this is in the nature of emotions, the importance of philosophical attempts to define emotions decreases. From this approach, the answer to the question "What is an emotion?" should be a description of a typical emotion. In this regard, I claim that typical emotions are generated by perceived significant changes and that their focus of concern is personal and comparative. Typical emotional characteristics are: instability, great intensity, partiality, and brief duration. Basic components are cognition, evaluation, motivation, and feelings.

## 2.1.1 The typical emotional cause: Change

Emotions typically occur when we perceive positive or negative *significant changes in our personal situation*, or in the situation of those related to us. A major positive or negative change significantly improves or interrupts a stable situation relevant to our concerns. Like burglar alarms going off when an intruder appears, emotions signal that something needs attention. When no attention is needed, the signaling system can be switched off. We respond to the unusual by paying attention to it. A change cannot persist for a very long time; after a while, the system construes the

---

[2] Lakoff, 1987; Rosch, 1977, 1978.
[3] See, e.g., Russell, 1991; Shaver et al., 1992.

change as a normal state and it excites us no more. Accordingly, sexual response to a familiar partner is less intense than to a novel partner. Indeed, the frequency of sexual activity with one's partner declines steadily as the relationship lengthens, reaching roughly half the frequency after one year of marriage compared with the first month of marriage, and declining more gradually thereafter. Decline has also been found in cohabiting, heterosexual couples and in gay and lesbian couples.[4] Our psychological reality consists of both stable and unstable events. The successful combination of the two gives us emotional excitement as well as a sense of calmness and security; both are crucial for a happy and healthy mental life.

The hypothesis that emotions arise when we perceive a significant change in our situation can be challenged on various accounts.[5] I would like to focus here on the claim that many of our emotions do not arise in response to an emotion-eliciting event but are rather concerned with "the life of the mind"—that is, with what we remember or imagine—and as such they do not relate to an event that constitutes a change in our situation.[6]

I agree that there is no need for an actual physical event in order to elicit an emotion, but there is a need for a change in our psychological environment, which is the environment relevant to emotional experiences. Human life concerns not only—or even mainly—the present but rather, and to a significant extent, the realm of imagined possibilities in both past and future circumstances. It is difficult to act without considering the infinite possibilities—what may be and what might have been. The imaginative capacity forces us to be concerned not only with the present circumstances but also with past and future circumstances. Indeed, people think about the future more than about the past or the present. Many potential events are more pleasurable to imagine than to experience.[7] The "road not taken" is as significant as the one we ultimately choose.

The past and the future are part of our present psychological situation and hence changes that might have occurred or that may still occur in past and future circumstances are highly relevant to our present well-being; hence they have a significant emotional impact upon us. Accordingly, when describing the various intensity variables, I divide them into two major groups, one referring to the perceived impact of the event eliciting the emotional state and the other to the background circumstances of the agents involved in the emotional state. The second group is significant in realizing whether the situation could have been prevented and whether we deserve to be in such a situation. Although the reference to the background circumstances may seem to be redundant in our current situation, it has a great functional value in preventing or

---

[4] Buss, 1994; Metts et al., 1998.
[5] Ben-Ze'ev, 2000: 41–4.
[6] Goldie, 2004.
[7] Gilbert, 2007: 17–18; Roese & Olson, 1995.

encouraging future similar experiences. Indeed, the major variables constituting the background circumstances—that is, accountability, readiness, and deservingness—are of great importance in generating emotional experiences and determining their intensity.

## 2.1.2  The typical emotional concern: A comparative personal concern

Emotions occur when a change is evaluated as relevant to our personal concerns. Concerns are our short- or long-term disposition toward a preference for particular states of the world or of the self. Emotions serve to monitor and safeguard our personal concerns; they give the eliciting event its significance.[8] An important difference between general and emotional changes is that the latter are of great personal significance. Our attention may be directed to any type of change, but in order for the change to generate emotions it must be perceived as having significant implications for us or for those related to us. An emotional change is always related to a certain personal frame of reference against which its significance is evaluated.

Emotional meaning is mainly comparative. The emotional environment contains not only what is and what will be experienced but also all that could be or that one wishes will be experienced. For the emotional system, all such possibilities are posited as simultaneously available and are compared with each other. The importance of the comparative concern in emotions is also connected with the central role of changes in generating emotions. An event can be perceived as a significant change only when compared against a certain background framework.

The comparison underlying emotional significance encompasses the mental construction of the availability of an alternative situation. The more available the alternative—that is, the closer the imagined alternative is to reality—the more intense the emotion. Thus, the fate of someone who dies in an airplane crash after switching flights evokes a stronger emotion than that of a fellow traveler who was booked on the flight all along. Greater availability indicates greater instability and the presence of significant changes. In fact, a crucial element in intense emotions is the imagined condition of "it could have been otherwise".

---

[8] Nussbaum, 2001.

## 2.1.3  Typical characteristics

Instability, great intensity, a partial perspective, and relative brevity can be considered as the basic characteristics of typical emotions. This characterization refers to "hot emotions", which are the typical intense emotions. The more moderate emotions lack some of the characteristics associated with typical emotions.

*Instability.* In light of the crucial role that changes play in generating emotions, instability of the mental (as well as the physiological) system is a basic characteristic of emotions. Emotions indicate a transition in which the preceding context has changed but no new context has yet stabilized. Emotions are like storms and fire—they are unstable states that signify some agitation; they are intense, occasional, and limited in duration. The opposite of being emotional is being indifferent. Contrary to emotional people, indifferent people are unresponsive to and detached from changes in their situation; they remain stable in the face of such changes. The life of people low in emotional intensity is characterized by endurance, evenness, and lack of fluctuation. The life of people high in emotional intensity is characterized by abruptness, changeableness, and volatility.[9]

*Great intensity.* One of the typical characteristics of emotions is their relatively great intensity. Emotions are intense reactions. In emotions, the mental system has not yet adapted to the given change, and, due to its significance, the change requires the mobilization of many resources. No wonder that emotions are associated with urgency and heat. In emotions there is no such thing as a minor concern; if the concern is minor, it is not emotional. A typical characteristic of emotions is their magnifying nature: everything looms larger when we are emotional. The fact that our colleague earns 2 percent more than we do is not a minor issue in the eyes of envious people: it is perceived to reflect the undeserved inferior position in which they are situated. Similarly, the slightly smaller size of a woman's breast is not considered a minor imperfection by the many women who undergo breast implants. Every emotional concern is perceived to be a profound one.

*Partiality.* Emotions are *partial* in two basic senses: they are focused on a *narrow* target, such as one person or very few people, and they express a *personal* and interested perspective. Emotions direct and color our attention by selecting what attracts and holds it; in this sense, emotions are similar to heat-seeking missiles, having no other concern but to find the heat-generating target. Emotions address practical concerns from a personal perspective. We cannot assume an emotional state toward everyone or toward those with whom we have no relation whatsoever. Focusing upon fewer objects increases the resources available for each and hence increases emotional intensity, just as a laser beam focuses upon a very narrow area and consequently achieves high intensity at that point. Emotions express our values and preferences; hence, they cannot be indiscriminate.

---

[9] Larsen & Diener, 1987: 27.

The partial nature of emotions is expressed in romantic love in the demand for exclusivity of the beloved. We cannot be indiscriminate in whom we love. We cannot love everyone; our romantic love must be directed at one or a few people. Since romantic love, like other emotions, necessitates limiting parameters such as time and attention, the number of its objects must be limited as well. We have greater resources to offer when we limit the number of emotional objects to which we are committed. The beloved has emotional significance that no other person has; the beloved fulfills much of our emotional environment. This limitation in the number of possible emotional objects forces us to focus upon those who are close to us. When we hear of the death of thousands of people in an earthquake occurring in a remote (that is, from our vantage point) part of the world, our emotional response comes nowhere near the intensity of our grief at the death of someone close to us, nor does it even approach the level of feeling we experience in watching the suffering of a single victim of that same earthquake on television (thereby establishing some affinity with that particular victim). Television news coverage maintains our emotional interest by describing global situations in terms of particular stories about individual people or families.

In light of the partial nature of emotions, we may reduce emotional intensity by broadening our scope, and increase the intensity by further limiting it. Counting to ten before venting our anger enables us to adopt a broader perspective, which may reduce anger. A broader perspective is typical of people who can calmly consider multiple aspects of a situation; it is obviously not typical of people who experience an intense emotional reaction to the situation. Emotional partiality does not diminish emotional complexity and diversity; a focused and partial attitude may express complex phenomena and be conveyed in multiple forms.

*Brevity.* Typical emotions are essentially states with relative brevity. The mobilization of all resources to focus on one event cannot last forever. A system cannot be unstable for a long period and still function normally; it may explode due to continuous increase in emotional intensity. A change cannot persist a very long time; after a while, the system construes the change as a normal and stable situation. If emotions were to endure for a long time regardless of what was occurring in our environment, they would not have an adaptive value. The exact duration of an emotion is a matter for dispute: depending on the type of emotion and the circumstances, it can last from a few seconds to a few hours and sometimes even longer. The fact that emotions are transient states does not imply that their impact is merely transient—a brief emotional state can have profound and long-lasting behavioral implications.

## 2.1.4  Basic Components

In addition to the typical characteristics discussed in the previous section, that is, instability, intensity, partiality, and brevity, there are other relevant features which might help us to understand emotions. One such feature is the division of emotions into four basic components, namely, cognition, evaluation, motivation, and feeling. The difference between typical characteristics and basic components is that characteristics are properties of the whole emotional experience, whereas components express a conceptual division of the elements of this experience. It is arguable that one could perhaps find a few relevant characteristics other than those I have discussed; however, the conceptual division of emotions into four components is more comprehensive and is supposed to cover all possible components.

I consider intentionality and feeling to be the two basic mental dimensions. Intentionality refers to a subject–object relation, whereas feeling expresses the subject's own state of mind. When a person is in love with someone, the feeling dimension surfaces in a particular feeling, say a thrill, which is experienced when they are together; the intentional dimension is expressed in the person's cognition of her beloved, her evaluation of his attributes, and her desires toward him. Intentionality is the relation of "being about something". It involves our cognitive ability to separate ourselves from the surrounding stimuli in order to create a meaningful subject–object relation. The intentional dimension includes several references to objects, such as those involved in perception, memory, thought, dreams, imagination, desires, and emotions.

The intentional dimension in emotions can be divided into three components: cognitive, evaluative, and motivational. The cognitive component consists of information about the given circumstances; the evaluative component assesses the personal significance of this information; the motivational component addresses our desires, or readiness to act, in these circumstances. Neither of these three intentional components nor the feeling dimension are separate entities or states. Emotions do not entail the separate performance of four varieties of activity: knowing, evaluating, desiring, and feeling. All four are distinct aspects of a typical emotional experience.

The cognitive component supplies the required information about a given situation. No emotional attitude toward something can emerge without some information about it. The cognitive component in emotions is often *distorted*. This is due to several related features typical of emotions: (a) partiality, (b) closeness, and (c) an intense feeling dimension. Emotional partiality contradicts the broad and impartial perspective involved in intellectual and scientific knowledge. When one does not see the whole picture, distorted claims may be adopted. The partial nature of emotions is compatible with great closeness, which in turn often distorts the cognitive content in emotions. When we look at someone from a short distance, our vision is fragmented and often distorted. We need some distance in order to achieve a perspective that encompasses multiple aspects of the object and thereby makes the perspective less fragmented. However, keeping a distance is contrary to the involved and intimate perspective typical of emotions. The intense feeling dimension in emotions often tends to override our ability to make sound cognitive assessments. In intense feelings, some of our intellectual faculties no longer function normally. All the above may function as obstacles to adequate knowledge of our emotional context. However, the unique nature of emotions has also some cognitive advantages. While being close, you may understand better some aspects of the situation you are in. Moreover, emotional arousal increases attentional capacity. Accordingly, emotions typically increase memory.[10]

The evaluative component is extremely important in emotions. Every emotion entails a certain evaluation. In a state devoid of an evaluative component, or one in which its weight is marginal, we are indifferent. In emotions we are not indifferent, as we have a significant personal stake. The evaluative component appraises the "cold" information presented by the cognitive component, in terms of its implications for personal well-being. The presence of an evaluative component is what distinguishes the emotion of hope from that of expectation: we do not hope for something unless we evaluate it as being somehow favorable, whereas our expectation of something entails no comparable evaluation. For similar reasons, surprise, when considered merely as a cognitive state, is not an emotion.[11] The distinction between cognition and evaluation should not, however, be overstated. Quite often we are unable to separate the cognitive and evaluative components from a certain belief, for example, from the belief that the situation is dangerous for us.

The *evaluative component* intrinsic to a certain emotional state should not be confused with *moral evaluation of the entire state*. Thus, pleasure-in-others'-misfortune involves a positive evaluation of the misfortune of others, and hence its feeling component is agreeable. However, this emotion is often evaluated as negative from a moral viewpoint. Similarly, pity involves a negative evaluation of others' misfortune, and hence its feeling component is disagreeable, even though it is often considered to be morally positive.

The motivational component refers to the desire or readiness to maintain or change present, past, or future circumstances. In some emotions, such as anger and sexual desire, the desire is typically manifested in overt behavior; in other emotions, such as envy and hope, the behavioral element is less in evidence and appears merely as a desire. Emotions are not theoretical states; they involve a practical concern, associated with a readiness to act. Since emotions are evaluative attitudes, involving a positive or a negative stance toward the object, they also entail either taking action or being disposed to act in a manner which is compatible

---

[10] Ben-Ze'ev, 2000: 57.
[11] Bedford, 1957; Ortony et al., 1988.

with the evaluation. Emotions typically express our most profound values and attitudes; as such, they often express not merely superficial involvement but deep commitment.

The feeling dimension is a primitive mode of consciousness associated with our own state. It is the lowest level of consciousness; unlike higher levels of awareness, such as those found in perception, memory, and thinking, the feeling dimension has no meaningful cognitive content. It expresses our own state, but is not in itself directed at this state or at any other object. Since this dimension is a mode of consciousness, one cannot be unconscious of it; there are no unfelt feelings. One indication for the absence of the intentional dimension in feelings is that we cannot speak of our reasons for experiencing a feeling, as we can in the case of emotions. There is no point in asking people about their reasons for having a toothache, although it does make sense to ask about the causes of such feelings. It is therefore futile to try to justify or criticize feelings in the same way as we do with emotions. We cannot reason people out of their toothache as we might reason them out of their hatred. Unlike emotions, feelings are not subject to normative appraisal.

The homogeneous and basic nature of feelings makes it difficult, though perhaps not impossible, to describe them. Indeed, there are few words for feelings, and we often have to resort to metaphors and other figures of speech in referring to them. Many feelings have only an "as if" recognizability ("It feels as if it is a lemon"; "It feels as if a knife stabbed me").[12] It is not easy to identify the varying characteristics of the feeling component. No doubt feelings have intensity, duration, and some have location as well; but what about other qualities? The qualities of being painful or pleasurable are obvious. Some level of pleasantness or unpleasantness, albeit often of low intensity, is experienced by most people most of the time. In addition to pleasure and displeasure, the continuum of arousal may be a common aspect of the feeling dimension.

Typical mental states in human beings consist of both intentional and feeling dimensions. Thus, seeing something often evokes pleasant or unpleasant feelings relating to the content of what we see. The relationships between the two dimensions vary in type and degree for different mental states. Whereas in emotions both dimensions are central, in most mental states only one of these is dominant. For example, the feeling dimension is dominant in painful experiences, thirst, hunger, and in affective disorders. In this sense, emotional experiences are more complex than other mental experiences.

Sometimes two different emotions, such as grief and pride, can be distinguished by virtue of the feeling component bound up with them. In other instances, the feeling component may be inadequate in this respect. The same emotion, such as love, may share a variety of feelings, and the same feeling may be shared by different

---

[12] Solomon, 1993: 10.

emotions, like shame, remorse, regret, and guilt. Although many emotions embrace a variety of feelings within their scope, their range is generally restricted to a particular set of characteristic feelings; in any case, not every feeling can be linked with every emotion. Moreover, feeling cannot be the basis for distinguishing the precise nature of the emotional object. When I hear my favorite music and greet my beloved at the same time, the feeling of a thrill cannot by itself identify the emotional object; we need some intentional aspects to be involved—in particular, the evaluative one. The feeling component may serve to distinguish between some emotions, for example, between negative and positive components, but empirical studies indicate that it is impossible to discriminate reliably between the emotions on the basis of the feeling dimension alone. For example, in one study, disappointment, envy, and shame were found to have a similar proportion of pleasure and arousal, yet they are clearly different emotions.[13]

The above description of causes, focus of concern, characteristics, and components of emotions provides a general picture of a typical emotion. In order to complete this picture, I would like to describe two further major emotional aspects: variables of emotional intensity and the various phenomena that, together with emotions, constitute the broader realm of affective phenomena.

## 2.1.5 Variables of emotional intensity

Emotional intensity is determined by several variables that may be divided into two major groups, one referring to the perceived impact of the event eliciting the emotional state and the other to background circumstances of the agents involved in the emotional state. The major variables constituting the event's impact are the strength, reality, and relevance of the event; the major variables constituting the background circumstances are accountability, readiness, and deservingness.

The event's *strength* is a major factor in determining the intensity of the emotional experience. It refers, for example, to the extent of the misfortune in pity, the extent of our inferiority in envy, the level of damage we suffer in anger, or the extent of beauty of the beloved. A positive correlation usually exists between the strength of the event as we perceive it and emotional intensity: the stronger the event, the more intense the emotion. Though positive, the correlation is not always linear: a stronger event may result in a more intense emotion, but the increase in intensity is not always proportional to the increase in the event's strength. In very strong events, an additional increase in their strength will hardly increase emotional intensity, which is anyway quite high and almost at its peak.

[13] Reisenzein, 1994.

This kind of correlation is also typical of other variables. The typical curve of emotional intensity rises up to a point with increases in the given variable; from this point on, emotional intensity hardly changes with an increase in the given variable.

The second major variable constituting the event's impact is its degree of *reality*: the more we believe the situation to be real, the more intense the emotion. The importance of the degree of reality in inducing powerful emotions is illustrated by the fact that a very strong event, which may be quite relevant to our well-being, may not provoke excitement if we succeed in considering it as fantasy: the emotional intensity decreases accordingly. Thus, despite the horrifying impact of a potential nuclear holocaust, many people do not allow this to upset them, since they do not consider the event to be a real possibility.[14] In analyzing the notion of "emotional reality" two major senses should be discerned: (a) ontological, and (b) epistemological. The first sense refers to whether the event actually exists or is merely imaginary. The second sense is concerned with relationships of the event to other events. The first sense expresses the "correspondence criterion" of truth where a claim is seen as true if its content corresponds to an existing event in the world. The second sense is related to the "coherence criterion" of truth in which truth is determined in light of whether the given claim is coherent with other claims we hold. In analyzing the perceived reality associated with our emotional experiences, the ontological sense is expressed in the actual existence of the emotional object, and the epistemological sense is typically expressed in its vividness. The degree of reality is highest when the object is real in both senses. Interesting cases are those with a conflict between the two senses, for example, when a fictional character is more vivid than a person we have just met. Both persons are real for us, and it is not obvious as to who may induce greater emotional intensity.

The third major variable constituting the event's impact is its *relevance*: the more relevant the event, the greater the emotional significance and hence the intensity. Relevance is of utmost importance in determining the significance of an emotional experience. What is irrelevant to us cannot be emotionally significant for us. Emotional relevance typically refers either (a) to the achievement of our goals, or (b) to our self-esteem. Goal relevance measures the extent to which a given change promotes or hinders our performance or the attainment of specific significant goals. In light of the social nature of emotions, our self-esteem is an important emotional issue. We do not envy trees for their height or lions for their strength, since these are irrelevant to our personal self-esteem. The relevance component restricts the emotional impact to areas which are particularly significant to us.

---

[14] Frijda, 1988: 352; 1986: 206.

Emotional relevance is closely related to *emotional closeness*. Events close to us in time, space, or effect are usually emotionally relevant and significant. Characterizing the relationship between relevance and closeness is not a straightforward task. Some may perceive them as different headings for the same thing. Others may conceive either relevance or closeness to be the basic factor. I believe that relevance is more directly connected with emotional significance than closeness. Relevance is defined as "having significant and demonstrable bearing upon the matter at hand"; closeness is defined as "being near in time, space, effect, or degree".[15] A close object is usually emotionally significant because it is often relevant to our well-being. However, not everyone who lives in our neighborhood is of great emotional significance to us. Spatial proximity does not always lead to emotional significance.

*Accountability* (or *responsibility*), which is the first variable of the group constituting background circumstances of the emotional event, refers to the nature of the agency generating the emotional encounter. Major issues relevant here are: (a) degree of *controllability*, (b) invested *effort*, and (c) *intent*. The greater the degree of controllability there was, the more effort we invested, and the more intended the result was, the more significant the event usually is and the greater the emotional intensity it generates. Thus, people feel more entitled to (or frustrated by) an outcome they have helped to bring about than to (or by) an outcome resulting from the whim of fate or other powerful agents. Quite often a greater degree of accountability does not merely increase emotional intensity but also increases the complexity of emotions because other emotions, such as guilt or regret, also become part of the emotional state.[16]

The variable of controllability, referring to our past control over the circumstances that generated the given emotion, should not be confused with our present control of the emotional circumstances. Whereas a positive correlation exists between emotional intensity and past control, the correlation between emotional intensity and present control is negative. When an event is perceived to be under our personal control, it does not produce as much stress as one perceived to be uncontrollable.[17] A threatening event is perceived to be stronger when we are unable to control its course. The relevant intensity variable here is not controllability, which refers to background circumstances but the event's strength, which refers to the present impact of the event upon us.

The variable of *readiness* measures the cognitive change in our mind; major factors in this variable are unexpectedness (or anticipation) and uncertainty. *Unexpectedness*, which may be measured by how surprised one is by the situation, is widely recognized as central in emotions. Since emotions are generated at the time of sudden change, unexpectedness is typical of emotions and is usually

---

[15] *Webster's New Collegiate Dictionary.*
[16] Folger, 1984; Spinoza, 1677/1985, II49s; Smith & Ellsworth, 1985.
[17] Taylor, 1989: 75–6.

positively correlated with their intensity, at least up to a certain point. We are angrier if we happen to be expecting a contrary result, just as the quite unexpected fulfillment of our wishes is especially sweet. Unexpectedness may be characterized as expressing the gap between the actual situation and the imagined alternative expected by us. When the actual situation is better, pleasant surprise occurs; when it is worse, disappointment or remorse occurs.[18]

A factor related to, but not identical with, unexpectedness is *uncertainty*. We can expect some event to happen but may not be certain of its actual likelihood. Uncertainty is positively correlated with emotional intensity. The more we are certain that the eliciting event will occur, the less we are surprised at its actual occurrence and the lesser the emotional intensity accompanying it. In situations of certainty, the alternative to the situation is perceived as less available and hence emotions are less intense. Spinoza emphasizes this variable, arguing that the wise man "who rightly knows that all things follow from the necessity of the divine nature, and happen according to the eternal laws and rules of nature, will surely find nothing worthy of hate, mockery or disdain, nor anyone whom he will pity".[19] An apparent exception to the positive correlation between uncertainty and emotional intensity is the fear of death. The intensity of this fear seems not to be diminished, and perhaps is even increased, by the certainty of our inevitable death. The explanation of this phenomenon is bound up with the event's highly negative impact on us. Such a significant impact reduces, if not eliminates, the weight of other variables.

The perceived *deservingness* (equity, fairness) of our situation or that of others is of great importance in determining the nature and intensity of emotions. No one wants to be unjustly treated, or to receive what is contrary to one's wish. Even though people disagree about what is just and unjust, most people would like the world to be just. Most people believe, whether explicitly or implicitly, that the world is a benevolent and meaningful place and that the self is a worthwhile person.[20] Accordingly, the feeling of injustice is hard to bear—sometimes even more so than actual hardship caused. When we perceive ourselves to be treated unjustly, or when the world in general is perceived to be unjust, this is perceived as a deviation and generates emotional reactions. The more exceptional the situation, namely, the more the situation deviates from our baseline, the more we consider the negative situation to be unfair or the positive situation to be lucky. In such circumstances, the issue of deservingness is crucial and emotions are intense. In some emotions, such as pity and envy, the variable of deservingness is very important; in others, such as fear, its role is less significant. The characterization of

---

[18] Aristotle, *Rhetoric* 1379a22; Frijda, 1986: 273, 291–5; Lyons, 1980: ch. 7; Ortony et al., 1988: 64–5; Spinoza, 1677/1985: IIIdef.aff.; Vp6s.

[19] 1677/1985: IVp50s.

[20] Aristotle, *Nicomachean Ethics*: 1136b6; Ortony et al., 1988: 77; Spinoza, 1677/1985: IVapp.XV.

deservingness is complex due to its similarity to, yet difference from, moral entitlement. Claims of desert, such as "I deserve to win the lottery", are based on our sense of the value of our attributes and actions; claims based on moral right, such as "she is entitled to receive a raise in her salary", often refer to obligations constitutive of the relationships with other agents. Claims of desert are not necessarily grounded in anyone's obligations but rather in the value persons perceive themselves to deserve.

In assessing the significance of an emotional change, and hence emotional intensity, our *personal make-up* should be taken into consideration. Factors such as personality traits, world views, cultural background, and current personal situation are crucial for determining emotional intensity. Differences in personal make-up may result in assigning different significance to given events, but they do not undermine general regularities concerning a certain intensity variable and emotional intensity. For example, different people may evaluate differently the reality of a given event: some consider the event to pose a real threat to their self-image, while others consider it to be imaginary. Thus, trivial social conversations between married women and other men may be perceived differently by their husbands depending on their personalities and cultural backgrounds. One man may perceive the situation as posing a real threat for him, while another will consider it as posing no real threat at all. The differences in attached significance will result in differences in the intensity of jealousy. However, in both cases the general correlation between the degree of reality and emotional intensity is maintained; the more real the event is perceived to be, the greater the emotional intensity it provokes.

## 2.1.6 The affective realm

In addition to emotions, the affective realm includes other phenomena such as sentiments, moods, affective traits, and affective disorders. As I assume that intentionality and feeling are the two basic mental dimensions, in characterizing the mental aspects of the affective realm, a reference to these basic dimensions is in order. Accordingly, I characterize an affective phenomenon as having an inherent positive or negative evaluation (this is the typical intentional feature) and a significant feeling component. The combination of a valenced aspect, namely, an inherent evaluation, with a significant feeling component is what distinguishes affective phenomena from nonaffective ones. A mere positive or negative evaluation, as is expressed for example in verbal praise, is not an affective attitude; similarly, a mere feeling, such as a tickle, which is devoid of an inherent type of evaluation, is not included within the affective spectrum.

The two suggested characteristics, namely, inherent evaluation and a significant feeling component, may serve not only to distinguish affective from nonaffective phenomena but also to discern the various phenomena within the affective realm. Accordingly, I suggest characterizing the differences between the major types of affective phenomena by referring to (a) the specific or general type of evaluation involved, and (b) the occurrent or dispositional nature of the given phenomenon. An evaluation is an intentional state; one difference between various evaluations concerns the degree of specificity of their intentional object. Some evaluations may focus on a specific object, and others may be more diffuse having quite a general intentional object. The distinction between *occurrent* (actual) and *dispositional* (potential) properties is crucial for describing mental states, as many mental features are not actualized at any given moment. Intentional states, such as beliefs and desires, can be dispositional in the sense that, even if at the moment I do not attend to this belief or desire, I can still be described as having them. This is not the case concerning feelings. I do not have feelings which at the moment I do not feel; feelings do not have such a dispositional nature.

The two suggested criteria for distinguishing the various affective phenomena (that is, the intentional nature of the evaluative stand, and the occurrent or dispositional nature of the given phenomenon) form four possible combinations which can be considered as the basic types of affective phenomena:

1. Specific intentionality, occurrent state—emotions, such as envy, anger, guilt, and sexual desire;
2. Specific intentionality, dispositional state—sentiments, such as enduring love or grief;
3. General intentionality, occurrent state—moods, such as being cheerful, satisfied, "blue", and gloomy;
4. General intentionality, dispositional state—affective traits, such as shyness and enviousness.

Emotions and sentiments have a specific intentional object, whereas the intentional object of moods, affective disorders, and affective traits is general and diffuse. Emotions and moods are essentially occurrent states; sentiments and affective traits are dispositional in nature. These differences are expressed in temporal differences. Emotions and moods, which are occurrent states, are relatively short, whereas sentiments and affective traits, which are essentially dispositional, last for a longer period. Emotions typically last between a few minutes and a few hours, although in some cases they can also be described as lasting seconds or days. Moods usually last for hours, days, weeks, and sometimes even for months. Sentiments last for weeks, months, or even many years. Affective traits can last a lifetime.[21] Affective disorders, such as depression and anxiety, do not clearly fit in

---

[21]  Rosenberg, 1998.

either group of affective phenomena; their intentionality is not as specific as that of emotions, nor as general as that of moods. Furthermore, with regard to the dispositional and occurrent nature, affective disorders are in an intermediate position between emotions and moods, on the one hand, and sentiments and affective traits, on the other hand. I suggest that we explain affective disorders as extreme, or pathological, instances of the above typical cases. For example, when fear takes a very extreme form, it may turn into anxiety and, in a similar vein, sadness may turn into depression.

The proposed description of typical emotions answers, in a sense, the classical question of "What is an emotion?" An emotion is something that is generated by perceived significant changes; its focus of concern is personal and comparative; its major characteristics are instability, great intensity, partiality, and brief duration; and its basic components are cognition, evaluation, motivation, and feelings. In addition to the influence of contextual and personality variables, a typical emotion is usually influenced by variables such as the event's strength, reality, and relevance, and our accountability, readiness, and deservingness in regard to the event. An emotion is part of a greater affective realm, which also includes sentiments, moods, affective traits and affective disorders. Although I find this is a relatively illuminating answer, it still lacks an explanation of the nature of this thing called "an emotion" that is at the essence of all these properties. For this reason, I would like to answer the above question by employing the classical philosophical method—that is, by defining the essence of emotions.

## 2.2 EMOTION AS A MENTAL MODE

The very complexity of emotions has made attempts to define them notoriously problematic. Some definitions of emotions that have been proposed include: mental entities, states, dispositions, capacities, types of intentional reference, and feelings. Furthermore, lay people differ systematically in their implicit theories of emotion: some view emotions as fixed (as do entity theorists), whereas others view emotions as more malleable (in line with incremental theorists).[22] I do not want to get into a discussion concerning the difficulties of each proposal. All these proposals are adequate in the sense that emotions do indeed involve those elements. However, in light of the complexity of emotions, I believe that no single mental element can adequately define emotions. Accordingly, I think that we should define emotions as a general mode of the mental system.

---

[22] Tamir et al., 2007.

The term "mode" has various meanings. The meanings closest to the view presented here are those of a manner of being (*"this is a novel mode of education"*) or doing (*"an emergency mode of operation"*). Mode involves a complex arrangement (*"a mode of living"*) and functioning (*"railroads are an important mode of transportation"*) over time. It is a dynamic, structured form or style of the system, expressing how the mental experience is organized or occurs. A mode indicates the way in which something takes place or is done. It includes a combination of qualities and relationships. A mode is always a manner of something—a certain entity, a living being, a system, and so forth.

An emotion is a general mode (or style) of the mental system. A general mental mode includes various mental elements and expresses a dynamic functioning arrangement of the mental system. The kinds of elements involved in a certain mode and the particular arrangement of these elements constitute the uniqueness of each mode. The emotional mode involves the activation of certain dispositions and the presence of some actualized states. It also includes the operation of various mental capacities and the use of different kinds of intentional references. This mode involves cognition, evaluation, motivation, and feeling.[23]

Other possible modes are the perceptual, imaginative, and intellectual modes. A given mental mode is not necessarily the complete opposite of another mode; they may differ in a few but not all features. For example, perception is found in all modes—although in different forms. Similarly, while feelings are intense in the emotional mode, they are not essential for the perceptual and intellectual modes. Thinking dominates the intellectual mode, but has less influence over the perceptual, imaginative, and emotional modes.

Over the various periods of our life and of the evolutionary development of human beings, each mental mode grows or decreases in dominance. The perceptual mode is dominant in our early childhood and in the primitive stages of human development. The emotional mode might also have been present during these periods, but in a less complex though more intense manner; while this mode is

---

[23] I use the term "mode", which may be considered as archaic, for lack of a better term. In a sense somewhat similar to the one suggested here, Margaret Donaldson (1993) also proposes that the mind consists of various modes. She distinguishes between four modes, which are defined by their loci of concern:

Point mode—locus "here and now"
Line mode—locus "there and then"
Construct mode—locus "somewhere/sometime" (no specific place or time)
Transcendent mode—locus "nowhere" (that is, not in space–time).

Donaldson further distinguishes four major mental components: perception, action, emotion, and thought. In my view, I do not define the various modes in light of their focus of concern but in light of their psychological nature. Nevertheless, the first two modes in Donaldson's view are related to the perceptual mode in my view, and the other two modes in her view to the intellectual mode suggested here. While I believe that perception and thought are mental capacities that are on the same conceptual level, emotions (and probably action as well) are on a different level.

more dominant during our late childhood and adolescence, it is present through-out our life. The intellectual mode is characteristic of more advanced stages of personal and evolutionary development.

Mental modes are not isolated entities but prototypes of various mental phe-nomena: one prototype is typical of our usual everyday situation, the second is typical of abstract thinking associated with scientific, detached calculations, and another is typical of intense, stormy mental experiences. There are many types of phenomena that do not fit perfectly into any of the three prototypes. Moreover, some of the features constituting a mental mode admit of degrees and hence no precise borderline is possible between the various modes. Nevertheless, the description of the prototypes of mental modes has a great explanatory value.

A distinction may be made between general and specific mental modes. A general mode is comprehensive in the sense that it involves most types of mental elements; a specific mode involves only a few mental elements. I believe that the emotional mode is the most comprehensive mode since it typically involves more types of mental elements than any other mode. The perceptual mode is probably the least comprehensive as it does not involve the activation of several mental capacities. The imaginative and intellectual modes are in between. The intellectual mode may not include, for instance, mental elements such as perception, feelings, motivation, and evaluation. Certainly, these elements may be found in some occurrences of the intellectual mode, but they are not constitutive or even typical of it. Similarly, thinking is not constitutive in the imaginative mode.

We may distinguish between elements that are constitutive of a certain mode and elements that are frequently associated with it. Examples of constitutive elements of the emotional mode are cognition, evaluation, motivation, feeling, instability, great intensity, partiality, and brief duration. Specific actions are typically asso-ciated with emotions but are not constitutive elements of it; but action readiness is a constitutive element. Thinking is a constitutive element of the intellectual mode; feeling, motivation, and evaluation are sometimes associated with this mode, but this mode is sometimes present without them.

A mental mode is typically complex, structured, episodic, and dynamic.[24] It is complex since it involves many elements; it is structured in the sense that the elements are arranged in a certain organized manner; and it is dynamic as it typically undergoes changes in the particular manifestations of its constitutive elements, in the kinds of associated elements involved, or in the relationships among them. A mental mode is also episodic since its duration is limited.

The various mental modes can be distinguished on the basis of a few categories, such as basic psychological features, basic types of information-processing mech-anisms, and basic logical principles of information processing. The category of

---

[24] See also Goldie, 2000: 12–13.

psychological features may be divided into characteristics such as complexity, instability, and intensity, and into components such as evaluation and motivation. Schematic mechanisms and deliberative mechanisms are examples of information-processing mechanisms. Logical principles are those determining the significance of events—for example, whether change or stability is of greater significance. The number and types of the general mental modes are open to dispute, since classification can be arranged in various ways. I propose to categorize these modes as the perceptual, imaginative, emotive, and intellectual modes.

The initial mental mode is the perceptual one, which includes sensation and sense perception. Sensation may be considered as the most primitive form of mental capacity. In sensation we are only aware of changes in our own body. Sensation may be characterized as a sign rather than a cognitive description: it does not describe the changes we are undergoing but merely indicates their presence. Despite the primitive nature of sensation, its survival value is enormous. Sensory awareness of changes in our body is crucial for survival as it forces us not to be indifferent to changes. Indeed, those very few people who, because of illness, lack sensation are in real danger every moment of their lives. Sensation is not an intentional capacity since it is not directed at some object and has no cognitive content. Intentional capacities emerged later when the organism was able to be aware not only of changes in its own body but also of the circumstances responsible for these changes. The first intentional capacities to emerge are perceptual abilities in which we separate the stimuli impinging on our sensory receptors and create a perceptual environment as a mental object. While possessing merely perceptual capacities, we are restricted to the limits of our body. The development of further intentional capacities, such as memory, imagination, and thought, enables us to be aware of things which are not present and to consider factors beyond our immediate environment.[25]

The main mental mode that evolves after perception is imagination. Imagination presupposes not merely perceptual capacities, which provide the raw materials for the imaginary content, but also the ability to retain this content when the actual object is no longer, or never has been, present. In this sense, perception logically precedes imagination.

Imagination may be broadly characterized as a capacity to consider possibilities that are not actually present to the senses. In this broad characterization, memory and thinking are types of imagination, since in both we consider such possibilities. A narrower characterization of imagination takes it to extend the perceptual content beyond the limits of the present, considering also past, future, and possible circumstances. The evolutionary advantages of being able to respond to imaginary events are obvious. For example, it enables us to avoid dangers rather than merely reacting to their effects upon us and to pursue positive goals rather

[25] Ben-Ze'ev, 1993; Ben-Ze'ev & Goussinsky, 2008.

than waiting for them to occur. In the narrower sense of imagination, in which imagination is a type of extended perception, imagination is essentially passive—we envision the event, not present for our perception, as if it is present to our mind's eyes.

Thinking, which is the central capacity in the intellectual mode, is different from the other imaginary capacities in the sense that it does not merely look at a perceptual content but rather analyses it. Whereas in imagination the active part of the agent was extending the framework in which the perceptual content is present, in thinking we also find the critical examination of this content. This capacity involves higher and more complex cognitive processes.

The emotive mode is the most comprehensive and complex mode, in part because that it is the only mode in which all (or almost all) the constitutive capacities of the other modes are also part of its own constitutive capacities. Thus, the most primitive capacity of sensation is expressed in the capacity of feeling, which is a type of sensation and is constitutive of emotions. As emotions are extended over time, the emotive mode comprises the mental capacities of perception, imagination, and thinking. The emotive mode is also the most dynamic mode as it involves all activities typical of the other modes. Such a variety of activities and attitudes make the equilibrium of this mode extremely fragile; hence its dynamic and episodic nature.

As the emotional mode consists of capacities constitutive of all other modes, it has developed alongside the other modes. We can observe emotional reactions even in creatures that have hardly any imaginative or intellectual capacities. However, those emotional experiences are substantially different from human experiences, where thoughts play a crucial role. There are certain human emotional experiences that probably do not exist in animals (or exist in such a primitive form that they could scarcely be given the same name); examples of these include emotions such as regret, pleasure-in-others' -misfortune, and perhaps romantic love as well. Even emotions such as anger and fear, which appear to be common to humans and animals, are quite different in the two cases.

The role of the agent is most significant in the emotional mode, as the agent has to decide between various, often conflicting possibilities and the criteria that should be used for such decisions are not always precise.

## 2.3 SUMMARY

I have suggested two ways of answering the question "What is an emotion?" In the first, which involves a lengthy and detailed process of description, all the basic features, characteristics, and components of emotions are described. Here, an emotion is described as being generated by perceived significant changes; its focus of concern is personal and comparative; its major characteristics are instability, great intensity, partiality, and brief duration; and its basic components are cognition, evaluation, motivation, and feelings. The intensity of a typical emotion is determined by variables such as the event's strength, reality, and relevance, and our accountability, readiness, and deservingness with regard to the event. Contextual and personality variables impact upon emotional intensity as well. An emotion is part of a greater affective realm, which also includes sentiments, moods, affective traits, and affective disorders.

The second way of answering the question tries to indicate more of the general essence of emotions. Here I suggest considering emotions as a general mental mode. This mode is the most complex, comprehensive, and dynamic of all other mental modes.

Both these ways of answering the question give us an initial comprehensive framework for understanding that thing called emotion, a framework that can be useful in every circumstance in which emotions occur. Thus, it can assist us in describing and explaining emotions generated in cyberspace.[26] Although this framework is valuable in explaining emotional experiences, we still have a long way to go to fill in this framework with many other specifics about these experiences.

# REFERENCES

ARISTOTLE, *The Complete Works of Aristotle: The Revised Oxford Translation*. (J. Barnes, ed.) Princeton: Princeton University Press (1984).

BEDFORD, E. (1957). "Emotions". *Proceedings of the Aristotelian Society*, 57, 281–304.

BEN-ZE'EV, A. (1993). *The Perceptual System: A Philosophical and Psychological Perspective*. New York: Peter Lang.

—— (2000). *The Subtlety of Emotions*. Cambridge, MA: MIT Press.

—— (2004a). *Love Online: Emotions on the Internet*. Cambridge: Cambridge University Press.

—— (2004b). "Emotion as a subtle mental mode". In R. Solomon (ed.), *Thinking about Feeling: Contemporary Philosophers on Emotion*. New York: Oxford University Press, 250–68.

—— & GOUSSINSKY, R. (2008). *In the Name of Love: Romantic Ideology and its Victims*. Oxford: Oxford University Press.

BUSS, D. M. (1994). *The Evolution of Desire: Strategies of Human Mating*. New York: Basic Books.

DONALDSON, M. (1993). *Human Minds: An Exploration*. London: Penguin.

---

[26] Ben-Ze'ev, 2004a.

FOLGER, R. (1984). "Perceived injustice, referent cognitions, and the concept of comparison level". *Representative Research in Social Psychology*, 14, 88–108.

FRIJDA, N. H. (1986). *The Emotions*. Cambridge: Cambridge University Press.

—— (1988). "The laws of emotion". *American Psychologist*, 43, 349–58.

GILBERT, D. (2007). *Stumbling on Happiness*. New York: Vintage.

GOLDIE, P. (2000). *The Emotions*. Oxford: Oxford University Press.

—— (2004). "The life of the mind: Commentary on 'Emotions in Everyday Life'", *Social Science Information*, 43, 591–8.

LAKOFF, G. (1987). *Women, Fire, and Dangerous Things*. Chicago: University of Chicago Press.

LARSEN, R. J. & DIENER, E. (1987). "Affect intensity as an individual difference characteristic: A review". *Journal of Research in Personality*, 21, 1–39.

LYONS, W. (1980). *Emotion*. Cambridge: Cambridge University Press.

METTS, S., SPRECHER, S., & REGAN, P. C. (1998). "Communication and sexual drive". In P. A. Andersen, P. A. & L. K. Guerrero (eds.), *Handbook of Communication and Emotion*. San Diego: Academic Press, 343–77.

NUSSBAUM, M. C. (2001). *Upheavals of Thought: The Intelligence of Emotions*. Cambridge: Cambridge University Press.

ORTONY, A., CLORE, G. L., & COLLINGS, A. (1988). *The Cognitive Structure of Emotions*. Cambridge: Cambridge University Press.

REISENZEIN, R. (1994). "Pleasure-arousal theory and the intensity of emotions". *Journal of Personality and Social Psychology*, 67, 525–39.

ROESE, N. J. & OLSON, J. M. (eds.) (1995). *What Might Have Been: The Social Psychology of Counterfactual Thinking*. Mahwah: Erlbaum.

ROSCH, E. (1977). "Human categorization". In N. Warren (ed.), *Advance in Cross-Cultural Psychology*. London: Academic Press, 1–72.

—— (1978). "Principles of categorization". In E. Rosch and B. B. Lloyd (eds.), *Cognition and Categorization*. Hillsdale: Erlbaum, 27–48.

ROSENBERG, E. L. (1998). "Levels of analysis and the organization of affect". *Review of General Psychology*, 2, 247–70.

RUSSELL, J. A. (1991). "In defense of a prototype approach to emotion concepts". *Journal of Personality and Social Psychology*, 60, 37–47.

SHAVER, P., WU, S., & SCHWARTZ, J. C. (1992). "Cross-cultural similarities and differences in emotion and its representation". *Review of Personality and Social Psychology*, 13, 175–212.

SMITH, C. A. & ELLSWORTH, P. C. (1985). "Patterns of cognitive appraisal in emotion". *Journal of Personality and Social Psychology*, 48, 813–38.

SOLOMON, R. C. (1993). "The philosophy of emotions". In M. Lewis & J. M. Haviland (eds.), *Handbook of Emotions*. New York: Guilford Press, 3–15.

SPINOZA, B. (1677/1985). *Ethics*. In E. Curley (ed.), *The Collected Works of Spinoza*. Princeton: Princeton University Press.

TAMIR, M., JOHN, O. P., SRIVASTAVA, S., & GROSS, J. J. (2007). "Implicit theories of emotion: Affective and social outcomes across a major life transition". *Journal of Personality and Social Psychology*, 92, 731–44.

TAYLOR, S. E. (1989). *Positive Illusions: Creative Self-Deception and the Healthy Mind*. New York: Basic Books.

# CHAPTER 3

# DESCRIBING THE FORMS OF EMOTIONAL COLOURING THAT PERVADE EVERYDAY LIFE

## RODDY COWIE

## 3.1 INTRODUCTION

Understanding the nature of emotion is the kind of challenge that attracts people immediately. The aim of this chapter is to highlight a challenge that has less instant appeal but which is none the less fascinating once it is accepted. Roughly speaking, the challenge is to develop good ways of describing what happens in the parts of people's lives where emotion in a broad sense plays a significant role. It is useful to have a name for the sum of those parts, and 'emotional life' seems appropriate. There is an abundance of material to draw on. The challenge is to organize it into an intellectually satisfying instrument.

The raw material comes from familiar sources—psychology, philosophy, and everyday understanding. However, the incentive to reconsider the topic comes from a newer development, research on 'emotion-oriented computing'. To people outside the discipline, the term tends to suggest fantastic and frightening creations like HAL from *2001*; and the philosophical issues that come to mind are ethical. In reality, the research is much more prosaic, and the philosophical issues that it highlights are more technical—but not obviously easier. This section gives a brief introduction to the area, and some of the key issues that it raises, for readers who are not yet familiar with it. The perspective is derived from the HUMAINE network, which was tasked to establish sound conceptual foundations for emotion-oriented computing over a four-year period. The HUMAINE handbook, which emerged from the project, provides a fuller introduction (Petta in press).[1] At the time of writing, the key sources for research reports are conferences such as *Affective Dialogue Systems* (André et al. 2004) and *ACII* (Paiva et al. 2007).

The driving force behind emotion-oriented computing is the fact that emotional colouring is an intrinsic part of everyday human interaction. That fact has become increasingly difficult to ignore as computing has become progressively more integrated into everyday life. Computing is no longer confined in boxes that people of a particular type keep on their desktops. It drives systems at the other end of a phone or a camera, which may communicate with people through speech and/or a simulated face, via headphones or the TV; or may alert a care agency or security agencies; or may simply turn on the central heating. Computers already handle telephone enquiries; offer us information in our cars and regulate our driving; provide psychological therapies (Proudfoot et al. 2003); and assist patients in hospital.[2] It is likely that they will play increasing roles in security monitoring; helping elderly people to remain in their own homes (Paganelli et al. 2008); delivering educational programmes (Graesser et al. 2001); facilitating communication (Stock et al. 2008); enriching work environments (Combetto 2006); and much more. So long as computing is confined to a box in a special room, it is acceptable for it to be blind to the emotional colouring that characterizes everyday human communication. But the more it moves into everyday life, the less acceptable that limitation becomes. There is also pleasure in life, and as computing touches more and more of life, the more designers are tempted to think of ways that their creations might add to the pleasure. Gaming is an obvious area, but topics like computational humour are also being pursued actively, and in some senses seriously (Stock and Strapparava 2003).

---

[1] The seminal book in the area is 'Affective Computing' by Picard (2000), and the term 'affective computing' has wide currency. This article prefers 'emotion-oriented computing' because of reservations about using the term 'affect' in this context, which are explained in later sections.

[2] <http://www.techshout.com/general/2006/06/receptionist-porter-robots-replacing-humans-at-japanese-hospital/> (accessed 9 July 2009).

In most of these areas, the challenges related to emotion revolve around a simple schema. When a person is interacting with a system, and the person's communication is emotionally coloured, the system has to detect the signs that convey the emotional colouring; to use them to form an assessment of the person's emotional state; to identify the best stance for it to adopt in response to that state; and to generate signals that express the relevant stance. In most applications, the challenge is to reach at least a coarse approximation of what any person would do automatically: computers able to detect signs too subtle for the human senses belong in fantasy not foreseeable reality.

Every step of that schema entails huge intellectual challenges. It is enormously difficult to write programs to detect that a person's eyes have just flicked to a significant object in the environment, or that the flow of speech has just broken in an informative way. It is no less difficult to frame rules that conclude what a system should do if it registers that the person interacting with it is troubled about something that is happening just below eye level on the left-hand side. It is a massive technical challenge to synthesize facial and vocal gestures that convey awareness of the problem, together with a judgment that it is not insuperable. But although it is less obvious, the problem at the focus of this chapter is probably not less difficult and certainly not less important. Progress in all the other areas depends on adequate ways of describing the emotion-related states that have to be registered and responded to.

It is easy to assume that very little needs to be said about description. Everyday language incorporates a default method of describing emotions, based on stock labels—happiness, anger, shame, and so on. Early research in the area tended to equate describing emotion with recognizing images or extracts of speech to which labels like that could unequivocally be applied. Over the past decade, that approach has unravelled in several different ways, exposing the need for a concerted effort to address descriptive issues.

The problem has been particularly clear in the context of databases. Databases are central to the area because modern computing systems often depend on rules that are not planned explicitly by a designer. Instead, the designer selects a machine-learning algorithm; applies it to a database containing an appropriate set of examples; and leaves the algorithm to infer the rules that are needed. The databases most relevant to this chapter contain records of emotionally coloured episodes (typically audio-visual, often with information about the context). Associated with each episode are descriptions of the states that human raters believe are likely to underlie those signs. The job of the learning algorithms is to discover rules that reflect associations between particular combinations of signs and particular descriptions of states.

Early databases were constructed by asking actors to generate episodes corresponding to standard emotion terms (Ekman and Friesen 1975; Kienast and Sendlmeier 2000). Around the same time, several teams independently explored what seemed the natural next step, and tried to collect comparable records of naturally occurring emotion. They converged, unexpectedly, on the conclusion that that the phenomena that they expected to find did not naturally occur at all frequently (Douglas-Cowie et al. 2003). What did occur was something very different. In the terms that have already been used, they found emotionally coloured action and interaction. Labelling everyday emotionally coloured episodes with terms like 'angry' or 'happy' fell short in multiple ways.

First, events that fit the standard category terms precisely are surprisingly rare. For instance, the Belfast Naturalistic Database was produced by searching chat shows and reality TV for clear-cut (and apparently genuine) episodes of emotion, and the selected clips were presented to three raters who assigned the best-fitting category label from a list of 16, with the option of adding a secondary label from a longer list if the first was not sufficient. There were 308 cases where the first label assigned to an episode was 'angry', 'sad', 'worried', 'pleased', or 'happy'. In only 18 of these cases was the first label judged to be sufficient (Cowie and Cornelius 2003). The finding is not isolated. Around the same time, the Leeds–Reading project began with the expectation that pre-existing interviews on emotive topics would yield speech that showed clear-cut, strong emotions, and found so little that they turned to other sources (Douglas-Cowie et al. 2003). More information on prevalence is given later in the chapter. Unsurprisingly, when people are required to assign standard category labels to naturalistic material, agreement is rather low (Douglas-Cowie et al. 2005).

On the other hand, what has been called 'emotional colouring' is common. In a study described later, observers watched videos of people filmed during several hours of outdoor activity, and reported whether they appeared emotional in the fullest sense of the word; truly emotionless; or in an intermediate state, involving some elements of emotion but not emotion in the full sense. The people were judged truly unemotional less than 10% of the time. Taking the two together, it appears that most of human life is touched by something to do with emotion, very little of which conforms neatly to the standard emotion category words.

Even when the standard category words do apply well, the computing context quickly makes it clear that, to be useful, they need to be embedded in a richer description. To respond appropriately, a system needs to know not only *that* the user is angry but also *how* angry; whether the anger is 'hot' or 'cold'; whether the anger is a diffuse mood or directed at something; if it is directed, what it is directed *towards*; whether the anger is ingrained or relates to something that can be dealt with; and so on. The term 'angry' needs to be embedded in a network that sets out the implications of being angry—risk of attack, tendency not to listen, responsiveness to signs of submission or retreat, and so on. Nor can categories be treated literally as discrete primitives. If a system assigns the descriptor 'irritation', it also needs to have a deeper descriptive system in which it is apparent that irritation is next door to anger and far from happiness.

The problems with relying on everyday categories are not confined to the technical domain. They also involve communication to the wider world. One of the major threats to the field is precisely that people misunderstand its goals when everyday categories, such as 'angry', happy, and 'emotion' itself, are used in an unsophisticated way to describe them. People are, reasonably, sceptical of the idea that computer scientists should concern themselves with the rare occasions when these terms apply in the fullest sense; and that is often seen as a reason to oppose research in the area. The argument is very hard to counter unless the use of everyday categories can be put properly in perspective.

These issues are highlighted by emotion-oriented computing but not created by it. The ways that people commonly talk and think about emotion are sufficient for most of the practical purposes that most people have had until recently. The development of emotion-oriented computing shows that there are practical purposes for which they are not sufficient. The limitations were always there, but it is human nature not to be unduly concerned about them until we encounter a situation where they matter. The emergence of emotion-oriented computing creates such a situation and provides an incentive to overhaul our descriptive machinery.

More specifically, working on emotion-oriented computing highlights several qualities that a good descriptive system ought to have. As one might expect in the context of computing, one is systematic structure. Wonderful though literary evocations of emotion may be, their free structure limits their use in a computing context. A second desideratum, also not surprising, is inclusiveness. A satisfactory system should provide the means to describe any part of emotional life. Perhaps more surprisingly, it emerges as an important issue that the system should be intuitive. The last two points are taken up more fully in later sections.

Again, these targets are highlighted by emotion-oriented computing but not created by it. They correspond to a natural task, which would be intellectually challenging and worthwhile even if emotion-oriented computing did not exist. A rough but useful way to characterize the task is optimizing everyday means of description. The most tangible part of it is optimizing everyday language, but the issues are not restricted to language. They involve the way emotion-related language is used and thought about, and the way it facilitates or obstructs access to underlying conceptual resources. Talking about 'means of description' is meant to reflect that broad agenda.

To pre-empt obvious objections, 'optimizing' is always used modestly. It refers to ensuring that the means of description are the best we can make them, not the best in all possible worlds. Similarly, it is taken for granted that one optimizes for some purpose; and what is optimal for one purpose may not be optimal for others. The purpose in the background throughout this chapter is facilitating emotion-oriented computing. However, it seems a sensible working hypothesis that descriptive systems optimized for that purpose would serve a great many others too.

## 3.2 OPTIMIZING EVERYDAY MEANS
## OF DESCRIPTION

This section expands the idea of optimizing everyday means of description, and comments on its relationship to other tasks. It would be preferable in a chapter like this to touch quickly on the general issue of optimizing description, and move on to the particular task of describing emotion. Unfortunately, there does not seem to be a ready-made framework that can be used to guide work on the particular task. It is surprising how much needs to be said to specify what is involved in what, on the surface, seems a very mundane kind of problem. It is some consolation that clarifying what is needed in the context of emotion may be useful in other areas. For instance, decades of teaching psychology suggest that similar efforts would be very useful in other areas of the subject.

Optimized everyday language can be thought of as a layer between raw everyday language and the kind of formal language that Schröder et al. (2007) call an EARL— an 'Emotion Annotation and Representation Language', formalized fully enough to be used directly by machines. As such, it can help to address problems with the related systems on either side. On one side, raw everyday emotion language has various deeply frustrating qualities (some have already been mentioned). Access to optimized everyday language is integral to handling them (or even articulating them). On the other side, experience in emotion-oriented computing highlights interesting reasons for working to optimize everyday language, rather than moving directly to a wholly formal system (such as an EARL). Key examples are communication with non-specialists, and access to important kinds of intuitive understanding. There are analogous reasons in other research areas: emotion-oriented computing exposes general issues rather than raising unique ones.

Communication with non-specialists is a not a challenge to be taken lightly. For emotion-oriented computing, key groups are funders of research, potential buyers, and users. They cannot be expected to master a language that is peculiar to specialists; and yet, raw everyday language can easily give seriously misleading impressions. For instance, its terms often have a broad and narrow sense, and so a description of a system's competence may be quite misleading if it is true when terms are taken in the narrow sense (which experts tend to favour) but false in the broad sense (which may well be the only way a funder or user is likely to construe them). There are ethical as well as practical reasons to be sure that non-experts are not given false expectations by that kind of linguistic mismatch. Optimized everyday language seems to be the key to dealing with such issues. Note that they are not at all unique to emotion.

Access to intuition is an intriguing issue. Some everyday words seem to function as privileged access routes to important areas of intuitive understanding. For example, arguments often hinge on the intuition that certain phenomena belong together—so that, for instance, it is cause for concern if a scientific account seems to fit some of them but not all. Some words have a special relationship to that kind of intuition. Competent language users know when they apply. It is not a conclusion that they reach by referring to some list of more basic tests: the judgement is psychologically primitive. Many emotion-related words seem to be like that. What is *ennui* but *ennui*? Of course we can give lists of features, but the adequacy of a list is judged against the unanalysed intuition that this is *ennui*, and this is *ennui*, but that is not.

Words like that have an irreplaceable role in accessing intuitions about natural boundaries. If emotion-oriented computing, or any other discipline, wants to access those intuitions, then it cannot dispense with the language that provides access routes to the intuitions. That is precisely what technical disciplines tend to do when they formulate definitions: they offer an alternative basis for judging whether or not a word applies in a particular case, with the intention of rendering unanalysed intuition obsolete, and eventually inaccessible. That may be to the good if the redefinition preserves what is valuable in the everyday use, and discards noise; but, at best, it is not proven whether that applies in the case of emotion language. A recent debate between Scherer (2005) and Reisenzein (2007) illustrates these issues well.

On the other hand, everyday language sets its own obstacles to accessing potentially important intuitions. Words shift their meanings according to context. If people are not fully aware of that property of language, and equipped to control it, they may find that intuitions that they want to access are obscured because the context brings other meanings to the fore. Part of optimizing description is to establish more control than we usually have over the access routes that it offers at any given time.

These are key motives for trying to optimize everyday emotion language rather than moving directly to build a fully formal system. To do the work needs an appropriate evidence base, and that raises questions that have recently gained a high profile in the philosophy of emotion and philosophy generally (Sosa 2007, Williamson 2008).

It might seem that optimizing everyday descriptions was obviously an armchair exercise. It is (the argument runs) about mapping out conceptual resources; and therefore it needs nothing but access to the contents of a suitably furnished mind. However, that argument conceals a strong assumption about the way conceptual resources can be mobilized. The assumption is exposed by one of the key activities in emotion-oriented computing, which is collecting naturalistic recordings of people acting and interacting in various emotionally coloured ways.

Faced with these recordings, observers form rich, subtle impressions of a recorded person's emotional status. These impressions reveal the richness and subtlety of the conceptual resources that people bring to the comprehension of emotion. However, if people are asked to conjure impressions of emotional life out of the thin air around an armchair, they tend to generate descriptions that are much more categorical. The point is nicely illustrated by the pioneering work on collection of naturalistic data that has already been mentioned: the teams involved expected to find clear-cut categorical phenomena and discovered that they were vanishingly rare.

The underlying point here is a purely logical one. It cannot be taken for granted that an armchair is the only equipment needed for access to the contents of a suitably furnished mind. In particular, key resources may only be brought into play when the right external prompts are present—rather like asking a pianist to play in thin air only gives a caricature of the resources that he or she mobilizes at a real keyboard. For that reason, if the exercise is conducted in an armchair, the armchair should at least have access to a video system. More advanced virtual reality facilities may conceivably have advantages, but that is tangential to the main argument.

The issue of evidence leads naturally to questions about relationships to science. Considering what scientists in the area do exposes a deep and interesting contrast between their concerns and concern to optimize everyday conceptions.

Scientists studying emotion typically look for structures that are defined by nature per se, not by human conceptions of nature. The typical working hypothesis is that everyday words like 'emotion' point to a functionally distinct type of structure or mode of action—much as the everyday word 'water' points roughly to $H_2O$. However, it is not at all clear that emotion words have, so to speak, $H_2O$ equivalents. Scientists do sometimes appropriate words with complex use conditions to describe categories that make sense from their point of view, with results that seem bizarre to the layman—for instance, botanists use 'berry' in a sense that applies to avocados and tomatoes but not to raspberries or blueberries. There is no guarantee at all that any scientifically satisfying category comes closer to the everyday term 'emotion' than the class botanists call 'berries' comes to the everyday meaning of that term.

One of the key reasons for suspecting that emotion words may not have $H_2O$ equivalents is that they pose a radical problem of dual classification. It must be possible for both the person experiencing the emotion and an observer to use them. That kind of constraint would be expected to produce compromises—words that do not connect in a simple way to either internal or external events, but that can be used with fair success from either side.

It is not the job of this chapter to judge whether emotion words have $H_2O$ equivalents. The point is just that science is a very different enterprise from optimizing everyday means of description. Science usually starts from everyday concepts, and it may retain the words, but it reserves the right to attach very different concepts to the original terms. Optimizing everyday means of description is a different enterprise because it is about preserving the original concepts. There is room for both, and they work best in tandem.

It has been argued that optimizing everyday description is practically significant, intellectually interesting, and distinct from other recognized tasks. It is, of course, another question whether the task belongs to philosophy. The simple answer is that nobody else wants it or has the skills to do it. Descartes's room is probably not the right place to do it, but the equipment that needs to be installed is simple, and its function is one that philosophy embraced long ago, that is, assembling reminders. The work depends absolutely on the analytic skills that are philosophy's hallmark, and it can be understood as a development of characteristic twentieth-century movements in philosophy, the linguistic turn and the conceptual turn. The enterprise does not seem alien to philosophy. The only issue would appear to be whether philosophers have better things to do.

## 3.3 INCLUSIVENESS

Inclusiveness was mentioned as a key requirement in the introduction. This section explains why, and deals with a key matter arising under that heading. The term 'inclusiveness' is used here to refer to a family of considerations. These include ability to describe any part of emotional life, not just parts that are conveniently well behaved; ability to describe all the significant features of any given part; and ability to express any significant intuition about the groupings into which individual parts of emotional life naturally fall.

Identifying these as goals may look like labouring the obvious. However, research can easily be pulled in the opposite direction unless clear markers are laid down. In particular, an appealing way to achieve linguistic precision is to insist that words should only be used in a particular, narrow sense. 'Emotion' itself is a key example, as has already been hinted. When the everyday vocabulary that describes a domain is reformed in that way, the result is often far from inclusive: parts of the domain are covered by terms with admirably precise definitions, but others are bereft of any descriptor at all.

That kind of selective coverage may not be a problem for some enterprises. Psychologists in a laboratory can legitimately control conditions to ensure that they obtain only states which conform to a particular, narrow description. However, emotion-oriented computing has different obligations. Machines are likely to be of very little use unless they can respond to states that do not conform to the obvious types of precise specification, because states that do are rare. There is also an ethical dimension. A machine (unlike a psychologist) cannot manipulate a human into the emotional states that it favours. The emotional states that humans confront it with are the states it has to deal with; and those who design machines have to ensure they do not respond in grossly inappropriate ways when the states that the systems encounter are not what was expected. That places an onus on the designer to have an overview of human emotion-related states that does not leave blanks where well-defined words fail.

A key first step towards inclusiveness is to consolidate access to the inclusive sense of the word 'emotion'. Stocker and Hegman (1992) argued that emotion pervades human life, and it is common to find statements to that effect. That view is generally what leads people to become involved in emotion-oriented computing. It suggests that, as computing touches more and more of human life, it has more and more obligation to consider the emotional nature of the people it touches. Conversely, one of the main threats to the field is the argument, mentioned earlier, that emotion is an occasional phenomenon, which generally can and should be set aside when people interact with machines, and, therefore, there is no reason for computing to be distracted by it.

The issue arises because the term emotion has both inclusive and exclusive senses. The inclusive sense describes what advocates of emotion-oriented computing want to consider; the exclusive sense describes what opponents discount. Raw everyday language invites misunderstanding because different parties to a conversation may be using it in different senses. Clearly it is practically important to find ways of avoiding the misunderstanding.

Many specialists propose to avoid misunderstanding by restricting 'emotion' to the narrow sense. The problem is that leaves no way to refer to the domain containing everything that is called 'emotion' in the broad sense. Given that people appear to believe the broad sense captures something important enough to shape career choices, that is an option that should be avoided if possible.

Subjectively, highlighting negative forms—such as 'unemotional'—seems to offer a solution. People appear to understand that they denote absence of emotion in the broad sense rather than the narrow one. Empirical studies lend weight to the idea. A study touched on earlier used several hours of film made by TV crews following people through daily activities (in preparation for the series 'Castaway'). Four observers watched them and noted instant by instant which of three categories best described the person being followed by the camera at that time: emotional in the fullest sense of the word; truly emotionless; or in an intermediate state, involving some elements of emotion but not emotion in the full sense. Exact numbers are not important, but, broadly speaking, states perceived as outright unemotional made up less than 10% of the total; states perceived as emotional in the strong sense made up about 15%; and the remaining 75% was perceived as intermediate, with elements of emotionality, but not emotion in the strong sense. All four observers showed broadly similar divisions. Again, the exact numbers are not important.

The studies confirm that the term 'emotion' has a broad sense according to which most of life is somewhat coloured by emotion, and that that sense can be brought to the fore by focusing on negative forms of the word. In that sense, the word marks a boundary on which people broadly agree, and it can be used to access the boundary that people intuitively draw.

If we believe it matters to have access to that boundary, and to communicate about it, what is needed is to find a way of retaining the word, but avoiding the confusion that raw everyday language engenders. Simple conventions seem to be reasonably effective. In the context of HUMAINE, 'pervasive emotion' proved a generally acceptable way of describing what is present when a person is not truly unemotional. 'Emergent emotion' appeared to be the least problematic way of describing the exclusive phenomenon, emotion in the narrow sense.

Many empirical research teams favour an alternative strategy, which is to use the term 'affect' to identify emotion in the broad sense. That would be thoroughly reasonable either if 'affect' had no prior meaning, and could simply be assigned the job of referring to what is present when a person is unemotional, or if it already had that meaning. However, neither seems to be true. 'Affect' has been assigned a great many different meanings by various academic disciplines and sub-disciplines (in philosophy, psychology, and medicine); and to assign it yet another is to address one confusion by deepening another. The move also conveys a message which is far from trivial, which is that experts need not be overly concerned with the divisions of mental life implicit in everyday words. Defining their research in terms of words like 'affect', which are extremely loosely defined in common use, effectively asserts their right to stipulate their own boundaries. Several reasons why that right might not be conceded have already been sketched.

Once terms are agreed, it is easy to say things that otherwise can cause endless confusion. The domain that interests most people who enter emotion-oriented computing is emotion in the sense of pervasive emotion rather than emergent emotion. The term 'emotional life', which has already been introduced, is related to it: it refers to the sum total of phenomena, events and processes that involve pervasive emotion—the parts of human life that distinguish it from the life of a being who, like *Star Trek*'s Mr Data, is always unemotional.

It bears repeating that this kind of linguistic housekeeping is not science, and should not be confused with it. But it is not irrelevant to science. Without it, it is difficult to know how well science has met the challenges that intuition suggests it should—particularly challenges that hinge on inclusiveness. Many challenges do hinge on inclusiveness because it is notoriously easy to fit a function to a small number of points. It is right and proper to ask whether a scientific theory is credible if it deals beautifully with emergent emotion but does not relate it convincingly to the broader domain of pervasive emotion. The question cannot be asked unless the housekeeping is done.

Finding ways to speak clearly about such things is at the heart of optimizing description. But there are limits to how much can be done without assembling tools at other levels. That is what the next section does.

# 3.4 DESCRIBING FRAGMENTS
# OF EMOTIONAL LIFE

This section moves to the task of describing individual parts of emotional life. The approach is heavily influenced by a core task in the construction of databases for emotion-oriented computing, which is taking a recording, for instance a video clip, and annotating it (hence the 'A' for 'annotation' in Schröder's EARL). The annotation task is about describing the emotion-related content of a sample at much the same level as any reasonably sensitive person might. The main difference is that annotation uses labels from a prespecified set and places them at appropriate positions on a timeline, observing appropriate constraints on the way labels may be combined (if x is present, y must be specified, for instance). A chapter in the HUMAINE handbook (Petta in press) provides an extended discussion of annotating emotional material.

Annotation systems are underpinned by intuitive ideas about what needs to be said to capture what is happening in a given situation. This section is concerned with articulating those ideas, bearing in mind the general considerations that have already been outlined. There is abundant material to draw on, mainly from psychology. The task is to extract from it a structure that is reasonably compact, coherent, and inclusive, and also remains reasonably intuitive.

The resources that psychology provides are often presented in the context of claims that a particular formulation captures the nature of emotion. Those claims are intensely debated. But whether or not they define the essence of emotion, they clearly incorporate acute observations about the issues that are relevant to describing what one can expect to find in an emotionally coloured situation. That is the way they are presented here.

## 3.4.1 Units

Description depends on subdividing emotional life into units to which descriptors can be attached. Three levels of unit are set out here as a basis for what follows. Others are considered later.

'Segment' is a natural term for the smallest kind of unit that a description considers. What counts as a segment depends on the granularity of the description. In some applications, a word will be treated as a segment. In others, it may be a fixed time period, and that may be short (a few milliseconds) or long (seconds or even minutes).

Beyond segment level, emotional life is typically divided into two major types of unit, which are illustrated by standard examples: William James's urgent reaction to a bear in the woods, on one hand (James 1884); and Lord Jim's lifelong shame at jumping ship as a young man, on the other. The term 'emergent emotion', which has been introduced already, was coined to describe units like James's sudden fear. A unit like Lord Jim's shame will be called an 'established emotion'.

That distinction draws in several others. 'Emotional episode' is a natural and standard name for the interval through which an emotion like James's persists, when the person's mental state changes briefly but deeply. The interval through which Lord Jim's shame persists, which may easily be most of a lifetime, will be called an 'emotional era'. The times when shame moves abruptly from the background to the focus of mental life will also be called episodes: there seems no good reason to invent a separate term. It is in line with standard terminology to call James's fear a state, but there is strong resistance to using the term 'state' to describe anything as intangible Lord Jim's shame between acute episodes. 'Condition' seems a reasonably safe alternative.

These units are individuated by features of various different types. Some are components (that is to say, processes or structures in their own right); others are attributes (that is to say, properties of processes or structures). The rest of this section is concerned with setting out the key types of component and attribute that give an individual unit its character.

Fixing names for units like these is rather a trivial exercise in itself, but it paves the way for quite a substantial shift of focus. The unit most often considered in discussions of emotion is the kind of concept expressed by global labels like fear, anger, etc. Describing actual segments of emotional life is a different task and has a fair claim to be considered more basic.

## 3.4.2 Dimensions

It may or may not be theoretically profound, but it is certainly often natural and useful to describe emotion in terms of a few dimensions. Three dimensions are standard. *Valence* describes the value (positive or negative) of the feelings involved. *Activation* describes the strength of the individual's disposition to act. *Potency* describes the individual's sense that he or she has the power to deal with relevant events.

Many other dimensions have been proposed, of which three will be mentioned here. *Unpredictability* is included because it emerges as a key factor in a particularly well-constructed study (Fontaine et al. 2007). The next was described by Ortony (2002) as 'caring'. *Engagement* (as opposed to detachment) may be a more neutral term. It is rarely mentioned in the psychological literature, and yet it is arguably the dimension on which Mr Data would be most distant from any human. The point is well established in research on 'presence' in virtual reality, where it is acutely important whether people have the sense of being materially engaged with the virtual surroundings rather than essentially distanced from them. In that context, it is widely assumed that emotional responsiveness and engagement are inseparable (Huang and Alessi 1999). Finally, *intensity* is clearly important. One might assume that it could be derived from the other dimensions, but that would only be so if they were all known and they combined in a straightforward way. Those are non-trivial conditions.

Dimensions do not exist *in vacuo*. It is natural to think of them as specifying how something is coloured. The question of what they colour is taken up below as the relevant candidates are considered.

## 3.4.3 Feeling

Feeling is intimately bound up with emotion, but the exact nature of the relationship is hotly debated. However, the debates are rarely critical for the task of description. It is reasonably straightforward to identify a good deal of what an inclusive description should say about the feelings involved in a particular emotional segment.

James (1884) famously observed that emotion is associated with visceral feeling—that is, awareness of physical changes that tend to accompany emotion such as a racing heart, tightness of breath, hairs standing erect, and so on. These are phenomena whose place in an adequate description of emotion is not in question. Note that they are mainly relevant to emergent emotion.

It is also generally accepted that emotion involves feelings linked to the dimensions described above. There are different conceptions of the relationship. Russell and his colleagues (Russell and Feldman-Barrett 1999; Russell 2003) use the term 'core affect' to describe emotional feelings associated with the dimensions of valence and (secondarily) activation, and propose that they function as a generalized barometer of the person's state (summarizing well-being and preparedness for action respectively). On that conception, valence and activation colour a global sense of the subject (relative to his or her situation, of course).

An obvious problem with that conception is that it struggles with mixed emotions, which the evidence shows are common if not the norm. A variant formulation due to Watson et al. (1988) allows a limited kind of mixing: it describes feeling in terms of two activation levels, one for positive feelings and one for negative. Hence it implies that two valences can coexist. More radical options, which allow for the co-occurrence of many valences, are considered later.

The differences between these options have prompted intense theoretical debate. However, from a descriptive point of view, it is hard to see them as anything but differences in level of resolution. Sometimes it is enough to attach a single valence label to a situation, sometimes it is not.

Theories that appeal to valence in any way are subject to a standard criticism, which is that people may evaluate a situation without feeling any emotion at all. The simple response is that what matters for emotion is felt valence, not rationally assessed valence. From a descriptive stance, all that is needed is to ensure that the two can be described separately, for instance, when we meet somebody that we know rationally is admirable, but who nevertheless makes us recoil emotionally. The same kind of move applies to the other dimensions (arousal, potency, etc).

Terms like felt valence are useful but still not ideal. The problem arises when the negative evaluation of the person from whom we recoil is part of an established emotion. There is then a sense in which it is present even when it is not felt—part of our constitution even when it is not expressed. It is rather paradoxical to use the term felt valence in that context; unfortunately, the obvious alternatives bring their own problems. Related issues were raised many years ago in a large body of work by Osgood and his collaborators (Osgood et al. 1967). They showed that concepts have what they called a 'feeling tone' which can be summarized reasonably well in terms of three dimensions (which they called evaluation, potency, and activity). It would be perverse to deny that the feeling tone was attached to the concept even when it was not felt.

An alternative way of describing feeling is in terms of particular emotional states—as in 'I feel angry'. Descriptive systems can reflect that kind of statement in two ways. One is clearly needed. 'I feel angry' expresses a conscious recognition that the speaker is in a state that involves distinctive feelings, and a conscious categorization of the state. It is practically important for emotion-oriented computing that feeling may or may not be recognized and classified. One of the applications that has been envisaged is warning people who need a cool head (in contexts such as negotiation or driving) that they are becoming emotional. Hence descriptions relevant to that application need to mark whether or not emotional feelings have been recognized and categorized.

A second way of taking these statements is more problematic. It assumes that there is a distinctive anger feeling, which is not simply feeling negative, active, relatively powerful, and so on. Some versions of the view add that that not all global emotion terms correspond to distinctive feelings—jealousy and righteous anger may feel the same, for instance (Sabini and Silver 2005).

In most respects, the issue seems to be of a type that is very familiar in psychology, where two essentially equivalent descriptive spaces are available (these issues are at the heart of techniques like factor analysis). In one, the axes are dimensions like valence, activation, and so on. In the other, the axes correspond to primitive types of feeling state, and an individual segment is located by co-ordinates which specify how much of each primitive type is present. At present, the first version has several practical advantages. The main axes are well established and they are almost independent, whereas nobody has identified a convincing set of category-related axes, and the obvious candidates are not independent. Various developments might shift the balance in future. However, it remains a practical matter, not least because it is relatively straightforward to translate information from one format into the other.

It is difficult not to ask what feeling is, and some conjectures are eminently natural, such as the idea that the felt elements of emotional life arise from activity in brain systems with a different style of operation from the predominantly cortical ones involved in reflective thought. Such ideas have been developed elegantly by writers like Panksepp (2003). But there are alternatives (one is considered shortly). As usual, the scientific proposal is separate from the descriptive issue—otherwise it could not be an empirical question whether the systems that (for instance) Panksepp considers are reliably associated with the presence of emotion-related feelings.

## 3.4.4 Appraisal

Recently there has been strong interest in the idea that emotion is closely linked to perception. Ben Ze'ev's (2000) phrase 'partial perception' captures neatly what happens: emergent emotion in particular involves a selective grasp of a situation, highlighting what is relevant to the subject's 'weal or woe' (Arnold 1960). The major psychological developments of that idea propose relationships between emotional states and value-oriented 'appraisals' of the situation.

There are many specific descriptions of appraisal. A particularly well-developed example is due to Scherer's group (Sander et al. 2005). It describes a sequence of 'stimulus evaluation checks' which makes sense logically and fits data collected by the group. It proposes that the onset of emergent emotion involves a series of checks, in the following sequence:

- Relevance (including sub-checks for novelty, intrinsic pleasantness, and relevance to the subject's goals and needs)
- Implications (including sub-checks for causal attribution, outcome probability, discrepancy from expectations, goal conduciveness, and urgency)
- Coping potential (including sub-checks for the controllability of the event and the subject's power to affect its course and/or to adjust to its consequences)
- Normative significance (including sub-checks concerned with the way outcomes relate to one's own values and to society's).

One of the analyses that has had most impact in technology, proposed by Ortony et al. (1988), is also rooted in appraisal theory. It was designed to articulate what emotion words mean, and does so elegantly. Scherer's version is more fully described here because it is easier to apply to segments of emotional life.

Scherer's categories imply that something—an object, in the traditional terminology—is perceived as (for instance) pleasant, conducive to the person's goals, within the person's power to control, morally acceptable, etc. Scherer's own descriptions tend to focus on cases like James's bear in the woods, where there is a single, obvious object. In cases like that, the idea of a fixed sequence makes sense. However, the categories apply readily to situations where many objects are involved, some in the immediate surroundings, some remembered, some antici-pated, some goal-obstructive, some goal-conducive, and so on. Making that kind of extension provides a systematic way to move beyond the idea that emo-tion-related descriptors are at least mainly about global states of the organism (in the way that Russell and others envisage them).

It is natural to extend the ideas about feeling outlined earlier to appraisal, and say that what matters for emotion is (for instance) felt goal conduciveness rather than rationally assessed goal conduciveness. Scherer appears to suggest another line of attack, which is that what makes emotional appraisals different is not that the individual components have a special quality but that they are bound together in a synchronized whole. That avoids the awkward conclusion that there are rational and felt versions of each appraisal category, implying massive duplication in the brain. On the other hand, it is not obvious how the emphasis on synchrony applies to a person in an armchair musing emotionally about past problems and anticipated pleasures. Conceptually, it is unclear what the best resolution is. It is not a great difficulty practically, though. It matters that appraisals are felt rather than calculated.[3] However, one can say that without specifying whether they have a distinctive quality because they arise in a distinctive system or because they have distinctive relationships to each other.

## 3.4.5 Action tendency

There is a long-standing recognition that emotion tends to close the gap between having an impression of the situation and acting on the impression. For instance, Aristotle cited the impulses to/for revenge as a defining feature of anger (1941, p. 1380). Frijda (1986) reintroduced a related concept in the modern era, and his term 'action tendencies' is widely used. He argued that tendencies to act in particular (biologically significant) ways were integral to emotion and were central to distinguishing among emotions with a direct biological significance—tendency to approach is the kernel of desire, tendency to avoid is the kernel of fear, tendency to reject is the kernel of disgust, and so on.

---

[3] More exactly, it matters that there *is* a felt appraisal. The appraisal may arise as a result of calculation—for instance, working out painfully that one has been exploited—and acquire emotional force. What makes it emotional is that it is felt, not—as sometimes happens—registered purely and simply as an abstract fact.

It is clear that an optimized descriptive system should provide for describing the action tendencies inherent in emotional situations. It is less clear that existing accounts offer anything like a full account of the tendencies that may arise. In contrast to appraisal categories, there seems to have been no systematic attempt to apply them to bodies of naturalistic data, partly because the task looks difficult.

## 3.4.6 Expression

Actions with a communicative element are among the most characteristic components of emotional episodes—smiling, weeping, screaming, and so on. Theorists from different traditions have understood these in substantially different ways.

Simplifying grossly, accounts that appeal to evolution (epitomized by Ekman 1973) have tended to assume that expressions of emotion are produced by innate mechanisms which automatically generate external signs of significant internal states, with socially defined operations (display rules) capable of concealing or mimicking the innate patterns (though not usually perfectly). In contrast, social psychologists argue that the patterns are fundamentally communicative: smiles are directed to people, not automatic externalizations of an inner state (Ruiz-Belda et al. 2003). The two lead to different descriptive strategies. For expression theorists, signs are simply emitted. For social theorists, the signs are directed to recipients, and an adequate description should specify the recipients. Note that both may be true for different signs and/or different situations. From a descriptive point of view, the obvious solution is to include a recipient in the description of signs, with the proviso that the slot may be filled by 'nonspecific'.

## 3.4.7 Emotional modes of action and cognition

Emotion affects not only what people do but also the way they do it (of course, the line is often blurred). Some of the effects flow from underlying shifts in the way people perceive and think under the influence of emotion. There are well-documented examples at many levels of cognition.

A practically important example of effects on attention is called 'weapon focus'—exclusive concentration on a single, focal detail of a scene (the gun) to the exclusion of other features which are actually important (the gunman's face). The effect seems to be due to the perceptual processes that evoke emotional responses (Laney et al. 2004). There is a substantial literature on the way anxiety affects perceptual and related process—attentional control, depth of processing, and speed of processing. Eysenck's work on anxiety illustrates a well-developed analysis of the issues surrounding these effects (1997; Eysenck et al., 2007). Positive conditions tend to generate extensive and well-organized memories, and positive affect promotes their recall later. It also fosters flexible and creative thought, can speed decision-making, and affects risk-taking, not necessarily in obvious ways (Isen 1998). Negative moods tend to increase people's impression of the effort that a task requires (Gendolla and Krüsken 2002). Marked emotion tends to reduce coherent verbal communication (Cowie and Cornelius 2003).

These effects are practically important for emotion-oriented computing. Consider, for example, the implications of ability to recognize when emotion is impairing a driver's perception of risk, or a pupil's ability to learn, or a manager's ability to communicate clearly, or a worker's readiness to sustain effort, and so on. Hence an inclusive description needs to specify them.

## 3.4.8 Connectedness

Usually (perhaps always) describing an emotional episode depends on referring beyond the person who has an emotional experience to various significant objects and significant others. That is already implicit in several of the points above, but deserves to be drawn out. An appraisal is an appraisal *of* people, events, or things; and expressions of emotion tend to be directed *to* particular people in the context of an audience (couples know how dramatically the sudden appearance of a child or an in-law can affect the expression of various emotions).

Writers have stressed that a great variety of connections may be involved in an emotional episode (e.g. Goldie 2000). It may be about one thing (mortality, for instance); prompted by another (a poetry reading, perhaps); with causal roots in events long past (such as a bereavement). Shame before an audience which approves of an action may arise because another audience (present in the mind rather than in reality) would not approve. There is no obvious end to the permutations. In addition, mixed emotions often involve connections with multiple different events, bearing different emotional colourings—gladness that a gap in life is to be filled, sadness about the loss that created the gap, concern that it might still not work out, and so forth. An inclusive descriptive system needs ways of specifying these things.

## 3.4.9 Impressions of emotion

Emotional episodes typically involve more than one person, and, when they do, describing how signs of emotion are being registered is as essential as describing how they are being emitted. There are several ways of conceptualizing registration.

Detection paradigms consider whether an objectively verifiable state is identified correctly. That approach is clearly appropriate in certain application areas—emotional intelligence tests based on perception of others' emotions, for instance, and lie detection (where emotion-related signs are assumed to be pivotal).

Experiential paradigms are broadly comparable to certain areas of psychophysics, where it is accepted that subjective experience may have its own dimensions. In a parallel way, it makes sense to consider whether, for instance, dimensional descriptions capture the way we perceive other people's emotions under certain circumstances, whether or not they capture the intrinsic nature of our own, and so on.

Control paradigms consider how variables affect behaviour rather than experience. The two can be very different. For instance, it is well known in perception that the behaviour of visually guided grasping is not affected by variables that distort conscious reports of size and distance. There is evidence that, in a parallel way, responses to others' emotion may reflect variables that are not reflected in conscious impressions of the other.

Timing needs to be considered alongside these distinctions. Taking time to identify a single static state is not the same as registering in real time how a person's emotional balance and focus is shifting, which is what people have to do when they participate in an emotionally coloured interaction. Perceived flow of emotion seems an apt term for the kind of impression that underpins real-time interaction.

People perceive (or fail to perceive) their own emotions as well as other people's. That would seem to involve forming explicit representations of changing flows and pressures that are at work in their own heads, so to speak. Helping people to perceive their own emotions is one of the application areas that is regularly considered for emotion-oriented computing.

There is a close relationship between the perception of emotion and the task of optimizing description. One way to think of an intuitive, inclusive description of an emotional episode is that it should capture all the qualities that a sensitive observer seeing and hearing the episode could register. That is certainly a simplification but it is a useful simile.

## 3.4.10 Global labels

This section has listed various kinds of resources that are relevant to describing a particular fragment of emotional life. It has deliberately left until last the resource that people typically consider first, that is, words like 'mood', 'anger', and so on. The reason is that people find it very easy to think of emotional life as a collection of events that are close to category archetypes, leaving the mass of everyday phenomena that are far from the archetypes sidelined.

The sequence in this section is designed to put everyday category labels in context. Attaching the label 'anger' to a segment of emotional life conveys information in some of the areas that have been considered, but only some; and the resources that have been set out seem capable of describing states for which there is no stock global label. That provides a context for asking what part category labels play in optimized descriptions; and that is what the next section considers.

# 3.5 GLOBAL EMOTION-RELATED CONDITIONS

For most people, terms like 'fear' and 'anger' are the obvious way to describe emotion. For that reason, an optimized descriptive system has to include them. However, they are subtle, complex constructs that exert an active pull on the way people think about emotion rather than simply allowing us to describe it. The core aim of this section is to highlight the problems that they pose and to suggest ways of keeping the terms under control rather than being controlled by them.

It is even tricky to find an acceptable way of referring to them. The term global has been used to reflect the fact that they encompass many elements of the kinds described in the last section. One might say that they describe global states, but that risks introducing a selective focus because there is a fairly standard use of the term in which established emotions, for instance, are not states. 'Global condition labels' avoids that commitment and will be preferred here even though it sounds rather clumsy.

Global condition labels have a structure that looks at first glance like a taxonomy, with terms like 'anger' in the role of species, episodic emotional states a level above (genera), and conditions involving pervasive emotion a level above that (family). The metaphor of a taxonomy breaks down, but it provides a useful way of organizing the discussion.

Inclusiveness is at the centre of the discussion again. Ideally, we would like a system of global condition labels that covered the whole of emotional life. That is more difficult than it sounds. To some extent, the problems can be remedied by using terms carefully and introducing new ones. Other problems seem to be too deep-rooted to remedy and the only option is probably to be aware of them.

## 3.5.1 Mindsets and personal conditions

Conferences on emotion-oriented computing often discuss concepts like interest, politeness, expressiveness, dominance, and stress. People are sceptical, and reasonably so, when the term emotion is stretched to cover these. The domain that includes both these and pervasive emotion has no agreed name, but 'mindsets' seems as good as any. Included at that level might be social states (dominance, deference, and so on) and cognitive states (confusion, interest, etc.). A broader domain still, including, for instance, states of health and well-being (ill, vigorous, and so on) as well as mindsets, might be called 'personal conditions'.

These terms are not particularly satisfactory, but it is not important for this chapter since their function is mainly to acknowledge the existence of areas it does not cover. They allow, for instance, people who are working on classification of states observed in meetings to say that they are interested in states which are mindsets but not, in the main, emotional. If the distinction is used, it should be understood that it is not clear-cut. For example, Lazarus (1999) has pointed out that it is unrealistic to discuss stress without reference to emotion, even though they can be separated conceptually: where there is stress there is almost always emotion. Precisely because emotion is pervasive, it is likely to be an issue in most real situations. The issue is simply how much of an issue it is and whether (Gestalt-like) descriptions make it the figure or part of the ground.

## 3.5.2 Generic emotion-related conditions

On the taxonomic metaphor, moods, emergent emotions, and so forth are genera which go to make up a family. 'Emotion-related conditions' describes the family in a way that does not raise too many objections. It is clearly of interest to emotion-oriented computing to know which kinds of state are actually common since, other things being equal, it makes sense to orient systems to common phenomena rather than rare ones.

A core list of conditions at this level is a fairly standard—emotions, moods, attitudes, and dispositions. In that context, emotion tends to be used in the sense of emergent emotion; mood implies a global shift of valence without an object; attitude is an enduring valence attached to a concept; and disposition is what makes a person more or less likely to enter a particular type of emotional state.

By now, it is automatic to ask whether the list is inclusive. There may be a domain that it covers fully, which would be something like pure conditions where valence is definitive and which can be identified by their quality at an instant. However, the list is far from sufficient to describe all the kinds of emotional colouring that appear in recordings of everyday action and interaction. As with the word emotion itself, it may be possible for psychologists to consider only cases which are in some sense pure; but that is not an option that emotion-oriented computing can take.

The literature identifies a number of states which are more complex in one way or another. Established emotion has already been considered: it is temporally complex. Siemer (2005) has highlighted another temporally complex phenomenon where the pure valence that defines mood in the classical sense locks intermittently onto objects or people: he argues that what people call mood is often that kind of oscillation between mood and emergent emotion rather than pure objectless valence. Another type of complexity occurs when emotion is bound up with social inclinations (such as 'friendly'): using a term from Bruner, Scherer (2005) has called these interpersonal stances. Last but not least, emergent emotion is often suppressed or controlled rather than allowed to take a full-blown form.

Logic also points to simple states that should be considered. If mood is defined by altered valence, it is not obvious why there should not be analogous states for the other major dimensions (excluding intensity)—altered arousal, altered potency, and so on.

These ideas were followed up by simple empirical studies. Pilot work asked people to describe experiences that fell into the a priori categories. The results prompted revisions. Descriptions of stances towards people seemed to divide into two categories, one describing short-term (and usually shallow) engagements, the other describing long-term (and often deep) engagements: the latter were classified as a separate category, called bonds. The term 'attitude' causes confusion because in everyday language it does not signify what psychologists have in mind. The concept seems to be captured better by using Bruner's term again and talking about stance towards an object or situation. Note that the issue here was intelligibility: it matters that the categories are likely to be understood by non-experts. It is noticeable that the term 'attitude' has also acquired quite different meanings in different academic literatures, taking on one technical sense in a literature derived from Ajazen and his colleagues (1988) and another in linguistics (O'Connor and Arnold 1973), which has sometimes been equated with Scherer's term 'interpersonal stance' (Wichmann 2002). Like 'affect', 'attitude' seems to have a facility for picking up multiple meanings; and it needs to be used cautiously for that reason.

Table 3.1 Prevalence of generic emotion–related conditions in an ambulatory study

| Condition | % |
| --- | --- |
| Established emotion | 0.9 |
| Emergent emotion (suppressed) | 1.7 |
| Emergent emotion (full-blown) | 1.5 |
| Mood/Emergent emotion oscillation | 1.5 |
| Mood | 36.1 |
| Stance towards object/situation | 25.6 |
| Interpersonal stances | 2.4 |
| Interpersonal bonds | 4.1 |
| Altered state of arousal | 21.9 |
| Altered state of control | 3.9 |
| Altered state of engagement | 0.4 |
| Emotionless | 0.0 |
| None of the above | 0.0 |

The revised list was used in a type of study described as 'ambulatory' (Wilhelm et al. 2004). The categories were explained to ten participants. Each of them was then contacted by phone 50 times at random times over a period of weeks. They responded by identifying the generic descriptor that best reflected their state at the time. The main results are summarized in Table 3.1.

A list like this is obviously not final. However, it gives a concrete illustration of something that an optimized descriptive system should contain—a list at the generic level that covers all the conditions that make up emotional life. Note also that the numbers reinforce the case for worrying about the term 'emotion'. Emotion in its archetypal sense—full-blown emergent emotion—does seem to be a rare event. If emotion-oriented computing were drawn by the vicissitudes of language into addressing that kind of event, there would indeed be reason to doubt how much effort should be devoted to it. Emotion is pervasive but not in that form.

## 3.5.3 Specific emotion terms

Words like anger, joy, etc.—what is being called the species level here—clearly have a kind of priority in the domain of emotion. In the phrase coined by Rosch (1978), they appear to be the basic level in this domain—as 'dog' or 'cat' are in the domain of animals. They are also what a huge proportion of the literature on emotion is about. Obviously this section cannot review all of that literature. It confines itself to the issues that are most directly relevant to optimizing description.

It is interesting to notice that in contrast to higher levels of the taxonomy, specific emotion terms are entrenched in a way that gives very little leeway for revising them or introducing new terms. In that context, what can be done to optimize description is mainly to provide protection against misunderstanding the kind of instruments that they are. At least five practically important kinds of misunderstanding can be identified:

(a) *The domain of specific emotions can be reduced to a fixed list*

There is a long history of attempts to produce a short, definitive list of emotions which underlie all the surface complexity of emotional life. Until the mid-twentieth century, the emotions on the hypothetical list were called primary, with the implication that they mixed like primary colours; in the late twentieth century, they were called basic, with the implication that they were associated with discrete biological systems.

The idea of such a list has a powerful hold on the imagination, but despite intense efforts, and irrespective of the formulation, no credible list has ever been formulated. Various authors have compiled tables that show how little agreement there is among the various lists that have been proposed. Probably the best known of the lists is the 'big six' proposed by Ekman and Friesen (1975), and it is salutary to read Ekman's own rejection of the standard list (1999).

The consequence for description is straightforward. It should not be assumed either that short lists of specific emotion terms will support satisfying descriptions of the emotion that occurs in everyday life, or that samples covering the emotions on such a list adequately represent emotional life.

(b) *Emotional life is composed of instances of the states named by specific emotion terms*

Even when quite a long list is used, naturalistic data tends not quite to fit any single specific emotion term. That point has already been made in the first section of this chapter using data from Cowie and Cornelius (2003), showing that, even with samples selected to approximate archetypes, raters were rarely content to use a single emotion word.

The consequence for description is that descriptive formats should allow multiple terms to be used. The format that has become increasingly standard in emotion-oriented computing uses 'soft vectors': these list several emotion terms, and associate with each a number indicating how much of that element is present. It is not an ideal solution conceptually, but it is not obvious how else category labels can be fitted to phenomena that elude classification.

(c) *All states that can be described by the same specific emotion term are essentially similar*

This kind of proposition is implicit in work that studies a given emotion in a particular context, and adduces claims about the emotion in general. There is ample evidence that that is misguided. Words like anger and love can famously refer to many different states—hot and cold anger, sexual and nurturant love, and so on (Russell and Fehr 1994; Sternberg 1988). They can also refer to one-off emergent episodes (anger at a rude shop assistant) or established emotion (anger at government policy in Iraq). Linked to that, there is evidence that there are material differences between the anger evoked by things that are physically present and the anger evoked by remembering past events (Stemmler et al. 2001). Beyond that, the signs of emotion will clearly depend on context—one is likely to find different expressions of happiness on a football terrace and in a boardroom. The implication for description is that an adequate descriptive system needs ways of supplementing descriptions based on specific emotion words. That is one of the roles of the descriptors discussed in the previous section.

(d) *Specific emotion terms describe internal states*

This kind of proposition also tends to be implicit, notably in claims about the difficulty of knowing true emotions and in the idea that finding the 'ground truth' about emotions ultimately requires measurements of brain states.

In reality, specific emotion words do not simply refer to inner affective states (however varied). Their meaning is bound up with a variety of complex judgements, many related to the fact that words in everyday language must allow people other than the subject to apply them (otherwise they could not form part of a common language). Sabini and Silver (2005) provide nice illustrations of the point. They argue that terms like jealousy and anger, shame and embarrassment may refer to the same affective state. The difference lies in factors surrounding that affective kernel, some internal to the subject experiencing the emotion, some external; some factual, others involving moral judgements.

(e) *The categorical structure of emotion language reflects categorical structure in emotional life*

Linnaeus, the father of taxonomy, is credited with coining the phrase *Natura non facit saltus*—Nature does not make abrupt jumps. Introspectively, it is difficult to imagine that emotion is an exception to the rule: people seem to move smoothly between emotional and emotion-related states. Evidence cited above underscores the point from a different angle. In contrast language, of necessity, works with categories. It is hard to see how the fit between them can be anything other than approximate.

There is a good deal of support for prototype theories of emotion language (for discussions, see Fehr and Russell 1984; Shaver et al. 2001). They suggest a useful image of the relationship. Specific emotion terms correspond to landmarks in the landscape of emotional life—mountain peaks, so to speak. The nearer a point lies to a given peak, the better the corresponding word fits; but fit is rarely perfect, and parts of the terrain are relatively distant from any landmark. The image is by no means perfect, but it is certainly a useful counterweight to the assumption that emotion terms partition emotional life much as national boundaries partition a political map into abutting regions of uniform colour.

These considerations are not abstruse entertainment for the philosophically minded. Emotion-oriented systems have to use everyday words for global emotion conditions, but they should be used with due care and attention. That means they need to be used in accordance with the complex considerations that actually govern their use in natural languages. Basic to that is recognizing that, although it is often convenient to think of specific emotion words as labels for species of states, it is only an approximation.

# 3.6  EMOTION-RELATED PROCESSES

Emotion is strikingly dynamic, and it is quite paradoxical that descriptions of it are so often static—couched in terms of what seem to be steady states whose only time-related property is being off or on. An optimized descriptive system needs to include ways of describing key processes as well as states. There is less of a systematic framework to draw on in this area than in the other broad areas that have been covered, and the section restricts itself to a preliminary sketch of the kind of framework one might develop. It recognizes systematically that emotion-related processes tend to have two aspects, private (relating to mental events within the subject of the emotion) and public (relating to signs that another agent may register and respond to).

*Forming and activating emotional connections*

The term 'emotional connections' is meant to describe linkages between emotion and ideas about people, objects, situations, and so on. It is fundamental to emotional life that things, people, and situations take on emotional significance, which may be brief or enduring. Correspondingly, an optimal description needs to identify when, for instance, a task is becoming aversive, and whether the aversion is transient or enduring. It is not obvious what signs convey to an outsider that these things are happening, but a good deal of teaching and persuasion, for instance, depend on the fact that these processes can be detected.

It is also a feature of emotional life that enduring connections are not necessarily active. For instance, it is a key finding in the literature on attitude that attitudes do not affect choices unless they are activated. Correspondingly, an optimized description needs to mark the fact that a connection is becoming active. Again, there clearly are often signs that that is happening, but it is far from clear what they are.

*Perceiving, thinking, and acting emotionally*

Some processes in this area have already been mentioned—emotionally coloured ways of perceiving and thinking, and action tendencies. These are small parts of a vast area. Emotion affects the way people carry out all sorts of routine activities, from driving to playing music, and, not least, talking. As the case of Phineas Gage famously illustrated, what we regard as normal competence may depend on emotion-related inputs that usually go unnoticed (Damasio et al. 1994). Perception and thought are more or less private processes which sometimes yield public evidence of emotion, sometimes not. Action is generally public, but that does not necessarily mean people can detect when it is influenced by emotion.

A key point about this area is that understanding the effects of emotion is intimately connected with understanding the activity affected. One needs to know something about hammering to register that the way someone is hammering indicates that he is angry. It is also important that the relationship between activities and emotion is bidirectional: activities change the emotions that are present when they begin (it is hard to stay happy through an hour of proofreading).

### Relating emotionally

There are particularly intimate links between emotion and social functioning. It seems appropriate to note here that social interactions, long- and short-term, are intricate processes, in which emotion is deeply involved. It would be a poor description that failed to register that a particular set of emotional interactions constituted forming a friendship, or stretching one.

### Talking and thinking about emotional life

It is important for emotion-oriented computing to recognize that assigning everyday emotion-related words as humans do is an intricate process. At least eight types of consideration appear relevant to the task (Cowie 2005). Some are more directly relevant to the subject of the emotion, others to an observer. One type of consideration involves the internal feeling state. But assigning emotion terms also depends on the objective events which prompt an emotion (if a successful person has genuinely insulted an unsuccessful one, the latter's emotional response would be called anger; if the latter has perceived an insult in quite innocent behaviour, it would be called envy). It depends too on evaluation of the person's character (the word 'shame' is applied when a person accepts that negatively evaluated actions reflect a genuine deficiency in themselves, 'embarrassment' when he or she does not). Similar points can be made about the other types of consideration: these involve the person's appraisal of circumstances; the involuntary signs that he or she gives; his or her choice of action; the manner in which the action is undertaken; and the observer's evaluation of action.

Related but distinctive problems arise over deciding who has the right to use particular words. A parent may describe a child as sulking. A machine which attached the same label to the child would be presuming a right to make moral judgements which the recipient might dispute, and might expect to be smashed. That highlights a problem with wide-ranging implications for emotion-oriented computing: it is not at all obvious what rights people might attribute to computers; and that means there are open questions about the emotion words they could or should use.

Beyond the assignment of words, thinking about emotion is an extraordinarily complex process. It is, of course, one of the themes of this chapter that the systems we use to think and talk about emotion are subtle, powerful, and tricky—prone to simplify and direct us in ways that we do not notice. It is the basic contention of the chapter that it is greatly to the advantage of emotion-oriented computing, or any other area dealing with emotion, to be alert to those properties.

Obviously these observations are scratching the surface of a huge subject. However, it seems important to lay down a marker that descriptions are missing something critical if they do not set segments of emotional life in the context of larger processes to which the emotion is harnessed.

# 3.7 Conclusion

The attempt to optimize everyday descriptions of emotion is an ongoing project, and it has only gradually become clear how substantial it is. At the beginning of HUMAINE, it was assumed that terminological confusions could be cleared up early in the project by producing a glossary. By the end, the kind of conception outlined here had begun to consolidate from a series of discussion papers and meetings, often stormy. The ideas outlined here underpin the formal annotation scheme used in the HUMAINE database.

The most important aspect of the conception is the project. This chapter has offered a sketch of the resources needed to describe emotional life in a reasonably intuitive and inclusive way. It is clearly possible to improve on the details, and it would be disappointing if improved schemes did not emerge. However, it seems true that there is a need to develop descriptive systems that reflect everyday intuitions about emotional life in an orderly way, so that those intuitions can be brought effectively into play when other tasks are addressed. If we cannot describe what we are studying, it is difficult to see how we can expect to achieve a deep understanding of it, scientific or philosophical.

## References

Ajazen, I. (1988). *Attitudes, Personality and Behavior*. Chicago: Dorsey Press.

André, E., Dybkjaer, L., Minker, W., and Heisterkamp, P. (eds). (2004). *Proceedings of Affective Dialogue Systems: Tutorial and Research Workshop, ADS 2004, Kloster Irsee, Germany, June 14–16, 2004* : Lecture Notes in Computer Science 3538. Berlin: Springer.

Aristotle (1947). *The Rhetoric*, Book II. In R. McKeown tr., *The Basic Works of Aristotle*. New York: Random House, 1379–1434.

Arnold, M. (1960). *Emotion and Personality 1.* New York: Columbia University Press.

Ben Ze'ev, A. (2000). 'I only have eyes for you': The partiality of positive emotions. *Journal for the Theory of Social Behaviour* 30 (3), 341–51.

Combetto, M. (2006). Affective Systems in Human-Centric Intelligent Environments. In *Proceedings of WP9 Workshop on Innovative Approaches for Evaluating Affective*

*Systems*, Kristina Höök, Jarmo Laaksolahti (eds.) HUMAINE deliverable D9e <http:// emotion-research.net/projects/humaine/deliverables/d9e> accessed 3 November 2008.

COWIE, R. (2005). What are people doing when they assign everyday emotion terms? *Psychological Inquiry* 16 (1), 11–18.

—— and CORNELIUS, R. (2003). Describing the emotional states that are expressed in speech. *Speech Communication* 40 (1–2), 5–32.

DAMASIO H., GRABOWSKI T., FRANK R., GALABURDA A. M., and DAMASIO A. R. (1994). The return of Phineas Gage: Clues about the brain from the skull of a famous patient. *Science* 264 (5162), 1102–5.

DOUGLAS-COWIE, E., CAMPBELL, N., COWIE, R., and ROACH, P. (2003). Emotional speech: Towards a new generation of databases. *Speech Communication* 40 (1–2), 33–60.

—— DEVILLERS, L., MARTIN, J., COWIE, R., SAVVIDOU, S., ABRILIAN, S., and COX, C. (2005). Multimodal databases of everyday emotion: Facing up to complexity. *Interspeech-2005*. Lisbon, Portugal, 813–16.

EKMAN, P. (1973). *Darwin and Facial Expression: A Century of Research in Review*. New York: Academic Press.

—— (1999). *Basic Emotions*. In T. Dalglish and M. Power (eds.) *Handbook of Cognition and Emotion*. Chichester: John Wiley and Sons, 45–60.

——, and Friesen, W. (1975). *Pictures of Facial Affect*. Palo Alto, CA: Consulting Psychologists' Press.

EYSENCK, M. (1997). *Anxiety and Cognition: A Unified Theory*. Hove, UK: Psychology Press.

——, DERAKSHAN, N., SANTOS, R., and CALVO, M. G. (2007). Anxiety and cognitive performance: Attentional control theory. *Emotion* 7 (2), 336–53.

FEHR, B. and Russell, J. A. (1984). Concept of emotion viewed from a prototype perspective. *Journal of Experimental Psychology: General* 113, 464–86.

FONTAINE, J., SCHERER, K., ROESCH, E., and ELLSWORTH, P, (2007). The world of emotions is not two-dimensional. *Psychological Science* 18 (12), 1050–57.

FRIJDA, N. (1986). *The Emotions*. Cambridge: Cambridge University Press.

GENDOLLA, G. H. E. and KRÜSKEN, J. (2002). Mood, task demand, and effort-related cardiovascular response. *Cognition and Emotion* 16, 577–603.

GOLDIE, P. (2000). *The Emotions: A Philosophical Exploration*. Oxford: The Clarendon Press.

GRAESSER, A. C., VANLEHN, K., ROSÉ, C. P., JORDAN, P. W., and HARTER, D. (2001). Intelligent tutoring systems with conversational dialogue. *AI Magazine* 22 (4), 39–51.

HUANG M. P., ALESSI N. E. (1999). Presence as an emotional experience. In J. D. Westwood, H. M. Hoffman, R.A. Robb, D. Stredney (eds.), *Medicine Meets Virtual Reality: The Convergence of Physical and Informational Technologies Options for a New Era in Healthcare*. Amsterdam: IOS Press, 148–53.

ISEN, A. M. (1998). On the relationship between affect and creative problem solving. In S. Russ (ed.), *Affect, Creative Experience, and Psychological Adjustment*. Ann Arbor, MI: Braun-Brumfield, 3–17.

JAMES, W. (1884). What is an emotion? *Mind* 9, 188–205.

KIENAST, M. and SENDLMEIER, W. F. (2000). Acoustical analysis of spectral and temporal changes in emotional speech. In R. Cowie, E. Douglas-Cowie, and M. Schröder (eds.), *Speech and Emotion: Proceedings of the ISCA Workshop*. Newcastle, Co. Down, September 2000, 92–7.

LANEY C., CAMPBELL H. V., HEUER F., and REISBERG D. (2004). Memory for thematically arousing events. *Memory and Cognition* 32, 1149–59.

LAZARUS, R. S. (1999). *Stress and Emotion: A New Synthesis.* Springer, New York.

O'CONNOR. J. D. and ARNOLD, G. F. (1973). *Intonation in Colloquial English.* (2nd edn). London: Longman.

ORTONY A (2002). On making believable emotional agents believable. In R. Trappl, P. Petta, and S. Payr (eds.), *Emotions in Humans and Artifacts.* Cambridge, MA: MIT Press. 189–212.

—— CLORE, G. L., and COLLINS A. (1988). *The Cognitive Structure of Emotions.* New York: Cambridge University Press.

OSGOOD, C., SUCI, G., and TANNENBAUM, P. (1967). *The Measurement of Meaning.* Urbana: University of Illinois Press.

PAGANELLI, F., SPINICCI, E., and GIULI, D. (2008). ERMHAN: A Context-Aware Service Platform to Support Continuous Care Networks for Home-Based Assistance. *International Journal of Telemedicine and Applications* Vol. 2008, Article ID 867639 <http://www.hindawi.com/journals/ijta/q2.2008.html> accessed 3 November 2008.

PAIVA, A., PRADA, R., and PICARD, R. (2007). *Proceedings of the Second International Conference on Affective Computing and Intelligent Interaction, Lisbon, Portugal, September 12–14, 2007.* Lecture Notes in Computer Science Vol. 4738. Berlin: Springer Verlag.

PANKSEPP, J. (2003). At the interface of the affective, behavioral, and cognitive neurosciences: Decoding the emotional feelings of the brain. *Brain and Cognition* 52, 4–14.

PETTA, P. (ed.) (in press). *The HUMAINE Handbook.* Berlin: Springer Verlag.

PICARD, R. (2000). *Affective Computing.* Cambridge, MA: MIT Press.

PROUDFOOT, J., SWAIN, S., WIDMER, S., WATKINS, E., GOLDBERG, D., MARKS, I., MANN A., and GRAY J. A. (2003). The development and beta-test of a computer-therapy program for anxiety and depression: Hurdles and lessons. *Computers in Human Behavior* 19 (3), 277–89.

REISENZEIN, R. (2007). What is a definition of emotion? And are emotions mental-behavioral processes? *Social Science Information* 46 (3), 424–8.

ROSCH, E. (1978): Principles of categorization. In E. Rosch and B. Lloyd (eds.), *Cognition and Categorization.* London: Lawrence Erlbaum Associates, 27–48.

RUIZ-BELDA, M.-A., FERNANDEZ-DOLS, J.-M., CARRERA, P. and BARCHARD, K. (2003). Spontaneous facial expressions of happy bowlers and soccer fans. *Cognition and Emotion* 17 (2), 315–26.

RUSSELL, J. A (2003). Core affect and the psychological construction of emotion. *Psychological Review* 110 (1), 145–72.

—— and FEHR, B. (1994). Fuzzy concepts in a fuzzy hierarchy: Varieties of anger. *Journal of Personality and Social Psychology* 67, 186–205.

—— and FELDMAN-BARRETT L. (1999). Core affect, prototypical emotional episodes, and other things called emotion: Dissecting the elephant. *Journal of Personality and Social Psychology* 76, 805–19.

SABINI J. and SILVER M. (2005). Why emotion names and experiences don't neatly pair. *Psychological Inquiry* 16, 11–48.

SANDER, D., GRANDJEAN, D., and SCHERER, K. (2005). A systems approach to appraisal mechanisms in emotion. *Neural Networks* 18, 317–52.

SCHERER, K. (2005). What are emotions? And how can they be measured? *Social Science Information* 44 (4), 695–729.

SCHRÖDER, M., DEVILLERS, L., KARPOUZIS, K., MARTIN, J.-C., PELACHAUD, C., PETER, C., PIRKER, H., SCHULLER, B., TAO J., and WILSON I. (2007). What should a generic emotion markup language be able to represent? In A. Paiva, R. Prada, and R. Picard (eds.),

*Proceedings of the Second International Conference on Affective Computing and Intelligent Interaction, Lisbon, Portugal, September 12–14, 2007.* Lecture Notes in Computer Science Vol. 4738. Berlin: Springer Verlag, 440–51.

SHAVER, P., SCHWARTZ, J., KIRSON, D. and O'CONNOR, C. (2001). Emotion knowledge: Further exploration of a prototype approach. In W. G Parrott (ed.), *Emotions in Social Psychology: Essential Readings.* Philadelphia: Psychology Press, 26–56.

SIEMER, M. (2005). Moods as multiple-object directed and as objectless affective states: An examination of the dispositional theory of moods. *Cognition and Emotion* 19 (6), 815–45.

SOSA, E. (2007). Experimental philosophy. *Philosophical Studies* 132 (1), 99–107.

STEMMLER G., HELDMANN M., PAULS C., and SCHERER T. (2001). Constraints for emotion specificity in fear and anger: The context counts. *Psychophysiology* 69, 275–91.

STERNBERG, R. J. (1988). Triangulating love. In R. J. Sternberg, M. L. Barnes *The Psychology of Love.* Yale: Yale University Press, 119–38.

STOCK, O. and STRAPPARAVA, C. (2003). Getting serious about the development of computational humor. *Proc. International Joint Conference on Artificial Intelligence, Acapulco, Mexico 2003*, 59–64.

STOCK, O., ZANCANARO, M., KOREN, C., ROCCHI, C., EISIKOVITS, Z., GOREN-BAR, D., TOMASINI, D., WEISS, P. (2008). A co-located interface for narration to support reconciliation in a conflict: Initial results from Jewish and Palestinian youth. *Proceedings 26th SIGCHI Conference on Human Factors in Computing Systems* 1583–92.

STOCKER, M. and HEGMAN, E. (1992). *Valuing Emotions.* Cambridge: Cambridge University Press.

WATSON, D., CLARK, L.A., and TELLEGEN A. (1988). Development and validation of brief measures of positive and negative affect: The PANAS scales. *Journal of Personality and Social Psychology* 54, 1063–60.

WICHMANN, A. (2002). Attitudinal intonation and the inferential process. *Proceedings of the Speech Prosody Conference 2002.* 11–16.

WILHELM, P., SCHOEBI, D., and PERREZ, M. (2004). Frequency estimates of emotions in everyday life from a diary method's perspective: A comment on Scherer et al.'s survey-study 'Emotions in everyday life'. *Social Science Information* 43 (4), 647–65.

WILLIAMSON, T. (2008). *The Philosophy of Philosophy.* Oxford: Blackwell.

..............................................................................

# CHAPTER 4

# THE MIND'S BERMUDA TRIANGLE: PHILOSOPHY OF EMOTIONS AND EMPIRICAL SCIENCE

..............................................................................

## RONALD DE SOUSA

## 4.1 INTRODUCTION

..............................................................................

My broad concern in this chapter is with the fruitfulness of intercourse between science and philosophy. I will approach this by focusing more narrowly, first, on a sampling of approaches adopted by practitioners of emotion science, and, secondly, on two specific sample problems. Of those two, one represents a time-worn philosophical puzzle, while the other is relatively new. The verdict will be mixed. Throughout the history of our subject, philosophers have claimed certainty for propositions regarded as necessarily true, but contradicted with equal aplomb by other philosophers. In this respect, philosophy's record is only slightly better than that of theology. It's time to say *Nostra Culpa*, and to start emulating the more tentative stance of science. On the other hand, we will find that philosophers have often done quite well at anticipating or framing, by dint of careful analysis, the scientific findings most relevant to our conclusions. Scientific findings sometimes come not to establish so much as merely to flesh out a picture already drawn fairly lucidly by philosophers.

Some empirical facts, if established, must have consequences for our philosophical views. If, for example, it could be shown that *all* of our behaviour is robotically determined by universal dispositions triggered by specific circumstances—with or without some room for play generated by randomness—then our notion of moral responsibility would require some reconstruction.

Conceptions of emotions, like other aspects of the philosophy of mind, are particularly liable to be affected by empirical discoveries. Sometimes we may find ourselves driven to trade off definitional axioms against empirical claims. Commonplace observations appear to contradict conventional assumptions and definitions. One example: we think emotions are grounded in articulable intentional states, and yet we ascribe emotions to infants and animals. We could define the latter away by speaking of "proto-emotions". Or we could amend the original assumption in the light of the homologies between the physiological and behavioural dispositions of humans and other animals. Similarly, starting with the fact of "recalcitrant emotions"—such as fear of flying—that appear to embody judgements inconsistent with those we rationally endorse, we can give up the doctrine that emotions embody judgements, or give up the axiom that we can't simultaneously endorse contradictory judgements. I shall argue that a third option should be preferred: we can try to construct an empirically adequate model that removes the apparent contradiction. A baseline constraint on a satisfying explanation is that it rest on empirically ascertainable mechanisms.

A promising framework for understanding many of the puzzles generated by the role of emotions in motivation and behaviour, I shall suggest, is to be found in the idea of the "two-track mind". This is the hypothesis that our behaviour derives from two relatively independent processing systems with different evolutionary origins in the brain. This approach is currently widely endorsed: a 2004 book lists some two dozen versions (Stanovich 2004, 30), and it is being applied to a surprisingly diverse range of problems including mathematical reasoning and knowledge ascription (Dehaene 1997; Nagel 2009). If indeed there are two types of mental processing, the fact that they sometimes yield incompatible verdicts ceases to be surprising.

## 4.2 BLURRING THE BOUNDARIES

Philosophy's traditionally lofty self-image rests on two props. One is the idea that philosophy's job is conceptual analysis; the other is that by virtue of being a native speaker I have privileged access to the concepts I set about to analyse. On these two grounds, we don't have to pay too much attention to non-linguistic facts. I shall call "conceptual autonomy" the presupposition, going back to Hume, that all truth claims can be classed into one of two groups. Those that pertain to "relations of ideas" comprise the *necessary,* the *analytic,* and the *a priori.* Science, by contrast, is in the business of inquiring into "matters of fact", consisting in *contingent, synthetic, a posteriori* truths. Curiously, it seems Hume didn't ask in which category the distinction itself is to be placed, though he urges that whatever is not one or the other we should "commit . . . to the flames: for it can contain nothing but sophistry and illusion" (Hume 1975, §12 Pt III). Sure enough, the two groups have not maintained their apparent orderly coherence. In Hume's stark version all and only relations of ideas are analytic, necessary, and knowable a priori. For Kant, some necessities, such as those of arithmetic, are a priori but synthetic. More recently Saul Kripke has argued that some contingent truths might be known a priori, and that some necessary truths are known a posteriori (Kripke 1980). In illustration of the former, he cites the Standard Metre Bar deposited at the Paris Bureau of Weights and Measures. Although it has now lost its status, this was once the object by reference to which the metre was defined. Any other thing was a metre long if it was *the same length* as the Meter Bar. Contrary to Wittgenstein, who alleged that it made no sense to ascribe a particular length to the Standard Metre Bar (Wittgenstein 1953, §50), Kripke plausibly maintained that, at any particular time under specific conditions, the fact that the Standard Bar is just *that length* remains contingent; it is known a priori and true by definition, however, that *that length* is one metre. A necessary truth known a posteriori is that water is essentially $H_2O$. Essences are necessary, but since they must be discovered they are not analytic.

The dogma of privileged access to meaning is neatly captured by Descartes's claim that I may not always know what I see, but what I *seem* to see "cannot be false" even when I am dreaming (Descartes 1986, Med. II, 29). And, Descartes assumes, I must know what I mean when I say that. This is the germ of the programme of Husserl's Phenomenology, which aims to identify essences by attending to pure experience, stripped bare by "epoche" or suspension of ontological assumptions (Husserl 1960).

In the light of recent philosophical and scientific work, both conceptual autonomy and privileged access must be abandoned. Since Quine's 1951 "blurring of the supposed boundary between speculative metaphysics and natural science" (Quine 1980, 20), many philosophers of mind have been keen to recover philosophy's kinship with science. Quine rejected the absolute distinction between synthetic and analytic propositions. Semantics evolve in the service of pragmatic ends. Making adjustments in our understanding of words is sometimes more expedient than changing our beliefs about empirical facts. Particular observations and general principles are tested against one another, and adjustments can go either way. Others have explored the significance of this blurring of boundaries. Ruth Millikan has attacked "meaning rationalism", the doctrine that we have incorrigible access to our own meanings—specifically meaning identity and difference, univocity, and meaningfulness (Millikan 1993). In the spirit of that work, but omitting much detail, I now sketch two arguments against the programme of phenomenology, interpreted as the doctrine that skilled introspection can give reliable access to the character and meaning of one's own mental states or dispositions.[1]

## 4.3  Two arguments against phenomenology

It is standard procedure in "conceptual analysis" to rely on intuitions about "what we would say". We might ask: "What would you say to someone who was sincerely convinced that she had seen a round square?"; "If someone had committed a crime under the influence of a post-hypnotic suggestion, would you say she was responsible for that crime?"; or perhaps: "What would we say if we were being addressed in English by a living and apparently ordinary tortoise?" This procedure raises many questions, not least of which are whom we should choose to ask, and why we should care about the answer. But the problem that goes to the heart of the phenomenological method is that the answer you get to the hypothetical question "if p, would you say (or do) q?" may not be indicative of what you would actually do or say if p were known to be true. Assenting to "if p, I would assent to q" does not establish that one would, on learning that p, actually assent to q. This simple point suffices to establish that correct answers to such hypothetical questions about

[1] The arguments in the next section are narrowly targeted at phenomenology as a method capable of yielding certainty about mental states and meanings. They are not intended to impugn the usefulness of introspection as an adjunct to cognitive science. It is clear that paying careful attention to the features of experience might disclose constraints on the possible physiological or computational explanations of those experiences, just as those physiological processes themselves limit the possible interpretations of those experiences. There are active debates about the role of phenomenology in the cognitive sciences. See Gallagher and Varela (2001), and contributions to a special issue of *Phenomenology and Cognitive Science* (notably Roy 2007; Siewert 2007; Thompson 2007; Dennett 2007). Among the disputed aspects of phenomenology are the irreducibility of the first person, and the question of whether phenomenologists expect the analysis of experience to yield knowledge of the underlying mechanisms. I take no position here on those broader issues. (But see de Sousa 1999.)

one's mental dispositions are not reliably accessible to consciousness. Our systematic inability to gauge our past and future evaluations is but one aspect of our ignorance of our motives and dispositions, a lacuna in our conscious life which cognitive science has abundantly established (Gilbert 2006; Wilson 2002).

It might be objected that the limitations just noted concern only our *future* emotions and behaviour. We might still have incorrigible insight into our *present* states, if only these could be adequately delimited. But the second argument disposes of that possibility, showing that we don't even have incorrigible access to the meaning of our current beliefs. The referential content of a belief depends on the meaning of the terms in which I would express it. That in turn depends on factors that are beyond my knowledge or control. This thesis of "externalism"—in one of several senses that have been the topic of philosophical controversy—was first put forward by Hilary Putnam in an influential paper (Putnam 1975) in which he famously argued: "Meanings ain't in the head." The meaning of a speaker's utterance depends in part on causal or referential facts that may be unavailable to that speaker. In particular, the denotation of a term commonly depends on the identity of the thing or stuff to which other speakers first intended to apply it. If so, then I can have no incorrigible knowledge of that referent's nature. To the extent that the referent's original nature partly determines the meaning of what I have "in mind", then, I do not have incorrigible knowledge of my own meaning.

Here is a different way of making the same point. Meaning presupposes some idea of function: the meaning of a term relates to the function that the term serves in our linguistic economy. But we can identify a function only in the context of the larger environment in which that function is effected. Inspection of a pair of scissors in isolation would not reveal their function. We need to see them at work with paper, thread, or dough. Similarly, any meaning function presupposes a context that includes, for each word used, contrastive and distributive sets. The meaning of "blue" depends in part on all the colour words that might fit in the same contexts, as well as on the sorts of sentential contexts in which "blue" and its contrasts could figure (Ziff 1964). Not all of that is necessarily available to me right now. I cannot have present experience of the larger context that provides my experience with its full meaning. Indeed, if I did have access to it, understanding the functional role of that context would presuppose a still larger context and so generate a regress. The experience of meaning is not in general capable of revealing the fullness of meaning.[2]

The foregoing arguments are not examples of empirical facts affecting philosophy. Instead they are conceptual arguments for admitting the empirical into

---

[2] It is worth noting that the same argument refutes rather than supports any type-identity of brain states and meanings. A neural state does not wear its own history on its face. But that history might be crucial to the determination of its function. The function and meaning of a state S might be different, for example, depending on whether S is reached on the way from A to B or from B to A.

philosophy. They are of particular relevance to emotions because emotions are typically *felt*. One might therefore assume that they are best explored from the subjective point of view. But insofar as an emotion's nature involves meanings, the arguments just sketched entail that what emotions feel like cannot give us full access to their nature. Emotions are also characteristically the most obviously embodied of our mental states. Their manifestations are both mental and physical, and theories of emotion over the last century and a half have distributed themselves along the path of a pendulum swinging between the physiological and the intentional poles. The first is represented by William James (1884) and recently by Damasio (1999); the other by "cognitivists" such as Robert Solomon (1984, 2007) or Martha Nussbaum (2001) whose views of emotions stress judgement, intentionality, and even choice. But emotions are also historically determined; and we have just seen that the reason we don't have full access to the meaning of our own mental states is precisely that they are in part historically determined. It follows that emotions are not altogether knowable on the basis of what is available only in the moment's consciousness. Indeed, emotions are shaped by history on at least two levels: that of individual development from zygote through infant to adult, but also on the phylogenetic scale of our evolution into the animals we are. Consequently it is not surprising that emotions are not entirely transparent to consciousness.

## 4.4 EMOTIONS AND THE TWO-TRACK MIND

The traditional view of emotions as *disruptive* gives them a central role to play in the experience of inner conflict, which in turn has motivated some of the best-known models of the dynamics or structure of the person in philosophy and science. Plato posited three parts of the soul, arguing that emotion could not be identified with either reason or desire since it sided sometimes with one and sometime with the other (Plato 1997, Bk VII). Freud also favoured a three-part model, but did not assign a clear place for emotions, which span all three of Id, Ego, and Superego (Freud 1923). We get yet another three-part model in neuroscientist Paul MacLean's (1975) "triune brain". MacLean suggested that the structure of our brains reflects a phylogenetic development in which successive layers partly replaced but also partly reduplicated functions established in earlier structures. A primitive "crocodile" brain controls basic autonomic bodily functions and is homologous with that of even distant vertebrate cousins; the limbic system, which we have in common with close mammalian relatives, is responsible for the more instinctual dispositions built into our emotional repertoires; and our uniquely developed neo-cortex takes care of so-called "higher" functions. The limbic system is commonly assimilated to the "emotional brain", and there is plenty of evidence for the importance of those brain regions to at least "basic" emotions or "affect programs" (Griffiths 1997). But emotions more loosely defined involve cortical regions as well. Another version of the "divided brain" is the two-hemisphere theory that Gazzaniga (1970) and others inferred from the effects of commissurotomies undertaken to impede the progress of particularly devastating epileptic episodes. Commissurotomy patients appeared in some respects literally to have "two minds". There is some evidence that left-hemisphere dominance was associated with a propensity to depression, while right-hemisphere dominance in the presence of a left-side lesion has been reported to leave a person more cheerful (Taylor 2006). But none of that work gives us reason to attribute a more significant role to one hemisphere in emotions generally.

The lack of clean fit between any of those models and the great variety of what we are wont to call emotions suggests that emotions are too diverse to be pinned to a specific part of the brain. Many of the features we associate with the modus operandi of emotions, however, can be classified as belonging to the First or Intuitive Track in the two-track model mentioned above. The contrast between an "intuitive" and an "analytic" mode of processing is reminiscent of the Freudian distinction between primary and secondary processing (Freud 1911). For Freud, however, primary processing was something we needed to get over very quickly, because it was driven exclusively by the "pleasure principle", dominated by the search for instant gratification. It was guided by fantasy rather than by any ability to track the outside world. In modern formulations of the two-track mind, both the intuitive and the analytic types of mental functioning are vital parts of our normal adult life. Intuitive processes are sometimes thought to be modular; they are typically associative, holistic, relatively fast, parallel, automatic, cognitively undemanding, highly contextualized, and organized around stable, "short-leashed" goal structures. Analytic processes, by contrast, are rule-based, controlled, serial, cognitively demanding, relatively slow, decontextualized, and organized around "long-leashed" and frequently updated goals.[3] The analytic system is typically dependent on explicit linguistic or at least digital representation. This explains why computers are much more easily programmed to perform the latter class of tasks, including ones we find very hard, such as complex analytic calculations. Tasks we find easy—walking, catching a ball, recognizing a face, reading handwriting—have turned out to be hardest to programme. This would greatly have surprised Descartes, who thought that animal functions would be easy to replicate in automata, whereas anything resembling reason would be impossible. But to us it should not seem surprising, remembering that arithmetic and other analytic

---

[3] See Stanovich (2004); also Strack and Deutsch (2004), whose "Impulsive" and "Reflective" systems correspond roughly to my "Intuitive" and "Analytic".

systems are recent inventions, whereas the intuitive systems that mostly keep us alive from day to day have evolved over millions of years, albeit often in a "klugey" way (Marcus 2008), and we don't in general know exactly how to reverse-engineer them. Notice, however, that while we, like Descartes, continue to regard explicit thinking as essentially human, most of our life skills are governed by the intuitive track. As Paul Churchland has remarked,

We are able to discriminate and recognize faces, colors, smells, voices, spatial relations, musical compositions, locomotor gaits, the facial expression of emotions, flowing liquids, falling bodies, and a million other things besides, where the exercise of these discriminative skills is once again largely or wholly inarticulable. (Churchland 2007, 90)

## 4.5 MODELS OF EMOTION

Emotions have been fitted into these and other models in a bewildering variety of ways. Some start from terms familiar to us from folk psychology: desire, belief, will. Others start with what are taken to be simpler component states such as arousal or activation, and valence or degree of pleasantness or unpleasantness (Russell 2005). Robert Plutchik (2001) arranges terms from the repertoire of folk psychology onto a concentric wheel, generating complex emotions as blends of simpler ones, comprising surprise, fear, sorrow, disgust, anticipation, anger, joy, and acceptance. The same list, minus "anticipation" and "acceptance", forms the six "basic emotions" that have, according to Ekman and Friesen (1975), a claim to universality of both experience and recognition. Yet another approach, based on a number of different dimensions of appraisal, is represented by Klaus Scherer (2005), who recently offered the following definition of emotion:

an episode of interrelated, synchronized changes in the states of all or most of the five organismic subsystems in response to the evaluation of an external or internal stimulus event as relevant to major concerns of the organism.

Scherer's five systems are: *evaluation of objects and events; system regulation; preparation and direction of action; communication of reaction and behavioural intention;* and *monitoring of internal state and organism-environment interaction.* In experience, these correspond respectively to the cognitive component; neurophysiological events; motivation; a motor expression component; and subjective feeling. (Scherer 2005, 697–8). For Jaak Panksepp's (2001), there are four major systems controlling emotion: a "seeking system", corresponding to joy; an "attack system", and two more, "fear" and "panic", which common speech doesn't distinguish very clearly but which differ as threat of harm differs from threat of abandonment in roughly the sense of Bowlby (1969–80). These cut across Scherer's five "components": each system comprises a coordinated set of genetically designed hormonal modulators and neural circuits, involving specific regions of the brain, as well as characteristic behavioural and experiential aspects.

It should be clear from this partial sampling that, while there is not one single scientific approach to the modelling of emotions, emotions theory has not unequivocally emerged from the methodological chaos that entitles it to be called philosophy. The diversity of these models suggests a need, in Locke's apt phrase, for conceptual "under-labourer[s] . . . removing some of the rubbish that lies in the way to knowledge" (Locke 1975, 9–10). Nevertheless it seems unpromising to philosophize about emotions without an eye on what those various scientific approaches can teach us. I shall suggest that the complications entailed for our conception of emotions will bring some gain in our potential understanding, but also some risk of loss.

## 4.6 FREE WILL

I move now to the first of my illustrative puzzles: the problem of the will in science and philosophy. The will presents us with the classic case of inner conflict in "weakness of the will" or *akrasia*, which motivated Plato and others to postulate the "divided soul" models mentioned above. But I focus not on conflict but on the very idea of a will.

Sartre (1993) famously said that we are "condemned to be free". If I ask you to wag your finger, you might or might not comply, but you cannot avoid deciding. If you wag your finger, that is a decision; if you refuse, it is one too. And if you simply ignore me, that too is a decision. Anyone observing you can just wait and see what the random processes or causal chains that govern your behaviour will determine you to do; but you yourself cannot.

Nevertheless, Daniel Wegner (2002) has presented a number of ingenious experiments to demonstrate that conscious will is an illusion. Some of his manipulations replicate table turning, in which agents act while entirely convinced of having merely "followed" the table's movements without any causal input whatever. Wegner also devised experiments to generate the opposite illusion, in which subjects are convinced they are doing something which in actual fact is entirely out of their control. This shows that the subjective sense of control is not always veridical. Further evidence for this has come from the now well-known experiments of Benjamin Libet (Libet et al. 1979), which showed that in situations like the simple finger-wagging case above, the consciousness of deciding lags almost a whole second behind the activation of the readiness potential that signals that the machinery of motion has already been triggered, and about 200–300ms after the activation of the brain's motor centres. We are forced to conclude—on pain of giving up the axiom that causes precede their effects—that free will cannot be assimilated to the causal efficacy of conscious decision. On the contrary, "deciding" is no less an effect of something else than the act itself. In one more illustration of the self-ignorance already noted, Wegner surmised that the consciousness of having willed something is often a confabulation, devised after the fact on the basis of common-sense assumptions about what would justify behaviour of that kind.

Some more news from neuroscience, however, may mitigate this demotion of the role of consciousness in the elaboration of voluntary behaviour. Patrick Haggard successfully replicated Libet's result, but suggested that, while the overall planning of an act undoubtedly precedes consciousness, we can ascribe to the latter a monitoring and predictive role in the detail of the plan's execution: "Conscious intentions are at least partly preconstructions, rather than mere reconstructions" (Haggard 2005, 293). This idea is supported in Shariff and Peterson (2008), who argue that we can keep as much free will as anyone ought to want providing we recognize two different mechanisms in the brain, one of which executes a plan elaborated in the longer term by the other. The executive phase, which does not involve consciousness, is a First Track process, even when it has been set up by Second Track deliberation (see also Clark 2007). This fits the phenomenology of action nicely. If you are a skier, Shariff and Peterson point out, you look not at the tip of your skis but several yards beyond you. What your skis are doing now was determined by your look ahead a few fractions of a second ago. Indeed, in new work by John-Dylan Haynes and his colleagues at the Max Planck Institute, using fMRI, the brain has been found to have embarked on an action as much as 10 seconds before the moment of conscious "decision" (Soon et al. 2008). In effect, then, what we interpret as the present is really the future: subjective experience misconstrues what is actually an anticipation and reads it as present consciousness. The awareness of a stimulus is attributed to the present, but it actually targets the future and is referred back. Conscious time is out of step with real time.

The experiments just cited are impressive, and it is hard to deny that they must have philosophical consequences. But it isn't easy to say what these are. To begin with, they don't suffice to establish that "there is no free will": that depends on just what that term is taken to imply. It need not, in particular, include the requirement that the moment of conscious decision must be the determining causal factor in ordinary action. That cannot be the case since it takes place after the whole mechanism of action has been set in motion. But we could know that by just thinking about it. A classic argument runs as follows. Libertarians require that a free will must be either independent or fully conscious of any determining factor.

If I claim sole responsibility for an action, I should be entitled to affirm that I originated or consciously took account of all the factors that have determined that decision. If my origination of the act was unrelated to any previously existing wants, inclinations, or prior intentions, then it cannot count as mine. If, on the other hand, my act did have immediate causal antecedents in my states of mind and character, then those states in turn may have been determined by others of which I am not and could not possibly be aware. In short, the libertarian requirement is incoherent.

In the light of that argument, we didn't need the science to tell us that conscious will or decision cannot be the uncaused origin of action. Once again, the brain data may be little more than interesting elaborations of a point already worked out correctly by philosophy—in this case by Hume, who pointed out that chance, not freedom, is the opposite of necessity (Hume 1975, §VIII Pt I). Chance is not what libertarians want. They think there must be room here for absolute origination by the self, a pure act of uncaused creation that is neither determined nor random. Hume couldn't understand what this amounted to; I can't understand what it means either. Libertarians think they can make sense of it (Wiggins 1987; van Inwagen 1983). To avoid mere invective or accusations of irrationality, it is perhaps best to concede that both sides may be manifesting differences of philosophical temperament which will not be bridged by argument alone. This attests to the reality of intellectual temperament, which remains at the root of many differences of opinion even if one has abandoned the theological certainty I deplored above.

The mutual incomprehension of compatibilist and libertarian also affords an entry point into my last illustrative case, by providing a little-noticed example of an *inability to imagine* how someone could hold a given position. Several related phenomena have been discussed under the heading of "imaginative resistance". The ones I shall focus on are very different; but it is well to keep in mind the parochial case of mutually unimaginable philosophical positions.

## 4.7  IMAGINATIVE RESISTANCE

Imagination is a tool for the exploration of the possible. But what is possible and what is imaginable are not the same. Imaginary numbers, for example, despite their name, are not imaginable. Neither are higher dimensionalities. Yet both are well conceived mathematical realities. The converse is also false: to some extent, we can imagine some impossible things. When you are telling a story, the imagination is not limited to what is possible physically, or chemically, or even logically. Most impossibilities, if not all, can at least be "conceived", if only well enough for their impossibility to be clearly grasped. Imagination connotes *imaging*, though it isn't always understood to require it; hence the importance of sensory content when we imagine what exactly imagining might be. And yet there are limits to what can be imagined, as the case of philosophical incomprehension has just shown. To raise the question of the possibility of imagination is to presuppose that imagination can fail: the limits of imagination are set, in part, by what counts as *successful* imagination (Morton 2006). If I am asked to imagine an object specified in a self-contradictory formula, for example, I might claim to comply by listing successive observations of the inconsistent properties. Yes, I can imagine a round square: it's all smooth and uniform, and then I can feel the sharpness of the four corners. I might even be able to imagine seeing that a box is empty and that it contains a carved figurine (Priest 1997). Escher's prints represent impossible spatial relations and so can be thought to imagine them. And in Roy Sorensen's amusing challenge to provide a picture of an impossible object, he is at pains to preclude bogus entries such as this dot "." as a picture of an impossible object viewed from very far away (Sorensen 2002).

The general question of the limits of imagination is therefore complex, and too hard for me to sort out. My interest here is much narrower, and is motivated by my general concern with the contributions of science to the philosophy of emotion. The puzzle I want to focus on poses not so much problems of definition or logic but a specific form of the problem of will—it is, roughly speaking, a problem about the constraints on wanting and emoting at will. The puzzle I am concerned with is commonly said to have originated in a much cited passage where Hume describes our response to writings about other ages or places:

There needs but a certain turn of thought or imagination to make us enter into all the opinions, which then prevailed, and relish the sentiments or conclusions derived from them. But a very violent effort is requisite to change our judgment of manners, and excite sentiments of approbation or blame, love or hatred, different from those to which the mind from long custom has been familiarized. And where a man is confident of the rectitude of that moral standard, by which he judges, he is justly jealous of it, and will not pervert the sentiments of his heart for a moment, in complaisance to any writer whatsoever. (Hume 1965, §33)

The thought is that it is easy to imagine strange people doing extremely strange things, but that "a very violent effort" is needed to imagine oneself *approving* of what they do. What is not clear from Hume's remarks, however, is whether his allusion to effort implies that we may sometimes be literally *unable* to imagine endorsing certain judgements, or rather that we *ought* not do so: "I cannot, nor is it proper I should, enter into such sentiments", he writes in the preceding paragraph. If his claim is that we *should* not imagine certain things, he may be endorsing Plato's reason for banishing art, namely that art enlists the imagination in the promotion of bad behaviour. The tradition that rehearses this argument is alive and well even now (Inderscience 2008). Alluring though it is, I shall make every effort to evade that debate. Since "should" is often held to imply "can", some have taken the view that imaginative resistance is exclusively a matter of unwillingness rather than inability (Gendler 2000, 2006). In that guise, the puzzle raises questions about what we *want* to imagine; but it also invites us to ask whether there are constraints on *what we can want* to imagine. That aspect of it connects with a classic problem about the compatibilist conception of free will: whether some of my wants are deeper or more deeply "mine" than others, and how to tell which those are. And that, in turn, evokes a certain model of the self—as a sort of onion, perhaps, with endless concentric layers. Purely on the basis of conceptual analysis, then, even that narrow form of the puzzle leads us far afield.

Although Hume's discussion invoked specifically moral attitudes, the difference between moral and non-moral attitudes will be marginal to my concerns. I shall also ignore the question of the aesthetic value of immoral art or pleasure, except to acknowledge that the purest aesthete may find it difficult to circumscribe the aesthetic domain. Even the most hedonistic gourmet's pleasure in eating chocolate may be spoiled by the thought of the conditions under which cocoa beans are harvested. But that sort of interference may have more in common with distraction than with imaginative resistance—best compared to the difficulty of concentrating on your reading in a noisy environment. The difficulty that attends the sort of cases I am looking for is unlike this, and also unlike the difficulty I might find in imagining four-dimensional objects. What I am unable to do is not to frame the *content* of an imagined situation but to *respond* in certain ways to certain imagined prospects. That crucial distinction is nicely elucidated by Peter Goldie (2003, 57), who gives the following illustration: "The disgust and horror I now feel at my [imagined future] self, old, decrepit and senile, is a *response* to what I imagine; it is not part of the *content* of what I imagine."[4]

Two cases will most clearly make my point: *sexual arousal* and *amusement*. I know of, and to some extent can visualize (with or without the assistance of the *News of the World*) sexual practices that others enjoy, but which entirely fail to arouse me. Similarly, the same joke or event can move one person to laughter which, although I can see the point, leaves me quite cold.[5]

---

[4] See also Moran (1994). Goldie also rightly notes, borrowing an important distinction from Richard Wollheim (1984), that the same event can be either centrally or acentrally imagined, even where I cast myself as a protagonist in the imagined event. Depending on whether I am imagining centrally or acentrally, I might feel fear or compassion (ibid.).

[5] The target of the amusement doesn't have to be a joke. Here is a case where the target of laughter is an actual event. It is reported that, at a performance by child acrobats attended by Chairman Mao, one young boy fell and was badly hurt. The crowd cried out in horror—except for Mao, who laughed (Mirsky 1994, quoting Li Zhisui 1994).

Here is a joke, related to Jenny Diski by a South African acquaintance:

*"An Englishman, a Thai and an African were all together at Oxbridge. After some years the Englishman goes to visit the Thai who is hugely rich. How come? asks the Englishman. See that road? I own 10 per cent of it, the Thai tells him. The Englishman goes to visit the African, who is also hugely rich. How come? See that road? says the African. What road? the Englishman asks."* Moira waited for me to burst out laughing, but it was a minute or two before I could make anything at all of this story. Besides, what were the overseas students doing in Oxbridge in the first place if they weren't rich already? (Diski 2008)

Given a minute or two, Diski sees the point, and there is no obstacle to imagining the scene, set up as in any classic joke. But what she doesn't do is *find it funny*. Finding it funny *in that context* would require sharing the teller's perceived attitudes, including the assumption that making money out of failing to build a road is typical of Africans, and also perhaps contempt and resentment towards Africans in general. Suspension of disbelief is easy; but it is powerless to induce the attitude that is required to find something funny.

The qualifier "in that context" is important; Diski might have laughed if she had heard it from an African whose attitudes were subtly different. And one sometimes laughs at a joke for its sheer cleverness, despite one's disapproval of the underlying attitude. One may laugh at a joke one disapproves of, and one can even approve of laughing at jokes one disapproves of (Jacobson 1997). But the crucial point here is, using Goldie's useful distinction again, that our power to imagine a given *content* is virtually unlimited regardless of context, whereas our emotional *response* is not equally under our power.

What is true of amusement is also true of sexual arousal. Most people can think of *something* they find disgusting that some others—and perhaps even themselves, in other moods or other contexts—find arousing or actually do for pleasure. For those people, or in those moods, it might seem impossible to imagine *enjoying* the joke or the sexual practice. But what is really going on in these cases is not so much an inability to imagine but to experience a certain *emotional response* (or an absence of emotional response) to something imagined. A further complication is that one's imagination of the sexual scene (whether central or acentral) can include arousal in its *content*. And—as Peter Goldie has pointed out to me—while imagining one's own arousal may itself be arousing, a failure of response in the present might make it more difficult to imagine the arousal response as part of the content.

## 4.8 Lessons from psychopathy

As in all cases where likings or tastes are in question, we can wonder about the separability of cognitive and emotional responses. Psychopaths are widely reputed to be capable of reasoning impeccably and arriving at correct moral judgements, while altogether failing to be moved to act or care. We can describe the psychopath in either of two ways. One says that his avowals are merely insincere. The other, while deploring his failure to be moved, grants that he may be competent and sincere, since he can articulate the implications of the statement as well as anyone else. There is no cognitive content he is intentionally withholding. Each description appears to beg the question against the other. The second ignores the reasonable requirement of a condition of sincerity, where sincerity implies caring. But that claim itself assumes without proof that evaluative emotions supervene on the character of their cognitive base. It is at least logically possible that two people might have qualitatively identical sensations and cognitions in all respects except for the fact that one responds with liking and the other with dislike or indifference.

Whether and to what extent natural facts under-determine value judgements remains a live if somewhat metaphysical dispute. But recent findings about the brains of normals and psychopaths, as well as about normal brain activity under different circumstances, argue for a genuine gap between fact and value, or at least between cognition and caring. There are also differences in moral opinions between individuals belonging to different cultures and different times. At least it seems that way: the anthropological evidence is never wholly conclusive, however, since no sufficiently exhaustive descriptions could ever be given to show that the "situational meanings" of a belief or attitude were the same for two individuals (Moody-Adams 2002). No observation could conclusively refute the hypothesis that, for values as for tastes, approval and disapproval supervene uniquely on qualitative experiences: *If you don't like (or approve of) it then it doesn't taste (or look or seem) the same to you as it does to me.*

Even the evidence about psychopaths' brains remains inconclusive. At first sight, true psychopaths appear to be capable of saying all the right things; they simply fail to have the physiological responses associated, for "normal" subjects, with fear and empathy. They fail to be *moved* by their apparently evaluative endorsements (Blair et al. 2005). Here again, there seems to be room for a battle of intuitions about the limits of philosophical imagination (Dennett 1991). A zombie is a creature that gets full marks on the Turing test. A zombie's utterances are perfectly convincing as human utterances, even when discussing the most subtle shades of experience, but the zombie has no consciousness and experiences nothing. The psychopath seems to qualify as a *moral zombie*: able to manifest all the verbal signs of moral consciousness without any of the expected emotional responses. He says things that would normally indicate conscious moral experience, or *conscience,* while actually having none at all.[6]

In fact, however, the psychology and neurology of real psychopaths spare us the stalemate over the conceivability of moral zombies. True psychopaths do not actually pass the moral Turing test. They betray themselves in a subtle and curious way, in that their moral judgements reveal their deficit in the very act of trying to conceal it. Most subjects—from fairly early childhood—distinguish between prohibitions that derive from social convention such as etiquette and those that derive from the avoidance of harm and suffering (Turiel 2002). But when psychopaths are asked to classify different prohibitions, they tend to rank them all, even those that most clearly derive from social convention, with absolute prohibitions of harm. They do so, apparently, precisely because they are attempting to conceal their inability to feel the force of prohibitions based on harm (Prinz 2007, 44). Neuroscience has begun to identify the brain peculiarities that underlie those differences. Physiological measures show that the psychopath lacks distress responses in the face of others' suffering or his own imminent pain, correlated with a failure of the mechanisms of negative learning (Blair et al. 2005)

Neither can we refute, however, the theoretical presumption that the relation between the qualitative experience and the emotional response is contingent—that judgements of value do not supervene on perceptions of fact. No necessity, logical, physical, or psychological, precludes different emotional responses from being aroused by the very same qualitative experience. Although the psychopath's brain is differently wired, his experiences might be qualitatively identical to others' in all respects *except* for emotional response and motivation. We seem to be up against a stalemate. Can we do better?

Recall that in discussions of the puzzle of imaginative resistance some see genuine *inability* to imagine, while others see merely *unwillingness* to do so. I have tried to isolate two robust types of cases involving genuine inability or extreme difficulty. I venture to surmise that the temptation to view these cases as involving unwillingness springs from the fact that *we cannot want at will.* Given the independent reasons I have sketched for regarding the "will" as a concept too murky to shed light on anything at all, I propose, following hints offered by both Matravers (2003) and Currie (2002), that many of the phenomena under discussion can be explained in terms of the adaptive role of imagination in planning.

Our faculty to imagine counterfactual situations enables us to explore alternative scenarios and possible outcomes, in a process akin to computer "simulation" (Oatley 1999). This, in the happy phrase often attributed to Karl Popper, "allows

---

[6] Jesse Prinz makes this point by adapting Frank Jackson's famous thought experiment about colour scientist Mary, who has never been exposed to an actual colour experience. Prinz's variant is an ethical expert who has never previously had the emotional experience of responding in a way that is appropriate to the judgements she expertly makes (Prinz 2007, 38 ff.).

our hypotheses to die in our stead" (Dennett 1996). Such exploration has the function of providing information about a course of action's likely outcome, but also, crucially, about the significance of that outcome for the agent. If I were to abandon my attitudes when I explore the space of possibilities, the simulation would not serve its purpose. Hence we should not be surprised that our attitudes are more difficult to modify at will than the purely representational aspects of imagination.

The difficulty in question may, however, be a matter of degree. We've seen that our attitudes are not absolutely inflexible: they can vary according to context. We should be able to learn something from the nature of those variations. Simple observation, as well as some indirect evidence from brain studies, suggests that our attitudes are most resistant to change in the light of counterfactual imaginings when they are most likely to require us to *do* something. In fiction, our attitudes are safe from commitment: we can't be expected to do anything about it, and so we can allow ourselves a broader range of sympathies than we can in active life. But the same applies to cases of actual belief about remote events. Plato's thought experiment about the ring of Gyges would be ineffectual if the average person could not fantasize without too much guilt about enjoying the powers it conferred, but we might not feel comfortable doing the same with a real tyrant closer in time and space. Fiction can indeed serve to broaden our sympathies as well as our imagination; but the more extreme the divergence between our own and the imagined attitudes, the more secure we need to be in the thought that "there is [no] risk of being drawn into action" (Goldie 2003, 68). One consequence of this, as Goldie noted, is that we may sometimes care less about real people one personally knows than about fictional ones. A related point, yet sufficiently different to complicate the matter further, is made by the character of Pegeen in the climactic scene of Synge's *Playboy of the Western World*. Pegeen, who thought she admired Christy for murdering his father, changes her mind entirely when he actually splits his father's skull. "And what is it you'll say to me," he cries, "and I after doing it this time in the face of all." "I'll say," she replies, "a strange man is a marvel, with his mighty talk; but what's a squabble in your back-yard, and the blow of a loy, have taught me that there's a great gap between a gallous story and a dirty deed" (Synge 1911, III/223–4). Her answer underlines the essential unreliability, noted above, of assent to conditionals as an indicator of conditional assent. It also shows that the difference doesn't line up neatly with the distinction between fiction and practical imagination. In the case of real life, it is more important to protect our enduring attitudes through the thought experiment. Fiction, by contrast, can explore outlandish situations that might entail radical changes in our own values. Thus fiction can indeed take us to mental places closed to ordinary practical deliberation. This important fact tends to be forgotten by crusaders against violent and sexually aggressive games or films. Many who enjoy fantasy games as fiction would be repelled by the prospect of acting them out in real life.

Functional MRI explorations of the brain lend some credence to this view of what causes our resistance to shifts of attitudes. When subjects consider different versions of the "trolley problem", their response is driven more purely by emotion in proportion as their own involvement in the envisaged scenario gets more personal. Most people say they would flip the switch that would divert a trolley from a track where it will kill five people to one where only one will be killed; but the same subjects are mostly reluctant to effect the same result by physically pushing a single fat man onto the track. With few exceptions, they reject the consequentialist solution—save five lives at the cost of one—when their personal involvement is more immediate. Different parts of the brain are active when one is making the utilitarian calculation than when responding to the "deontological" prohibition against causing harm (Greene et al. 2001). Antonio Damasio and his colleagues confirmed this when they compared subjects suffering from a lesion in the Ventro Medial Prefrontal Cortex (VMPFC) with controls with intact brains. In those with damage to the VMPFC, an area crucial to emotion processing, the aversive character of personal intervention failed to overcome the utilitarian calculation of overall benefit. A brain lesion in the area responsible for controlling emotional response made subjects more "rational", that is, more consistently consequentialist (Koenigs et al. 2007). Ironically, in the light of Kant's disdain for emotions as motivators of authentically moral acts, this suggests that only con-sequentialists are moved by reason, while strict Kantians are responding purely to emotion (Haidt and Bjorklund 2008).

## 4.9 CONCLUSION

Jerry Fodor (1983) argued that certain functions of the mind were "modular", or encapsulated, that is, relatively immune to correction from other channels. Thus we see the stick as bent at the surface of the water even when we know it isn't, and we do not make visual illusions go away by ascertaining that we are not seeing them as they are. Perceptions are modular in this sense, but Fodor insisted that general cognition is not. In terms of the two-track model, this could be rephrased to say that First Track processes are modular, whereas Second Track ones are not. Efficient and speedy responses are produced without elaborate deliberation. Modularity can be plausibly explained in terms of a selective advantage conferred to encapsulated First Track processes. Some First Track functions belong to general cognition, however, although they work fast and automatically. In some slightly revised sense, cognition is also to some extent modular (Carruthers 2003). The results of brain observation in the two cases I have discussed—the will and imaginative resistance—support the idea that a certain lack of conscious control may be adaptive. Once the preparatory work of the deliberative function is done, the will must be kept from interfering with the efficient functioning of the executive function. In the course of imaginative simulation, we need to protect our value commitments in counterfactual situations in proportion to the extent that we are personally committed to acting.

Natural selection explains why certain functions are encapsulated, and psychology tells us something about how we might nevertheless modify our responses in the light of changing circumstances. The efficiency of our First Track functions would be at risk if they were too easily influenced by external information; and the phenomena I have discussed strengthen the practical relevance of imaginative simulations by anchoring our evaluations of hypothetical outcomes in present values. To some extent, these explanations are still couched in the vocabulary of folk psychology. But neuroscience demonstrates the mutual independence of mechanisms we thought of as forming a single function. Thus deliberation and execution seem to be united in the will, but they turn out to be distinct and empirically separable. Similarly, imagination and emotional response seem to function as one in the exploration of counterfactual futures, but they draw apart, sometimes usefully so, when the link between imagination and potential action is loosened.

Nevertheless, we must not forget the limits of our intuitive self-understanding, particularly concerning our own motivations and our own emotions (Wilson 2002). We are subject to massive self-deception and confabulation (Hirstein 2005). The rationale I have postulated for keeping values constant through counterfactual deliberation actually works rather poorly: we tend to err in both our predictions and our memories of our own responses (Gilbert 2006). The way out of this predicament is not by way of first-person introspection but on the contrary by treating ourselves as objects, not as subjects. Introspection needs to be supplemented, if perhaps not replaced, with "heterophenomenology" (Dennett 2003). In doing that, however, we diminish the hold on our conceptual scheme of the traditional categories of emotion. If our emotions are modular, they don't necessarily function in the ways our existing emotional concepts lead us to expect. When we unravel the causal mechanisms that make it possible to act, we may lose sight of our notions of free will, of motivation, and of emotions, not because we are puppets of determinism but because the mechanisms involved are just too *complicated*. Like ships in the Bermuda triangle, our emotions might seem to disappear because they were never really there.

## References

BLAIR, J., D. MITCHELL, and K. BLAIR (2005). *The Psychopath: Emotion and the Brain*. Oxford: Blackwell.

BOWLBY, J. (1969–80). *Attachment and Loss*. New York: Basic Books.

CARRUTHERS, P. (2003). The mind is a system of modules shaped by natural selection. In *Contemporary Debates in the Philosophy of Science*, C. Hitchcock (ed.). Oxford: Blackwell.

CHURCHLAND, P. M. (2007). What happens to reliabilism when it is liberated from the propositional attitudes? In *Neurophilosophy at Work*, 88–112. Cambridge: Cambridge University Press.

CLARK, A. (2007). What reaching teaches: Consciousness, control, and the inner zombie. *British Journal for the Philosophy of Science* 58: 563–94.

CURRIE, G. (2002). Desire in imagination. In *Conceivability and Possibility*, T. Gendler and J. Hawthorne (eds.), 201–21. Oxford: Oxford University Press.

DAMASIO, A. R. (1999). *The Feeling of What Happens: Body and Emotion in the Making of Consciousness*. New York, San Diego, London: Harcourt Brace.

DEHAENE, S. (1997). *The Number Sense*. Oxford: Oxford University Press.

DE SOUSA, R. (1999). Twelve varieties of subjectivity. In *Proceedings of the Sixth International Colloquium on Cognitive Science*, ICCS., J. Lazarrabal (ed.).

DENNETT, D. C. (1991). *Consciousness Explained*. Boston, Toronto, London: Little, Brown.

—— (1996). *Kinds of Minds: Towards an Understanding of Consciousness*. New York: Basic Books.

—— (2003). Who's on first? heterophenomenology explained. *Journal of Consciousness Studies* 10(9/10), October: 19–30.

—— (2007). Heterophenomenology reconsidered. *Phenomenology and the Cognitive Sciences* 6(3): 247–70.

DESCARTES, R. (1986). *Meditations of First Philosophy, with Selections from the Objections and Replies*. Trans. John Cottingham, intro. Bernard Williams. Cambridge: Cambridge University Press.

DISKI, J. (2008). Diary: On not liking South Africa. *London Review of Books* 30(13), 2003 July: 41.

EKMAN, P. and W. FRIESEN. (1975). *Unmasking the Face: A Guide to Recognizing Emotions from Facial Expressions*. Englewood Cliffs, NJ: Prentice-Hall.

FODOR, J. (1983). *The Modularity of Mind*. Cambridge, MA: MIT Press.

FREUD, S. (1911). Formulations on the two principles of mental functioning. In *Standard Edition of the Complete Psychological Works*, vol. 12, J. Strachey (ed.), 213–26. London: Hogarth Press.

—— (1923). The Ego and the Id. In *Standard Edition of the Complete Psychological Works*, vol. 19, J. Strachey (ed.), 3–68. London: Hogarth Press.

GALLAGHER, S. and F. VARELA (2001). Redrawing the map and resetting the time: philosophy and the cognitive sciences. *Canadian Journal of Philosophy*. Supplementary Volume 29: 93–132.

GAZZANIGA, M. (1970). *The Bisected Brain*. New York: Appleton Century Crofts.

GENDLER, T. S. (2000). The puzzle of imaginative resistance. *Journal of Philosophy* 97(2): 55–81.

—— (2006). Imaginative resistance revisited. In *The Architecture of the Imagination: New Essays on Pretence, Possibility, and Fiction*, S. Nichols (ed.), 149–73. Oxford: Oxford University Press.

GILBERT, D. T. (2006). *Stumbling on Happiness.* New York: Knopf.

GOLDIE, P. (2003). Narrative, emotion, and perspective. In *Imagination, Philosophy and the Arts*, M. Kierans and D. Lopes (eds.), 54–68. London: Routledge.

—— (2005). Imagination and the distorting power of emotions. *Journal of Consciousness Studies* 12(8–10): 130–42.

GREENE, J. D., E. B. SOMMERVILLE, L. A. NYSTROM, J. M. DARLEY, and J. D. COHEN (2001). An fMRI investigation of emotional engagement in moral judgment. *Science* 293 (14 September): 2105–8.

GRIFTHS, P. E. (1997). *What Emotions Really Are: The Problem of Psychological Categories.* Chicago: University of Chicago Press.

HAGGARD, P. (2005). Conscious intention and motor cognition. *Trends in Cognitive Sciences* 9(6): 290–5.

HAIDT, J. and F. BJORKLUND (2008). Social Intuitionists answer six questions about moral psychology. In *Moral Psychology*, vol. 2, W. Sinnot-Armstrong, 181–217. Cambridge, MA: MIT.

HIRSTEIN, W. (2005). *Brain Fiction: Self-Deception and the Riddle of Confabulation.* Cambridge, MA: MIT.

HUME, D. (1965). *Of the Standard of Taste and Other Essays.* Intro. by J. W. Lenz (ed.). The Library of Liberal Arts. Indianpolis: Bobbs-Merrill.

—— (1975). *Enquiries: Concerning Human Understanding and Concerning the Principles of Morals.* 3rd ed. Intro. by L. A. Selby-Bigge (ed.). Revised by P. H. Nidditch. Oxford: Oxford University Press.

HUSSERL, E. (1960). *Cartesian Meditations: An Introduction to Phenomenology.* Trans. D. Cairns. The Hague: Martinus Nijhoff.

INDERSCIENCE (2008). Could videogames reduce rather than increase violence. *Science Daily*, 15 May. ScienceDaily. Retrieved March 20, 2009, from <http://www.sciencedaily.com/releases/2008/05/080514213432.htm>.

JACOBSON, D. (1997). In praise of immoral art. *Philosophical Topics* 25(1): 155–200.

JAMES, W. (1884). What is an emotion? *Mind* 9: 188–205.

KOENIGS, M., YOUNG, L., ADOLPHS, R., TRANEL, D., CUSHMAN, F., HAUSER, M., and DAMASIO, A. (2007). Damage to the prefrontal cortex increases utilitarian moral judgements. *Nature* 05631: 1–4.

KRIPKE, S. A. (1980). *Naming and Necessity.* Cambridge, MA: Harvard University Press.

LI ZHISUI. (1994). *The Private Life of Chairman Mao: The Memoirs of Mao's Personal Physician.* Tai Hung-chao and A. F. Thurston. New York: Random House.

LIBET, B., E. WRIGHT, Jr., B. FEINSTEIN, and D. PEARL (1979). Subjective referral of the timing for a conscious experience: A functional role for the somatosensory specific projection system in man. *Brain* 102: 193–224.

LOCKE, J. (1975). *An Essay Concerning Human Understanding*, P. Nidditch (ed.). Oxford: Oxford University Press.

MACLEAN, P. D. (1975). Sensory and perceptive factors in emotional functions of the triune brain. In *Emotions: Their Parameters and Measurement*, L. Levi (ed.). New York: Raven Press.

MARCUS, G. (2008). *Kluge: The Haphazard Construction of the Human Mind.* New York: Houghton Mifflin.

MATRAVERS, D. (2003). Fictional assent and the (so-called) "puzzle of imaginative resistance", *Imagination, and the Arts*, 91–106. London: Routledge.

MILLIKAN, R. G. (1993). White Queen psychology; or the last myth of the Given. In *White Queen Psychology and Other Essays for Alice*, 279–363. Cambridge, MA: MIT Bradford Books.

MIRSKY, J. (1994). Unmasking the monster: The memoirs of Mao's personal physician. Review of *The Private Life of Chairman Mao*. Li Zhisui. *New York Review of Books* 41(19), 1919. November: Online: <http://www.nybooks.com/articles/2080>. accessed 25 July 2008.

MOODY-ADAMS, M. (2002). *Fieldwork in Familiar Places: Morality, Culture, and Philosophy.* Cambridge, MA: Harvard University Press.

MORAN, R. (1994). The expression of feeling in imagination. *Philosophical Review* 103(1): 75–106.

MORTON, A. (2006). Imagination and misimagination. In *The Architecture of the Imagination: New Essays on Pretence, Possibility, and Fiction*, ed. S. Nichols, 57–71. New York: Oxford University Press.

NAGEL, J. (2008). Knowledge ascriptions and the psychological consequences of thinking about error. Forthcoming in *Philosophical Quarterly*. Doi : 10.111/j.1467–9213.2009.624x.

NUSSBAUM, M. (2001). *Upheavals of Thought: A Theory of the Emotions.* Gifford Lectures. Cambridge: Cambridge University Press.

OATLEY, K. (1999). Why fiction may be twice as true as fact: Fiction as cognitive and emotional simulation. *Review of General Psychology* 3(2): 101–17.

PANKSEPP, J. (2001). The neuro-evolutionary cusp between emotions and cognitions: Implications for understanding consciousness and the emergence of a unified mind science. *Evolution and Cognition* 7(2): 141–63.

PLATO. (1997). Republic. In *Complete Works*, J. M. Cooper and D. Hutchinson (eds.). Indianapolis: Hackett.

PLUTCHIK, R. (2001). The nature of emotions. *American Scientist* 89(4): 344–50.

PRIEST, G. (1997). Sylvan's box: A short story and ten morals. *Notre Dame Journal of Formal Logic* 38(4): 573–82.

PRINZ, J. (2007). *The Emotional Construction of Morals.* Oxford, New York: Oxford University Press.

PUTNAM, H. (1975). The meaning of meaning. In *Mind, Language and Reality*, vol. 2. Philosophical papers, 215–71. Cambridge: Cambridge University Press.

QUINE, W. V. O. (1980). Two dogmas of empiricism. In *From a Logical Point of View: Nine Logico-Philosophical Essays.* 2nd revised ed. Cambridge, MA: Harvard University Press.

ROY, J.-M. (2007). Heterophenomenology and phenomenological skepticism. *Phenomenology and the Cognitive Sciences* 6(3): 1–20.

RUSSELL, J. A. (2005). The circumplex model of affect: An integrative approach to affective neuroscience, cognitive development, and psychopathology. *Development and Psychopathology* 17: 715–34.

SARTRE, J.-P. (1993). *Being and Nothingness: An Essay on Phenomenological Ontology.* Trans. & intro. H. E. Barnes. New York: Washington Square.

SCHERER, K. R. (2005). What are emotions? And how can they be measured? *Social Science Information* 44(4): 695–729.

SHARIFF, A. F. and J. B. PETERSON (2008). Anticipatory consciousness, Libet's veto and a close-enough theory of free will. In *Consciousness and Emotion: Agency, Conscious Choice, and Selective Perception*, R. D. Ellis and N. Newton (eds.), 197–214. Amsterdam: John Benjamins.

SIEWERT, C. (2007). In favor of (plain) phenomenology. *Phenomenology and the Cognitive Sciences* 6: 201–20.

SOLOMON, R. C. (1984). *The Passions: The Myth and Nature of Human Emotions*. New York: Doubleday.

—— (2007). *True to our Feelings: What our Emotions Are Really Telling Us*. Oxford, New York: Oxford University Press.

SOON, C. S., M. BRASS, H.-J. HEINZE, and J.-D. HAYNES (2008). Unconscious determinants of free decisions in the human brain. *Nature Neuroscience* 11 (13 April): 543–5. Doi:10.1038/nn.2112.

SORENSEN, R. A. (2002). The art of the impossible. In *Conceivability and Possibility*, T. Gendler and J. Hawthorne (eds.), 337–68. Oxford: Oxford University Press.

STANOVICH, K. E. (2004). *The Robot's Rebellion: Finding Meaning in the Age of Darwin*. Chicago: University of Chicago Press.

STRACK, F. and R. DEUTSCH (2004). Reflective and impulsive determinants of social behavior. *Personality and Social Psychology Review* 8(3): 220–7.

SYNGE, J. M. (1911). *The Playboy of the Western World*. Boston: J. W. Luce. Bartleby.com. 2000. <http://www.bartleby.com/1010/>. Accessed 2008/07/24.

TAYLOR, J. B. (2006). *My Stroke of Insight*. New York: Penguin.

THOMPSON, E. (2007). Look again: Phenomenology and mental imagery. *Phenomenology and the Cognitive Sciences* 6: 137–70.

TURIEL, E. (2002). *Culture and Morality*. Cambridge: Cambridge University Press.

VAN INWAGEN, P. (1983). *An Essay on Free Will*. Oxford: Oxford University Press.

WEGNER, D. M. (2002). *The Illusion of Conscious Will*. Cambridge MA: MIT Press.

WIGGINS, D. R. (1987). Towards a reasonable libertarianism. In *Needs, Values, Truth*, 269–302. Oxford: Basil Blackwell.

WILSON, T. D. (2002). *Strangers to Ourselves: Discovering the Adaptive Unconscious*. Cambridge, MA and London: Harvard University Press, Belnap.

WITTGENSTEIN, L. (1953). *Philosophical Investigations*. Trans. G. E. M. Anscombe. New York: Macmillan.

WOLLHEIM, R. (1984). *The Thread of Life*. Cambridge: Cambridge University Press.

ZIFF, P. (1964). *Semantic Analysis*. Ithaca: Cornell University Press.

# PART II

## THE HISTORY OF EMOTION

# CHAPTER 5

...........................................................

# EMOTIONS IN PLATO AND ARISTOTLE

...........................................................

## A. W. PRICE

# I

...........................................................

The Greeks had no word equivalent to our Latinate 'emotion'. The term they commonly use in its place, *pathos*, had the most general meaning '*that which happens* to a person or thing' (Liddell and Scott, 1940); I shall render it by 'affection'. It came commonly to be applied to experiences to which a person is subject, and also lasting states manifested in such experiences, or initiated or alterable by them. Hence it became the term standardly applied to emotions, occurrent or dispositional, if also to many other mental states.

Greek treatments have attracted recent attention as anticipations of current views that are *cognitive* in stressing not just the *intentionality* of emotion, its directedness upon an object that may be real or imaginary, but its *propositionality*, its dependence upon ways in which things are or may be. Human emotions, at any rate, commonly have a propositional core: one is angry, say, *that* so-and-so has acted unjustly. Which raises the question how the emotion relates to associated beliefs. Can I sincerely be angry that such-and-such is the case without *believing*, truly or falsely, that it is? And, to capture the *emotionality* of an emotion, is it enough to refine its propositional content, or do we need to identify some further element?

Greek views of the emotions give a central role to cognitions in a broad sense. What we meet in the writings of Plato and Aristotle are developing conceptions of the relevant cognitions. These can exemplify for us the need to be reflective about the nature and role of cognition within emotion.

# II

In Plato's *Protagoras*, Socrates asks an explicitly definitional question: 'Is there something that you call apprehension (*deos*) and fear (*phobos*)? . . . I mean by this a certain expectation of evil (*prosdokian tina kakou*), whether you call it fear or apprehension' (358d5–7). Interestingly, his interlocutors disagree: 'Protagoras and Hippias thought that that's what apprehension and fear are, while Prodicus thought it was apprehension, but not fear' (d7–e1). Ammonius (an Alexandrian grammarian of the 4th century AD) was to distinguish apprehension as a 'lasting anticipation of evil' (*poluchronios kakou huponoia*) from fear as 'immediate excitement' (*parautika ptoēsis*).[1] Though Prodicus is frequently cited in Plato for making fine verbal distinctions, we do not know that he made that one. Yet it is tempting to read it into the background: allusion to it makes excellent sense as a recognition of a less (or less purely) cognitive conception of the emotion. Socrates maintains his own view in treating the two sentences 'No one goes for what he fears' (358e3) and 'No one goes for what he considers fearful' (359d5–6) as equivalent. That equation leaves open alternatives that Socrates proceeds to restrict:

If what has just been said is true, will any man be willing to go for what he fears, when he can go for what he doesn't fear? Or is that impossible, according to what we have agreed? For if anyone fears something, it was agreed that he thinks it bad; and no one who thinks anything bad goes for it or takes it of his own free will (358e2–6).

The reference is not just to the definition of fear but to previous argument that going for what one really knows to be bad can only come of an error of perspective by which, for example, an evil that is salient (say, by being immediate) both appears, and *is taken to be*, larger at the time of action than an evil that is less present (356c5–d7). The present implication is not just that no one fears what he does not consider *bad* and so fearful *in a way*, but that he cannot fear what he takes to be *best in context*.[2] Socrates thus excludes *a priori* what we may accept as a datum

---

[1] *De adfinium vocabulorum differentia* (ed. Nickau), 128.

[2] Socrates recognizes that one's choice may be between two evils (*Prot.* 358d2–4). However, he assumes that, in any situation, the agent has an option that counts as *acting well*, which cannot itself be an evil—nor therefore, on his account, a proper object of fear. Cf. Taylor (2008: 281–4).

of experience: an agent thinking it best to $\phi$, given his options in the circumstances, may still be afraid to $\phi$ because of some danger (say, to his life) that saliently attaches to his $\phi$'ing. It will follow that fear is possible for a man, but not strictly *qua* agent: he may fear the death that may come of acting bravely, but he cannot be afraid to act bravely for that reason. Within the compass of intentional action, fear is impossible.

Yet elsewhere we find Plato's Socrates well aware of 'immediate excitement' of a kind that Prodicus may have identified with fear. At the sight of the beautiful Charmides, all are amazed and confused (*Charm.* 154c3); Socrates himself 'blazes' as he glances inside his garment, in a manner that reminds him (through a literary allusion) of a lion about to snatch a portion of meat (155d3–e1). In Diotima's description, to the body already full to bursting there comes an intense excitement (*ptoiēsis*, the same term as in Ammonius) in the presence of the beautiful that brings on an act of procreation (*Symp.* 206d5–e1). Such responses have a felt intensity that is not reducible to the confidence of a belief. That Socrates could surely grant. (It would not exclude his central thesis that knowledge is sufficient for virtue.) One might further take their spontaneity to imply an independence of judgement. However, Socrates could appeal to what I have already noted in the *Protagoras*. The proximity of an erotic stimulus must be presumed to distort the subject's evaluations, so that it suddenly takes on overwhelming importance for him that he make love to this boy or woman.

And yet, in the *Charmides*, though Socrates admits to losing his head (d4), he 'somehow with difficulty' carries on with the conversation (e3), and gradually recovers his equanimity (156d1–3). For all the intensity of his emotion, he surely never assents to an act of sexual assault. Does this not illustrate the distinctness of emotion and judgement? Maybe. Yet, when Plato shifts his position in order to accommodate such cases, he prefers to distinguish the judgements of head and heart than to change his conception of emotion as centrally involving judgement. Take a passage of the *Phaedo* describing how the heart (or a lower organ) may corrupt the head: 'Each pleasure and pain . . . makes the soul corporeal, so that it believes that whatever the body affirms is true. As it shares the opinions and pleasures of the body, it is compelled to share its diet and habits' (83d4–8). Here a soul that takes on the pleasures of the body also, and (it appears) *thereby*, takes on its evaluations as well. A soul that resists the contagion contradicts the body, 'conversing with its desires and passions and fears as if it were a distinct thing' (94d5–6). As body and soul trade their own assertions, conflict becomes a form of self-contradiction.

Given that the body that has its own pleasures and opinions is a *living* body, that is, a body animated by a soul, Plato is rather drawing a corollary than changing his mind when, in the *Republic*, he divides not soul from body but a rational soul, competent to assess what is best for the whole soul (4.441e3–442c7), from a non-rational soul, which he further divides into 'appetite' and 'spirit'.[3] He appeals to what is itself a logical principle (a subject-predicate version of the law of non-contradiction): 'It is evident that the same thing will never do or suffer opposites simultaneously in the same respect and in relation to the same thing' (4.436b9–10). He takes the principle to imply that, if a man simultaneously desires to $\phi$ and desires not to $\phi$, his soul must be divided: the desires are to be ascribed to different parts of his soul (not that the term 'part' is often used). But to what effect? This is debated. On one interpretation, the agent's soul contains different subjects of desire, one of which desires that he $\phi$, another that he not $\phi$. On another, he remains the subject of his desires, but qualifiedly: it is in respect of one part of his soul that he desires to $\phi$, and of another that he desires not to $\phi$.[4] In either case, the logic is puzzling. Is Plato carelessly confusing at once desiring to $\phi$ and desiring not to $\phi$ (a familiar predicament) with at once desiring to $\phi$ and not desiring to $\phi$ (a self-contradictory description)?

It rather seems that he has a distinctive conception of desires and emotions oriented towards an option (4.437b1–c9). He contrasts opposing attitudes dynamically (as opposing forces), quasi-spatially (what the one 'draws to' itself, the other 'thrusts away'), and intentionally (what one 'aims at', the other 'rejects'). While I can be attracted in a way by something that in another way repels me, I cannot, in imaginative anticipation of action, move something towards myself (or move towards something) at the same time as I move it away from myself (or move away from it). It seems that Plato's conception of desire identifies it with psychic action of a kind: to desire to $\phi$ is to start $\phi$'ing in one's mind, if not yet in actuality. This makes desires (or emotions) that conflict in relation to a single option (that of $\phi$'ing) not just a discomfort, but a paradox—one whose solution demands no less than a partitioning of the soul (however precisely we interpret that).[5]

Appetite is the home of 'a certain class consisting of desires' (*epithumiai*), of which the 'clearest' members are hunger and thirst (4.437d1–3). This part is called 'desirous' (*epithumētikon*) on the ground of 'the intensity of its desires for food and drink and sex and their accompaniments' (9.580e2–5). Intense desires, though not themselves emotions, are accompanied by emotion: it is in respect of its appetite that the soul 'loves, hungers, thirsts, and feels the excitement (*eptoētai*) of other desires'.[6] Even appetite is cognitive in a way. It desires the *pleasures* of nutrition and generation and the like (4.436a10–b2); it is 'a companion of certain repletions and pleasures' (439d8). To desire something, in this mode, is to desire it *as* pleasant;

---

[3] A matching threefold division of attachments was already made in the *Pdo* (68c1–2, 82c2–8).

[4] Price (1995: 53–7) finds Plato ambivalent. Bobonich (2002: 219–35) and Lorenz (2006: 18–34) take his arguments for different psychic parts to commit him to distinct psychological subjects; *contra*, see Price (2009).

[5] The same difficulty does not attach to desiring to $\phi$ and to $\chi$ when, as a matter of contingent fact, I cannot actually accomplish both.

[6] Cf. *ptoiēsis*, already cited from *Symp.* 206d8 and Ammonius.

such desiring, Plato assumes, involves thinking *to be* pleasant. To an extent, this is not new. We already read in the *Charmides* that *epithumia* is for pleasure, as wish (*boulēsis*) is for some good (167e1–5). Yet that drew no dichotomy between rational desire (*boulēsis*) for the good, and non-rational desire (*epithumia*) for the pleasant; for it added that love is of something beautiful (*kalos*), and fear of something fearful (*deinos*, 167e7–168a1), thus leaving open that the pleasant might be a part or aspect of the good, just as the fearful is a part or aspect of the bad. Now, in the *Republic*, a contrast is drawn. We are not to accept that 'everybody desires not drink but good drink and not food but good food, on the ground that all men desire good things' (438a2–4); for, in truth, 'the soul of the thirsty, in so far as it thirsts, wishes nothing else than to drink' (439a9–b1, with—as is common in Plato, in contrast to Aristotle—a *bouletai* not distinguished from *epithumei*).

The point of Socrates' insistence is not transparent. It would actually suit his view that reason and appetite contradict each other if he allowed them to disagree about the application of the term 'good', thirst asserting that it is good to drink since it is pleasant, reason denying that it is good to drink in a case where, say, it is unhealthy (cf. 439c2–d2). As it is, he has appetite 'prescribing' that the man drink (*keleuon*, c7), and reason 'preventing' him from drinking (*kōluon*, c6, 8). Strictly, *keleuein* is illocutionary, *kōluein* perlocutionary, but Plato is doubtless less influenced by meaning than by alliteration: the contrast resumes an earlier one between 'assent' and 'dissent' (437b1). The conflicting judgements might be 'It is good to drink' and 'It is bad to drink', asserted from different points of view, each of which claims priority.

When Socrates makes not good drink, but simply drink, the object of thirst, he may have the following in mind. There are two contexts that exclude an obstinate conflict of judgements. One is that the judging faculty is a unity, like the soul that is opposed to the body in the *Phaedo*: it will never judge simultaneously that a thing is to be done, and not to be done. Another is that the judgement applies a concept with a single criterion of application. If 'good' applied to a drink meant 'pleasant to taste', reason would not contradict appetite; if it meant 'healthy to taste', appetite would not contradict reason. As it is, we may take the argument at *Republic* 4.438–9 to intend this: thirst, as a specific kind of desire, has an object that does not so fall under the competence of reason that thirst must come into being, or cease to be, at reason's behest.

If this is typical of appetite, the emotions of the appetitive life are non-rational since they arise from frustrations and satisfactions that are independent of any rational assessment of what is best. More equivocal are the emotions of Plato's third part, which he introduces by citing an emotion. Socrates takes a line of Homer about Odysseus, 'He smote his breast and chided thus his heart', to represent 'that in us which has reflected about the better and the worse as rebuking that which feels unreasoning anger as if it were a distinct and different thing' (441b7–c2). Anger shares with hunger and thirst an aspect of physiological disturbance: it boils (440c7, cf. *Tim.* 70b3). As such, it is already manifest in infants and lower animals (a7–b3). In its distinctively human form, it has a double intentionality: Odysseus is rightly angry with what he sees when he returns home, though wrongly tempted to attempt revenge too soon.[7] And yet anger's appropriate objects, present and prospective, make it more receptive than appetite of rational discipline, so that it becomes reason's natural ally (440b3–4). Indeed, this varies with innate disposition: 'When a man thinks that he doing wrong, is it not true that, the nobler he is, the less he is capable of anger though suffering hunger and cold and whatsoever else at the hands of him whom he believes to be doing this justly' so that 'his spirit refuses to be aroused'? (c1–5). The noble are angry only when they are indignant, and indignation, being a response to an appearance of injustice and a prospect of revenge, is liable to inhibition by the correction of such perceivings or imaginings.

Though it is by way of anger that Socrates introduces spirit as a distinct part of the soul, his conception of it is soon extended and civilized. It is inhibited by the thought of being in the wrong, and exercised by that of being wronged (440c7–8). When its anger is directed at oneself (e.g., b1–2), this gives rise to a new emotion, one of shame (*aidōs*, 8.560a6–7). It is sooner provoked by wrongs to be resisted than stimulated by goods to be achieved; thus it speaks rather in terms of 'just' and 'unjust', 'ought' and 'ought not', than of 'good' and 'bad'. This further explains why it is by nature reason's ally (4.441a2–3): it is receptive of another's values, translating them into its own terms (cf. 442c1–3). Its temperament also inclines it to values of its own: being naturally belligerent and competitive, it is set on honour (for the pugnacious love honour, 9.583a8) and victory (e.g., 8.545a2–3). It takes on the emotive attitudes of admiring, honouring, and taking pride in (8.553a4–6).

It can then become tempting to interpret Plato's spirit very widely as *the* emotive part of the soul. Yet his own conception, though to a degree open-ended, is more distinctive. I have mentioned emotions that are ascribed to it: anger, shame, pride, admiration. Though various, these can all be placed within the development of a part of the soul whose role is analogous to the defensive and policing role of the auxiliaries within Plato's utopia (and anticipatory of Freud's superego). Fear may be a possible corrective, but would seem out of place within spirit. What of grief? This is neglected until *Republic* 10, where the mental conflict of a decent man who has lost his son but tries to moderate his grief instances how opposed impulses betray a division of the soul (604a9–b2). Here Plato does not advance explicitly beyond a division between a rational and non-rational soul, and this may indicate an awareness that many emotions do not fit well within his tripartition.[8] However,

---

[7] Plato anticipates Aristotle over both the materiality and intentionality of anger (cf. *DA* 1.1403a29–b1, *NE* 7.6.1149a25–34, *Rhet.* 2.2.1378a30–2).

[8] Plato lists as affected by poetry 'the emotions of sex and anger, and all the desires and pains and pleasures of the soul which we say accompany all our actions' (*Rep.* 10.606d1–3), where only mention of sex and anger remind us of appetite and spirit. He then mentions 'the bad elements in us' without specifying them as two (603a7).

his treatment of grief respects it in two ways.[9] First, it is the presence of his equals that best inhibits a bereaved father's displays of grief, since he is *ashamed* to be overheard (604a1–7). Hence it is plausibly his spirit, in alliance with 'the best element in our nature' (606a7), that restrains him. Secondly, it is in the nature of the part that needs to be restrained to *hunger* for the tears in which it finds *pleasure* and *satisfaction* (a3–7). Though grief is not in origin a desire for pleasure of a kind, it becomes appetite-like in pursuing its own satisfactions. When we read that 'it cannot get enough' of lamentation (604d8), we are reminded that appetite has been described as typically insatiable (8.562b4–5, 9.590b8). If grief is by nature like that, 'the plaintive part' (10.606a8–b1) may be nothing else than appetite itself; if it can become like that, then we have still to discover where in the soul it was originally at home.[10] Plato leaves his options open.

In later Plato, we find two distinct developments. Tripartition is first loosened, and then neglected. Spirit is conceived more broadly. The *Timaeus* discards any sustained political analogy, and localizes the parts within the body—reason in the head, spirit in the breast, appetite in the belly and below. As a psychic domain grounded in one area of the body, spirit can accommodate the less spirited ethical and emotional dispositions: timidity alongside rashness, cowardice alongside courage, modesty alongside boastfulness, and so on. Then the *Laws* introduces a new simile (1.644d7–645b1). Our affections are like sinews or cords pulling against one another. The leading string of reasoning is soft and golden; other strings are hard and steely, and so useful in its assistance. Thereafter, there are traces of tripartition, but no regimentation. What does the work in explaining conflict is no longer that structure, but a looser conception of mental forces that, operating independently of one another, are not automatically in the service of rational reflection.[11]

What governs the cognitive states that are integral to non-rational emotions and desires? Socrates adduces visual illusions (*Rep.* 10.602c7–603a7). Take the Müller-Lyer illusion, in which, through varying diagonals, two parallel lines (call them *a* and *b*) *appear* unequal in length, though they *measure* as equal.[12] Socrates distinguishes a part of the soul that forms an opinion contrary to measurement, and a part that forms an opinion according to it; the best part trusts calculation, while a bad part opposes it (603a1–7). Does he suppose that to *perceive a* as longer than *b* is to believe, in some part of one's soul, that *a is* longer than *b*? If so, perception is proprietary to some part of the soul—which would make little sense,

---

[9] Cf. Burnyeat (2006: 18), Lorenz (2006: 62).

[10] Compare the dilettantish hedonism that drives the democratic man's alternation between philosophy and politics (and other things besides, *Rep.* 8.561c6–d8). Philosophy is properly a rational project, and politics a spirited one; yet they fall within cycles of depletion and repletion within the soul of the man who has become a creature of appetite.

[11] On the *Tim.*, see Price (1995: 82–9); on the *Laws*, Price (1995: 89–94), Bobonich (2002: 260–7).

[12] Wikipedia illustrates this, and offers possible explanations.

and is not supported by the evidence.[13] Instead, he might suppose that non-rational parts of the soul, as Hendrik Lorenz puts it, are 'at the mercy of how things appear through the senses' (2006: 68). Take a case of simple desire (which can stand in for more complex cases involving emotion): suppose my appetite desires the longer in length of two strands of unhealthy food (liquorice, say). My mouth may well water more at the prospect of what *looks* like the longer strand: I have to *hunger* for it more, even if I know, rationally, that the lengths are equal.

And yet there are problems. Suppose that, in need of maximal nutrition, I rightly prefer what I *know* to be the longer strand of spaghetti to what *looks* the longer. That could be interpreted as a victory of reason over appetite. But what if, greedy for liquorice—though I know *any* of it to be bad for me, and *more* of it to be worse—I choose what I know to *be* the longer strand over what *looks* the longer? I can then be acting neither on reason (since it prefers less to more when it comes to liquorice), nor on appetite (since it takes the strand that looks longer to be longer).

A more tenable view must be more complex.[14] Hunger and thirst, being primitive aspects of appetite, may be helpless slaves of the appearances. But in respect of other desires, appetite may make use of reason's calculations in order to satisfy its own preferences. Plato supposes that a dominant appetite allows reason 'to calculate and consider nothing but the ways of making more money from a little' (8.553d3–4). It must then form desires in accordance with rational calculation. This allows more intelligence to the lower parts of the soul in respect of most of their desires and emotions. It also alerts us to another possibility: nothing is gained, either in simplicity or in plausibility, by supposing that hunger and thirst are channelled towards particular objects (*this* food or drink) only through the formation of *beliefs*; surely, in their case, *perception* (and imagination) can suffice.[15] Directed hunger is a creature of the perceptual imagination, and an animal that was simply a creature of hunger (a sea anemone, say) would respond directly to perceptual input.

Once this is granted, it throws open whether, so far, Plato's account of the cognitive aspect of desires and emotions has in general been too *doxastic* (that is, belief-related), rather than *perceptual*. This becomes an issue after the *Republic*. The *Timaeus* appears to claim that the appetite possesses 'pleasant and painful perception together with desires', but lacks 'belief, reasoning and understanding' (77b5–6).[16] To the mortal, incarnate soul in general are still ascribed 'dread and

---

[13] See Price (1995: 70–1).

[14] Cf. Aristotle's distinction between two types of appetite (*epithumia*), one that comes of persuasion, the other determined by the body's needs and uninfluenced by supposition (*Rhet.* 1.11.1370a19–27).

[15] Thus, a castaway suffering thirst in a longboat may be subject to an obstinate desire to drink sea water because he *imagines* it as thirst-quenching, though he *knows* (and believes) it to be thirst-intensifying.

[16] Lorenz connects this with a more demanding conception of belief (such as we probably find in the *Theaet.*) that requires even for simple perceptual beliefs a grasp of abstract intelligibles such as

necessary affections: first pleasure, the strongest lure of evil; next, pains that take flight from good; confidence moreover, and fear, a pair of unwise counsellors, anger hard to entreat, and hope too easily led astray' (69c8–d4). To spirit's indignation, unjust action can result 'from the desires within' (70b3–5); yet, in the production of action, these may connect with perceptions rather than beliefs. Reason can convey corrective thoughts to appetite, but by way of impressions that, received by the liver as if it were a mirror, are reflected as images (71b3–5). Plato is at last doing justice to the phenomenology of appetite by recognizing its dependence on the sensory imagination, and its responsiveness less to thoughts than to images.[17]

Spirit remains more akin than appetite to reason. Placed in the breast, where it is separated from the head only by the isthmus of the neck, it is housed close enough to reason to overhear the *logos* even before the *logos* addresses it (70a2–b5). It thus comes to *believe* the very things that reason *knows*—still very much as, in the *Republic* (4.442b10–c2), a brave spirit preserves what reason prescribes to it as to be feared or not to be feared. There is no indication in the *Timaeus* that 'confidence and fear' (69d2) is not still to be understood centrally as a matter of expectation and belief. Hence the emotions of spirit—now more inclusively conceived as including fear as well as anger—may still be centred upon beliefs, even if the emotions of appetite, such as sexual excitement, are not.[18]

being, difference, and opposition (2006: ch. 6). Hence he finds, *contra* Bobonich (2002: 296–7, 318–20), that what has changed is that Plato's conception of belief has become more demanding, and not that his conception of the non-rational soul has become more demeaning (2006: 95–9). However, I am not certain that the composite phrase 'belief, calculation and understanding' is not a hendiadys equivalent to 'rational belief' (cf. *Phdr.* 253d7–e1, where *keleusma kai logos* means 'rational command'); there would be nothing new in appetite's being denied *that*. (Note that there was already an association between understanding, reasoning, and *right* belief in *Rep.* 4.431c5–6. *Laws* 10.896c9–d1 specifically associates reasonings and *true* beliefs.) If so, the *Tim.* may not be taking over from the *Theaet.* a new general notion of belief. It then fits that the *Soph.* calls *phantasia* a mixture of perception and belief (264b1–2); for it is by phantasms that appetite is led (see my next note). Against Bobonich, who doubts whether the phantasms available to appetite are representative at all (2002: 556–7 n. 43), see Carone (2007).

[17] The relation of appetite to the rational *logos* is equivocal. Its desires need constraint if they are not willing to obey reason's prescription and *logos* ( *Tim.* 70a5–7)—which apparently permits that they *may* be willing (so Lorenz, 2006: 98, against Bobonich, 2002: 317.) Yet appetite cannot understand *logos*; and, if it were to receive some perception of *logoi*, it would not naturally care for them, but would be led by images and phantasms (71a3–7). I infer that appetite *can* comply with rational *logoi*, *once* they have been translated into seductive or inhibiting images.

[18] Here I disagree with Bobonich (2002: 320–1) and Lorenz (2006: 97). What of grief (supposing that its traditional association with the heart places it within an expanded spirit)? It is possible, if *Rep.* 10 was right, that it tends to take on some of the features of appetite even as it retains the intelligence of spirit. Price (1995: 72) argues that Plato needs to allow that emotions and desires may constitute compromise formations deriving from different parts of the soul.

In the *Timaeus*, reason still communicates with spirit by means of a *logos*, overheard (70a4–5) or imparted (b3–4), whereas it communicates with appetite by means of images (71b5). This may happily contrast fear or anger with hunger or thirst, but sits awkwardly with certain ascriptions of emotions to one part or another: why, say, should rashness and timidity (which are placed within spirit) be more comprehending of *logoi* than peevishness and despondency (which are apparently placed within appetite, 87a2–6)? Plato's position seems unstable. It is more happily that the *Philebus* finds a role within our souls for two metaphorical figures, a scribe and a painter: memory inscribes words in our souls, true or false, but also forms images as illustrations of them (39a1–c5). Such pictures help explain the pleasures of anticipation: 'Someone often envisages himself in the possession of an enormous amount of gold and of a lot of pleasures as a consequence; and in addition, he also pictures himself, besides himself with delight' (40a10–12). Such picturing can help to explain how emotion can take pleasure, or find pain, in experiences not actually present: it simulates them. Images become not just a *faute de mieux* in the absence of intelligence, but the very stuff of felt emotion.

Imagining oneself as rich as Croesus is a daydream. More serious emotions, in the *Philebus*, involve belief: 'Expectation before the actual pleasure will be pleasant and will inspire confidence, while the expectation of pain will be frightening and painful' (32c1–2). Yet for quasi-experiential vividness we need experiential memory, which is the 'preservation of perception' (34a10). Desires and emotions typically involve a mixture of pleasure and pain. In the keenest cases, there is a surplus of pleasure, with a small admixture of pain that, causing a tickle and mild irritation, accentuates the intensity of the anticipation (47a2–9). Even anger offers marvellous pleasures: Socrates cites two lines of Homer (familiar also to Aristotle) that allude to the anticipation of revenge (e5–9). So do lamentation and longing: tragedy provokes 'laughter mixed with the weeping' (48a1–6). What the *Republic* asserted of grief is now extended into a general conception of emotions as involving mixtures of pleasure and pain (47e1–5, 50b7–d6). It is to this complexity that they owe their seductive intensity.

Thus we find in Plato a double development out of Socratic simplicity. Emphasis is still placed upon the cognitive aspect of emotions, whether or not this involves the presence of actual belief. What emotions typically lack in rationality, they make up for in a phenomenology that comes of imaginative recall or anticipation, and combines pleasure and pain.[19] Plato is opening up a path that Aristotle will follow. Nowhere else is their continuity so apparent.

---

[19] According to the *Phdr.*, reason itself is subject to passions that prepare it for a fuller rationality; see Price (1995: 80–2, 1997: 63–7).

# III

Aristotle connects the passivity of the affections with their physicality:

It seems that all the affections of the soul involve the body—anger, good temper, fear, pity, confidence, and, further, joy and both loving and hating; for at the same time as these the body is affected in a certain way. (*DA* 1.1.403a16–19)

He at once offers an example of an emotion: 'Being angry is a particular motion of a body of such and such a kind, or a part or potentiality of it, as a result of this thing and for the sake of that' (a26–7). This links anger to a definitional schema for any emotion. Distinguishing aspects are then given as follows: there is 'a desire for retaliation or something of the sort', which interests the dialectician as the form of anger, and 'the boiling of the blood and hot stuff round the heart', which interests the student of nature as its matter (a29–b2). The occasion of anger is doubtless some offence inviting retaliation, its goal is retaliation, and the physical motion is a boiling of the blood round the heart. The specifics are familiar to us from Plato: a boiling of the blood (which is doubtless a discomfort), and a prospect of revenge (which is a consolation).[20] The schematic definition attempts to relate the form/ matter distinction—central to Aristotle's general account of how soul relates to body—to a particular mental state. (Not very happily, one may complain: blood hardly boils *for the sake of* retaliation.)

It is to the *Rhetoric* that we turn for a full account of the formal, intentional aspect of emotions. An orator hardly needs the philosophical understanding that we still lack of how the mental and physical relate intelligibly. He does need enough of a knowledge of how emotions connect occasions and goals so that he can excite or exploit them in whatever ways suit his purposes at the time (cf. 2.1.1378a22–6). His grasp can be less than scientific (and *Rhetoric* 2 mentions neither the physiology of the emotions, nor the division between a rational and non-rational soul). Yet it must be more than 'dialectical' (in Aristotle's sense of depending uncritically upon common conceptions).[21] Aristotle need offer no single theory even of the affections that are relevant to the kinds of oratory that concern him (political and forensic, but not eulogies or memorials); yet he must characterize each of the affections that he does consider correctly. Unfortunately, for all the concrete details that enrich his accounts, the terminology of his definitions is ambiguous and its interpretation debated. An early statement in Book 2 at once raises questions: 'The affections are things through which, changing, men differ in their judgements, and which are followed by pain and pleasure, such as anger, pity, fear, and other such

[20] For more metabolic details, see Knuutila (2004: 34).
[21] For a variety of views, see Nussbaum (1994: 82), Cooper (1999b: 407–10), Striker (1996: 206–8), Nieuwenburg (2002: 86–7).

things, and the opposites of these' (2.1.1378a19–22). 'Which are followed by' (*hois hepetai*) could signify a subsequent state, but may well signify a current aspect, essential or accidental: alternative renderings are 'which are accompanied by', and even 'to which there attach'. 'Through which' (*di'hosa*) could signify a consequence of the emotion, either simultaneous or subsequent; but it may instead signify an aspect of the complex change involved in an occurrence of emotion.[22]

Such issues might be clarified by the precise account of anger that follows. So let us first attend to that, and then to its ambiguities, in a translation that hugs the Greek:

2.2.1378a30: Let anger (*orgē*) be a desire (*orexis*) with pain for an apparent (*phainomenos*) revenge because of an apparent slight by people for whom it was not fitting to slight oneself or someone close to one.

a32: If this is anger, the man who is angry must always be angry with an individual, such as Cleon, and not with man [sc. in general], and because of what he has done, or aims to do, to oneself or someone close to one.

b1: And every occurrence of anger must be accompanied (*hepesthai*) by a certain pleasure, that which arises from the expectation (*elpis*) of taking revenge; for it is pleasant to expect to achieve what one aims at (*hōn ephietai*), and no one aims at things that appear impossible for him.

b4: So it has well been said of anger (*thumos*), 'It is much sweeter than dripping honey, and spreads through the breasts of men.' For a certain pleasure attends it, both because of this, and because men dwell upon taking revenge in thought.

b9–10: So the imagining (*phantasia*) that then arises causes pleasure, as it does in dreams.

Some incidental points first. The word for 'desire' is *orexis*, Aristotle's most generic term. Talk of *epithumia* would be less apposite, since revenge is not desired *as* something pleasant, though, since it is desired, it is pleasant to look forward to achieving it. Also inapposite would be 'wish' (*boulēsis*), for two reasons: wish is rational desire, while one can be angry contrary to one's own best judgement (cf. *NE* 7.6.1149a24–b3); and one can wish for what knows to be impossible (*NE* 3.2.1111b22–3), whereas Aristotle supposes that one can only be angry if one has a prospect of taking revenge. The associated pleasure attaches to an imagining that is integral to the desiring.

The quotation from Homer is *post* if not *propter* Plato (cf. *Phil.* 47e5–9). Aristotle has inherited a conception of emotions as typically involving a mixture of pain and pleasure: the prospect of revenge compensates for the memory of a slight (*NE* 3.8.1117a6–7).[23] Yet, in each case, one or the other is primary: pain (*lupē*) is primary within the definition of anger (see also 1379a10–12), and many other emotions are

---

[22] Leighton (1996) is well aware of such variations.

[23] On this point, D. Frede (1996) well relates Plato and Aristotle. It even applies to desire (*epithumia*) itself (listed as a *pathos* in the *Ethics*, and at *Rhet.* 2.12.1388b32–3): cf. *NE* 3.11.1119a4 (on pain) with *Rhet.* 2.2.1378b1–10 (on pleasure in the imaginative expectation of fulfilment). Striker (1996:

defined as special cases of pain: fear (2.5.1382a21–2), shame (2.6.1383b12–14), pity (2.8.1385b13–16), indignation (2.9.1387a9), envy (2.10.1387b23–5), and emulation (2.11.1388a32–5).[24] The pains that constitute fear and shame are, or may be, accompanied by 'disturbance' (*tarachē*, 2.5.1382a21, 2.6.1383b13), while the pain of envy is itself characterized as 'disturbance-like' (*tarachōdēs*, 2.9.1386b18). As in Plato, emotional pains tend to run to turmoil, perhaps in part *because* they are typically accompanied by a pleasure that is taken in the uncertain anticipation of relieving one's fears or achieving one's desires.

The two *Ethics* introduce pleasure *or* pain, or pleasure *and* pain, in order to generalize from lists of affections. Thus we read, 'By the affections I mean desire (*epithumia*), anger, fear, confidence, envy, joy, love, hatred, longing, emulation, pity, and in general things that are accompanied by pleasure or pain' (*NE* 2.5.1105b21–3);[25] but also, 'By the affections I mean such things as anger, fear, shame, desire, and in general things that, as such, are accompanied for the most part by perceptual pleasure and pain' (*EE* 2.2.1220b12–14). Presumably it is not a coincidence that the *Eudemian Ethics* adds both the qualification 'for the most part' and the specification 'perceptual': Aristotle must think that a special kind of pleasure or pain attaches to most affections, though not all. The *Physics* identifies the affections with changes in the soul's perceptual part (*to aisthētikon morion*) that involve bodily pleasures and pains excited by action, memory, or anticipation (7.3.247a3–9). Such pleasures and pains are excited by sensible things through perception or imagination (a9–17). They arise from their location within that part of the soul which Aristotle elsewhere calls 'the perceptual and desirous' (*EE* 2.2.1219b23): they are not merely sensible because conscious, but sensory in that they connect closely with sense-perception and imagination within the affective soul (*to pathētikon morion*, *Pol.* 1.5.1254b8). Many of the affections involve imagination (*phantasia*) in the service of memory and expectation; this connects them with the pleasures that follow on imagination as a weak form of perception (*Rhet.* 1.11.1370a27–32).

Cognate with the abstract noun *phantasia* is the participle *phainomenon*, which I rendered by 'apparent' in qualification both of the occasion of anger ('an apparent slight'), and of its goal ('an apparent revenge', 2.2.1378a30–1). This qualification recurrently qualifies the objects of affections.[26] What is its point? There are

---

301 n. 14) suggests a nice definition of *epithumia* as a *pathos*: 'a desire with pain for an apparent pleasure'.

[24] Why is anger not defined as pain of a kind, on the analogy of fear? Because Aristotle supposes that it is part of anger to intend revenge, whereas it is not part of fear to intend safety. While anger must have good hopes of revenge if it is to intend it, it is confidence, not fear, that has good hopes of safety or success (2.5.1383a16–21, b8–9).

[25] At *NE* 2.6.1106b18–20, Aristotle writes as if all affections of the soul are species of pleasure and/or pain.

[26] Cf. calmness (2.3.1380a11), shame (2.6.1383b13), pity (2.8.1385b13), indignation (2.9.1387a9), envy (2.10.1387b23), emulation (2.11.1388a32).

multiple possibilities. Certainly one implication is that anger is possible even if nothing has happened that can really count as a slight, and nothing is intended that could really count as revenge. Hence we should not use *factive* language (such as 'the fact that...') in specifying the occasion and goal of an emotion. That is very likely *all* that Aristotle means when he specifies that 'no one aims at things that appear impossible for him' (b3–4, cf. 1.11.1370b13). Generally, however, the term *phainomenos* serves to bring out further that, for there to be an occurrent affection, its occasion must *strike* its subject in a way that combines intentionality and phenomenology. Affections are creatures of perception and imagination, and in that manner peculiarly painful and/or pleasant (as is instanced at 2.2.1378b9–10, and I shall shortly discuss in relation to 2.1.1378a19–21). So one possibility is that the occasion and goal must be 'apparent' to the subject in that he perceives them, or imagines them vividly to himself; otherwise, whatever he believes, there will be no affection, no troubling of the stream of his consciousness (nor indeed, if we recall the physiology of the *De Anima*, of the flow of his metabolism).[27]

In the particular case of anger, there is an alternative. One form of slighting is 'insolence' (*hubris*), which consists in 'doing and saying things that cause shame (*aischunē*) to the victim' (*Rhet.* 2.1.1378b23–4); and shame is defined as 'a certain pain or disturbance concerning bad things that appear to lead to discredit' (2.6.1383b12–14). Thus a slight, at least if it is to merit anger, must be manifest to *others* than the slighter and the slighted. Equally, an act of revenge is imperfect if its success is unknown either to the agent or his victim, *or* to others whose lowered opinion of him the agent wishes to redress. Elsewhere, however, it is to the subject of the emotion that the occasion needs to be apparent.[28]

What then of the relation of an affection to relevant *beliefs*? As we saw, this was a central issue for Socrates and Plato. Whereas Socrates defined fear in the *Protagoras* as 'a certain expectation of evil' (358d5–7), Plato may suppose in the *Timaeus* that at least the lowest part of the soul is capable of emotions but not of beliefs (77b5–6). Several interpreters take Aristotle's conception of the affections to identify them with certain perceivings or imaginings, which may or may not be prompted or seconded by beliefs.[29] I doubt whether the *Rhetoric* envisages a separation of emotion from belief.

---

[27] This may be why, in the *DA*, a brief listing of 'affections of the soul', 'being angry, confident, desiring', is brought under the heading 'perceiving in general' (1.1.403a7), not because they are species of perceiving but because perceiving (or imagining) is integral to all of them.

[28] This is the one good reason that Cooper gives (1999b: 419 n. 23) for dismissing Roberts's rendering, in the Oxford translation, of *phainomenos*, in qualification of occasion and goal, by 'conspicuous'. Others, while accepting that there may be an allusion to others than the subject, might prefer to keep with 'apparent' since this would not imply facticity. W. D. Ross excised the 'apparent' attaching to 'revenge'; it is omitted in the otherwise very similar definition of anger in *Top.* 8.1.156a32–3.

[29] So Cooper (1999b: 416–17), Striker (1996: 291), Nieuwenburg (2002); *contra*, Nussbaum (1994: ch. 3), D. Frede (1996: 270–2), Fortenbaugh (2002: 96–103), Knuutila (2004: 36–8). Aspasius argued

One context where such a conception *is* at home is the lives of infants and lower animals. For Aristotle ascribes anger to non-rational creatures (*NE* 3.2.1111b12–13, *EE* 2.10.1225b26–7), but denies them belief on the ground that they all lack conviction (*pistis*), though many possess imagination (*DA* 3.3.428a20–2, cf. 3.10.433a11–12).[30] In their case, imagination must suffice to fuel emotion, desire, and action. Moreover, Aristotle writes of the human soul, 'Imagination and belief are not present in the same part of the soul' (*EE* 7.2.1235b28–9). However, we should not infer that, because we share an affective soul with the lower animals, our emotions do not involve an interaction with belief. For Aristotle also remarks that *both* parts of the soul that partake of reasoning, whether their role is to prescribe or obey (cf. *NE* 1.13), are peculiar to the human soul (*EE* 2.1.1219b37–8). The non-rational soul 'is in a way persuaded' by reason (*peithetai pōs, NE* 1.13.1103a33–4), and it is because they *cannot* be persuaded that lower animals lack conviction and so belief (*DA* 3.3.428a22–3).[31] Hence articulate human emotions may involve an interaction between perception, imagination, and belief of which inarticulate creatures are incapable, even if belief is never, strictly speaking, a *component* of emotion.[32]

Let us return to the *Rhetoric*: 'The affections are things through which, changing, men differ in their judgements, and which are followed by pain and pleasure' (2.1.1378a19–21). Implicit in this, in the central cases (such as anger), is an act of perception or imagination viewed as a change to which a man is subject. Which is consistent with both the passivity of an affection, and the acuity of its pains and

---

against Andronicus that *phantasia* can generate emotion without 'supposition' (*In NE* 44.33–45.16, translated in Sorabji, 2000: 134)—but with a Stoic conception of belief as initiated by a voluntary act of assent (*sunkatathesis*), whereas Aristotle denies that believing is up to us (*DA* 3.3.427b20).

[30] *DA* 3.3.428a22–4 even make having been persuaded a precondition of *each* state of belief; but there is reason to excise them (see Ross, 1961: ad loc.).

[31] Lorenz (2006: 189 n.11) reads the phrase 'in a way' as equivalent to a pair of scare-quotes around 'is persuaded', since the non-rational soul cannot appreciate a reason or follow an argument; yet we meet an unqualified 'readily persuadible' (*eupeithes*) at *NE* 3.2.1119b7. The sense of 'persuade' here must fall within a spectrum of possibilities: (i) directing attention; (ii) imparting information; (iii) convincing by giving reasons. Lorenz rightly excludes (iii); we may take (iv) to create a state in the irrational soul that does not amount to belief but depends upon it.

[32] Cf. Lorenz (2006 ch. 13). When Aristotle writes of agents acting on their *phantasiai* 'because their understanding is sometimes obscured by *pathos* or disease or sleep' (*DA* 3.3.429a5–8), or 'contrary to their knowledge' (*DA* 3.10.433a10–11), or impetuously not awaiting the *logos* (*NE* 7.7.1150b25–8), he leaves it open whether they act without relevant beliefs, or without rational ones. More indicative is his treatment of spirited and appetitive acrasia in *NE* 7.6. When anger 'reasons as it were that one must fight against such a thing' (1149a33–4), it impulsively mistakes what the agent really believes, which adds the *caveat* that this depends on the circumstances (cf. the analogue of servants who rush into action before hearing *all* that they are told, a25–8). And *logos* or perception *tells* appetite, more simply, that a thing is pleasant (a35). We may indeed ask whether one cannot be angry with a man whom one knows rationally to be innocent of any slight. I believe that Aristotle would qualify that by insisting that, as in cases of acrasia, one's knowledge is occluded (cf. *NE* 7.3.1147b6–17).

pleasures.[33] The first part of the sentence *could* express a generalization: affections often influence men's subsequent judgements—which is why the orator needs to attend to them (cf. 1.2.1356a15–17). But that makes the statement a bizarre mismatching of contingent generalization and essential characterization—with the generalization coming first. And it does not fit the examples that were spelled out shortly before (2.1.1377b31–1378a5): those were of thoughts of a kind *always* to come *with*—and not *sometimes* to come *after*—different emotional states. If some of those were stated in the language of 'appearing' (*phainetai*, 1377b31, 1378a4), there was also talk of 'seeming' (*dokei*) that was connected with making a judgement (*krisis*). While the terms *dokein* and *krisis* are themselves equivocal, it is the *krisis*, in the sense of decision or verdict, that his hearers may reach that is the speaker's ground for taking an interest in these things (1377b20–2). It is true that there is no explicit mention of belief in the initial definition of anger (2.2.1378a30–2); but belief is implicit in mention of desire (*orexis*), given that such *orexis* is equated with 'aiming at' (*ephiesthai*), which is taken to presuppose *believing*, and not just *imagining*, that an end is attainable.[34]

It was already indicative in the *Topics* that it could be said equally that anger presupposes the supposition (4.5.127b30–1, 6.13.151a15–16), or the appearance (8.1.156a32–3), of an injury. In the *Rhetoric*, anger is felt 'because of an apparent slight' (2.2.1378a31), but also when one *thinks* one is despised (1379b6), or that one is suffering unfittingly (2.3.1380b17–18). Fear comes of a *phantasia* of a coming evil (2.5.1382a21–2), but also of its expectation (*prosdokia*, b29–30, cf. *NE* 3.5.1115a9); no one fears what he does not think (*oiesthai*) will happen to him (b31).[35] Confidence, the opposite of fear, is defined as 'expectation, together with *phantasia*, of the nearness of what brings safety' (1383a17–18). It becomes evident that Aristotle's thought is not that human emotion does not require belief but that the beliefs that feed into it are commonly creatures of appearance.[36]

I have already indicated (with reference to 2.1.1378a19–21) why Aristotle emphasizes the role of imagination in fuelling emotions. It is not just, though it is partly,

---

[33] It is thus intelligibly that Aristotle allows that one thing that makes for calmness is the passage of time, when the subject is no longer 'fresh' (*hupoguios*) in anger (*Rhet.* 2.3.1380b5–6). Here he anticipates a feature of Stoic accounts of pleasure and distress, that they involve 'a fresh opinion' that something good or bad is present (LS 65B). He might rather appeal to the physiological aspect in explanation of another observation: men also become calm when they have spent their anger in another context (1380b10–11).

[34] The language of *Rhet.* 2.2.1378b3–4 is equivocal (with a *phainomenos*); but, if *every* case of anger is attended by pleasure, it must involve *thinking* that one will realize one's intention (b1–3).

[35] The word 'think' (*oiesthai*) is recurrent in discussion of fear (*Rhet.* 2.5.1382b31–1383a12), and of pity (2.8.1385b17–1386a1). Fortenbaugh (2002: 99 n. 1) notes that *EN* 5.8 associates an *apparent* wrong with *thinking* one is being wronged (1135b28–1136a1).

[36] That is, they are not merely *realized* in images, as Aristotle believes *all* occurrent thoughts are (e.g., *DA* 1.1.403a8–10). However, any theory of the emotions needs to recognize that, in any particular case, emotionality comes in degrees: a state of emotion may in part rest upon, or recruit, reflective beliefs or goals.

that this confirms that emotions can arise through misconceptions. It is more that, in emotion, one is subject to an exercise of one's imagination (or perception) that can take one over, causing intense pleasure or pain (or pain-*cum*-pleasure), and changing how one thinks of things. Those who are best at exciting pity 'make the evil appear close, bringing it before our eyes' (2.8.1386a33–4, cf. 3.11.1411b22–5). Aristotle is emphasizing the spontaneity of emotional beliefs: they need not be contrary to reason, and may be discriminating and sophisticated in content; yet one does not adopt them as a result of reflection upon reasons.[37] His attitude towards emotions becomes ambivalent. In *Rhetoric* 2 he is putting his reader in a position to exploit them; and yet he has remarked that to induce emotion in a juror is to 'pervert' him, likening it to bending the mason's rule that one is about to use (1.1.1354a24–6). Elsewhere he applies the same term (*diastrephein*) to the effect of anger upon even the best rulers (*Pol.* 3.16.1287a31–2), and of wickedness upon one's conception of the end of action (*NE* 6.12.1144a34–6). Yet it is virtue of character, not practical wisdom or its *logos*, that gives an agent the right end in action (a7–9, a20–2; *EE* 2.11.1227b22–5); and such virtue is the best condition of one's desires and emotions.[38]

Aristotelian deliberation is a process of calculation and reflection that ideally leads the agent from a provisional goal, suggested by one's character in the circumstances as perceived, to a way or means that acceptably achieves it. It does not follow, and Aristotle certainly does not believe, that deliberation is nothing but the calculation of effective means. The ultimate end is acting well, which demands an open receptivity to the emergence of *pros* and *cons*. If there are alternative ways of achieving one's more concrete goal, considerations of facility and fineness come into play (*NE* 3.3.1112b16–17). And the practical wisdom that is exercised within deliberation tests the goal *in the circumstances* by discovering whether they permit it to be achieved acceptably (which is how best sense is to be made of 6.9.1142b31–3). Yet the initial selection of a goal, at once of deliberation and of action, emerges out of the agent's perception of his situation. And this is a matter not just of his identifying the neutral facts of the case, but of his being attracted and repelled by the possibilities that pleasant or painful perception presents to him (*DA* 3.7.431a8–11). The practical eye is the eye of the heart, not just of the head.

Thus practical wisdom is rooted in educated affective responses. Education takes place through experience which habituates the agent in choosing and acting well *through* training him aright in his responses of pleasure and pain (*NE* 2.3). Achieving the *mean* in relation to an affection is a matter of being inclined to it not indiscriminately, but as is apt and best from situation to situation. How is this brought about? Aristotle's emphasis in the *Ethics* is dictated by an initial distinction between intellectual virtues, imparted by teaching, and ethical ones, imparted by habit (*ethos*, 2.1.1103a14–18). It is a *single* process of habituation that moulds acting

---

[37] Cf. Cooper (1999a: 242–4), Nehamas (1992: 297–300).
[38] Cf. Striker (1996: 297–9).

and feeling in circumstances of danger (b16–17). Yet this must ideally involve not just practice in action, but affection for a mentor: what a father says and does has more force than the laws of a city because of his consanguinity and beneficence; so his children start with a natural tendency to love and obey (10.9.1180b3–7). Building on that foundation, lawgivers can fruitfully invite and inspire obedience by appeal to the *fine* as a motive of action (a6–8). Ethical education in Aristotle is emotional education.

Yet its upshot, of course, is true belief as well as good desire (cf. 6.2). Whether an exercise of *phantasia*, perceptual or imaginative, generates a corresponding belief is no doubt a matter of content and context. The sun may obstinately continue to look one foot across even when one knows that it is much larger (*DA* 3.3.428b2–4; cf. *Insomn.* 1.458b28–9a 2.460b18–20). John Cooper cites that (1999*b*: 417), but not an earlier observation: 'When we form an opinion about something terrible or fearful, we are at once affected appropriately, and similarly in the case of something reassuring; but in respect of *phantasia* we are in the same condition as if we were looking at terrible or reassuring things in a picture' (*DA* 3.3.427b21–4). It is true that Aristotle is there considering the active imagination, which is under our control as belief is not (b17–21); and what one imagines may generally affect one's emotions less when the imagining is subject to one's will than when one is subject only to one's imagination. But that is because imagining at will is commonly less revealing about oneself than the imaginings that come upon one (especially in dreams). Can I really be angry with someone because I find myself imagining him having slighted me when I fully believe that he has not? (I might still become angry because I take it that what disposes me to imagine him so is that he despises me—but that gets us to a belief eventually.)[39]

One advantage in tying emotion to imagination rather than to conviction is that it is then unproblematic how we can be emotionally affected, even intensely, by what we take to be fictitious. (This remains a debated question within contemporary aesthetics.) We would also then *expect* plays and films that represent sufferings graphically to have more effect upon us than factual reports. Our resultant emotions will be like, and unlike, those whose objects are taken to be actual—yet with enough commonality in feelings, symptoms, and imaginings to make it apt to apply the language of real-life emotion. Such an approach could appeal to Aristotle as a writer on epic and tragedy. A first point to make is that this phenomenon tells more clearly against a pure doxastic view (such as Socrates') than the mixed view

---

[39] A more plausible claim might be that *phantasiai* are sufficient to produce emotions in a human subject, even if he does not judge that things *are* so, just so long as he does not judge that they are *not*. But consider two passages in the *Insomn.*: 'We are easily deceived concerning perceptions when we are excited by emotions' (2.460b3–4); 'In general, the *archē* affirms what comes from each sense, unless another and more reliable sense denies it' (3.461b3–5). They suggest that *phantasiai* that are not disbelieved are believed. Note also how the *DMA* counts movements, as of heart and penis, as *in*voluntary when 'these are moved when something appears, but without the command of thought' (11.703b5–8). Yet Aristotle counts action upon emotion as voluntary.

which I have ascribed to Aristotle. On my reading, the audience's imagination may be fully involved, with accompanying pleasure and pain, even though an awareness that they are observing the re-enactment of a fiction inhibits a forming of the beliefs that cause unetiolated emotion. A second observation is that Aristotle, without explicitly addressing the problem, appears to incline towards a factive solution: what moves one in a play is not particular fiction but egocentric truth, that is, not what *does* happen *to a character* in a play, but what one knows *might* happen *to oneself.* He famously holds that the poet presents not what *has* happened, but what *would* happen, expressing universals where history states particulars (*Poet.* 9.1451a36–b7). Pity is inspired by 'someone who is suffering undeservedly', fear by 'someone who is like ourselves' (13.1453a5–6).[40] As Alexander Nehamas has put it, 'When I sympathize with Oedipus, I feel an imaginative fear for myself, one which is based on seeing myself as someone relatively similar to Oedipus—indeed, Oedipus *is* a type, and one to which we may recognize ourselves as belonging' (1992: 302). Accordingly, Aristotle advises the poet to set out his plot in universal terms before supplying the names and turning the story into episodes (17.1455a34–b13). Even emotionally, human reality is the core; fictitious characters are a covering. Here one may feel that, while there is some truth in what Aristotle says, he is failing to make the best use of his own theory: it could have helped him more to keep in mind the connection between emotion and imagination, whether or not self-regarding beliefs play a subsidiary role.[41]

As it is, Aristotle's strategy is to retain an emphasis upon belief, while changing its content from the particular and fictitious to the general and factual. If this is how he accommodates aesthetic emotion, it is hardly likely that he adopts a view of real-life emotion that permits a subject of belief to count as fully and genuinely angry though he does not *believe* that he has cause. In another class of case he is explicit about belief, and silent about imagination. His lists of affections in the *De Anima* (1.1.403a16–18) and the *Nicomachean Ethics* (2.5.1105b213) include loving (*philein* or *philia*) and hatred (*misein* or *misos*). Both are duly treated in the *Rhetoric* (2.4), but in ways that differentiate in kind them from anger and fear.[42] Loving is defined as 'wishing (*boulesthai*) to someone what one thinks to be good things, for his sake and not one's own, and bringing them about to the best of one's

---

[40] This marks no contrast between the two. In the *Rhet.*, Aristotle says that we pity in others what we fear for ourselves, and vice versa (2.5.1382b25–6, 1386a27–9), and, in his definition of pity, that pity is excited by what happens to someone who does not deserve it, 'and which one might expect to befall oneself or someone close to one' (2.8.1385b13–15).

[41] More precisely, Aristotle needs to recognize that I can imagine *being* Oedipus, and so fully empathize with him, even if I not only am not Oedipus (in this, or any possible, world), but have little in common with him beyond a shared humanity. His view of imagination, though unduly imagistic, can accommodate at least something very like the phenomenon of imagining looking at Oedipus' situation through Oedipus' eyes.

[42] See Cooper (1999b: 410–14, 417–19).

ability' (2.4.1380b36–1381a1). In fact, Aristotle holds that *all* incarnate thinking involves *phantasia*. Yet there is no mention of a *phantasia* that connects with a pain or pleasure that is in part somatic; instead, loving is defined in terms of 'wishing' (*boulesthai*), which is rational desire, and acting. Pleasure comes in a little later: 'A friend shares one's pleasure in good things, and one's grief in painful things' (a3–4). That brings loving within his bare general formulations (*NE* 2.5.1105b21–3, *Rhet.* 2.1.1378a19–22), but with a difference: loving, in the present case, is a disposition upon which pleasure 'follows' (*hepetai*) not as an accompaniment but as a later manifestation or sign (cf. *sēmeion*, 1381a7).[43] Aristotle actually specifies that hatred is without pain (1382a12–13, *Pol.* 5.10.1312b33–4); by which he must mean not that hatred does not dispose one to certain pains (and indeed pleasures), but that one could not say that to hate someone *is* to feel pain. This connects with the equating of loving and a species of 'wishing'; for wishing is said to be free of pain (*Top.* 6.146b2). The same must be true of kindness (*charis*), which is defined as activity for a certain goal, which is benefiting another (2.7.1385a17–19), and for his sake (cf. b1); it therefore involves goodwill (*eunoia*), which is *wishing* another goods for his sake (*NE* 8.2.1155b31). Unlike anger (see n. 31), hatred is not cured by time (*Rhet.* 2.4.1382a7–8). Such variations doubtless explain the bareness of the general formulations: Aristotle could have enriched those by mention of *phantasia*, and the distinctive (and partly somatic) pleasure or pain that it can fuel, if he had intended a restriction to such affections as anger and fear. Instead, he prefers a determinable definition that applies to a wide range of affections that are heterogeneous, but all of interest within ethics and rhetoric.

# IV

Without separating off emotions as such, Plato and Aristotle alert us to their compositional intricacy, which involves body and mind, cognition and desire, perception and feeling. Even the differences of interpretation to which scholars are resigned focus our minds upon the complexity of the phenomena, and their resistance to over-unitary definitions. Emotions, after all, are things that we *feel*; at the same time, emotionally is how we often *think*. Discarding too simple a Socratic focus upon contents of thought, Plato and Aristotle embrace the interconnections, within the emotions, of body and soul, and of perception, imagination, feeling, and thinking. Theirs was not the last word, but, after them, there was no going back to

---

[43] Cf. *NE* 8.5.1157b28–9, where Aristotle remarks that *philēsis* is like a *pathos*, *philia* like a state (*hexis*). Yet it is *philia* that he treats in the *Rhet.* (2.4.1380b35).

first words. We should still read them, for the reason that what demands clarification *in them* demands clarification *in itself*. The questions that they bring alive for us are our questions.[44]

## References

### Ancient

| | |
|---|---|
| Plato | *Charmides* (*Charm.*) |
| | *Laws* |
| | *Phaedo* (*Pdo*) |
| | *Phaedrus* (*Phdr.*) |
| | *Philebus* (*Phil.*) |
| | *Protagoras* (*Prot.*) |
| | *Republic* (*Rep.*) |
| | *Sophist* (*Soph.*) |
| | *Symposium* (*Symp.*) |
| | *Theaetetus* (*Theaet.*) |
| | *Timaeus* (*Tim.*) |
| Aristotle | *De Anima* (*DA*) |
| | *De Insomniis* (*Insomn.*) |
| | *De Motu Animalium* (*DMA*) |
| | *Eudemian Ethics* (*EE*) |
| | *Nicomachean Ethics* (*NE*) |
| | *Physics* |
| | *Poetics* (*Poet.*) |
| | *Politics* (*Pol.*) |
| | *Rhetoric* (*Rhet.*) |
| | *Topics* (*Top.*) |
| Aspasius | *In ethica Nicomachea commentaria* (*In NE*) |
| Ammonius | *De adfinium vocabulorum differentia* |

### Modern

BOBONICH, CHRISTOPHER (2002), *Plato's Utopia Recast: His Later Ethics and Politics* (Oxford: Clarendon Press).

BURNYEAT, MYLES (2006), 'The Truth of Tripartition', *Proceedings of the Aristotelian Society* 106: 1–23.

---

[44] This chapter has benefited from the comments of the editor, and a lecture in Oxford by Christof Rapp.

CARONE, GABRIELA R. (2007), 'Akrasia and the Structure of the Passions in Plato's Timaeus', in C. Bobonich and P. Destrée (eds.), Akrasia in Greek Philosophy (Leiden: Brill), 101–18.

COOPER, JOHN M. (1999a), 'Some Remarks on Aristotle's Moral Psychology' (first published 1988), in his Reason and Emotion: Essays on Ancient Moral Psychology and Ethical Theory (Princeton: Princeton University Press), 237–52.

—— (1999b), 'An Aristotelian Theory of the Emotions' (revised from a piece first published in 1993, first printed in Rorty [ed.] 1996), in Reason and Emotion, 406–23.

FORTENBAUGH, W. W. (2002), Aristotle on Emotion, 2nd edn (London: Duckworth).

FREDE, DOROTHEA (1996), 'Mixed Feelings in Aristotle's Rhetoric', in Rorty (ed.) (1996), 258–85.

KNUUTILA, SIMO (2004), Emotions in Ancient and Medieval Philosophy (Oxford: Clarendon Press).

LEIGHTON, STEPHEN R. (1996), 'Aristotle and the Emotions' (abridged from an article printed in 1982), in Rorty (ed.) (1996), 206–37.

LIDDELL, HENRY GEORGE and SCOTT, ROBERT (1940), A Greek-English Lexicon, revised by Henry Stuart Jones (Oxford: Clarendon Press).

LONG, A. A. and SEDLEY, D. N. (1987), The Hellenistic Philosophers, 2 vols (Cambridge: Cambridge University Press).

LORENZ, HENDRIK (2006), The Brute Within: Appetitive Desire in Plato and Aristotle (Oxford: Clarendon Press).

NEHAMAS, ALEXANDER (1992), 'Pity and Fear in the Rhetoric and the Poetics', in Rorty (ed.) (1992), 291–314.

NIEUWENBURG, PAUL (2002), 'Emotion and Perception in Aristotle's Rhetoric', Australasian Journal of Philosophy 80: 86–100.

NUSSBAUM, MARTHA C. (1994), The Therapy of Desire: Theory and Practice in Hellenistic Ethics (Princeton: Princeton University Press).

PRICE, A. W. (1995), Mental Conflict (London: Routledge).

—— (1997), Love and Friendship in Plato and Aristotle, expanded edn (Oxford: Clarendon Press).

—— (2009), 'Are Plato's Soul-Parts Psychological Subjects?', Ancient Philosophy 29: 1–15.

RORTY, A. O. (ed.) (1992), Essays on Aristotle's Poetics (Princeton: Princeton University Press).

—— (ed.) (1996), Essays on Aristotle's Rhetoric (Berkeley: University of California Press).

ROSS, W. D. (1961), Aristotle De Anima (Oxford: Clarendon Press).

SORABJI, RICHARD (2000), Emotion and Peace of Mind: From Stoic Agitation to Christian Temptation (Oxford: Oxford University Press).

STRIKER, GISELA (1996), 'Emotions in Context: Aristotle's Treatment of the Passions in the Rhetoric and his Moral Psychology', in Rorty (ed.) (1996), 286–302.

TAYLOR, C. C. W. (2008), 'Wisdom and Courage in the Protagoras and the Nicomachean Ethics', in his Pleasure, Mind, and Soul: Selected Papers in Ancient Philosophy (Oxford: Clarendon Press), 281–94.

CHAPTER 6

# STOICISM AND EPICUREANISM

## CHRISTOPHER GILL

STOICISM and, to some extent, Epicureanism are striking examples of (what we now call) 'cognitive' theories of emotion, which stress the role of belief and intention in shaping emotional reactions. This feature has sometimes been seen as a ground of criticism of the theories, especially of the Stoic version, both in antiquity and in some modern discussions. But contemporary interest in cognitive theories of emotion has given fresh relevance to these ancient ideas, along with the cognitive dimension in some other ancient ideas of emotion, including those of Plato and Aristotle.

In this discussion, I bring out the cognitive dimension in the Stoic and Epicurean theories of emotion, while also locating this feature in a more comprehensive account of their thinking about emotion. Their theories of emotion are analysed here in terms of the intersection of four, partly overlapping, categories or branches of theory. These are (1) an account of human psychology, (2) an account of human physiology, (3) an account of natural functioning and value, and (4) an account of interpersonal or social relations. The analysis of emotions in the two theories presupposes a distinctive set of ideas in all four areas and a specific way of understanding the relationship between these areas. The cognitive dimension of their thinking about emotion falls primarily into the first area (their account of human psychology). But this feature of their thought is also linked with their distinctive views under the other three headings, and it cannot be understood fully without reference to those views.

My primary concern here is with historical interpretation and not with advancing the theory of emotion, which is the objective of other parts of this volume. But it is worth suggesting that the approach adopted here may have larger theoretical implications. Although (as is clear from other contributions here) there is no single current canonical account of emotions, one possible way of analysing emotions is in terms of the four categories noted here and of their interplay. The approach adopted here also offers a possible means of assessing theories of emotion, namely by reference to two related criteria, those of adequacy and consistency. A theory of emotion can be considered as adequate—in the first instance at least—if it analyses emotions under all four headings (rather than ignoring certain headings). A theory of emotion can be regarded as consistent if the analysis offered under any one heading is consistent with that offered under the other three headings. Of course, those criteria might be explored further and elaborated. For instance, there is scope for argument about what should count as an adequate account under each heading and about how we should understand the proper interrelationship between the four headings. Also, one might question the validity of the headings chosen; the coupling of natural functioning and value may seem particularly surprising or tendentious, though it corresponds to important features of Stoic and Epicurean thought, as I bring out later. But, even taken in its most basic form, this framework offers some advantages as compared with some other approaches. For instance, it enables us to assess a specific theory not just by whether it deploys a category we do or do not favour—for instance, a cognitive conception of emotions. Rather, we can assess a specific theory by reference to the adequacy with which it analyses emotions under these four headings (or others chosen) and by the consistency of the analysis under the various headings. Exploring the full theoretical implications of this suggestion would require a fuller and differently organised type of discussion than I can offer here. But, though my focus is on applying this framework to these two ancient theories, some broader theoretical implications may also emerge, as is suggested in the Conclusion.

Stoicism and Epicureanism originated in Athens at about the same time (the late fourth and early third century BC) and remained important and influential theories for the remainder of the Hellenistic age (until 31 BC) and, especially in the case of Stoicism, until the second century AD and beyond.[1] As with much Hellenistic philosophy, the main treatises of the original theorists have been largely lost, and the theories need to be reconstructed by reference to subsequent writings.[2] For the Stoic theory of emotion, in particular, we rely on later ancient summaries of doctrine, and on (often critical) discussions of the Stoic theory, which preserve quotations and key features of the views of leading Stoic thinkers.[3] However, in recent years, there has been intensive scholarly work on reconstructing the original

---

[1] The founder of Stoicism was Zeno (334–262) and the most important theorist was Chrysippus (c.280–c.206); Epicurus lived in 341–271 (all dates BC).

[2] See further Mansfeld 1999.

[3] See *S.V.F.* (= von Arnim 2004), III.377–490 and Long and Sedley (1987) (=LS) 65.

theories and analysing their content, especially in the case of Stoicism. So, although there is continuing debate on many specific points, we now have the basis for a broadly acceptable account of the theories, which can bring out their significance within the larger history of the philosophy of emotion.[4]

# STOICISM

Stoicism was famous in antiquity for its theoretical consistency and systematic character; and this feature is strikingly evident in Stoic thinking on emotions. Of the four headings under which I examine the theory here, that of natural functioning and value is, arguably, the most important and underpins Stoic thinking on the other aspects of emotion. Ethical naturalism, in one or other sense, is typical of most ancient theories, by contrast with at least some modern ones.[5] But both these Hellenistic theories draw a particularly close connection between human nature and ethical value, and this linkage justifies coupling these notions together to form one heading. As brought out later, the key ideas relevant for this linkage in Stoicism constitute part of their distinctive conception of development as 'appropriation' or 'familiarization' (*oikeiōsis*). The crucial Stoic underlying thought is that, although emotions (as normally conceived) in some ways express natural patterns of human functioning and development, they also show that something has gone badly wrong in human development and in the understanding of what is really valuable. However, I begin with two other headings, those of human psychology and physiology, since these bring out other important features of Stoic thinking that fall more obviously within the scope of the philosophy of emotion and also provide a good basis for comparison with Epicurean ideas under the same headings.

In terms of Stoic thinking about human psychology, the concept of emotion falls under the broader category of motivation. By contrast with Plato or Aristotle (or with much modern theory), motivation is not defined by reference to the concepts of perception, belief, and desire. Rather, it is explained in terms of 'appearance' or 'impression' (*phantasia*) and 'impulse' (*hormē*), which is perhaps better translated as 'motive'. A crucial underlying assumption, informing the Stoic use of these terms, is that human beings and other animals are naturally drawn to objects or actions which benefit their human character or 'constitution'. Thus, when an object or action 'appears' to an animal to be beneficial, this automatically generates an

---

[4] See Knuuttila 2004: 47–87 for an overview of both theories, viewed within the history of ancient and medieval philosophy.

[5] On some relevant features of ancient ethics, and for comparison with modern ethics in this respect, see Gill 2005; see also text to n. 73 below.

'impulse' to have the object or perform the action in question. However, the Stoics also see human motivation—more precisely, adult human motivation—as having certain distinctive characteristics. One is that adult human impressions, by contrast with those of human children or non-human animals, are constitutively rational. A second is that adult humans need to give 'assent' (*sunkatathesis*) to the content of their impressions before these impressions issue in 'impulse' or motivation to act. The rationality of human impressions consists, in the first instance, in the impressions having content that can be expressed in linguistic form, more specifically, in their having propositional content ('that $x$ is the case'). Hence, the assent consists in accepting the thought 'that $x$ is the case'. However, what underpins this stipulation is the more general idea that adult humans are constitutively (and distinctively) capable of an interrelated set of complex, advanced, and structured activities such as communicating through language and formulating propositions about their experience. To recast their view in slightly different terms, the fact that adult human motivation has these additional or special features (rational impressions, assent) reflects the role played by belief-sets in shaping adult human experience and action.[6]

The Stoic account of emotions reflects this larger pattern of thought about adult human motivation. The crucial mark of an emotion (*pathos*) is assent to the rational impression that it is appropriate to react in a certain way to a given situation. Assent is taken necessarily to bring with it the corresponding impulse, namely to react in that way. This point applies both to what are conventionally regarded as emotions (anger, grief, and so on) and the contrasting class of 'good emotions' (*eupatheiai*) which are characteristic of the experience of the normative wise person or ideal human being. Both sets of emotions are subdivided into four (or in the case of 'good emotions', three) broad types, correlated with the present or future (in time) and with good or bad (in value). Thus, in the case of conventional types of emotion, desire is correlated with good in the future and fear with bad in the future, whereas pleasure is correlated with good in the present and pain is correlated with bad in the present. In the case of 'good emotions', wish is correlated with good in the future and caution with bad in the future, whereas joy is correlated with good in the present. (There is no equivalent among 'good emotions' for the conventional response to what is bad in the present, because the only bad thing in Stoic ethics is ethical vice and the wise person has no experience of this.) Different definitions of emotions survive, which reflect the various aspects of the Stoic conception of emotion including the role of certain types of belief or impulse and the 'irrationality' (in a sense to be explained) of these responses. But these various definitions express the core psychological pattern of motivation, in

---

[6] See further Brennan 1998: 22–9, 2003: 260–9, Gill 2006: 138–41, Graver 2007: 24–8.

which assent to the impression that it is appropriate to react in a given way necessarily triggers that reaction.[7]

Here, for instance, is a formulation of one of the four basic emotions, in the conventional sense, namely of pleasure (*hēdonē*): 'pleasure is an elevation of psyche which is disobedient to reason, and its cause is a fresh believing that some bad thing is present at which it is appropriate to be elevated.'[8] The definition of the equivalent good emotion, joy (*chara*) is similar in basic structure, but salient differences include the fact that the response is 'well reasoned' and not 'disobedient to reason' and that it is based on knowledge and not belief or opinion.[9] The Stoics think that a wide range of conventionally recognized emotions can be regimented under the four basic types of emotion (or three types of good emotion), with the proviso that the latter type of emotion is only experienced fully by the ideal normative wise person.

Two other distinctive features of Stoic thinking about emotion can be linked with this account of the psychological pattern involved. One is that, as already indicated, emotions form a subgroup of the motivation of adult human beings, as distinct from human children or animals. This claim aroused much criticism in antiquity, but it is wholly consistent with the Stoic definition of emotions in terms of advanced and structured rational activities of a type that are characteristic of adult human beings. Stoic thinkers also identify types of reaction which are experienced by adult humans but which fall short of being full-scale (rationally based) emotions. For instance, one later Stoic thinker, Posidonius (*c*.135–*c*.50 BC), seems to have deployed the idea of 'emotional movements', which are sub-rational in character and are experienced by animals as well as humans; and there were probably equivalent ideas in earlier Stoicism.[10] Other sources identify reactions, sometimes called 'pre-emotions' (*propatheiai*), which include, alongside involuntary or instinctive reactions, other responses which are only provisionally entertained, such as the imaginative engagement of the audience in the theatre.[11] The salient common feature is that such responses do not depend on rational assent to an impression about the appropriateness of the relevant response, and thus do not generate the emotional response in its full form, which includes disobedience to reason and a correlated overwhelming psychological force.

---

[7] The necessary or automatic link between assenting to an impression and experiencing the relevant affective reaction reflects a strongly unified or 'holistic' view of human psychology, in which emotions are tied very closely to beliefs. See further Brennan 1998: 30–9, 2003: 269–79, Sorabji 2000: 29–54, Graver 2007: 35–60. For sources, see *S.V.F.* III.377–420 and LS 65A–F.

[8] Stobaeus II.90.16–18, translation based on Graver 2007: 42; see also Inwood and Gerson 1997: 218.

[9] See references in *S.V.F.* III.431–42, esp. 431 (Diogenes Laertius VII.115) (=LS 65 F); also Brennan 1998: 34–6.

[10] See Cooper 1998. Cooper, along with Tieleman 2003: 198–287, and Gill 2006: 266–90, seeks to correct the impression given by Galen that Posidonius made more radical revisions to Stoic psychological theory, which brought it closer to the tripartite psychology of Plato's *Republic*.

[11] See Graver 2007: 85–108, referring especially to Seneca, *On Anger* II.2.1–3.3.

These features of Stoic thinking are the ones which most obviously anticipate modern cognitive theories of emotion in stressing the role of beliefs and (what we call) intentionality in shaping emotion. The upsurge of contemporary interest in such theories is one of the factors that have led to a more positive appraisal of the Stoic theory than was common until recently. Martha Nussbaum, for instance, presents her theory as a modern version of the Stoic cognitivist approach.[12] The Stoic theory stands in pointed contrast to certain aspects of earlier ancient thinking, notably the association of emotions and desires in Plato and Aristotle with a non-rational part (or parts) of the psyche. The contrast is particularly stark with the argument in Book IV (435–41) of Plato's *Republic* in which desire and 'spirit' (the location of anger) are presented as constituting different 'parts' (or competing sources of motivation) from reason. In later antiquity, especially the first and second centuries AD, thinkers such as Plutarch and Galen highlighted the contrast with the Platonic–Aristotelian view, and used this as a basis for criticism of the Stoic theory. The Stoics were presented as denying what were taken to be obvious facts of psychological experience, which earlier thinkers had recognized, including the fundamentally non-rational character of emotions.[13] Whether the Stoics, in formulating their view of emotion, were consciously or explicitly marking a difference from previous philosophical ideas, is not clear from the kind of sources we have for early Stoicism.[14] In any case, their approach has certain points in common with earlier thinking. The Stoic stress on the role of beliefs (or, in the case of the wise person, knowledge) in shaping emotions is very close to ideas in, for instance, Plato's *Protagoras* and *Gorgias*, often taken to reflect the thinking of the historical Socrates.[15] Also, the idea that motivational patterns can appropriately be analysed in terms of propositions and logical reasoning is prefigured in Aristotelian ideas about the 'practical syllogism'.[16] So the Stoic approach to emotions may have been seen by them as constituting a selective development of earlier thought, rather than as marking a radical break (towards a radically intellectualist view), as it is presented by Plutarch and Galen.

What is clear, however, is that Stoic ideas about the psychology of emotion are closely and systematically linked with other aspects of their thought, including their ideas about human physiology and about natural facts more generally. The Stoics, like the Epicureans, adopt what we would regard as a physicalist or materialist position on psychology. Psychological processes are conceived as part of a larger scale of natural entities, all of which are outcomes of the interaction of active and passive principles in the universe. Thus, all aspects of the psychological

---

[12] See Nussbaum 2001: chs. 1–2.
[13] Plutarch *On Ethical Virtue* (*Moralia* 440 D–452 D), Galen *On the Doctrines of Hippocrates and Plato* (*PHP*) IV–V; see further Gill 2006: 219–66.
[14] See Gill 2006: 136–7, 212–13.
[15] See Plato *Protagoras* 352b–360e and *Gorgias* 466b–468e; also Gill 2006: 142–3.
[16] See further Inwood 1985: 9–17.

processes involved in emotions, including assent to rational impressions and the resulting impulse, are conceived as physical events. The only specifically non-physical aspect in the Stoic theory is that the intelligible content of thoughts or knowledge (*lekta*) is presented as non-material.[17] In Stoic accounts of emotion, the impulse or motive is often presented in strongly physical terms, namely as 'contraction' or 'elevation' of the psyche, or as 'reaching' or 'withdrawal'. 'Pre-emotions' are also sometimes characterized in physical terms, such as 'bitings', though full-scale emotions can also be described in this way.[18] However, the purpose of such language is not to suggest that these aspects of the psychology of emotion are physical in nature whereas other aspects (such as the assent to rational impressions) are not. In part, the aim of such language seems to be convey what we might describe as the phenomenology of emotions, or what it feels like to have emotions. In principle, Stoics assume that such felt emotions also have a physical expression and one of which the person concerned may be aware, such as the pounding of the heart in anger. But it does not seem that the Stoics attempted to establish a systematic correlation between specific forms of impulse, for instance, contraction or elevation, and specific physiological processes, for instance, types of heart movement. To this extent, the Stoics (like Aristotle, for instance) deploy—at least sometimes—two kinds of language for emotions such as anger, a psychological one, as in the definitions of emotions cited earlier, and a physiological one.[19]

However, the linkage between psychological and physiological analysis of emotion is sometimes drawn more closely and explicitly together, both on specific points and the overall structure of the theory. For instance, Stoic thinkers including Chrysippus, the main Stoic theorist, cite the felt presence of anger in the region on the breast as a ground for accepting the traditional location of the psychological centre in the heart, rather than the brain. This line of argument assumes a direct correlation between a subjectively experienced feeling and a physiological process, even if the feeling is not taken to provide a scientifically exact account of the location and nature of the process involved.[20] The line of argument may perhaps be connected with an idea found in one late but orthodox Stoic source, namely that the animal is in some sense aware of her own body as a psychophysical system or unit, an idea sometimes linked with the modern notion of 'proprioception'.[21] At a more general level, there is a direct and explicit link between the Stoic unified or holistic account of psychological processes and their account of the physiology of

---

[17] On the physicalism of Stoic psychology, see Annas 1992: 37–43, and Long 1999: 560–72; on *lekta*, see LS 33.

[18] See Graver 2007: 28–30, 88–92.

[19] Thus, for Aristotle, the 'dialectical' account of anger is the desire for retribution and the 'physical' one the boiling of blood around the heart (*On the Soul* I.1, 403a29–b1); for the analogy with Stoic thought on this point, see Graver 2007: 16–17, also 31–2.

[20] See Galen, *PHP* II.7.8; cf. Tieleman 1996: 148–50, Sorabji 2000: 38–9.

[21] See LS 53 B (Hierocles); cf. Long 1996: ch. 11, Graver 2007: 31–2.

psychological processes. At the psychological level, as we have seen, emotions are conceived as depending on rational processes (assent to rational impressions) and not as constituting an independent or potentially conflicting source of motivation. In physiological terms, all rational processes, including emotions, are explained as functions of a unitary psychological agency, the 'control-centre' (*hēgemonikon*), which is seen as located in the heart. There is no attempt to allocate different psychological processes (such as emotions or reasoning) to different centres and parts of the body, as Plato does in the *Timaeus* (followed by Galen). In this respect, the distinctive Stoic unified, or cognitive, account of emotions at the psychological level has a correlative in a distinctive account of human physiology.[22]

The features of Stoic thought discussed so far (under the headings of human psychology and physiology), though important, do not explain the most crucial—and controversial—aspect of Stoic thinking on this topic, namely the idea that emotions, as normally understood, are defective, 'irrational, or 'diseased' states of mind. To make sense of this point, and the way these defective states are characterized, we need to refer to their thinking about natural functioning and about value. The Stoics see ethical values as grounded in 'nature' in a number of ways. In particular, they think that human beings are naturally constituted to develop towards virtue through a process they describe as 'appropriation' or 'familiarization' (*oikeiōsis*). Development is subdivided in their theory into two, linked aspects, individual and social, and both aspects are relevant for making sense of Stoic thinking on emotion. The Stoics hold that all animals, including human beings, are constitutively attracted to what benefits their nature, such as things that promote health or material well-being. In non-human animals and human children, this process is an instinctive or automatic one; but as humans become adult, it is informed by their emerging rationality. Adult humans learn to select what is beneficial and to reject the opposites; and, if their development proceeds properly, they do so with increasing regularity and consistency. The culmination of the process is that the adult human recognizes that what matters is not so much securing beneficial things, such as health or wealth, but doing so in a completely appropriate way, which the Stoics identify with acting virtuously. At this point, the person realizes that, in comparison with virtue, which is the only real good, the objects previously sought, such as health and wealth, are 'matters of indifference' (*adiaphora*), even if they are still appropriately regarded as 'preferable' to the alternatives. The notions of 'indifference' and 'preferable' might seem to a modern reader to imply a kind of subjectivism about value; however, this impression would be quite misleading as the Stoics assume a strongly objectivist position. The Stoics think that we are naturally drawn to what are (objectively) beneficial things, such as those that promote our health, which they characterize as 'preferable' things. They

---

[22] See Long 1999: 562–72. For the contrast with Galen (*PHP* II–III), see Gill 2006: 242–3, 296–304.

also think we are naturally adapted to develop towards recognition of the objective truth that virtue is the only good, and that this recognition brings with it the realization that 'preferable' things are merely 'matters of indifference' in compari-son with virtue. This recognition is only complete when the person concerned achieves complete wisdom or ethical perfection, though all human beings are constitutively capable of achieving this state and should treat this as their overall goal in life.[23]

The theory of value involved, especially the radical contrast between virtue and 'indifferents', was a central and controversial feature of Stoic ethics. It is also one that underpins their thinking about emotions and their view of the contrast between emotions as most people experience them and the 'good emotions' that form part of the experience of the normative wise person. Both types of emotion, as we have seen, involve the belief that a specific thing is good or bad and that it is appropriate to react accordingly (for instance, to be elevated or contracted, to reach towards or withdraw from the thing in question). But most emotions depend on a false or misguided belief-set, in which 'indifferents' such as health or wealth, sickness or poverty are treated as if they were good or bad, instead of merely preferable or the opposite. The people concerned have not made the crucial, culminating move in ethical development, namely recognizing that only virtue is really good and only vice (moral defectiveness) is really bad. The Stoics believe that the emotions normally recognized, both the four basic types (pleasure and pain, desire and fear) and the sub-species, depend on this type of misevaluation. In these emotions, undue importance is being attached to things such as health, property, sexual pleasure, or status, thus generating responses such as fear, envy, (undue) erotic desire, or anger. By contrast, the good emotions of the wise person reflect correct valuations and express positive attitudes towards virtue (in the present or future) and caution as regards ethical wrongdoing.[24]

This point goes some way towards explaining why the Stoics characterize most emotional states as 'irrational' (though they also express adult human rationality, as explained earlier). The pattern is implied in this definition of desire (*epithumia*): 'a reaching (*orexis*) which is disobedient to reason, and its cause is believing that a good is in prospect in the presence of which we will flourish, the belief itself including a disorderly and fresh motive element as to that being genuinely a thing to reach for.'[25] This definition indicates another feature of emotions (as normally understood) which the Stoics accentuate, namely that they are powerful or overwhelming in their impact, even when they conflict with what the person

---

[23] On the Stoic theory of development as 'appropriation', see LS 57 A and 59 D. On the way in which this theory links value and nature, see Annas 1993: 135–41, 159–79, and Gill 2006: 129–66. On ancient 'objectivism' about ethics, see Gill 2005, esp. part 2.

[24] See Brennan 1998: 30–2, 2003: 269–71, and Graver 2007: 41–51.

[25] Stobaeus II. 90.7–10. Translation by Graver 2007: 42; see also Inwood and Gerson 1997: 218.

concerned, as well as others, sees as an appropriate response. Hence, unlike other kinds of misjudgements, the person concerned cannot rid herself of the emotion, even when she acknowledges that it rests on a mistaken valuation. A related feature, also stressed by the Stoics, is that emotions often conflict with each other (as well as with other, more well-grounded judgements); partly for this reason, emotions are described as 'fluttering', 'feverish', and taken to involve certain kinds of internal conflict.[26]

Ancient critics such as Plutarch and Galen dispute that the Stoics can explain these features of emotions without recourse to the Platonic or Aristotelian idea that there are distinct non-rational parts in the psyche which naturally conflict with the judgements of reason.[27] However, this criticism may not be justified. Stoic thinking about the factors involved in development in fact provide a rather rich repertoire of ideas to explain the overwhelming character of emotions and the phenomenon of internal conflict. Important considerations include the fact that the things that typically arouse emotions, including health or sickness, wealth or poverty, are ones towards which (in Stoic theory too) we are naturally drawn. The Stoics also recognize the role of social influences, such as those of family and friends, in promoting the mistaken belief that these things are really good or bad and not simply matters of indifference by comparison with virtue or vice. Also important is the Stoic view that all human beings constitutively possess the mental and psychological equipment to enable them to develop towards full ethical perfection, even if in practice almost nobody does so. This set of ideas provides the basis for explaining that fact that the kinds of judgements involved in emotions exercise powerful psychological force, even in cases when the people concerned can recognize that the emotions are misguided and rest on defective beliefs. The Stoics also explain in this way the kinds of internal conflict that emotions often generate, as the person's natural capacity for grasping sound ethical beliefs conflicts with the emotions based on erroneous judgements she has also formed. Thus, in one of Chrysippus' favourite examples, even Medea, about to kill her children, can recognize that what she is about to do is bad, even though she also sees that at this moment she is 'mastered' by the anger (the desire to take revenge on her unfaithful husband) that drives her to infanticide.[28]

The last example leads on to the fourth topic that is relevant for understanding the Stoic theory of emotions, namely that of interpersonal and social relationships. In Aristotle's account of emotions, notably in Book 2 of the *Rhetoric*, the content of the belief linked with a given emotion often relates directly to interpersonal

---

[26] See LS 65 A, G, J.

[27] Plutarch *Moralia* 446 E–448 F, 450 B–451 B, Galen *PHP* IV.2.8–44, 4.1–34. See also Gill 2006: 225–7, 249–50.

[28] See Euripides *Medea* 1078–81, and Galen *PHP* IV.2.27, 6.19–22. See further Gill 2006: 251–60, Graver 2007: chs. 3 and 7.

relations. For instance, Aristotle defines anger as 'a desire, accompanied by pain, for revenge at what is taken to be an insult to oneself or those close to one, in a situation where insult is not appropriate'. He adds: 'Every case of anger must be accompanied by a certain sort of pleasure, namely that which derives from the hope of taking revenge.'[29] Stoic definitions of anger are similar in this respect, for instance, 'anger is a desire to take revenge on someone who appears to have wronged you contrary to what is appropriate'.[30] However, there is the crucial difference that the Stoics, unlike Aristotle, see the judgement underlying the emotion as misguided in regarding the insult done as a genuinely bad thing (and not merely 'dispreferable') and thus justifying the motivation to revenge. Indeed, it is sometimes thought that Stoic ethics advocates some kind of radical detachment from interpersonal relationships and that this detachment is designed to protect one's own peace of mind and freedom from emotion (*apatheia*). Although there are some passages which might seem to support this interpretation, it is also clear that this is a misinterpretation or simplification of the Stoic position. A better way of putting their view is that forming a correct understanding of what is appropriate in interpersonal and social relationships is an integral part of a virtuous life and this life will be characterized by good emotions (and absence of bad emotions).[31]

Here too the Stoic theory of development as appropriation (*oikeiōsis*) is relevant in both of its main aspects, individual and social. It seems clear that individual ethical development, outlined earlier, is conceived as informing one's interpersonal and social relationships too. These relationships should be conducted with an increasing awareness that what matters, ultimately, is not securing 'preferable indifferents', such as health or wealth either for oneself or other people, but doing so virtuously. Since virtuous action is often characterized as benefiting other people by securing such 'indifferents' for them, careful discrimination is needed to draw and apply the relevant distinctions, as Stoic theory recognizes.[32]

Apart from the social implications of this side of ethical development, Stoicism also outlines a distinct programme of social development. Fundamental here is the idea that benefiting others ('appropriating' them to oneself) is a basic human (and animal) motive, parallel to the basic motive to benefit oneself, and exemplified above all in the natural instinct of parents to love and care for their offspring. As in the case of individual development, the theory envisages progressive movement from this basic motive. This leads (among other outcomes) to the recognition that any given human being may become an object of moral concern and someone whom one appropriately benefits. It is tempting to see here the expression of the

---

[29] Aristotle, *Rhetoric* II.2, 1378a30–2, b1–2, my translation.
[30] Stobaeus II.91.10–11 (=*S.V.F.* III.396). Translation by Inwood and Gerson 1997: 218.
[31] For this view, see also Graver 2007: ch. 8.
[32] On the relationship between social and individual appropriation, see Reydams-Schils 2002 and 2005: ch. 2.

idea that social ethical development consists in shifting one's concerns from specific people, such as one's own children, to humankind in general. However, a more plausible interpretation is that developing rationality enables one to extend one's ethical concern to more complex and structured forms of relationship, both within one's own specific community and in the larger 'community' or 'kinship group' of humankind as a whole. It also seems clear that we are intended to draw ever closer links between the two kinds of ethical development, individual and social. Thus, our advancing understanding of the radical distinction in value between virtue and 'indifferents' should inform our engagement in progressively more structured social relationships, and vice versa.[33]

The implications of these aspects of Stoic ethical development for our experience of emotions are drawn out especially in teachings on practical ethics by Epictetus, for instance. These discussions can help to counter the impression, noted earlier, that Stoicism advocates radical detachment from interpersonal relations with a view to maintaining one's own peace of mind. For instance, Epictetus insists that the appropriate (or 'natural') response for a father with a sick daughter is to assist at her bedside rather than to be so consumed by anxiety about her health that he has to get away from his home.[34] (This insistence on the appropriateness of beneficial action co-exists with a reminder that, when you kiss your child or friend goodnight, you should be aware that their death—or yours—may prevent another meeting.)[35] Epictetus also commends the response of a senator who recognizes that playing his social role properly may require his death at the hands of an emperor—and a readiness to do so 'without grieving'.[36] Marcus Aurelius, a Stoic writer and emperor, reminds himself that thinking of his troublesome companions as fellow members of the brotherhood of humankind can help to counteract the (unworthy) emotions of resentment and irritation that might otherwise be aroused.[37] What underlies all these comments, I think, is the attempt to bring out the point that ethical development, at the individual and social level, has profound implications for our affective experience and for the extent to which we can succeed in avoiding (bad) emotions and move towards a state where we only experience 'good emotions'. Thus, this fourth topic brings out from another direction a point I have stressed throughout this discussion, namely the high level of consistency between the different aspects of Stoic thinking that bear on their conception of emotions.

---

[33] See LS 57 D-G, esp. Cicero On Ends III.62–8 (=LS 57 F). See also, on Stoic commitment to family and community, Reydams-Schils 2005: chs. 3–5, and, stressing the commitment both to 'cosmopolitanism' and one's local community, Annas 1993: 302–11, and Vogt 2008: ch. 2.

[34] Epictetus Discourses I.11, esp. 5–15; see also Long 2002: 77–9 (also 231–8).

[35] Epictetus Discourses III.24.84–8; see also Long 2002: 248–9.

[36] Epictetus Discourses I.2.19–24, esp. 21.

[37] Marcus Aurelius Meditations II.1. See also Gill 2000: 607–15.

# EPICUREANISM

As in Stoicism, our evidence for Epicurean thinking on emotion causes difficulties. Although we have more surviving writings from Epicurus himself than from early Stoic thinkers, very little is directly on emotions; also most of his writings on related topics are relatively non-technical, consisting of short statements or letters summarizing key ideas. The most important Epicurean sources on emotion are partly surviving works of practical ethics (for instance, on the management of anger and the fear of death) by Philodemus, along with parts of Lucretius' verse account of Epicureanism, both produced in the first century BC. As with the Stoic theory of emotion, there has been recent intensive scholarly work on the topic, and debate continues vigorously on several key questions. The theory is examined here under the same four broad headings as in Stoicism; and it is clear that Epicureans have determinate ideas on all four topics and that there is a good deal of consistency between their views on these topics, though it is less clear than in Stoicism that there was a sustained attempt to establish a systematic theory. It is also evident, I think, that the Epicurean view of emotions is revisionist, as compared with conventional ideas; what is more open to debate is just how revisionist it is and how close the revised account is to the Stoic treatment.[38]

In Stoicism, there are clear indications of a highly worked-out psychological account of emotion, strongly focused on the cognitive dimension. Epicurean ideas are more informally presented; there is also a clear cognitive dimension, though there is less emphasis on this aspect than in Stoicism. The role of beliefs in generating emotions, such as anger, grief, or erotic passion, is presented as central; as brought out later, emotions are evaluated as 'natural' or 'empty' according to the quality of the beliefs involved.[39] There is also, as one might expect, an affective or 'feeling' dimension in emotions. This is sometimes characterized by the term 'bites', used in Stoicism mostly for *pre*-emotions but in Epicureanism signifying full-scale emotions.[40] In Stoicism, it is made very clear that the affective response *depends* on the cognitive content (assent to a rational impression triggers an impulse). This is rather less explicit in Epicurean writings, but it does seem to be strongly implied. The central component in the Epicurean therapy of the emotions (as in Stoic therapy)[41] lies in revising people's belief-sets with a view to changing their patterns

---

[38] Armstrong 2008 argues that the Epicurean view was relatively close to Aristotelian (and conventional) thinking on emotions. Annas 1993: ch. 7 and Warren 2004 suggest that the Epicurean approach was more revisionist.

[39] See Annas 1992: 193–9.

[40] See Tsouna 2007: 44–51.

[41] On the Stoic therapy of the emotions, which is highly cognitive in approach, see Tieleman 2003: chs. 4 and 6 (reconstructing Book 4 of Chrysippus' 'therapeutic' book 4 of *On Emotions*). See also Nussbaum 1994: chs. 9–11, Sorabji 2000: ch. 11–13, Knuuttila 2004: 71–80.

of emotion; and this in turn implies that the affective response depends on the belief involved.[42]

A feature that might seem to run counter to the idea that emotions are belief-based is a suggestion (in Lucretius) that an underlying (and often unrecognized) fear of death creates a whole series of secondary emotions and desires including self-hatred, greed, and craving for honour. However, what underlies this suggestion is that this underlying fear and the secondary emotions thus produced depend on erroneous ('empty') beliefs; and Lucretius' aim is to bring the emotional effect of these beliefs into the open and so help people to change them and thus rid themselves of the fear of death and the other emotions this generates.[43] Certainly, we do not find in Epicurean writings any analogue for the Platonic argument (*Republic* IV.435–41) that reason and desire or appetite are distinct, and potentially conflicting, sources of motivation. Although we find in some sources the contrast between 'rational' and 'non-rational' parts of the psyche, this does not seem to refer to a Platonic (or Aristotelian) type of division between rational and non-rational motives. What seems to be involved is the contrast between the psychological centre (the 'ruling part' or 'mind') and other psychological operations or functions, a contrast described by Lucretius as that between *animus* ('mind') and *anima* (other body-based psychic functions). Lucretius also makes plain that the 'mind' (*animus*) is the seat of both rational deliberation and emotions.[44]

The picture of psychological functions suggested by these features of Epicurean thought is consistent with Epicurean thinking about human physiology and the physical dimension of human psychology. The Epicureans, like the Stoics, hold a physicalist or materialist position on psychology;[45] thus Epicurus, in one important passage replaces the Platonic–Aristotelian contrast between psyche and body with that between psyche (presented as one part of the body) and the rest of the psycho-bodily aggregate.[46] The mind (*animus*) is taken to be located in the heart, whereas the *anima* links the mind with other functions including sensation and movement. The combination of a unitary mind, coordinated with other body-based psychic functions, resembles the Stoic picture. In another way, it is close to the modern picture of a combination of a unitary brain (the seat of reason and emotion) and a central nervous system operating throughout the body as a whole.[47] The Epicurean view is combined with their atomic account of nature; the psyche is regarded as made up of certain kinds of atoms, composed in a

---

[42] This point is compatible with the fact that the means of therapy are themselves highly emotional in character; the aim is still change in beliefs. On Epicurean therapeutic techniques, see Nussbaum 1994: ch. 4, Sorabji 2000: 233–4, and Tsouna 2007: 74–87.

[43] Lucretius III.59–86, 1053–79, also II.14–61; see Gill 2006: 114.

[44] Lucretius III.136–44; see also Annas 1992: 144–7, and Gill 2006: 52–3.

[45] See Annas 1992: 123–34, and Everson 1999.

[46] Epicurus, *Letter to Herodotus* 63–4 (=LS 14 A); cf. von Staden 2000: 81–5.

[47] See Lucretius III. 136–76; for the Stoic picture, see LS 53 G–H; also Gill 2006: 55.

distinctive way.[48] Animal species, and individual human beings, are supposed to have certain emotional tendencies or predispositions according to their atomic make-up. However, it is also maintained that human beings, unlike (at least wild) animals can modify their congenital make-up, a process explained in atomic terms by reference to the contrast between (atomic) 'developments' and the original 'first nature'.[49] Hence, Epicurus argues, human beings are properly held responsible for their emotional dispositions.[50] Also, Epicurean therapy can in principle help people to revise their congenital make-up and to replace 'empty' beliefs and emotions with 'natural' ones, as discussed later.

These features of Epicurean thinking about emotions (as part of the human psychological and physiological make-up) are broadly similar to the Stoic ideas discussed earlier. However, the most distinctive and striking features of Epicurean thinking on emotion emerge in connection with the third heading considered here, natural functioning and value. The Epicureans, like the Stoics, see ethical value as, in some sense, grounded on natural facts, though on a very different view of what is 'natural' and what values are thus validated. The Epicureans, like the Stoics, think that human beings and other animals display from birth certain primary motives that reflect their nature or 'constitution'. But for the Epicureans, the key motive is the inclination towards pleasure, rather than towards benefiting themselves or others. Also, this inclination is taken to be a life-long one, and not one that evolves into a substantively different motivational pattern (directed at virtue or the good) as in the Stoic picture. Pleasure is conceived, unusually, in negative terms, as the absence of pain in the body and absence of disturbance in the mind (*aponia* and *ataraxia*). These states are also sometimes defined as 'static' or dispositional pleasures, by contrast with the 'kinetic' pleasures which involve movement towards these states or variation in the way they are experienced. The negative characterization of the nature of pleasure, as absence of pain or disturbance, in fact implies a positive idea: namely, that simply *being alive* and exercising one's natural functions is inherently pleasurable. Pleasure does not require intense or heightened experiences; the most we need or can hope for is the normal state of the human organism. This conception of pleasure is fundamental for the Epicurean view of what it means to lead a good and worthwhile human life. It is taken to provide the basis for a revisionist account of ethics (or what is meant by happiness and virtue) and of the best way to conduct interpersonal and social life.[51]

This conception of a good human life gives rise to a number of important distinctions in the area of desires and emotions. As regards desires, Epicurus

[48]  LS 14 C–D.
[49]  LS 20 B–C (extracts from Epicurus' lost work *On Nature*), and Lucretius III. 262–322 (=LS 14 D).
[50]  See further Bobzien 2000, O'Keefe 2005, and Gill 2006: 56–66.
[51]  See LS 21, esp. A, O–P. See further Annas 1993: 188–200 (who stresses that Epicurean ethical theory involves a strongly revisionist account of what 'nature' means); also Sedley 1998, Erler and Schofield 1999, Gill 2006: 109–112.

distinguishes between those which are natural and necessary, natural but not necessary, and neither natural nor necessary but the product of 'empty opinion'. The first type of desires is for those things needed to achieve the goal of an Epicurean life (freedom from pain and disturbance); the second type is for objects which give variety to those pleasurable states, and the third is for objects which make no contribution to these ends, including symbols of status and perhaps also specific types of food or sexual pleasure.[52] A related distinction is drawn between 'natural' and 'empty' emotions, such as anger. Broadly, natural anger is consistent with a correct understanding of the nature and proper objectives of a human life whereas empty anger reflects erroneous beliefs about this. Modern scholars have debated whether Epicurean thinking on emotions is closer to the Aristotelian view (that they are natural human reactions to specific types of situations) or the Stoic one (that most emotions reflect misguided beliefs about what is really valuable). Indeed, debate of this type seems to have taken place at quite an intense level within the Epicurean school itself in the first century BC, to judge from the evidence of Philodemus.[53] Different aspects of Epicurean thinking seem to answer to these two types of position, though perhaps a consistent intermediate view emerges overall.

On the one hand, natural anger is defined, by Philodemus, for instance, as a response that is correctly matched to the situation: thus, 'it arises from insight into the nature of things and from avoiding false opinion in calculating the disadvantages and in punishing those who do harm'.[54] We are also told that gratitude, anger, and resentment are activated by the voluntary nature of the actions involved.[55] These aspects of Epicurean thinking on 'natural' anger evoke the Aristotelian view of anger (which reflects conventional Greek thinking) noted earlier. However, one clear and emphatic point of contrast with the Aristotelian type of view is that natural anger, by contrast with empty anger, regards taking revenge as a painful necessity rather than a source of pleasure.[56] There is also evidence, some going back to Epicurus, that (certain kinds of) grief are natural though painful responses to loss of life, an idea sometimes formulated as being that they are 'bites' imposed necessarily on us. Similarly, there is at least some evidence that points to the view that sexual or erotic desire is a natural one.[57]

[52] LS 21 I; also Annas 1993: 192–3, and Gill 2006: 112–13.

[53] Thus Nicasicrates takes a Stoic-style position, while Timasagoras takes an Aristotelian-style one; see Fowler 1997: 24–30, Procopé 1998: 186–9, and Armstrong 2008: 112–15.

[54] Philodemus On Anger 37.52, translated by Procopé 1998: 18.

[55] Philodemus On Anger 46.28–35. Emotions, as so understood, are close to the 'reactive attitudes' identified by Strawson 1974; on Strawson 1974 and Epicurean thinking on emotion, see further text to n. 65.

[56] Contrast the Aristotle passage cited in text to n. 29 above. On this point of contrast, see Annas 1993: 194–5, and Armstrong 2008: 80–1.

[57] See Armstrong 2008: 94–7, 106–7, also Tsouna 2007: 44–7.

On the other hand, a very central part of Epicurean philosophy consists in sustained and fully argued critiques of emotions based on false beliefs about natural facts and values, especially unnecessary fear of death, 'empty' anger, and erotic desire based on illusory ideals. This feature forms a crucial part of the Epicurean therapy of emotions.[58] Is this consistent with the view that at least some versions of these emotions are 'natural'? The underlying thought may be this. Emotions such as anger and grief or sexual desire are, at a basic level, instinctive responses as mechanisms of defence or expressions of natural need in humans as well as other animals. However, whether or not they should count as fully 'natural', within the framework of a human life, depends on whether or not they are informed by a correct pattern of beliefs about the real nature of human existence and about what is really valuable.

This complex, but intelligible, line of thought goes some way towards explaining the seemingly ambivalent presentation of emotions in Epicureanism, including their characterization of the ideal wise person in this respect. However, to make full sense of their views, we need also to refer to Epicurean ideas about the proper conduct of interpersonal and social relations. Ancient critics maintained that, in taking (one's own) pleasure as the overall goal in life, Epicureans ruled out a proper recognition of the importance of benefiting other people.[59] And, certainly, Epicureans take a very guarded view about the value of most conventional forms of human association, including family life and communal involvement. On the other hand, from Epicurus onwards, a very high value was placed on friendship (*philia*), and friends were presented as a source of positive emotions such as joy as well as objects of genuine, even intense, concern. Exactly how one should reconcile this valuation of friendship with regarding pleasure as the goal of life was a question debated within the school as well as by ancient and modern commentators on the theory. But one key factor is that the kind of friendship that is primarily validated is that which is shaped by distinctive Epicurean objectives and ideals and which enables the friends to help each other to lead a properly Epicurean life.[60] Hence, as we see vividly in Philodemus' *On Frank Criticism*, social life in first-century BC Epicurean communities was marked by a high level of mutual criticism and encouragement, as friends helped each other in 'consciousness-raising' and in ensuring that their actions and feelings matched the school norms.[61]

This set of ideas, together with their thinking on emotions, may serve to make sense of the presentation of the emotional reactions of the wise person (or of

[58] See, e.g., Lucretius III (against fear of death), IV.1037–287 (against erotic illusions), and Philodemus *On Death* and *On Anger*; also Nussbaum 1994: chs. 4–7, and Warren 2004.

[59] See, e.g., Cicero, *On Ends* II.73–85.

[60] See esp. Cic. *On Ends* 1.68: 'Therefore the wise person will have the same feelings towards his friend as himself and will undertake the same labour for his friend's pleasure as he would for his own'; also Gill 1996: 391–4. See also LS 22, taken with Annas 1993: 236–44, and Warren 2004: ch. 5.

[61] See Konstan et al. 1998, esp. introduction; also Nussbaum 1994: 115–36, Tsouna 2007: 91–121, and Armstrong 2008: 97–100.

Epicurus, the exemplary figure for the school). As regards anger, we have what seem to be competing features. On the one hand, we are told that he 'neither falls into such intense emotions as these [empty desires for revenge] . . . nor is impelled to punishment as something enjoyable . . . but approaches it as something most unpleasurable, as he would the drinking of [bitter medicine] or the doctor's knife'.[62] This matches the ideal of 'natural' anger, experienced as a necessary and appropriate pain, rather than a source of pleasure (as in 'empty' anger). We also hear that such a person will not be harmed by other people (in a way that provokes natural anger) because 'he is not even susceptible to great troubles in the presence of great pains, and much more is this so with anger'.[63] On the other hand, Philodemus is, clearly, aware of a good deal of evidence suggesting that Epicurus was, or appeared to be, 'irascible' (with a strong disposition to anger). He tackles this feature head-on, suggesting that this behaviour did not derive from a tendency to anger (whether natural or empty) in the ordinary sense but formed part of Epicurus' deeply felt desire to urge his friends and students towards the best way of life. Hence, 'out of friendship there is frequent rebuking of all or most of his disciples, and quite intense, often even (amounting to) reviling'.[64] Epicurus' apparent anger, or irascibility, derived from his frequent use of 'frank criticism' (*parrhēsia*), an activity that is in fact compatible with genuine (Epicurean) friendship, and also with a natural, but rather complex, type of anger. This explanation can be characterized in terms of Peter Strawson's distinction between 'objective' and 'reactive' attitudes. Although Epicurus' anger (or irascibility) appeared to be of a 'reactive' kind, which Aristotle takes as normal, it is better seen as expressing a more detached ('objective') attitude, that of a teacher intent on urging his students in a direction that he is best placed to recognize.[65]

Another, very famous, passage which illustrates the link between proper forms of emotion and interpersonal relations is Epicurus' death-bed letter to his friend Idomeneus:

I wrote this to you on that blessed day of life which was also my last. Strangury and dysentery had set in, with all the extreme intensity of which they are capable. But the joy (*echaron*) in my mind at the memory of our past conversations was enough to counterbalance this. I ask you, as matches your life-long companionship with me and with philosophy: take care of the children of Metrodorus.[66]

---

[62] Philodemus *On Anger* 44.5–35 (extracts), translated by Armstrong, cited by Fish 2004: 114–15.

[63] Philodemus *On Anger* 41.28–42.14, translated by Annas 1989: 158–9.

[64] Philodemus *On Anger* 35.18–40, translated by Armstrong 2008: 112.

[65] See Strawson 1974; Strawson's examples of 'objective' attitudes are those of parent towards child or psychotherapist towards patient. For the use of the 'objective–reactive' distinction to illustrate the contrast between Aristotelian and Epicurean (or Stoic) ideas of acceptable forms of anger, see also Gill 2003: 208–16, and 2006: 451–3.

[66] Diogenes Laertius X.22 (=LS 24 D, their translation modified).

This passage illustrates a number of central features of Epicurean ethical thinking, including the ideas that the wise person 'will always have a supply of tightly-knit pleasures' and that mental pleasures can counterbalance physical pains.[67] But the most important points in this context relate to the relationship between the right kind of emotional experience and the right kind of friendship. Epicurus' life-long companionship with friends such as Idomeneus and their shared philosophical activity have produced a kind of 'joy' that counteracts any fear of death, as well as outweighing Epicurus' intense physical pain. It also creates a bond of shared experience and ideals that makes it appropriate for Epicurus (in spite of his hedonistic ideal) to be concerned about the future of the children of his friend and fellow philosopher Metrodorus, and for Idomeneus to respond to this concern. The self-consistency both of Epicurus' courageous equanimity and his disinterested concern for the future welfare of a friend's children have been called into question by ancient and modern critics.[68] But there are grounds for arguing that the letter bears out a consistent, if highly revisionist, set of ideas about ethics, emotion, and interpersonal relationships, as well as illustrating vividly their potential practical force.[69]

# CONCLUSION

In this discussion, my main aim has been to offer a plausible interpretation of these Hellenistic accounts of emotions and, in particular, to bring out the coherence of each of them when taken as a whole. But it is worth asking what larger implications follow from this study for the analysis of theories of emotion more generally. More specifically, what are the merits and demerits of examining and assessing theories of emotion in the way adopted here, in terms of the interplay between four categories (psychological, physiological, natural functioning and value, and interpersonal relations) and of the degree of consistency achieved in the theory between the views expressed in each category?

I think that this approach has proved much more satisfactory than the one sometimes deployed by ancient or modern critics of the Stoic account. Critics such as Plutarch or Galen maintain that the Stoic theory is defective because it ignores or rejects what are taken to be obvious psychological facts, such as that reason and

---

[67] See Cicero *Tusculan Disputations* V.95 (=LS 21 T).

[68] See, e.g., among ancient writers, Cicero, *On Ends* II. 96–103, Plutarch *Moralia* (*Moral Essays*) 1089 F–1090 A, 1099 D–E.

[69] See further Gill 2006: 122–4, and on the consistency of Epicurus' concern with events after his own death with his hedonistic ethics, Warren 2004: ch. 5.

desire or emotion constitute independent and potentially conflicting sources of motivation.[70] Also, it has often been thought that the Stoic account of the ideal emotional state was humanly unacceptable because it gives no place for emotions (as conventionally understood).[71] The appeal to supposedly obviously psychological facts seems to me a highly questionable one because the nature of these 'facts' and the basis for establishing them is strongly contested. There is also ample scope for dispute about what kinds of emotions should or should not be included in a credible account of the ideal character-state. An advantage of the method followed here is that it enables the theory to be considered fully and in the round (at least, as regards the four categories selected), before attempting to make judgements about the views offered in any one category. Not only does this enable more comprehensive coverage of the theory but it also allows us to consider the implications of each part of the theory for the others instead of taking each one in isolation. The primary mode of assessment of a given theory proposed here is by reference to the consistency between the views expressed on each of the categories. But taking the theory as a whole in this way enables us to make better sense of its views in any one area, and to consider how adequately each area is dealt with.

However, there are at least two possible objections to the method followed here, which need to be considered to see if they can be countered. One is that the criterion of self-consistency is too broad or inclusive to be useful in considering such theories. It might be argued that virtually any theory of emotion is likely to meet this criterion, and so this method serves little useful purpose as a way of discriminating between more or less convincing theories. However, I do not think that, in fact, all theories of emotion do meet this criterion. Galen, as noted earlier, is one of the most prominent ancient critics of the Stoic theory; but, if we examine his own ideas about emotion, there are good grounds for questioning their internal consistency. In particular, his account of human physiology (based on anatomical study of the brain and nervous system) presupposes a much more unified account of psychological functions than is expressed in the tripartite account of psychological functions he adopts from Plato.[72] In the case of Stoicism and Epicureanism, by contrast, there is a high degree of consistency between the four aspects of the theories. This is because the theories, especially Stoicism, have been thought through in a cogent and systematic way, as well as because they express a distinctive and coherent vision of what counts as a worthwhile human life. The counter-example of Galen, whose contribution to the understanding of emotions is, in various ways, also very substantial, suggests that the criterion of self-consistency is more searching than it may seem initially.

---

[70] See n. 27 above.
[71] See, e.g., Sorabji 2000: 173, and Nussbaum 2001: 12.
[72] See Gill 2006: 243–4, 2007: 108–10.

A second, and perhaps more serious, objection is that the four categories chosen, while they work well in the case of the two Hellenistic theories, are not generally or universally applicable. For instance, one might argue that the idea that accounts of natural functioning and value are closely connected is a characteristic only of certain kinds of 'naturalistic' theories.[73] Also, there are a number of theories of emotion (both ancient and modern) in which we cannot find a distinct account of the physiological dimension of emotions.[74] There are several possible lines of response to these objections. One is that the categories adopted here represent a starting-point at least for examining any given theory. If, on consideration, we find that a given theory has nothing to say under one or other heading, or that the headings need to be varied significantly, this serves to bring out the distinctive character of the theory being considered, which can then be correlated more precisely with the kind of theory offered by the Hellenistic philosophers. Another possible move, which may not be incompatible with the first, is to suggest some rather broader and inclusive headings, for instance 'body-related', rather than the more narrow or technical category of 'physiological'. We might also want to expand the third category into the 'anthropological' (expressing a specific picture of human nature and value); or this category might need to be expanded yet further to cover theories, such as the Platonic or Neoplatonic, which claim to identify the 'divine' dimensions of human nature and value. A more robust response to these objections might be to maintain that a given theory is defective precisely in so far as it fails to offer ideas under any one of these headings, though this response would need to be backed up with independent argument for the framework adopted here.

At the very least, I think this discussion has shown that the method adopted has distinctive advantages, as a vehicle for exploring and assessing the specific theories involved and perhaps others. It also exemplifies a certain methodology for analysing theories of emotion that has a prima facie plausibility and merits further consideration.

---

[73] This idea runs counter to the view common in European moral theory between Kant and G. E. Moore that natural facts and values belong to fundamentally different categories. Stoicism and Epicureanism, by contrast, assume both that ethics is in some sense grounded on nature and that we can establish close links between the way human beings naturally function and ethical value. See further Annas 1993: part 2, and, on ancient and modern forms of ethical naturalism or objectivism, Gill 2005.

[74] This is the case, for instance, in Plato's thinking about emotion (if we exclude the *Timaeus*). A distinct—though related—point is that, even if some theories offer accounts which can be organized under these four headings, the accounts are not integrated in the way they are in Stoicism and Epicureanism. There are also questions about what counts as a unified theory of emotions, as distinct from a set of localized observations or ideas.

## REFERENCES

ALGRA, K., BARNES, J., MANSFELD, J., and SCHOFIELD, M. (eds.) (1999), *The Cambridge History of Hellenistic Philosophy* (Cambridge: Cambridge University Press).

ANNAS, J. (1989), 'Epicurean Emotions', *Greek, Roman and Byzantine Studies* 30: 145–64.

—— (1992), *Hellenistic Philosophy of Mind* (Berkeley: University of California Press).

—— (1993), *The Morality of Happiness* (Oxford: Oxford University Press).

ARMSTRONG, D. (2008), '"Be Angry and Fear Not": Philodemus versus the Stoics on Natural Bites and Natural Emotions', in J. T. Fitzgerald (ed.), *Passions and Moral Progress in Greco-Roman Thought* (London: Routledge): 79–121.

ARNIM, H. von (ed.) (2004), *Stoicorum Veterum Fragmenta* (4 vols.) (Reprint of first edition 1903–24) (Munich: Sauer).

BOBZIEN, S. (2000), 'Did Epicurus Discover the Free Will Problem?', *Oxford Studies in Ancient Philosophy* 19: 287–337.

BRENNAN, T. (1998), 'The Old Stoic Theory of Emotions', in Sihvola and Engberg-Pedersen: 21–70.

—— (2003), 'Stoic Moral Psychology', in B. Inwood (ed.), *The Cambridge Companion to the Stoics* (Cambridge: Cambridge University Press): 257–94.

COOPER, J. M. (1998), 'Posidonius on Emotions', in Sihvola and Engberg-Pedersen: 71–111. Reprinted in *Reason and Emotion: Essays in Ancient Moral Psychology and Ethical Theory* (Princeton: Princeton University Press): 449–84.

ERLER, M. and SCHOFIELD, M. (1999), 'Epicurean Ethics', in Algra et al.: 642–74.

EVERSON, S. (1999), 'Epicurean Psychology', in Algra et al.: 542–59.

FISH, J. (2004), 'Anger, Philodemus' Good King, and the Helen Episode of *Aeneid* 2.567–589: A New Proof of Authenticity from Herculaneum', in D. Armstrong, J. Fish, P. A. Johnston, and M. Skinner (eds.), *Vergil, Philodemus, and the Augustans* (Austin: University of Texas Press): 111–38.

FOWLER, D. (1997), 'Epicurean Emotions', in S. M. Braund and C. Gill (eds.), *The Passions in Roman Thought and Literature* (Cambridge: Cambridge University Press): 16–35.

GILL, C. (1996), *Personality in Greek Epic, Tragedy, and Philosophy: The Self in Dialogue* (Oxford: Oxford University Press).

—— (2000), 'Stoic Writers of the Imperial Era', in C. Rowe and M. Schofield (eds.), *The Cambridge History of Greek and Roman Political Thought* (Cambridge: Cambridge University Press): 597–615.

—— (2003), 'Reactive and Objective Attitudes: Anger in Virgil's *Aeneid* and Hellenistic Philosophy', *Yale Classical Studies* 32: *Ancient Anger: Perspectives from Homer to Galen*, S. M. Braund and G. Most (eds.) (Cambridge: Cambridge University Press): 208–28.

—— (ed.) (2005), *Virtue, Norms, and Objectivity: Issues in Ancient and Modern Ethics* (Oxford: Oxford University Press).

—— (2006), *The Structured Self in Hellenistic and Roman Thought* (Oxford: Oxford University Press).

—— (2007), 'Galen and the Stoics: Mortal Enemies or Blood Brothers?', *Phronesis* 52: 88–120.

GRAVER, M. R. (2007), *Stoicism and Emotion* (Chicago: University of Chicago Press).

INWOOD, B. (1985), *Ethics and Human Action in Early Stoicism* (Oxford: Oxford University Press).

—— and GERSON, L. P. (1997), *Hellenistic Philosophy: Introductory Readings* (2nd edn.) (Indianapolis: Hackett).

KNUUTTILA, S. (2004), *Emotions in Ancient and Mediaeval Philosophy* (Oxford: Oxford University Press).

KONSTAN, D., GLAD, C. E., THOM, J. C., and WARE, J. (1998), *Philodemus: On Frank Criticism*, Translated with introduction and notes (Atlanta: Society of Biblical Literature, Texts and Translations 43, Graeco-Roman).

LONG, A. A. (1996), *Stoic Studies* (Cambridge: Cambridge University Press).

—— (1999), 'Stoic Psychology', in Algra et al.: 560–84.

—— (2002), *Epictetus: A Stoic and Socratic Guide to Life* (Oxford: Oxford University Press).

—— and Sedley, D. N. (1987), *The Hellenistic Philosophers* (2 vols.) (Cambridge: Cambridge University Press).

MANSFELD, J. (1999), 'Sources', in Algra et al.: 3–30.

NUSSBAUM, M. C. (1994), *The Therapy of Desire: Theory and Practice in Hellenistic Ethics* (Princeton: Princeton University Press).

—— (2001), *Upheavals of Thought: The Intelligence of Emotions* (Cambridge: Cambridge University Press).

O'KEEFE, T. (2005), *Epicurus on Freedom* (Cambridge: Cambridge University Press).

PROCOPÉ, J. (1998), 'Epicureans on Anger', in Sihvola and Engberg-Pedersen: 171–96.

REYDAMS-SCHILS, G. (2002), 'Human Bonding and *Oikeiōsis* in Roman Stoicism', *Oxford Studies in Ancient Philosophy* 22: 221–51.

—— (2005), *The Roman Stoics: Self, Responsibility, and Affection* (Chicago: University of Chicago Press).

SEDLEY, D. (1998), 'The Inferential Foundations of Epicurean Ethics', in S. Everson (ed.), *Ethics: Companions to Ancient Thought* 4 (Cambridge: Cambridge University Press): 129–50.

SIHVOLA., J. and ENGBERG-PEDERSEN (eds.) (1998), *The Emotions in Hellenistic Philosophy* (Dordrecht: Kluwer).

SORABJI, R. (2000), *Emotion and Peace of Mind: From Stoic Agitation to Christian Temptation* (Oxford: Oxford University Press).

STADEN, H. von (2000): 'Body, Soul, and the Nerves: Epicurus, Herophilus, Erasistratus, the Stoics, and Galen', in J. P. Wright and P. Potter (eds.), *Psyche and Soma: Physicians and Metaphysicians on the Mind-Body Problem from Antiquity to Enlightenment* (Oxford: Oxford University Press): 79–116

STRAWSON, P. F. (1974), 'Freedom and Resentment', in *Freedom and Resentment and Other Essays* (London: Methuen): 1–25.

TIELEMAN, T. (1996), *Galen and Chrysippus on the Soul: Argument and Refutation in the De Placitis, Books II–III* (Leiden: Brill).

—— (2003), *Chrysippus' On Affections: Reconstruction and Interpretation* (Leiden: Brill).

TSOUNA, V. (2007), *The Ethics of Philodemus* (Oxford: Oxford University Press).

VOGT, K. M. (2008), *Law, Reason, and the Cosmic City: Political Philosophy in the Early Stoa* (Oxford: Oxford University Press).

WARREN, J. (2004), *Facing Death: Epicurus and his Critics* (Oxford: Oxford University Press).

# CHAPTER 7

# EMOTIONS IN MEDIEVAL THOUGHT

## PETER KING

No single theory of the emotions dominates the whole of the Middle Ages. Instead, there are several competing accounts, and differences of opinion—sometimes quite dramatic—within each account. Yet there is consensus on the scope and nature of a theory of the emotions, as well as on its place in affective psychology generally. For most medieval thinkers, emotions are at once cognitively penetrable and somatic, which is to say that emotions are influenced by and vary with changes in thought and belief, and that they are also bound up, perhaps essentially, with their physiological manifestations. This 'mixed' conception of emotions was broad enough to anchor medieval disagreements over details, yet rich enough to distinguish it from other parts of psychology and medicine. In particular, two kinds of phenomena, thought to be purely physiological, were not considered emotions even on this broad conception. First, what we now classify as drives or urges, for instance hunger and sexual arousal, were thought in the Middle Ages to be at best 'pre-emotions' (*propassiones*): mere biological motivations for action, not having any intrinsic cognitive object. Second, moods were likewise thought to be non-objectual somatic states, completely explicable as an imbalance of the bodily humours. Depression (*melancholia*), for example, is the pathological condition of having an excess of black bile. Medieval theories of emotions, therefore, concentrate on paradigm cases that fall under the broad conception: delight, anger, distress, fear, and the like.

The enterprise of constructing an adequate philosophical theory of the emotions in the Middle Ages had its counterpart in a large body of practical know-how. The medical literature on the emotions, for instance, was extensive, covering such subjects as the causal role of emotions in disease and recovery, the nerves as connecting the brain to the organs involved in the physiological manifestations of the emotions, and the effect of diet and nutrition on emotional responses. Many Arabic philosophers in the Middle Ages were also physicians, and their discussions of the emotions centre on such medical questions. Another fund of practical know-how is the penitential and confessional literature: topics as diverse as how to induce a proper feeling of repentance, how to comfort a grieving widow, how to defuse anger, and the like are touched on. Christian doctrine, of course, gives a central role to the emotions; not only are people enjoined to love one another and to love God, complex emotional states like contrition and compassion are key elements in leading a Christian life.

As rich and interesting as medieval practical knowledge about the emotions may be, however, we are concerned here with medieval attempts to understand the emotions as psychological phenomena in their own right. This effectively limits our focus to the philosophically inclined theologians of the Latin Christian West. The Arabic philosophers dealt with such matters largely as physicians; the Byzantines were scholiasts rather than systematic thinkers; the Christian laity, and much of the clergy, were content with folk psychology rather than trying to construct speculative psychological theories of the emotions. Hence the task was left to the only intellectuals left standing in the Middle Ages: Christian theologians with an interest, and possibly training, in philosophy.

The starting-point for later medieval discussions of the emotions was Augustine (§1), whose treatment of the emotions allowed for divergent interpretations. One strand of Augustine's account, the notion that emotions are closely bound up with volition, was initially explored in the twelfth century by Anselm and Abelard (§2). With the 'Aristotelian revolution' of the thirteenth century came a new impetus to systematic speculation, picking up a different strand from Augustine and developing it into a organized scheme (§3), eventually given its masterful exposition in the writings of Aquinas (§4). In contrast to this, an alternative inspired by the thinkers of the twelfth century was formulated at the end of the thirteenth and the beginning of the fourteenth centuries, most notably by Franciscan thinkers, including Scotus and Ockham (§5). Later scholastic thought tended to recapitulate the earlier debates, incorporating advances in medical knowledge, but also betrayed an increasing impatience with the earlier systematic classificatory schemes, preparing the way for their eventual rejection in Renaissance and early modern philosophy (§6).

A final warning. Research in medieval thinking about the emotions is in its early days. The survey sketched here is up-to-date with current knowledge, but it will, no doubt, need to be revised as our knowledge increases.

## 7.1 THE BEGINNINGS: AUGUSTINE

Augustine (354–430) offers an extended treatment of the emotions in his late work *The City of God*, in Book 9.4–5 and throughout Book 14. His target there is the Stoic theory of the emotions, at least as presented by Cicero, Seneca, and other Latin authors; while Augustine's knowledge of Stoicism is neither scholarly nor technical, it is enough to convince him that it clashes with Christian doctrine. In its place Augustine advocates an eclectic mix of ancient theories of the emotions.

Augustine endorses Cicero's claim that the Stoic account of the emotions differs from the Platonist and Peripatetic accounts merely in terminology, at least to the extent that it is correct (*City of God* 9.4). His syncretistic conviction that there is a core of truth in theories of the emotions which is common to Platonists, Aristotelians, and even the Stoics dominates his discussion. Thus he adopts Stoic terminology, often calling the emotions 'disturbances' or 'upheavals' (*perturbationes*) when not using the neutral 'affections' (*affectiones*) or the Peripatetic 'passions' (*passiones*), and agrees with the Stoics that emotions are often contrary to reason and upset the mind—at least, in *this* life, as part of the punishment for original sin (*City of God* 14.9). The Stoics are mistaken, however, in thinking that this is true of all emotions, even in this life, and drawing from their mistake the mistaken conclusion that the ideal condition is to be free of emotions, the 'emotionlessness' (*apatheia*) of the Sage. At the least, this encourages insensitivity (14.9), but more than that some emotions should not be extirpated, for instance compassion (9.5). Christian doctrine bids us to feel emotions: to love enemies, be angry at sinners, fear God, be distressed when faced with temptation (9.5 and 14.9). Even Jesus wept; His emotion, Augustine maintains, was not feigned but a function of His assumption of human nature, and as such his emotions must be altogether fitting and appropriate (14.9). Nor do the Stoics really believe that all emotions are objectionable, Augustine points out, for they allow that some emotions are not contrary to reason, the so-called 'good-feelings' (*eupatheiai*). Augustine argues that these are neither special emotions nor restricted to the Sage: 'when affections are exhibited where they are appropriate, they are in accordance with right reason, and who would then dare to declare that emotions are "diseases" or objectionable?' (14.9). The fear of God is to be cultivated, not overcome.

Augustine generally endorses the Stoic fourfold classification of the emotions in which the fundamental kinds of emotions are distinguished on the one hand by their objects, directed at something good or something evil, and on the other hand by their temporal orientation, directed at either a present object or a future object (14.5–6).

These emotions—delight (*laetitia*), desire (*libido/cupiditas/appetitus*), distress (*aegritudo/dolor*), and fear (*metus*)—are the basic types; all other emotions may be classified as subtypes of these. Despair, for example, is the emotional response to

|      | Present  | Future |
|------|----------|--------|
| Good | delight  | desire |
| Evil | distress | fear   |

an unavoidable future evil, and hence is one of the varieties of fear. According to this typology, emotions are intrinsically objectual, bound up with a conception of their targets as good or evil. We are not merely distressed but distressed *by* (or 'at' or 'over') something. Furthermore, whatever is distressing must be something taken as a present evil; it literally makes no sense to speak of the object of distress in any other way.

Augustine makes regular use of the fourfold division when writing about the emotions. When he asks which emotions are natural to human beings, for instance, he recasts the question as whether Adam and Eve in their prelapsarian condition experienced delight, distress, fear, and desire (14.10–26). He replies that fear and distress are not part of sinless human nature, and are therefore not present in Heaven (14.10); it is with original sin that humans have become 'disturbed by conflicting and fluctuating affections' (14.12), most notably by the emotions of lust and anger (14.19). Prior to the Fall, all emotions, even these, were in our control; sexual arousal involved feelings no stronger than those felt nowadays in seeding crops (14.23). Since all emotions are included in the Stoic fourfold division, Augustine's answer is complete and exhaustive.

Augustine identifies a common element in the four basic emotions: 'willing is in them all, or rather, they are all nothing other than kinds of willing' (14.6). Accepting the Stoic thesis that the agent has the ability to assent, or to refrain from giving assent, to impressions, and the further claim that emotions are the result, Augustine concludes that emotions are intimately bound up with the will: 'what is desire and delight but willing with consent the things we will for? What is fear and distress but willing in dissent from the things we will against?' (14.6). The endorsement or rejection of an object as good or bad is, at least in part, an act of the will, and hence the corresponding emotional response depends on an act of will. And this in its turn is simply an expression of the kinds of loves that the agent has. Hence, Augustine concludes, rather than joining the Stoics in condemning all emotions we need to look at the will's choice of object to see whether it is appropriate: the uprightness or perversity of the will is at stake in moral assessments of the emotions, not the mere fact of having an emotion (14.7).

The burden of Augustine's extended treatment of the Stoic theory of the emotions has been to purge it of elements it does not share with what he takes to be the core tradition, common to Platonists and Peripatetics. The corrected Stoic theory is grafted on to a Platonic–Peripatetic distinction among the kinds of emotions. In a discussion of shame, Augustine writes: 'those philosophers who have come closer to the truth than others have acknowledged that anger and lust are the vice-ridden parts of the soul, in that they are turbulent and disorderly emotions, inciting us to acts which reason forbids' (14.19). Anger (*ira*) and lust (*libido/concupiscentia*) make up the irrational part of the soul, providing an alternative classification of emotions—at least, of irrational emotions—into 'irascible' or 'concupiscible', a distinction stemming ultimately from Plato (*Republic* 436A–441C) and adopted by Aristotle (*Nicomachean Ethics* 1.13 and *Rhetoric* 1.10). Augustine does not try to reconcile this distinction among emotions with the Stoic fourfold division; he accepts them both, though he is careful to say that the former is adopted by 'philosophers who have come closer to the truth'.

Augustine's discussion of the emotions in his *City of God* was not only authoritative for later thinkers, it was the only extended discussion inherited by the Latin Christian West. The few comments of a theoretical nature about emotions made by others with a direct knowledge of ancient philosophy, such as Origen and Boethius, were sketchy and, as far as could be told, compatible with Augustine—a compatibility that was all the easier to find given Augustine's eclectic belief in a core tradition he never described in detail. Later medieval thinkers made of Augustine what they could, often in strikingly different ways.

# 7.2 THE TWELFTH CENTURY: ANSELM AND ABELARD

The disintegration of the social institutions of the classical world, and the slow forging of a new social structure to replace it, left little room for speculative psychological enquiry. When things finally settled down again, many centuries had passed, and a new monolingual and religiously homogenous culture had come into being: the Latin Christian West. By the middle of the eleventh century, a large measure of social stability and prosperity had been regained, and the establishment of monastic centres of learning, soon to be followed by the founding of universities, gave a new impetus to intellectual activity. At first this was little more than reclaiming the heritage of antiquity. William of St-Thierry (1075?–1148), in his work *The Nature of Body and Soul*, repeats without elaboration Augustine's presentation of the Stoic fourfold division of emotions and the Platonic–Aristotelian distinction between the concupiscible and the irascible powers (2.88–89). The latter had been given additional support in the discussion of emotions in the work *On Human Nature* by Nemesius of Emesa (c.400), translated from Greek into Latin in the second half of the eleventh century; some of this material was used by John Damascene (676–749) in his *The Orthodox Faith*, likewise translated from Greek into Latin in the middle of the twelfth century. Forging a single coherent account from Augustinian materials was a challenge taken up in short order. Isaac of Stella (1100?–1169), in his *Letter to Alcher on the Soul*, offered a solution that was widely adopted. There are four kinds of affections, Isaac declares, which depend in good Augustinian fashion on what we love or hate: things we love may be present (delight) or future (hope), and things we hate may be present (distress) or future (fear). Hence 'delight and hope stem from the concupiscible power, whereas distress and fear stem from the irascible power' (1878D). Isaac's substitution of hope for desire was thought to be a mere terminological refinement: 'hope' is the emotional response to a future good, which includes the desire for it as part of taking it as a good. The reconciliation was not perfect; why hate is correlated with anger is not clear, for instance. But Isaac's solution worked well enough to give many philosophers a single unified scheme that could reasonably be presented as what Augustine had in mind, as well as a starting-point for further investigation of the types and subtypes of emotions.

Anselm of Canterbury (1033–1109) and Peter Abelard (1079–1142) took a different approach to Augustine's legacy. Putting aside the disputed question of how to reconcile the classificatory schemes presented in the *City of God*, Anselm and Abelard each focus on Augustine's suggestion that emotions are forms of willing (*uoluntates*). More exactly, they each take Augustine to be making a general claim about the nature of emotions, not about the relation of psychological faculties. For neither Anselm nor Abelard take Augustine's remarks to describe the relation between the psychological faculty that is the will, the faculty responsible for choice and decision, and individual acts of will, but instead to be making the claim that all emotions have motivational force: they are forms of 'wantings', broadly speaking, a claim we would express by saying that emotions are fundamentally desires motivating the agent's actions. Then their accounts diverge.

Anselm, in his work *The Fall of the Devil* 12–14, argues that an agent has to be given a *uoluntas*, a motivation, in order to act at all. He proposes a thought-experiment. If God were creating an angel and endowed it with a will (and hence the bare capacity to initiate action), but had not yet supplied it with any motivation, then that angel would never initiate action, since it would have no reason to act in one way rather than another. Hence agents must be equipped with a motivational structure. Fortunately, most creatures are given the motive to seek their own happiness or well-being, which Anselm generally terms their 'advantage'. The individual emotions are instances of this generic template. I fear something that appears to conflict with what I take to be my happiness, whatever that may be, which therefore counts as an evil; hence fear is the emotional response to the threat of a thwarted motivation. Anselm argues further that moral agents need to have two distinct kinds of motivations. In addition to being motivated by one's happiness, a moral agent must also be capable of being motivated by moral concerns, or, as Anselm puts it, by 'justice'. We are *moral* agents because these two types of motivations may conflict: delight in my happiness may be tempered by shame at attaining it unjustly, for instance. Anselm clarifies his view in his later work *The Harmony of Grace, Predestination, and Foreknowledge with Free Choice*, where he explicitly calls these motivations 'affections' (Augustine's preferred term for the emotions) of the will, roughly permanent dispositions to choose certain objects as goods, and to reject others as evils. The upshot is a reconceptualization of human emotions as volitional phenomena of two distinct types, which are broadly speaking moral and non-moral.

Like Anselm, Abelard refers to all forms of motivation as 'wantings' (*uoluntates*). In his *Ethics* Abelard sketches the following account. An agent is equipped with a variety of emotions, each of which, by definition, has motivational force. An agent then may give assent (*consensus*) to one or another of these emotions, which will generate an *intention* to act in a certain way. (In his *Commentary on 'Romans'* §§207–9 Abelard spells out the details a bit more fully: any emotion involves desire for an object and pleasure when it is attained, and the approval of an emotion simply *is* intending to act so as to attain its pleasurable object.) For Abelard, unlike Augustine or Anselm, emotions have no intrinsic moral value, no matter how independent of reason they might be. Moral assessment rides strictly on the agent's intentions, not on the emotions as such, or even the actions the agent actually performs. We are constructed in such a way, Abelard declares, that feeling delight is inevitable in certain situations, and therefore cannot be morally objectionable or the penal consequence of original sin, as Augustine had claimed. If sexual pleasure in marriage is not sinful, for instance, then the pleasure itself, inside or outside of marriage, is not sinful; if it is sinful, then marriage cannot sanctify it—and if the conclusion is drawn that such acts should be performed wholly without pleasure, then Abelard remarks they cannot be performed at all, and it was unreasonable (of God) to permit them only in a way in which they cannot be performed (*Ethics* 20.1–6). Emotions are natural to human beings.

Anselm and Abelard each explore Augustine's suggestion that emotions form a single natural kind of psychological phenomenon, namely motivational states. Neither wrote systematically on the emotions, preferring to keep their discussions on a general plane. Their contributions, though innovative, were initially swamped by the wave of 'new philosophy': the recovery of Aristotle, which begins a new phase in the history of theories of the emotions.

# 7.3 THE EARLY THIRTEENTH CENTURY: JEAN DE LA ROCHELLE

The intellectual resources of the Latin Christian West were occupied from roughly the middle of the twelfth century to the middle of the thirteenth century with a dual project: finding and translating the works of Aristotle into Latin, with accompanying materials; and attaining philosophical mastery of them. It is important to recognize that, from the inception of this project, medieval thinkers understood that they were engaged in critical assimilation. Aristotle provided a wealth of philosophical tools and a methodological approach that were adopted because of their power and flexibility. That is quite different from adopting the contentful philosophical views he held, which were not automatically endorsed. Because of the depth and difficulty of Aristotle's work, the first order of business was to sort out what he was claiming; because of the profundity of his philosophical insight, his views were given a measure of presumptive authority. But Aristotle's positive philosophical doctrines were only as good as the arguments he gave for them, and they were variously accepted, rejected, or revised. In short, the cultural consensus in the Latin Christian West on Aristotelianism as its intellectual framework neither entailed nor enjoined consensus on Aristotle's particular doctrines.

This fact is all the more apparent in the case of the emotions, where Aristotle provides a theoretical context, namely a sketch of the science of psychology, but no ready-made doctrine of the emotions; indeed, he has little more than the bare Platonic distinction between the concupiscible and the irascible, fleshed out with unsystematic remarks about particular emotions in his *Nicomachean Ethics* and *Rhetoric*. Here the native medieval tradition stemming from Augustine, supplemented by medical information from the Arabic commentators, were combined to produce a unique and comprehensive theory of the emotions. It was given its highest expression by Thomas Aquinas, who built on the work of many predecessors, most notably Jean de la Rochelle and Albert the Great.

For Aristotle, psychology is the branch of natural philosophy dealing with things whose nature it is to be alive. From the sketchy remarks in *On the Soul* 1.1, medieval philosophers understood Aristotle to be engaged in constructing a 'faculty psychology', explaining psychological phenomena in terms of quasi-independent interacting principles and capacities whose interaction causes or constitutes the phenomenon under investigation. In the case of human psychology, medieval philosophers read Aristotle as proposing two cross-cutting distinctions: (a) a distinction between the cluster of principles and capacities that account for movement and sensation, known as the *sensitive* part of the soul, and the cluster of principles and capacities that account for thought and volition, known as the *intellective* part of the soul; (b) a distinction between the apparatus of powers whereby information about the world is acquired and assimilated, known as the *cognitive* or *apprehensive* potencies, and the apparatus of powers whereby one engages the world, known as the *appetitive* potencies. Now (a) and (b) have to be combined: the intellective and sensitive parts of the soul each have cognitive and appetitive faculties; cognition and appetition take place in both the intellective and sensitive parts. There are thus four fundamental departments into which psychological experience is divided. The principle of cognition in the intellective part of the soul is the intellect itself, where thinking and reasoning take place. The principle of appetition in the intellective part of the soul is the will, responsible for volition and choice; the will is literally 'intellective appetite'. The principle of cognition in the sensitive part of the soul is called 'sensing', where sensation and perception occur. The final department of psychological experience encompasses the principles of appetition in the sensitive part of the soul, namely the emotions (*passiones animae*). The task of a theory of the emotions, like that of any Aristotelian branch of knowledge, is to organize the subject by a taxonomic classification of its fundamental principles.

The earliest efforts to formulate a theory of the emotions along Aristotelian lines, then, gave pride of place to organizing the apparent chaos of emotional life into proper genera and species. John Blund, whose *Treatise on the Soul* (1210) was one of the first, if not the first, to attempt this task, proposed to divide emotions by their contrary objects. On this score, the basic distinction among emotions is that some are oriented toward good and others toward evil. Following Isaac of Stella, Blund aligns the distinction of contrary objects with the distinction between the concupiscible and the irascible, so that the concupiscible emotions of love, delight, and desire are directed at the good, and the irascible emotions of hate, distress, and aversion are directed at evils. Blund did not explain why we should classify opposed emotions (love/hate, delight/distress, desire/aversion) as belonging to fundamentally different kinds, a failing that perhaps explains why his proposal was not widely adopted, Alexander Neckham (1157–1217), an early follower of Anselm, being his most noteworthy convert.

The impulse to systematize, and hence understand, the emotions persisted. A breakthrough came in the *Summary Treatise on the Soul* (1235) by Jean de la Rochelle. Jean suggested, first, that distinction between the concupiscible and the irascible emotions could itself be understood as a matter of the distinct formal objects to which they are oriented, the former being directed at *the pleasureable or painful*, the latter at *the difficult* (2.107), a distinction that apparently originated in the 1220s and employed before Jean by Phillip the Chancellor (1160?–1236). Now Jean's reasoning seems to be that we may be either straightforwardly attracted or repelled by something, in the manner of simple 'push/pull' Lockean affective psychology, or our attraction and repulsion may involve some sort of effort on our part, and hence not be immediately explicable in terms of simple attraction and repulsion. For example, a dog will straightforwardly be attracted to a bone; if Smith holds the bone away, teasing the dog with it, at some point the dog will shift the focus of his activity from the bone (the desired object) to the obstacle to attaining the bone (Smith), attacking Smith even if Smith drops the bone. Any obstacle or effort in the pursuit or avoidance of something will fall under *the difficult*. Second, Jean suggested that emotions can be grouped in contrary pairs as part of their taxonomic classification. Under the generic heading of the concupiscible, for instance, we find conjugate pairs of contrary emotions such as love/hate, desire/avoidance, delight/distress, and three further pairs; under the irascible we find hope/despair, pride/humility, reverence/contempt, two further pairs, and two that have no contrary, namely anger and generosity. In neither case are contrary emotions grouped into coordinate species which are exclusive and exhaustive, defined by opposite differentiae; instead, Jean puts forward a multiplicity of criteria that allow several pairs of contraries at the same level. In point of fact Jean does not offer strict criteria that produce his list and no others. He often appeals to the medical literature, and above all to Avicenna, for physiological grounds to underpin his classifications.

Jean de la Rochelle at a stroke laid out the basic elements of a solution to the challenges facing the construction of an Aristotelian taxonomic theory of the emotions. Bonaventure and Albert the Great, to name only two, adopted Jean's suggestions and much of his positive account. Albert in particular tried to further systematize Jean's classification of the emotions by compounding it with physiology and physics (*Treatise on the Good* 3.5).

# 7.4 AQUINAS

It was left to Albert's student, Thomas Aquinas (1224/5–1274), to think through Jean de la Rochelle's discoveries in his lucid and compact 'treatise on the emotions' (*Summary of Theology* 1a2ae qq.22–48), a treatment so masterful that it eclipsed the works of his predecessors. Aquinas's particular improvement on Jean's work was to take the variety of disorderly principles on which Jean based his classification and underwrite them with clear and careful argumentation.

Aquinas identifies eleven essentially distinct types of emotion, sorted into two kinds and for the most part occurring in pairs of contraries: the six concupiscible emotions love/hate, desire/aversion, delight/distress; the five irascible emotions hope/despair, confidence/fear, and anger (as with Jean having no contrary). Each type is a genuine kind, including a variety of subtypes. Anger, for example, includes wrath, rancour, and vindictiveness; love is divided into friendly (*amor amicitiae*), which seeks the good of its object, and covetous (*amor concupiscentiae*), which seeks the object for one's own good. In contrast to Jean de la Rochelle, Aquinas holds that the formal object of concupiscible emotions is *the sensible good*, although he accepts a modification of Jean's view about the formal object of the irascible emotions, which he takes to be *the sensible good as difficult* (1a q.80 art.2). Not too much emphasis should be put on 'sensible': Aquinas means only that, as the sensitive appetite depends on sensitive apprehension (perception), its object must be capable of being perceived. He certainly does not mean to exclude non-present targets of the emotions, and he permits some passions to be directed at things simply in virtue of the kind of thing they are.

Aquinas opens his discussion of the emotions by asking about their nature, in particular whether they are cognitive or appetitive (1a2ae q.22 art.2). Citing Augustine's discussion in his *City of God* 9.4 as precedent, Aquinas argues that emotions can only motivate action, as they unquestionably do, if representations of their objects occur in a context in which they move the agent (as in the appetite) rather than one in which such representations are merely assessed for the information they convey (as in cognition). Hence the passions must belong to the appetitive part of the soul. Now earlier Aquinas had drawn a distinction between two ways in which the bodily organs used by the soul may undergo change (1a q.78 art.3): immaterially, when it receives the representation (*intentio*) of the object in the organ, and materially, when the organ itself undergoes a physical change. In visual perception the immaterial reception of the representation is essential, but any change in the eye is merely incidental (the eye does not itself become coloured). Emotions are disanalogous to perceptions on this score, however. An emotion—that is, an actualization of the sensitive appetite—is 'essentially an instance of the second type of change; accordingly, in the definition of the movements of the appetitive part, some natural change in an organ is materially given, so that anger, for example, is said to be the boiling of blood around the heart' (1a2ae q.2 art.2 *ad* 3). For Aquinas, the somatic manifestations of an emotion are essential to it. More precisely, Aquinas argues that the formal element in an emotion is a motion of the appetitive power as defined by the formal object of the emotion, so that fear, for instance, is the response to a future evil difficult to avoid, whereas its material element is the physiological change, such as trembling and chattering teeth. Unlike sense-perception, the emotions are not associated with bodily organs (with the possible exception of sexual lust); the somatic manifestations of an emotion are an essential part of the emotion, but what the manifestations are is not essential but accidental. (Aquinas argues that male impotence proves that sexual desire is distinct from bodily arousal.) It is no proper function of the teeth to chatter any more than it is of the eye to become tired after long exercise; it is merely a concomitant side effect. Aquinas examines the somatic reactions associated with each emotion in considerable detail. The effects of fear, for instance, are a matter of the vital spirits being concentrated in the higher region of the body, deflected from the heart, which is contracted; this chills the rest of the body and may produce trembling, teeth-chattering, and fluttering in the stomach. Depending on the kind of fear, blood may rush into the head to produce blushing if the object is shameful, or away from the head to produce paleness if the object is terrifying. Should the onset of fear be sudden and sharp, control over bodily limbs and functions will be lost, resulting in shuddering, knees knocking, difficulty in breathing, or worse, perhaps even general paralysis, so that one is 'frozen with fear' (1a2ae q.44).

Having established that emotions are psychophysical objectual states, Aquinas then turns to the distinction he inherits from Augustine (among others), namely the concupiscible and the irascible. Unlike many of his predecessors, Aquinas sets out to establish the distinction on a firm philosophical basis. His treatment in 1a2ae q.23 art.1 hearkens back to his earlier examination of the distinction in 1a q.81 art.2, in which he offers three arguments that the concupiscible emotions and the irascible emotions 'are not reducible to a single principle':

- *The Interference Argument.* The two kinds of emotions must be different in kind because they can interfere with one another: stirring up anger lessens lust, and conversely stirring up lust can lessen anger.
- *The Submission Argument.* Sometimes the soul 'submits' to distress against the inclination of desire, so that it may fight against things opposed to it.
- *The Champion Argument.* The irascible emotions arise from the concupiscible emotions and terminate in them; anger, for example, may be born from distress and, in taking revenge, end in delight.

Each calls for comment. The Interference Argument, ultimately derived from Plato's *Republic,* turns on the fact that the distinct kinds of emotions can be directed at one and the same real thing while nevertheless differing in their formal (intensional) objects: someone can be simultaneously alluring and annoying, features that interfere with one another. While we do speak of the relative strength of the different emotions, such talk is clearly metaphorical. It is not at all like two desires of the same sort in competition, as for instance when I have to choose between chocolate ice cream and vanilla ice cream; in this case all that matters in making the choice is the relative strength of the desires for each. But that does not seem to be the case when concupiscible and irascible emotions interfere with one another, as Aquinas notes.

The Submission Argument is further clarified by Aquinas in *On Truth* q.25 art.2. Sometimes the sensible good taken as difficult is such that the difficulty is an intrinsic feature of the good in question: we want to win the race, earn the Nobel Prize, master quantum physics. But sometimes not: the difficulty is in the surrounding circumstances, not inherent in the object itself. In such cases, Aquinas declares, the end can be unproblematically desired and enjoyed, independent of the difficulties associated with it. In such cases, we can speak of 'submitting' to the difficulties for the sake of the object to be attained. The force of the Submission Argument should be clear. Aquinas charges that we cannot understand all behaviour in terms of simple 'push/pull' desires, in particular instances of submission to present pain, which involve not merely weighing the relative strength of the desires but at least rudimentary means–ends calculation. On this score, Aquinas notes in his *Commentary on the 'Sentences'* 3 d.26 q.1 art.2 that the irascible emotions are 'closer to reason' since they involve a more complex cognitive stance toward their objects than do concupiscible emotions.

The Champion Argument turns on the fact that the concupiscible emotions are comprehensible in their own terms, whereas the irascible emotions make sense only against the background of the concupiscible emotions. Aquinas presents this as partly a logical claim, partly a causal claim. Overcoming the difficulties means attaining the sensible good, which prompts the emotional response of delight; so much is simple logic. But other connections among the emotions, such as distress, anger, and revenge, are causal rather than logical in nature. Aquinas's point is that in such causal connections, the irascible emotions 'come to the aid' of the concupiscible emotions, the former being 'champions' of the latter. They can do so in virtue of being a different kind of emotion, for otherwise they would be a constitutive part of the initial (concupiscible) emotional response to the object, not something further than can come about.

Aquinas's discussion of the causes, effects, and often the remedies for each passion are wide-ranging, penetrating, and occasionally humorous, as when he considers whether youth and inebriation are causes of hope in 1a2ae q.40 art.6 (they are), or whether anger notably interferes with the ability to reason in 1a2ae q.48 art.3 (it can). Aquinas investigates serious questions of all sorts, such as whether ecstasy and jealousy are necessary effects of love (1a2ae q.28 art.3–4), whether someone can hate himself (1a2ae q.29 art.4), whether sympathy from friends can help alleviate distress (1a2ae q.38 art.3), whether love is the cause of fear (1a2ae q.43 art.1), and more.

Once he has established the distinction between concupiscible and irascible emotions, Aquinas turns to the principles underlying the differentiation of the six concupiscible and five irascible emotions into pairs of associated contraries (1a2ae q.23 art.2–4). The details are complicated, since Aquinas makes the differentiation of the emotions rational by recourse to principles taken from Aristotle's natural philosophy, on the grounds that emotions are, literally, 'motions' of the sensitive appetite. Aquinas therefore mobilizes the resources of the science of motion to explain the complex types of contrariety found among the emotions. Very roughly, the first contrary pair of each type of emotion, love/hate (concupiscible) and hope/despair (irascible) are simple tendencies of the sensitive appetite toward its objects; they are 'emotional attitudes' toward the object, pure and simple. The second contrary pairs, desire/aversion and confidence/fear, involve some kind of movement in respect of the object, desire toward and aversion away from it, confidence to confront and fear to shrink from the difficulties facing one. The final group includes the concupiscible contrary pair delight/distress and the solitary irascible emotion of anger; here the appetitive power has attained its object and 'rests' in it, taking the full measure of the good or evil (for the concupiscible emotions) or the difficulty (for anger).

This brief discussion only scratches the surface of Aquinas's theory of the emotions. One topic not considered here is the extent to which our emotional responses are in our control. This is a pressing issue for Aquinas, since he identifies emotions formally as passive potencies of the sensitive appetite—that is to say, as things that happen to us, rather than as something in which we are active:

'passions' in the etymological sense. Aquinas recognizes the difficulty, and tries to blunt the edge of it by pointing out that we have a measure of indirect control over our emotional responses: unlike sneezes or digestion, emotions are cognitively penetrable, and so may be influenced by (habits of) thought and belief. Nor are all the emotions equally controllable: desire is simply voluntary, according to Aquinas, whereas fear is involuntary (1a2ae q.6 art.7). This is not to say that fear is unaffected by cognition; we can bring other considerations to bear on a situation and thereby lessen our fear through the exercise of what Aquinas calls 'particular reason', that is, reason applied to a particular case (1a q.81 art.3).

Aquinas's presentation of the theory of the emotions, while clearly indebted to earlier thirteenth-century thinkers, was widely acknowledged as a classic treatment; both eclipsing earlier work and casting a long enough shadow that later thinkers could do no better than to begin with Aquinas's account, even when they disagreed with it. Often the disagreements were a matter of details. But there was also a systematic alternative, one that looked back to the twelfth century and earlier to Augustine, that won its share of adherents at the end of the thirteenth century and the beginning of the fourteenth century.

# 7.5 THE EARLY FOURTEENTH CENTURY: SCOTUS AND OCKHAM

John Duns Scotus (1265?–1308) and William of Ockham (1285?–1349) did not write treatises on the emotions, or even discuss them extensively, but their differences with Aquinas are deep and principled, to the point where they can be seen as offering a systematic alternative to his views (which is indeed how later medieval philosophers understood them). Begin with the last point mentioned about Aquinas, namely the extent to which emotions are in our control. Both Scotus and Ockham reject Aquinas's general claim that all emotions are at best only indirectly in our control. Rather, they see at least some emotions as having an active, perhaps volitional, component: they are actions of the will, not mere passions of the will. Scotus explicitly cites Augustine's reduction of the Stoic fourfold division of emotions to kinds of willing, and therefore to love, as an intellectual precedent; while it may not be entirely up to us to experience pleasure or distress, we can choose to love someone, which shows that at least some emotions are in the scope of the will (*Ordinatio* 3 d.15 q.1). Earlier thinkers, such as Bonaventure and Henry of Ghent, had spoken of concupiscible and irascible acts of the will, but Scotus seems to have been the first to offer a complete theory of the emotions that rejected the sharp division of psychological faculties assumed by Aquinas and earlier thinkers.

For Scotus, emotions were no longer confined to the sensitive appetite; emotions are a feature of the appetitive power generally, intellective appetite (the will) as well as sensitive appetite (*Ordinatio* 3 d.33 q.1). Ockham accepted this view, and argued further that 'passive' emotions, such as pleasure or distress, are the causal by-products of 'active' emotions of the will unless they are explicitly suppressed by other actions or mental events (*Ordinatio* 1 d.1 q.3). Both Scotus and Ockham claimed to be following Anselm's theory of affections of the will, each accepting Anselm's claim that the will has intrinsic motivational structure. Scotus identifies the first active emotions of the will to be 'taking a liking to' (*complacentia*) or 'taking a dislike to' (*displicentia*), traditional terminology found in Bonaventure and Jean de la Rochelle, which are not quite choices but not mere reactions either (*Ordinatio* 3 d.33 q.1). They are a kind of hybrid phenomenon, partly volitive and partly perceptual.

Scotus, and Ockham in his train, found the psychological boundaries among the faculties more fluid than Aquinas in part because they held a different view about the metaphysics of the mind. Aquinas argues at length in his *Questions on Aristotle's 'On the Soul'* that the soul is really distinct from its faculties and the faculties from one another, or, to put the point another way, that cognitive and affective psychology are distinct disciplines that require distinct foundations. His main line of argument for this conclusion is as follows. If thinking or willing belonged to the real essence of the soul rather than to distinct subordinate psychological faculties, then from the mere existence of the soul it would follow that it (always) thinks and wills, which is manifestly false; likewise for the separate faculties (*Summary of Theology* 1a q.77 art.1). Scotus rejects Aquinas's argument, however, arguing that the faculties of the soul are not really distinct from one another and from the soul itself but are only what he calls 'formally' distinct. Very roughly, this amounts to the claim that different psychological faculties can have causal powers they only exercise in virtue of the kinds of objects to which they are directed, so that intellect and will, or perception and emotion, can differ in terms of their formal objects. We need not pause to iron out the details here, because William of Ockham argued that they were simply not needed; after stating at length and refuting the views of Aquinas, Henry of Ghent, and Duns Scotus, Ockham concludes that the 'parts' of the soul are only conceptually distinct from one another (*Reportatio* 2 q.20). That is, it is one and the same soul that thinks, feels, wills, and perceives. There is no need to postulate a plurality of entities when one entity can perform many functions, which is one formulation of Ockham's Razor. The upshot for a theory of the emotions is this. If psychological faculties are not really distinct from one another in the world, then there is no reason to think that psychological phenomena need be confined to the boxes in which Aquinas put them. Some emotions might be a function of the sensitive appetite, others of the intellective appetite; since the underlying subject is one and the same thing, there is no ground for insisting on their sharp separation.

Emotions, then, should be investigated on their own terms. One aspect of this conviction was the rejection of Aquinas's attempt to give a general theoretical grounding for his taxonomy of emotions through Aristotelian natural philosophy. Scotus, and to some extent Ockham, instead preferred the view of Albert the Great, according to which emotions are understood as qualities or forms inherent in the soul, not as types of motion. Without the substructure of the theory of motion, though, there is no reason to adopt Aquinas's particular classification of the emotions more than any other. Neither Scotus nor Ockham gives such a classification, in fact, perhaps as a consequence of their open-mindedness about psychological faculties.

Given all the other points on which they disagree, it is no surprise to find that Scotus rejects Aquinas's claim that the irascible emotions have the common formal object *the sensible good as difficult*. Scotus proposes instead that irascible emotions have instead the common formal object *the offensive* (*Ordinatio* 3 d.34 q.1). He reasons as follows. The action performed by an irascible emotion is to be angry, and 'its object is therefore *to overcome*, or more exactly *what can be overcome*, which can be called the "irascitive" or, in more ordinary language, *the offensive*'. It is not simply a variant, or a variant object, of the concupiscible emotions; it is different in kind. Concupiscible emotions either pull one toward or push one away from their objects. But that is not what happens with irascible emotions, which, on the contrary, try to 'overcome' or defeat their objects, neither pursuing nor fleeing them, but treating them as something that ought to be righted; hence it is *the offensive*.

The alternative view staked out by Scotus and Ockham was a popular alternative to Aquinas's account. For instance, Jean Buridan, an influential Master of Arts at the University of Paris in the first half of the fourteenth century, adopted it and made extensive, though not uncritical, use of it in his *Questions on Aristotle's 'Nicomachean Ethics'*—a work that was still used in universities in the early seventeenth century. More than anything else, it coloured the development of Late Scholasticism, with the followers of Scotus and the followers of Ockham (Ockhamists or Nominalists).

It should be noted that there were many individual philosophers who wrote about the emotions and who offered powerful criticisms and alternatives to Aquinas, Scotus, Ockham, and other established thinkers. To mention only one case among many: Adam Wodeham (1300?–1358), a close associate of Ockham, argued for a cognitivist view of the emotions, maintaining that emotions are essentially acts of intellectual evaluation that bring in their train acts of volition, much like an up-to-date version of Abelard's view about intentions. On this score he was opposed by Gregory of Rimini (1300?–1358) and Pierre d'Ailly (1351–1420), who argued that no amount of cognition could ever have intrinsic motivational force, as emotions clearly do. This is, of course, to beg the question; Wodeham was careful to link his cognitive acts of evaluation with acts of volition, so that emotions, on his account, do have motivational force, though not intrinsically.

# 7.6 LATE SCHOLASTICISM: SUÁREZ

The general story told about medieval philosophy in the Later Middle Ages is that it is 'scholastic' in the narrow sense; organized into self-identified schools of thought, largely exegetical and polemical, it became increasingly hermetic and ultimately intellectually stale, degenerating into a caricature of itself. There is some truth to the stereotype, to be sure, but it overlooks the vitality of many parts of the later tradition. Psychology in particular was a central subject of interest all the way through the Renaissance, the Reformation, and the Counter-Reformation, and affective psychology, including the theory of the emotions, remained a lively subject for exploration and debate.

One of the most widely respected figures of Late Scholasticism, Tommaso de Vio, better known as Cajetan (1469–1534), wrote in 1511 a detailed and careful commentary on Aquinas's 'treatise on the emotions'. In the course of analysing and expounding Aquinas, Cajetan regularly describes and attacks Scotus's alternative account of the emotions, with an eye to showing the philosophical superiority of Aquinas's views. At no point does Cajetan engage with the later Scotist tradition, even when later Scotists had replied to the points he was pressing against Scotus. For all the evidence in his commentary, Cajetan could have been writing two centuries earlier. This is not to say that his objections are without merit. He is sharply critical of Scotus's claim that the proper formal object of the irascible emotions is *the offensive* rather than, as Aquinas had it, *the difficult*. Cajetan declares that Scotus merely asserts his claim rather than proving it, and that once it is examined carefully it will be seen that it presupposes Aquinas's view, since *the offensive* is worthy of attack only if it involves a difficulty; otherwise it would be simply avoided (commentary on 1a2ae q.23 art.1). Later thinkers, such as Bartolomé de Medina (1527/8–1580), take Cajetan to have proved Aquinas's point against Scotus, though again without considering the arguments and rebuttals offered by later Scotists.

Cajetan does occasionally disagree with Aquinas. For instance, he doesn't take Aquinas's distinction between the formal objects of the concupiscible and irascible emotions to support further subdivision into species; the emotions are only diversified from one another, not differentiated in the technical sense. This has the further consequence that putative subtypes of a given emotion, such as irritation and rancour with respect to anger, are not its species; instead, they are different degrees of anger, not different in kind from one another.

In general, Cajetan's criticism of Aquinas is guarded. Other late medieval thinkers, even those who identified themselves as followers of Aquinas, were not so restrained. Take, for example, the last great scholastic philosopher, Francisco Suárez (1548–1617), as vociferous a supporter of Aquinas as might be found. Suárez wrote extensively on the emotions, once treating them independently (*Lectures on the Soul*) and once by way of discussing Aquinas's specific views (*On Aquinas's 'Treatise on the Emotions'*). In each work he begins his analysis by describing the 'old theory' that puts forward the 'most popular division of the emotions', namely the division into the concupiscible and the irascible. He also runs through a series of arguments to support the distinction, including the Interference Argument and the Submission Argument, in more or less the form in which Aquinas presents them. Nevertheless, Suárez holds that the distinction should be discarded.

His reasoning is instructive. First, Suárez argues that these arguments do not entail that there is a real distinction between the concupiscible and the irascible powers, 'since it could easily be held that there is a unique sensitive power directed at the good apprehended by sense, and that it has acts by which it pursues the sensible good (and as such is called "concupiscible"), and again acts by which it protects the sensible good against things contrary to it (in which case it is labelled "irascible")' (*Lectures on the Soul* 5.4.3). Indeed, Suárez argues, this is the correct way to think of the matter. The sensitive appetite, he maintains, should be taken as a single unified whole, which may have two distinct though related functions, namely to pursue the good or to overcome obstacles to the good. In the former capacity the emotions are concupiscible; in the latter, irascible. There is no need to postulate a real distinction here. Just as one and the same person can discharge two different tasks, as (say) bank president and scout leader, so too the same sensitive faculty can have two different functions. Suárez proposes that concupiscible and irascible emotions share a common formal object, namely *the sensible good*. The pursuit of a good might involve overcoming an obstacle, or it might not, but that hardly seems a sufficient ground for insisting that two kinds of pursuit must be at stake. Suárez, it turns out, does not put much weight on the distinction of formal objects; he tells us that it is not an important issue since the concupiscible and the irascible are not really distinct, though since they are conceptually distinct we can treat them as though they were, if we please (5.4.8). Finally, Suárez rejects the Interference Argument, on the grounds that it cannot establish a distinction among powers from an incompatibility among acts, as he puts it (5.4.4).

Suárez has made a powerful case that we should give up the real distinction between the concupiscible and the irascible—a view in keeping with Scotus and Ockham more than Aquinas, it seems. But if we give up their real distinctness, what grounds are there for retaining their conceptual distinctness? Surprisingly, Suárez concludes that there really are none, and, furthermore, that the identification of eleven fundamental kinds of emotions is arbitrary (*On Aquinas's 'Treatise on the Emotions'* 4 disp.1 §12.2). He offers instead four criteria that are pragmatically useful in dealing with the emotions: by their general tendencies; by the most basic kinds of acts; by the distinctive movements they involve; by their individual merits. Applying these criteria yield different accounts of the number of emotions. The first, Suárez tells us, leads us to six emotions: love, desire, and pleasure, directed to the good; hate, fear or avoidance, and pain or distress, directed to evil. The second produces an indeterminate number, since there are, for example, an unlimited number of subdivisions of love or desire (§12.3). The third results in Aquinas's set of eleven emotions. The last depends on the authority consulted. The upshot, for Suárez, is that questions about the taxonomic structure of the emotions are purely instrumental: 'From all of this it is clear that the division into eleven passions is largely accommodated to the scheme of a [given] theory and isn't necessary' (§12.5). But as the distinction between the concupiscible and irascible emotions goes, so go all other distinctions among the emotions. Suárez concludes that there are no hard facts about the emotions, or, more precisely, there are no facts that do not depend on the purposes being served. We can continue to privilege Aquinas's scheme to preserve continuity with the tradition, though the grounds for doing so are purely pragmatic; it is 'the most common and the easiest for explaining the affections' (§12.6).

## 7.7 CONCLUSION

The internal critique of earlier medieval theories of the emotions, brought to the brink by Suárez, was mirrored by the emergence of other philosophical movements that dissociated themselves from their medieval heritage. The best known of these movements is usually called 'Renaissance Humanism', which advertised a return to the models of classical antiquity. For affective psychology, this often meant adopting a Stoic, or neo-Stoic, account of the emotions: figures as diverse as Juan Luis Vives (1492–1540) and Justus Lipsius (1547–1606) enthusiastically turned to Stoic sources in preference to the detailed tradition of medieval thinking about the emotions.

Cutting the moorings out from under the medieval theories of the emotions, as Suárez did, however, finally brought consensus on the emotions among late medieval thinkers: the unitary single soul, having no real distinctions within itself, need not be split up in order to accommodate affective psychology. Furthermore, the taxonomic model of scientific explanation, so successful in various branches of biology, ultimately fails in psychology. The best thing to do is to treat all the hard-fought distinctions and insights about the emotions won throughout the Middle

Ages as raw data still in need of a unifying theory. Thus was the ground cleared for the modern revolution in affective psychology initiated by Descartes, Locke, and others.

## FURTHER READING

### Surveys and Anthologies

*Klassische Emotionstheorien* (2008). Hilge Landweer and Ursula Renz (eds.). Walter de Gruyter.

Knuutila, Simo (2004). *Emotions in Ancient and Medieval Philosophy.* Oxford University Press.

*Les passions antique et médiévale* (2003). Bernard Besnier, Pierre-François Moreau, and Laurence Renault (eds.). Théories et critiques des passions, tom. 1. Paris: Presses Universitaires de France.

*Emotions and Choice from Boethius to Descartes* (2002). Henrik Lagerlund and Mikko Yrjönsuuri (eds.). Studies in the History of Philosophy of Mind. Kluwer Academic Publishers.

### 1 Augustine

BYERS, SARAH (2003). 'Augustine and the Cognitive Cause of Stoic "Preliminary Passions"', in *The Journal of the History of Philosophy* 41: 433–48.

BRACHTENDORF, JOHANNES (1997). 'Cicero and Augustine on the Passions', in *Revue des études augustiniennes* 43: 296–99.

IRWIN, TERRY (2003). 'Augustine's Criticisms of the Stoic Theory of Passions', in *Faith and Philosophy* 20: 430–47.

SORABJI, RICHARD (2000). *Emotion and Peace of Mind: From Stoic Agitation to Christian Temptation.* The Gifford Lectures. Oxford University Press.

VAN RIEL, GERD (2004). '*Mens immota mota manet*: Neoplatonic Tendencies in Augustine's Theory of the Passions', in *Augustiniana* 54: 507–31.

### 2 The Twelfth Century

BROWER, JEFF (2004). 'Anselm on Ethics' in Brian Davies and Brian Leftow (eds.), *The Cambridge Companion to Anselm.* Cambridge University Press.

LOTTIN, ODON (1943–1960). *Psychologie et morale aux XIIe et XIIIe siècles.* Gembloux.

MARENBON, JOHN (1997). *The Philosophy of Peter Abelard.* Cambridge University Press.

PERKAMS, MATTHIAS (2001). *Liebe als Zentralbegriff der Ethik nach Peter Abaelard.* Aschendorff.

### 3 The Early Thirteenth Century

HASSE, DAG (2000). *Avicenna's 'De anima' in the Latin West: The Formation of a Peripatetic Philosophy of the Soul 1160–1300.* Warburg Institute Studies and Texts.

VECCHIO, SILVANA (2006). 'Il discorso sulle passione nei commenti all'*Etica Nicomachea*: da Alberto Magno a Tommaso d'Aquino', in *Documenti e studi sula tradizione filosofica medievale* 17: 93–119.


## 4 Aquinas

BRUNGS, ALEXANDER (2002). *Metaphysik der Sinnlichkeit*. Akademische Studien und Vorträge 6. Hallescher Verlag.

DROST, MARK (1991). 'Intentionality in Aquinas's Theory of Emotions', in *International Philosophical Quarterly* 31: 449–60.

GOREVAN, PATRICK (2000). 'Aquinas and Emotional Theory Today: Mind-Body, Cognitivism, and Connaturality', in *Acta Philosophica* 9: 141–51.

KING, PETER (1998). 'Aquinas on the Passions' in Scott MacDonald and Eleonore Stump (eds.), *Aquinas's Moral Theory*. Cornell University Press: 101–32.

MARMO, COSTANTINO (1991). '*Hoc etiam etsi potest tollerari . . .* Egidio Romano e Tommaso d'Aquino sulle passioni dell'anima', in *Documenti e studi sula tradizione filosofica medievale* 2: 281–315.

SPEER, ANDREAS (ed.) (2005). *Thomas von Aquin: De Summa theologiae. Werkinterpretationen*. Walter de Gruyter.


## 5 Scotus and Ockham

BOLER, JOHN (1993). 'Transcending the Natural: Duns Scotus on the Two Affections of the Will', in *The American Catholic Philosophical Quarterly* 67: 109–26.

ETZKORN, GERALD (1990). 'Ockham's View of the Human Passions in Light of his Philosophical Anthropology', in *Die Gegenwart Ockhams*, Rolf Schönberger and Wilhelm Vossenkuhl (eds.). Wiley-VCH Acta humaniora: 265–87.

HIRVONEN, VESA (2004). *Passions in William Ockham's Philosophical Psychology*. Studies in the History of the Philosophy of Mind. Kluwer Academic Publishers.

HOLOPAINEN, TAINA (1991). *William of Ockham's Theory of the Foundations of Ethics*. Luther Agricola Society.

KENT, BONNIE (1995). *Virtues of the Will: The Transformation of Ethics in the Late Thirteenth Century*. Catholic University of America Press.

LEE, SUKJAE (1998). 'Scotus on the Will: the Rational Power and the Dual Affections', in *Vivarium* 36: 40–54.

PERRIAH, ALAN (1998). 'Scotus on Human Emotions', in *Franciscan Studies* 56: 325–45.


## 6 Late Scholasticism

JAMES, SUSAN (1997). *Passion and Action: The Emotions in Seventeenth-Century Philosophy*. Oxford University Press.

# CHAPTER 8

# A SENTIMENTALIST'S DEFENSE OF CONTEMPT, SHAME, AND DISDAIN

## KATE ABRAMSON

PHILOSOPHERS have recently appropriated the anthropologist's distinction between so-called "guilt-centered" and "shame-centered" moral practices to tell a dubious tale about some of the affective attitudes that play a crucial role in our moral assessments, and about the place that these attitudes held in early modern moral theories. The historical part of this story runs as follows. Certain emotional attitudes—disdain, shame, and contempt—are said to have a natural home in the kind of virtue and spectator-centered moral theories proffered by Hume and his sentimentalist contemporaries. In contrast, we are told, guilt, resentment, and indignation have a natural home in act and agent-centered theories like those of Kant and his descendants.[1]

---

[1] See, e.g., Baier (1994); Blackburn (1998); Gibbard (1990); Nussbaum (2004); Taylor (1985); Wallace (1996); Williams (1993).

This purported difference between sentimentalist and Kantian attitudes of negative moral assessment—one drawn by contemporary Humeans and Kantians alike—would be little more than an historical curiosity were it not commonly coupled with a further set of claims, namely, that the supposedly "sentimentalist" attitudes of disdain, shame, and contempt are morally objectionable in ways that resentment, indignation, and guilt are not. In this light, objections to the moral propriety of "shame-centered" emotions are taken not only as demonstrations that the sentimentalists were wrong to endorse such affective attitudes but as telling signposts pointing us toward fundamental flaws in their respective moral theories.

It is certainly true that Kant himself resoundingly condemned at least one member of the "shame" family of emotions—contempt—and that his sentimentalist predecessors in various ways, and to various extents, endorsed them all. But the purported links between endorsing these affective attitudes and advocating a sentimentalist, virtue and/or spectator-centered moral theory, as well as the canonical objections to these attitudes, both dissipate on close examination.

Or so I will contend. In the discussion that follows, I take contempt as my paradigmatic example of an attitude in the "shame" family for a number of reasons. First, contemporary objections to contempt arguably have the longest history, one dating back to Kant himself. Second, to a remarkable extent, the standing objections to contempt highlight the ways in which the presumed links between certain sorts of moral theories and the endorsement of emotions in the "shame" category is woven into even the objections to these attitudes. Third, whatever reasons the sentimentalists may have had for endorsing contempt, shame, and disdain as potentially appropriate moral responses, focusing on contempt will allow us to see that there is no good reason for even the most ardent of Kantians not to do so as well.

Moreover, in this context, contempt can plausibly serve as a "stand in", at least in some measure, for shame and disdain as well. For one, there is the simple fact that ethicists who object to the attitudes in question treat shame as either the self-directed (or *a* self-directed) counterpart of contempt, and similarly treat disdain as either a kind of generalized or slightly mitigated version of contempt.[2] In the same vein, the objections to contempt with which I'll here be concerned are also objections that have been brought to bear in one way or another against shame and disdain. This is not to say that I myself take the view that all forms of shame, contempt, and disdain stand in such elementary relations to one another, or that they do so per se as the kind of attitudes that they are. In fact, I doubt very much

---

[2] See Blackburn (1998), pp. 17–18; Darwall (2006), p. 71; Gibbard (1990), p. 51; Wallace (1996), p. 237; Williams (1993), pp. 89–90.

that this is the case. But my goal here is not conceptual analysis; it is rather to defend certain forms of the so-called "shame-centered" emotions, and the sentimentalists' invocation of them, against the charge that any such affective attitudes are necessarily and deeply morally problematic.

I'll proceed as follows. Section 8.1 is devoted to a discussion of some of the most intractable objections to contempt and the parallel objections to shame and disdain. In laying out these objections, I'll explore the ways in which they have been answered by those few others who, like myself, have seen even contempt as worthy of defense. In section 8.2, I'll sketch the outlines of an improved account of moralized contempt, together with its self-directed counterpart (a form of shame) as well as its generalized counterpart (a form of disdain). Finally, in section 8.3, I'll offer reasons for thinking that Shaftesbury, Hume, and Smith were all principally interested in what I will identify as the morally innocent forms of contempt, shame, and disdain. Here, too, the scope of my argument will be limited. It would be impossible in this context to examine every invocation of contempt, shame, and disdain in the works of all three sentimentalists, and determine thereby whether any of them ever implicitly endorses a morally objectionable form of some shame-centered attitude in some particular passage. But there are good reasons, I'll argue, to think that, if there is any such passage, it ought to be regarded not—as the philosophical opponents of sentimentalism would have it—as the natural outgrowth of sentimentalist moral theory but rather as an unfortunate misstep.

# 8.1 Objections to contempt and its affective allies

The most familiar objection to any of the shame-centered attitudes is undoubtedly Kant's objection to the evaluative presentation of contempt. Kant famously complains that to hold another in contempt is to deny her "all moral worth" (6:464). If someone has *no* moral worth, Kant continues, he "could never be improved either", which is objectionable on the grounds that persons as such can "never lose all predisposition to the good".

It's not hard to see why one would suppose that if contempt presents a person as worthless in Kant's sense, then it also presents her as incapable of moral improvement.[3] The difficulty lies in trying to figure out why one should suppose that

---

[3] See Mason (2003) See also Bell (2005)., As Mason points out (p. 258), Jean Hampton raises a similar, and in my view telling, objection about hatred of persons in *Forgiveness and Mercy* (1988).

contempt denies another's fundamental moral worth. Contempt certainly involves a negative judgment of value: the judgment that the object is inferior, fails to live up to some basic standard, or is of no worth at all.[4] And to be sure, a failing must be significant to earn our contempt. But it is simply not the case that even very strong forms of contempt always present their objects as worthless. I have such hearty contempt, for instance, for *Fox News* as an instance of what it is supposed to be, namely *news*, that I occasionally contemplate installing a channel blocker to prevent myself from even accidentally catching sight of it as I flip channels. Yet had I no other avenue for news, I would turn it on in the hopes of gleaning something about current events. I cannot claim, then, to regard *Fox News* as strictly worthless, qua news program. I see no reason to presume that the case is any different when it comes to contempt for persons.

But why, then, do so many suppose otherwise in objecting to contempt? Michelle Mason hypothesizes that the real worry behind the claim that contempt presents its object as worthless is the thought that contempt has a troubling globalizing tendency, one that "mistakenly equates the person [himself] with certain traits or wrongly assumes that characters are monolithic".[5] In other words, when ethicists complain that the evaluation implicit in moralized contempt is that a person is worthless, the underlying thought runs as follows: to adopt an attitude of contempt is to regard a person as irredeemable (herself a moral failure) on the grounds that she has some particularly horrific character trait. But, however horrific a particular trait may be, say contempt's detractors, the value of someone's character as a whole cannot be properly reduced to the value of any particular trait, and it is only the monsters of an infantile fantasy whose entire character is comprised of all and only contemptible character traits.

Mason's hypothesis is plausible not only because—as she herself argues—it accounts for so much of what philosophers say in the voice of complaint about contempt's evaluative presentation but also because many see shame as having this

---

[4] I am deliberately ambiguous here about the precise role of this judgment in contempt, e.g. whether contempt involves an evaluative presentation of its object in the sense of which contemporary virtue ethicists sometimes speak, or whether contempt possesses propositional content in a more traditional sense.

[5] Mason (2003), p. 258. Mason in fact offers two responses to this complaint. Her other line of defense begins with the speculation that perhaps Kantians view contempt as a denial that another has any moral worth because they suppose that, in viewing another with contempt, the appraiser imagines herself entitled to use the person thought contemptible "merely as a means" to her own ends (p. 265). I agree with Mason that the attitude of contempt need not have this character, but I also find Mason's speculation troubling as an account of the Kantian objection at issue. Denying a wrongdoer all moral worth may or may not lead us to also think ourselves entitled to treat the wrongdoer as a mere means, but regarding another as lacking all moral worth would surely be objectionable even if it did not lead us to imagine ourselves entitled to treat her as a mere means to our ends.

same kind of troubling globalizing tendency. Martha Nussbaum, for instance, writes that "shame, as is generally agreed by those who analyze it, pertains to the whole self, rather than to a specific act of the self" (Nussbaum, 2004, p. 184). For those who take shame to be the self-directed counterpart (or *a* self-directed counterpart) of contempt, the link between such worries about shame on the one hand and contempt on the other is clear. And for those who, like Darwall or Blackburn, tend to treat shame as the self-directed counterpart of disdain, raising such worries about shame is—albeit indirectly—a way of raising the same set of worries about disdain.[6]

What, then, are we to say with regard to such claims about the purportedly globalizing nature of "shame-centered" attitudes? Mason argues that global contempt—contempt for a person's character as a whole—can be appropriate, even if someone has redeeming qualities, provided only that we are warranted in "giving greater weight" to the "bad" quality (Mason, 2003, p. 259). Although she is concerned specifically with contempt, the same response might equally well be given on behalf of shame and disdain, e.g. that it is entirely appropriate for me to be ashamed of myself as a person, provided only that I am warranted in giving greater weight to whatever may be the grounds for my shame (e.g. my cruelty) than I am to my less unsavory traits (say, my punctuality).

This response troubles me. An interlocutor might easily grant the premise that we are sometimes warranted in "giving greater weight" to a person's vices in our evaluation of her character as a whole, or even in our evaluation of the significance of some particular vice of hers, and yet still balk at the notion that global contempt is ever warranted. In fact, one might think it a mark of moral maturity to be able to sincerely say of even the most manipulative, dishonest, egomaniacal, power-hungry, and cruel character that her dedication to worthy political causes, though grotesquely outbalanced by her vices, is no less part of her moral persona than her terrible vices. This last point seems necessarily lost insofar as we hold another *person* in contempt, for our affective response in that case just is one of contempt. So too with shame: insofar as I am ashamed of myself because I'm chronically weak-willed in the face of alluring food, rather than simply being ashamed of being weak-willed in this way, I cannot appreciate my more redeeming qualities, what-ever they may be.[7]

Note that the worry at issue isn't about "mistakenly *equating* a person with certain traits", i.e. a worry about making some kind of mistaken judgment. Rather,

---

[6] Darwall (2006), p. 71, Blackburn (1998), p. 18.

[7] As others note, the phrase "to be ashamed" is colloquially used in a fashion that sometimes refers to embarrassment, sometimes a kind of moral sanction, occasionally something on the order of humiliation, and only sometimes *shame* itself. To prevent confusion, I note that throughout this article I use this phrase to refer to one's bearing an attitude of shame; unfortunately, there simply is no alternative phrase that is more exact without being unwieldy.

the worry is that to hold a person in contempt, or to be ashamed of oneself as a person, is to adopt an attitude that precludes appreciation of another's or one's own redeeming qualities. If I hold a person in contempt, I may *recognize* that she has redeeming qualities, in the sense of making the judgment that her dedication to worthy political causes deserves appreciation. But I cannot *appreciate* her dedication at the same time that I hold her as a person in contempt. It is just such appreciation that an attitude of global contempt precludes. Talk of someone's vices outweighing their virtues simply doesn't address this concern, one that turns centrally on the fact that contempt is not merely a belief but an affective attitude or form of regard.

Perhaps realizing this, Mason alternatively proposes that global contempt may be warranted only when it is the case both that a person's vices outweigh their virtues, *and* that the condemner stands in a special relationship to the condemned in the context of which the condemned's vices provide their (most) salient point of contact. To persuade us of this, Mason imagines a case in which a man, Paul, who regularly volunteers his time for charitable causes, has been egregiously ill-treating his spouse, Camille. When Camille reacts to Paul with contempt, he protests, "well, yes, dear, I was hoping to parlay your beauty and sex appeal for an opportunity to make my way to Hollywood; but how can you say I'm a wretched louse? What about all those weekends at the soup kitchen?" "Such a response," writes Mason, "would in fact count in favor of a worse assessment of Paul precisely because he fails to appreciate its irrelevance" (Mason, 2003, pp. 259–60).

Here's the tricky part. The take-away lesson Mason needs is that Paul's response is irrelevant *in the sense that*, given their relationship, Camille has no reason to regard Paul as anything but contemptible. Yet what makes Paul's retort outrageous is not that he's wrong about his redeeming qualities being worthy of appreciation—even by Camille—but that his response tries to deflect, rather than account for, his behavior. It is in *that* sense irrelevant. The same would be true if, say, Paul had failed to pick up Camille's mother at the airport as promised, and responded to her anger by exclaiming, "but, just last month I weeded her garden!" The latter is indeed worthy of appreciation: it's just no way of accounting for his broken promise.

The central worry at issue here thus remains: globalizing attitudes preclude appreciation of someone's redeeming qualities.[8] Save for barely conceivable cases of monolithically shameful, contemptible, and/or disdainful characters, it seems reasonable to think that the global forms of these attitudes—those directed toward a person as a whole, or the whole of their character—are always morally inappropriate. And contempt, shame, and disdain only come in the global form, or so the thought goes.

---

[8] It also and for the same reason precludes appreciation of other qualities that may be worthy of anger or resentment *rather than* contempt.

A second set of complaints focuses on the fact that contempt, shame, and disdain are all typically expressed in withdrawal or avoidance. Advocates and critics of these attitudes alike agree that withdrawal is the "behavioral manifestation" of contempt, that disdain motivates disengagement rather than engagement, and that shame is classically expressed in "concealment", a desire to "hide ourselves from the gaze of others", or in Bernard Williams' somewhat melodramatic description, a "wish that the space occupied by me should be instantaneously empty".[9] But there are varying accounts of what makes this feature of shame, contempt, and disdain objectionable.

One such objection has to do with what withdrawal says about how we see the contemptible or our shameful selves qua members of the moral community. Thomas Hill, for instance, writes that:

> contempt is a deep dismissal, a denial of the prospect of reconciliation, a signal that the conversation is over. Furious argument and accusation, and even sharp-tongued deflation of hypocrisy and self-deception, leave some space to resume communication; but cold, silent contempt does not. [ ... ] Moral argument, however impassioned, is addressed to a person, acknowledged as "one of us": perhaps delinquent, misbehaving, outrageously deviant from our common standards, but still "one who can be reached", or so we presume.[10]

Mason reads Hill as concerned with the possibility of reconciliation and forgiveness, and as calling upon us to recognize a "positive requirement of an active form of engagement". In response, she argues that contempt does not foreclose reconciliation, that forgiveness cannot be demanded, and that we have no "duty of active engagement" (268–9).

I don't have any quarrel with Mason's views about forgiveness, reconciliation, etc. But all this strikes me as peripheral to Hill's main concern. What Hill is really worried about is whether contempt precludes us from seeing another as an *ongoing* member of the moral community. Openness to reconciliation and forgiveness are but prima facie indications of whether, in Hill's words, the "conversation is over" in a way tantamount to exiling another from the community of mutually accountable agents. In this light, the core problem with contempt is that insofar as its expression involves withdrawal, it seems to communicate the message that one is neither interested in what another might say in defense of herself, nor willing to be held accountable for one's own contempt. Take the colloquial response, "talk to the

---

⁹ On contempt, here see, e.g., Hill (2000); Mason (2003); and Bell (2005); on disdain, see Darwall (2006) (esp. pp. 70–1) and Blackburn (1998), pp. 17–18; on shame, see Nussbaum (2004); Darwall (2006) and (1999), and the quote from Williams (1993), p. 89.

¹⁰ Hill (2000), p. 60. I take it that Christine Korsgaard has partly this worry in mind when she writes that the temptation to "write someone off" "seems disrespectful" (Korsgaard (1996), p. 200).

hand". The gesture alone seems to say, "I am not answerable to you for regarding you with contempt". That I might later be reconciled to the object of my contempt is beside the point. If holding another in contempt involves an appraiser's denial of accountability to the contemptible, it is for that reason alone objectionable, for in so denying our accountability to another we necessarily treat her as outside the community of mutually accountable agents. The possibility of reconciliation then amounts only to the possibility that her exile from the moral community may be temporary.[11]

This seems no less true of shame than it is of contempt. If, or to the extent that, I hide from the view of those with regard to whom I take myself to have reason to be ashamed, I preclude the possibility of their forgiveness, as well as, more darkly, the possibility that I might find myself on the receiving end of a reactive attitude which, for whatever personal or other reason, is more difficult for me to bear than is my shame. Remember Mason's case of Camille and Paul, and imagine that Paul hid, ashamed, thereby cutting off any possibility that Camille might express righteous, infuriated, indignation at Paul. Shame, one might worry, is in this manner a way of excluding oneself from the moral community, and a potentially morally pernicious way at that.

A second worry about contempt's characteristic expression in withdrawal focuses even more directly on its role as part of an accountability relation. What reactive attitudes *do*, in the first instance, is hold someone responsible for her conduct or character. Anger, for instance, is often expressed by literally calling another to account for her conduct—e.g. "what were you thinking!?" In Darwall's words, our reactive attitudes seem to come with an "rsvp" (2006, p. 42 n.5). In no other case do we hold people accountable by *withdrawing* from them. Thus, as Darwall points out, the question remains as to why we should suppose that, in contempt or shame, "withdrawal is a way of holding its object accountable and not a non-"reactive' response like, say, disgust" (2006, p. 67 n.4, p. 71)

One might hope to get some mileage here by trading on the common claim that, whereas resentment and guilt are action-focused, contempt and shame are person-focused: I resent what you did to me and am guilty for what I have done, but I find *you* contemptible, and I am ashamed of myself.[12] Resentment, on this conception, is a response to another's failure with regard to some demand we can make on her

---

[11] Thus understood, the worry about contempt's expression in withdrawal is inseparable from the worry that contempt is a refusal of recognition respect. This is not, as Mason suggests, because Kantians implicitly assume that recognition respect involves or entails previously unrecognized duties, such as a duty of active engagement with others. Rather, the worry at issue here just is that, precisely insofar as we express our disapproval of someone by withdrawing from her, we reject her status as an *ongoing* member of the moral community.

[12] Mason (2003), p. 246; Bell (2005), pp. 83–4; Nussbaum (2004), pp. 207–8. Bell is more reticent than Mason about the flip side of this hypothesis, i.e. that resentment is essentially action-focused. See Bell (2005), p. 92 n.4.

conduct, while properly focused contempt and shame are responses to a failure in light of a "demand to live up to an ideal" of character (Mason, 2003; Bell, 2005; Wallace, 1996, pp. 237–8). In fact, on some views, contempt and shame's person-focus is so thoroughgoing that "a wrong need not have been committed" in order for these attitudes to be appropriate.[13] Perhaps this difference between resentment and guilt, on the one hand, and contempt and shame, on the other, can explain the parallel difference that troubles Darwall.

The fundamental problem with this proposal is that it is not clear how or why an attitude's person-focus could be connected to its expression in withdrawal such that it would make sense to think of withdrawal as a way of holding someone accountable for her dismal character. To put it another way: if I need not wrong anyone within the context of my interpersonal interactions in order to become the proper object of your contempt or my shame, then why would your withdrawal from those interactions with me (or my withdrawal from you) make sense as a way of holding me accountable for my bad character?

One last complaint about contempt traces the problem to the standpoint from which contempt is felt. This objection has been made most forcefully by Darwall, and has not yet been addressed by contempt's defenders. The basic idea, I take it, is this. Reactive attitudes, as I've already noted, do not merely claim *that* someone is responsible; they *hold* her responsible. But to hold someone morally responsible, as Korsgaard puts it, is itself to "plac[e] yourself in a relationship with her", a relationship within which—at minimum—we see her as accountable to us for her conduct.[14] As such, the reactive attitudes must be felt from the standpoint of one participant in ethical life addressing another. Hence one reason for the title of Darwall's recent monograph: the standpoint from which reactive attitudes are felt is the second-person standpoint.

In contrast, we are told, contempt is felt—like disdain and shame—from a spectator's standpoint, the standpoint of an observer of ethical life, rather than a participant in it. While this is an evaluative standpoint, it is not the kind of standpoint from which one can hold another responsible, for that can only be done interpersonally.[15] Again as Darwall puts it,

[13] Mason (2003), p. 254, pp. 248, 252n, 257; Bell (2005), p. 83, 92n1–3; Wallace (1996), pp. 237–8. In spite of this, the examples Mason and Bell use to argue their case for the moral appropriateness of contempt in fact involve someone's (egregiously) wronging another.

[14] Korsgaard (1996), pp. 198, 189, see also p. 205; also Darwall (1999), pp. 161–3. The thought that practices of holding one another accountable are interpersonal in this special sense is hardly unique to Kantians. The same thought is captured, for instance, by Strawson's remark that the characteristic feature of reactive attitudes is that they "involve, or express, a certain sort of demand for inter-personal regard" (Strawson (1982)). Darwall (2006) traces the development of this thought from natural law theorists to the present day.

[15] These are major themes in both Darwall (1999) and Darwall (2006). Of course contempt involves a particular way of relating to its object, if only that, as Hume says, "we commonly keep at a distance" the contemptible [T 2.2.10.9; SBN 392–3]. The problem is that contempt's spectatorial standpoint

We don't deserve praise, our own or others', of course, unless our motives and character are proper. But we are not accountable before others for general impropriety. Imprudently wasting my fortune may rightly make me subject to disesteem, but not to any emotion, like resentment or anger, that makes a claim on how I should act. (1999, p. 163)

Following this, one might say that, while disdain and contempt can take persons as objects, they are not responses to individuals *as* responsible agents.

## 8.2 OUTLINE OF AN ALTERNATIVE

Let me begin my outline for an alternative account by addressing the complaint that the apparent person-focus of contempt, shame, and disdain—their globalizing nature—is itself morally objectionable. The problem with such globalizing attitudes—contempt for a person, being ashamed of oneself, holding a third party in disdain (the generalized or impersonal form of the former two attitudes)—is that such attitudes preclude appreciation of a person's redeeming qualities, and (save for barely conceivable cases of monolithically rotten characters) are therefore always morally inappropriate.

But why presume that contempt, shame, and disdain must always be global in their scope? Why assume that, for instance, contempt *necessarily* takes as its focus the whole toward which it is directed, rather than some particular feature thereof?[16] Where persons are concerned, this amounts to the thought that contempt always takes as its focus the whole of someone's character, rather than, say, some particular trait of hers.

I can find only two indications for how the presumptive global focus of contempt might be defended. Some suggest that localized contempt or shame is psychologically impossible (Mason, 2003, pp. 234–72, p. 240 n.30). Others explain the presumptive global focus of contempt by reference to other apparently similar

---

seems to entail that, if it does involve a particular way of relating to its object, it does so in the manner of what Strawson calls an "objective" attitude, an attitude that involves viewing another as "a subject for what, in a wide range of sense[s], might be called treatment; as something certainly to be taken account, perhaps precautionary account, of; to be managed or handled or cured or trained". In Abramson (2008), I argue that the more general complaint about Hume at issue in the passage from Darwall quoted above, namely that in general the Humean attitudes of disapproval have this problematically spectatorial character, misses its target. In that article, I left open the possibility that such a complaint might find an apt target in contempt. Here I show otherwise.

[16] Mason (2003), for instance, makes this assumption in her defense of contempt; as does Bell (2005) in her defense; as does Hampton in her critique of hatred and related attitudes in Murphy and Hampton (1988).

attitudes. Contempt is often seen, for instance, as a close ally to disgust. We are told, among other things, that both attitudes are felt from a spectator's standpoint, and are typically expressed in avoidance.[17] If contempt and disgust are as closely allied, as commonly thought, and shame is simply the self-directed counterpart of contempt, then it would not be implausible to think that understanding something about how disgust works might illuminate parallel features of both contempt and shame. Imagine, then, a moldy, slimy slab of rotten meat rediscovered in the fridge. The mold will surely *cause* disgust, but, just as surely, our disgust is not disgust for some particular feature of it, like its slimy texture. It is, rather, disgust for "that rotten piece of meat". Similarly, one might think that while we may be led to be contemptuous of someone because of her dishonesty, the object of our contempt is always "that liar", not "that woman's dishonesty". I might become ashamed of myself, the argument would go, because I'm a layabout, but the object of my shame would be *me*, not my slacker tendencies.

Yet neither of these defenses of contempt and shame's purportedly global focus can withstand scrutiny. The most an analogy to disgust can give us is a prima facie reason to suspect that the other two attitudes are inherently or ineliminably global. And both the psychological claim and the analogy to disgust are susceptible to refutation by example.

Consider, for instance, the following. Some years ago, the president of the National Organization for Women, Patricia Ireland, was called upon to justify NOW's continuing political support for Bill Clinton in spite of his appallingly sexist treatment of some of the women in his personal life. Ireland responded:

Women voters elected Clinton, and the majority of women still approve of his performance in office [ . . . ] Clinton's administration worked hard and successfully on the Violence Against Women Act, the Freedom of Access to Clinic Entrances Act, the Family and Medical Leave Act, the earned income tax credit, women's health and other issues that affect us and our families; he has appointed more women and women's rights supporters to positions of power than ever before. Still, he seems to be a man who divides women into two unfortunate traditional categories: women he must treat with respect like Janet Reno, Madeleine Albright and Ruth Bader Ginsburg, and those he can use and toss aside like tissue paper.[18]

The final lines of this passage ring with contempt. Yet it is equally clear that Ireland *admires* Clinton's attitudes and conduct toward women as a class, and toward the

---

[17] See, e.g., Miller (1997); Nussbaum (2004). Even Bell, whose project it is to defend the moral propriety of contempt, at moments tries to elucidate features of contempt by deploying analogies to disgust (e.g. Bell, 2005, p. 84). My thanks to David Sussman for the suggestion that one might argue for contempt's global scope by analogy with disgust.

[18] National Organization for Women (1998). The sentiments Ireland expresses here were, by all reports, shared by thousands who—like myself—voted for Bill Clinton, *twice*.

women with whom he interacts professionally. Ireland's contempt is limited to another aspect of Clinton's character, namely, his attitudes and conduct toward the women with whom he interacts as mere ego-boosting sexual conquests. This is enough to show the psychological possibility of localized contempt, and we have but to imagine Clinton (or rather, a better version of him) taking the attitude toward himself that Ireland expresses in order to envision the relevantly similar attitude of localized shame, i.e. shame focused on a single aspect of a person's character.

I hasten to note that there is, of course, a difference between bearing attitude x toward a person on account of some feature of their character or conduct, and bearing attitude x toward some particular feature of a person's character or conduct. For a variety of reasons, it can be difficult to tell in situ with which of these two phenomena one is dealing when it comes to contempt and shame. At times it is the form of words which makes discerning the difference problematic: we cannot know if a phrase like "you ought to be ashamed" or "contemptible little man" expresses a local or global attitude without an account of the context in which they are uttered. At other times, the difficulty in discerning whether a given case is one of a local or global attitude is psychological, and discovering the truth of the matter may require conversational cooperation of friends and/or therapeutic professionals. But in these respects, contempt and shame are no different from other reactive attitudes. "I'm so furious with you" does not tell us whether the object of anger is a person's conduct, a character trait, or the person (e.g. anger verging on hatred), and the usual psychological phenomena of deflection, projection, internalization, and so on can make proper discernment of what is in fact the object of one's own or another's anger just as knotty a psychological matter as it can be in the case of shame or contempt. Indeed, just as psychologists and analysts often make it part of their work to help patients first discover and then refocus their anger on its proper object, so too in the case of shame and contempt, when such attitudes are, for instance, improperly global. It would make no sense for analysts to undertake such tasks were shame or contempt ineliminably global.[19]

---

[19] My thanks to Peter Goldie for pressing me to say a bit more here about the sometimes vexed relationship between global and localized contempt, and in particular pointing out that we can make the mistake of taking a global attitude of shame or contempt where a local one is appropriate, that bringing people to see that they have made such a mistake is often the concern of psychologists and analysts, and that none of that would make the least bit sense if shame and contempt were ineliminably global attitudes.

In correspondence, Goldie also raised the possibility that there may be a form of these attitudes that is neither strictly localized, nor global in the sense to which I object, but rather something in between, namely, an attitude that is "directed towards the person, but only insofar as they have that trait". It seems to me exactly right to suppose that we can (and do) have such attitudes. Goldie suggests we call these "pro-tanto" attitudes. I hesitate slightly about so naming the affective attitude Goldie describes, for "pro-tanto attitude" suggests to me yet a further possibility: that of bearing an attitude towards a

On the other hand, as Ireland's remarks about Clinton show, sometimes it is not the least bit difficult to tell that the phenomenon at issue is one of local, rather than global contempt, and for our purposes here, really, that's all we need.

Perhaps, however, it will be said that talk of the psychological impossibility of localized contempt, or localized shame, is only the surface of a deeper worry that admitting *localized* contempt into our moral repertoire would in some way force us to treat virtues as isolable traits, not united by the moral reasoning apart from which the virtues are in fact unintelligible as such. Or, in less polysyllabic terms, an interlocutor might object to the thought that Bill Clinton's supposed virtues could be unpolluted by what are so evidently his vices.

This is no place to debate the unity of the virtues. Fortunately, we don't have to for we can grant a strong version of those ancient theses without undermining the case for localized contempt.[20] We might stipulate, for instance, that Clinton's attitudes and conduct toward women as a class will inevitably be infected in some way by the contemptible side of his character, and yet maintain that the pollution of the former redeeming attitudes need not be so thoroughgoing as to warrant the assessment that those apparently redeeming attitudes are in fact contemptible. Clinton's political virtues will never reach their full perfection so long as he remains plagued by "private vices", but the former qualities can be quite laudable nonetheless. In other words, localized contempt is compatible with the thesis that if one lacks one virtue, then to some extent one lacks them all; it is only incompatible with the rather extreme thesis that, to the extent one lacks one virtue, *to that extent* one lacks them all.

Finally, one might worry that accepting the possibility of such localized contempt would make contempt's expression in withdrawal from its object seem problematic. If we avoid someone, an interlocutor might say, we are avoiding that whole person—not just a particular aspect of her character. Yet our avoidance of, or withdrawal from, persons for whose character traits we bear contempt need not be any more global than our contempt. In the Bill Clinton case, for instance, the relevant form of avoidance can be captured by something like the thought that Clinton is to be admired as a president and accordingly reelected, though one ought to avoid intimate contact with the guy.

---

person (as a whole) pending further information. We might imagine, for instance, that all I know about Joe is that he has x contemptible trait, and so that I adopt a pro-tanto attitude of contempt for *him*, which would transform into a form of localized contempt should I learn of his redeeming qualities. In contrast, it seems to me that the kind of attitude Goldie describes could persist without becoming fully globalized in the sense that most troubles me, even were I to learn of Joe's redeeming features.

[20] What is typically called the thesis of the "unity of the virtues" is in fact a nexus of more or less strong positions about the relationship among the virtues, some of which are properly called "reciprocity theses" rather than "unity theses". On the difference between these two ancient theses see Annas (1993), pp. 75–82.

This brings me nicely to the second set of objections to contempt—those having to do with the fact that contempt as well as shame and disdain are typically expressed in avoidance or withdrawal. I don't wish to deny this. In fact, in the case of contempt and the species of shame that is the counterpart to contempt, I wish to make a stronger claim: avoidance and/or withdrawal are essential features of the normative force of these attitudes. Contempt presents its object as "to be avoided". Consider in this light the difference between contemptuous and patronizing attitudes. I might avoid those toward whom I feel patronizing. But I might also be the sort of person who deliberately seeks out such people, precisely because I enjoy feeling superior to them. There are people of this sort, and they are no less recognizable *as* patronizing because they do so. Contempt can also involve pleasurable feelings of superiority. But even in cases where the affect of contempt is dominated more by pleasurable feelings of superiority than pain, we regard those for whom we have contempt as "to be avoided" nonetheless. We would not recognize contempt as such in the absence of any disposition to distance oneself from the object of one's contempt.

If, for instance, I tell you that I'm contemptuous of Joe but spend a good deal of time with him, you would likely begin to wonder whether I really find him contemptible. I might be able to produce a satisfying explanation for my behavior, but it would need to have the character of an explanation for why I spend so much time with him *in spite of* the fact that I find him contemptible.[21]

Contempt differs in this way not only from patronizing attitudes but also crucially from disgust. Like contempt, disgust is typically expressed in avoidance. Unlike contempt, however, there's nothing unintelligible about being fascinated with something one finds disgusting, precisely because it is disgusting.[22] This

---

[21] One implication of this view is that one cannot be "indifferent" to the object of one's contempt in the sense of not caring—crudely speaking—whether it is present in one's life. I think we'd begin to doubt either the sincerity or self-awareness of a person who declares her contempt for fashion trends, but who is perfectly happy to wear them when her spouse purchases all the latest styles for her. If she really is *contemptuous* of fashion, we'd expect her at some point to ask her spouse to express generosity in another way.

As Peter Goldie reminded me, the same is not true of fictional characters—we indulge an apparently strange passion for reading about contemptible characters, precisely because they are so contemptible. This parallels the famous problem concerning tragedy that is the subject of (among many other things) Hume's essay by that name, insofar as we seem to seek—in both cases—that in literature which we avoid in life. But there is an additional problem with our apparent fascination with contemptible literary characters, namely, that we are there seeking out the immoral *for that reason*. There is an enormous and ever-growing literature devoted to explaining such apparent differences between our responses in the aesthetic and moral and/or practical realm, as well as a closely overlapping literature on the sometimes troubling relationship between these two types of responses (i.e. work on so-called "immoralism" in literature). The latter too was an issue with which Hume was very much concerned, in, e.g., the final three pages of his essay "Of the Standard of Taste" (in *Essays, Moral and Political*).

[22] See, e.g., Miller (1997) for a discussion of this aspect of disgust.

makes it nearly impossible to see how *any* form of disgust could qualify as a reactive attitude; surely, responding to someone's moral failure with fascination cannot count as a way of holding her as accountable for it. In contrast, the fact that contempt presents its object as "to be avoided" makes it plausible to think that contempt might sometimes qualify as a reactive attitude: at least avoidance is a negative response.

Yet Kantians like Hill are nevertheless wrong to worry that such disengagement as is necessarily involved in contempt leaves no space for mutual accountability, and thereby exiles the contemptible from the moral community. Even if we literally withdraw from the object of our contempt, there are concomitant ways of indicating that mutual accountability remains in place. Imagine, for instance, someone whose parting words are "Call me if you ever realize what you've done". Moreover, we need not be so literal in thinking about what it means to say that contempt presents its object as "to be avoided". On occasion, simply expressing contempt can do the work of relevantly distancing oneself. If I refer to George W. Bush as "the former occupant of the White House", the contemptuous message I thereby express is that of distancing myself and my country from a man who once held the office of president. At the same time, however, the very use of such a phrase practically invites anyone within earshot to call me to account for my use of that phrase, and/ or to defend Bush.

Indeed, expressions of contempt can be quite complex on this score. As a child, for instance, I once responded to the command that I play with my younger brother by declaring that we would play "library". My brother would be a staff worker, my sister a student, and I the librarian. I proceeded to remove all the books from my shelves, pile them on the floor, and tell my brother to alphabetize them, while my sister and I continued to read the books we had been reading. In addition to being spiteful toward my brother, my conduct clearly exhibited contempt for the command I'd been given. I could have flatly refused, snapped that I didn't want to play with my brother, or responded in any number of other ways that would have indicated anger. Instead, I chose contempt: by constructing the game as I did, I managed to "follow" the command while at the same time distancing myself from even the appearance of having actually obeyed it. None of this prevented my beleaguered brother from objecting that I wasn't "really" playing with him, nor did it exclude the opportunity for those who'd given me the command to call me to account for my attitude toward it.

There are similar variations in the ways we express the form of shame that is the natural counterpart of contempt. I might be so ashamed as to think of myself as someone who is "to be avoided" in the sense of "kept out of decent company", and so either refuse all companionship or deliberately seek the companionship of those I hold in equally low regard. Those whose self-contempt reaches its nadir do terrible things to themselves, including suicide. Toward the other end of the scale, if I think myself, say, as weak-willed about standing up to one particular person, I might express my shame in ways as deceptively small as showering after every encounter, as though I might literally wash away that part of myself.

In fact, *literal* avoidance or disengagement is often the last of many ways in which contempt or shame are expressed. Someone who has come to feel contempt for a spouse might express this by saying something like "You are not the person I thought you were". We use remarks of this sort as a way of distancing ourselves from those with whom we were formerly intimate. But such contemptuous comments also function as final opportunities for those toward whom the remark is directed to complain that our contempt is unjustified. The same can often be said of exchanges in which someone invokes the phrase "talk to the hand". With hand raised, and face averted, the offended party typically remains firmly in place, awaiting a response. Only if she is met with silence or what she takes to be inadequate excuses does she then turn and walk away.

All this still leaves us with the question Darwall raises about the fact that these attitudes are paradigmatically expressed in withdrawal. Again, whereas reactive sentiments like anger characteristically demand a response from the wrongdoer—whether an apology, contrition, or an accounting—I have argued that contempt and shame present their objects as "to be avoided". Disdain is then the impersonal counterpart (in Strawson's sense) of the former two attitudes. But how can avoidance or withdrawal be a way of holding someone accountable? And even supposing that it can, what reason could there be for holding another accountable by disengaging or avoiding her, rather than demanding a response from her and sticking around to hear it?

To address this question, we need to return to the issue of contempt's proper focus. While agreeing with earlier defenders of contempt that this attitude is typically character- rather than action-focused, I have also argued that properly focused contempt is local rather than global, that is, focused on aspects of an agent's character rather than her character as a whole. I now wish to suggest that we ought to be even more specific about the focus of properly focused contempt, and by extension, the forms of shame and disdain with which I am here concerned. For ease of discussion, I'll focus simply on contempt, but everything that follows could, I believe, be equally said, without loss, of at least some forms of shame and disdain, and for my purposes here, this will suffice.

Let me begin by highlighting two claims about contempt that both Bell and Mason make in their own defenses of contempt. First, they claim that one must fail to live up to ideals of character that are seen by the condemner as *important* before one becomes eligible for properly focused contempt. Second, at the same time, both insist that "a wrong need not have been committed for contempt to be properly focused".[23] The first of these claims strikes me as too ambiguous to be

---

[23] See Mason (2003), pp. 241, 254; 248, 252n, 257; Bell (2005), pp. 83, 92nn.1–3.

illuminating, and the second is, I think, mistaken, for reasons that become clear when one tries to disambiguate what is meant by "important" in the first claim.

Generosity, mercifulness, courtesy, justice, honesty, and fidelity are all *in some sense* important. But ask yourself: which of these do we regard as important in the sense that falling short of those ideals to any extent is marked as a grave moral failing? Not generosity—for while we regard generosity as important, we all also willingly acknowledge ourselves to be less than perfectly generous and do not for that reason alone haul ourselves off to the corridors of self-flagellation. Neither does incomplete virtue with regard to the Kantian duty of self-perfection, or courteousness, or mercifulness raise substantial opprobrium until the gap between the virtue and an individual's character becomes great. So, for instance, we could all do more to perfect ourselves, and be more attentive to those around us in the ways that qualify as courtesy. But it is only the wholly indolent and the astoundingly rude who earn our ire. Contrast these cases with matters of justice, honesty, and fidelity. One lie may not make one dishonest, but a pattern of lying or adultery generates grave disapproval far more readily than does a pattern of lazy weekends.

Such differing responses are, I think, at least partly explained by the different relationships these vices bear to the obligations we have toward one another *within* the context of our interactions. One might argue that we are under a general obligation to be generous, to perfect our character, and to be merciful. I cannot plausibly contend, however, that my neighbor who fails to act generously toward me by, say, giving me a thousand dollars for a vacation, has thereby violated an obligation he has toward me. I may properly demand that you treat me with fairness, equity, respect, justice, that you do not lie or dissemble to me, and that you do not betray me; I may not properly demand that you perform particular generous acts for me, or demand that you show me mercy when I have wronged you.

Contemptuous attitudes toward persons are at least sometimes focused on the kind of traits we see not only as failures to live up to legitimate interpersonal ideals but also as dispositions to engage in morally prohibited conduct—e.g. dishonesty. In a slogan to which I will return, properly moralized contempt stands at the nexus of our moral responses to vice and our reactions to prohibited conduct. Consider in this light how common it is for novelists to use the manipulator and liar as examples of contemptible persons. Consider as well how racist, sexist, and heterosexist forms of contempt commonly work. Contempt in these cases appears (and is in fact) directed toward a group of persons held in low esteem simply as persons. Nevertheless, such bigots often try to justify their contempt by speaking in terms of purportedly morally prohibited conduct. For instance, bigots not infrequently regard those toward whom their contempt is directed as under an obligation to be, or remain, hidden from public view. When I was young, a local neo-Nazi group targeted a number of high-profile local Jewish personalities, eventually murdering the radio talk-show figure Alan Berg. They could have easily attacked many more members of the ethnically Jewish community by looking up certain surnames in the phone book. Most of us, after all, were not wary of stalkers in the way that public figures are. The primary objects of these neo-Nazi's contempt, however, were not all persons of Jewish surnames but rather those who dared to be publicly visible (and audible).

Of course, I have argued that avoidance or withdrawal is essential to contempt's normative force. And the neo-Nazis didn't avoid Alan Berg; they killed him. And yet, as I've said, bigots often try to justify their contempt by speaking of how the objects thereof have violated some imagined obligation to remain out of sight and out of earshot. This, coupled with the thought that avoidance is essential to contempt's normative force, actually quite nicely explains Berg's murder, and why he was targeted as opposed to the rest of us less famous Jews of Colorado. The neo-Nazis in question thought Alan Berg had an obligation to "not force" his Jewish ethnicity on other people, and understood this supposed obligation in such a way that even his appearance on the radio was taken to be a violation of it. Then there were the advertisements for the Alan Berg show on TV, radio, and buses. One can almost hear the neo-Nazis shout "You can't avoid that [epithet]! He's everywhere". So they killed him: it was, in their minds, the only way they could avoid him.

It is, in fact, the same mindset that in more recent days has led the "advice", frequently given to gay men and lesbians, "not to force it on other people". That peculiar locution (given what is here at issue) is all too often proffered as advice in contexts that often amounts to a warning never to so much as mention one's partner, or wear a wedding ring. Indeed, this "advice" is sometimes given even when everyone in the relevant community already knows that said person is a gay man or lesbian. Under such circumstances, the thought seems to be that one makes oneself subject to contempt (and one ought to be ashamed) insofar as others find it difficult to avoid interacting with one *as* a gay man or lesbian. In other words, the heterosexist in fact takes simply being a gay man or a lesbian as a shameful matter, but such is the force of moral propriety that even they find themselves contorting matters so as to at least try to describe the object of shame as here the violation of an obligation "not to force 'it' on other people".[24]

I don't doubt that contempt and shame may take other aspects of character as objects. Indeed, I don't doubt that there are cases of global contempt and/or shame. These examples are intended only to show that moralized contempt commonly takes for its object those vices which cannot be understood apart from their tie to morally prohibited conduct, and is often understood as an appropriate attitude only insofar as there is such a tie.

The link between the trait and prohibited conduct that is at issue in these cases is a conceptual link. An ungenerous person, for instance, may or may not as a result engage in morally prohibited conduct insofar as that trait gains expression.

---

[24] Cf. Velleman (2001).

A dishonest person, by definition, does so every time her dishonesty is expressed. I now wish to suggest that contempt is *properly* focused when it takes the latter sort of trait as its object. Again, to use the slogan I earlier mentioned: contempt stands at the nexus of our moral responses to vice and our reactions to prohibited conduct. So conceived, contempt is a morally appropriate response to—and is focused on—traits whose exercise always involves the violation of significant obligations that we have to others within the context of our interactions with them. A person who regularly violates such obligations becomes blameworthy in a special way for she violates a special demand that others properly make of her *character*, namely, that she be the sort of person on whom we may generally and safely rely to meet the legitimate moral demands that may arise within our interpersonal interactions with her. (By "safely" here, I mean that we may rely upon a person in this way without injudiciously imperiling either our own well-being, or the well-being of any other person.) So, for instance, someone who refuses to help a friend in need violates an obligation of friendship and should expect to be met with anger or resentment. Someone who never helps friends in need—a fair-weather friend, as they say—is someone who cannot be *relied upon* as a friend and may well be appropriately greeted with contempt. When I get angry at Bush for lying, I react to him as one who has violated his obligation to be truthful; when I am contemptuous of him, I react to him as someone who has violated his obligation to be the sort of person on whom we may appropriately *rely* to tell the truth.[25] Moralized contempt is a reaction to the violation of this special character-focused obligation.

Seen in this light, contempt's presentation of its object as "to be avoided" makes perfect sense as a reaction—in the Strawsonian sense—to the breach of an obligation, namely, the obligation to be the sort of person on whom we may generally rely to meet legitimate moral demands made of her within the context of our interactions. Avoidance makes sense as a way of holding people accountable for violating this obligation, because we cannot enter into the specifically moral relationships within which we legitimately make demands of one another without relying on one another to meet those demands. For instance, a person who interacts with her friend as one who can never be relied upon in times of need does not, in that respect, interact with her *as a friend*. If I believe that someone cannot be generally relied upon to tell the truth, I will not ask him any questions—certainly not any to which I want an answer; in so doing, I interact with him *as* someone of whom I will not make the most ordinary demands for truth-telling. Moralized contempt says, in short, "I will hold you accountable for not being reliable about meeting your obligations to me or others, by not relying on you". To refuse to rely on another in

---

[25] Whether or not it is appropriate to bear toward another person some form of localized contempt cannot be a matter determined simply by which vices she exhibits. The scope and depth of her vice and the agent's role obligations, for instance, are surely also relevant.

this way necessarily involves withdrawal from or avoidance of those morally laden interactions within which one could not but rely upon that person.

Finally, then, we are in a position to address the complaint about the very standpoint from which contempt is felt. The objection, recall, is as follows. Moral sentiments are, by their very nature, responsibility-conferring. When we are angry or resentful toward someone, we do not simply make a claim about her responsibility; rather, in being angry or resentful, we hold her accountable. To do so is to assume the standpoint of a participant in ethical life—the standpoint of one member of the moral community addressing another; in Darwall's words, we adopt a second-person standpoint. The relevant contrast here is with aesthetic judgments of persons or spectator's judgments about the participants in ethical life. To regard someone as "ugly" I need not think of myself as someone who does, or even could, interact with her.

The standpoint from which properly moralized contempt is felt is *not* spectatorial in this way. Properly moralized contempt presents someone as "to be avoided" with respect to specific sphere(s) of interpersonal interactions—as a potential friend, romantic partner, or authority figure like a president. To regard someone as "to be avoided" with respect to some sphere of interpersonal interactions, I must adopt the standpoint of someone who *could* have those interactions *with* her.[26] This is the standpoint of a participant in ethical life responding to the character and conduct of another participant as such.[27] Part of what makes contempt a participant's attitude is hence one of the very facts about contempt that has made its critics so nervous, namely, the fact that its normative force consists in disengagement.


# 8.3 The sentimentalists' bad attitudes

The only question that remains at this point is whether we have reason to think that the sentimentalists advocated the morally innocent forms of contempt, shame, and

---

[26] This way of stating the point has the advantage of making it clear why moralized contempt is not an "objective" attitude. Consider the difference between the way moralized contempt presents the disloyal, and the way in which a psychiatrist would regard that same person were she a patient. In adopting the attitude of moralized contempt, we hold this person in contempt on account of her disloyalty, regard her as someone who could have those interpersonal relationships in which disloyalty would be particularly problematic, and see her as someone "to be avoided" with respect to those interactions. The psychiatrist, in contrast, insofar as she takes the patient's "disloyalty" as a subject for treatment must regard her not as someone "to be avoided" with respect to those interactions but as *ineligible* for them.

[27] There are respects in which moralized contempt as I have characterized it is not a "second personal" attitude in Darwall's (2006) sense. Most notably, it does not "essentially include an rsvp" (p. 40). My contention is that contempt need not be a second-personal in this sense in order to qualify as a full-fledged reactive attitude.

disdain that I have here identified, rather than the highly objectionable counterparts that have been the subject of so much Kantian critique.

Minimal principles of generosity in interpretation might suggest that the burden of argument has at this point shifted to the critic of sentimentalism to show otherwise. Nevertheless, I want to go further and offer some positive reasons for thinking that the primary forms of contempt, shame, and disdain endorsed by the sentimentalists are morally innocent.

To begin with, all three of our sentimentalists are terribly attentive to the mixed nature of persons' characters. To see this, we need only remind ourselves of Shaftesbury's *Soliloquy* discussions of how one can improve one's character through a kind of "inward anatomy" in which one turns one's own virtuous dispositions against the more vicious ones, of Hume's many discussions in the *Histories* of persons whom he explicitly marks as of mixed character, and of Smith's discussions of the varying effects that persons' social circumstances have on their characters—such as the softening of men's self-command in civilized societies and the deepening of their other virtues. The consistent recognition of the mixed nature of most persons' character across all three sentimentalists ought alone make the possibility of localized contempt appealing to each of them.

Second, I have argued that there are forms of contempt and shame that are peculiar reactive attitudes in that they stand at the nexus of our responses to vice and our responses to morally prohibited conduct. This fits remarkably well with both Shaftesbury and Smith's conception of moral judgment itself, for while both are ultimately concerned with the cultivation of virtues, the standpoint of Smithean and Shaftesburian moral judgment is that of agent and patient in situ, contemplating particular courses of conduct and reactions thereto. The same admittedly cannot so easily be said of Hume's conception of moral judgment. But consider that the following is a complete list (*Histories* included) of all the character traits that Hume indicates anywhere may make one deserving of localized contempt: malice, a total lack of social virtues, dishonesty, iniquity, miserly avarice, infidelity and/or disloyalty, meanness or "abjectness", cowardice with respect to the defense of one's own country, impudence, a disposition to abandon oneself entirely to "dissolute pleasures and womanish superstition" once in the safety of high office, and being at once "indolent, profuse and addicted to low pleasures".[28] And what is the

---

[28] As is now standard practice, citations to David Hume's *A Treatise of Human Nature and Enquiries* are provided for both the recent Fate-Norton and Selby-Bigge editions (*A Treatise of Human Nature*, ed. David Fate-Norton and Mary Norton [Oxford University Press, 2000], and *A Treatise of Human Nature*, ed. L. A. Selby-Bigge, rev. P. H. Nidditch [Oxford: Clarendon Press, 1992]). Citations to Hume's *Treatise* appear as follows: T. book.part.section.paragraph in the Fate-Norton edition; SBN. page number of the Selby-Bigge edition. Citations to Hume's *Enquiry Concerning the Principles of Morals* are similarly provided for both the recent standard editions (*An Enquiry Concerning the Principles of Morals*, ed. Thomas Beauchamp [Oxford: Clarendon Press, 1998], *Enquiries Concerning Human Understanding and Concerning the Principles of Morals*, ed. L. A. Selby-Bigge, rev.

*single* vice that Hume explicitly mentions in the *Treatise* as being deserving of shame? Infidelity (T3.2.12, SBN.571). Virtually every vice on this list fits my earlier, and quite narrow, description of the kind of vices that are the appropriate objects of moralized contempt. That is, nearly every vice on Hume's list can be understood as a disposition to engage in morally prohibited conduct (the only possible exceptions being "miserly avarice", and, depending on one's role obligations and understanding thereof, cowardice with respect to defense of one's own country). To some extent, the same is true of Smith. Perhaps most interestingly, Smith, in the midst of his discussion of justice, in the very section devoted to critique of Hume's purportedly utility-based account of justice, altered the text of *Theory of Moral Sentiments* between the fifth and the sixth editions in order to substitute contempt for the respect-based reactive attitude of resentment.[29] To say that this emendation would make no sense if Smith shared Kant's view of contempt would be putting it mildly. To say that the emendation would make perfect sense if Smith adopted the view of contempt for which I have argued here is, on the other hand, no exaggeration.

Thus, not only do our three sentimentalists have good reason to endorse localized contempt, but all three also have reason to endorse the thought that properly focused and morally appropriate contempt takes as its objects those vices that can be understood as dispositions to morally prohibited conduct. That is, all three have reason to see properly moralized contempt as standing at the nexus of our responses to vice, and our responses to prohibited conduct.

Finally, then, there is the issue of the role of contempt, shame, and disdain as responsibility-conferring attitudes—as attitudes through which we hold one another accountable for our character and conduct. I have proposed that these attitudes make perfect sense as part of an accountability relation, for to adopt such an attitude is to hold someone responsible for not being reliable in some particular sphere of interpersonal relations by not relying on them. Would our three sentimentalists think so? Would they care? Again, I suggest the answer to both questions is yes, though for differing reasons in the case of Shaftesbury and Smith, on the one hand, and Hume, on the other. Shaftesbury and Smith were both explicitly concerned with the role of moral attitudes in conferring responsibility.

---

P. H. Nidditch [Oxford: Clarendon Press, 1992]). Citations to Hume appear as follows: EPM.section. part (where appropriate).paragraph in the Beauchamp edition, SBN.page number in the Selby-Bigge edition. See, e.g., HENG Vol. 5 Ch 59 p. 537; EPM.2.1.3, SBN 177; EPM.6.1.13, SBN 238; *Essays*, p. 480; EPM.7.10&n.42, SBN 253&n; EPM Appendix 4.5, SBN 315; HENG Vol. 2 Ch 16 p. 253; HENG Vol.1.Ch. 3 p. 110, HENG Vol. 1 Ch 6 p. 258; HENG Vol. 2 Ch 17 p. 305.

[29] "When the happiness or misery of others depends in any respect upon our conduct, we dare not, as self-love might suggest to us, prefer the interest of one to that of many. The man within immediately calls to us, that we value ourselves too much and other people too little, and that, by doing so, we render ourselves the proper object of the contempt and indignation of our brethren" (TMS III.3.5, p. 138; NB: in editions 2–5, Smith had "resentment and indignation" in the final line of this passage for which he substituted "*contempt* and indignation in the 6th edition).

Indeed, Smith explicitly treats this responsibility-conferring power as the distinguishing feature of moral sentiments (as opposed to affective attitudes that are merely aesthetic) and, rightly or wrongly, criticizes what he takes to be the aestheticized nature of the Humean moral sentiments on just this score. "So far as the sentiment of approbation arises from the perception of this beauty or utility", writes Smith, "it has no reference of any kind to the sentiments of others", and as such cannot make us "exult from the notion of deserving reward in the one case, nor tremble from the suspicion of meriting punishment in the other". (*TMS*, IV.2.12, p. 192) Without conceding that Smith was right in so criticizing the Humean moral sentiments, we can certainly agree that Hume does not speak at length of accountability relations (to put it mildly). But what Hume does do is lay out a criteria of virtue according to which the virtues just are those traits that make a person especially well suited for some particular sphere of interpersonal interactions, and the vices are those traits that make a person especially ill suited for some particular sphere of interpersonal interactions.[30] To move to my claim about when contempt and shame are morally appropriate responses to vice, one need only add the thought that one way of being egregiously ill suited for a particular sphere of interpersonal interactions is to be the sort on whom one may not reasonably *rely* to meet legitimate moral demands made of her within the context of those interactions.

# 8.4 CONCLUDING NOTIONS

It is worth remembering at this point that the story which has been my target in this chapter is one on which contempt, shame, and disdain have their natural home in certain moral theories insofar as those theories are sentimentalist, virtue-centered, and spectatorial. Without rehearsing territory covered, it should by now be obvious how the central assumptions of this popular story are woven into the objections commonly proffered against the "shame-centered" attitudes. But notice: the forms of contempt, shame, and disdain that I have here defended against the canonical objections, and which I have contended are forms of the "shame-centered" attitudes the sentimentalists had reason to endorse, are neither "virtue-centered" nor "spectatorial" in any interesting respect. While the forms of contempt, shame, and disdain that I have defended do take character traits as their objects, the character traits in question are ones which are properly

---

[30] I argue for this interpretation of the Humean criteria of virtue in "Sympathy and Hume's Spectator-Centered Theory of Virtue" (2008).

understood as dispositions to prohibited conduct—precisely the point at which the dividing line between acts and traits ceases to be of much philosophical interest. And the attitudes in question are certainly not "spectatorial" for, as I have argued, they are attitudes that are necessarily felt from the standpoint of a participant in ethical life who views another participant (or herself, in the case of shame) as "to be avoided". Are these particularly "sentimentalist" attitudes? Well, they are affective, so, to be sure, they are sentiments. But if that alone makes an attitude the special province of the sentimentalists, it is not the sentimentalists who are in trouble.

## References

### Primary:

HUME, DAVID (1983). *The History of England in Six Volumes* (Indianapolis: Liberty Press).
—— (1990). *Essays: Moral, Political and Literary*, ed. Eugene Miller (Indianapolis: Liberty Press).
—— (1992a). *Enquiries Concerning Human Understanding and Concerning the Principles of Morals*, ed. L. A. Selby-Bigge, revised by P. H. Nidditch (Oxford: Clarendon Press).
—— (1992b). *A Treatise of Human Nature*, ed. L. A. Selby-Bigge, revised by P. H. Nidditch (Oxford: Clarendon Press).
—— (1998). *An Enquiry Concerning the Principles of Morals*, ed. Thomas Beauchamp (Oxford: Clarendon Press).
—— (2000). *A Treatise of Human Nature*, eds. David Fate Norton and Mary Norton (Oxford: Oxford University Press).
KANT, IMMANUEL (1797/1983). *Metaphysical Principles of Virtue in Kant's Ethical Philosophy*, tr. James W. Willington, Introduction by Warner A. Wick (Indianapolis: Hackett).
SHAFTESBURY, ANTHONY ASHLEY COOPER (1999). *Characteristics, of Men, Manners, and Times*, ed. Lawrence Klein (Cambridge: Cambridge University Press).
SMITH, ADAM (1976). *A Theory of Moral Sentiments*. eds. D. D. Raphael and A. L. Macfie (Indianapolis: Liberty Classics).

### Secondary:

ABRAMSON, KATE (2008). "Sympathy and Hume's Spectator-Centered Theory of Virtue", *A Companion to Hume* (Malden: Blackwell): 240–56.
ANNAS, JULIA (1993). *The Morality of Happiness* (Oxford: Oxford University Press).
BAIER, ANNETTE (1994). "Moralism and Cruelty", *Moral Prejudices* (Cambridge, MA: Harvard University Press).
BELL, MACALESTER (2005). "A Woman's Scorn: Toward a Feminist Defense of Contempt as a Moral Emotion", *Hypatia* 20.4 (Fall): 80–93.
BLACKBURN, SIMON (1998). *Ruling Passions* (Oxford: Clarendon Press).
DARWALL, STEPHEN (1999). "Sympathetic Liberalism", *Philosophy and Public Affairs* 28: 139–64.

—— (2006). *The Second Person Standpoint* (Cambridge, MA: Harvard University Press).

GIBBARD, ALAN (1990). *Wise Choices Apt Feelings* (Cambridge, MA: Harvard University Press).

HAMPTON, JEAN (1988). *Forgiveness and Mercy* (Cambridge, MA: Cambridge University Press).

HILL, THOMAS (2000). *Respect, Pluralism and Justice: Kantian Perspectives* (New York: Oxford).

KORSGAARD, CHRISTINE (1996). *Creating the Kingdom of Ends* (Cambridge, MA: Cambridge University Press).

MASON, MICHELLE (2003). "Contempt as a Moral Attitude", *Ethics* 113: 234–72.

MILLER, WILLIAM IAN (1997). *The Anatomy of Disgust* (Cambridge, MA: Harvard University, Press).

MURPHY, JEFFRIE G. and JEAN HAMPTON (1988). *Forgiveness and Mercy* (Cambridge: Cambridge University Press).

NATIONAL ORGANIZATION FOR WOMEN, "Statement of NOW President Patricia Ireland in Response to Clinton Testimony", 17 August 1998. http://www.now.org/press/08–98/08–17–98.html. (accessed 8 July 2009).

NUSSBAUM, MARTHA (2004). *Hiding From Humanity* (Princeton: Princeton University).

STRAWSON, P. F. (1982). "Freedom and Resentment", in Watson ed. *Free Will* (Oxford: Oxford University Press).

TAYLOR, GABRIELE (1985). *Pride, Shame and Guilt* (Oxford: Clarendon).

VELLEMAN, DAVID J. (2001). "The Genesis of Shame", *Philosophy and Public Affairs* 30.3: 27–52.

WALLACE, R. J. (1996). *Responsibility and the Moral Sentiments* (Cambridge: Harvard University Press).

WILLIAMS, BERNARD (1993). *Shame and Necessity* (Berkeley: University of California Press).

CHAPTER 9

# EMOTIONS IN HEIDEGGER AND SARTRE

## ANTHONY HATZIMOYSIS

## 9.1 EMOTIONS IN PHENOMENOLOGY

Phenomenology has done more than any other school of thought for bringing emotions to the forefront of philosophical enquiry. The main reason for the interest shown by phenomenologists in the nature of emotions is perhaps not easily discernible. It might be thought that phenomenologists focus on emotions because the felt quality of most emotional states renders them a privileged object of enquiry into the phenomenal properties of human experience. That view, in its turn, might lead one to think that phenomenologists attend to emotional experience for its highly subjective character. On the contrary, it is the ability of emotions to engage with reality that makes them crucial for phenomenological analysis. Emotional experience is an opening to the salient features of a situation; undergoing an emotion is a way—and, for some phenomenologists, the principal way—in which the world manifests itself to us. The exact character of that manifestation will be the main topic of discussion in the present chapter.

We shall look at the two major accounts of the way in which that manifestation is structured. The first account is due to Martin Heidegger, and the second is articulated in the writings of Jean-Paul Sartre. The choice of focus on Heidegger and Sartre is guided by several considerations. They treat emotion as a distinct topic of philosophical research rather than as a side-issue upon which a ready-made theory of mind is to be applied. They are both primarily interested in the nature of emotion in general rather than in the particularities of a few cases. They both formulate important challenges to the picture of emotions as 'blind' or 'ineffable feelings', closed within themselves. Finally, it is those two phenomenologists who have attracted most interest in recent years—and for good reason since it is in their work that we find not only perceptive answers to some classic questions but also a new way of approaching emotional phenomena.

The theories articulated by Heidegger and Sartre build upon a view of emotional states variously defended by Brentano, Husserl, and Scheler, and further developed by Merleau-Ponty, Levinas, and Ricoeur. Among the several representatives of that tradition in the English-speaking world, one should not fail to mention Robert Solomon, whose rich and insightful work in that area was crucial in bringing phenomenological theories to the attention of contemporary philosophers of emotion.

In the next section I identify some of the difficulties in making proper sense of Heidegger's approach to affective phenomena. Then I offer a reading, which, in my opinion, saves most of the textual phenomena, while bringing to the fore the significance of Heidegger's account not just for the analysis of emotion but for the philosophical conception of self-awareness as a whole. In section 9.3 I introduce Sartre's view of affectivity, and in sections 9.4 and 9.5 I reconstruct his phenomenologically rich account of emotional activity.

The choice of presentation for the work of two major philosophers poses its own methodological concerns. Some scholars might have opted for an overview of their system; my presentation, on the other hand, is based on a rather close reading of specific paragraphs. We shall focus on parts of the philosophical texts that have rightly exerted considerable influence in analytic discussions over the nature of emotional phenomena.

# 9.2 READING HEIDEGGER ON EMOTION:
## SOME DIFFICULTIES

Heidegger's writings share with some classic texts of German philosophy the curious fate of being judged very influential, yet highly obscure. Among the influential points attributed to his work we should include the claims that: (i) in affective experience we are somehow attuned to the world; (ii) moods are, in some sense, prior to emotions; (iii) we are always in some mood; and (iv) there is a small set of fundamental moods, attendance to which reveals important truths about human existence.

Those claims purport to summarize the theory of emotion put forward in *Being and Time* (1927). In the central sections of that work Heidegger presents an account which brings together points pursued in some of his earlier work and which is elaborated upon, without major changes, in most of his subsequent writings.[1] Yet a careful reading of those three sections appears to generate more questions than answers. I would like to take the standpoint of someone who comes to that text for the first time, and, equipped with some basic understanding of current work on emotions, wishes to make sense of what they read, especially in the crucial §29, of Heidegger's *magnum opus*.

The common modern German terms for emotion, *Gefühl* and *Affekt*, are used by Heidegger sparingly, and mainly in the course of clarifying his attitude towards the views of his philosophical predecessors. Instead, in *Being and Time* we read mostly about *Stimmung*, a term often translated as 'mood'. It might be thought that this is not a real issue; it simply indicates that, when it comes to the details of his account, Heidegger's concern is not with emotion proper but with moods. However, this reasonable suggestion does not offer an easy way out of our interpretative difficulties. Consider, for a start, the fact that when Heidegger attempts to illustrate his view of moods, he discusses *fear*, which has always been taken as a paradigmatic case of *emotion*. It would not help either to think that, for Heidegger, the traditional taxonomy of affective states has got it wrong, and that fear is a mood and not an emotion, since Heidegger attributes to fear precisely those characteristics (specificity of intentional target, limited duration of relevant experience, explicit concern about our well-being in view of an identifiable threat), which mark fear not as a mood but as an emotion.

We may see our way through this issue by examining a term Heidegger devises for referring to the relevant phenomena: *Befindlichkeit*.[2] Derived from the reflexive verb *sich befinden*, which in the present context means 'to find oneself' (in a place, or a situation), *Befindlichkeit* can at a first approximation be translated by the phrase 'that one is found' (in a place, or a situation).[3] We might thus be helped in our reading by considering both moods and emotions as exemplifications of the

---

[1] Of particular importance are Sections 28, 29, 30, and 40. Heidegger's account of emotion is clarified or partly elaborated in subsequent writings, without, in my view, undergoing any major changes. Some of the new claims Heidegger brings into his discussion concern mainly his original and insightful interpretation of other philosophers' views, especially those of Plato and Nietzsche; cf. his remarks in *Was ist das-die Philosophie?* (Pfullingen: Günther Neske, 1956) and in *Nietzsche: Der Wille zur Macht als Kunst* (Frankfurt a.M.: Klostermann, 1984), pp. 53–9.

[2] 'Fear', as Heidegger often repeats, 'is a mode of *Befindlichkeit*'. See *Being and Time* (Oxford: Blackwell, 1962), a translation by John Macquarrie and Edward Robinson of *Sein und Zeit* (Tübingen: Max Niemeyer Verlag)—henceforth cited as *SZ*—pp. 134, 140.

[3] The passive grammatical construction is intended to convey the sense of being thrown into being in a place or a situation, a phenomenon aptly expressed by Heidegger's notion of *Geworfenheit*.

overarching phenomenon of finding ourselves in some situation. This interpretation sounds more plausible if we connect Heidegger's technical noun with the colloquial phrase 'Wie befinden Sie sich?', which can be translated as 'How do you find yourself?', or more naturally as 'How do you feel?', while an answer to that question expresses 'wie einem ist und wird', 'how one is [or feels], and how one becomes [to be or to feel]'.[4]

However, the fusing together of the meanings implicit in colloquial phrases might make us suspect that what we are offered is not a secure bridging of, but a quick glossing over the difference between 'how one is' and 'how one feels that one is'. We may attempt to connect the two by invoking a psychological process that links one's *cognition* or, at least, one's *perception* of 'how one is' to the arising of a *feeling* about that which is cognized or perceived.

Going down that route, however, will take us even further away from Heidegger's programme. On the one hand, the appeal to such a psychological process is at odds with Heidegger's statement that *Befindlichkeit* is precisely not just another psychological state—next to cognition, presentation, or volition—a state to be added or subtracted from our mental economy; indeed, his ardent critique of the mind–world dichotomy entails that, for Heidegger, *Befindlichkeit* is anything but a 'state of mind'.

On the other hand, neither *Befindlichkeit* nor *Stimmung* should be thought of as picking out something that arises *after* cognitive or perceptual awareness: the 'affective' is either fully fused (and, thus, *simultaneous*) with the cognitive and the perceptual, or arises *prior* to them.[5] Heidegger expresses the former point by asserting that the 'affective' is involved in our perceptual and cognitive engagement with the world, present in even our most abstract intellectual endeavours: 'even the purest theory has not left all *Stimmungen* behind it' (*SZ* 138). Heidegger's point, though, is not identical to a similar-sounding claim, popular both within and outside phenomenological circles, that the awareness of an object brings with it an affective quality. His claim is not that, in seeing or intuiting something, we (simultaneously) experience certain feelings or passions. Rather, his view is that unless we approach a thing with a certain *Stimmung*, that thing will not reveal itself to us as it really is.[6] That is certainly an important claim, but some care is needed in how we interpret its role in the present context. Heidegger is not arguing for that

---

[4] *SZ* 134: 'wie einem ist und wird': literally, 'how it is and becomes for one'.

[5] I place the 'affective' in quotes because it has not been specified, yet, in what sense *Befindlichkeit* and *Stimmung* should count as affective phenomena.

[6] A point that applies equally to our scientific and philosophical inquiries, as noted by Aristotle in Book A of his *Metaphysics*, and quoted approvingly by Heidegger: '[the thing will] not show itself purely as it looks unless the *theoretical look* lets it come towards us in a *tranquil* tarrying alongside . . . , in *comfort* and *recreation*' (*SZ* 138). The terms in italics are given in Greek in Heidegger's free rendering of Aristotle's text: they are all taken from *Met* A2, 982b 22.

claim, but from it: he simply asserts that this is how things are, invoking Aristotle's authority in its support.

It might be retorted that Heidegger does not need to argue for a claim that merely describes the affective dimension of intellectual activity. After all, what sort of phenomenologist would Heidegger be (the retort goes), if he did not take ordinary experience at face value? The problem is that, at other parts of that text, Heidegger appears to do anything but accept the verdict of the 'average everyday understanding' of the relevant phenomena. In the second paragraph of §29, for instance, he lists a number of possible counterexamples to his thesis that one is always already in a mood (*ist gestimmt*), but he then promptly dismisses them: 'the undisturbed equanimity', as well as 'the pallid, evenly balanced lack of mood [*Ungestimmtheit*]' are in fact...moods (*SZ* 134). A different approach to Heidegger's text is needed, if we are to save it from apparent inconsistencies of this kind.

Note that these difficulties will not go away just by replacing the standard translation of *Stimmung* as 'mood' with that of 'attunement'. The etymological analysis of the word indicates that *Stimmung* can mean the tuning of an instrument. It may thus be reasonably suggested that the previous objections to Heidegger's account of *Stimmung* miss their mark, given that what Heidegger is proposing is not an account of moods, but of the very different phenomenon of somehow 'being attuned to' the world in general, or with the particular situation in which one is found. That reading is certainly closer to the spirit of Heidegger's approach. However, it cannot, by itself, resolve some of the interpretative difficulties already encountered, while it gives rise to some new ones. The above-mentioned, apparent inconsistency remains: what the phenomenology of ordinary experience presents as being *ungestimmt* ('being out of tune', according to the new translation) is, according to Heidegger, a case of *Gestimmtsein* ('being attuned'). Secondly, the claim about the alleged fusion of *Stimmung* with every instance of cognitive or perceptual awareness increases in plausibility, but also loses a lot of its significance. What Heidegger seems to be saying is that someone cannot see some thing as it is, and for what it is (or, to use the phenomenologically correct turn of phrase: someone cannot let some thing manifest itself to them, as it is and for what it is), unless someone is somehow attuned to that thing. That claim sounds correct (at least to my philosophical ear), but the worry is that part of its appeal is that it is a claim so vague that one might appear foolish to deny it. That vagueness is I think due to two reasons. First, the claim is not argued for but is blandly asserted (invoking, as already mentioned, Aristotle's authority). Secondly, it is not explicated how or why the so-called 'attunement' relates to the topic of our discussion: the nature of emotional phenomena. The expression 'being attuned to' (the world etc.) does not on its own indicate how it bears upon anything that might fall under the heading of affect. At the very least, the attempted connection between attunement and emotion leaves open four very different options: (i) emotion and attunement are two independent occurrences, but the presence of the former facilitates the success of the latter; (ii) emotion is dependent on attunement in the sense that one is not able to experience an emotion about anything unless one is attuned to that thing (where: 'attuned to' is not emotionally loaded, on pain of circularity); (iii) being attuned is dependent on emotion, in the sense that unless one is emotionally engaged with some thing, one cannot 'tune oneself to' that thing (whatever that 'tuning oneself to' might mean); (iv) 'emotion' and 'attunement' denote exactly the same occurrence: what Heidegger's analysis aims to show is that what traditionally goes under the name of 'emotion' is really the attunement of oneself to the world.

The last point is of course the most interesting. Unfortunately, though, in the absence of a proper cashing out of the 'attunement' metaphor, it is also the hardest to defend. In the next section we shall tread a different path through the Heideggerian maze with the hope of reaching a better understanding of *Befindlichkeit*, as well as a clearer view of the motivation for the attempted identification of *Stimmungen* with emotions.

## 9.3  HEIDEGGER ON EMOTIONAL AWARENESS OF BEING IN THE WORLD

As you might have noticed, our presentation has not yet employed Heidegger's most famous term: *Dasein*. Let us see how a basic grasp of that notion might relieve some of the interpretative difficulties identified in the previous section.

*Dasein* is translated as 'being-there', but *Dasein*'s 'there' is inclusive of, not contrasted to, its 'here'. The prefix *Da* points both to a 'here' (*Hier*) and to a 'yonder' (*Dort*) (*SZ* 132). Depending on the analytical context, Heidegger switches emphasis from the 'yonder' to the 'here', while constantly reminding us that *Dasein* is not a thing for which 'here' and 'yonder' refer to two independently existing points in absolute space but a totality whose 'here' and 'yonder' are two intrinsically related aspects, given Dasein's way of existing as directed towards 'ready-to-hand things', which are encountered 'within-the-world', and with which *Dasein* is constantly engaged.[7]

Heidegger proceeds from these basic observations to make a twofold claim, a claim that, in Heidegger's characteristic manner, is both transcendental and phenomenological. As a transcendental claim, it states the condition for the possibility of something—in this case, the possibility of 'here' and 'yonder'. As a

---

[7] This basic analysis applies to the relation of 'concern' characteristic of 'being alongside the world'; 'solicitude' has a different structure in so far as it denotes Dasein's relation to being-with (others).

phenomenological claim, it identifies that condition with a phenomenon, i.e., with something that 'shows-itself-in-itself' (*SZ* 31). Heidegger's claim is that 'here' and 'yonder' are possible because there is a being whose way of existing discloses simultaneously the 'being-yonder' of the world, and the 'being-here' of itself. That being has to be an entity whose way of being is necessarily that of 'being-there'. And that, of course, is *Dasein*: the being whose essence is that of being-in-the-world.[8]

The question now arises as to what exactly that 'being-in' consists in. It would be misleading, according to Heidegger, to present the 'being-in' as what may come in 'between', and thus conjoin, two self-subsistent entities; or even to think of it as the contingent agreement of, for example, an immaterial subject, and a material object. It would be no less false to conceive of 'being-in' as the extant relationship of two differently sized present-at-hand things, e.g. of a smaller box *being-inside* a bigger box. But if *Dasein*'s 'being-in' the world is neither a 'between' (*Zwischen*), nor an agreement (*convenientia*), nor insideness (*Inwedigkeit*), what is it? The brief answer is: *Befindlichkeit*. Or, more precisely, 'being-in-the-world' is Dasein's mode of existing, as that mode is disclosed in the phenomenon of *Befindlichkeit*.

The importance of *Befindlichkeit* for the ontology of *Dasein* is hard to miss. What is less evident, though, is why anyone would think that that notion is relevant to a philosophical enquiry into human emotions. Part of the explanation, I think, is found in the origins of that notion in Heidegger's reading of a classic text in emotion theory. In the summer of 1924, Heidegger gave a series of lectures on Aristotle's philosophy, addressing the pioneering view of emotions expounded in the Second Book of *Rhetoric*. The Aristotelian analysis pays special attention to how an audience is *disposed towards* (διάκειται προς) the speaker. The affective disposition [διάθεσις] is one of the senses of 'Stimmung', when that word is used to highlight one's tendency or readiness to engage with something or someone emotionally, not unlike the English term 'mood' employed with a subjunctive object, e.g., 'I am in the mood for love' (as the song would have it). That dimension of one's affective engagement with beings encountered within the world, in general, is underplayed in the *Aristotle Lectures* but is brought to the fore in *Being and Time*. However, what is really significant for our enquiry is that when Heidegger discusses the famous paragraphs on the *passions* (πάθη, *Affekte*) experienced by the audience in attending to the orator's speech, Heidegger's term of choice for rendering both πάθη and διαθέσεις is *Befindlichkeit*.[9]

We have so far seen, very briefly, some of the ontological grounds for bringing *Befindlichkeit* into the analysis of *Dasein*, as well as some philological evidence for

---

[8] 'The entity which is essentially constituted by being-in-the-world is itself in every case its there' (*SZ* 132).

[9] *Grundbegriffe der aritotelischen Philosophie*, Gesamtausgabe, vol. 18, edited by M. Michalski. Frankfurt a.M.: Klostermann, 2002; see especially the discussion on pages 176–7.

Heidegger's penchant for that notion when he discusses affective phenomena. But are there any good grounds for connecting the two? Why would a notion expressive of affective experiences be the key to the ontological puzzle over the awareness of being-in-the-world? Let me reconstruct part of the Heideggerian response to our query.

Heidegger's enquiry is a search for the meaning of being. He wants to understand how being itself can be revealed, outside the conceptual strictures of scholastic metaphysics. Among the various notions he employs for characterizing *Dasein's* coming to the truth of being, it is 'disclosure' (*Erschlossenheit*) that he seems to reserve for the bringing to light of the being of the world itself, as distinguished from the appearing of inworldly entities, which 'manifest themselves' or 'show-themselves-in-themselves'.[10] More precisely, Heidegger is at pains to identify a phenomenon of disclosure which meets the following desiderata: (i) it discloses the *Da* of *Dasein*, the fact of its *being-in-the world*; (ii) it discloses entities encountered *within-the-world*; (iii) (i) and (ii) are achieved simultaneously, in equal measure, and with no metaphysical priority, i.e., 'equiprimordially'; (iv) the disclosure is not deliberately brought about, it is not the outcome of voluntary effort, but it is something that 'befalls' *Dasein*; (v) it is a disclosure that should be sharply contrasted with any kind of cognition or observation, including 'theoretical intuition', 'perceptual understanding', 'beholding', 'looking at', 'staring', 'reflecting', 'cognizing', and 'knowing'.[11]

According to Heidegger, the awareness enabled by affective experience meets all of the above desiderata. Consider the main example he presents for illustrating his case: 'fearing about something, as being afraid in the face of something, always discloses equiprimordially entities within-the-world and being-in—the former as threatening and the latter as threatened. Fear is a mode of *Befindlichkeit*' (*SZ* 141).

As that quotation makes clear, *fearing* meets conditions (i), (ii), and (iii). It also meets condition (iv) in the sense that one does not, *normally*, exert special effort to become afraid of something one does not consider fearful: the emotion 'befalls', 'comes' or 'arises into' one, when one encounters the fearful. Not all emotions follow the same pattern of arousal. Yet, none, according to Heidegger, make us aware of things in the world through a two-step programme of first cognizing a neutral entity, and then (voluntary, deliberately, or otherwise) projecting onto it a

---

[10]  (*SZ* 132) 'Unhidness', 'Uncoveredness', and 'Openness' are some of the notions Heidegger uses in discussing being's self-revelation. With a direct allusion to a traditional philosophical metaphor, Heidegger invokes yet another term, *Lichtung*, to illustrate how *Dasein* itself 'is "illuminated" [erleuchtet], meaning: lightened [gelichtet] in itself as being-in-the-world, not by another entity but in being itself the lightening' (*SZ* 133). In what follows, for the sake of brevity, I reconstruct Heidegger's reasoning employing only the core term 'disclosure', instead of the variety of similar (though, by no means identical) technical terms.

[11]  Sections 28, 29, and 30 abound with Heidegger's warnings against the confusion of *Befindlichkeit* or *Stimmungen* with any kind of cognitive or perceptual awareness, but see especially *SZ* 134, 136.

psychical colouring. In fearing, for example, 'we do not first ascertain a future evil and then fear it. But neither does fearing first take notice of what is drawing close; it discovers it beforehand in its fearsomeness' (*SZ* 141).

And so we reach what in my view is the most crucial condition: that the disclosure effected in emotional experience is not of a cognitive or observational nature. Here we need to distinguish among different levels of analysis. The obvious way of interpreting the claim that condition (v) is met by emotional experience is to contend that, as a matter of phenomenological fact, emotions disclose in a non-cognitive, non-observational manner. That contention can be further substantiated by the ontological claim that, in emotional experience, ourselves and the world are disclosed in a way that *precedes* and *grounds* any perceptual, theoretical, reflective, or cognitive grasp of both the 'here' of ourself and the 'yonder' of the world (*SZ* 134–6). 'Fearing', for instance, 'as a slumbering possibility of the affectively found [befindlichen] being-in-the-world, . . . has already disclosed the world, in that out of it something like the fearsome may come close [to us]' (*SZ* 141, tr. changed).

However, Heidegger's extant discussion of those issues seems to create a serious problem that appears to slip easily under the scholarly radar. Let me explicate what the problem is by focusing on the 'here' side of emotional disclosure.

For Heidegger's argumentation to work, his claim should be not only that the emotional awareness of ourself is non-cognitive, pre-reflective, or non-observational but also that the non-cognitive, pre-reflective, non-observational awareness of ourself is emotional. Heidegger makes a case (in my view, a very strong case) for the claim that emotions disclose *Dasein* to *itself* as being-in-the-world, in a pre-reflective etc. manner. To identify, though, *Dasein's* pre-reflective etc. disclosure with emotional experience, we need a case to be made for the claim that *Dasein* cannot pre-reflectively etc. be disclosed to itself, unless it is in some emotional mode. And that is something for which Heidegger's text does not seem to provide adequately.

It is worth revisiting, at this point, an issue we touched upon at the beginning of our presentation. Section 29 opens with a declaration of the ever-present *Stimmungen* in our life. Heidegger maintains that apparent counterexamples to his thesis should be dismissed. We can now see why Heidegger is adamant on this issue: dispensing with *Stimmung* would amount to no less than losing our primordial (non-observational, pre-reflective, first-person) awareness of our own self. The stakes on this issue are sufficiently high for Heidegger to momentarily slip into a less than perfect attention to terminological detail. Recall that a counterexample to his approach is that there is such a thing as 'pallid, evenly balanced lack of mood [Ungestimmtheit], which is . . . not to be mistaken for a bad mood [Verstimmung], is far from nothing at all. Rather'—the standard English translation continues—'it is in *this* that Dasein becomes satiated with itself. Being has become manifest as a burden' (*SZ* 134). The translation makes it sound as if it is the 'lack of mood' which is revealing of the being as a burden. The original, though, clarifies that it is 'bad mood' that offers that manifestation: 'Das Sein des Da ist in solcher Verstimmung [not: Ungestimmung] als Last offenbar werden'.[12]

Perhaps one should not dwell on such terminological issues. What matters is that Heidegger's illuminating discussion of the disclosive capacity of emotional experience in all its varied forms does not as such preclude the availability of being attuned to oneself and to the world in an emotion-free mode.

The belief in the availability of a pre-reflective, non-observational, yet emotion-free first-person awareness of oneself as being (located) in the world is by no means antithetical to a phenomenological enquiry. After all, it is what Husserl argued for, in exhaustive detail. It is also the view of a phenomenologist who, despite his stated admiration for Heidegger, presents a methodologically more conservative, or, at least, less ambitious theory of emotional awareness. Sartre did not dig as deep as Heidegger into the foundations of being; neither did he grapple with some borderline cases of emotional experience, with the intellectual fortitude that characterizes Heidegger's discussion of one's awareness of one's own being and non-being. Yet Sartre offers something that was to prove crucial in all subsequent discussions of emotion: that 'action' is no less an important aspect of emotional phenomena than 'passion'.

## 9.4 SARTRE ON EMOTIONAL CONSCIOUSNESS

Emotions make their appearance in every single philosophical text written by Sartre. Beginning with his seminal paper on Intentionality,[13] and moving through his pioneering study of the Ego,[14] the treatises on Imagination,[15] and his *magnum opus* in the ontology of our concrete relations with others,[16] through his rich observations in the posthumously published *Notebooks on Ethics*,[17] and concluding

---

[12] Literally: 'The being of there becomes manifest as a burden in such bad mood.'

[13] 'Intentionality: A Fundamental idea in Husserl's Phenomenology' *Journal of the British Society of Phenomenology* 1(2) (1970): 4–5, a translation by Joseph Fell of 'Une Idée fondamentale de la phénoménologie de Husserl: l'intentionnalité', in *Situations I* (Paris; Gallimard, 1947), pp. 31–4.

[14] *The Transcendence of the Ego* (London: Routledge: 2004), a translation by Andrew Brown of *La Transcendance de l'Ego* (Paris: Librairie Philosophique, 1988)—first published in *Recherches Philosophiques* (1937).

[15] *L'Imagination* (Paris: Presses Universitaires de France, 1936) and esp. Parts III and IV of *The Imaginary: A Phenomenological Psychology of the Imagination* (London: Routledge, 2004), a translation by Jonathan Webber of *L'Imaginaire: psychologie phénoménologique de l'imagination* (Paris: Gallimard, 1940).

[16] *Being and Nothingness* (Oxon: Routledge Classics, 2003), a translation by Hazel Barnes of *L'Être et le néant: Essai d'ontologie phénoménologique* (Paris: Gallimard, 1943); see Part III, 3.

[17] *Cahiers pour une morale* (Paris: Gallimard, 1983).

with his voluminous biography of Flaubert,[18] Sartre observed with an unflinching eye the moving generosity and the common duplicity, the existential revelations and the mundane self-deceptions, all the highs and the lows of our emotional involvement with each other. His most famous book, after all, illuminates the epistemic, normative, and ontological aspects of a unique affective experience: *nausea*. It is not on that novel, however, that we shall focus here but on a short, and tightly argued, treatise published in the same year.[19] The *Sketch* presents a detailed critique of subjectivist feeling-based theories, and challenges some reductionist versions of cognitivist and psychoanalytic models of emotion.[20] The book's influence, though, lies not in its critical agenda but in its positive programme, which often, in the secondary literature, gets summarized with the catch phrase 'emotions are actions'. We shall see that this way of presenting the Sartrean view is inaccurate, since—selective readings to the contrary—Sartre actually denies that emotions are actions. The analysis of these issues requires a clear grasp of the Sartrean conception of psychological states. I shall accordingly begin with a brief account of the Sartrean view of those states. I will then present Sartre's views on the relation between emotional awareness and behavioural reaction, and shall conclude with his interpretation of action out of emotion. Our discussion will be informed by the Sartrean idea that the philosophical analysis of emotions should enquire about what an emotion *signifies*: what it indicates for the life of the person that experiences the emotion, and which aspect of reality is indicated when the person is emotionally directed towards the world.

Sartre maintains that affective states, such as boredom, jealousy, or hatred, appear as psychical objects when we reflect on our past mental or physical activities. Take for instance the relation between the feeling of revulsion and the state of hatred. Feeling revulsion at the sight of a particular person is an experience absorbed with the detestable qualities of that individual. Experienced as a direct engagement with the world, the upheaval of a particular feeling towards someone marks the intentional connection between my consciousness and that being. The feeling of revulsion is a conscious activity occurring instantaneously or through a limited time span, and one that meets Sartre's absolute principle of consciousness, i.e., to *be* an instant of revulsion and to *feel* as an instant of revulsion are one and the same thing: there is no gap within the 'consciousness (of) revulsion' between appearing and being.[21]

The genitive construction 'consciousness *of* revulsion' might give the impression that, in the course of ordinary encounter with the world, there is a thing called

[18] *L'Idiot de la famille. Gustave Flaubert de 1821 à 1857*, t. I-III (Paris: Gallimard, 1971–72).

[19] 1938 sees the publication of both Sartre's 'sketch' on emotion, in the series *Actualités Scientifiques Industrielles*, and of his first novel with *Librairie Gallimard*.

[20] *Sketch for a Theory of the Emotions* (London: Routledge Classics, 2004) – henceforth cited as *STE* – a translation by Philip Mariet of *Esquisse d'une théorie des emotions* (Paris: Hermann).

[21] Cf. *Transcendence of the Ego*, pp. 22–3.

'revulsion' to which consciousness pays attention. That view is false. Revulsion is not an object for consciousness; it is consciousness itself as it experiences its intentional object. The genitive participle 'of' is put in brackets so as to signal that the grammatical construction purports to characterize what a particular consciousness *is* (namely, revulsion), not what the consciousness is *about* (its intentional object, the particular person who just started addressing a political rally). Similarly, the locution 'consciousness (of) despair' denotes, in the present context, a 'despairing consciousness'—*how* an agent experiences a world where all possibilities are barred—not that his experience is *about* a certain object called 'despair'.

However, if we were to move from the plane of emotional encounter with the world to the higher level of reflection upon that type of encounter, our consciousness could take in its purview the emotion-consciousness. At that level, revulsion or other emotional experiences would themselves become an object of conscious examination and, thus, the locution 'consciousness of revulsion' (free of internal brackets) would denote the second-order activity of consciousness focusing upon its conscious activities. The confusion of the first-order level of the (revulsive, despairing, or joyous) experience of the world, with the second-order level of the consideration of such an experience by the (reflective) subject is a major source of difficulties for the adequate analysis of emotional phenomena.

The confusion of levels is itself the outcome of two kinds of pressure. The first stems from the unobjectionable claim that people are aware of having various emotions. That claim is taken to entail that what people are conscious of during an emotional episode is their own feelings. However, the latter claim is much stronger than, and it does not on its own follow upon, the former claim. To effect the transition one should draw on the dubitable principle that one cannot be aware of x, unless x is the explicit object of conscious attention. Sartre repudiates this view on two grounds. On the one hand, it falls foul of the phenomenology of conscious experience. On the other hand, it entangles consciousness in an infinite recurrence of reflective acts on pain of rendering conscious experience unconscious. The issues raised by the last contention cannot be taken up here.[22] Suffice it to note that consciousness' (non-reflective) awareness of itself need not be cast in conceptual terms. Hence, it is not a consequence of the Sartrean approach that, to be aware of feeling a particular way towards someone, one should conceive of his feeling under a particular heading. All that the present view implies is that *for an experience to be conscious it need not take itself as its intentional object*. For Sartre, a particular experience of revulsion is simply a conscious experience that is appropriately focused on a detestable person, that is, on something other than the experience itself.

---

[22] Cf. *Being and Nothingness*, 'Introduction' and Part I ch. 1, as well as *Transcendence of the Ego*, Part A.

However, the alleged importance of reflective activity is apparent not only in the context of theoretical debates but also in the way that we usually think and talk about emotional phenomena. In ordinary discourse about psychological phenomena, emotional states are marked by a fixity and duration that transcends the fleeting nature of emotional feelings. The state of hatred may extend well beyond the instantaneous encounter with the repulsive person, as it underpins past feelings of disgust, aversion, or anger towards him over a period of days, weeks, or even years. It is thus thought to continue to exist even when I am absorbed in different activities, and to make its appearance each time it finds an expression at the prompting of events that present me with the detestable person. Hatred is not exhausted by a particular episode of feeling revulsion: the state was here yesterday when the feeling was not, and it might be here tomorrow well after my feeling has ceased to exist. To move from the claim 'I am feeling revulsion while looking at him' to the claim 'I hate him' is to perform a 'passage to infinity': to state that you hate someone is, in essence, to give your verdict on what your feelings towards him meant in the past and to express a commitment as to how you are to think, feel, or act towards that person in the future.

According to Sartre, any 'psychic state'—including 'emotional states' such as hate—does not denote a fixed entity awaiting to be discovered but the product of our attempt to make sense of our experience, by setting our mental and physical activities into some intelligible order. At the ordinary, pre-reflective stage one is absorbed in things one encounters, or in the tasks at hand; there is feeling, seeing, thinking, or acting, but no psychic state that allegedly precedes and causes any of those activities or experiences; the psychic state appears when a reflective consciousness turns its attention on past conscious activities and purviews those consciousnesses under the heading of a particular concept.

According to Sartre, the state is a relative being, depending for its existence on the reflective gaze upon the ordinary conscious experience of things or events in the world. However, in a reversal of actual priorities, the reflectively created state is taken to underlie one's feelings, thoughts, and actions. The state appears as the principle that ties together various activities of consciousness, and holds the meaning of one's relation to the world. The analysis of that relation thus becomes an exploration of the allegedly hidden meaning of conscious experience. Our feelings, thoughts, and actions provide clues to the mechanics of each psychic state that acts upon the agent as a physical force, accounting for their past attitude and conditioning their future stance. Hence, the aim of the scientist of psychic states is to try to uncover the meaning of the state through the psycho-analysis of verbal and physical behaviour, viewed as the external mantle of inner psychic entities. On this point, some trends in contemporary cognitive psychology and in classical psychoanalysis concur in their view of emotional states as entities to which the agent can have only restricted access, and over which he or she may enjoy very limited control. The vocabulary of passivity that permeates much of the folk and scientific discourse on emotions reflects a conception of human beings as governed by entities dwelling somewhere between the spontaneous activities of the stream of consciousness, on the one hand, and the bodily constitution of our interaction with the world, on the other. The space in between the mental and the physical is that of the psychological, whose dual character speaks to the paradoxical nature of emotional states: passive yet purposive, involuntary but intentional, evaluative no less than physiological.

The occurrence of paradox might be a warning against setting psychic states as the starting point of a philosophical enquiry into emotional phenomena. However, that is not the main objection that Sartre reserves for the standard view of emotions. The real problem, for Sartre, is that zooming in on psychic states produces theoretical short-sightedness: psychic states cannot be studied independently of human nature and the world in general since the psychic facts that we meet in our research are never prior: 'they, in their essential structure, are reactions of man to the world: they therefore presuppose man and the world, and cannot take on their true meaning unless those two notions have first been elucidated' (*STE* 7–8).

## 9.5 SARTRE AND THE BEHAVIOURIST APPROACH TO EMOTION

Among the various aspects of emotion examined by Sartre, the behavioural manifestations of emotional experience are of particular importance for him. The initial attraction of a behaviourist approach to emotion is that, in contradistinction to traditional subjectivist accounts, it is an approach that leaves the private chambers of bodily sensations for the public space of human interaction. Behaviourism purports to analyse emotion in terms of the behaviour exhibited by a subject in the grip of an emotion (*STE* 17–26). We may identify three features of that theory that appeal to Sartre: it is a theory that views emotion as an integral part of a subject's interaction with his or her environment, it purports to highlight aspects of emotional phenomena that are amenable to objective description, and it offers a method of understanding the occurrence of emotional reactions that might otherwise appear unnecessary or counterproductive (*STE* 18). I will reconstruct the analysis of emotional behaviour offered by the present model before I address some methodological questions about the Sartrean critique, and eventual rejection, of behaviourism.

A subject encounters a situation that calls for a certain type of action, A1. What makes the performance of A1 the appropriate type of response is determined by the goal the subject is to achieve, in the light of his or her particular role, as this is set by the implicit or explicit (cultural, social, family, etc.) rules that—ought to—govern his or her behaviour in the relevant context. However, in some circumstances, the cost of performing A1 is too dear for the subject to incur. He or she therefore opts for a different response, A2, whose enactment transforms the shape of the situation in a way that the subject is released from the obligation of performing A1. Because A2 falls short of achieving the declared goal, it signals a kind of failure or 'defeat' on the part of the subject. That behaviour of defeat is the emotion (*STE* 19).

The above paragraph outlines the sequence of events that, according to the theory examined by Sartre, constitutes an emotional episode. However, what makes that theory of emotion behaviourist is not its analysis of emotion in the terms of that sequence but the particular way that sequence is interpreted. The behaviourist understands that sequence as a continuous process that leads seamlessly from the presentation of a demand to the subject, to the subject's responding in a sub-optimal fashion. The mechanics of that response is a focal point of discussion within the behaviourist school of thought. One can invoke the existence of nervous or psychic energy which is discharged according to the mechanical law of least resistance. Which action is performed is a matter of which channel is followed by the nervous energy that governs one's organic and bodily processes. Opting for one response over another is thus explained as the 'switching of the liberated nervous energy on to another line' (*STE* 18, 19, 21). Alternatively one can appeal to the activity of biologically grounded reflexes. When the sophisticated patterns of behaviour developed in our adult life fail to meet the demands generated by threatening or otherwise troublesome situations, we automatically revert to a response set off by the nerve circuit that conditioned our reactions at the early stages of our development. Locating the source of emotion in the 'primitive circuit' of reflex behaviour operative in very early childhood, allows the 'pure behaviourist' to conceive of emotions as basic and universally valid modes of adaptation (*STE* 20). Contemporary neurobiological theories provide elaborate versions of this approach that identify basic emotions with a small set of reflex mechanisms. However the details of the relevant mechanism are filled out, the main point is that emotion constitutes a fall-back option for an organism when 'all the ways are barred' and the going gets tough (*STE* 39).

The plausibility of this account can be challenged in a number of ways some of which are less effective than others. Sartre, for one, avoids a wholesale attack on behaviourism, arguing instead that as a theory it fails to deliver on its promise of restoring the reality of emotional phenomena by looking beyond the narrow confines of bodily perturbations at the meaning of our transactions with the world. For those transactions to be meaningful two criteria should be met. The first is that the emotional transaction should be an adaptation of the organism to the situation. If this condition is to be met, then the organism should be aware of the behaviour conducive to the declared goal, the difficulties involved in behaving that way, the availability of adopting an alternative behaviour, and the opting for that alternative as (in a sense a sub-optimal, but nevertheless, functional) way out of an impasse. Hence, the occurrence of the alternative behaviour should be something other than a mechanical process of switching nervous energy channels. Thus, the second criterion is that the account should not leave behaviour proper out of its picture. Nervous energy discharged at random is not just sub-optimal behaviour: it is no behaviour at all. Analysing emotive behaviour as a set of arbitrary organic diffusions 'would be less like a behaviour of defeat than a lack of behaviour' (*STE* 19).

Sartre's main argument against behaviourism is that it fails on its own terms. Note, though, that an analogous problem is faced by the functionalist account, propounded by Gestalt Psychology – and *partly* endorsed by Sartre (*STE* 27). Emotional reaction is here interpreted as an abrupt solution to a problem, whereby the prescribed form of behaviour is substituted by *behaviour that cancels the demands made on the subject through changing the shape of his or her situation*. However, the mere affirmation of the occurrence of a form of behaviour does not amount to an explanation of that occurrence. If the explanation to be sought in the end is brought about by the occurrence, then an account is owed of how and why a particular end calls for, and brings forth, a particular form of behaviour. What we are offered, instead, is the description of the break up of one form of behaviour followed by the reconstitution of another form of behaviour. The result is an account of a succession of forms that sounds true but incomprehensible. The missing ingredient, according to Sartre, is an explication of the *meaning* of the forms that, according to Gestalt theorists, constitute an emotion.

Behaviourism fails to interpret emotion as a meaningful aspect of our being in the world. Emotion is meaningful because it is a *conscious* adaptation of the agent to his or her situation. The exact nature of adaptation involved in an emotional episode will be discussed in the next, and final, section of this chapter. We should stress, though, that the discussion that follows grants Sartre an important assumption: that it is not possible for emotions to acquire their significance through a process from which consciousness is absent. Sartre, in other words, rejects the belief in the reality of unconscious emotion. Talk of the unconscious, in the context of the Sartrean exploration of emotions, refers mainly to two things. It can denote an emotion whose *existence* is not in any way present to consciousness. Or, it can refer to emotional phenomena whose *meaning* lies in the unconscious. It is the latter issue that occupies Sartre in the *Sketch for a Theory of the Emotions*. Although his philosophy is inhospitable to unconscious states in general, it is important not to mistake his critique of the psychoanalytic view of emotions for a simplistic affirmation of the alleged *omniscience* of self-consciousness. In particular, the signification of a conscious event need not be explicit: 'there are many possible degrees of condensation and of clarity' (*STE* 41). Sartre's refusal to appeal to unconscious causes in interpreting emotional experience is based on the methodological *credo* that 'we should not interrogate consciousness from outside, but from within: that we should look into it for its signification' (*STE* 42). Elsewhere we have offered a reconstruction and qualified defence of the rejection of unconscious emotional states.[23] Here we shall focus on Sartre's positive account of how affective awareness relates to emotional action.

## 9.6 SARTRE ON EMOTIONAL ACTION

A common way of presenting Sartre's view is with the catchphrase: 'emotions are actions'. That claim expresses the metaphysical thesis that emotion itself is a type of event that falls under the category of action. However, a careful reading of Sartre's text indicates that the catch phrase is misleading. The core of the Sartrean view is that during an emotional episode one's relation to the world is 'magically' transformed by means of one's body (*STE* 39–41). Let me explicate what this claim means.

The world is understood as a totality of phenomena linked by a complex network of references to each other. The way in which each phenomenon relates to others defines the type of world encountered by the subject. In the world of daily activity we experience reality as a combination of demands (for projects awaiting completion, bills to be paid, walls to be decorated) and affordances (given by fast computers, bank transfers, or DIY shops). The link between demands and affordances is itself experienced as ruled by deterministic processes between causes and effects. The 'instrumental world' of action is captured in the 'pragmatic intuition' of the situation that makes certain moves available for the subject, while denying him or her others (*STE* 39). And this relates to a crucial contrast between action and emotion: for Sartre, the world encountered in emotional experience—what we variously characterize as a 'hateful', 'joyful', or 'bleak' world—far from being identical to the world of action is clearly distinguished from the instrumental world (*STE* 35). The distinction is twofold. On the one hand, the 'emotional apprehension' of the world hooks on to those qualities or aspects that carry affective meaning for the agent, while the 'pragmatic intuition' focuses on features of the situation that make or not possible the execution of a task, the realization of an objective, or the creation of a product. On the other hand, the agent's response in an emotional episode engages the overall stance and physiology of the body *not so as to effect material changes in the world* but so as to alter his or her perception of reality, and, through that, his or her relation to the world: 'during

---

[23] 'The Case Against Unconscious Emotions' *Analysis* 67 (2007): 292–9.

emotion, it is the body which, directed by the consciousness, changes its relation-ship to the world so that the world should change its qualities' (*STE* 41). That change in qualities is called by Sartre 'magical' (*STE* 40, 43, 59). What makes the transformation of the word magical is precisely that what changes is *not the material constitution of reality but how reality appears to the agent* and, consequent-ly, how the agent will respond to a thus transformed reality.

The notion of 'emotional response' is rather ambiguous, so a few clarifying remarks are in order. The analysis propounded by Sartre highlights the *functional* character of emotional response, not only in the case of 'active emotions' (as when one's shouting reduces the chances of properly listening to what the other person says) but also in the case of 'passive' emotions (as when one's bowed head and bent posture limits the range of one's vision so that as little as possible of the cruel world is taken in). There is, though, a notion of 'emotional response' that attaches to action which, while it can be described independently of the occurrence of emo-tion, is thought to be somehow better accounted for by reference to the emotion preceding the particular action.

Let us distinguish among the following scenarios regarding one's running away from a dangerous-looking bear. Case One is where the agent weighs his or her options, and after relevant deliberation, decides to create quickly a sufficient distance between him- or herself and the bear. Case Two is as in the previous scenario, but with the emotion of fear preceding the thought and action process described in Case One. Case Two can be subdivided into Case Two (a), whereby the fear experienced and the resulting action are temporally successive but otherwise unconnected; and Case Two (b), whereby the fear causes the deliberating process that results in the relevant action. In Case One, the running away is rationalized by reference to the thought process (usually taken to include the putting together of one's beliefs and desires) that aims to lead the agent out of danger. In Case Two (b), the running away is accounted for (at the level of explanation) and also rationalized (at the level of justification) by invoking the emotion of fear, because it is that emotion that initiates the relevant thought and action processes. However, *none* of the above Cases satisfies Sartre's description of fleeing as an emotional response.

Case One is a non-starter in the present context because, on the one hand, it includes no reference to emotion, and, on the other hand, it implies an analysis (in terms of reflective consideration and manipulation of one's own beliefs and desires) that is false to the phenomenology of normal human activity (which, according to Sartre, is a non-reflective, outward-looking engagement with the objects, tools, and tasks of a situation).[24]

Case Two (b) offers a more interesting and arguably correct account of the phenomena involved. What it presents, though, is not an analysis of emotional

---

[24] An intentionalist view consistently discussed and defended by Sartre; see esp. *STE* 36–8, *BN* III, 2, i.

response but of prudential action—and the two types of event are markedly different. Running out of prudence is acting according to a plan; emotional fleeing, on the other hand, is a 'magical behaviour which negates the dangerous object with one's whole body, by reversing the vectorial structure of the space we live in and suddenly creating a potential direction on the other side' (*STE* 43). It is not a case of reaching for shelter (as in prudential behaviour) but of 'forgetting' or 'negating' the threat. The dangerous object is the focal point of fear, and—contrary to the case of prudential action—the *faster* one runs (the louder one shouts, the further one withdraws) the *more* afraid (or angry, or sad) one feels.

The Sartrean analysis of emotion ranges over a wide variety of phenomena that could not be reviewed in the present chapter—not least because several of his points are simply acute observations made in the course of his unique narration of human phenomena, for which there is no substitute other than reading Sartre's text itself. I would like to conclude the discussion by drawing attention to some parts of the text that highlight the Sartrean approach to affective phenomena.

First, behaviour on its own (including one's overall conduct or particular actions vis-à-vis a situation) forms an important and integral part of emotional phenomena but is not, and should not be conceived as, exhaustive of what an emotion really is: 'behaviour pure and simple is *not* emotion, any more than is the pure and simple awareness of that behaviour' (*STE* 48). Secondly, emotional experience cannot be dissociated from the body on pain of 'falsity' of the professed emotion: 'the physiological phenomena . . . represent the *genuineness* of the emotion, they are the phenomena of belief' (*STE* 50). Thirdly, what the agent believes is not some reflective statement about his or her own thoughts or bodily processes but the reality of the affective meanings that make up the object upon which the emotion feeds: 'Consciousness does not limit itself to the projection of affective meanings upon the world around it: it lives the new world it has thereby constituted—lives it directly, commits itself to it, and suffers from the qualities that the concomitant behaviour has outlined' (*STE* 51).

The active dimension of affective phenomena is important even in cases where ordinary discourse emphasizes passivity. Moods, especially those of a negative valence, are commonly thought of as passive states that are not directly related to the world outside the subject. We saw, in section 9.3, how Heidegger resisted that view by underlining the capacity of *Stimmungen* to disclose the very being of the world in general. For Sartre, the world's involvement in the constitution of moods is more specific, and, in that sense, more prominent. Consider *tristesse passive*, a mood that bears passivity on its sleeve. Passive sadness is characterized by paleness, muscular relaxation, and 'withdrawal', whereby one prefers solitude in small spaces to lecture halls and public squares: ' "To be alone", as they say, "with one's sorrow". But that is not true at all: it is good form, of course, to appear to meditate deeply over one's grief. But cases in which a sorrow is really cherished are rather rare' (*STE* 43). In most cases, Sartre maintains, passive sadness arises when one of the (e.g., material) conditions of my activity is no longer there, yet the demands placed by my situation are still here. I am therefore required to substitute that to which I am accustomed, with means new to me—and that is precisely what I cannot bear to do. Passive sadness, according to Sartre, is not the causal imprint of the world on my soul but *my response* to my predicament: 'my melancholy is a method of suppressing the obligation to look for [new means], by transforming the present structure of the world, replacing it with a totally undifferentiated structure' (*STE* 44). What distinguishes the emotive response from a practical response is that the desirable transformation is not effected by altering the shape of things but by altering *myself*, e.g., by 'dimming the lights' (*mettre en veilleuse*) of our daily life (*STE* 44).

I think that, despite the differences in their ontology, Sartre is in fundamental agreement with Heidegger on what sustains the phenomenological importance of emotional awareness. For Heidegger, affective experience enables the primordial apprehension of the concrete reality that is our being-in-the-world. Similarly, for Sartre, affective experience is neither blind nor self-referential: 'Emotion is a specific way of apprehending the world' (*STE* 35).

## FURTHER READING

### General

CERBONE, DAVID (2006), *Understanding Phenomenology* (London: Acumen).

MICKUNAS, ALGIS (1997), 'Emotion' in *Encyclopedia of Phenomenology*, ed. Lester Embree et al. (Dordrecht: Kluwer Academic Publishers): 171–7.

MORAN, DERMOT (2000), *Introduction to Phenomenology* (London: Routledge).

SCHROEDER, WILLIAM (2005), *Continental Philosophy: A Critical Approach* (Oxford: Blackwell).

SOKOLOWSKI, ROBERT (2000), *Introduction to Phenomenology* (Cambridge: Cambridge University Press).

### Heidegger

CARMAN, TAYLOR (2003), *Heidegger's Analytic* (Cambridge: Cambridge University Press).

DREYFUS, H. and WRATHALL, M. (eds.) (2004), *A Companion to Heidegger* (Oxford: Blackwell).

GUIGNON, CHARLES (ed.) (2006), *Cambridge Companion to Heidegger* (Cambridge: Cambridge University Press).

HARR, M. (1992), 'Attunement and Thinking' in H. L. Dreyfus and H. Hall (eds.), *Heidegger: A Critical Reader* (Oxford: Blackwell).

INWOOD, MICHAEL (1999), *A Heidegger Dictionary* (Oxford: Blackwell).

MULHALL, STEPHEN (1996), *Routledge Philosophy Guidebook to Heidegger and Being and Time* (London: Routledge).

RATCLIFFE, MATTHEW (2002), 'Heidegger's Attunement and the Neuropsychology of Emotion' *Phenomenology and the Cognitive Sciences* 1: 287–312.

STAEHLER, TANJA (2007), 'How is a Phenomenology of Fundamental Moods Possible?' *International Journal of Philosophical Studies* 15(3): 415–43.

## Sartre

BARNES, HAZEL (1967), An *Existentialist Ethics* (New York: Alfred A. Knopf).

HATZIMOYSIS, ANTHONY (2009), *The Philosophy of Sartre* (London: Acumen).

HOWELLS, CHRISTINA (ed.) (1992), *Cambridge Companion to Sartre* (Cambridge: Cambridge University Press).

McBRIDE, WILLIAM LEON (ed.) (1996), *Sartre and Existentialism: Philosophy, Politics, Ethics, the Psyche, Literature, and Aesthetics*, 8 Vols. (London: Routledge).

McCULLOCH, GREGORY (1994), *Using Sartre* (London: Routledge).

MURPHY, JULIEN S. (ed.) (1999), *Feminist Interpretations of Jean-Paul Sartre* (University Park: Pennsylvania State University Press).

PRIEST, STEPHEN (2000), *The Subject in Question* (London: Routledge).

SOLOMON, ROBERT C. (2001), *Phenomenology and Existentialism* (Lanham, MD: Rowman & Littlefield).

WIDER, KATHLEEN (1997), *The Bodily Nature of Consciousness* (Ithaca, NY: Cornell University Press).

# REINSTATING THE PASSIONS: ARGUMENTS FROM THE HISTORY OF PSYCHOPATHOLOGY

## LOUIS C. CHARLAND

Passion became an active, persistent, emotionally-laden tendency towards a goal, strong enough eventually to dominate the whole mental life.

Pierre Pichot
'The Passions in French Psychiatry', p. 72

This article is dedicated to Professor Stanley G. Clarke (1939–2008), friend and mentor, who first introduced me to the philosophy of emotion. Special thanks to Tom Ban, Thomas Dixon, Jennifer Radden, and Peter Goldie for their comments on earlier versions of this chapter.

# 10.1 THE CONCEPTUAL DOMINION
## OF EMOTION

The passions have vanished. After centuries of dominance in the ethical and scientific discourse of the West, they have been eclipsed by the emotions. To speak of the passions now is to refer to a relic of the past, the crumbling foundation of a once mighty conceptual empire that permeated all aspects of Western cultural life. Philosophical and scientific wars continue to be fought in these ruins; new encampments are built, rebels plot in the catacombs, and bold victors plant their flags on the highest peaks. But it is hard to escape the conclusion that now it is the emotions which reign supreme in affective science. It is in their terms that conflicts are fought and settled.

In this conceptual transfiguration, the ancient passions have not simply been marginalized. They have also been desacralized and stripped of their ethical and spiritual connotations. Opinions vary as to what exactly has been lost or gained in this transformation. While some rejoice, others grieve. Some see a philosophical liberation where the old passive states of the soul are replaced by inner motions that can guide and determine action (Rorty 1982). Others lament the fact that a once rich and complex spiritual category has been replaced by a crude secular amoral substitute (Dixon 2003). Whatever the verdict may be, philosophically and scientifically, we now live in the age of emotion – even though the English term arguably has no mono-lexical or conceptual equivalent in many other world languages (Russell 1991; Wierzbicka 1999).

In reflecting on these developments, it worth remarking that there are those who would urge us to remember the sentiments (Be'en Ze'ev 2000; Evans 2001). But these posits were never serious contenders. The majority opinion has always been to relegate them to the wayside. Yet in one way the sentiments are worth noting. They fill an important theoretical gap between the alleged passivity of the passions and the new emotions as actions in the mind. Part of what is supposed to make the sentiments distinct is their duration. They are affective orientations that endure over long periods of time. Perhaps because of this, they are less amenable to scientific inquiry and experiment, with its focus on measurement in the here and now.

Moods must also be included among the constituents of the affective realm. Curiously, despite their central role in modern psychopathology, these last posits fail to capture much philosophical interest. They usually receive rather perfunctory attention as feeling states of long duration, affective states that lack intentionality, emotions without discrete objects, or emotions with more global as opposed to discrete objects (Goldie 2000, 143–51; Griffiths 1997, 248–57; Prinz 2004, 185; Solomon 1993, 3–4). Indeed, moods are rarely the primary focus of interest in philosophical discussions of affectivity. They are also largely absent from the history of passions to emotions (Dixon 2003; Rorty 1982). Consequently, although they are obviously posits of great theoretical importance in some sectors of affective science, they will play no part in what follows.

# 10.2 A LOST OPPORTUNITY

This then is the age of emotion. Emotion is now the central and supreme theoretical posit of the philosophy of emotion and large segments of affective science. Obviously, it would be folly to deny that remarkable progress has been made under the banner of 'emotion' in both these areas. However, at the same time, under this conceptual dominion, a large expanse of affective life that was once fertile ground for scientific and philosophical inquiry has been forgotten.

There is some philosophical recognition that our current category of emotion cannot do everything that is asked of it (Griffiths 1997, 242–7). One particularly acute problem is the need to recognize the existence of complex affective states of long duration (Goldie 2000, 104–6). These more complex and enduring affective states are often accompanied by short-term episodes of emotion (Goldie 2000, 12–16). Strictly speaking, then, those more enduring states should perhaps not be called 'emotions'. A better solution is to call them 'passions'. This indeed is what they would have been called in nineteenth-century French medical science. The point is not merely semantic but theoretical. It has to do with the *kinds* of posits involved and not merely their labels.

There are in fact good reasons for positing complex affective states of long duration called 'passions' and contrasting these with emotions. But those reasons do not figure in the accepted history of passions to emotions (Dixon 2003; Rorty 1982). They lie in French medical science of the nineteenth century, a period that saw the birth of psychiatry as a rigorous clinical discipline (Goldstein 2001; Pichot 1983; Pigeaud 2001; Weiner 1999). It has been said that these developments represent a 'lost opportunity' for present-day psychopathology of affectivity (Berrios 1985, 1996, 295). They also represent a significant lost opportunity for present-day philosophy of emotion and affective science.

Perhaps one reason why this segment of history is ignored in the Anglo-Saxon 'newspeak' of modern emotion theory is that most of its heroes are French – Philippe Pinel (1745–1826), Jean-Étienne Dominique Esquirol (1772–1840), and Théodule Ribot (1839–1916). But there are also other pivotal figures whose absence from the relevant historical and philosophical scholarship is harder to understand; for example, Immanuel Kant (1724–1804) and Sir Alexander Crichton (1763–1856).

In any case, it is clear that additional chapters must be added to our current histories of the transformation from passions to emotions. Therefore, to the history of passion *to* emotion, I propose to add the history of passion *and* emotion.

None of this is to deny that there is an important linguistic and conceptual transition from 'passions to emotions' that takes place in Western history between the seventeenth and nineteenth centuries. What seems to have escaped notice is that there are large segments of that history where the battle for the emotions was never won and the passions still reign supreme (but see Dixon 2003, 108, note 47 and Dixon 2006). In what follows, I offer several vignettes from this forgotten history in order to motivate the thesis that the passions must be reinstated. My argument, which can only be sketched in general form, is that we must reinstate the passions if we are to have any theoretical hope of achieving a satisfactory comprehensive scientific theory of affective life. I begin with a selective review of some central figures who are conspicuous in their absence in the favored histories of passion to emotion. The discussion closes with a selective overview of the work of Théodule Ribot, probably the most able and sophisticated defender of the passions in psychopathology and psychology generally. His views are certainly still relevant today.

# 10.3 René Descartes: Conflating Passion and Emotion

In 'The Passions of the Soul' (*Les Passions de L'Âme*), Descartes famously relabeled the passions (*passions*) and called them 'emotions' (*émotions*). However, in doing so, he arguably conflates two very different posits that many later thinkers argue require an independent elaboration. At the same time, he innovates by highlighting the fact that the passions are active and not simply passive states of the mind. In addition, by ostensibly attempting to reconcile science and morals in his theory of the passions – or at least lay them side by side – Descartes also throws down a gauntlet for future medical theorists of the passions, most of whom aspire to a psychopathology of the passions that is strictly scientific. I will refer to this challenge as 'Descartes's Gauntlet'.

Descartes starts by noting that while the passions (*passions*) resemble perceptions (*perceptions*) and sensations (*sentiments*) in being largely passive, calling them emotions (*émotions*) is even better (*encore mieux*), since it emphasizes the fact that these thoughts (*pensées*) also agitate and disturb the mind, and so are also active

(Descartes 1650/1990, Article 57; James 1997, 95). A consequence of this definition is that, contrary to tradition and etymology, the passions are no longer merely passive states of the mind. They are also active (1650/1990, Article 1; James 1997, 96; Rorty 1982). Descartes tells us that the passions both incite and contribute to actions that help conserve and improve the body (Article 137). Their primary function is to help direct and move the mind: to 'dispose the soul to want the things which nature deems useful to us, and to persist in this volition' (James 1997, 100; Descartes 1650/ 1990, Articles 40, 137). This is consonant with the etymology of the new 'emotions' (French: *emouvoir*; Latin: *emovere*).

A crucial aspect of Descartes's view is that it is in virtue of their physiologically embodied character that the passions move the body and the mind. They are a species of mental state (*pensées*), namely, feelings (*sentiments*), which are caused and sustained by animal spirits that course throughout the body (*les esprits*), which in turn impact on the brain, especially the pineal gland (Articles 27, 31, 32, 36, 40). It is important to note that while the passions can disturb the mind and cause it many harms (*le mal*) and bitterness (*amertume*), they are not necessarily nor invariably pathological. On the contrary, it is on them that all the good in this life (*le bien*) depends (Article 212). It is the use (*usage*) of the passions that is especially relevant in this regard. Properly deployed, the passions are all good in themselves: '*toutes bonnes de leur nature*' (Article 211). Troubles arise when they are excessive and are not managed properly (Article 212). In such cases, we must endeavor to control our passions, a moral task that requires both strength of the will and knowledge of the truth (Articles 45, 48, 49, 50). This implies a recognition that the physical health and conservation of the body requires the moral health and perfectibility of the soul (Articles 138, 139).

There is an irony to this last point. In a prefatory letter to his treatise, Descartes states that his 'intention was to explain the passions only as a natural philosopher, and not as a rhetorician or even as a moral philosopher' (Cottingham et al. 1985, 327). Despite this disclaimer, he arguably delivered an ethical treatise nonetheless (Levi 1964, 248). Descartes's uncompromising rigor and commitment to the theoretical exigencies of his task apparently forced him to acknowledge the link between science and morals in his account of the usage of the passions. This being his last major work, he left the details to posterity. Any psychopathology and psychotherapy of the passions or emotions that aims to be scientific must still pick up this gauntlet in order to determine the true nature of its professed scientific credentials. The challenge becomes especially pertinent when assessing the credentials of popular forms of emotional regulation and psychotherapy for contemporary personality disorders; interventions which profess to be 'scientific' but are arguably forms of 'moral treatment' that are primarily ethical in nature (Charland 2004, 2006, 2007).

# 10.4 DAVID HUME: CONFUSING
# PASSION AND EMOTION

In his *Treatise on Human Nature*, David Hume routinely refers to emotions in his account of the passions. For example, he writes about 'the passions, and the other emotions resembling them' (Norton and Norton 2000, 181, Sec. 1). It has been suggested that the appearance of the term 'emotion' in the work of Hume is an innovation that is probably due to Descartes (Dixon 2003, 108). Indeed, Hume may be the first major philosopher to grant significant theoretical status to the term 'emotion' in English. Evidently, he sometimes felt a need to refer to 'passions' and 'emotions' in his new science of the mind. What exactly he intended by that distinction is still subject to debate. Yet that he did employ both terms in a manner that suggests *some* distinction is indisputable. His central posit though appears to be 'passion'. After all, Book 2 of the *Treatise* is entitled 'Of the Passions'. Apparently, emotions play a secondary role in Hume's theory.

Some commentators suggest that that by 'emotion' Hume means 'a feeling that may attend a passion' (Norton and Norton 2000, 575). This is consistent with Descartes's conception of emotions as agitations or disturbances of the mind. Emotions in this case appear to be rather simple posits; relatively primitive forms of feeling. Passions are also a species of feeling on Hume's account. They are 'secondary' impressions, or 'impressions of reflection' (Norton and Norton 2000, Sec. 1.2).

Hume's account and classification of the passions is notoriously complex and subject to varying interpretations (Fieser 1992). At one point, he states that the passions have 'not any representative quality' (Norton and Norton 2000, 226, 2.3.3.5). This would seem to imply that some passions, at least, are relatively primitive forms of feeling. That arguably may be true of 'direct' passions which 'arise immediately from good or evil, from pain or pleasure' (Norton and Norton 2000, 182, 1.4). However, the role of feelings in 'indirect' passions is substantially more complex. These arise from a 'double relation of impressions and ideas' in a manner that strongly suggests that the objects to which those passions 'direct their view, when excited' are also part of the 'content' of these passions (Norton and Norton 2000, 281, 2.3.9.4; 183, 2.1.2). On this view, indirect passions are not simply feelings but rather combinations of feelings and ideas that function as a unified causal whole in explanations of mental processes and the generation of behavior. Thus indirect passions are complex affective states that inextricably implicate ideas in a manner that goes beyond the primitive feelings involved in token instances of emotions.

There is therefore some evidence that passions and emotions differ markedly in their nature and complexity in Hume's account. Nonetheless, there exist scores of commentators who treat passion and emotion as if they were equivalent terms and notions in Hume's work (Lyons 1980; Solomon 2003). Thus Hume's role in the history of passion and emotion turns out to be slightly ironic. He arguably confused the distinction between passion and emotion at the same time that he popularized it.

## 10.5  ALEXANDER CRICHTON: DEFINING PASSION AND EMOTION

A far more explicit and precise account of the distinction between passion and emotion is found in the work of Hume's contemporary, Sir Alexander Crichton. Unlike Hume, who chooses to eschew questions of anatomy and physiology in formulating his science of the mind, Crichton adopts a brazen physiological medical stance. His approach is predominantly physiological, largely inspired by German sources (Weiner 1990). However, this does not stop the Scottish doctor from highlighting the relevance of the contributions of Hume and other 'psychologists' like Locke to his new physiological theory of the passions (Porter 1987, 191). Crichton is a pivotal turning point in our history of passion and emotion. He is without a doubt one of the most interesting and influential medical scientists of the passions of the eighteenth century (Charland 2008a).

In his *Enquiry Into the Nature and Origins of Mental Derangement*, Crichton acknowledges that 'the word *emotion* is often used, not only in conversation, but also in philosophical works, as an equivalent expression for passion' (Crichton 1798, III.1.115). Yet he insists that the two must be distinguished. Crichton conceives of emotions as 'animal' or 'involuntary' effects of the passions (III, I, 126). He notes that 'every passion has its emotions, as every disease has its symptoms' and that 'the relationship which exists between them is similar to the general one of a cause producing its peculiar effect' (II. 4. 345). This seems consistent with the view that emotions are feelings which can attend a passion.

Passions, on their side, are more complex affective states. First, they have 'objects'. Second, unlike emotions, they are subject to volition. In Crichton's words:

Sorrow and grief are terms which are often indiscriminately applied to many kinds of painful emotions; and hence it appears that they cannot, with propriety, be considered as distinct passions. Indeed, sorrow scarcely has a claim to be classed with the passions, as that word is commonly employed, for in many cases of sorrow, and anguish, the will is not excited into action by any distinct object. But, in the painful passions, strictly so called, such as anger and rage, jealousy and envy, there is always an object of aversion which excites volition into powerful action (Crichton 1798, III.3.177).

We apparently have come full circle. In Crichton's account, it is the emotions which are passive and the passions which are active, rather than the reverse. Note also that on his account the passions are also feelings. They are feelings at the praecordia (Crichton 1798, III.1.113). However, passions are not simply feelings. They are 'complex affections' that are felt at the praecordia.

Crichton is important for our history because of the manner in which he attempts to sharply distinguish passion from emotion. While he did not have much to say about emotions, he certainly made influential contributions to the physiological theory of the passions. His is a physiology that focuses primarily on the form rather than the content of the various passions in assessing their role in psychopathology (Charland 2008a). It is interesting that, contrary to Descartes, who attempts to accommodate morals in his theory of the passions, Crichton lays down a gauntlet of his own. At the start of his *Enquiry*, he brazenly asserts that he is only concerned with the passions as 'natural phenomena'. He declares:

The passions are to be considered, in a medical point of view, as part of our natural constitution, which is to be examined with the eye of the natural historian, and the sprit and impartiality of a philosopher. It is of no concern in this work whether the passions be esteemed natural or unnatural, or moral or immoral affections. They are mere phenomena, the natural causes of which are to be inquired into (Crichton 1798, III. 1. 99).

This manifesto resonated with the aims of the next two figures in our history of passion and emotion; namely, Philippe Pinel and Jean-Étienne Esquirol. Certainly, both were very influenced by Crichton's physiological theory of the passions. What is seldom noted, however, is that both also found it impossible to entirely expunge 'moral' considerations from their respective psychopathological theories of the passions.

# 10.6 Philippe Pinel: Curing Passion with Emotion

Like Crichton, Pinel believes that passions and emotions both can and must be distinguished. Perhaps the best way to introduce his conception of the passions is to contrast these with his other favored affective posit, namely, the emotions. In his main publication on the psychopathology of affectivity, the *Traité médico-philosophique sur l'aliénation mentale*, Pinel pays careful attention to emotions (*émotions*). According to him, emotions are sudden and intense commotions (*commotions*) of the mind. As such they can sidetrack or disturb reason and the imagination (Pinel 1809, 155, 180; see Hickish, Healy, and Charland 2008 for a full English translation of Pinel's 1809 *Traité*). Because of their sudden onset and short duration, emotions can also play a positive role in treating mental illness.

Accidentally or through artificial induction, they can help to shock patients back to reason (150, 372). This they do by snapping or breaking the fixed chains of ideas and faulty associations that underlie and sustain delusions.

Unlike passions, which can grow and endure for months or even years, emotions are affective states of short duration, with sudden onset and extinction (155, 179). In contrast, passions can manifest as processes that ebb and flow and vary in intensity over long periods of time. However, passion can also sometimes suddenly appear and disappear and sometimes even share names with their cognate emotions.

Pinel argues that passions are implicated in forms of mental illness like melancholia. He defines melancholia as a fixed and exclusive delusion directed at a single idea (*délire exclusif*) which in turn is linked to a dominant passion (*passion dominante*). Thus melancholia has two components. There is an intellectual component; namely, the fixation on a single idea. And there is a dominant passion that accompanies and sustains that intellectual fixation. What a sudden emotional shock can do in such a case is to disrupt and break one or more of the ties that bind these components together. In other words, an emotion can be used to alter or break the hold of a passion. Therefore, passions and emotions are different.

Consider now the list of states which Pinel considers to be passions. It reflects an important departure from the enumeration of emotions and passions provided by Descartes, Hume, and Crichton. Behind this change lies an important shift in emphasis, away from mono-lexical names taken from natural language as a basis for classification to more complex states and processes inspired by the etiology of psychopathology.

At first sight, many of Pinel's passions resemble traditional affective categories for which there are ready-made names. For example, he mentions anger (*colère*), hate (*haine*), wounded pride (*orgueil blessé*), desire for vengeance (*désir de vengeance*), extreme disgust with life (*dégoût extrême de la vie*), and an irresistible tendency to suicide (*penchant irrésistible au suicide*) (Pinel 1809, 81). But note already that some of the items on this list are not easily identifiable with or traceable to distinct *names* for passions. Other examples of passions that do not appear to be directly tied to discrete names include domestic chagrins (*chagrins domestiques*), impediments to marriage (*obstacles à un marriage fortement désiré*), consequences of the revolution (*événements de la revolution*), fanatical zeal (*un zèle fanatique*), and terrors of the afterlife (*terreurs de l'autre vie*) (Pinel 1809, 457).

Clearly, Pinel does not feel compelled to restrict himself to traditional names or categories for passions in formulating his psychopathology the passions. Neither does he mind stretching the term 'passion' to include them. Nonetheless, all the states he enumerates are meant to be serious scientific posits. In fact, they are among the major causes of mental illness (Pinel 1809, 28, 34). Pinel's list of passions is largely etiological in nature. He is attempting to enumerate affective states that cause and degenerate into mental illness. This happens when the states or passions in question get too stormy (*orageuses*), or vehement (*véhémentes*), generate too much ardor (*fougueuses*), get too lively (*vives*), fleeting (*fugaces*), or carried away (*emportées*). The manner in which Pinel individuates the passions by looking to etiology looks like a precursor of the suggestion that we should individuate affective states by homology rather than analogy or resemblance (Charland 2002; Griffiths 1997; Elster 1999; Panksepp 1998). It is the beginning of a recognition that the posits of affective science may not be recoverable from simple names taken from ordinary language. Crichton, Esquirol, and Ribot also adopt this methodological stance. Descartes, Hume, and Kant do not. Perhaps this is because the former are all primarily interested in the psychopathology of the passions, while the latter are more interested in their relevance to philosophy.

Pinel defines passions rather vaguely. He states that 'the passions in general are a set of unknown variations in physical or mental sensitivity which we can only untangle and to which we can only allocate distinctive characters through external signs (Pinel 1809, 25). But why 'unknown'? The reason is that Pinel considers the term 'passion' (*passion*) to be a complex general term which is built by theoretical abstraction from primitive sensory observable data. Like all medical diagnostic and nosological terms and categories, both its true meaning and constituents must be carefully reconstructed and derived from clinical observation and experience. In adopting this stance, Pinel is undoubtedly influenced by the epistemology of Condillac (Riese 1969; Goldstein 2001). The goal here is to ground all clinical diagnostic terms and categories in sense experience, building complex general terms by abstraction, out of simpler terms derived form notions that have a clear basis on observation. This is called the method of 'analysis' (*analyse*). It is because of this philosophical commitment that, in the title of his *Traité*, Pinel characterizes its method as 'medico-philosophical' (*médico-philosophique*). His goal is to reconcile the descriptive clinical method of Hippocrates (*méthode descriptive*) with the analytical philosophical epistemology of Condillac (*analyse*).

Because of their elusive nature and largely unobservable mental and physiological characteristics, the passions prove recalcitrant to the method of analysis. It is hard to distinguish their specific characteristics (*caractères spécifiques*) from what is merely accessory and correlated, or accidental. Admittedly, Pinel does present many detailed clinical descriptions of the observable behavioral and physiognomic signs that accompany the expression of the affective states, sometimes even noting their history over days and weeks. However, at the same time he considers it an important clinical discovery that passion and other affective posits prove so hard to define. A plausible explanation is that he believes that a complete formal medical definition of the passions and emotions is impossible in the early stages of his new medico-philosophical psychopathology (Goldstein 2001, 94, note 103).

One final aspect of Pinel's doctrine of the passions is his stance on the relation between science and morals and his response to the challenge posed by Descartes's Gauntlet. It is commonly thought that Pinel follows Crichton on this question. After all, he is a determined medical scientist. And at one point he even explicitly professes to consider the passions only in their physiological capacity, in abstraction from any questions of morals: '*les considérant en abstraction de toute question de moralité*' (Pinel 1809, p. xxij). However, the use of the term 'moral' in this context can easily mislead and result in gross exegetical error. The term Pinel uses in the above passage is 'morals' (*moralité*). But in Crichton's manifesto, 'moral' has a much wider intended meaning. It refers to what is mental or psychological in a very wide sense; a meaning that is also associated with '*moral*' in French, where it also connotes mental phenomena in a very wide sense.

As one of the founding figures of 'moral treatment' (*traitement moral*), Pinel obviously disagrees with Crichton that affective psychopathology and clinical therapy can proceed without alluding to the mental and psychological characteristics of the passions and other affective posits; namely, emotions (*émotions*) and feelings (*sentimens*). His stance on whether moral treatment must also invoke questions that have to do with morals is much harder to ascertain. Is he, like Descartes, theoretically prepared to reconcile science and morals in his psychopathology of the passions and their treatment? To this crucial but complicated exegetical question, I will simply answer in the affirmative. Unfortunately, the reasons for that answer are too onerous to review in this discussion. Suffice it to say that, if this conclusion is correct, the scientific credentials of Pinel's moral treatment need to be revisited, along with most of its accepted history (Charland forthcoming).

# 10.7 JEAN-ÉTIENNE ESQUIROL: MONOMANIACAL PASSION

Crichton's physiological theory of the passions had a marked influence on both Pinel and his equally famous student and successor, Jean-Étienne Esquirol (Weiner 1999). Like Pinel, Esquirol believed that passions were directly implicated in the etiology, symptomatology, and treatment of mental illness. In fact, he went even farther, arguing that each species of mental illness (*alienation*) could be traced to an analogous primitive passional type, or form (Esquirol 1805/1980, 21). Thus maniacal fury is a prolonged and extreme form of anger; erotomonia is form of love that is carried to excess; and suicide is a form of chronic or acute despair pushed beyond its limits (Esquirol 1838, 14). There is also lypemania, Esquirol's proposed new category for melancholia, which is a chronic and prolonged form of sadness. When the passions become excessive in this way they turn into a kind of delirium (*délire*). The delirium is partial and centered around a fixed idea. Indeed, there are different kinds of these partial forms of delirium, each associated with different passional form. For example, pyromania, which Esquirol calls 'incendiary monomania' (*monomanie incendiare*) derives from acute or chronic jealousy or vengeance (1838, 84). Different kinds of monomania (*monomanie*) can be traced back to primitive passional forms where they have their origins. Sometimes, the delirium in question can be broken by sudden emotional shocks (*secousses*). Like Pinel, Esquirol maintains that emotions can be employed as therapeutic agents.

Esquirol is famous for introducing the concept of 'monomania' into psychopathology (Goldstein 2001). According to him, delirium (*délire*) in monomania has a single aim or object, as the prefix 'mono' suggests. This is a crucial turning point in the psychopathology of the passions. The new concept builds on Pinel's observation that the passions often manifest as affective processes of long duration, organized in accordance with a fixed idea (*idée fixe*). Recall that for Pinel melancholia is a selective form of delirium organized around a fixed idea. What Esquirol does is extend this observation to the passions in general. He claims that his concept of monomania is inseparable from the passions. He also claims that it has all the characteristic signs of the passions. Thus 'the delirium of monomaniacs is exclusive, fixed and permanent, like the ideas of a passionate man'.

The passions, then, are not simply affective states that can endure for long periods of time. They are affective states of long duration organized around a fixed idea. In this scheme, the fixed idea acts as an organizing force, a magnetic core, that directs attention and behavior, causing the organism to prefer and seek some things while avoiding and rejecting others. Passions then are affective states tied to fixed ideas. For example, ambition (*ambition*) is a passion organized around the fixed idea that one must be successful (Esquirol 1838, 726). And avarice (*avarice*) is a passion that is organized around the fixed idea that one should seek and conserve riches. When these ideas attain an all-consuming hold on the individual that cannot be broken or redirected, they acquire the character of monomania.

Clearly, ambition and avarice are not simply momentary affective states, nor are they reducible to their short-term emotional analogues. Passions of this sort are better described as projects or goals that can extend over a lifetime. They are centered on a fixed idea but they are not simply ideas. They are ideas sustained by affective force and motivation, which is what makes them passions. Note that passions in this sense are not assimilable or reducible to dispositions. The mechanisms are different. This is because of the cumulative manner in which passions grow and feed on themselves as they evolve. In their development, passions alter their own constitution at the same time as they alter the world in order to achieve their stated goal. Dispositions are not usually thought of in this way (but see Goldie 2006; Wollheim 1999, 2–9, 11–17). The progress of a passion is analogous to an avalanche. There is a 'snowball effect' that is not normally associated with the concept of disposition. The disposition of salt to dissolve in water remains the same. Not so with the progress of a passion. In this case there is not only repetition but also growth of a specific, cumulative kind.

We have come a long way from emotions: momentary and sudden affective states of short duration and extinction. It seems impossible to deny that any psychopathology of affective life that aspires to be comprehensive must incorporate the passions in addition to emotions. There are several key differences between the two posits that have emerged. First, unlike emotions, which have a sudden onset and relatively rapid extinction, passions can endure for long periods of time. Second, while passions have a significant intellectual component, emotions have limited intellectual elements, or even none at all. And third, while passions are complex affections that evolve in a cumulative manner over time, emotions are relatively simple responses that remain the same.

## 10.8 IMMANUEL KANT: PASSION WITH REASON

Immanuel Kant is a major philosophical figure in the history of passion and emotion. Like Hume, he believes that philosophy and science require passions and emotions. But Hume, you will recall, fails to give any clear or consistent account of the difference between these two posits. Not so with Kant. He addresses the distinction between passion (*leidenschaften*) and emotion (*affekte*) with uncompromising rigor and clarity.

At the beginning of his discussion of the Faculty of Desire (*appetitio*) in the *Anthropologie*, Kant states:

Emotion works like water that breaks through a dam; passion works like a river digging itself deeper and deeper into its bed. Emotion works upon health like a stroke of apoplexy; passion works like consumption or atrophy . . . Emotion is like an intoxicant that can be slept off; passion is to be regarded as an insanity which broods over an idea that is embedding itself deeper and deeper (Kant 1798/1996, 156–7).

According to Kant, 'emotions are generally morbid occurrences' (Kant 1798/1996, 160). Thus 'whoever is customarily seized by emotion with rapture, no matter how good-natured he may be, still resembles a deranged person' (157). Apparently, Kant does not hold the emotions in high esteem. However, not all emotions are blatantly morbid. Neither are they all self-defeating. Some emotions, like laughter and weeping can 'strengthen health' (167–8). This perhaps is one reason why people sometimes wish for certain emotions.

The situation with passions is notably different. Kant says that these are states that 'no man wishes for himself' (Kant 1798, 1996, 157). With respect to the passions, he asks rhetorically: 'who wants to have himself put in chains when he can be free?' (157). Passions are like chains. They do the 'greatest harm to freedom' (172). Thus 'passions are not, like emotions, merely unfortunate moods teeming with many evils, but they are without exception bad' (174). In other words: 'Emotion produces a momentary loss of freedom and self control. Passion surrenders both, and finds pleasure and satisfaction in servile disposition' (174).

Reason plays a special role in the case of passions that is absent in the case of emotions. While 'want of reflection' and a transitory form are both characteristic of emotions, the passions 'must take roots gradually and even be able to coexist with reason' (Kant 1798, 1996, 159, 172). Indeed, passions are usually assisted by reason. They always 'presuppose a maxim of the subject, namely, to act according to a purpose prescribed to him by his inclination' (173). Thus passion 'is always associated with the purposes of reason, and one cannot attribute passions to animals' (173). Some passions have an innate character and derive from our 'natural inclinations', for example, freedom and sex. Most other passions are acquired culturally. These include ambition, lust of power, and avarice (175).

Kant views both passions and emotions as largely pathological. He tells us that 'to be subject to emotions and passions is probably always an illness of the mind because both emotion and passion exclude the sovereignty of reason' (Kant 1798, 1996, 155). Most of the figures we have considered would agree with Kant that the passions can indeed cause and degenerate into mental illness. But none of them would agree that the passions are always or necessarily negative in the manner he describes. Théodule Ribot would also disagree with this last claim, although he would undoubtedly agree with our other psychopathologists that the passions can both cause and degenerate into mental illness. Ribot is the last and most important figure in our brief history of passion and emotion.

# 10.9 THÉODULE RIBOT: PASSION AS EXAGGERATED TENDENCY

Théodule Ribot is the founder of experimental psychology in France (Nicolas and Charvillat 2001). He had a long and illustrious career and made major contributions to the study of heredity, memory, attention, personality, and especially psychopathology (Nicolas and Murray 1999). Although William James and other contemporaries of Ribot respected and cited his work, he remains almost completely unknown in present-day psychological and philosophical circles outside of France (but see Berrios 1985, 1996; Dixon 2003, 108. note 470). Yet his work on affectivity is remarkable in its rigor and originality, especially on the topic of the passions. He wrote a total of five books on affectivity, one of which is specifically devoted to the passions. His contribution to the theory of the passions, and indeed many other aspects of his thought, are still relevant today (Nicolas 2005).

Ribot begins his 'Essay on the Passions' (*Essai sur les Passions*) by remarking how the term 'passion' (*passion*) has fallen into oblivion and disrepute (Ribot 1907/2007, 1). He points out that while the term was once stretched to include anything and everything in matters affective, it has been replaced by the term 'emotion' (*émotion*), which is now plagued by exactly the same abuse and laxity (v–vii, 2–3). All this is a mistake, Ribot says. After reminding readers of Immanuel Kant's famous distinction between passion and emotion in the *Anthropologie*, he proceeds to distinguish those two posits in his own manner. In doing so he builds importantly on Kant's observations. However, he also tells us that we must reject Kant's 'excessive thesis' (*thèse excessive*) that the passions are always pathological (4).

According to Ribot, the passions have their origin in primitive tendencies (*tendances*) and movements (*mouvements*) of the organism. He endorses the definition of passion as an 'exaggerated tendency': '*exagération d'une tendance*' (Ribot 1907/2007, 13). Contrary to both common sense and etymology, which suggest that the passions are primarily passive (Greek: *pati, pathe*; Latin: *passi, passiones*), Ribot argues instead that the passions are fundamentally active (43, 55). His main thesis is that the passions are a form of motor activity (*activité motrice*). Specifically, they are a form of motor activity based on two kinds of movement: initiation of movement (*impulsion*) and cessation of movement (*arrêt*).

The above two forms of movement – impulse and arrest – give rise to 'dynamic passions' (*passions dynamiques*) and 'static passions' (*passions statiques*), respectively (Ribot 1907/2007, 25, 31, 43). Dynamic passions tend to build on impulses (*impulsion*) and are expansive (135). Ribot sometimes labels these 'positive' (184). Static passions build on repulsion (*repulsion*) and are concentrated and inhibitory (135). These Ribot sometimes labels 'negative' (185).

Examples of dynamic passions include love, ambition, avarice, gambling, and some passional forms of religious and political devotion and fanaticism (Ribot 1907/2007, 184). Examples of static passions include hate, jealousy, and some passional forms of religious and political persecution (184). Ribot is careful to note that there can be passions with alternating and mixed (*mixtes*) dynamic and static features. Such intermediate cases are probably more numerous than the pure types (44).

In addition to their motor element (*élément moteur*) the passions also have an intellectual element (*élément intellectuel*). In dynamic passions the motor element is stronger and the intellectual is weaker, while in static passions the reverse is true (Ribot 1907/2007, 43–4). The intellectual element of passions is absolutely fundamental to their nature. Each individual passion is defined by a goal (*but*) or ideal (*idéal*) that is manifest as a fixed idea (*idée fixe*). The passion in question is organized around this fixed idea, which gives it a unique, exclusive direction (15–16).

Passions often begin insidiously in the unconscious and then grow to the point where their fixed idea comes to dominate and absorb the whole life (Ribot 1907/2007, 17–18, 138). Ribot likens the growth of a passion to an avalanche – a kind of cumulative summation that feeds back on itself and grows as it progresses. Passions can end in five different ways (138). Either (1) the passion eventually burns itself out through exhaustion (*épuisement*); or (2) it is transformed (*transformé*) into another passion which shares a common core; or (3) it is replaced by a different passion though substitution (*substitution*); or (4) it leads to madness (*folie*) due to excess; or finally (5), it ends because it causes the death of its bearer (142). Ribot devotes an entire chapter to how the passions end: '*comment les passions finissent*' (136–80). This discussion is one of the most interesting aspects of his theory.

Formally speaking, passions are constituted by three elements. They have motor, intellectual, and affective elements (Ribot 1907/2007, 20–1, 182). By itself a fixed idea is not a passion. It is simply an idea. In order to move us, that fixed idea requires motor elements. However, passions are not simply motor tendencies with a specific intellectually defined goal or direction. They are complex states and processes. Thus passions also have an affective element. Feelings and other affective states (*états affectifs*) must be present for there to be passion. Sometimes passion can arise from or give rise to emotion (127–34). But most often passions organize emotions and 'passion is organized emotion' (Shand 1907, 488).

The notion of organization is central here. Alexander Shand, one of Ribot's most astute critics, explains the point this way: 'in every passion there is a system of self-control regulating more or less efficiently the intensity and behavior of its emotions; whereas when emotions act independently there is at most the restraint which one exerts on the others, there is no system of self-restraint within the emotion' (Shand 1907, 488). Passions thus represent the highest level of organization in our affective life. Emotions are simpler, and feelings yet even simpler, forms of affective experience. Other affective states that can accompany passions are affective memories and evaluative judgments. Creative imagination (*imagination créatrice*) is also often involved. Among contemporary philosophers of emotion, only Peter Goldie comes close to recognizing the existence of such complex emotional states of long duration. His distinction between *emotions* and *emotional episodes* nicely captures the fact that the passions are often accompanied by discrete individual emotional episodes and responses, which are connected to the aim and intellectual content of those passions (Goldie 2000, 12–16, 104). In a related point, Bennett Helm appears to recognize the importance of emotional organization that both Shand and Ribot attribute to the passions. He argues that emotions can sometimes be linked to other emotional states and responses in patterns that are organized around a shared *focus* (Helm 2001).

Feelings are a crucial ingredient of Ribot's theory. They provide the backdrop of our affective life. According to him, our affective life is populated by fleeting affective feeling states of momentary duration. These are the foundation of affective life. Those affective feeling states express appetites (*appétits*), needs (*besoins*), tendencies (*tendances*) that are inherent to our psychophysiological organization (Ribot 1907/2007, 4). Feelings at this level are states of feeble and moderate intensity. Some are pleasurable and displeasurable and linked to the satisfaction of basic needs and elementary sensory processes. Ribot admits that at this level language is largely inadequate. Most such feeling states elude linguistic and scientific description. They are largely impossible to seize (*insaisissable*). Ribot's characterization of this dimension of affective life bears an interesting resemblance to what some contemporary affective scientists have called 'background feelings' or 'core affect' (Damasio 1994; Russell 2003).

Emotions are another important posit in Ribot's affective psychology. Much of what he says regarding emotions and how they differ from passions reiterates themes we have already encountered in our history of passion and emotion. Thus emotions are said to be states of sudden onset, short duration, and quick extinction, while passions are said to endure for months or years. One interesting new criterion for distinguishing the two which is proposed by Ribot is that passions are stable while emotions are unstable (Ribot 1907/2007, 15, 129). It is the presence of a fixed idea – an intellectual component – that makes the passions stable compared to emotions. Passions also have additional intellectual components that make them unlike emotions. They involve imagination, memory, logic, and judgments, to an extent that emotions do not (29, 33, 35, 37). Ribot also makes the interesting observation that while emotions exist only in the present, the passions also live in the future and the past (33). They feed on affective memories of the past and reach into anticipated affective states in the future. Finally, passions are also said to differ from emotions in their intensity, although clearly this is a criterion that needs to be treated with caution, since it is often differentially applicable, not only to passions but even some emotions (20, 25–7). Ribot is careful to underscore that all of his criteria are nuanced and that nothing is entirely rigid and determinate in the affective realm.

In sum, passions are organized and enduring affective–motor–intellectual complexes that alter and filter the environment through mechanisms of association and dissociation, imagination and evaluative judgment, motor attraction and repulsion, impulse and inhibition, in accordance with a fixed idea. Unlike emotions, which are 'preformed' responses, passions are social and cultural products. Because of their intellectual limitations, children are incapable of sophisticated passions and animals have no passions at all (Ribot 1907/2007, 25).

Some highlights in Ribot's list of passions include: drunkenness (*ivrognerie*), gluttony (*gourmandise*), love (*amour*), will to power (*volonté de puissance*), gambling and play (*jeu*), ambition (*ambition*), avarice (*avarice*), antipathy (*antipathie*), patriotism (*patriotisme*), and various forms of political fanaticism and religious devotion (Ribot 1907/2007, 25, 26, 42, 44, 120, 139, 157). Collecting is a passion, on his view, and one with innumerable varieties (122–127). He frequently cites Napoleon's ambition as an example of a 'great passion' (*grande passion*) that absorbs the individual's entire life. Such passions have an almost universal character (9). Passions of shorter duration are '*passionettes*' (141). These are often closer to emotion than passion. And we must not forget 'small passions' (*petites passions*) which are limited and bizarre or rare (122). Note that many of these passions give rise to yet other passions.

Ribot is careful to trace each passional form to its origins in primitive instincts and tendencies of the organism: nutrition, conservation, attraction, expansion etc. He offers not a classification or description of the passions but rather a genealogy (Ribot 1907/2007, 45–136). Contemporary readers may balk at some of his examples. But Ribot himself would undoubtedly admit that his list needs revising in light of new scientific developments. Because of this, his own list is meant to be very flexible and open-ended. Suffice it to say that, once again in our history of passion and emotion, we have a derivation of affective posits that is based on considerations of origins and homology, rather than analogy based on adherence to names in natural language. This and the general manner in which Ribot attempts to distinguish among passions, emotions, and feelings, is what is primarily interesting about his account.

There remains the matter of Ribot's stance on the psychopathology of the passions. Are the passions all necessarily pathological? (Ribot 1907/2007, 162). We have seen that they do not all end in madness. But could they still all be morbid in character? Certainly, passions are sometimes closely allied with mental illness (167). But there are also differences. The madman often has no insight into his madness, whereas the bearer of a passion is normally aware of his passion (166). And while passions are always associated with a fixed idea that dominates the personality, many forms of mental illness have no such intellectual element (165). In the end, Ribot says that he is inclined to side with a pathological view of the passions (*thèse pathologique*). At the same time, he maintains that the passions cannot all be completely identified with individual forms of mental illness (170). This is true despite the fact that they are made of the 'same stuff' (*taillés dans la même étoffe*).

Ribot's final position on the question whether the passions are all pathological is that there is no one-to-one correspondence between different types of passion and existing varieties of mental illness (Ribot 1907, 170). He continues to reject Kant's 'excessive thesis' that the passions are all and always 'pathological' (*pathologique*) and 'morbid' (*morbide*). However, he concedes that the passions are ultimately 'abnormal' (*anormal*) states and processes (174). That is not the same as pathological.

Due to their stable and enduring nature, passions interrupt and impede the normal ebb and flow of psychic life. They represent a rupture (*rupture*) in psychic life. According to Ribot, as a rule (*règle*), our psychic life is defined by constant change and perpetual adaptation (Ribot 1907/2007, 165). Thus, in its 'normal' (*normal*) – or baseline – state, psychic life is characterized by a high degree of plasticity (*plasticité*). The passions interrupt this momentary flux of change and adjustment. They polarize consciousness in a single and unique direction, as they feed off and subjugate other goals and projects of the individual and consciousness generally (174). Ribot sometimes goes so far as to say that the passions are comparable to parasitic growths, or tumors, of consciousness (*une excroissance, un parasitisme*). But this general formula needs to be understood in a nuanced way. 'Abnormal' in the above explanation sometimes means only 'unusual' and not necessarily 'destructive' or wholly 'pathological'. In the end, we must look at particular cases and there is no absolute answer to the question whether the passions are pathological (175).

## 10.10 THE NATURAL KIND STATUS OF PASSION

The theoretical developments reviewed here strongly suggest that 'passion' is a necessary theoretical posit and category in affective science. The onset, growth, and various endings of the passions constitute a distinct explanatory domain within affective science, a system that is governed by its own special explanatory principles and regularities. Therefore, it makes sense to say that passion is a natural kind (Charland 2002, 2005). This point is implicit in all of the major thinkers in our history of passion and emotion. All of them treat the passions as a unified 'coherent category' representing a distinct explanatory domain of mind, which is different from, say, the understanding or the will (Dixon 2003, 4).

Combined with our other two affective posits, namely feelings and emotions, the passions constitute the affective realm, the domain of 'affectivity' (Berrios 1985). In our account, affectivity also constitutes a distinct, but wider, explanatory domain of its own. There is an important sense in which it, too, is a natural kind. Ribot is very clear on this question of the distinct theoretical status of affectivity. In his 'Problems of Affective Psychology' (*Problèmes de Psychologie Affective*) he explicitly argues that affectivity is theoretically distinct from the intellect. While he is careful to acknowledge their interdependence and interaction, he is adamant that the two are theoretically distinct. He also argues that affectivity is primordial in our mental life: '*la conscience primordiale est donc purement affective*' (Ribot 1910, 8). There are important lesson here for contemporary 'cognitive' science, which continues to favor the study of cognitive phenomena over affective ones. The situation is much the same in psychopathology, where affectivity continues to be treated as the 'poor relation' of the intellect (Berrios 1985, 1996).

With affective science and affectivity more firmly theoretically in place, we are left with the challenge posed by Descartes's Gauntlet. Descartes himself left the problem to posterity. But he did talk about both science and morals in his treatise on the passions. Pinel also tackled the issue directly in his clinical theory of 'moral treatment'. He proposed psychological interventions (*le moral*) that often had ethical implications or overtones (*la morale*). Whether Pinel succeeded in this endeavor remains open to debate (Charland forthcoming). On their side, Hume and Kant clearly embraced the perspectives of both science and morals in their respective theories of the passions. But such a combined perspective proved unacceptable to medical theorists like Crichton and Esquirol, who were arguably more consistent on the matter than Pinel. On his side, Ribot ignores morals altogether. He limits his discussion of 'moral' matters to what is psychological (*le moral*), setting ethics and morals (*la morale*) aside. Neither the psychology or psychopathology of affectivity have much to do with ethics and morals on his view. Not surprisingly, by 'moral' (*moral*) he means only what is mental or psychological as opposed to what is physical (Ribot 1907, 186).

This issue in the history of passion and emotion – Descartes's Gauntlet – is still with us today, as modern scientific accounts of 'emotional regulation' and psychotherapy continue to profess to be scientific and largely value-free (Healy 1990). On this question, it is perhaps the experience of Pinel that is the most philosophically interesting and enlightening. It shows that it is clinically impossible to completely eschew matters of ethics and morals in psychotherapy, scientific or otherwise (Charland 2008*b*; forthcoming). If true, this means that the professed scientific credentials of large segments of the psychology and psychopathology of affectivity may need to be rethought.

## References

BEEN ZEEV, AARON (2000), *The Subtlety of Emotions* (Cambridge, MA: MIT Press).
BERRIOS, G. E (1996), *The History of Mental Symptoms: Descriptive Psychopathology since the Nineteenth Century* (Cambridge: Cambridge University Press).

—— (1985), 'The Psychopathology of Affectivity: Conceptual and Historical Aspects'. *Psychological Medicine* 15: 745–58.

CHARLAND, LOUIS C. (Forthcoming) 'Pinel's Passions: Science and Morals in the Affective Psychopathology of Philippe Pinel'. *History of Psychiatry.*

—— (2008a), 'Alexander Crichton's Psychopathology of the Passions'. *History of Psychiatry* 19(3): 275–96.

—— (2008b), 'Technological Reason and the Regulation of Emotion'. In Jim Phillips (ed.) *Psychiatry and Technology* (Oxford: Oxford University Press), pp. 61–9.

—— (2007), 'Benevolent Theory: Moral Treatment at the York Retreat'. *History of Psychiatry*, 18(1): 61–80.

—— (2006), 'The Moral Nature of the Cluster B Personality Disorders'. *Journal of Personality Disorders* 20(2): 116–25.

—— (2005), 'The Heat of Emotion: Valence and the Demarcation Problem'. *Journal of Consciousness Studies* 12 (8–10): 82–102.

—— (2004), 'Moral Treatment and the Personality Disorders'. In Jennifer Radden (ed.) *The Philosophy of Psychiatry: A Companion* (Oxford: Oxford University Press) pp. 64–77.

—— (2002), 'The Natural Kind Status of Emotion'. *British Journal for the Philosophy of Science* 53: 511–37.

CRICHTON, ALEXANDER (1798), *An Inquiry into the Nature and Origin of Mental Derangement* (London: Cadell & Davies).

COTTINGHAM, JOHN, STOOTHOFF, ROBERT, and MURDOCH, DUGALD (trans.) (1985), *The Philosophical Writings of Descartes.* Vol. I. (Cambridge: Cambridge University Press).

DAMASIO, ANTONIO (1994), Descartes' Error: Emotion, Reason and the Human Brain (New York: Putnam & Sons).

DESCARTES, RENÉ (1650/1990), *Les Passions de l'âme* (Paris: Librairie Générale Française).

DIXON, THOMAS (2006), 'Patients and Passions: Languages of Medicine and Emotion, 1789–1850'. In Fay Bound Alberti (ed.) *Medicine, Emotion, and Disease, 1750–1950* (Palgrave), pp. 22–52.

DIXON, THOMAS (2003), *From Passion to Emotion: The Creation of a Secular Psychological Category* (Cambridge: Cambridge University Press).

ELSTER, JON (1999), *Alchemies of the Mind: Rationality and the Emotions* (Cambridge: Cambridge University Press).

ESQUIROL, JEAN-ÉTIENNE (1838), *Des Maladies mentales considerées sous les rapports médical, hygiénique, et médico-légal* (Paris: Baillière).

—— (1805/1980), *Des Passions considérées comme causes, symptômes et moyens curatifs de l'aliénation mentale* (Paris: Librarie des Deux Mondes).

EVANS, DYLAN (2001), *Emotion: The Science of Sentiment* (Oxford: Oxford University Press).

FIESER, JAMES (1992), 'Hume's Classification of the Passions and its Precursors'. *Hume Studies* 18: 1–17.

GOLDIE, PETER (2006), 'Wollheim on Emotion and Imagination'. *Philosophical Studies* 127(1): 1–17.

—— (2000), *The Emotions: A Philosophical Exploration* (Oxford: Clarendon Press).

GOLDSTEIN, JAN (2001), *Console and Classify: The French Psychiatric Profession in the Nineteenth Century* (Cambridge: Cambridge University Press).

GRIFFTHS, PAUL E. (1997), *What Emotions Really Are: The Problem of Psychological Categories* (London and Chicago: University of Chicago Press).

HEALY, DAVID (1990), *The Suspended Revolution: Psychiatry and Psychotherapy Re-Examined* (London and Boston: Faber and Faber).

HELM, BENNETT (2001), *Emotional Reason: Deliberation, Motivation, and the Nature of Value* (Cambridge: Cambridge University Press).

HICKISH, GORDON, HEALY, DAVID, and CHARLAND, LOUIS C. (trans.) (2008), *Medico-Philosophical Treatise on Mental Alienation* (New York: Wiley-Blackwell).

JAMES, SUSAN (1997), *Passion and Action: The Emotions in Seventeenth-Century Philosophy* (Oxford: Oxford University Press).

KANT, IMMANUEL (1798/1996), *Anthropology from a Pragmatic Point of View*. Translated by Victor Lyle Dowdell. Revised and edited by Hans H. Rudnick (Carbondale and Edwardsville: Southern Illinois University Press).

LEVI, ANTHONY (1964), *French Moralists: The Theory of the Passions 1585 to 1649* (Oxford: Clarendon Press).

LYONS, WILLIAM (1908), *Emotion* (Cambridge: Cambridge University Press).

NICOLAS, SERGE (2005), *Théodule Ribot: Philosophe breton, fondateur de la psychologie française* (Paris: L'Harmattan).

NICOLAS, SERGE and CHARVILLAT, AGNES (2001), 'Introducing Psychology as an Academic Discipline in France: Théodule Ribot and the College de France (1888–1901)'. *Journal of the History of the Behavioral Sciences* 37(2): 143–64.

NICOLAS, SERGE, and MURRAY, DAVID J. (1999), 'Théodule Ribot (1839–1916): Founder of French Psychology: A Biographical Introduction'. *History of Psychology* 2(4): 277–301.

NORTON, DAVID F. and NORTON, MARY J. (eds.) (2000), *David Hume: A Treatise on Human Nature* (Oxford: Oxford University Press).

PANKSEPP, JAAK (1998), *Affective Neuroscience: The Foundations of Human and Animal Behavior* (Oxford: Oxford University Press).

PICHOT, PIERRE (2000), 'The Passions in French Psychiatric History'. In Ernest Franzek, Gabor S. Ungvari, Eckhart Ruther, and Helmut Beckman (eds.), *Progress in Differentiated Psychopathology* (Wurzburg, Germany: International Wernicke-Kleist-Leonard Society), pp. 72–7.

—— (1983), *Un Siècle de psychiatrie* (Paris: Roche).

PIGEAUD, JACKIE. (2001), *Aux Portes de la psychiatrie* (Aubier: Paris).

PINEL, PHILIPPE (1809), *Traité médico-philosophique sur l'aliénation mentale* (Paris: Brosson).

PORTER, ROY (1987), *Mind-Forg'd Manacles: A History of Madness in England from the Restoration to the Regency* (London: Athlone).

PRINZ, JESSE (2004), *Gut Reactions: A Perceptual Theory of Emotion* (Oxford: Oxford University Press).

RIBOT, THÉODULE (1910), *Problèmes de psychologie affective* (Paris: Félix Alcan).

—— (1907/2007), *Essai sur les passions* (Paris: L'Harmattan).

RIESE, WALTER (1969), *The Legacy of Philippe Pinel: An Inquiry into Thought on Mental Alienation* (New York: Springer).

RORTY, AMELIE (1986), 'The Historicity of Psychological Attitudes: Love Is Not Love Which Alters When It Alteration Finds'. *Midwest Studies in Philosophy* 10: 399–412.

—— (1982), 'From Passions to Emotions and Sentiments'. *Philosophy* 57: 175–88.

RUSSELL, JAMES, A. (2003), 'Core Affect and the Psychological Construction of Emotion'. *Psychological Review* 110(1): 145–72.

—— (1991), 'Culture and the Categorization of Emotion'. *Psychological Bulletin* 10(3): 426–50.

SHAND, ALEXANDER, F. (1907), 'Mr. Ribot's Theory of the Passions'. *Mind* 16(64): 477–505.

SOLOMON, ROBERT C. (1993), *Not Passion's Slave* (Oxford: Oxford University Press).

—— (2003), 'Nothing to be Proud Of'. In Robert C. Solomon, *Not Passion's Slave: Emotions and Choice* (Oxford: Oxford University Press), pp. 42–56.

WEINER, DORA. (1999), *Comprendre et soigner: Philippe Pinel (1745–1826.) La médecine de l'esprit* (Paris: Fayard).

—— (1990), 'Mind and Body in the Clinic: Philippe Pinel, Alexander Crichton, Dominique Esquirol and the Birth of Psychiatry'. In G. S. Rousseau (ed.), *The Languages of Psyche: Mind and Body in Enlightenment Thought* (Los Angeles: University of California Press), pp. 331–402.

WIERZBICKA, ANNA (1999), *Emotions Across Languages and Cultures* (Cambridge: Cambridge University Press).

WOLLHEIM, RICHARD (1999), *On the Emotions* (New Haven and London: Yale University Press).

# PART III

## EMOTIONS AND PRACTICAL REASON

C H A P T E R   1 1

················································································

# EMOTIONAL CHOICE AND RATIONAL CHOICE

················································································

## JON ELSTER

## 11.1 INTRODUCTION

················································································

The relation between emotion and *reason* has been a major topic in Western philosophy since its inception. The topic of this chapter, the relation between emotion and *rationality*, is a more recent concern, reflecting the fact that the idea of rationality is itself a fairly new one. I shall not here explore the distinction between reason and rationality (see Elster 2009), except to note that while the idea of reason has a normative purpose, that of rationality serves to *explain* behavior.

Strictly speaking, the idea of rationality, too, is primarily normative. It tells an agent what he or she should do to realize his or her aims as well as possible. The explanatory use arises when we adopt the hypothesis that the agent has taken the normative advice and test it by confronting the prescribed behavior with the observed behavior. In economics, rational-choice explanations of behavior, based on the assumption that

This chapter overlaps to some extent with my chapter on emotion in the *Oxford Handbook of Analytical Sociology* (Elster 2009*a*). Readers who want to pursue the empirical issues briefly discussed here are referred to that chapter for a fuller treatment.

agents maximize expected utility, was the staple until about 1980, when they began to be subject to criticism from a number of scholars who also, crucially, replaced them with other models of behavior. Broadly speaking, these alternative models constitute the loosely unified field of *behavioral economics*. The main postulates in this approach are probably those of loss aversion (Kahneman and Tversky 1979) and hyperbolic time discounting (Ainslie 1975).

Emotions, too, have a place within behavioral economics, but a secondary one compared with the two mechanisms just mentioned. The influential work of George Loewenstein (1996) on "visceral factors" includes the emotions, but only on a par with pain, thirst, intoxication, and drug cravings, thus ignoring the cognitive antecedent of emotions as well as their action tendencies. Often, "emotion" simply means "affect" or "arousal", thus precluding fine-grained distinctions such as, say, that between guilt and shame. One aim of the present chapter is to persuade both philosophers of social science and practicing social scientists that a systematic account of the impact of emotion on the mental antecedents of action can improve our understanding of many forms of behavior. I shall also consider the thorny question of whether emotions can have a direct impact on action.

Although I shall be comparing emotions and rationality as causes of choice and action, one might also ask whether the emotions themselves are or can be rational. I have argued elsewhere (Elster 1999a, Ch. IV) that the answer, by and large, is negative. Emotions can be instrumentally *useful* and biologically *adaptive*, but since (i) they are typically unchosen and (ii) rationality can be a feature only of choice, I conclude that they cannot be *rational*. Below I address the slightly different question whether emotions might enhance rationality and answer, once again, in the negative.

Section 11.2 provides the foil for the analysis by presenting the standard model of rational choice. In Section 11.3 I present a model of emotional choice that involves the same basic elements as the rational-choice model, differing only in the causal relations that obtain among them. In Sections 11.4 through 11.7 I then consider the impact of emotion on each of the basic elements: action, desires, beliefs, and information-gathering.

## 11.2 A MODEL OF RATIONAL CHOICE

What I take to be the standard model of rational choice is defined in terms of the relation among four elements: action, beliefs, desires (or preferences), and information (Fig. 11.1).

The arrows in the diagram have a double interpretation: they stand for relations of causality as well as of optimality. The desires and the beliefs of a rational agent

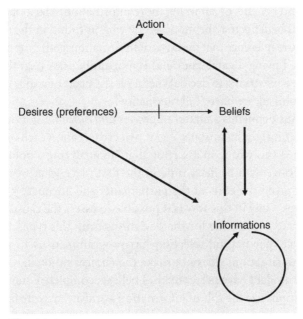

**Fig. 11.1**

cause him or her to choose the course of behavior that they rationalize.[1] In this Humean approach, no arrows lead to the desires: they are the unmoved movers of behavior. This is not to say, of course, that desires are uncaused, only that they are not the result of any optimizing operation.[2]

The rational agent optimizes in three separate dimensions. He or she chooses the action that best realizes his or her desires, given their beliefs about what their options are and about the consequences of choosing them. I shall refer to this condition as "minimal rationality". The beliefs are themselves inferred from the available evidence by the procedures that are most likely, in the long run and on average, to yield true beliefs. The blocked arrow reflects the fact that desires are not allowed to have any direct impact on beliefs, as they have in wishful thinking or in counterwishful thinking (see Section 11.6). Finally, prior to belief formation the agent may gather more evidence in an amount that is optimal in light of the agent's desires and the

---

[1] To avoid Davidsonian problems of non-standard causal chains, we should add "cause in the right way".

[2] In some cases, an agent may want to modify her desires, e.g. if she finds that her all-things-considered preferences are too easily reversed. Because we generally lack the technology, the change may not be feasible; and even if it were, the fact that most technologies are costly can be a deterrent. In practice, I believe that rational change of desires is extremely rare and can safely be disregarded for purposes of moral psychology. In other cases, rationality may require a change in derived or induced preferences, as when knowledge about the effects of smoking, combined with the fundamental preference for good health, causes a preference reversal.

expected costs and benefits of gathering more information. The loop reflects the fact that the expected benefits may be modified by what is found in the search itself. We may note for future reference that the costs of information-gathering are of two kinds: direct costs (e.g. buying a catalogue) and opportunity costs (e.g. the risk of being bitten by a snake while trying to decide whether it is a snake or a stick). When all three conditions are fulfilled, we have "full rationality".

Rationality thus defined is a matter of *process and outcome*, not only of outcome, since one may get it right by mistake, e.g. if two errors cancel each other out. Hence Weber (1968, p. 6) was wrong in asserting that "in analyzing a political or military campaign it is convenient to determine in the first place what would have been a rational course, given the ends of the participants and adequate knowledge of all the circumstances. Only in this way is it possible to assess the causal significance of irrational factors as accounting for the deviations from this type." Similarly, as we shall see, the fact that natural selection has programmed us to make the right choices in certain situations does not make the choices rational.

Although the model I have presented is, I believe, completely standard, it may be worthwhile to emphasize the role of information acquisition. Note first that whereas a direct influence of desires on beliefs is inconsistent with rational belief formation, an indirect influence mediated by information-gathering is not necessarily irrational. A person who cares little about the future, for instance, is rationally unmotivated to invest resources in determining the expected life span of different car makes. He will form his beliefs about this aspect of the cars on the basis of whatever information he already happens to possess. This being said, some desire-information links are proof of irrationality, as when a person stops looking when and because the evidence collected so far supports the belief he would like to be true.

In many contexts it can be hard to determine the (unique) optimal investment in information. As was noted first, I think, by Sidney Winter (1964–65), one may run into an infinite regress if the determination itself requires information about the costs and benefits of the search. Yet it is often possible to fix lower and upper bounds on the investment. A doctor called to the scene of an accident has to do some preliminary tests before deciding on diagnosis and treatment, but not so many that the patient dies at his hands. When looking for mushrooms in an unfamiliar forest, general knowledge about the distribution of mushrooms tells us that we should try out a few sites before settling on one as the most profitable,[3] but at the same time we know we should not keep looking until nightfall. As we shall see below, emotional choice often induces, by two distinct mechanisms, too little investment in information. More conjecturally, it may sometimes induce excessive investment.

I use "desires" and "preferences" more or less interchangeably. Although each term seems more natural than the other in some situations, translations from one into the

---

[3] If we strike rich at the first attempt, however, there is no need to look further; this illustrates the loop in Fig. 11.1.

other are usually possible. The main difference is that desires, unlike preferences, do not necessarily have the feature that two options are simultaneously present to the mind. In the face of danger, a desire to flee does not imply a preference for fleeing over standing fast, since the latter option may not appear on the mental screen of the agent. Similarly, the desire to get a coveted object immediately may not be rooted in a structure of time preferences, not even in a short-lived structure. At the same time, the desire to do x may always, given specific circumstances, be overridden by a desire to do y. Following Gary Watson (1999), I believe there are no such things as irresistible desires. If these circumstances are not present, the idea of y may not come to mind. I do not think these mild ambiguities affect any of the substantial arguments I make below.

It will prove useful to distinguish between two kinds of preferences: substantive preferences and formal preferences or, as I shall call them, *propensities*. Substantive preferences relate to specific pairs of options, such as a preference for vanilla ice cream over chocolate or for one political candidate over another. Instances of propensities are the rate of discounting of the future, risk aversion, loss aversion, and the like. Although propensities may be somewhat domain-specific – a person may use different discount rates for future health and future income – they have a wider scope than substantive preferences. The final choice is often defined by the interaction between substantive preferences and propensities, as when I prefer chocolate today over vanilla tomorrow.

Rationality differs from intelligence as well as from wisdom. Broadly speaking, rationality is consistent with making many cognitive mistakes, provided that they have no systematic bias.[4] Intelligence, by contrast, is reasonably defined as the ability to make few cognitive mistakes. Wisdom may, perhaps, be defined as the ability to make choices that tend to make one's life as a whole go well. In this perspective, propensities such as a high rate of discounting of the future, a very high degree of risk aversion or a tendency towards risk-seeking may all be seen as unwise, although none of them detract from rationality. These remarks underline the idea that a rational agent *does as well as he or she can according to his or her own lights*, that is, given the cognitive resources and the propensities with which they find themselves endowed.

## 11.3 A MODEL OF EMOTIONAL CHOICE

Although my main concern is with the effects of emotions on other mental states and on behavior, I begin with a brief comment on their causes. I shall assume that

---

[4] Traditionally, it was assumed that these biases would have to be "hot", e.g. emotional. An important insight of the "behavioral economics revolution" is that we are also prone to systematic "cold" biases, which are more akin to optical illusions.

**Table 11.1**

| BELIEF | EMOTION |
|---|---|
| A imposed an unjust harm on B | B feels anger towards A |
| A imposed an unjust harm on C in the presence of B | B feels "Cartesian indignation" towards A |
| A is evil | B feels hatred towards A |
| A is weak or inferior | B feels contempt towards A |
| B shows contempt towards A | A feels shame |
| A has behaved unjustly or immorally | A feels guilt |
| A has something that B lacks and desires | B feels envy |
| A is faced with impending danger | A feels fear |
| ??? | B loves A |
| A suffers unmerited distress | B feels pity towards A |
| A enjoys undeserved good fortune | B feels "Aristotelian indignation" towards A |
| A has helped B | B feels gratitude towards A |

emotions arise from beliefs, that is, that they have cognitive causal antecedents. Although in human affairs this is the typical and most important case, it is not the only one. A mere perception without any propositional content can also trigger emotion, as is especially well known from the study of fears and panics (LeDoux 1996). I return to this issue below. Here, I only want to note that when perception occurs together with cognition, it can magnify the impact of the latter. A sign on the wall "Smoking is dangerous for your health" causes greater emotional arousal when accompanied by a color picture of a cancerous lung.

The relations between beliefs and the emotions they generate are remarkably fine-grained. (As we shall see shortly, the relations between the emotions and the desires to which they give rise are equally fine-grained.) Table 11.1 offers a sample of important cases:

Whether love has cognitive antecedents seems to be an open question (Soble 1990). According to Stendhal, love can arise only when there is a belief that it might be requited. This condition is, however, at most necessary, and surely not sufficient. As we shall see, many of the beliefs about the loved person that might seem to cause the emotion are in fact its effects. The other conditions seem broadly plausible. Novelists and moralists have, to be sure, offered finer distinctions and proposed numerous exceptions. If B's show of contempt towards A is perceived by A to be motivated by the desire to shame A, the reaction of A may be one of anger rather than shame. When A helps B, the latter may feel resentment rather than gratitude. B may feel angry merely because A inadvertently frustrated his desires, as automobile drivers can get furious when forced to slow down by a bike rider. As Descartes noted, when B loves C the reaction of B to A's unjust behavior towards C may be one of anger rather than indignation.

In Table 11.1, the belief-emotion connections are one-to-one. In more complex cases, there can be an element of indeterminacy in the triggering of emotion. If a parent gives an ice cream to a daughter and not to her brother, the latter may either feel anger towards the father or envy towards his sister. If the Resistance in a German-occupied country killed German soldiers in order to provoke retaliations against civilians, the latter may react either (as expected by the Resistance) by turning against the Germans or by turning against the Resistance. In World War II, both patterns were observed. Such cases of one-to-many relations are probably common.

For my purposes here, these summary comments on the causes of emotions will have to do. I turn now to the central issue of the effects of emotions. In discussing this question, I shall rely on the following model of emotional choice:

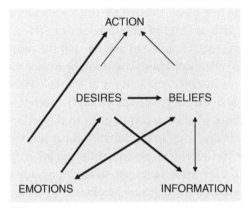

**Fig. 11.2**

The thinly drawn lines represent (as in Fig. 11.1) causal relations that are also optimality relations. The heavily drawn lines represent causal relations that are not optimality relations. Some of these causal influences violate optimality, as when desires directly shape beliefs. Others are independent of the question of optimality: given a certain belief, for instance, the idea of the optimal emotion arising from it is not well defined. The heavily drawn line from desires to information may be viewed as superimposed on the thin line connecting them in Fig. 11.1.

As shown in Fig. 11.2, beliefs can be the effect of emotions as well as their causes. This fact can generate a runaway feedback process or "emotional wildfire" (Ekman 1992a), as instantiated notably in fear. In the discussion in later sections, beliefs will in fact have a crucial role. In many cases, emotional choice will be minimally rational: the action performed will be the best means to realize the agent's desire, given his belief. If the belief is induced by emotion, however, the action will not be fully rational. (On my Humean premises, the fact a *desire* is induced by emotion need not undermine the full rationality of the action.) In the next section I discuss whether emotions can induce actions that are not even minimally rational.

## 11.4 WEAKNESS OF WILL

Consider, then, whether emotion can have a direct impact on action, bypassing the desire-belief mechanism. There is a venerable tradition in philosophy for arguing that emotions can cause agents to behave contrary to what, *at the time of action*, they believe would be the best thing to do, all things considered (e.g. Davidson 1969). "I do not do the good I want, but the evil I do not want is what I do" (St. Paul). "I see the better, and approve it, but follow the worse" (Medea). The claim is not that emotion is a necessary condition for weakness of will but that it can be a sufficient one. Although I do not want to deny the possibility of weakness of will in this synchronic sense, the idea is open to three objections (Elster 1999*b*).

It seems hard, in the first place, to envisage this combination of extreme passion and extreme lucidity, such as that found in Medea or in Racine's *Phèdre* (Bénichou 1948, p. 230). It is often more plausible to assume that the emotion that induces the desire to do wrong also clouds or biases cognition by one of the mechanisms I shall discuss later. This is, for instance, the pattern of Racine's Hermione (ibid.). In the second place, how could one distinguish empirically between this synchronic case and one in which a preference reversal occurred prior to the action, perhaps only a few milliseconds before? Finally, what is the causal mechanism by virtue of which the emotion bypasses the considered judgment of the agent? References to an alleged "partition of the mind" (Davidson 1982) are, so far, little more than hand waving.

Many purported instances of synchronic weakness of will may instead be due to a temporary *preference reversal* (Elster 2006, 2007*a*). A person who has volunteered for army service and then deserts under the influence of fear does not necessarily act against his preferences at the time of deserting, but might act in accordance with emotionally induced new preferences. Later, when the danger has abated and his original preferences are reinstated, he might regret deserting and even return to the army. The pattern, in other words, is the following:

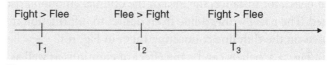

**Fig. 11.3**

I believe that this pattern has greater intuitive appeal than the idea of synchronic weakness of will, at least when emotions are involved. There may be "cold" cases of synchronic weakness of will, as when I find a full wallet in a deserted street and, against my better judgment, decide to keep the money. I remain skeptical (or agnostic) as to the existence even of such cases, but at least they are not vulnerable to the first of the three objections I canvassed above.

## 11.5 THE IMPACT OF EMOTION ON
## SUBSTANTIVE PREFERENCES

Each emotion has associated with it a characteristic *action tendency* (Frijda 1986), which is an incipient action, a state of readiness of the organism, including a desire to act in a certain way. In Fig. 11.2, the action tendencies are included among the desires. Table 11.2 shows the typical action tendencies for the emotions enumerated in Table 11.1.

As Table 11.1 shows, the relations between an emotion and an action tendency can be one-to-many rather than one-to-one. Fear, for instance, may cause either fight or flight. If a guilty person is unable to "redress the moral balance of the universe" by undoing the harm he has caused, he may try to achieve the same result by imposing a comparable harm on himself. If we combine the indeterminacy of the relations between beliefs and emotions with that of the relations between emotions and action tendencies, the overall scope for ambiguity is considerable. Which of the several possible emotions and action tendencies that will be triggered depends on contextual factors that may be hard to capture explicitly (Elster 1999*a*, Ch. I).

When action tendencies lead to actions, these may be minimally but not fully rational, depending on the rationality of the beliefs. For an example, consider the distinction between actions inspired by visceral (emotional) fear and those inspired by prudential fear (Gordon 1987, p. 77). An example of the effect of visceral fear is provided by the estimated 350 excess deaths caused after 9/11 by Americans using their car instead of flying to wherever they were going (Gigerenzer 2004). They may have conformed to the first part of La Fontaine's observation, "We believe easily what we fear and what we hope." By contrast, it appears that no excess deaths were caused by people switching from train to car after the attacks in Madrid on March

### Table 11.2

| EMOTION | ACTION TENDENCY |
| --- | --- |
| Anger, Cartesian indignation | Cause the object of the emotion to suffer |
| Hatred | Cause the object of the emotion to cease to exist |
| Contempt | Ostracize or avoid the object of the emotion |
| Shame | "Sink through the floor"; run away; kill oneself |
| Guilt | Confess; make amends; hurt oneself |
| Envy | Destroy the envied object or its owner |
| Fear | Fight; flight |
| Love | Approach, touch, help, or please the object of the emotion |
| Pity | Console or alleviate the distress of the object of the emotion |
| Aristotelian indignation | Confiscate the fortune of the object of the emotion |
| Gratitude | Help the object of the emotion |

11, 2004 (López-Rousseau 2005). The Spanish may have been habituated to terror by decades of ETA actions, and come to adopt an attitude of prudential fear.

Action tendencies are not "knee-jerk" automatic responses. They can be kept in check or tempered by prudential concerns or by countervailing action tendencies. As an example of the former, consider the Ultimatum Game:

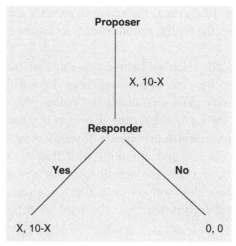

**Fig. 11.4**

In this game, one subject (the Proposer) offers a division of ten dollars between himself and another subject (the Responder). The latter can either accept it or reject it; in the latter case neither gets anything. A stylized finding is that Proposers typically offer around (5, 5) and that Responders reject offers that would give them 2 or less (see Camerer 2003, Ch. 2, for details and references). If Responders were motivated only by anger (an emotional response to unfair treatment), they would not accept anything less than 5. If they were motivated only by material self-interest, they would accept any positive amount. The experiments show that their motivation results from a parallel-ogram of forces with anger and prudence as the two components.

An illustration of how one action tendency may be kept in check by a countervailing one is provided by the fact that many people refrain from acting on a destructive envious urge, even when there is no risk of detection, because of the guilt they would feel if they gave full rein to the emotion. An alternative reaction can take the form of the transmutation of envy into Aristotelian indignation or anger (Elster 1999, Ch. V), as happens when people "rewrite the script" to make it appear as if the envied subject acquired his possession by immoral means and perhaps at one's own expense.

These emotion-based action tendencies are often claimed to have three proper-ties: quick decay, a cold-to-hot empathy gap, and a hot-to-cold empathy gap. For the first, I refer to Ekman (1992b); for the last two one may consult Loewenstein (1996, 2005). I shall briefly describe these claims and then point to some exceptions.

The quick decay of emotion is what enables us, in many cases, to refer to the emotion-induced preference reversal as a *temporary* one. In some cases, the emotion disappears together with its cause. When you flee from a danger, the fear abates because you have removed yourself from the threat. In other cases, the emotion simply loses momentum even though the cause is still present. The short half-life of anger, for instance, underlies the advice of counting to ten. (Whether an angry person could remember that advice is another matter.) In countries that had been occupied by Germany during World War II, the collaborators that were tried shortly after Liberation were sentenced more severely, for the same crimes, than those who were tried one or two years later. It seems very likely that the spontaneous abatement of emotion was a major cause of this trend (Elster 2004, Ch. 8).

If emotion induces immediate action, it may sometimes be reversed later when the emotion abates. Some of the severe sentences for collaborators who had been tried early were commuted in the light of the more lenient practice that developed later. In some cases, however, action taken on the basis of emotion-induced temporary preferences is irreversible. Some collaborators who received the death penalty were executed before the tide turned. When young men and women enlist in a guerilla movement in a moment of enthusiasm and later want to leave it, they may find that this option is closed to them (a lobster-trap situation).

While these and other examples show that emotion-induced preference reversals can be relatively short-lived, there are counterexamples. Unrequited love and unsatisfied desires for revenge may endure for decades (Elster 1999a, p. 305). Hatred and envy seem more impervious than anger to spontaneous decay. The emotion may also stay alive for very long if the abstract knowledge of injustice done to oneself or to one's ancestors is reinforced by constant perceptual reminders. Although we might think that killings would leave stronger memories than confiscation of property, the opposite can be the case. Referring to the 20th-century descendants of those who had their property confiscated in the French Revolution, one historian writes that "Generations forget more quickly spilled blood than stolen goods. By their continued presence under the eyes of those who had been despoiled of them, the fortunes providing from the national estates maintain an eternal resentment in the souls" (Gabory 1989, p. 1063).

A cold-to-hot empathy gap arises when an agent, in a non-emotional state, is incapable of anticipating the impact of an emotion he might experience on some future occasion. A hot-to-cold empathy gap arises when the agent, in an emotional state, is incapable of anticipating that it may not last forever. Both effects may be illustrated by the example of the six Frenchmen who killed themselves in June 1997 after they had been exposed as consumers of pedophiliac materials. Had they been able to anticipate the devastating impact of shame, they might have abstained from becoming consumers in the first place. Had they been able to anticipate that their shame (and the contempt of others) would decay with time, they might not have killed themselves.

In some cases, people have been able to anticipate the decay of their emotions and to act on the basis of that anticipation. During World War II, the desire to contribute to the American war effort was strong only immediately after hearing radio appeals for funds. A study of contributors revealed that some listeners telephoned at once because they wished to commit themselves to a bond before their generosity waned (Cowen 1991, p. 363, citing Merton 1946, pp. 68–9). A similar case arose in the Belgian war trials after World War II. On the basis of the experience from World War I, it was believed that after a while the popular willingness to impose severe sentences on the collaborators would give place to indifference. Hence some Belgians wanted the trials to proceed as quickly as possible, before anger was replaced by a more dispassionate attitude (Huyse and Dhondt 1993, p. 115). In these cases, the anticipation of decay produced the same effect as urgency: a desire for immediate action. In other cases, it may counteract urgency. In Holland after 1945, some jurists argued that the death penalty was to be avoided because "in collaboration cases the court, and the public, tended to become less severe as the memories of the occupation faded" (Mason 1952, p. 64).

## 11.6 The impact of emotion
### on formal preferences

Among formal preferences (or propensities), I include risk aversion, impatience, and urgency. Whereas the first two have been widely discussed, the third is relatively marginal in the literature. Yet I believe it is of comparable importance in its impact on behavior.

In many psychological studies of emotions, *valence* (position on the pleasure–pain dimension) is used as the independent variable. In this paradigm, it has been found that positive emotions tend to make people more risk-averse (Isen and Geva 1987), whereas negative emotions cause them to be more risk-seeking (Leith and Baumeister 1996). At the same time, positive and negative emotions generate, respectively, optimistic and pessimistic cognitive biases (Isen and Patrick 1983). Hence when subjects are not explicitly told the odds of winning and losing, but have to assess them from the evidence available to them, cognitive bias and risk attitudes work in opposite directions. Thus happy people assess the odds as more favorable, but for given odds are less willing to risk their money. The net effect is in general indeterminate.

Compared with the fine-grained classifications of emotions based on cognitive antecedents or action tendencies, valence is a coarse-grained category. In studies that use cognitive antecedents as the independent variable, the impact of emotion on risk attitudes appears in a different light. Lerner and Keltner (2001) found that, whereas fearful people expressed pessimistic risk estimates and risk-averse choices, angry people expressed optimistic risk estimates and risk-seeking choices. In this case, emotion-induced risk attitudes and emotion-induced cognitive bias work in the same direction.

I define *impatience* as a preference for early reward over later reward, i.e. some degree of time discounting. Although this preference can exist in "cold" unemotional states, it can be enhanced by emotion. I define *urgency*, which arises only as the effect of emotion, as a preference for early action over later action. The distinction is illustrated in Table 11.3.

In each case, the agent can take one and only one of two actions, A or B. In case 1, these options are available at the same time, in cases 2 and 3 at successive times. In case 2, the rewards (whose magnitude is indicated by the numbers) occur at the same later time, in cases 1 and 3 at successive later times. Suppose that, in an unemotional state, the agent chooses B in all cases, but that in an emotional state he chooses A. In case 1, the choice of A is due to emotionally induced impatience. In case 2, it is due to emotionally induced urgency. In case 3, it could be due to either or to the interaction of the two. In practice, the tendency for early action to be correlated with early reward makes it hard to isolate the two effects. One can, however, imagine experiments that would allow one to do so. It might be more difficult, however, to isolate the urgency effect from the anticipation of the decay of emotion.

In impatience, there is a two-way trade-off between the size of the reward and the time of delivery of the reward. In urgency, there is a three-way trade-off: the urge to act immediately may be neutralized if the size of the reward from acting later is sufficiently large or if that reward is delivered sufficiently early.

There is scattered evidence (e.g. Tice et al. 2001) and some speculation about how occurrent emotions may cause increased rate of time discounting. The change in the formal preferences of the agent may, in turn, induce a reversal of substantive

**Table 11.3**

| $T_1$ | $T_2$ | $T_3$ | $T_4$ |
|-------|-------|-------|-------|
| A | 3 | | |
| B | | 5 | |
| | | Case 1: Impatience | |
| A | | 3 | |
| | B | 4 | |
| | | Case 2: Urgency | |
| A | | 3 | |
| B | | | 6 |
| | | Case 3: Impatience and/or urgency | |

preferences, causing the agent to prefer front-loaded options, in which the benefits are delivered first and the costs come later, over options that have the opposite pattern.

The case of urgency is more complicated. The first to have clearly stated the idea may have been Seneca: "Reason grants a hearing to both sides, then *seeks to postpone action*, even its own, in order that it may gain time to sift out the truth; but anger is precipitate" (*On Anger* I.xvii). Seneca praises the Roman general Fabius, called the Cunctator (hesitator) for his delaying tactics, asking

How else did Fabius restore the broken forces of the state but by knowing how to loiter, to put off, and to wait – things of which angry men know nothing? The state, which was standing then in the utmost extremity, had surely perished if Fabius had ventured to do all that anger prompted. But he took into consideration the well-being of the state, and, estimating its strength, of which now nothing could be lost without the loss of all, he buried all thought of resentment and revenge and was concerned only with expediency and the fitting opportunity; he conquered anger before he conquered Hannibal. (*On Anger* I. xi)

Although the emotion-induced tendency to prefer immediate action to delayed action has not been much discussed or recognized by psychologists, it has long been recognized in proverbial wisdom: "Marry in haste, repent at leisure". I believe the tendency also underlies what has variously been called "commission bias" (Groopman 2007, p.169) or "action bias" (Bar-Eli et al. 2007) – an *inability to tolerate inaction*. It is hard to do nothing when we are under the sway of emotions. In Elster (2009*b*) I offer numerous other illustrations of the tendency (and suggest an experiment by which it might be elicited). Here, I shall only cite a striking example of the tendency of angry individuals to retaliate immediately, even when waiting is costless. In a dissenting opinion in the trial of General Yamashita after World War II, Justice Frank Murphy wrote that "in all this needless and unseemly haste there was no serious attempt to charge or prove that he committed a recognized violation of the laws of war" (Yamashita v. Styer, 327 U.S. 1 [1946]). The crucial fact is that the haste was *needless*: I return to this point.

Urgency can be highly adaptive. In threatening situations, immediate reaction is often crucial. The opportunity costs of urgency are often far less than the opportunity costs of waiting. In many cases, however, waiting is costless. After the enemy has been defeated, haste in condemning and executing him is indeed "needless". In typical cases, delaying a proposal of marriage cannot harm and might help. Whatever the causes of maladaptive urgency, it seems clear that it exists and matters. The reasons it has been ignored are probably that the effects of urgency are easily confused with those of impatience and that urgency is easily assumed to be adaptive in all cases simply because it is adaptive in some cases.

A contentious but important example is provided by the reactions of Western governments after the attacks on September 11, 2001. The unprecedented haste in which the antiterrorist laws were adopted (Haubrich 2003) suggests that emotion may have been at work. It is not clear which emotion dominated: anger or fear. Nor is it clear whose emotions were in play: those of the executive and legislative leadership or those of the population at large. Bracketing these issues, and assuming that the urgency of the measures that were taken had some emotional source, were they adaptive or maladaptive? I shall return to that question in the next section.

## 11.7 THE IMPACT OF EMOTION ON BELIEF FORMATION AND INFORMATION-GATHERING

As suggested by Fig. 11.2, emotions can affect beliefs in two ways: directly and indirectly via the gathering of information. The results are, respectively, biased beliefs and low-quality beliefs. I shall consider them in turn. Before I do so, let me express some skepticism towards the currently fashionable idea that emotions can enhance the rationality of belief formation. While it is clear, as I argue below, that emotionally induced belief formation can be adaptive, this effect is not due to the epistemically superior nature of the beliefs but to the opportunity costs of achieving epistemic superiority.

Earlier I cited La Fontaine: "We believe easily what we fear and what we hope." The second part of the statement refers to the well-known phenomenon of emotion-induced wishful thinking. In a state of "amour-passion" a person will find all sorts of wonderful qualities in the object of the emotion. As Stendhal says, "From the moment he falls in love even the wisest man no longer sees anything *as it really is*. [ . . . ] He no longer admits an element of chance in things and loses his sense of the probable; judging by its effect on his happiness, whatever he imagines becomes reality" (Stendhal 1980, Ch. 12). As a different kind of example, one may cite the numerous rumors, among Napoleon's followers, about his impending return after his two defeats in 1814 and 1815 (Ploux 2003).

This familiar effect is entirely unsurprising. The phenomenon of emotion-induced "counterwishful thinking" is more puzzling. Why should we believe that a danger is greater than it actually is? Why, for instance, would a husband believe that his wife is unfaithful to him when both the evidence and his desires point in the opposite direction? What's in it for the organism? The outcome is dissonance production, not reduction. This "Othello effect", as we might call it, does not seem to have attracted the attention of psychologists, although a few philosophers (e.g. Mele 1999) have offered some (to my mind unconvincing) speculations. Yet the phenomenon is undeniable, as shown by many cases of panicky rumor formation. After the insurrection of the workers in Paris in June 1848, for instance, two men who were observed on the side of a country road became first 10, then 300, and 600 in the telling and retelling, until finally one could hear that 3,000 "levelers" (*partageux*) were looting, burning, and massacring. Thirty thousand soldiers were sent out to counter the threat. An investigation revealed that one of the two was insane and that the other was his father who was in charge of him (Ploux 2003).

I now turn to the impact of emotion on belief that is mediated by information-gathering. One crucial mechanism is that of urgency. The preference for early action over delayed action may prevent the agent from gathering the amount of information that would have been optimal from a rational point of view. In itself, this mechanism does not induce biased beliefs, only low-quality beliefs. It may, however, *prevent de-biasing* of beliefs. Often, bias and urgency coexist. In love, we observe both the bias described by Stendhal and the urgency described by the proverb about marrying in haste. If it had not been for the urgency, the agent might have gathered more information about the other person that would have made it harder to sustain the rose-tinted perceptions. The same interaction between bias and urgency can occur in fear and anger. After September 11, 2001, emotion may both have induced an exaggerated perception of the danger and prevented the gathering of information that would have produced a more accurate perception.

Typically, urgency generates low-quality beliefs by causing the agent to ignore long-term consequences of present choice, because *the calculation of long-term and indirect effects is itself a time-consuming process.* One reason why legislatures scrutinize bills for a long time – sometimes several years – before enacting them into law is the desire to identify possible indirect or "perverse" effects. If they focus on the immediate – and more quickly identifiable – short-term effects only, they run the risk of making serious mistakes. After September 11, 2001, Western governments may have done exactly this. It has now become a commonplace to observe that the violation of human rights symbolized by Guantánamo Bay and Abu Ghraib led to more terrorists being recruited than were deterred or apprehended. As Minister of the Interior Nicholas Sarkozy opposed the French law banning the veil in schools on these grounds. In an interview with *Le Nouvel Observateur* on October 19, 2003, he stated his "fear that a law adopted in such a hurried way (*dans l'urgence*) would be viewed by the Muslim community as a punishment or a humiliation. This would only produce the opposite of the desired effect, and might risk triggering confrontation or radicalization. [ ... ] Let us not open up a new war of religion."

Emotion may also shape information-gathering by the need for cognitive *closure* (Kruglanski and Webster 1996). For some individuals, the state of not having a definite opinion on a given topic can be intensely unpleasant (see also Neurath 1913). Hence they may end the search for information prematurely and jump to poorly justified conclusions. Whereas urgency causes suboptimal investment in information because of the need to *act*, the induced need for closure is dissociated from action. At the same time, of course, beliefs shaped by the need for closure may serve as premises for action.

The need for closure can have several causes. Albert Hirschman (1986) has said that most Latin American cultures "place considerable value on having *strong opinions* on virtually *everything* from the *outset*". In such societies, to admit ignorance is to admit defeat. The emotional root of this tendency is *pridefulness*, induced by the belief that one is a superior kind of person. In other cases, the need for closure may be induced by the diffuse anxiety induced by the belief that one doesn't know what to believe. Montaigne (1991, p. 1165) said: "Many of this world's abuses are engendered – or to put it more rashly, all of this world's abuses are engendered – by our being schooled to be afraid to admit our ignorance and because we are required to accept anything which we cannot refute." The mind abhors a vacuum.

As noted earlier, an impatient person is rationally unmotivated to invest resources in determining long-term consequences of present action. Urgency and the need for closure may cause the agent to be irrationally unconcerned with the same effects. Hence, as shown in Fig. 11.5, urgency, impatience and the need for closure may interact to produce a strong tendency to invest few resources in gathering information about long-term consequences.

I conclude by a speculative remark about the tendency for emotions to cause *overinvestment* in information. I have in mind what I have elsewhere (Elster 2007b, Ch. 11) referred to as *hyperrationality*: the propensity to search for the abstractly optimal decision, that is, the decision that would be optimal if we were to ignore the costs of the decision-making process itself. By virtue of causal mechanisms similar to those underlying the need for closure, we often feel a need to have

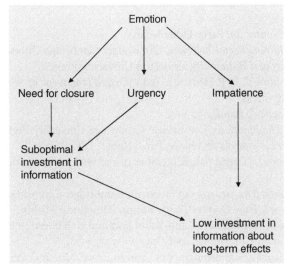

**Fig. 11.5**

*sufficient reasons* for our choices (Shafir et al. 1993). Even in situations where a rational agent would choose among the available options by flipping a coin or tossing dice rather than investing in information that would design one option as clearly superior, we are often reluctant to do so (Neurath 1913; Elster 1989, Ch. II).

## References

AINSLIE, G. (1975), "Specious reward", *Psychological Bulletin* 82, 463–96.

BAR-ELI, M. et al. (2007), "Action bias among elite goalkeepers: The case of penalty kicks", *Journal of Economic Psychology* 28, 606–21.

BÉNICHOU, P. (1948), *Morales du grand siècle,* Paris: Gallimard.

CAMERER, C. (2003), *Behavioral Game Theory,* New York: Russell Sage.

COWEN, T. (1991), "Self-constraint versus self-liberation", *Ethics* 101, 360–73.

DAVIDSON, D. (1969), "How is weakness of the will possible", reprinted in D. Davidson, *Essays on Actions and Events,* Oxford: Oxford University Press 1980.

—— (1982), "Paradoxes of irrationality", in R. Wollheim and J. Hopkins (eds.), *Philosophical Essays on Freud,* Cambridge: Cambridge University Press, 289–305.

EKMAN, P. (1992a), *Telling Lies,* New York: Norton.

—— (1992b), "An argument for basic emotions", *Cognition and Emotion* 6, 169–200.

ELSTER, J. (1989), *Solomonic Judgments,* Cambridge: Cambridge University Press.

—— (1999a), *Alchemies of the Mind,* Cambridge: Cambridge University Press.

—— (1999b), "Davidson on weakness of will and self-deception", in L. Hahn (ed.), *The Philosophy of Donald Davidson,* Chicago: Open Court 1999, 425–42.

—— (2004), *Closing the Books,* Cambridge: Cambridge University Press.

—— (2006), "Weakness of will and preference reversal", in J. Elster et al. (eds.), *Understanding Choice, Explaining Behavior: Essays in Honour of Ole-Jørgen Skog,* Oslo Academic Press.

—— (2007a), *Agir contre soi,* Paris: Odile Jacob.

—— (2007b), *Explaining Social Behavior,* Cambridge: Cambridge University Press.

—— (2009), *Reason and Rationality,* Princeton University Press.

—— (2009a), "Emotions", in P. Hedstrom (ed.), *Oxford Handbook of Analytical Psychology,* Oxford University Press.

—— (2009b), "Urgency", *Inquiry* 52, 1–13.

FRIJDA, N. (1986), *The Emotions,* Cambridge: Cambridge University Press.

GABORY, A. (1989), *Les guerres de Vendée,* Paris: Robert Laffont.

GIGERENZER, G. (2004), "Dread risk, September 11, and fatal traffic accidents", *Psychological Science* 15, 286–7.

GORDON, R. M. (1987), *The Structure of Emotions,* Cambridge: Cambridge University Press.

GROOPMAN, B. (2007), *How Doctors Think,* Boston: Houghton Mifflin.

HAUBRICH, D. (2003), "September 11, anti-terror laws and civil liberties: Britain, France and Germany compared", *Government and Opposition* 38, 3–28.

HIRSCHMAN, A. O. (1986), "On democracy in Latin America", *New York Review of Books* 33 (6).

HUYSE, L. and DHONDT, S. (1993), *La répression des collaborations,* Bruxelles: CRISP.

ISEN, A. and GEVA, N. (1987), "The influence of positive affect on acceptable level of risk and thoughts about losing", *Organizational Behavior and Human Decision Processes* 39, 145–54.

ISEN, A. and PATRICK, R. (1983), "The effects of positive feeling on risk-taking", *Organizational Behavior and Human Performance* 31, 194–202.

KAHNEMAN, D. and TVERSKY, A. (1979), "Prospect theory", *Econometrica* 47, 263–92.

KRUGLANSKI, A. and WEBSTER, D. (1996), "Motivated closing of the mind: 'seizing' and 'freezing'", *Journal of Personality and Social Psychology* 103, 263–83.

LEDOUX, J. (1996), *The Emotional Brain*, New York: Simon and Schuster.

LEITH, K. and BAUMEISTER, R. (1996), "Why do bad moods increase self-defeating behavior? Emotion, risk-taking, and self-regulation", *Journal of Personality and Social Psychology* 71, 1250–67.

LERNER, J. S. and KELTNER, D. (2001), "Fear, anger, and risk", *Journal of Personality and Social Psychology* 81, 146–59.

LOEWENSTEIN, G. (1996), "Out of control: visceral influences on behavior", *Organizational Behavior and Human Decision Processes* 65, 272–92.

—— (2005), "Hot-cold empathy gaps and medical decision-making", *Health Psychology* 24, S49–S56.

LÓPEZ-ROUSSEAU, A. (2005), "Avoiding the death risk of avoiding a dread risk. The aftermath of March 11 in Spain", *Psychological Science* 16, 426–8.

MASON, H. L. (1952), *The Purge of Dutch Quislings*, The Hague: Martinus Nijhoff.

MELE, A. (1999), "Twisted self-deception", *Philosophical Psychology* 12, 117–37.

MERTON, R. K. (1946), *Mass Persuasion*, Westport, Conn.: Greenwood.

MONTAIGNE, M. de (1991), *Essays*, Harmondsworth: Penguin Books.

NEURATH, O. (1913), "Die verirrten des Cartesius und das Auxiliarmotiv", translated in his *Philosophical Papers* vol. I, Dordrecht: Reidel 1913.

PLOUX, F. (2003), *De bouche à oreille: Naissance et propagation des rumeurs dans la France du XIXe siècle*, Paris: Aubier.

SHAFIR, E. SIMONSON, I., and TVERSKY, A. (1993), "Reason-based choice", *Cognition* 49, 11–36.

SOBLE, A. (1990), *The Structure of Love*, New Haven, Conn.: Yale University Press.

STENDHAL (1980), *De l'amour*, ed. V. Del Litto, Paris: Gallimard.

TICE, D., BRASLASVKY, E., and BAUMEISTER, R. (2001), "Emotional distress regulation takes precedence over impulse control", *Journal of Personality and Social Psychology* 80, 53–67.

WATSON, G. (1999), "Disordered appetites", in J. Elster (ed.), *Addiction: Entries and Exits*, New York: Russell Sage.

WEBER, M. (1968), *Economy and Society*, Berkeley: University of California Press.

WINTER, S. (1964–65), "Economic 'natural selection' and the theory of the firm", *Yale Economic Essays* 4, 22572.

..........................................................................................

# CHAPTER 12

# WHY BE EMOTIONAL?

..........................................................................................

## SABINE A. DÖRING

## 12.1 INTRODUCTION

..........................................................................................

What would it mean for agency if we could fully control our emotions, or even had no emotions at all? I shall defend the thesis that this would not be a gain but a loss. As will be shown in the following, the emotions are significant and even indispensable for agency, albeit not in terms of control or guidance. Instead, they are an indispensable source of practical knowledge.

I shall start from the idea and ideal of agency emphasized by Donald Davidson (2004, pp. 196–7) and many others: that it is constitutive of being an agent to comply with the requirements of rationality, so that to violate them is, at the limit, to cease to be an agent (cf. also, e.g., Korsgaard 1996; Helm 2001; Jones 2003). According to this ideal, agents are set above the brutes, so to speak, by virtue of their rationality; they are attributed the 'role of Rational Animal' (Davidson 1963, p. 8). As traditionally understood, an agent is practically rational to the extent to which he complies with his judgements about what is best for him to do in a given situation. In order to be practically rational, an agent must, in other words, guide and control his actions via his normative judgements which provide him with at least 'subjective reasons' for action. (A subjective reason may but need not be also objective. I shall explain this important distinction in the next section.)

Emotions are traditionally distinguished from cognitive judgements (or beliefs).[1] Theories of action and of practical rationality typically subsume them within the wide array of conative (rather than cognitive) states, of which the most obvious examples are desires. Technically speaking, emotions thus are 'pro-attitudes' which function as an arational source of practical deliberation by constituting goals for action.[2] It may however happen that an emotion gets out of the agent's rational control and then inappropriately interferes with the rational pursuit of goals, and, if this is a distinct category, with the exercise of practical reasoning in general. In the worst case, this leads to irrational action, a prime example of which is akrasia, or 'weak will'.[3]

Challenging the traditional picture of agency, some philosophers have recently defended the claim that akrasia can be rational if caused by emotion.[4] Nomy Arpaly

---

[1] For the purpose of this chapter, I shall not distinguish between judgement and belief.

[2] I am here referring to the standard belief-desire theory of intentional action. This theory's attraction goes far beyond philosophy; it is the standard model of the explanation of action in all the sciences and derives from folk psychology. Underlying it is a picture of the mind that divides all intentional mental states into two distinct and mutually exclusive classes, namely into cognitive beliefs on the one hand and conative desires on the other hand. Traditionally, philosophers make the distinction between cognitive beliefs and conative desires in terms of the notion of direction of fit: conative desires are said to have a characteristic 'world-to-mind direction of fit' in contrast to the 'mind-to-world direction of fit' characteristic of cognitive belief. As opposed to beliefs which are held to aim at truth, i.e. at fitting the world, it is claimed of desires that they aim at bringing about goals, and that is, conversely, at changing the world in such a way that it fits the desire. By virtue of their characteristic direction of fit or goal-directedness (rather than truth-directedness), desires are considered to be indispensable to the explanation of action whereas beliefs are regarded as incapable of motivating: it is the desire, and not the belief, that provides an end for action. The desires agents have are claimed to dispose them to act in such way that their goal is brought about, where the desired goal constitutes the end to which the action is intended as a means (cf., in particular, Smith 1987; 1994, ch. 4). Given this picture of the mind, emotions must be either desires, or beliefs, or non-intentional states. Because of their motivational force, they are typically treated as desires. Robert H. Frank's (1988) 'commitment model', which is meant to establish the rationality of emotional choice, may serve as an example, regardless of the fact that the non-comparative notion of desire is replaced with the comparative notion of preference. As Ronald De Sousa (2003, p. 261) points out, this model does not involve emotions 'in any sense in which emotion might not be simply reducible to *preference*'. Another example is Michael Smith's (1998) account of expressive action in which the expressed emotion is reduced to a mere disposition to act in a certain way. More recent are attempts to analyse emotions as beliefs (or judgements) of a special kind, or as combinations of beliefs and desires, and perhaps some non-intentional bodily sensation. As many have argued, such attempts are neither satisfactory nor compatible with the cognitive–conative divide characteristic of the belief-desire theory (cf., in particular, Goldie 2000; Helm 2001).

[3] Christine Korsgaard (1986, p. 13), for instance, mentions as paradigmatic causes of practical irrationality emotional states such as rage, passion, depression, or grief.

[4] Ronald de Sousa's influential book *The Rationality of Emotion* (1987) paved the way for this claim by pointing to the fact that emotions are not just factors which tend to interfere with reason but can be rational in themselves.

(2003), for one, argues that there are cases of so-called 'inverse akrasia', which she (at p. 75) defines as cases in which the agent acts rationally and even morally but does so against his better judgement (cf. also Arpaly 2000). In support of this argument Arpaly and others point to the famous example of Huckleberry Finn.[5] After having helped his friend Jim to run away from slavery, Mark Twain's character Huckleberry Finn decides to turn him in. But when he is given the opportunity to do so, Huck finds himself doing just the contrary. Instead of turning Jim over to the slave hunters, he lies in order to protect his friend. It is his sympathy for Jim which causes Huck to act this way, even though he does not endorse his emotion but castigates himself for his weakness. According to Arpaly, we here have a perfect illustration of 'inverse akrasia'. After all, Twain gets the reader to believe that his protagonist actually did the right thing and even deserves moral praise for his action.[6]

Implicit in arguments for 'inverse akrasia' is often the assumption that emotions cannot be reduced to conative desires (cf. Jones 2003; Tappolet 2003). Instead, proponents of 'inverse akrasia' typically rely on an insight shared by almost all contemporary emotion theorists: that emotions can provide us with information about the world and thus are cognitive states, but of a different kind than judgements.[7] Starting from this assumption, it is claimed that emotions are susceptible to reasons and are sometimes more reliable than judgements in telling an agent what he has reason to do. The term 'reason' here refers to 'objective reasons' which exist because of some feature of the agent's actual situation.

Let us grant that in cases of so-called 'inverse akrasia' there is an objective reason for the akratic action. I shall argue in the following that this does not suffice to establish the rationality of akrasia. An akratic action is not shown to be rational merely by pointing to the fact that there is an objective reason for it. Even if it is conceded that, as a matter of fact, there is a reason for Huck to protect his friend Jim from the slave hunters (although this, for example, involves a lie), Huck's akratic action fails to be rational. As will become clear, to claim that akrasia can be rational is to confuse objective with subjective reasons, or, as we may also put it, to confuse 'reasons' with 'rationality'.

---

[5] Jonathan Bennett (1974) introduced this example into the philosophical literature; it is also discussed, for example, in de Sousa (1987), McIntyre (1990), Jones (2003), and Tappolet (2003).

[6] I shall leave open whether this interpretation is what Twain had in mind as it is of no consequence for the argument.

[7] First, this does not imply that emotions must have a 'mind-to-world direction of fit', rather than a 'world-to-mind direction of fit' (cf. footnote 2 above). As many have argued, the emotions cannot be forced into the direction-of-fit mould (cf., e.g., Helm 2001). Secondly, even those emotion theorists who claim that emotions are judgements do not identify them with ordinary judgements but conceptualize emotions as judgements of a special and irreducible kind (cf., e.g., Nussbaum 2004; Solomon 2004).

At the same time, to maintain the rationality of emotional akrasia is to block the insight that agency amounts to more than rational guidance and control. In order to deserve the predicate, an agent must also be capable of discovering new reasons and improving his existing ones. In this ongoing enterprise, which is the search and the striving for practical knowledge, the emotions play an indispensable role by virtue of their being non-inferential evaluative perception.

## 12.2 AKRASIA AND THE GUIDANCE CONDITION

According to a common definition, akratic (or weak-willed) actions are done intentionally but 'against one's better judgement'. Provided that akrasia in this sense is possible, we may characterize it in the following way: in doing x, an agent is akratic if and only if he judges that, all things considered, it is better for him here and now to do some alternative action y rather than action x, and yet he intentionally does x, although he believes himself to be able to do y.[8] On this definition, the akratic agent seems to be too 'weak' to make his judgement, as the expression of his 'real will', motivationally effective. The agent thus fails to guide and control his action, and this is what we accuse him of. His akratic action is irrational in that it is not under his control. This is already indicated by the Greek word 'akrasia' which Aristotle introduced for the phenomenon in question and which may be translated as 'lack of self-control'.

The accusation of a lack of self-control rests on the ideal and normative picture which we have of ourselves as agents. As pointed out above, it is by no means only Kant and his followers who never weary of emphasizing that we do not regard ourselves as mere playthings of causes but believe ourselves to be capable of guiding our actions via reasons. We thus arrive at what is called the 'guidance condition' for agency. To quote R. Jay Wallace (1999, p. 219):

---

[8] The possibility of akrasia under this description is prominently defended by Davidson (1969). Christine Tappolet (2003) criticizes Davidson—and de Sousa (1987), following him—for supposing that, in addition to his better judgement, the akratic agent must also make the judgement that it is better to perform the action he actually performs. It seems quite false to suppose that the akratic agent must judge it better to perform the akratic action. Davidson is forced to suppose this (so to speak), since he has it that, to qualify as intentional, the akratic action must be caused by a suitable belief-desire pair on the part of the agent. Instead of analysing akrasia as a conflict between two judgements, Tappolet suggests that what happens in akratic action is that the agent judges that another course of action is better, but the non-judgemental motive for the akratic action turns out to be more forceful. I agree with Tappolet, presuming for the present that, *pace* Davidson, the akratic action is nonetheless intentional (cf. also Döring 2003).

It is important to our conception of persons as rational agents . . . that [their] motivations and actions . . . are guided by and responsive to their deliberative reflection about what they have reason to do. Unless this guidance condition (as we may call it) can be satisfied, we will not be able to make sense of the idea that persons are genuine agents, capable of determining what they shall do through the process of deliberation.

The guidance condition commits us to act for reasons seen as such. In order to act, understood as behaving rationally, the agent must act for a reason which is transparent to him, i.e., which he sees as a reason for him to act. This means that he must have a self-conception, and that he must possess the concept of a reason as something that justifies, rather than merely explains, an action. Due to the comparative nature of practical justification he is committed to prefer better reasons to worse ones.

In the introduction to this chapter I distinguished between objective and subjective reasons. This distinction is between what *is* a reason because of some objective feature of the agent's actual situation, and what the agent *justifiably sees* as a reason because of the contents of his actual mental states. We are trying to act for what are reasons for us, and, ideally, our subjective reason is also objective. But the only path of access to objective reasons is through subjective assessment, and it may well happen that subjective and objective reasons come apart. As Niko Kolodny (2005, p. 509) puts it, the normativity of rationality is not straightforwardly that of objective reasons. Following Kolodny, I shall presume here that rationality can be explained in terms of reasons, so that subjective reasons are derivative of objective ones and do not constitute a second class of normative reasons beyond the class of objective reasons. Subjective reasons are what justifies an action from the first-person or personal standpoint. It is only from the third-person or impersonal standpoint that subjective and objective reasons come apart. For it is only from a standpoint other than the agent's that it is possible to distinguish between what he is justified to see as a reason and what is a reason.

The guidance condition implies that an account of practical rationality—as opposed to an account of objective practical reasons—must be given in terms of subjective reasons: an agent is rational to the extent to which he is guided by his subjective reasons. What is important for my argument here is that acting on an objective reason may even be irrational. Consider the following example by Garrett Cullity and Berys Gaut (1997, p. 2): your doctor tells you to take a certain medicine, but he is mistaken, and the medicine will harm you. In this example, you will see it as a reason to take the medicine, and you are justified in doing so. There is a clear sense in which your doctor's advice provides you with a normative reason for action, in spite of the fact that the medicine will harm you. Doing what you have most objective reason to do—not to take the medicine—would be irrational.

This is similar in the case of Huckleberry Finn. Huck is irrational when he protects his friend Jim from the slave hunters. At the moment of choice, he judges that, all things considered, it is better for him to turn Jim in rather than to protect him, and he believes himself to be able to turn Jim in; therefore he must turn Jim in. From his personal perspective, Huck is justified in judging that he ought to turn Jim in, so that his judgement gives him a subjective reason for turning Jim in, thereby requiring him to guide and control his behaviour accordingly. Huck's lack of self-control is not affected by the fact that not his judgement but his emotion is appropriate to the situation, so that, from the impersonal perspective of an objective observer, there is an objective reason for protecting Jim from the slave hunters. Even if Huck himself should recognize in retrospect that it was right not to turn Jim in, this would not make his behaviour a rationally controlled action. When he acts, he does not do so for the reason that he relies on his sympathy. His emotion plays the role of a 'blind instigator', to borrow Robert Musil's evocative phrase. At the moment of choice, Huck does not see his sympathy as a reason, or at least considers it to be a comparatively bad reason. His sympathy resists, and refuses to comply with, his better judgement, and in view of his lack of self-control one may even dispute whether his behaviour deserves the predicate 'action' at all.

Insisting that, from an objective point of view, our emotions sometimes give us better reasons than our judgements does therefore not suffice in order to establish that emotional akrasia can be rational. To question this is either to ignore the normative picture of human agency or to reject it. To take up a distinction introduced by Karen Jones (2003, p. 188 ff.), the sceptic treats us as mere 'reason-trackers', as opposed to the 'reasons-responders' as which we see ourselves. A reason-tracker is a creature which passively registers and reacts to environmental stimuli much as a thermostat registers and reacts to changes in temperature. By contrast, a reason-responder actively relates himself to and reflects about the information which he gains about his environment so as to treat informational inputs as reasons for judgement and action.

Since our self-conception is not that of a thermostat, or a mere reason-tracker, but that of a reason-responder, Jones rejects Arpaly's account.[9] Trying to preserve

---

[9] If this picture is to be preserved, emotional akrasia can also not be shown to be sometimes rational simply by the empirical proof that the emotions constitute a cognitive subsystem which sometimes does better in registering and reacting to environmental stimuli than the system of judgement. Even the most sophisticated neuroscientific, psychological, or other scientific theory will not do. One might object that the normative picture of human agency is not empirically sustainable and is therefore just an illusion. But this does not seem promising, especially so as the picture in question may well be compatible with a naturalistic view of the world. It is not implausible to assume that our capacity to 'reason-track' is improved by virtue of our normative self-conception as rational agents. It may be an empirical truth that we are better reason-trackers *because* we are reason-responders. Attempting to 'reason-respond', to guide and control one's actions via reasons seen as reasons, may bring it about that we reflect on the reliability of our reason-tracking capacities so as to improve those capacities by cultivating and exercising them. Jones relies on exactly this instrumental argument in order to defend the normative picture of human agency against Arpaly and others.

the normative picture of human agency, she nonetheless wants to allow for the possibility of 'inverse akrasia'. The norm that always forbids akrasia is abandoned, but this is not meant to imply that we have to give up our normative self-conception as reason-responders. For this project to succeed, it must be possible in cases of supposedly 'inverse akrasia' to reconcile objective with subjective reasons, or to reconcile 'reasons' with 'rationality'. The crucial question is whether an action, for which there is an objective reason, can be done for that reason, even though the action is in conflict with the agent's better judgement. Only then will the guidance condition be satisfied.

We have seen that it does not suffice if, contrary to the agent's better judgement, there is an objective reason for the akratic action. Jones agrees with this. However, on her view it is also insufficient to accept exclusively the agent's judgement at the moment of choice as a reason for action. I take it that reason here means 'subjective reason'. Jones does not distinguish between subjective and objective reasons, but she is clear on that an agent can only guide his action via a reason, and thus act rationally, if the reason is transparent to him as a reason. Jones's point now is that the cognitive system of judgement is not the only system that can provide the agent with subjective reasons for action. The system of judgement is claimed to be just one cognitive subsystem among other such systems. This means that our judgements do not occupy a privileged role in the giving of reasons but have to share that role with other cognitive subsystems such as, in particular, the emotions. Therefore Jones does not regard it as necessary that an emotion like Huck's sympathy for Jim must first be authorized by a judgement in order to qualify as a subjective reason for action. Against this requirement Jones argues that all that is needed for acting for reasons is that the agent generally accepts some subsystem as reason-giving.

We thus get a third picture of human agency which neither sacrifices normativity nor relapses into the traditional picture, which Jones dismisses as 'intellectualist'. Within this third picture, Huck's akrasia is regarded as rational because his sympathy gives him a subjective reason and even his best subjective reason. According to Jones, this is possible because Huck generally accepts his emotions as a reason-giving system, where 'reason-giving' is understood as reason-tracking. Both judgements and emotions are introduced as reason-tracking first-order mechanisms, which the agent can guide and control through his second-order conscious reflective and self-monitoring capacities. Rational guidance here consists in 'regulative guidance': the rational agent directly guides and controls his different reason-tracking mechanisms, and indirectly his actions, by monitoring the mechanisms in order to step in when necessary, and where possible, to recalibrate them. The problem with Huck, as Jones describes it, then is just that, at the moment of choice, Huck's self-monitoring capacities do not function properly, with the result that he is mistaken about which reason-tracking system gives him the best reason. Mistakenly, Huck trusts his judgement instead of his sympathy. But, Jones says, this cognitive mistake does not make his akratic action irrational. By Jones's lights this action is guided via Huck's best reason, whether or not he is aware of this at the moment of choice.

## 12.3 WHY AKRASIA CANNOT BE RATIONAL

Does this suffice to meet the guidance condition for rational agency? The main problem of Jones's analysis seems to me that it remains obscure how, in the case of conflict between two reason-tracking subsystems, the agent may decide which system is to be given preference. If Huck is mistaken in the example, how could he have avoided the mistake? Clearly, it is not enough for him to accept that he may *generally* trust his emotions. Even if this should be true, it does not follow that Huck can trust his emotions *in each particular case*. After all, he also generally trusts his judgements. What Huck needs to know is whether he should here and now follow his sympathy or had better stick to his judgement.

This problem has a deeper source. Ultimately, it emerges because Jones is ambiguous about the notion of a reason. When she characterizes 'reason-responders' she seems to mean subjective reasons, whereas in defining 'reason-trackers' it appear to be objective reasons which she has in mind. Otherwise we could hardly make sense of thermostats being *reason*-trackers. A thermostat may be called a 'reason-tracker' in the sense that it registers and reacts to certain objective features of his environment and does so reliably under standard conditions. From a third-person standpoint we may thus metaphorically say that a thermostat tracks 'reasons'. But this does clearly not mean that the thermostat *has* reasons from a first-person standpoint. On Jones's view, the difference to agency seems to be that, by contrast with a thermostat, the cognitive subsystems of an agent track 'reasons' in the literal sense. These systems track reasons (in the literal sense) because the agent accepts them as reason-tracking, i.e., because he reason-responds, so that the objective reasons tracked by that system become also subjective reasons.[10]

However, when it comes to a conscious and explicit conflict between two reason-tracking subsystems, this explanation does not work. For it lies in the very nature of such conflict that at least one of the two systems must go wrong. As long as the agent is uncertain which of the two systems is mistaken (if not both), neither of them provides him with a subjective reason. To resolve the conflict: what other strategy could there be than one which reiterates on a meta-level the very problem of making a decision between different reason-tracking subsystems. In which other

---

[10] This is how I read Jones's (2003, p. 196) statement that 'our subsystems can reason-track because we, as agents, reason-respond'.

way could the conflict be resolved by Jones's higher-order reflective and self-monitoring capacities? In whichever way the decision is made, in the end, it will come down to a *judgement* about what one ought to do in the given situation.

Even if we accept Jones's claims, *first*, that our emotions are reason-trackers in the sense described, and, *secondly*, that, as agents, we accept our emotions as reason-trackers, this does not suffice to establish the possibility of rational (or 'inverse') akrasia. I agree with both claims, yet a closer look at how the emotions reason-track will make clear that, ultimately, it is judgements which provide us with subjective reasons for action.

In order to track *practical* reasons, emotions must be motives for action but neither in the form of neo-Humean conative desires nor in terms of Humean passions, if the latter are conceived as non-cognitive feelings.[11] Tracking objective reasons necessarily requires them to represent features of the agent's actual situation. If the emotions had no representational content,[12] they could not provide agents with subjective reasons either but merely cause them to act in certain ways. To say that Huck protected Jim against the slave hunters 'because' he felt sympathy for him is ambiguous. The 'because' may indicate either a merely causal or a rational explanation of the action.[13] The second possibility depends on Huck's sympathy being directed at Jim and representing him as being a certain way. To make it rational to protect Jim, Huck's sympathy must at least purport to contain the information, say, that Jim is in distress and '*merits*' sympathy, to put it in John McDowell's (1985, p. 207) words, which could then make it rational to protect Jim from the slave hunters.[14] Otherwise Huck's sympathy would be no more than a blind instigator, and it would be equally rational for Huck to take a drug that releases him from his emotion.

---

[11] I shall not deal here with the question of how the motivational force of emotion is to be explained. Elsewhere (2003) I have disputed the view that the emotions owe their motivational force to a 'world-to-mind direction of fit'. A similar point is made by Bennett Helm (2001).

[12] I am here using Christopher Peacocke's influential notion (see Peacocke 1992). Although representational content is also intentional, it differs from non-representational intentional content in being subject to a correctness condition. It is content that represents the world as being a certain way, and can thus be correct or incorrect.

[13] This is not to exclude that rational explanations of actions may also be causal.

[14] Alternatively, we may say with David Wiggins (1987, p. 228) that Huck's sympathy must represent Jim so as 'to make sympathy *appropriate*'. I cannot tell about Jones, but in my reading of it the claim that our emotions are reason-trackers which we, as rational and moral agents, accept as such, amounts to a sensibility theory (cf., in detail, Döring 2008). Sensibility theory is in contrast to projectivism, according to which we project our arbitrary and non-cognitive feelings onto a world which does not in itself have the properties in question. Projectivism could not help an agent with the question of whether he should rely on his emotions or better trust his judgement in the case of conflict. The projectivist may tell the agent at best that it is of evolutionary advantage to trust his emotions (this is exactly Frank's recommendation). But this 'hand-having about survival value' (Johnston 2001, p. 184) is of no use in a particular decision situation, when it comes to conflict between emotion and judgement. For a critique of projectivism cf. Johnston 2001; cf. also McDowell 1994.

In other words, to be capable of giving reasons, emotions must resemble judgements in being about some actual state of the world that they purport to represent. If, as presumed by Jones, they cannot *be* judgements, what else could they be? I shall not attempt here to define what an emotion is[15] but restrict myself to showing that the role of the emotions in the rationalization of other mental states and actions is different from that of judgements. The difference is such that it is hardly plausible to defend the thesis that emotions are judgements, not even if this is meant to say that emotions are judgements of a special and irreducible kind.

Many have insisted that the rationalizing role of emotion cannot be captured by a judgementalist model, pointing to the fact that, by contrast with judgements, emotions need not be revised in the light of the subject's better judgement and knowledge (cf., e.g., de Sousa 1987; Greenspan 1988; Roberts 1988; 2003; Goldie 2000; Tappolet 2000; Helm 2001; Prinz 2004). Hume (1739–40/1978, p. 148) provides a prime example: your fear of falling may persist and represent it as dangerous to be so high up above the ground although you judge and even know that you are safe. This kind of conflict between emotion and judgement is readily intelligible and happens all too often. It need not be a pathological case of vertigo, say, but occurs as an ordinary experience of ordinary people. And there are many more examples, including emotions such as indignation, resentment, shame, or sympathy. As illustrated by the very example of Huckleberry Finn, even emotions that cannot be had without considerable cognitive sophistication nonetheless display only partial integration with the subject's conscious and explicit judgement.

Let us be clear that it is not just the psychological phenomenon which is at stake here. The point at issue is the logical possibility of 'conflict without contradiction', as I have called it elsewhere (2007; cf. also Döring 2009). Conflicts between emotions and judgements are rational conflicts, i.e. conflicts in content about how the world actually is, and yet they differ from rational conflicts between judgements in that they do not involve contradictions. Of course, this is not to say that rational conflicts between judgements are always contradictory. But if, in the case of two conflicting judgements, one judgement predicates that a certain thing has a certain property, whilst the other judgement denies that the thing has that property, we are faced with a contradiction. Even if it were psychologically possible, it would clearly be contradictory to judge that you are safe whilst at the same time judging that you are in danger (not safe). By contrast, it is not contradictory to judge that you are safe whilst at the same time feeling fear, and that is: experiencing the situation as dangerous. Although judgement and emotion are about the same thing and seem to contradict each other in how they represent that thing, the subject does not contradict himself.

---

[15] Some would claim that this is impossible in any case, since there is no such thing as one single category of *the* emotions (cf., in particular, Rorty 1984; Griffiths 1997). Robert C. Roberts (2003, ch. 3) presents a defence of the coherence of the category 'emotion'.

This possibility suggests an analogy to perception. Consider perceptual illusions such as the famous Müller-Lyer illusion (cf., e.g., the illustration in Crane 1992). Just as, despite his better knowledge, the protagonist of Hume's example cannot help but see himself as in danger, the perceiver of the Müller-Lyer illusion cannot rid himself of seeing the two lines as being of different lengths even when careful study has convinced him that they are the same length. As in the case of an emotion–judgement conflict, in the case of a perception–judgement conflict it need not be the perception which gets things wrong. Like Huck's sympathy for Jim, a perception that rationally conflicts with the subject's better judgement need not be an illusion but may equally be adequate to what it purports to represent.[16]

The analogy to perception is also instructive with regard to Jones's idea of the subject's accepting a certain mental subsystem as reason-tracking. This idea applies very well to perception. In the default mode we rely on our perceptions; it does not occur to us to ask whether the conditions under which we perceive (such as, e.g., the lighting conditions) are normal. In the default mode we operate so as to take the representational content of our perceptions at face value, thereby making a corresponding immediate—non-inferential—perceptual judgement. A similar picture may be drawn of how we treat our emotions.[17] In the default mode we regard them as a reliable source of information and do not, for example, question our sympathy with a human or animal in distress or pain. As it does not count against the cognitive power of perception that it sometimes deceives us, occasional failures do not diminish the cognitive power of the emotions, by virtue of which an emotion may emerge the winner in a rational conflict with judgement.

This is not to say, however, that emotions and perceptions are like judgements in that the subject must necessarily regard their content as true. On the standard view, judgement, or belief, 'aims at truth': it is considered to be part of the very concept of belief that its content is regarded as true by the subject.[18] Neither emotion nor perception 'aim at truth' in that sense.[19] This need not, and does not, prevent the

---

[16] With the Müller-Lyer illusion I have chosen an example for a perception–judgement conflict in which the conflict cannot be resolved, because the perception in question resists calibration. Still, many perceptions can be calibrated. Here we may consider the train illusion example: when sitting in a train waiting to depart from the train station and watching a neighbouring carriage pulling out of the station, one gets the impression of moving oneself, even though it is in fact the train on the adjacent track that has just started to move. By contrast with the Müller-Lyer illusion, it is easy to correct one's perception in the train illusion by calibrating it. I deliberately chose an example for the case of perception as it is sometimes maintained that emotions are easier to calibrate than perceptions. As far as I can tell, this is wrong. The train illusion provides a counter example; and there are many more.

[17] On the non-inferentiality of both perception and emotion see, in detail, Döring 2007 and 2009.

[18] For example, this view lies behind Bernard Williams's (1970) argument on why there is no such thing as deciding to believe.

[19] In Scholastic parlance we may say with de Sousa (1987, p. 122) that '*truth* is the formal object of *belief*'; but it not the formal object of emotion: 'There are as many formal objects as there are emotion types' (where the formal object is the property which the subject must necessarily ascribe to the intentional object of his mental state in order to render the state intelligible).

subject from treating both his emotions and perceptions as generally reliable cognitive subsystems which are appropriate to the facts under standard conditions. But these systems provide merely prima facie reasons in the form of non-inferential beliefs, which emotions and perceptions cause in the default mode. If necessary and possible, these prima facie reasons should be held up to the tribunal of deliberative reflection.

This is how I understand what Roberts (1988, p. 191) has aptly called the 'verisimilitude' of our emotions. According to Roberts (1988, p. 191; cf. also 2003, p. 92), the content of an emotion is 'verisimilar' by which he means to say that, for the subject, the content has 'the *appearance* of truth, whether or not she would *affirm*' its truth. On my view, emotional representations have the appearance of truth because the subject recognizes the subsystem of emotion *as a whole* as a reason-tracking system. This does not imply that the subject must thereby regard the content of *each particular* emotion as true. In the default mode we affirm the truth of the contents of our emotions through non-inferential emotional judgements. But these judgements give us merely prima facie reasons that may well be rejected by deliberation.

The possibility of conflict without contradiction is then explained as follows (cf., in more detail, Döring 2009): conflict without contradiction between emotion and judgement arises when an emotion persists in spite of the subject's better judgement, where 'better' means 'deliberate' or 'all things considered'. In the default mode we rely on our emotions as a reason-tracking subsystem, but once we suspect that this system deceives us we are ready to leave the default mode and to switch into a different mode. When an emotion and the belief that is immediately (non-inferentially) generated by it in the default mode fail to pass the tribunal of deliberation, we withdraw our confidence in them. It comes to conflict without contradiction when the emotional belief vanishes but the emotion itself persists. This is possible because the subject only affirms the truth of his judgements' (or beliefs') content, whilst the content of his emotion merely appears to be true to him. Therefore no contradiction arises; and yet there is rational conflict because, in being accepted as a generally reliable reason-tracking system, the emotions are seen by the subject as being in the service of truth and knowledge, albeit in a different way than judgements are.

Like Roberts, I hold that conflict without contradiction is to be explained along the same lines in the case of perception.[20] This has two important consequences for

---

[20] Against this analogy Helm (2001, 41 ff.) objects that it explains away not only the contradiction but also the conflict. According to Helm, it is not at all irrational to have the two lines of the Müller-Lyer illusion look a different length even after one has found out that they are the same length. As the content of perception is genuinely and fully repudiated in this case, it is, by Helm's lights, regarded as a mirage. This is to say, the content of a perception known to be illusionary is regarded as merely fictitious, as opposed to both being regarded as true and to appear to be true, and Helm therefore compares it with the content of an imagination, such as imagining that there is a bar of

the question of 'inverse akrasia'. *First,* prior to practical conflict between emotion and judgement is rational conflict of a certain kind. Characteristic of this kind of rational conflict is that the subject regards the content of his judgement as true, while the content of his emotion merely appears to be true to him. If this is granted, it follows, *secondly,* that it does not suffice for an emotion to hold its ground against a conflicting judgement in the particular case if the subject sees his emotions as generally reliable reason-trackers. To return to the example of Huckleberry Finn: prior to practical conflict between Huck's better judgement and his emotion, which causes his akratic action, is rational conflict without contradiction. The latter is plausibly explained by Huck's not endorsing the content of his emotion. In feeling sympathy for Jim, it appears to Huck that he ought not to turn his friend over to the slave hunters. Yet he does not regard this as true, but dismisses the non-inferential belief corresponding to his emotion because of deliberation. Deliberation leads Huck to the judgement that he ought to turn Jim over to the slave hunters, and this judgement, or the belief in which it results, conceptually implies that its content is regarded as true, thereby providing Huck with an 'all-things-considered reason' (as opposed to a mere prima facie reason). In turn, this means that it is Huck's better judgement, rather than his emotion, which provides him with a subjective reason for action, so that his akratic action is and remains irrational.

*Pace* Jones, it is ultimately always judgement which provides the agent with subjective reasons for action. This is not to relapse into the 'intellectualist' view opposed by Jones that all action, including fast and habitual action, must consciously and explicitly be authorized by deliberative judgement. But in order to be rational, an agent must satisfy the condition that he *would* so authorize the action, were he asked to do so. In order to provide an agent with a subjective reason here and now, a motive for an action such as an emotion must at least be *hypothetically authorized* by the agent's deliberative reflection about what he has reason to do. Otherwise an action caused by it is irrational, for this action fails to meet the guidance condition; and this failure is independent of whether the emotion, as in the example of Huckleberry Finn, is appropriate to the agent's actual situation and thus presents an objective reason for action.

chocolate on the table. The 'Helm objection', as Roberts (2003, p. 91) calls it, confuses the attitude we take towards the content of an illusionary perception on the meta-level of judgement with how that perception's content appears when it is experienced. To be sure, once we are certain that the two lines of the Müller-Lyer illusion are the same length, we judge that our visual experience deceives us. But this does not prevent the experience itself from having the appearance of truth. The occurrent perception of the two lines as being of a different length puts forward this content as correct. The content is representational, or verisimilar, as Roberts puts it in his early writings. This is perfectly analogous to conflict between emotion and judgement. Once we are certain that an emotion is inappropriate we regard its content as a mirage in judgement. Yet in experiencing the emotion it still seems to us that the world really is as the emotion represents it to be. In the case of emotion this is more obvious than in the case of perception because emotional conflict entails practical as well as rational conflict (see below).

## 12.4 BEYOND GUIDANCE AND CONTROL

Nevertheless Huck's sympathy is, by virtue of being a reason-tracker, significant and even indispensable for him as an agent. It is one question whether Huck succeeds in guiding his actions via reasons seen as reasons; but it is another question whether his all-things-considered judgement or his emotion is appropriate to the situation. If emotions are neither merely conative desires nor non-cognitive feelings but can be true to the facts, then agency amounts to more than guidance and control via reasons seen as reasons. It also comprises the ongoing cultivation of one's practical reasons through discovering new reasons and improving one's existing reasons. In this epistemic respect, the emotions are indispensable for agency. As regards epistemic appropriateness, judgement and reason do not have the last word as their cognitive power is not superior to, but on a par with that of emotion. Accordingly, reason cannot set itself up as judge and jury when it comes to epistemic conflict with emotion; it is absolutely open whether reason or emotion (if any of them) will gain the victory. If reason here adopts the role of judge, then just as if it were refereeing a boxing match, say, in which case it cannot decide the match, but can merely declare the winner. Reason is entitled to this role precisely because its 'products', judgement, and belief, conceptually imply that their content is regarded as true by the subject, so that reason determines what the subject sees as a reason. But to be regarded as true is not to be true.

Because of his persistent sympathy, Huck may come to know later that he made an error in judgement (as he in fact does in Twain's novel). In retrospect, Huck may recognize that it was right to protect Jim, even though he did not see this at the moment of choice. That is, he may recognize in retrospect that it was his sympathy, rather than his judgement, which represented the situation correctly to him. Since this does not follow from the moral principles he had hitherto accepted, the occurrence of his emotion may lead him to question those principles and to formulate new, better, more comprehensive moral principles. Such a rational role can be played by any emotion, and this may, other than in the example of Huckleberry Finn, be so already at the emotion's first occurrence.[21]

---

[21] As should be clear from the above, this does not make it rational to adopt some meta-principle of practical reason according to which agents should better trust their emotions instead of their judgements (cf. also footnote 14 above). An emotion such as sympathy might well go wrong. Suppose you see someone struggling, late at night, with a heavy burden at the back door of the Museum of Fine Arts; your sympathy tells you that you ought to help that person out . . . (I owe this example to Barbara Herman). Again, to regard your emotions as a reason-tracking mental system means only that they are reliable under standard conditions; it does not follow from this that they can be trusted in *each particular case*.

To be able to play their rational role, the emotions must be beyond the agent's guidance and control. That is, they must to a certain extent occur uncontrollably by the agent's judgement and be able to persist despite the agent's better judgement. This is precisely what happens in the example of Huckleberry Finn. As explained above, it here comes to rational conflict, and yet Huck does not contradict himself, since he does not endorse his emotion. Therefore his sympathy for Jim can persist despite his better judgement that he ought to turn Jim in. The conflict is, so to speak, productive: in the end, Huck comes out of it with new and better reasons, by which he may then guide his actions. Only an omniscient agent could do with rational guidance alone. As humans we must accept conflicts between emotion and judgement, in order not to be 'caught up in ourselves'.

The sense in which the emotions must not be—and are not—fully controllable is that of not being subject to inferential constraints. In this respect, the emotions are like perceptions, and unlike judgements.[22] As I have argued elsewhere (2007; cf. also 2009), the possibility of conflict without contradiction implies that both emotions and perceptions are not inferentially related to other states (including other states of the same kind).[23]

For the case of perception, this is shown by Tim Crane (1992, p. 149 ff.). Perceptions, Crane argues, are not revisable in the light of better judgement and knowledge which shows that their logic is not the inferential logic of judgement, and that, therefore, perceptions are not judgements. I second this argument. Inferential relations holding between judgements include obvious logical relations. If you judge that $p$, you commit yourself to certain other judgements that are the obvious logical consequences of this judgement, among them the judgement that not($p$ & not-$p$). Hence you are not entitled to judge that $p$ and that not $p$ simultaneously. Even if it should be psychologically possible to make simultaneous contradictory judgements, from a logical point of view, you would certainly make a mistake, as illustrated by the fact that you would commit yourself to Moore-paradoxical utterances of the form '$p$, but I do not believe it. I believe that not-$p$'.[24] Perceptual illusions like the Müller-Lyer illusion show that

---

[22] As always, this is not to say that emotions *are* sense perceptions. There are a number of obvious disanalogies between emotions and sense perceptions. None of them undermines the analogy, since all that I am claiming is that both sense perceptions and emotions play a non-inferential role in the rationalization of other mental states and actions.

[23] This includes that emotions are not subject to a principle of coherence, as is maintained by Helm (2001, ch. 3). Requiring coherence of our emotions is incompatible with non-inferentiality (cf. also Crane 1992) and seems overintellectualizing in any case: may I not feel attracted by a person and, at the very same time, be repelled by her without contradicting myself (as I would do in judging that one and the same person is attractive and repellent)?

[24] Let me emphasize again that it is not the psychological possibility which is at stake here. Nor do I mean to say that people always draw the logical and material inferences which are available to them by what they believe. Like Crane, I am here skating over such complications, in order to make the general point clear.

there is no contradiction involved in having a perception that rationally conflicts with judgement. It is not paradoxical to say, for example, 'The two lines are the same length, but I do not see it. I see one line as longer than the other.' In the Müller-Lyer illusion Moore's Paradox does not apply, as perception is not subject to inferential constraints.

In the same way, Huck's sympathy may persist and represent Jim as meriting sympathy and protection even when Huck's better judgement is that he ought to turn Jim in. It is not contradictory for Huck to judge that he ought to turn Jim in whilst at the same time feeling sympathy for his friend, which shows that the logic of emotion is not that of inference. Accordingly, it is not paradoxical to say 'I ought to turn Jim in, but this doesn't feel right. I feel sympathy for Jim.'

If it is agreed that emotions are like perceptions, and unlike judgements, in that they do not enter inferential relations, we may then ask how this could be so. A natural answer, also given by Crane, is that non-inferentiality is to be explained by a state's having a content of a different kind than the content of inferential judgement. Lurking in the background is the notion of non-conceptual content. Assuming that 'concepts are the *inferentially relevant constituents of intentional states*', Crane (1992, p. 147) actually defines the content of non-inferential perception as non-conceptual. This seems quite plausible, but I shall not address non-conceptuality here. Instead, let me conclude by pointing to a difference between the content of emotion and the content of perception which is crucial to agency.

This difference consists in that, by contrast with perceptions, emotions contain evaluations of their intentional objects. They represent their objects in the light of the subject's concerns. On the one hand, this is why they have motivational force. Our emotional reactions are concern-based evaluations, and as such they reveal that we do not only look at the world under the aspect of how it is. We also assess things in light of our sense of how they ought to be (which does not entail that there is anything that the subject ought to *do*; as I argued elsewhere [2003], emotions do not necessarily provide goals for action). By contrast with the perceiver of the Müller-Lyer illusion, Huckleberry Finn is poised to act out of his sympathy for Jim, whether or not he considers his emotion to be appropriate. If an emotion which the subject believes to be inappropriate cannot be revised, i.e., if it resists calibration, its motivational force persists even when the subject comes to know that his emotion is mistaken. Therefore an arachnophobe, say, is in trouble and should see a therapist, whereas the perceiver of an illusion that resists calibration in spite of better knowledge, such as the perceiver of the Müller-Lyer illusion, normally manages to prevent his deceptive perception from distorting his thought and action, if simply by ignoring it. Due to their *inbuilt* motivational force, emotions pose a more severe problem to rational guidance than perceptions.[25]

---

[25] This explains why we do not normally say that the perceiver of the Müller-Lyer illusion is 'irrational' when he found out that, in fact, the two lines are of the same length, and yet continues to

Again, what appears as a weakness on the one hand, on the other hand constitutes a strength. Only because the emotions contain evaluations, do they have a rational impact on an agent's normative reasons for action. By presenting Jim as someone who merits sympathy, Huck's emotion does not *entail* that Jim ought to be protected from the slave hunters. But by contrast to a mental state with a purely descriptive content (like a colour perception, say), it can without further ado enter into a chain of reasoning which *justifies* this very conclusion (cf., in more detail, Döring 2007).[26]

To sum up, the ideal agent is guided by practical knowledge. But to go on to say that this ideal is to be achieved by barring the emotions from interfering with better judgement is to ignore that this attempt is both hopeless and counterproductive. What we ought to do instead, and can do, is to cultivate our emotions over time. The ongoing cultivation of our emotions is essential for us humans in order to gain and improve our practical knowledge, in order not to remain 'caught up in ourselves'.

# REFERENCES

ARPALY, N. (2000), 'On Acting Rationally against One's Best Judgement', *Noûs* 13, pp. 173–96.

——(2003), *Unprincipled Virtue. An Inquiry into Moral Agency*, Oxford: Blackwell.

BENNETT, J. (1974), 'The Conscience of Huckleberry Finn', *Philosophy* 49, pp. 123–34.

CRANE, T. (1992), 'The Nonconceptual Content of Experience', in T. Crane, ed., *The Contents of Experience: Essays on Perception*, Cambridge: Cambridge University Press, pp. 136–57.

CULLITY, G. and GAUT, B. (1997), *Ethics and Practical Reason*, Oxford: Clarendon.

DAVIDSON, D. (1963), 'Actions, Reasons and Causes', reprinted in his *Essays on Actions and Events*, Oxford: Clarendon 1980, pp. 3–19.

——(1969), 'How Is Weakness of the Will Possible?', reprinted in his *Essays on Actions and Events*, Oxford: Clarendon 1980, pp. 21–42.

see them as being of different lengths. This person is rational in the sense that he succeeds in keeping his illusionary perception under rational control.

[26] As should be emphasized again, all of this requires that the emotions are capable of representing actual states of the world. Otherwise they could not make other states and actions rational; nor could they rationally interact with judgements. I agree with Jones in that revising an emotion is a matter of calibration (cf. also footnote 16 above). This also explains why the content of an emotion or of a perception may or may not be revised in the light of better judgement and knowledge. If an emotion is revised in the light of better judgement and knowledge, this is not a matter of contradiction but of calibration. Still, the ease or difficulty of calibration need not be a matter solely of the causal mechanisms underlying our emotions and perceptions. Instead the explanation of why some emotions and perceptions resist calibration, whereas others are open to it, must also refer to their specific non-inferential logic.

DAVIDSON, D. (2004), 'Incoherence and Irrationality', in *Problems of Rationality*, Oxford: Oxford University Press, pp. 189–98.

DE SOUSA, R. (1987), *The Rationality of Emotion*, Cambridge, Mass.: MIT Press.

——(2003), 'Paradoxical Emotions: on *sui generis* Emotional Irrationality', in Ch. Tappolet and S. Stroud, eds., *Weakness of Will and Practical Irrationality*, Oxford: Oxford University Press, pp. 274–97.

DÖRING, S. (2003), 'Explaining Action by Emotion', *The Philosophical Quarterly* 211, pp. 214–30.

——(2007), 'Seeing What to Do: Affective Perception and Rational Motivation', *Dialectica* 61, pp. 363–94.

——(2008), *Gründe und Gefühle. Zur Lösung "des" Problems der Moral*, Berlin and New York: de Gruyter.

——(2009), 'The Logic of Emotional Experience: More on Conflict without Contradiction', in S. Döring and R. Reisenzein, eds., *Perspectives on Emotional Experience*, Special Issue of *Emotion Review*, 1(3) (July 2009), pp. 234–44.

FRANK, R. (1988), *Passions within Reason: The Strategic Role of the Emotions*, New York/London: W. W. Norton & Company.

GOLDIE, P. (2000), *The Emotions. A Philosophical Exploration*, Oxford: Oxford University Press.

GREENSPAN, P. (1988), *Emotions and Reasons: An Inquiry into Emotional Justification*. New York: Routledge.

GRIFTHS, P. (1997): *What Emotions Really Are. The Problem of Psychological Categories*, Chicago: Chicago University Press.

HELM, B. (2001), *Emotional Reason. Deliberation, Motivation, and the Nature of Value*, Cambridge: Cambridge University Press.

HUME, D. (1739–40/1978), *A Treatise of Human Nature*, L. A. Selby-Bigge and P. H. Nidditch, eds., Oxford: Clarendon Press.

JOHNSTON, M. (2001), 'The Authority of Affect', *Philosophy and Phenomenological Research* 63, pp. 181–214.

JONES, K. (2003), 'Emotion, Weakness of Will, and the Normative Conception of Agency', in A. Hatzimoysis, ed., *Philosophy and the Emotions*, Cambridge: Cambridge University Press (Royal Institute of Philosophy Supplement; 52), pp. 181–200.

KOLODNY, N. (2005), 'Why Be Rational?', *Mind* 114, pp. 509–63.

KORSGAARD, CH. (1996), *The Sources of Normativity*, Cambridge: Cambridge University Press.

MCDOWELL, J. (1985), 'Values and Secondary Qualities', reprinted in S. Darwall, A. Gibbard, and P. Railton, eds., *Moral Discourse and Practice. Some Philosophical Approaches*, New York: Oxford University Press 1997, pp. 201–13.

——(1994), *Mind and World*, Cambridge, Mass.: Harvard University Press.

MCINTYRE, A. (1990), 'Is Akratic Action Always Irrational?', in O. Flanagan and A. Rorty, eds., *Identity, Character, and Morality. Essays in Moral Psychology*, Cambridge, Mass.: MIT Press, pp. 379–400.

NUSSBAUM, M. (2004), 'Emotions as Judgments of Value and Importance', in R. Solomon, ed., *Thinking about Feeling*, Oxford: Oxford University Press, pp. 183–99.

PEACOCKE, CH. (1992), *A Study of Concepts*, Cambridge, Mass.: MIT Press.

PRINZ, J. (2004), *Gut Reactions: A Perceptual Theory of Emotion*, New York: Oxford University Press.

ROBERTS, R. (1988), 'What an Emotion Is: A Sketch', *The Philosophical Review* 97, pp. 183–209.

——2003, *Emotions: An Essay in Aid of Moral Psychology*, Cambridge: Cambridge: Cambridge University Press.

RORTY, A. (1984), 'Aristotle on the Metaphysical Status of *Pathe*', *Review of Metaphysics* 84, pp. 521–46.

SMITH, M. (1987), 'The Humean Theory of Motivation', *Mind* 96, pp. 36–61.

——1994, *The Moral Problem*, Oxford: Blackwell.

——1998, 'The Possibility of Action', in J. Bransen, ed., *Human Action, Deliberation and Causation*, Dordrecht: Kluwer Academic Publishers, pp. 17–41.

SOLOMON, R. (2004), 'Emotions, Thoughts and Feelings', in R. Solomon, ed., *Thinking about Feeling*, Oxford: Oxford University Press, pp. 76–88.

TAPPOLET, CH. (2000), *Émotions et valeurs*, Paris: Presses Universitaires de France.

——(2003), 'Emotions and the Intelligibility of Akratic Action', in S. Stroud and Ch. Tappolet, eds., *Weakness of Will and Practical Irrationality*, Oxford: Clarendon, pp. 97–120.

WALLACE, J. (1999), 'Three Conceptions of Rational Agency', *Ethical Theory and Moral Practice* 2, pp. 217–42.

WIGGINS, D. (1987), 'A Sensible Subjectivism', reprinted in S. Darwell, A. Gibbard, and P. Railton, eds., *Moral Discourse and Practice*, Oxford: Oxford University Press 1997, pp. 227–44.

WILLIAMS, B. (1970), 'Deciding to Believe', reprinted in *Problems of the Self. Philosophical Papers 1956–1972*, Cambridge: Cambridge University Press, pp. 136–51.

.............................................................................

# CHAPTER 13

# EMOTIONS AND MOTIVATION: RECONSIDERING NEO-JAMESIAN ACCOUNTS

.............................................................................

## BENNETT W. HELM

EMOTIONS are notorious for their irrationality, and nowhere does this irrationality show up more clearly than in their effects on motivation. Thus, to take some stereotyped examples, fear, anger, and jealousy frequently seem to move us to act contrary to our better judgment. Recently, however, there has been increasing emphasis on the rationality of emotions and their place in practical reason. Thus, while deliberating about what to do, although we may be able to articulate reasons for and against each option, we may not be able to say why the weight of these reasons favor one over the others; in such cases, we may simply go with the one that "feels" right—that resonates more fully with our emotional sense of our circumstances—and such an appeal to emotions seems appropriate.

My claim will ultimately be that emotions are fundamental to motivation and practical reasoning. In particular, I shall argue that emotions motivate not because they involve mere dispositions to behave but rather because they are rational responses to things we care about, responses that sometimes rationally demand intentional action. This, together with the way our linguistic concepts can inform these emotional responses, makes for rational interconnections with evaluative judgments that allow our emotions to play a significant role in our determining what to do. I shall argue for this by first, in §13.1, laying out a former orthodoxy in philosophical understandings of emotions and what I shall call "neo-Jamesian" responses to it. In §13.2, I shall argue that these neo-Jamesian accounts are inadequate, and that much more is demanded of an account of emotions and motivation. In §13.3, I shall offer the outlines of my positive account of how emotions motivate, an account I shall elaborate in §13.4 by a consideration of the connections between emotions and judgments.

# 13.1 COGNITIVIST AND NEO-JAMESIAN ACCOUNTS

In the 1970s and early 1980s, the prominent philosophical account of emotions was largely reductionist: emotions, it was widely thought, are to be understood in terms of antecedently intelligible beliefs and desires, together with some extra ingredient—a certain sort of bodily sensation, for example—that makes intelligible what is distinctively emotional about the subject's mental state. Thus, such *cognitivist* accounts of the emotions argued that fear is, roughly, a belief that something is dangerous, a desire to avoid the danger, and a sinking feeling in one's stomach. Such cognitivist accounts were an improvement on earlier "feeling" theories by acknowledging the intentionality and therefore potential rationality of emotions; they did so by understanding emotional intentionality and rationality to be parasitic on that of the beliefs and desires that, they theorized, composed the emotions.

At this point it can seem that what does all the work—at least all the positive work—of emotions is the underlying belief and desire. Emotions, it might seem, are irrational when the extra ingredient that accounts for the emotionality of emotions takes over, distracting us or having us put too much weight on the belief or desire, all with potentially disastrous consequences: we may freeze from fear or lash out from anger in ways that run contrary to what we think is best to do, thereby undermining our rationality as agents. Consequently, Jerome Shaffer confidently concluded:

From a rational and moral point of view, I can see no possibility of a general justification of emotion. And it is easy enough to imagine individual lives and even a whole world in which things would be much better if there were no emotion. (1983, 169)

And this seems right *if* emotions are understood on the cognitivist model, for on this model whatever is distinctive of the emotions themselves would seem to be pointless or worse. Emotions, we might think, are simply an evolutionary vestige, the mental equivalent of human appendixes or ostrich wings.

Of course, this conclusion is too hasty. The way emotions motivate action is distinctive and seemingly cannot be understood in terms of desire, as when we are motivated to tear at the photo of someone we hate or when we celebrate out of joy (Hursthouse, 1991; Döring, 2003). Moreover, Damasio (1994, 1999, 2003) has argued quite persuasively that the empirical evidence reveals emotions to have an important and distinctive function in our practical lives. Patients with damage to the ventromedial region of their prefrontal cortex—the classic example is Phineas Gage—often suffer from dramatic personality changes but do not tend to suffer any changes in their cognitive functioning as measured by standard IQ tests. Damasio argues that these changes can be traced to a loss of emotional responsiveness that are critical to practical reasoning, and to better understand this he develops a revised version of James' theory of emotions (1884, 1950).

According to Damasio's neo-Jamesian theory, when things go well or badly for us, our bodies are naturally tuned to respond in some way—including both overt behavioral responses and inner physiological responses; this bodily response is then felt, and the combination of response and feeling is the emotion.[1] Thus, when we are thrust into a dangerous situation, our bodies respond, pumping adrenaline into our bloodstreams, tensing our muscles, etc., and these bodily changes together with our perception of them constitute our fear.

It should be clear that the neo-Jamesian model is not a retreat to feeling theories; rather, emotions are understood to be about the type of circumstances in the world that cause them. This is clearest in Prinz's neo-Jamesian account of emotions as *embodied appraisals* (2004). According to Prinz, the bodily responses relevant to emotions are, as the result of evolutionary pressures, reliably causally connected to certain types of environments relevant to our well-beings. Following Dretske (1981), Prinz argues that such causal connections mean the bodily changes *represent* the corresponding "organism-environment relation" and given the bearing of this relation on our well-beings it is appropriate to understand these representations as *appraisals* (2004, 77). Indeed, the content of these appraisals—danger, offense, etc.—is part of what distinguishes one emotion type (fear) from another (anger).[2]

By understanding emotions to be appraisals, neo-Jamesians think they can explain how emotions motivate. The basic idea is that evolution guarantees that these bodily attunements to circumstances affecting our well-beings are themselves positively or negatively reinforcing of certain types of actions; Damasio calls these

---

[1] Technically, Damasio distinguishes the response, which he calls the 'emotion', from the perception of it, which he calls the 'feeling', though he often defers to common usage in calling the whole combination the emotion; cf. James (1950, 449).

[2] Other neo-Jamesian accounts of emotions include Robinson (2005) and, to a certain extent, LeDoux (1996).

reinforcers "somatic markers" (1994, Chapter 8), and Prinz calls them "valence markers" Prinz (2004, 173). Thus, Damasio says:

In brief, the [emotional] signal *marks* options and outcomes with a positive or negative signal that narrows the decision-making space and increases the probability that the action will conform to past experience. (2003, 148)

Or, as Prinz puts it, valence markers "serve as a command that says something like 'More of this!' [or] . . . 'Less of this!'", where "this" is the emotion itself: "Positive emotions are ones we want to sustain, and negative emotions are ones that we want to get rid of" (Prinz, 2004, 174). Consequently, "the somatic component of an emotion prepares us for action, and the valence marker disposes us to act" (Prinz, 2004, 194). In this way, emotions motivate actions both directly (as dispositions to behave) and indirectly (through their influence on our attention and practical judgments). This leads to Damasio's conclusion:

The emotional signal is not a substitute for proper reasoning. It has an auxiliary role, increasing the efficiency of the reasoning process and making it speedier. (2003, 148)

In short, emotions play a role in practical reasoning insofar as they are quick and dirty mechanisms that adapt us to features of our environments that bear on our well-being, thereby complementing our ability to reason slowly and carefully about what to do. As Horst (1998) describes it, emotions are the "junk-yard dog of the soul": quick to respond, but with many false positives.[3]

This is, surely, an improvement over cognitivist theories, which seem to leave no room for a distinctive emotional contribution to motivation and practical reason. But is it the right way to understand that contribution? In the next section, I shall argue that it is not.

## 13.2 AGENCY AND IMPORT

In order to assess the neo-Jamesian account of the place of emotions in motivation and practical reason, we need to be clear on what the problem about motivation is—about what the interesting questions in the area are. In particular, if the target is to understand human action, as it clearly is for Damasio and Prinz, we need to be careful to distinguish full-blooded action from mere goal-directedness.

---

[3] LeDoux (1996) supports this conception neurologically: the amygdala, central to our capacity for emotions, is what provides the quick and dirty response.

Now this demand may seem strange to anyone who buys into a broadly Humean conception of motivation. On the Humean view, what distinguishes cognitive states like belief from motivating states like desire is their respective directions of fit. Beliefs and other cognitions, the Humean claims, have *mind-to-world direction of fit* insofar as what they represent is the world as it is independently; when we notice a discrepancy between the world and what we believe to be the case, we rationally ought to change our beliefs to get them to conform to the world. Motivating states like desires do not work this way; rather, they have *world-to-mind direction of fit* insofar as, when we notice a discrepancy between the world and what we want, we rationally ought to change the world to get it to conform to our desires. Indeed, Humeans construe desires simply to be states with world-to-mind direction of fit (Smith, 1994, 116). Given this, no meaningful distinction can be made between having a desire and being in a state of goal-directedness—i.e., having a kind of disposition, mediated by cognitive states, to achieve a goal. Indeed, this Humean conception of motivation—of desire as simply goal-directedness—is implicit in neo-Jamesian understandings of the connection between emotion and motivation (Damasio, 2003, 34–7; Prinz, 2004, 196).

This is, I believe, fundamentally mistaken, for it implies that all practical rationality is instrumental rationality. Given a particular goal, we can understand actions to be rational insofar as they are instrumental to achieving that goal; but what makes it rational to pursue the goal in the first place? What reasons can we have for this desire? One answer might be that this goal is instrumental to other, superordinate goals, but this only pushes back the question one step further. Another answer might be that this desire is one we would continue to have under idealized conditions of perfect knowledge and rationality. But if desires are sharply distinguished from beliefs in terms of their direction of fit, then this idealization can only reveal possibly hidden, perhaps contingent conflicts among desires, e.g., that we cannot pursue both the desire for a third helping of chocolate cake and the desire to lose weight by eating healthier foods, and so given our preference for health we ought to drop our desire for more cake. Once again, however, this enables us to understand the rationality of desire only in terms of their coherence with other desires, but the rationality of any of these desires is simply presupposed.

What is missing from this Humean picture, I submit, is the idea that desires are for things that are *worth* pursuing, so that the rationality of desire is to be assessed in terms of whether their objects really are worth pursuing. In making this claim, I am of course sidestepping an enormous debate in metaethics concerning the source(s) of practical rationality. However, this claim seems phenomenologically correct and it enables us to make distinctions we want to make. Thus, chess-playing computers exhibit goal-directedness in virtue of representational states with world-to-mind direction of fit and structured by instrumental rationality, but we would not consider such goal states to be genuine desires precisely because these goals are not worth pursuing to the computer: they don't *matter* to it, it does not *care* about them. When genuine agents—whether persons or other animals—pursue goals we do so because we care, because they are worthwhile, because, as I shall say, these goals have *import* to us.

This suggests that we cannot understand motivation simply in terms of representational states that have world-to-mind direction of fit, as Humeans do, but rather must do so in terms of the subject's appreciation of import as a *reason* for acting. One central question of understanding the nature of motivation then becomes that of understanding how such an appreciation of import can, by providing us with reasons, move us to act.

It might be thought that neo-Jamesian accounts of emotions are able to accept and respond to this central question. After all, they understand emotions to be evaluations in light of the subject's well-being. Thus, fear provides a reason for hiding because fear is a bodily appreciation of the bearing some danger has on the subject's well-being; indeed, it is only because of this that emotions can play the role in practical reason they do. However, a closer look at how neo-Jamesians understand the nature of such evaluations reveals this is not the case. Thus, on Damasio's account, emotions are appraisals insofar as they involve positive or negative signals: they "signify optimal physiological coordination and smooth running of the operations of life" (Damasio, 2003, 137), a kind of homeostasis that constitutes our well-being (35).[4] Yet this tying of well-being, of emotional appraisals, to a biological notion of well-being is surely too narrow. For the point of the notion of well-being is to convey the idea that the relevant circumstances bear on what is in some sense worthwhile to the subject, but we need not suppose that the relevant notion of worth will always be something we can spell out biologically.[5]

Prinz recognizes this limitation and offers a more general and more sophisticated account. According to Prinz, things mattering or having import to us has two sources:

[Embodied] appraisals represent things that matter to us, but they do not represent the fact that they matter. That's where valence markers come in. When one couples an embodied fear appraisal with a state that serves as a negative reinforcer, one represents the fact that the situation inducing the fear matters. (Prinz, 2004, 178)

It should be clear, however, that valence markers are simply positive or negative *reinforcers*: "states that get associated with representation of stimuli" (Prinz, 2004, 173) that "increase [or decrease] the probability of response" (169). Consequently, the valence markers do not themselves provide *reasons* for responding in a particular way; that must fall to the embodied appraisal. Here Prinz claims that embodied appraisals are evaluative insofar as they represent in some way circumstances having a bearing on what we value. Thus, sadness represents the circumstances as

---

[4] See also LeDoux (1995, 220) for similar claims about the pleasantness or unpleasantness of emotions.

[5] Christine Tappolet (this volume) argues somewhat more carefully for a similar claim.

involving a loss, where a loss "is the elimination of something valued by an organism" (Prinz, 2004, 63). This certainly seems to provide an account of how emotions can involve an appreciation of import as a reason for acting and so play a role in motivation, and the key to this is the relation of one's circumstances to something valued.

The promise of this account is dashed, however, when we see what Prinz says about valuing: "If one represents something as valued, its being so represented constitutes its being valued" (2004, 63). It is not clear what this could mean or how this could help make sense of reasons for action. For if such a representation of value is under our control, as with a judgment, then simply judging something is valuable makes it be valuable, and we can generate whatever reasons we want at will. This implies that such "reasons" impose no normative standard over us at all. Yet if such representations of value are not judgments, then it is not clear what they are. Moreover, it is not clear how the emotion itself enters into the picture of providing reasons for action, for it would seem that could be done simply by making judgments about how one's circumstances bear on one's values. Why must this connection to motivation run through the emotions rather than through evaluative judgments directly? In short, Prinz's account, like other neo-Jamesian accounts of emotions, fails directly to address the central question of motivation, and it does so at its peril, or so I shall argue.

Before doing this, we first need an explicit account of import and of emotions and judgments in relation to import. It is to this that I now turn.

## 13.3 EMOTIONS, IMPORT, AND MOTIVATION

For something to have import to you—for it to matter to you, for you to care about it—is for it to have a kind of worth. Thus, for a goal to have import to you is for you to find it worth pursuing; but things other than goals can have import as well: objects, states of affairs, activities, relationships, causes, etc. In general, at least part of what it is for something to have import is for it to be worthy of attention and action. That something is worthy of attention means not merely that it is permissible or a good thing to pay attention to it; rather, it means that paying attention to it is, by and large, required on pain of giving up or at least undermining the idea that it really has import to you. Thus, it would not make sense to say that having a clean house has import to you if you never or rarely notice when it gets dirty. Of course, you might sometimes be distracted by other things that are more important and so sometimes not notice its getting dirty. What is required, however, is a consistent pattern of attending to the relevant object: in short, a kind of *vigilance* for what happens or might well happen to it. Similarly, that something is worthy of action means that acting on its behalf is required, other things being equal: for a clean house to have import requires not only vigilance for cleanliness but also a *preparedness* to act so as to maintain it.

The relevant modes of vigilance and preparedness necessary for import are primarily emotional, desiderative, and judgmental, and I shall argue that we can understand the sense in which objects of import are *worthy* of attention and action in terms of the rational interconnections among these modes. I begin with the emotions, which I shall understand to be intentional feelings of import.

Emotions have several kinds of objects. First is the emotion's *target*, namely that at which the emotion is intuitively directed: when I'm angry at my kids for tracking mud into the house, they are the target of my anger. Second, each emotion type has a characteristic way in which it evaluates the target: what makes fear be fear and distinct from anger is that in fearing something we implicitly evaluate it to be dangerous, whereas in being angry at something we implicitly evaluate it to be offensive. Such characteristic evaluations are these emotions' *formal objects*. Finally, and often overlooked, is the *focus* of emotions: the background object having import to which the target is related in such a way as to make intelligible the target's having the evaluative property defined by the formal object. For example, in being angry at my kids, what makes intelligible how they have offended me is the relation between them and my having a clean house, which has import to me; hence, having a clean house is the focus of my anger.

Given this, emotions are intelligible as *warranted* or not in terms of the implicit evaluation of their targets, where such warrant has two conditions. First, the focus must really have import to the subject: my anger at my kids would be unwarranted if having a clean house did not matter to me. Second, the target must be, or intelligibly seem to be, appropriately related to the focus so as to have the kind of import defined by the formal object: my anger would be unwarranted if the kids did not offend me by intentionally or negligently harming the cleanliness of my house (because someone else tracked in all that mud). Given these conditions of warrant, emotions are intelligible as a kind of sensitivity or responsiveness to the import of one's situation: emotions are essentially *intentional feelings of import.*

So far this sounds much like Prinz's understanding of emotions as responsive to "values". My claim, however, is that emotions are not simply responsive to import; they are a kind of *commitment* to import, as is revealed when we consider the rational interconnections they have to other mental states, including other emotions. Thus, to experience one emotion is in effect to commit oneself to feeling other emotions with the same focus in the relevant actual and counterfactual situations because of the import of that focus. If I am angry at my kids for tracking in mud, I ought also to be worried about whether I can get it cleaned up before our dinner guests arrive, relieved when I do (or embarrassed when I don't), and so on. Moreover, it would at first blush seem inconsistent with these emotions to be afraid of cleaning up or upset with my kids for picking up their toys without my asking because these latter emotions would seem to involve a contrary commitment to import.

Such emotional commitments define a pattern of emotions with a common focus, patterns that are both rational and projectible. Such patterns are *rational* in that, other things being equal, one rationally ought to have emotions belonging to the pattern, so that the failure to experience emotions that fit into the pattern when otherwise appropriate is a rational failure. Thus, my anger at my kids would be unwarranted unless I also felt the worry, relief, embarrassment, etc. Consequently, being such as to have these emotions in the relevant actual and counterfactual situations is rationally required, and the resulting pattern of emotions therefore ought to be *projectible.* Of course, one need not feel emotions every time they are warranted in order for the relevant pattern to be in place; isolated failures to feel particular emotions, though rationally inappropriate, do not undermine the rational coherence of the broader pattern so long as these failures remain isolated.

Insofar as each particular emotion is an intentional feeling of import by virtue of the conditions of its warrant, it may seem that import is conceptually prior to these emotions and therefore to the patterns they constitute. This would be a mistake. For if something is the focus of such a pattern of emotions, the projectibility of that pattern ensures that one will typically respond with the relevant emotions whenever that focus is affected favorably or adversely. In effect, the projectibility of the pattern of emotions is an attunement of one's sensibilities to the well-being of that focus, and this just is the sort of vigilance normally required for import. Moreover, such emotional vigilance is not merely a disposition to attend to the focus; insofar as the pattern itself is rational, one *ought* to have these emotions—one ought to attend to the focus—precisely because the past pattern of emotions rationally commits one to feel these subsequent emotions when otherwise warranted. Consequently, the projectibility and rationality of the pattern makes intelligible the sense in which to have import is to be *worthy* of attention, and so import itself presupposes this pattern of emotions: it is hard to make sense of someone as caring about something if he or she does not respond emotionally no matter what when it is affected favorably or adversely.

Of course, to have import is to be worthy of action as well. Once again this is intelligible in terms of the kind of commitment to import these patterns of emotions essentially involve. For if the commitment to import that emotions essentially involve is to be genuine, it must involve not merely a commitment to attend to that import but also to act on its behalf. Thus, other things being equal it would be rationally inappropriate for me to be afraid that my kids will track mud into the house again and yet not be motivated to act accordingly, and never or rarely to be motivated to act out of fear would bring into question whether I in fact have the capacity for fear.

It might be thought that fear motivates behavior arationally: by simply causing us to tremble, for example. Although this is possible, I set such *arational expressions* of emotions aside to focus on the more interesting cases in which emotions motivate action as a motive: by making the action intelligible within a broader context of rationality through the commitment to import they essentially involve.

Emotions can rationally motivate action either directly or indirectly and in ways that are goal-directed or not. Thus, emotions motivate us to act directly as when we duck out of fear, jump for joy, or cry out of sadness. Unlike cases of the arational expression of emotions, in these cases our actions have a point revealed to be worthwhile by the emotion itself through its commitment to import. Thus, the point of ducking is made intelligible by fear insofar as it is by ducking that I avoid the looming danger to which I respond in feeling fear: fear motivates ducking as a goal-directed intentional action. Similarly, jumping for joy or crying out of sadness each have a point—celebration or mourning—where the jumping or crying just are the celebrating or the mourning rather than means to it; in these cases, the jumping and celebrating are non-goal-directed intentional actions, which we can understand to be *rational expressions* of these emotions insofar as these emotions reveal their point to be worthwhile in light of their commitment to the import of their focuses. In each case, we can highlight this motivating role of emotional commitments through a more precise specification of their formal objects: to feel fear, joy, or sorrow is to find its target to be a danger worth avoiding, a good worth celebrating, or a loss worth mourning. Thus, it is a condition of the possibility of having a capacity for emotions that, through the exercise of this capacity, one normally both attends to the import of one's circumstances and is thereby motivated to act accordingly.[6]

Emotions also motivate us indirectly through their rational interconnections with desire. For the commitment to import involved in having an emotion, insofar as that commitment is to the focus as worthy of action, is not only to having other emotions with the same focus but also to having the relevant desires to act on its behalf. Thus, in fearing that my kids will track mud into the house, I ought to desire to take means to prevent this: by talking to them, posting notes, imposing rewards or punishments, buying a doormat, etc. As before, a failure to have such desires would be a rational failure, and consistently to fail to have such desires indicates that one is not prepared to act on behalf of that focus, thereby undermining one's commitment to its import and so the rationality of the pattern of emotions. Conversely, insofar as to desire something normally is not merely to be disposed to pursue it as an end but rather to find it *worth* pursuing,[7] desire itself is a commitment to import and so also to feeling the

---

[6] This understanding of the rational expressions of emotions provides an alternative to the common idea that emotions motivate us either to arational behavior or (via desire) to goal-directed action (see, e.g., Tappolet, this volume). Consequently, unlike Tappolet I see no reason to think that emotional motivation, insofar as it is rational, essentially involves desire.

[7] Of course it is possible to have a desire that is for what is not in fact worth pursuing—what does not in fact have this kind of import. Such desires will be defective in the same way emotions that respond to things that do not in fact have import to us are.

relevant pattern of emotions: if one did not normally feel fear when a desired end is threatened, relief when that threat does not materialize, anger at those who intentionally impede your progress, disappointment at failure, etc., it would be hard to make sense of that end as having import and so as being an appropriate object of desire. In short, the projectible, rational pattern of emotions with a common focus includes desires as well.[8]

This understanding of the way emotions and desires motivate through their commitments to import reveals (a) how the projectibility of such a pattern of emotions and desires with a common focus makes possible not only one's vigilance for import but also one's preparedness to act on its behalf, and (b) how the rationality of the pattern makes intelligible its focus not only as worthy of attention but also worthy of action. Because to have import is to be worthy of both attention and action, I conclude that *to have import just is to be the focus of a projectible, rational pattern of emotions and desires.* Emotions and desires thus not only respond to import but also thereby constitute that very import.

One might object that this account is viciously circular, for I have said both that import is constituted by our emotions and that it serves as a standard of warrant for our emotions. So which is it?—which comes first, import or the emotions? Indeed, it looks as though on my account emotions and desires exhibit both mind-to-world and world-to-mind directions of fit, which is impossible insofar as these are mutually exclusive. In reply, I reject the idea, implicit in the notion of a direction of fit, that one or the other of import or our emotions must be onto-logically or conceptually prior to the other, and so I reject this notion of direction of fit as it applies to import. Rather, on my account, import and the emotions emerge together as a holistic package all of which must be in place for any of it to be intelligible. The circularity of the account is therefore a normal part of such holism and is not at all vicious.

Several important implications of this account are worth drawing out. First, intentional action must be distinguished from mere goal-directedness in that action is essentially motivated by import; in particular, emotions and desires rationally motivate action because of the way they involve commitments to import. Indeed, such motivation by import is what distinguishes us as agents from things like chess-playing computers: to be an agent is to be a subject of import and so to have the capacities not merely for belief and desire but also for emotion.[9] Second, given the nature of such commitments to import, emotions are not, as neo-Jamesian accounts encourage us to think, states of feeling we can understand in isolation

---

[8] Indeed, I have argued elsewhere that emotions and desires are each species of the genus felt evaluations; see Helm (2002) for details.

[9] It is worth noting that there is no reason at all to think that what has import to you must always be yourself. This bolsters the argument Tappolet offers (this volume) against the thesis of motivational egoism.

from one another; rather, they are essentially interconnected with other emotions and desires so as to constitute import. Consequently, it is not possible to have the capacity for one emotion type without also having the capacity for many other emotion types and for desire: fear is unintelligible apart from other emotions like relief, disappointment, joy, anger, and hope, or apart from desire. Finally, it should be clear that emotions are not simply responses to already existing concerns to which they can provide epistemic access of a distinctive sort (namely, quick and dirty), as on neo-Jamesian accounts. Rather, emotions are at least partly constitutive of our concerns—of import—and, as I shall argue below, it is in part because of this that they are fundamental to practical reasoning in ways neo-Jamesian accounts cannot acknowledge.

It might be suggested that Prinz makes room for these interconnections among emotions with his notion of a sentiment (Prinz, 2004, 188ff.). According to Prinz, a sentiment (e.g., a like or dislike) is an "affective disposition": "If you like something, interactions with it should cause joy or other positive affects. Conversely for dislikes" (189). A sentiment, therefore, might seem to involve the kind of interconnections among emotions that I have just argued we need. However, Prinz has no clear understanding of what the relevant connections among emotions would be. Interactions with something I like *rationally ought* to cause positive affects *only if* the circumstances involve positive import; if instead my interaction with my prized Ming vase results in its shattering on the floor, joy or other "positive affects" would hardly be appropriate. Understanding which other emotions are interconnected here and why these emotions *ought* to come together as a group requires understanding a "sentiment" to be an evaluative attitude like caring: an attitude comprised of a projectible, rational pattern of emotions and desires, a pattern that is defined by the commitment to the import of its common focus—by its evaluative content—and that thereby both constitutes the import of its focus and rationally motivates the appropriate actions on its behalf. Nothing like this is in view from Prinz's neo-Jamesian account of emotions. Indeed, with merely biological, dispositional substitutes for a genuinely evaluative notion of import, neo-Jamesian accounts seem to assimilate all cases of emotional motivation to arational expressions. I shall return to this point below.

## 13.4 EMOTIONS AND EVALUATIVE JUDGMENTS

I have argued that emotions and desires motivate by virtue of being commitments to import—by virtue of their evaluative content, we might say. At this point, one might raise an objection I raised for Prinz at the end of §13.2 concerning the role of emotions in motivation: if the commitment to import that is implicit in our emotions and desires is what explains how they rationally motivate intentional action, why not think that evaluative judgments can motivate action directly? Cannot evaluative judgments be just as much commitments to import as emotions or desires are?

The short answer is yes: evaluative judgments can motivate us to act both directly and indirectly, in precisely the same way emotions and desires do, *if* they succeed in committing us to import. Understanding this requires delving more deeply into the rational interconnections among emotions, desires, and evaluative judgments and so into the place evaluative judgments have in constituting import. Of particular importance is the way, by virtue of these interconnections, the linguistic concepts of evaluative judgment come to inform our emotions, thereby making intelligible how emotions can play a much more substantial role in practical reason than the merely "auxiliary" role as quick and dirty adaptive mechanisms that neo-Jamesian accounts allow.

## 13.4.1 Single Evaluative Perspective

Emotions are commitments to the import of their focuses and thereby to their targets having the evaluative property expressed by their formal objects. Such evaluations made within the patterns of emotions and desires define what we might call the agent's *evaluative perspective*.[10] Of course, in making evaluative judgments, we also articulate an evaluative perspective, and my claim is that our evaluative judgments, emotions, and desires together define a single evaluative perspective: it is possible to make judgments with the same intentional content as our emotions and desires, and vice versa, such that each is a commitment to the same import. That this is so is revealed by the kinds of rational interconnections among them, as I shall now argue.

Consider first a simple example from Solomon (1976, 185): if I believe you have stolen my car, I am liable to get angry at you, thereby evaluating you, the target, as having offended me. If I subsequently discover that you did not steal it, my anger ought to disappear: this revised understanding of my circumstances ought to alter my emotional response, which is based on that same understanding. Consequently, if I continue to be angry even after making these new judgments in light of further information, then my anger is irrational, other things being equal.

---

[10] Of course, the notion of an agent's evaluative perspective must take into account not merely the various things that in fact have import to him or her but also the way in which such import is structured in light of preferences and priorities; for details on how I think this ought to be understood, see Helm (2001), especially Chapter 4. However, this complication is not relevant to my discussion here, and so I shall ignore it.

The claim here is not that if I judge you to have offended me then I ought to feel anger, and vice versa; there are, after all, other reasons I might have for not feeling anger, such as that other things here and now are more important so that such an offense is not worth attending to now. Moreover, the standards for the warrant of an emotion are appropriately less stringent than the standards of correctness of evaluative judgment, so that there need be no rational conflict involved in, for example, being afraid and feeling the target to be dangerous and yet failing to judge that it really is dangerous. Indeed, it may seem here that the idea of emotions as "quick and dirty" responses to one's circumstances has some applicability. Yet the claim is not simply that judgments can in some cases overrule emotions and reveal those emotions, if they remain, to be irrational. For we should not interpret the alleged "dirtiness" of emotional responses to indicate that in cases of conflicts between judgment and emotion it is always the emotion that is irrational. Surely this can be true in some cases, as with phobias, for example. Yet in other cases a rational conflict between emotion and judgment can cast doubt on the judgment itself. Thus, walking down an unfamiliar street late at night, I may feel afraid, even as I tell myself that everything is fine, that I'm perfectly safe. In this case, the persistence of my fear may reveal my judgment to be merely wishful thinking, such that I ought to resolve the conflict within my evaluative perspective by giving up (at least by withholding) on that judgment. Consequently, the rational interconnections between emotions and judgments are bi-directional.

This may make it sound as though the rational interconnections between emotions and judgments involve simply the avoidance of manifest conflict, that one's evaluative perspective on the world ought not to contain conflicting elements, such as the feeling that you have offended me together with the judgment that you have not. However, the demands of consistency across emotions and judgments are more rigorous than that. I have already argued that each emotion involves a commitment to the import of its focus (and of its target) and thereby to having other emotions with the same focus in the appropriate circumstances. Such commitments are in effect commitments to sustain a particular evaluative perspective on the world. Now particular emotions may be unwarranted precisely because their focus does not have import—because the relevant evaluative perspective is not sustained—and so the commitment to import they involve is a false commitment. When the relevant evaluative perspective is sustained by a projectible, rational pattern of emotions with a common focus, the commitment is *genuine*, a commitment that ought to be sustained within our evaluative perspective quite generally.[11] This has a couple of implications for the rational interconnections between emotions and evaluative judgments.

---

[11] It is important to distinguish two senses in which such a commitment "ought" to be sustained: one insofar as it is the rational continuation of a pattern of such commitments that constitute its focus as *in fact* having import to you; and another insofar as this focus is something that *ought* to have that

First, if something has import to me by virtue of a projectible, rational pattern of emotions with it as their common focus, then, other things being equal, in the appropriate circumstances I ought to judge that it has that import. For, an agent's perspective on the world is normally unified rather than bifurcated and so to fail to judge this is to fail in my genuine commitment to sustaining this evaluative perspective. Second, and conversely, to commit oneself in judgment to the import of something is, other things being equal, to commit one to sustaining the relevant evaluative perspective not only by making further evaluative judgments when appropriate but also by having the relevant emotions. This is true not merely when the judgment corresponds to the focus of an emotion but also when it corresponds to the emotion's formal object. Thus, suppose my daughter is asked to give a presentation of her science fair project to her whole school. She may initially find it frightening—a danger to her self-esteem and social standing given the risks of making a fool of herself. However, after thinking (and talking) it over, she comes to judge that this is an exciting opportunity to learn and grow rather than a danger, and such a judgment ought, other things being equal, to alter her emotions and, thereby, her motivation.[12] Indeed, without a general resonance between evaluative judgments and emotions, the commitment to import she undertakes in judgment or feels in emotion would be defective, such that there is no clear fact of the matter of what her evaluative perspective really is—what really has import to her.

The upshot is that emotions and evaluative judgments are rationally connected not merely insofar as they can come into conflict that the subject rationally ought to resolve by modifying one or the other but, more fundamentally, in that they together define what is normally a single view on the world—a single evaluative perspective—that can diverge only irrationally. For creatures like us with a capacity for evaluative judgment, then, import is constituted by projectible, rational patterns not merely of emotions and desires but also of evaluative judgment.

This conclusion is inconsistent with neo-Jamesian accounts of emotions. For neo-Jamesians understand the interconnections between emotions and judgments fundamentally in causal or dispositional rather than rational terms. Thus, Damasio, after asserting that "the *essence* of emotion [is] the collection of changes in body state", claims that:

---

import. My intent here is to appeal merely to the former. (For a detailed account of how to make sense of the latter partly in terms of the rational interconnections between emotions and evaluative judgments, see Helm [2001, especially Chapter 7].)

12 Of course, her emotions can be recalcitrant and fail to fall in line with this judgment. As I have argued, such a conflict between emotion and judgment is irrational and so ought to be resolved: either by giving up on or rethinking the judgment or, if she is convinced the judgment is correct, by exercising control over her emotions to conform. For details on how such control can be exercised, see Helm (1996).

emotion is the combination of a *mental evaluative process*, simple or complex, with *dispositional responses to that process*, mostly *toward the body proper*, resulting in an emotional body state, but also *toward the brain itself* (neurotransmitter nuclei in brain stem), resulting in additional mental changes. (Damasio, 1994, 139, emphasis in the original)

The problem here is the dispositional analysis: if our evaluative judgments merely dispose us to have the bodily process—the emotional essence—then it is hard to see how changes in judgment of the sort described above *ought* to result in changes in emotion, and it seems inconsistent with Damasio's understanding of the one-way connection between the two that the persistence of an emotion in the face of revised judgments should provide a reason for changing that judgment. Of course, Damasio would say that the emotion, as a somatic marker, can direct our attention to features of our environments that can influence our judgments. However, once these features are "marked" as relevant, and once we have taken them into account in judgment, there is for Damasio no further role for emotions to play our reasoning processes, and so Damasio is unable to make sense of how the persistence of one's emotions can itself either be irrational or impose rational pressure on one to revise one's conflicting evaluative judgments.[13] All of this means that Damasio cannot make sense of the role emotions and judgments each play as parts of a pattern of rationality that constitutes import, thereby assimilating all emotional motivation to arational expression.

One final consequence of this account is worth drawing out. I argued in §13.3 that emotions and desires motivate intentional action by virtue of the commitments to import they involve. I have just argued that evaluative judgments, like emotions, are commitments to import and so can affect our motivations indirectly through their rational interconnections with our emotions—and, it should be added, our desires as well. Yet it is a condition of the possibility of our being committed to import that, other things being equal, we are motivated to act in the appropriate circumstances, and this is true whether that commitment is emotional, desiderative, or judgmental. Consequently, by making evaluative judgments and thereby committing ourselves to import, we have the capacity directly to move ourselves to act; such a capacity just is the *will*. Of course, that we have such a capacity does not mean its exercise will be successful: weakness of will and listlessness are persistent possibilities, and the genuineness of one's judgmental commitment to import can be called into question by the failure of judgment to motivate.[14]

---

[13] Prinz's account of emotions is more subtle, for he makes room for the intentional content of emotions to be modified by the concepts we deploy in judgment; I shall come back to Prinz's view in §13.4.2.

[14] This is, of course, a controversial thesis. For a defense, see Helm (2001, especially Chapter 6).

## 13.4.2  Conceptually Informed Emotions

I have argued that emotions, desires, and evaluative judgments together form an evaluative perspective that is normally unified but can involve rational conflicts. Yet such harmony or conflict is intelligible as such only if what is judged and what is felt in emotion is potentially the same thing, and that requires that the linguistic concepts we bring to bear in judgment inform the intentional content of our emotions. Thus, by making evaluative judgments we commit ourselves in part to having certain emotions in the relevant kinds of situations: kinds of situations we define in judgment in terms of linguistic concepts. Consequently, in order for us to be properly emotionally responsive to the perspective on the world to which we are committed by judgment, our emotions must respond to kinds of situations delineated by these concepts: our emotions are shaped by the conceptual and inferential skills our capacity for judgment brings with it. Of course, this conclusion applies only to creatures that have a language and are capable of evaluative judgment; non-linguistic animals like dogs and cats do have the capacity for a variety of emotions and so are subjects of import without linguistic concepts. However, once we linguistic animals acquire the capacity for judgment, our emotions are transformed by virtue of these rational interconnections, so that our capacity for discrimination need be no less refined in our emotions than it is in our judgments.

All of this suggests that we should not be so impressed, as neo-Jamesians are, by the supposedly animal nature of emotional capacities—by the thought that emotions are merely "quick and dirty" responses that can have merely an "auxiliary" role in evaluative thought by virtue of the way they direct our attention. We should not think that because animal emotions are "quick and dirty" in this way that human emotions must be no different. For the biological grounding of our emotions does not preclude their transformation by capacities we develop through language and culture; indeed, it is only once emotions have been transformed by our linguistic concepts so as to acquire this refinement and discrimination that we can understand them to have a more fundamental rational role in evaluation and reason.

Prinz would surely object that I have given short shrift to neo-Jamesian accounts by failing to recognize the resources they have for understanding the relations between emotions and judgments and so the role that linguistic concepts can play in the emotions. For, Prinz argues, our linguistic concepts can come to inform our emotions through the mechanism of a calibration file. A *calibration file* is a set of representations—including but not limited to those we use in judgment—that each dispose us to have a particular bodily response the perception of which is an emotion. For example, my calibration file for anger may include judgments about lack of respect, and it is for this reason that we should understand my anger in these cases to be about lack of respect rather than some other feature of my circumstances. Thus, Prinz says, "by establishing new calibration files, an embodied appraisal can be said to represent something beyond what it is evolved to represent" (2004, 100), and this explains not merely how we can fear things like exams that do not pose any immanent physical danger but also how we can come to have non-basic emotions like jealousy, which is a particular refinement of our basic emotion of anger in light of its unique calibration file.

This understanding of the connection between emotions and judgments can be deepened when we consider not just emotions but sentiments like caring, which Prinz understands to be "disposition[s] to experience different emotions" (2007, 84). For judgments about import—that respecting others is good, for example—*express* sentiments in two respects.[15] First, in making a judgment of import, we describe the relevant dispositions that sentiments are, so that when I judge that some behavior exhibits a lack of respect, I am describing that behavior as apt to cause an emotional response in me. Second, such judgments themselves can cause me to have the relevant emotions, so that these judgments thereby come to be a part of the calibration file not just of the individual emotions but also, we might say, of the sentiment itself. Given that such judgments use linguistic concepts, we can now see that it is not just emotions but also sentiments that come to be shaped by the linguistic concepts we bring to bear in judgments. Neo-Jamesians like Prinz, therefore, may seem to make sense of the kind of transformation and refinement of emotions I have made so much of. Indeed, such an account can seem to grant emotions a significant role in practical reason, for Prinz argues for a form of motivational internalism that runs through the emotions: by making judgments that express sentiments, we cause ourselves to have emotions and thereby motivate ourselves accordingly (Prinz, 2007, 102; cf. Döring, 2003, 2007).

Nonetheless, there is considerable sleight of hand here, which can be revealed by thinking about cases in which things start to go wrong. Consider the example of Mary, which Annas (2005, 640) uses to criticize Doris' (2002) account of the moral relevance of situationist social psychology. "Mary", Annas writes, "treats her colleagues at work with respect and courtesy, is collegial and friendly to work with." One of Mary's colleagues, we might expect, would say that Mary cares about being respectful—has a positive sentiment towards respect—given the dispositions to a variety of emotions she reliably displays at work. Upon seeing Mary being "demanding and rude to shop assistants", this colleague would be surprised and puzzled—even "*shocked*", as Annas says (2005, 640)—but he might write it off as an aberration. However, upon discovering that Mary consistently "humiliates waiters in restaurants, screams at her son's soccer coach", and so on, he ought to revise his understanding of her: she does not, after all, care about respect, but some surrogate notion, understanding "respect" to mean something like politeness and courtesy owed to her social equals (or betters). At this point, assume Mary's colleague confronts her and convinces her that she has

---

[15] I am here generalizing Prinz's discussion somewhat, for Prinz in fact talks more narrowly about *moral* judgments expressing moral sentiments. It seems reasonable, however, to think he would say similar things about sentiments more generally being expressed by what I would call judgments about import.

misunderstood what respect is and should instead understand it in more Kantian terms. With her newfound understanding of respect, Mary is able reliably to distinguish respect from disrespect and so is able to apply the concept correctly, and she judges with apparent sincerity that she ought to respect all persons. However, let us assume, this does not change her emotional dispositions or her motivation: she continues to humiliate waiters, judges that she ought not, and still does not feel bad about it. This is, I submit, a live possibility, although something has clearly gone wrong with Mary. How are we to understand it?

One tack for Prinz to take is to understand the emotional responsiveness to be at fault: Mary has the disposition to respond emotionally to such judgments concerning respect, but for whatever reason this disposition fails to be activated. This approach would make sense of isolated failures to respond emotionally, but we cannot sustain the idea that she has *this* disposition—this pattern in the causal relationships between judging and feeling—when there is such a widespread pattern to the failures, as in Mary's case. Another tack is to say that Mary is simply mistaken in judging that she ought to respect all others given that this judgment does not accurately express the sentiment, for what she cares about is still just politeness to her social equals. The trouble here is that this seems to suggest that she ought to give up on her judgment that she ought to respect others in order accurately to describe the dispositions to emotions she finds herself with, which is clearly the wrong conclusion to draw. What we need to say instead is that she *ought* to change her sentiment, that the failure is a *rational* failure with her emotions. Once again, we are back to the conclusion that the interconnections between emotions and judgments must be understood in rational rather than dispositional terms.

On my account, this rational interconnection is straightforward, at least in its outlines. In judging that respect for others has import—and doing so not just as a matter of giving it lip service on one occasion but rather consistently as appropriate to a variety of situations—is to establish a rationally structured pattern of commitments to the import of respect that, other things being equal, ought to include emotions and desires as well. Of course, in Mary's case it does not, and the absence of emotional response in a wide range of cases reveals a troubling irrationality within her evaluative perspective. Now the question arises as to how this rational conflict can be resolved. Here, as I have argued, Mary can bring her explicit understanding of respect and the reasons for respect to bear on her perception of particular circumstances in an effort to come to feel, say, shame and remorse for her poor treatment of her waiter, thereby imposing rational pressure on herself to have these emotions, an effort that can be more or less successful.[16] Nonetheless, there is no guarantee that her lack of emotional response is the source of irrationality here: that failure may instead indicate that she ought to rethink her judgment and, in particular, the concept of respect it involves.

[16] Cf. note 12.

This is clear if we imagine that things went the other way around: Mary initially did exhibit proper respect for others, but was convinced by her colleague, through appeals to rational egoism, that she ought instead to care merely about politeness to her social equals. Now, faced with the rational conflict between her judgment that self-interest, not respect, is what matters and her recalcitrant emotions, it is much more plausible to suppose that her emotions have gotten things right, thereby correcting her faulty judgment.[17]

Now fleshing out the details of how such deliberation about import works is terrifically complicated, and I cannot do it here. But what I have said is enough to show that our emotional capacities involve a kind of sophistication and refinement that merits their having a significant role in practical reasoning and motivation: a role to which neo-Jamesian accounts are simply blind by their focus on bodily responses. Indeed, this is, in effect, the kind of emotional sophistication and refinement to which Annas appeals in her criticism of Doris. Empirical evidence about how people are disposed to respond to certain types of situations of the sort both Doris and the neo-Jamesians appeal to cannot so easily dislodge an understanding of these rational interconnections that, I have argued, are central to our ability to find things to be worthwhile and motivate ourselves to act accordingly. Of course we are embodied creatures and our emotional capacities must therefore be somehow grounded in our bodies. But to think that we can understand the emotions as such in terms of that bodily response is to ignore their manifest rationality.

## References

ANNAS, JULIA (2005). "Comments on John Doris's *Lack of Character*". *Philosophy and Phenomenological Research*, 71(3), 636–42.

BENNETT, JONATHAN (1974). "The Conscience of Huckleberry Finn". *Philosophy*, 49, 123–34.

DAMASIO, ANTONIO (1994). *Descartes' Error: Emotion, Reason, and the Human Brain* (New York, NY: Grosset/Putnam).

—— (1999). *The Feeling of What Happens: Body and Emotion in the Making of Consciousness* (New York, NY: Harcourt, Brace & Co.).

—— (2003). *Looking for Spinoza: Joy, Sorrow, and the Feeling Brain* (New York, NY: Harcourt, Brace & Co.).

DÖRING, SABINE A. (2003). "Explaining Action By Emotion". *The Philosophical Quarterly*, 53, 214–30.

—— (2007). "Seeing What to Do: Affective Perception and Rational Motivation". *Dialectica*, 61(3), 363–94.

---

[17] Such a case is similar to that of Huck Finn, who judges he ought to turn Jim in but finds himself emotionally unable to do so. For further discussion, see, e.g., Bennett (1974); McIntyre (1990).

DORIS, JOHN M. (2002). *Lack of Character: Personality and Moral Behavior* (New York, NY: Cambridge University Press).

DRETSKE, FRED (1981). *Knowledge and the Flow of Information* (Cambridge, MA: MIT Press).

HELM, BENNETT W. (1996). "Freedom of the Heart". *Pacific Philosophical Quarterly*, 77(2), 71–87.

—— (2001). *Emotional Reason: Deliberation, Motivation, and the Nature of Value* (Cambridge: Cambridge University Press).

—— (2002). "Felt Evaluations: A Theory of Pleasure and Pain". *American Philosophical Quarterly*, 39(1), 13–30.

HORST, STEVEN (1998). "Our Animal Bodies". *Midwest Studies in Philosophy*, 22(1), 34–61.

HURSTHOUSE, ROSALIND (1991). "Arational Actions". *The Journal of Philosophy*, 88(2), 57–68.

JAMES, WILLIAM (1884). "What Is an Emotion?" *Mind*, 9(34), 188–205.

—— (1950). *The Principles of Psychology*, Vol. Two (New York, NY: Dover).

LEDOUX, JOSEPH E. (1995). "Emotion: Clues from the Brain". *Annual Review of Psychology*, 46, 209–35.

—— (1996). *The Emotional Brain: The Mysterious Underpinnings of Emotional Life* (New York, NY: Simon & Schuster).

MCINTYRE, ALISON (1990). "Is Akratic Action Always Irrational?" In Owen Flanagan and Amélie O. Rorty (eds.), *Identity, Character, and Morality: Essays in Moral Psychology* (Cambridge, MA: MIT Press), 379–400.

PRINZ, JESSE J. (2004). *Gut Reactions: A Perceptual Theory of Emotion* (Oxford: Oxford University Press).

—— (2007). *The Emotional Construction of Morals* (Oxford: Oxford University Press).

ROBINSON, JENEFER (2005). *Deeper than Reason: Emotion and Its Role in Literature, Music, and Art* (Oxford: Clarendon Press).

SHAFFER, JEROME A. (1983). "An Assessment of Emotion". *American Philosophical Quarterly*, 20(2), 161–73.

SMITH, MICHAEL (1994). *The Moral Problem* (Oxford: Oxford University Press).

SOLOMON, ROBERT C. (1976). *The Passions* (New York, NY: Anchor Press).

TAPPOLET, CHRISTINE (2009). "Emotion, Motivation, and Action: The Case of Fear". In Peter Goldie (ed.), *Oxford Handbook of the Philosophy of Emotions* (Oxford: Oxford University Press).

# CHAPTER 14

# EMOTION, MOTIVATION, AND ACTION: THE CASE OF FEAR

CHRISTINE TAPPOLET

CONSIDER a typical fear episode. You are strolling down a lonely mountain lane when suddenly a huge wolf leaps towards you. A number of different interconnected elements are involved in the fear you experience. First, there is the visual and auditory perception of the wild animal and its movements. In addition, it is likely that, given what you see, you may implicitly and inarticulately appraise the situation as acutely threatening. Then, there are a number of physiological changes, involving a variety of systems controlled by the autonomic nervous system. Your heart races, your breathing becomes strained, and you start trembling. These changes are accompanied by an expression of fear on your face: your mouth opens and your eyes widen while you stare at the wolf. There is also a kind of experience that you undergo. You are likely to feel a sort of pang, something that might consist in the perception of the physiological changes you are going through. Moreover, a number

A first version of this chapter has been presented at the workshop *La Peur. Épistémologie, Éthique et Politique*, Paris 2007, organized by Bertrand Guillarme and Ruwen Ogien, whom I would like to thank. For discussions, I am grateful to Frédéric Bouchard, Luc Faucher, Bertrand Guillarme, Daniel Laurier, Vanessa Nurock, Ruwen Ogien, Cass Sunstein, and especially Ronnie de Sousa and Peter Goldie, whose comments greatly helped me to improve the chapter.

of thoughts are likely to cross your mind. You might think that the wild beast is about to tear you to pieces and that you'll never escape from this. In addition to this, your attention focuses on the wolf and its movement, as well as, possibly, ways of escaping or defending yourself. Last, but not least, your fear is likely to come with a motivation, such as an urge to run away or to strike back.

Whatever the details of the story, it is clear that a typical emotion episode involves a number of different components. Roughly, these components are (a) a sensory perception or more generally an informational component, (b) a kind of appraisal, (c) physiological changes, (d) conscious feelings, (e) cognitive and attentional processes, and (f) an action-tendency or more generally a motivational component. One central question in the theory of emotion is which, if any, of these components, constitute the emotion. For instance, is the fear you undergo a feeling, a thought, or an action-tendency? Or else, does it involve several or maybe all of the components on the list? What can we subtract without losing the emotion of fear? In other words, the question is what, if any, components are essential to fear. More generally, emotion theorists have tried to determine what, if any, are the essential components of emotions, regardless of the kind of emotion under consideration.

As is shown by the example of fear, it is natural to think that emotions are intimately related to motivation and action. The question I am interested in concerns the motivational component of emotions. What exactly is its nature? Is it a behavioural disposition? Is it a desire? Is such a motivational component necessarily present? And what is its relation with the other components of emotions?

These questions are closely related to the question of the rationality of emotions. Emotions have traditionally been considered as a threat to rationality, whether theoretical or practical. Our angers, envies, and fears have been accused of interfering with proper reasoning, to favour irrational behaviour, and to elicit immoral actions. Following the works of Ronald de Sousa and Antonio Damasio, a new consensus has established itself among emotion theorists, be they philosophers, psychologists, or neurologists.[1] Most theorists now claim that, far from constituting an obstacle to rationality and morality, emotions are both necessary to the proper functioning of theoretical and practical rationality, and essential to moral action. In brief, emotions would allow us to think and act more appropriately, both from the point of view of prudence and ethics.[2]

The question is whether or not the proposed revalorization of emotions is plausible. Clearly, some kinds of emotions, such as anger, envy, or fear, do not

---

[1] See de Sousa (1987) and Damasio (1994). Karen Jones speaks of a new pro-emotion consensus (Jones 2008).

[2] There are notable voices of dissidence to this consensus, such as Jon Elster (1999). Interestingly, the pro-emotion consensus also fails to be widely accepted by laymen, who seem much more ambivalent with respect to emotions.

easily fit such a rosy picture. These emotions often seem to trigger actions that fail to promote our self-interest, to say the least. And even when such actions happen to be in our best interest, they have little to boast about, morally speaking. Consider fear again. Insofar as this emotion seems to come with innate behavioural dispositions, which are automatically triggered by stimuli that constituted a threat to our ancestors but not for us, and which result in a narrow range of behaviours, one can doubt that fear can help us to act appropriately in the actual world. Moreover, it seems rather hopeless to claim that actions motivated by fear are morally admirable. The motivations that are involved in fear seem clearly self-interested. Thus, it would seem that it is at best by favouring behaviours that conform to what morality requires that fear, and in particular fear of punishment and of blame, can play a role in moral motivation. Fear thus appears to resist the current revalorization of emotions. And much the same could be said of emotions such as anger or envy, for instance.

The picture of emotions presupposed in these considerations is one that involves two theses. First, *the thesis of motivational modularity*, according to which emotional motivations are rigid and innate behavioural dispositions. Second, *the thesis of motivational egoism*, which claims that emotional motivations aim at the interest of the organism that experiences the emotion. Both theses can be questioned; or so I shall argue.

Note that instead of considering emotions in general I shall mainly concentrate on the motivational component of fear.[3] Fear is clearly a good candidate for both the thesis of motivational modularity and that of motivational egoism. My aim is to show that these two theses are problematic, even when applied to fear. As far as I can see, it is methodologically preferable to be prudent when making claims about emotions in general. It is likely that the relation to motivation can be tighter or looser depending on the kind of emotion. Thus, joy, hope, and awe seem to have a much looser relation to motivation, compared with other kinds, such as fear and anger.

My plan is the following. I start with some general points about fear. After that, I spell out and discuss the thesis of motivational modularity. We will see that, even though that thesis is plausible in cases of non-human fear, this is not so for human fear. This is why I turn to the claim that fear comes with some specific desire instead. In the last section, I discuss the thesis of motivational egoism. I argue that when we experience fear for someone else, the motivation involved is exactly as altruistic as when we feel compassion for that person.

---

[3] This is not to deny that many if not all emotional dispositions normally come in structured networks, which correspond to concerns or cares. To care for someone is to be disposed to a range of emotions that depend on how that person fares: fear if we think that things will go badly for her, happiness if we think that they will go well, hope if we think that there is a fair chance that they will improve, etc. See Shoemaker (2003), as well as Nussbaum (2001); Prinz (2004, pp. 188 ff.) and Helm (this volume).

## 14.1 FEAR AND THE PERCEPTION
## OF THE FEARSOME

.......................................................................................................................

Even if you restrict yourself to occurrent emotions, that is, episodes of emotions that are experienced at a certain time by a certain person, it is striking that there is a wide variety of terms related to fear.[4] This suggests that there are different kinds of fear. *Prima facie*, it seems we can distinguish between anxiety, anguish, apprehension, worry, phobia, fright, terror, panic, not to mention *megatu* of the Ifaluk people, an emotion which seems to be very close to our fear, but which is positively valued, as those who experience it are proud of themselves.[5] In addition to this, we often distinguish between fears on the basis of their objects: we speak of fear of heights, agoraphobia, arachnophobia, flying-phobia, etc., while the Chinese have a term for fear of the cold: *pa-leng*.[6]

What all these kinds of fear share, I propose, is that they are related to what is fearsome.[7] Indeed, the claim that fear and the fearsome are intimately related is certainly a good candidate for being a conceptual truth. More specifically, as many would agree, the object of fear appears to be represented as fearsome. According to some, this means that fear consists in or at least necessarily involves the evaluative judgement that something is fearsome.[8] However, there is reason to think that the representation in question is not a judgement or more generally a propositional attitude, that is, a state that requires the possession of concepts.[9] For one thing, fear can be experienced by beings that do not seem to possess concepts, such as animals and new-borns.[10] Another reason is that we often experience so-called recalcitrant fears: we can fear something even though we also judge that it is not fearsome.

---

[4] For the concept of occurrent emotion, see Lyons (1980), pp. 53–7. Another useful distinction to be made is between long-lived emotional states, such as Marcel's jealousy for Albertine, to borrow an example from Peter Goldie (2000), and shorter emotional episodes, such as the disgust you experience when seeing a rotten corpse. Both philosophers and psychologists have in general concentrated on such short-lived emotions and I will follow their lead.

[5] See Lutz (1988), ch. 7; Roberts (2003), pp. 197–8.

[6] Thanks to Jingsong Ma for information on this emotion. According her, it is not clear that pa-leng is a morbid fear of the cold, associated with a yin/yan imbalance (but see Prinz 2004, p. 135 and Kleinman 1980).

[7] A nice question is whether the so-called formal object of fear is the fearsome (D'Arms and Jacobson 2003), the threatening (Nussbaum 2001), the dangerous (Prinz 2004), the property of being an aversive possibility (Roberts 2003), or the frightening (de Sousa 1987). Depending on the preferred option, the formal object of fear will be either a relational property of the world or a response-dependent property, something which can nonetheless be perfectly objective (see Wiggins 1976). Though I am not arguing for this here, I think the latter option is the correct one.

[8] See Solomon (1976) and Nussbaum (2001), for instance.

[9] By 'concepts', I mean content elements that have to be postulated in order to account for the inferential relations between thoughts. See Evans (1982); Crane (1992); Tye (2006).

[10] See Morreall (1993); Deigh (1994).

If one assumes that fear involves a judgement about fearsomeness, one would have to attribute contradictory judgements to the person who experiences the emotion. But whatever irrationality is involved in recalcitrance, it seems to be a less acute species than what is involved in contradictory judgements.[11] To account for recalcitrance, one might suggest that the propositional attitude in question is one that fails to involve a commitment to the truth of the proposition. Thus, it has been claimed that fear involves construing things or seeing things as fearsome, something that is perfectly compatible with the conviction that the thing in question is not fearsome.[12] The problem, however, is that construing or seeing something as fearsome would not explain why, when we experience fear, we are nonetheless tempted to avoid what we fear. If I construe or see a cloud as a horse, I am not likely to be tempted to try to ride it.

Does this entail that fear does not involve any evaluative representation? If so, we would have to explain why we are prone to assess our emotions with respect to how they appear to fit evaluative facts. We criticize our fears when they are about things that are not fearsome, for instance. Fortunately, there is an alternative to the claim that emotions involve evaluative propositional attitudes. It consists in the claim that the appraisal involved in fear is a non-propositional representation, or, what is generally taken to be equivalent, a non-conceptual representation.[13] To fear something and hence to represent it as threatening, it is not necessary to judge that it is fearsome. Fear can involve a non-conceptual representation of the thing as fearsome. This idea is often formulated as the claim that emotions are perceptions of values, where it is understood that the perceptions in question are non-conceptual.[14] On this account, emotions involve a representational content in the minimal sense that they have correctness conditions. So, they can be assessed in terms of their fittingness. For example, fear would consist in the perception of its object as fearsome. Such a perception represents its object correctly when this object is really fearsome.

Much more would have to be said to spell out and defend the view that emotions are perceptions of values. Let me simply assume its truth. Now, if it is true that fear is the perception of something as fearsome, it will also be true that fear is the perception of something as having a negative value. This follows from the fact that to be fearsome is to be *pro tanto* bad. Now, as far as our fears are reliable, they will inform us about our practical reasons. For nobody would deny that we have

[11] See Rorty (1978); Greenspan (1988); Deigh (1994); D'Arms and Jacobson (2003).

[12] See Roberts (2003); and also Greenspan (1988) for the claim that emotions involve evaluative thoughts.

[13] See Tappolet (2000, ch. 6) and Tappolet (forthcoming); Tye (2006, pp. 13–14).

[14] Perceptual accounts of emotions are defended by Meinong (1917); de Sousa (1987), (2002); Tappolet (1995), (2000), (forthcoming); Charland (1996); Stocker and Hegeman (1996); Johnston (2001); Prinz (2004), (2008); and Deonna (2006).

*pro tanto* reason to avoid what is fearsome.[15] Thus, fear makes it possible to explain the action it causes in terms of practical reasons. But even if this gives us a better idea of how fear relates to action, this story leaves open the question of the relation between fear and motivation. In particular, it is neutral with respect to both the thesis of motivational modularity and the thesis of motivational egoism.

## 14.2 THE THESIS OF MOTIVATIONAL MODULARITY

When one thinks of the behaviour of the alpine marmot that has seen an eagle circling in the sky, or of that of the hare when a fox chases it, it seems plausible that fear comes with rigid behavioural dispositions, such as the disposition to flee or to freeze. Such dispositions seem to have the following characteristics:

(a) they are innate, in the sense that they are causally facilitated by our genes;[16]
(b) they are triggered by a narrow range of stimuli, such as the perception of a predator;[17]
(c) their manifestation is rapid and automatic, and it does not require the intervention of thought or decision;
(d) they result in a small number of specific behaviours, such as flight or freeze.

A motivational mechanism underlying such reactions can be characterized as modular, for it shares important traits with modular systems as described by Jerry Fodor (1983). Fodor defines modules as information processing systems that are (a) domain-specific, their responses being restricted to a specific class of stimuli, (b) mandatory rather than subject to the will, (c) opaque, in the sense that central cognitive processes have no access to the representations contained in the modules, (d) fast, (e) informationally encapsulated, in the sense that, in the processing of information, the systems' access to beliefs, desires, and utilities is restricted, (f) producing superficial outputs, which are framed in basic categories, (g) having a fixed neural architecture, and (h) corresponding to specific breakdown patterns.[18] Now, on the account under consideration, the motivations related to

---

[15] This is particularly obvious if one assumes with de Sousa (1987) that the proper object of fear supervenes on dangerousness.

[16] As Prinz notes, this does not exclude that dispositions' development depends in part on the social and natural environment. As Mineka et al. (1984) note, the Rhesus monkeys' disposition to fear snakes arises only when they see other monkeys manifesting fear when confronted with snakes (see Prinz 2004, p. 104).

[17] To make room for the fact that most beings can learn to fear new kinds of things, one would need to add that this claim only concerns what we fear without conditioning.

[18] For more details and for other concepts of modularity, see Faucher and Tappolet (2008).

fear manifest domain specificity, the reactions being restricted to the specific range of stimuli that are constituted by the fearsome. They are also characterized by being mandatory, by rapidity, as well as independence from higher cognitive systems, and innateness. So, it would seem that the mechanism that underlies fear reactions, though being an output rather than an input system, is modular.

In one form or another, the thesis of motivational modularity is widespread. First, many have insisted that fear comes with a limited number of motivations. For instance, Nico Frijda, who holds that emotions are in fact what he calls 'action-tendencies', claims that the action-tendency that characterizes fear is avoidance (1986, p. 88). In a similar way, Jon Elster suggests that '[f]ear has two action tendencies: fight or flight' (1999, p. 282).[19] Leda Cosmides and John Tooby have the same general conception, but they add two other types of motivation. They claim that fear, and more specifically the fear of being stalked, involves a range of fixed behaviours:

Behavioral decision rules are activated. Depending on the nature of the potential threat, different courses of action will be potentiated: hiding, flight, self-defense, or even tonic immobility [ ... ]. Some of these responses may be experienced as automatic and involuntary. (2000, p. 94)

The claim that such reactions are modular is explicitly made by Paul Griffiths (1997). Griffiths is interested in the evolutionary benefits of the modularity of emotions in general, but there is no doubt that he would be happy to make the same claim about fear and its related reactions:

[ ... ] the modularity of our emotional responses can be seen as a mechanism for saving us from our own intelligence by rapidly and involuntarily initiating essential behaviors. If central cognitive processes conform more or less closely to rational decision theory and implement plans designed to maximize expected outcomes, there may be evolutionary advantages in retaining more cautious and conservative mechanisms to handle certain vital responses. (1997, p. 95)

One point that speaks in favour of such an account is, given the changes that our environment has undergone since the period in which our emotional capacities became innate, the modularity of such mechanisms would nicely explain why our actual fears often result in inadequate behaviour. A great many of the threats we face in our contemporary world have little to do with the threats encountered by our hunter-gatherer ancestor of the Pleistocene (or of even more distant periods, depending on the evolutionary story one favours), and the behaviours that were adequate to meet those dangers are also quite different. Flight or freeze when confronted with nuclear weapons or global warming, say, is not particularly well adapted.

---

[19] Note, however, that later on Elster claims that emotions felt with respect to fiction lack behavioural tendencies (1999, p. 293).

To have a better understanding of what the account under consideration entails, it will be useful to say a bit more about animal fear.[20] Interestingly, there are many more fear reactions than philosophers usually suppose. In addition to the three 'fs' of flight, fight, and freeze commonly acknowledged, there is tonic immobility, a reaction that by contrast to the other ones involves a slowing down of cardiac activity and respiration, as well as a decrease in bodily temperature, and which results in a paralysis that is close to death, apart from the fact that consciousness is maintained. This kind of reaction, which is manifested once a predator has seized its prey, is quite frequent in the non-human animals. It has been observed in chicken, falcons, geese, ducks, mice, as well as, in a slightly different form, in snakes, fishes, crickets, water beetle, crabs, and spiders. Given that predators are in general only interested in live preys, tonic immobility often allows the prey to escape. Two other kinds of behaviour are common. The first one consists in adopting a protective position, such as the hedgehog that rolls into a ball. The other is simply to hide. To escape from their predators, some small mammals, the tundra voles, even go to the extent of digging their own holes in order to disappear into the ground. Finally, fear behaviour is often associated with expressive movements, sounds and odours—one can think of the skunk and the nauseous scents it produces when threatened.

In addition to this variety of fear behaviours, it is important to understand that there is a certain amount of flexibility even when one considers individuals of the same species. A marmot will freeze and whistle when its sees an eagle circling high up in the sky. When the eagle comes closer, it will run away in flight, try to hide in its terrier, fight back, and finally fall into tonic immobility when its gets caught. As the example shows, a crucial factor here is distance with respect to the fear stimulus. The nature of the stimulus also makes a difference. Experiments with rats show that a violent electric shock results in flight, while shocks of milder intensity trigger freezing. The animal's previous behaviour also makes a difference. The reaction of a chick to the same kind of stimuli (a bright light) differs depending on whether the chick stands still or moves around to pick up corn. In the latter case, the chick most often starts running and shrieking, while in the former case, it usually freezes. Moreover, studies suggest that hormones influence fear behaviour. Chickens that have received a testosterone injection have a stronger tendency to freeze, while those that did not receive the injection tended to run away. Finally, it would seem that gender plays a role. Female rats tend to react with active danger-avoiding behaviour, which involve running and jumping, while male rats more often have the tendency to stop moving and to defecate. In his survey, John Archer summarizes the role of the different factors as follows: 'There is some evidence [ . . . ] that the type of fear responses an animal shows depends on its immediately

---

[20] See Archer (1979) for a fascinating study of fear behaviours in animals.

preceding behaviour, its long-term internal state (e.g. its sex hormones make-up) and on the nature of the particular fear-evoking stimulus (e.g. on properties such as intensity and location)' (1979, p. 83).

Given the variety and the flexibility of danger-related behaviour, one might think that the thesis of motivational modularity is in trouble. However, there are two strategies to counter this worry. The first one consists in the suggestion that there are different kinds of fears, which are each related to fixed behavioural dispositions. The second one stresses the importance of contextual factors. Fear would involve the complex disposition to freeze when the predator is far away, to flee when the predator comes closer, to fight back when the predator is even closer, etc.

A number of authors have suggested that different kinds of fear are related to different kinds of motivation. According to Jaak Panksepp (2000, pp. 147–9), anxiety and panic depend on different neuronal mechanisms. One might thus expect that they also differ with respect to motivation. In a similar way, Richard Lazarus (1991, p. 122) distinguishes between anxiety and fright. Anxiety would correspond to an uncertain existential threat, whereas fright involves the appraisal that one faces an immediate and concrete physical danger. Again, this suggests that the motivation of anxiety and fright differ. According to Jesse Prinz (2004, pp. 152–3), who refers to Jeffrey Gray's work (1987), there are two main kinds of fears: anxiety and panic (or fright). Anxiety would usually come with freeze and would be caused by neutral stimuli, such as the ringing of a bell, and conditioning, by associating it with a painful stimulus. It would correspond to a coming danger instead of an immediate danger. Panic, by contrast, would be caused by a painful stimulus and would correspond to flight or else fight, when flight is not possible. There thus seems to be some agreement that two main kinds of fear have to be distinguished: anxiety and fright (or panic). What happens to our marmot, for example, is that it first experiences anxiety at the sight of the eagle and then fright when the eagle gets closer.[21]

It will be clear that the second strategy is needed even if we distinguish between different kinds of fear. Contextual factors, such as the possibility for flight, but also the kind of threat, etc., determine if fright results in flight or fight. In sum, a convincing version of the thesis of motivational modularity can allow for different kinds of fear associated with different behavioural dispositions. It also has to make room for contextual factors. But the advocate of motivational modularity will insist that even though fear motivation is more complex than it first appeared, the mechanism underlying those motivations are nonetheless modular.

---

[21] See also Robert Roberts (2003), who distinguishes between fear, anxiety, fright, terror or panic, horror, and spook and claims that each of these emotions involves a particular concern and hence comes with slightly different motivations. Fear, for instance, comes with the desire that the object, that is presented as an aversive possibility having a significant degree of probability, does not realize itself (or that its consequences do not come about), whereas fright comes with the desire that its object or its consequences are immediately avoided (2003, pp. 195–9).

Now, it should be clear that the thesis of motivational modularity seems plausible when applied to marmots and their likes. The question is whether it consists in a convincing description of human fear.[22] It is clear that we sometimes manifest the same kind of fear behaviours. It happens that we freeze or run away out of fear. Moreover, tonic immobility is a quite common reaction when we are confronted with acute dangers, such as an attack by a wild animal or the explosion of bombs.[23] But it is not necessary to consult psychological studies to realize that what we do when we experience fear is more varied than what marmots could ever dream of. Panic might make you run out of a building on fire, but it can also get you to call for help on your mobile phone. Your emotion is likely to influence the way you perform these actions. If you panic, you are likely to act in a frenzied and hurried manner. But your panic will not result in specific kinds of behaviour or action. This is why many theorists have claimed that the relation between fear and action is more distant than what the thesis of motivational modularity suggests. Fear would involve desires rather than behavioural dispositions.

## 14.3 THE DESIRE MODEL

According to the psychologist Gerald Clore, emotions facilitate action, but emotions would not involve behavioural tendencies:

[ ... ] it is common to assume that fear involves behavioral tendencies to escape. But [this link is] probably more indirect than is generally assumed. Such words as 'behavior', 'response' and 'action', even when qualified by such words as 'tendencies', 'readiness' or 'inclination' imply that specific muscle groups and motor circuits are activated when one is [ ... ] fearful [ ... ]. Such [a claim] suggests, rather implausibly, that one's legs are programmed to run when afraid [ ... ]. Of course emotions such as fear do involve a redistribution of blood from the viscera to the large muscle, and such effects would presumably enable one to engage in rapid action or extreme exertion. But such general activation is not at all the same thing as a specific action tendency or a motor program. (1994, pp. 110–11)

Clore distinguishes between what he calls 'motivational' and 'behavioural' effects and claims that:

---

[22] I leave aside the question of whether or not this account fits animals that are cognitively more complex, such as big apes.

[23] According to Suarez and Gallup (1979), more than 50% of rape victims manifest tonic immobility. See Marks (1987, pp. 68–9), reported by Cosmides and Tooby (2000, p. 113).

[ ... ] the direct effects of emotions are motivational rather than behavioral. One can achieve more agreement about the likely goals of [ ... ] fearful [ ... ] persons than about their likely behaviors. It seems clear, for example, that fear involves a desire to avoid harm or loss, but not at all clear whether achievement of this goal would necessitate selling one's stocks, listening to the weather report, or running away. Thus, the immediate effects of emotion may be more mental than behavioral. (1994, p. 111)

Jesse Prinz makes a similar suggestion. Prinz distinguishes between what he calls 'motivations', that is, dispositions that move us to action, or action-commands, and what he calls 'motives'. By contrast with motivations, motives give us reasons for action. According to Prinz, '[ ... ] emotions are motives. On can even describe emotions as motivating, because they drive us to select courses of action. In other words, emotions lead to motivations. But they are not to be identified with motivations' (2004, p. 194).[24] Like Clore, Prinz suggests that emotions facilitate action. The physiological changes and the positive or negative valence of emotions prepare us for action and increase the probability that certain type of actions, such as revenge when we are angry, are performed. But just like Clore, Prinz denies that emotions determine specific behaviour or action. What is needed for emotion to result in action is that the agent deliberates and chooses. Thus, fear would give the agent a reason to flee or fight, but even if fear increases the probability of and facilitates such behaviour, fear would not be constituted by a disposition to flee or fight.

Although there are some differences between the accounts proposed by Clore and by Prinz, they suggest a conception according to which fear involves a desire, understood as a state that influences the agent's deliberation by setting a goal. More precisely, what could be called the *desire model* involves the following features:

(a)  given its physiological underpinnings, fear facilitates but does not necessitate certain types of actions;

(b)  fear involves a desire that sets a goal, such as the avoidance of a specific harm or loss, and if it results in action, it does so only on the basis of the agent's deliberation.[25]

Now, this certainly seems to be a quite plausible conception of the motivational impact of human fear. It allows for the huge variety of actions that we perform when we experience fear by finding a place for emotion in rational deliberation. But given its stress on the physiological underpinnings of fear, it also makes room for the a-rational influence of this emotion.

In fact, the physiological component of fear does not only play a facilitating role. Fear can easily have a hampering effect. Fear of heights can be responsible for the shaky hand of the unexperienced alpinist, thereby colouring his actions whether

---

[24]  Cf. Helm (this volume) rejects Prinz' general framework, but nonetheless seems to agree with him on this point when he claims that emotions motivate action as a motive.

[25]  Alternatively, we might say that it is the emotion itself which sets a goal. The emotion would have to be considered to partly be a desire.

these are motivated by fear or not. So, we need to add a clause specifying this other a-rational influence:

(c)  fear colours the action of the agent.

Another point that needs to be added to this picture is that emotions have a further and very powerful way to have an a-rational influence on what we do. As has been pointed out by philosophers, neurologists, and psychologists, emotions influence attention.[26] As Ronald de Sousa, writes, an emotion '[ . . . ] limits the range of information that the organism will take into account, the inferences actually drawn from a potential infinity, and the set of live options among which it will choose' (1987, p. 195). Though there is reason to think that different types of emotions have a different impact on attention—positive emotions are thought to widen and not to narrow our attentional focus[27]—it is certainly plausible to claim that fear narrows the focus of attention. Although this influence is a-rational, it would be a mistake to infer that it necessarily leads to irrationality. Quite to the contrary, it often makes it possible for the agent to focus on what is important. As de Sousa underlines, emotions thus allow us to supply to the insufficiency of reason, which is unable to determine what we ought to attend to. According to de Sousa, emotions' role is to make up for the shortcomings of reason. Emotions would be '[ . . . ] one of Nature's ways of dealing with the philosopher's frame problem' (1987, p. 195). Thanks to fear, we are able to avoid the sad destiny of the robot that kept analysing infinitely many irrelevant data instead of running away from a ticking bomb.[28] In any case, we need to add a further clause to our list:

(d)  fear influences what we do by narrowing the agent's attentional focus.

A further point that has to be taken into account is that even though what we do when we experience fear often depends on our means–end beliefs, it also happens that we manifest instinctive behaviour. As I have noted, it happens that we instinctively freeze or else fall into tonic immobility. It would be clearly abusive to suggest that these reactions are the result of some quick deliberation. Of course, we would be hard pressed to explain why some frightened people freeze, say, while others do not, but what is clear is that both possibilities exist. It would seem that we all have a tendency to manifest such reactions, but some of us are better at controlling ourselves. In any case, it seems justified to add the following clause to our list:

(e)  even human fear can result in reactions that depend on modular behavioural dispositions.

Now, what should we think of the desire model? The question that has to be asked to assess this model is whether or not fear necessarily involves a desire that sets a

---

[26]  See de Sousa (1987); Damasio (1994); Wells and Matthew (1994); for a survey, see Faucher and Tappolet (2002).

[27]  See Frederickson (1998).

[28]  See de Sousa (1987, p. 195).

goal. According to Sabine Döring, there are cases of fear in which no goal is set: '[o]ne's fear may represent it as being dangerous to be so high up above the ground while one is travelling by plane and better off doing nothing at all' (2003, p. 227). But would it not be more plausible to say that, if you experience fear on this occasion, your fear involves the desire not to be there, high up above the ground? This desire gives you a goal, even though there is not much you can reasonably do about it—you certainly do not prefer to jump out the emergency door to quickly get down. Also, the goal in question might be overruled by some other goal of yours, such as the goal of crossing the ocean to get back home. But are not some fears completely cut off from possible actions? What has to be acknowledged is that fear does not necessarily come with any concrete goal which could lead to action. You might be afraid that the financial crisis will end in a meltdown, but have no directly related goal, for there is strictly nothing you can do to change the course of the events. Insofar as you desire, or rather as you wish that the financial crisis will not end in a meltdown, and thus that you wish to avoid the loss the meltdown would cause, however, there is something that is the object of a conative state of yours. And this justifies the ascription of what could be described as a kind of ideal goal. So, the desire model has to be broadened to include conative states such as wishes.[29]

More difficult questions arise from so-called expressive actions. As Rosalind Hursthouse (1991) has pointed out, emotions sometimes get us to do things that are hard to reconcile with the idea of aiming at a goal. Consider Hursthouse's example of Jane, whose hatred for Joan gets her to tear at Joan's photograph with her nails and to gouge holes in the eyes of the picture. Let us suppose that this action is intentional. The question, then, is what desire and belief could explain it. According to Hursthouse, no such desire-belief explanation can be given: though intentional, such actions are a-rational.[30] Now, it certainly seems that Jane wants to tear out the eyes in Joan's photograph.[31] The problem is that this suggestion does not account for the quite obvious relation between the action and the emotion. Why exactly would Jane want to scratch the eyes out, given that, as we can safely assume, she does not believe that this will harm Joan in any way? The desire in question does not seem to rationally depend on the kind of desire that seems involved in hatred, such as a desire to harm and destroy the person whom one hates. It thus seems that what we have here is the case of an intentional action, which is motivated by an emotion, but which is not rationally conducive to any goal set by the emotion. Do we have to reject the desire model, then?

The question is how exactly is Jane's action related to the emotion. It might be claimed that the emotion only has a causal role in the production of the action. The desire to scratch the eyes out would be caused by the hatred. This seems true, but it certainly appears that the emotion yields more than a causal explanation of the

---

[29] Thanks to Peter Goldie for suggesting that wishes might be involved.
[30] Döring concurs (2003).
[31] For such a suggestion, see Smith (1998); Goldie (2000).

action. Why is it that Jane scratches the eyes out instead of putting the picture into her pocket or boiling an egg while singing a song? Quite obviously, it is because she hates Joan. A more plausible suggestion is that some innate behavioural disposition is at work. Of course, scratching out the eyes in photographs cannot in itself be the manifestation of some innate behavioural disposition—our Pleistocene ancestors did not have cameras. But it might well be that the disposition to harm the object of one's hatred manifests itself in a variety of more or less efficient ways.[32] Given the visual similarity between the photograph and the person, harming the image comes quite close to harming the real person. That this is so is confirmed by the fact that looking at the photograph of someone you hate (or you love) often triggers a vivid experience of hate (or love).

The suggestion, then, is that so-called expressive actions are explained by the misfiring of behavioural dispositions. What does this entail for fear? There are many ways fear can result in so-called expressive actions. Döring gives the example of someone clinging tightly to her bag when she experiences fear of flying. This can plausibly be explained as the misfiring of the disposition to try and grasp something to hold onto when one is afraid of falling down. So, expressive actions can be accounted for by the clause about behavioural dispositions.

A more serious objection to the desire model comes from the fact that there is reason to believe that even an emotion like fear comes without any desires. In one of the most famous passages of contemporary philosophy, Kendall Walton describes the miseries of Charles:

Charles is watching a horror movie about a terrible green slime. He cringes in his seat as the slime oozes slowly but relentlessly over the earth, destroying everything in its path. [ ... ] The slime, picking up speed, oozes on a new course straight towards the viewers. Charles emits a shriek and clutches desperately at this chair. (1978, p. 5)

As Walton underlines, Charles seems terrorized. Yet, he appears to have no motivation resulting from this intense fear; he has no inclination to leave the theatre or to call the police, for instance. Walton concludes that Charles does not really believe that there is danger. This is certainly true. However, Walton is wrong to infer that Charles is not really afraid of the slime. As we have seen earlier, there are independent reasons to think that fear does not require any propositional attitude of that kind. It thus seems that what we have here is a case of purely contemplative fear, which has no motivational force whatsoever. Of course, it is not accurate to say that Charles does nothing at all: he cringes in his seat, shrieks, and clutches at his chair. But these reactions are just the more or less apt manifestations of behavioural dispositions. We do not need to postulate any desire to explain them. So, can fear be purely contemplative, in the sense that it does not involve a desire?

---

[32] As Döring (2003) notes, it is possible that the selection of the action—scratching the eyes out instead of trampling on the picture, say—might also be influenced by cultural norms.

Now, it might be suggested that had Charles really experienced fear, he would have run out of the theatre. The absence of motivation would show that Charles does not experience real fear. This seems difficult to believe, given that we can easily imagine that all the other elements of fear are in place: the physiological reaction, the subjective experience, the behavioural dispositions, etc. More plausibly, one could claim that Charles in fact has the fear-related desire, but this desire fails to manifest itself in action. Why would this be so?

One possibility is that Charles has another desire, such as the desire to watch the end of the film, which proves stronger. Charles' case would be akin to that of the bungee-jumper whose fear-related desire not to jump proves weaker than the desire to jump. The problem is that the suggestion that there is a conflict of desire, which could possible require some deliberation, does not seem to fit Charles' case. Charles seems far from torn between a desire to watch the film and a desire to run away. Also, one wonders how it could be that Charles' desire to watch the film could be stronger than the desire to avoid a horrible death.

Another possibility is that Charles' beliefs interfere with his fear-related desire. If Charles did not have the conviction that the green slime is just a fiction, and hence that there is no real danger, he certainly would have tried to escape. But the belief that he is watching a film prevents the manifestation of the fear-related desire. The problem is that it seems just as plausible to claim that Charles fails to have the fear-related desire, given his beliefs. We are asked to suppose that the belief that there is no danger interferes with the manifestation of the fear-related desire, but we can just as well suppose that the belief in question interferes with the desire itself. Thus, given the belief that he is watching a film, it would not be true of Charles that he has escaping from the slime as a goal. This seems to make more sense than to attribute to Charles the belief there is no slime *plus* the desire, and thus the goal, to escape from the slime.

If this is on the right track, we have to allow for cases of *contemplative fears*: full fears that do not involve any desire. So, proposition (b) has to be amended in the following way:

(b¹)  in the absence of a belief that the object of one's fear is a fiction, fear involves a desire, or more generally a conative state, that sets a specific or ideal goal, and if it results in action, it does so only on the basis of the agent's deliberation.[33]

But in what sense exactly is the desire involved: is the desire an essential ingredient of normal, non-contemplative fear or is it a causal and contingent effect of the emotion, which happens to be always present?[34] Given the cases of contemplative fears, what is clear is that desires are not essential ingredients of the emotion of fear as such. This suggests that, even in normal cases, the desire involved is only

---

[33] As Ronnie de Sousa pointed out to me, this could be too narrow: other circumstances might have the same effect as the belief that what one fears does not exist.

[34] Thanks to Peter Goldie for raising this question.

contingently related to the emotion of fear. Let me now turn to the question of whether or not the motivations of fear are necessarily self-interested.

## 14.4 THE THESIS OF MOTIVATIONAL EGOISM

When the frightened hare runs away from its predator, or when the hedgehog rolls into a ball, it is in order to try to save its life. When you are frightened by the wolf that leaps at you, your desire is to avoid what threatens you. Thus, the motivations involved in fear seem to aim at the well-being of the one who experiences the emotion.

What I called the thesis of motivational egoism is not often explicitly mentioned, but it is very generally assumed. Here are nonetheless a few explicit statements of this thesis. According to Nico Frijda '[f]ear, presumably, motivates actions to protect *oneself* from the event that caused it, or to prevent the event from actually materializing, or to suppress activity until the threat has passed (as in anxious freezing)' (1994, p. 114). And here is what Jesse Prinz writes: 'An appraisal is a representation of the relation between an organism and its environment that bears on well-being. I might appraise that the environment presents a physical danger *to me*' (2004, p. 51, my italics). It is of course tempting to relate this thesis to the idea that emotions, or at least some kinds of emotions such as basic emotions, are adaptations. Paul Griffiths, who argues that basic emotions are 'affect programs' in the sense that such emotions consists in a number of correlated reactions, claims that '[a]ffect programs are adaptive response to events that have a particular ecological significance for the organism. The fear response is adapted to dangers [ . . . ]' (1997, p. 89). Clearly, Griffiths assumes here that these dangers are dangers for the person who experiences the fear.

However, it is quite obvious that two kinds of fears have to be distinguished: fear for oneself and fear for others.[35] As John Morreall claims, a mother who sees her child disappear under a huge wave is likely to experience fear for her child. The fears we feel with respect to fiction are in fact often of that kind. We fear that Spiderman misses his jump and miserably gets squashed on the ground or that Anna Karenina attempts to kill herself. Moreover it would be wrong to believe that fear for others can only be found in human beings. It seems quite clear that animals fear for their offspring as well.

---

[35] See Morreall (1993) as well as Davis (1987); Nussbaum (2001, p. 28); Roberts (2003), pp. 197 and 201. As Ronnie de Sousa pointed out to me, one can ask whether these are really two variants of the same emotion instead of two different kinds of emotions. Given that fear for oneself and fear for others differ only with respect to their motivation, I think we have good reasons to believe that these are two variants of the same emotion kind.

It is worth noting that both human and non-human responses to what threatens offspring can be just as immediate as responses to threats to oneself. Here is how Hume describes the immediacy of such reactions, which he considers to be central to humanity and benevolence:

The social virtues of humanity and benevolence exert their influence immediately, by a direct tendency or instinct, which chiefly keeps in view the simple object, moving the affections, and comprehends not any scheme or system, nor the consequences resulting from the concurrence, imitation, or example of others. A parent flies to the relief of his child; transported by that natural sympathy, which actuates him, and which affords no leisure to reflect on the sentiments or conduct of the rest of mankind in like circumstances. (*Enquiry*, Appendix, III, Paragraph 2, p. 303)[36]

As Hume notes, fear for others motivates us to help those for whom we feel fear. In fact, fear for others might be stronger than the fear we feel for ourselves. Here is how Morreall puts it: 'To the extent that I feel fear for others, I want to prevent them from being harmed; in heroic cases I may fear for them more than for myself, and give up my own life to save theirs' (1993, p. 364). It thus seems that we have to reject the thesis of motivational egoism: someone who is motivated by fear for someone else acts not for his or her own good, but for the good of this other person; his or her motivation seems altruistic.

The advocate of the thesis of motivational egoism is likely to remain unconvinced. Is it so clear that the motivation to help others is altruistic? Is the final end of such a desire not to promote one's own interest? Psychological egoists are likely to insist that it is always to help oneself that one tries to help others. I am not convinced, but let me leave this question open and consider instead two less theory-laden arguments.

The first argument starts with the claim that fear is an adaptation. According to Cosmides and Tooby (2000, p. 92), for instance, the function of fear is to coordinate a number of reactions that help to deal with danger. Fear thus increases the chances that the organism survives, thereby increasing the probability that it has lots of offspring, spreading its genes. One might therefore be tempted to conclude that the motivation of fear must be egoistic. But this clearly would be a *non sequitur*. Natural selection does not have the same 'aim' as the organism. What promotes the spreading of your genes has little to do with what is in your interest. It could well be the case that having motivations that threaten your self-interest nonetheless promote the survival and spreading of your genes. For instance, it is certainly quite an advantage from the point of view of genes that you are inclined to sacrifice yourself for your offspring.

More convincingly, it could be argued that it is only insofar as you consider the well-being of someone else as being your own, i.e. that you identify with this other person to the extent of not making any difference anymore between your well-

---

[36] Thanks to Peter Goldie for this quote.

being and his or hers, that you will experience fear for that person. Thus, in helping this other person, you nonetheless promote your own interest. After all, the mother who fears for her child would certainly be devastated if her child drowned. According to Martha Nussbaum, who explicitly defends this view, all emotions are oriented towards our own flourishing.[37] She allows for fear for those whom we love, but she claims that the well-being of those for whom we experience fear is intimately related to our own well-being:

I do not go about fearing any and every catastrophe anywhere in the world, nor (so it seems) do I fear any and every catastrophe that I know to be bad in important ways. What inspires fear is the thought of damage impending that cut to the heart of my own cherished relationships and projects. (2001, pp. 30–1)

It is the thought of damage to *your* relationships and projects that is crucial in the fear you feel for others. Thus, it would be hard to deny that the motivation that comes with this emotion is fundamentally oriented towards you own well-being.

It is certainly true that in most cases it is for our closest and dearest that we feel fear. And it is when we become familiar with and start to care for some fictional character that our emotions are engaged. However, it would be a mistake to deny that we can experience fear for perfect strangers. Imagine that you see some stranger from quite a distance and from the back. When he crosses the street, a truck speeds around a curve and towards him, threatening to kill him. Quite certainly, you are likely to experience fear for that person even though he is a stranger, someone you have never met and are not likely to ever meet. It is of course true that your emotion shows that you in a sense care for the fate of this person. Your reaction is a way of caring for that person. But of course, the fact that you have this reaction does not mean that you quickly adopt the stranger as one of your closest and dearest or that you consider your own well-being to depend on his well-being. Thus, whatever motivation you have because of your fear seems to be purely altruistic.

Without assuming the falsehood of psychological egoism, what is likely to be uncontroversial is that the motivations involved in fear for others are exactly as other-regarding as the motivations that depend on compassion. Apart from the temporal factor, the conditions in which we experience fear for others are of the same kind as the ones in which we experience compassion for that person. You experience fear for someone when he or she is threatened by something and compassion when that threat has materialized and he or she is harmed. Consider the following statement: 'Speaking generally, anything causes us to feel fear that when it happens to, or threatens, others causes us to feel pity' (Aristotle, *Rhet.*, Book II, ch. V, 1382b). Aristotle was clearly right with respect to fear for oneself. But

---

[37] She writes: '[ . . . ] emotions appear to be *eudaimonistic*, that is, concerned with the person's flourishing' (2001, p. 30). Nussbaum denies, however, that this entails that all emotions are egoistic, for we can include the well-being of someone else into our ends (2001, pp. 53 and 31, note 23).

if one takes into account fear for others, what one would have to say is that what inspires fear for oneself are the events that inspire fear for others when they threaten others, and pity or compassion when others have been harmed. Thus, if you accept that pity or compassion come with altruistic motivations, you must also accept that fear for others involves altruistic motivations.

## 14.5  CONCLUSION

Fear does not fit well with the contemporary enthusiasm for emotions. In spite of this, I hope to have shown that fear is better placed than one might have initially thought. Fear need not come with ill-adapted and rigid behavioural dispositions or with egoistic motivations. Both the thesis of motivational modularity and the thesis of motivational egoism are wrong at least in the case of human fear. As I have tried to spell out, the relation of fear to action and motivation is complex. Insofar as emotions are perceptions of values, they can inform us about our practical reasons, such as the fearsome. Moreover, in addition to a number of important a-rational influences on motivation, an emotion like fear normally involves a desire that sets a goal. But as cases of fear for others show, this goal need not be related to the promotion of one's own well-being and flourishing.

## REFERENCES

ARCHER, J. (1979), Behavioural Aspects of Fear. In W. Sluckin ed., *Fear in Animals and Man* (New York: Van Nostrand Reinhold Company), 56–85.

ARISTOTLE (1924/2007), *Rhetorics*. Trans. by W. Rhys Roberts, originally published Oxford: Clarendon Press (University of Adelaide, South Australia: e-book@Adelaide, <http://www2.iastate.edu/"honeyl/Rhetoric/index.html>).

CHARLAND, L. (1996), Feeling and Representing: Computational Theory and the Modularity of Affect. *Synthese*, 105, 273–301.

CLORE, G. (1994), Why Emotions are Felt. In P. Ekman and R. Davidson eds., *The Nature of Emotion* (New York: Oxford University Press), 103–11.

COSMIDES, L. and TOOBY, J. (2000), Evolutionary Psychology and Emotions. In M. Lewis and J. Haviland-Jones eds., *Handbook of Emotions*, 2nd edn. (New York: The Guilford Press), 91–115.

CRANE, T. (1992), The Nonconceptual Content of Experience. In T. Crane ed., *The Contents of Experience*, Cambridge: Cambridge University Press.

DAMASIO, A. (1994), *Descartes' Error: Emotion, Reason and the Human Brain* (New York: Gossett/Putnam).

D'ARMS, J. and JACOBSON, D. (2003), The Significance of Recalcitrant Emotions; Or Anti-Quasi Judgmentalism. *Philosophy*. Suppl. vol. *Proceedings of the Royal Institute of Philosophy*, 127–46.

DAVIS, W. A. (1987), The Varieties of Fear. *Philosophical Studies*, 51, 287–310.

DE SOUSA, R. (1987), *The Rationality of Emotion* (Cambridge, MA: MIT Press).

DEIGH, J., (1994), Cognitivism in the Theory of Emotions. *Ethics*, 104, 824–54.

DEONNA, J. (2006), Emotion, Perception and Perspective. *Dialectica*, 60 (1), 29–46.

DÖRING, S. A., (2003), Explaining Action by Emotion. *The Philosophical Quarterly*, 53 (211), 214–30.

ELSTER, J. (1999), *Alchemies of the Mind: Rationality and the Emotions* (Cambridge: Cambridge University Press).

EVANS, G. (1982), *The Varieties of References* (Oxford: Clarendon).

FAUCHER, L. and C. TAPPOLET (2002), Fear and the Focus of Attention. *Consciousness and Emotion*, 3 (2), 105–44.

——(2008), Introduction: Modularity and the Nature of Emotions. In L. Faucher and C. Tappolet eds., *The Modularity of Emotions, The Canadian Journal of Philosophy*. Suppl. vol. 32, vii–xxxi.

FODOR, J. (1983), *The Modularity of Mind* (Cambridge, MA: MIT Press).

FRIJDA, N. H. (1986), *The Emotions* (Cambridge: Cambridge University Press).

——(1994), Emotions Are Functional, Most of the Time. In P. Ekman and R. J. Davidson eds., *The Nature of Emotion: Fundamental Questions* (New York: Oxford University Press), 112–22.

FREDRICKSON, B. L. (1998), What Good Are Positive Emotions? *Review of General Psychology*, 2 (3), 300–19.

GOLDIE, P. (2000), *The Emotions: A Philosophical Exploration* (Oxford: Oxford University Press).

GRAY, J. A. (1987), *The Psychology of Fear and Stress* (New York: McGraw-Hill).

GREENSPAN, P. S. (1988), *Emotions and Reasons* (New York: Routledge and Kegan Paul).

GRIFFITHS, P. (1997), *What Emotions Really Are* (Chicago: University of Chicago Press).

HUME, D. (1777/1975), *Enquiry Concerning Human Understanding and Concerning the Principles of Morals*. Ed. L. A. Selby-Bigge (Oxford: Oxford University Press).

HURSTHOUSE, R. (1991), Arational Actions. *Journal of Philosophy*, 88, 57–68.

JOHNSTON, M. (2001), The Authority of Affect, *Philosophy and Phenomenological Research*, 53, 181–214.

JONES, K. (2008), Quick and Smart? Modularity and the Pro-Emotion Consensus. In L. Faucher and C. Tappolet eds., *The Modularity of Emotions, The Canadian Journal of Philosophy*. Suppl. vol. 32, 3–27.

KLEINMAN, A. (1980), *Patients and Healers in the Context of Culture* (Berkeley: University of California Press).

LAZARUS, R. S. (1991), *Emotion and Adaptation* (New York: Oxford University Press).

LUTZ, C. A. (1988), *Unnatural Emotions: Everyday Sentiments on a Micronesian Atoll and Their Challenge to Western Theory* (Chicago: University of Chicago Press).

LYONS, W. (1980), *Emotion* (Cambridge: Cambridge University Press).

MARKS, I. (1987), *Fears, Phobias, and Rituals* (New York: Oxford University Press).

MEINONG, A. (1917), Ueber Emotionale Präsentation, *Kaiserliche Akademie der Wissenschaft in Wien*, 183, 2nd part, 1–181.

MINEKA, S., M. DAVIDSON, M. COOK, and R. KEIR (1984) Observational Conditioning of Snake Fear in Rhesus Monkeys, *Journal of Abnormal Psychology*, 93, 355–72.

MORREALL, J. (1993), Fear without Belief. *The Journal of Philosophy*, 90, 359–66.

NUSSBAUM, M. C. (2001), *Upheavals of Thought: The Intelligence of Emotions* (Cambridge: Cambridge University Press).

PANKSEPP, J. (2000), Emotions as Natural Kind within the Mammalian Brain. In M. Lewis and J. Haviland-Jones eds., *Handbook of Emotions*, 2nd edn. (New York: Guilford Press), 137–56.

PRINZ, J. J. (2004), *Gut Reactions: A Perceptual Theory of Emotion* (New York: Oxford University Press.)

—— (2008) Is Emotion a Form of Perception? In L. Faucher and C. Tappolet eds., *The Modularity of Emotions, The Canadian Journal of Philosophy*. Suppl. vol. 32, 137–60.

ROBERTS, R. C. (2003), *Emotions: An Essay in Aid of Moral Psychology* (Cambridge: Cambridge University Press).

RORTY, A. O. (1978), Explaining Emotions. Reprinted in A. O. Rorty ed., *Explaining Emotions* (Berkeley: University of California Press).

SHOEMAKER, D. W. (2003), Caring, Identification, and Agency. *Ethics*, 114, 88–118.

SMITH, M. (1998), The Possibility of Action. In J. Bransen ed., *Human Action, Deliberation and Causation* (Dordrecht: Kluwer).

SOLOMON, R. (1976), *The Passions* (Indianapolis: Hackett Publishing Company).

STOCKER, M. and E. HEGEMAN (1996), *Valuing Emotions* (Cambridge: Cambridge University Press).

SUAREZ, S. D. and G. G. GALLUP (1979), Tonic Immobility as a Response to Rage in Humans: A Theoretical Note. *Psychological Record*, 29, 315–20.

TAPPOLET, C. (1995), Les Émotions et les concepts axiologiques. In P. Paperman et R. Ogien eds., *La Couleur des pensées, Raisons Pratiques*, 4, 237–57.

——(2000), *Émotions et valeurs* (Paris: Presses Universitaires de France).

——(forthcoming), Emotion, Perception, and Perceptual Illusions, in C. Calabi and K. Mulligan eds., *The Crooked Oar, The Moon's Size and The Necker Cube. Essays on the Illusions of Outer and Inner Perception*, Cambridge, MA: MIT Press.

TYE, M. (2006), The Thesis of Nonconceptual Content. In C. Van Geen and F. de Vignemont eds., *The Structure of Nonconceptual Content, European Review of Philosophy*, vol. 6, 7–30.

WALTON, K. (1978), Fearing Fiction, *The Journal of Philosophy*, 75, 5–27.

WELLS, A. and G. MATTHEWS (1994), *Attention and Emotion: A Clinical Perspective* (Hove and Hillsdale: Lawrence Erlbaum Associates).

WIGGINS, D. (1976), Truth, Invention and the Meaning of Life. In D. Wiggins ed., *Needs, Values, Truth* (Oxford: Blackwell).

# PART IV

EMOTIONS AND
THE SELF

..............................................................................

# CHAPTER 15

# THE PHENOMENOLOGY OF MOOD AND THE MEANING OF LIFE

..............................................................................

## MATTHEW RATCLIFFE

## 15.1 INTRODUCTION
..............................................................................

In his book *The Passions*, Robert Solomon proposed that emotions are the 'meaning of life'. By this, he meant that they constitute the meanings *in* a life, frameworks of value and significance that are incorporated into the experienced world. I think there is something importantly right about his claim, and my aim in this chapter is to defend a somewhat revised version of it. I begin by outlining Solomon's conception of emotion, focusing on the phenomenological role assigned to emotion, the distinction drawn between emotions and feelings, and the claim that moods are generalized emotions (intentional states that have the whole world or a substantial chunk of it as their object). I go on to argue that Solomon, like many others who have written on the emotions, fails to appreciate the phenomenology of mood. It is a background of feeling more often referred to as a 'mood' than an 'emotion' that plays the meaning-

I am grateful to Peter Goldie and to an audience at Durham University for helpful comments on an earlier version of this chapter.

giving role emphasized by Solomon. Not all moods are generalized emotions. Some may indeed take this form but those that are responsible for the 'meaning of life' are not intentional states at all. Instead, they are part of the background structure of intentionality and are presupposed by the possibility of intentionally directed emotions. To illustrate this, I turn to Martin Heidegger's phenomenological analysis of boredom and then to descriptions of altered mood in depression. In so doing, I draw a distinction between the intensity or strength of an emotional state and its depth. An emotion can be quite intense but at the same time shallow, whereas a phenomenologically inconspicuous mood can be deep precisely by virtue of its inconspicuousness. This greater depth of a mood, I suggest, consists in its being responsible for a space of possibilities that object-directed emotions, however intense, presuppose. For example, to be able to experience fear, one must already find oneself in the world in such a way that being 'endangered' or 'under threat' are possibilities.

Having described the phenomenological *role* of deep moods, I go on to consider their *nature*. I argue that we experience the world through our feeling bodies, and that distinctions between internally directed bodily feelings and externally directed intentional states should be rejected. I distinguish between intentional and pre-intentional feelings, suggesting that most of those phenomena referred to as 'emotions' are comprised at least partly of the former, whereas those moods that constitute the experienced meaningfulness of the world consist entirely of pre-intentional feeling.

# 15.2 SOLOMON ON EMOTION AND THE MEANING OF LIFE

In his earlier writings, Solomon insists on a clear distinction between emotions and feelings. Emotions, he says, are judgements rather than feelings. Although feelings often or perhaps even always accompany emotions, the relationship is one of association rather than constitution. Feelings are *mere* bodily reactions, whereas emotions are conceptually sophisticated intentional states that have objects outside of the body. By claiming that emotions are judgements, Solomon does not mean to suggest that they are attitudes that we adopt on the basis of our experiences of the world. Instead, he says that emotional judgements are *constitutive* of world-experience. The world is experienced as a practically significant realm of norms, values, and enticements to act. Things appear to us as inviting, valuable, fascinating, threatening, dull, repulsive, proper, improper, comforting, terrifying, and so on. Emotions are responsible for our sense that things *matter* in these various different ways: 'The passions are judgments, *constitutive* judgments according to which our reality is given its shape and structure' (1993, p. xvii). Solomon also claims that emotions, although constitutive of the experienced world rather than explicitly and knowingly adopted by us, are in a sense chosen. As with beliefs, emotional judgements are often unreflective but we are still responsible for evaluating and revising them.

According to Solomon, emotions are the 'meaning of life', in the sense that they are a precondition for the intelligibility of all our goal-directed activities. If no actual or possible states of affairs were ever judged by us to be preferable to any other, we would have no grounds for action. Without emotions, we could have no projects, nothing to strive for, no sense of anything as worth doing:

I suggest that emotions are the meaning of life. It is because we are moved, because we feel, that life has a meaning. The passionate life, not the dispassionate life of pure reason, is the meaningful life. (1993, p. ix)

So emotions do not give life a meaning relative to some standpoint external to experience but are experienced as the significance of things *in* the world; they are the 'meanings *in life*' (1993, p. 7). As Solomon puts it, we do not experience a neutral, objective reality but live in a 'surreality' of purpose, value and significance (1993, p. 18). However, he is not very clear on what the relationship is between objective conceptions of reality and our everyday surreality. One possibility is that science succeeds in transcending the everyday world and replacing it with a description of things that is freed of emotional projections. Alternatively, it might be that the scientifically described world continues to obliviously presuppose the context of significance that we take for granted in everyday life. In the next section, I will suggest that the latter view is more plausible.

In his later writings, Solomon retreats from some of the more extreme claims made in *The Passions* and elsewhere. The emphasis on choice is toned down and he also acknowledges that the body makes an indispensable contribution to emotional experience. A problem with the early view is that it is not clear how an emotional judgement is to be distinguished from a non-emotional value judgement with the same content, without appealing to the fact that the former is *felt* while the latter is not. Solomon tries to deal with the problem by insisting that emotions are 'self-involved and relatively intense evaluative judgments' (1993, p. 127). But this seems to beg the question, as it is not clear what, aside from feeling, could make a value judgement intense. For this and other reasons, Solomon later concedes that our bodily phenomenology makes an important contribution to emotional experience. However, rather than accepting that emotions incorporate feelings, he widens the concept of judgement so as to accommodate at least some of what others might call feelings. He does this by drawing an analogy between emotional and kinaesthetic judgements (2003, 2004*a*, 2004*b*). When you walk up the stairs, you 'judge' the distance between the steps but this judgement is not separate from your activity. Such judgements are incorporated into activity; they are '*judgments of the body*', habitual and often skilful bodily responses to situations (2003, p. 191). Similarly, Solomon suggests, the bodily 'feelings' that others take to be partly or wholly constitutive of emotions can be reconceived as bodily judgements. As with experiencing the stairs while climbing them, these judgements are not feelings of bodily states but ways of experiencing things external to our bodies. The stairs appear as 'steep but climbable'; the bodily judgement is partly constitutive of how they are perceived.

Despite these concessions, Solomon continues to emphasize the *existential* role of emotion, by which I mean its role in constituting an experiential sense of belonging to a world, of *being there*, purposively immersed in a realm where things matter. In so doing, I think he recognizes an important aspect of experience that tends to be overlooked by philosophers and others. However, I will suggest that his account needs to be clarified and significantly revised in order to make it plausible. Most pressing is the need for a clear distinction between those emotions that constitute the sense of being part of a meaningful world and other emotions that presuppose it. If I am happy about a specific event, I experience myself as being happy within a pre-given world. My happiness does not constitute the entire framework of practical significance that I inhabit at the time of the event. Although Solomon frequently uses the term 'emotion' to refer to occurrent judgements such as being happy or angry about something, when he claims that emotions are the meaning of life he does also stress that they are not isolated, specifically focused episodes:[1]

> My emotion is a structure of my world, which may at times manifest itself in certain specific displays of feeling or behaviour. But my emotion *is* neither such displays nor the disposition to such displays. (1993, p. 100)

An emotion is thus an enduring aspect of world-experience. Between episodes of occurrent emotion, it remains in place as a system of meanings that we experience as integral to the world. Hence emotions '*set up*' the world that we live in; they '*constitute* the framework within which our knowledge of the facts has some meaning, some "relevance" to us' (1993, p. 135).

One might object that an emotion such as anger, even if it cannot be reduced to an occurrence or a disposition, surely does not 'set up' a world. Solomon addresses this concern by maintaining that emotions are holistically linked. Every emotion 'presupposes the entire body of previous emotional judgments to supply its context and its history' (1993, p. 137). Although no single emotion is responsible for the sense that one is part of a significant world, they do so when taken together.

However, it is not clear how a number of interrelated emotions, all of which individually presuppose experience of a meaningful world, combine so as to constitute that experience. No doubt it is possible to concoct an account along such lines but I think this is the wrong way to go. What is needed instead is a distinction between those emotional states that constitute (or at least partly

---

[1] Consider, for example, Solomon's example of mistakenly thinking someone has stolen one's car. The example is employed to illustrate that emotions are separable from feelings. When one realizes that the person did not steal one's car, one is no longer angry with him or her, even though the associated feelings remain. In this case, it is clear that the anger in question is an occurrent judgement directed at a particular person (1976, p. 123).

constitute) the sense of belonging to a meaningful world and those that we experience as occurring within the world. In everyday English language, the contrast between 'mood' and 'emotion' perhaps best approximates this distinction. It is certain moods, I want to suggest, that constitute the meaning of life.

Solomon claims that moods are just 'generalized emotions' (1993, p. 15), with the level of generality varying from case to case. Emotion is therefore the primary phenomenon and moods are a subset of emotions:

> To understand the nature of moods, one has to first understand the nature of emotions. Moods, in their indiscriminate universality, are metaphysical generalizations of the emotions. (1993, p. 71)

In taking emotions to be intentional states with specific objects and moods to be intentional states with generalized objects, Solomon loses sight of the aspect of experience that he refers to as the meaningfulness of life. A sense of participating in a realm where some things matter is not an intentional state, a collection of intentional states or a generalized intentional state but a pre-intentional background to intentional states. I say 'pre-intentional' rather than non-intentional because it is not wholly distinct from intentional states. Rather, it contributes to the structure of intentionally directed emotion, determining the range of emotions that one is capable of experiencing. For example, in the extreme case of a mood where the world appears utterly bereft of practical significance, *worrying* about whether a project will succeed and *hoping* that it will succeed would not be possible. Such emotions would be unintelligible without a presupposed set of mood-constituted concerns.

A failure to fully appreciate the phenomenology of mood is not specific to Solomon. Many discussions of emotion take moods either to be generalized emotions or to be states that add 'colour' to experience, analogous to the icing on a cake. For example, Goldie (2000, p. 141) states that the difference between moods and emotions is primarily down to the 'degree of specificity of their objects', and Roberts (2003, p. 115) similarly endorses the view that moods are generalized emotions, adding that mood is analogous to a colour or tone: 'depression and elation color the objects of our experience in hues of value'. This may well apply to some moods but what is needed, I will now suggest, is an account that also recognizes the greater phenomenological 'depth' of other moods.

## 15.3 THE PHENOMENOLOGY OF MOOD

Solomon acknowledges Heidegger as a source of inspiration for his account of emotion and world-meaning (e.g. Solomon, 1993, p. 50), and it is to Heidegger that I turn in order to draw a distinction between moods and emotions. For Heidegger

(1962, 1995), moods are phenomenologically deeper than emotions, by which I mean that emotions are only intelligible in the context of a mood. Heidegger does not actually draw a distinction between moods and emotions. However his discussion can, I think, be fruitfully couched in these terms, as he does want to distinguish intentional states (amongst which I include the majority of what we call 'emotions') from pre-intentional moods.[2] Those emotional states that we refer to ourselves as being *in* generally go deeper than those that we *have* (Cataldi, 1993). When we *have* an emotion, we are already *in* a situation. And, as Heidegger appreciates, this sense of being there depends upon mood.

Of course, the everyday terms 'mood' and 'emotion' do not map neatly onto two distinct phenomenological categories. Not all moods are pre-intentional and, as I will make clear in the next section, not all pre-intentional backgrounds are moods either. Nevertheless, 'mood' is more often employed than 'emotion' to communicate those states that are responsible for giving the experienced world its significance. Hence I use the term 'mood' for current purposes. However, when referring to mood, I restrict myself to 'deep' moods and thus depart from everyday usage, which is more wide-ranging. I will suggest towards the end of this chapter that, when it comes to further studying the relevant phenomenology, a term of art ('existential feeling') might be preferable to the term 'mood'.

Heidegger's conception of mood (*Stimmung*) is premised on the acknowledgement that we do not experience the world as disinterested spectators; we find ourselves *in* it. We are not *in* the world in the way that an object might be *in* a container. Experiencing oneself as part of the world is not principally a matter of registering one's spatiotemporal location in relation to other entities. Rather, we are situated in the world in the sense that we are purposively entangled with it. In any situation, certain things show up as practically significant. This is the case with items of equipment, for example, which knit together in holistic teleological frameworks that reflect potential activities (Heidegger, 1962, pp. 95–102). Consider perceiving a coffee cup. It is experienced as functional, as something for drinking from, and this function is interconnected with the functions of the bottle of milk in the fridge, the sugar bowl and spoon, the coffee jar, the kettle, the sink, the work surface, and so on. We do not perceive such objects in a neutral, detached,

---

[2] Throughout this chapter, I adopt a phenomenological conception of intentionality, which takes it to be the directedness of *experience*. Intentionality is sometimes conceived of as a non-phenomenological 'aboutness' and there is nothing to stop people from defining it as such. However, the intentionality of emotion is inextricable from the phenomenology of emotion. As I will argue later in this chapter, emotional feeling is intentional. See also Goldie (e.g. 2002, p. 241) for this view. Hence a non-phenomenological conception of intentionality would be inappropriate in this context. I also conceive of emotions (and moods) phenomenologically, unlike some authors who treat them as physiological changes that may or may not be experienced (e.g. Damasio, 2004; LeDoux, 1999). Separating emotion from experience is, in my view, counter-intuitive and unwarranted. But, if one insists on doing so, then we can simply call what I am addressing here 'feelings of emotions' rather than 'emotions'. The disagreement is merely terminological.

standoffish fashion. More often, our appreciation of them is practical in nature; we encounter them *as* tools that are seamlessly integrated into our activities. Thus, according to Heidegger, the world that we inhabit takes the form of a web of practical, purposive relations. We experience things in terms of what they *offer* in relation to our various projects.

However, it is important to appreciate that there are various different ways in which things appear to us as practically significant. For example, the potential activities offered by an object might present themselves as pleasant, unpleasant, required, pressing, enticing, interesting, boring, only for me, for us, for them but not for me, difficult, easy or impossible. Objects do not summon us to act in a single, homogeneous way. Furthermore, potential practical utility is not the only kind of significance that things have for us. We experience actual and potential *happenings* as significant in many different ways too. They might be threatening, dangerous, exciting, relevant to you, me, us or them, fascinating, boring, expected or unexpected, comforting, reassuring, safe or unsafe. And then there are other people too, who we relate to in all sorts of ways and who appear to us as offering a range of significant activities, happenings, and relations, from sexual gratification to a boring conversation to a punch in the face.

Hence we experience people, objects, events, and situations in the world in terms of different kinds of significant possibility, different ways of *mattering*. The range of emotions that we experience reflects this possibility space. All emotions presuppose an appreciation of certain possibilities as somehow significant. This clearly applies to what Gordon (1987) calls 'epistemic emotions', which are directed towards outcomes that are either non-actual or unknown. One fears, dreads, hopes for, or is excited by something that may or may not happen or have happened. But it also applies to many or perhaps even all of what Gordon calls 'factive emotions', emotions that are directed at things one knows to be the case. For example one might be sad, angry, or happy about an event. Here too there is an experience of salient possibilities. In disappointment, there is often the sense that the space of possibilities has narrowed, that certain significant possibilities are irrevocably gone. Much the same can apply to anger at something someone has done. In *mattering* to us, their deed has a significance that reaches out beyond the actual and impacts upon the likely shape of things to come. Not all of the salient consequences that provoke the anger are actualized.

Heidegger's proposal, as I interpret it, is that moods constitute the various different ways in which we are able to experience things as *mattering*. Hence they are presupposed by intentionally directed emotions. Take fear, for example. Heidegger claims that the experience of being afraid of something presupposes an appreciation on our part of distinctive kinds of possibility; 'different possibilities of Being emerge in fearing' (1962, p. 181). In order to be afraid, one must already find oneself in the world in such a way that being *in danger or under threat* are possibilities. Some being, perhaps oneself, has to matter in a certain kind of way for fear to be possible. The point applies more generally: different kinds of emotion presuppose a range of different ways in which things can matter to us, such as having practical significance, threatening us or being intriguing. According to Heidegger, mood determines the space of possible kinds of concern.[3]

It is surely uncontroversial to maintain that having an emotion with a specific *content* requires having a particular set of concerns. For example, the state of being thrilled at finding a rare stamp presupposes the kinds of value that a stamp collector might have. However, Heidegger's claim does not relate merely to the contents of emotions but also to the *kinds* of emotion that we are capable of experiencing, such as fearing, hoping, enthusing, regretting, or rejoicing. Take the appreciation of practical significance, for example. Some things appear to us as practically significant and others not, but consider the experiential changes that might occur if all *sense* of practical significance were removed from experience, if one were no longer able to entertain the possibility of anything having any consequence. Sartre's (1963) 'nausea' is a mood along such lines, where a background sense of purpose and function that pervades everyday experience is removed altogether, with the result that everything appears strangely alien and contingent. Things are experienced as bereft of their usual familiarity, appearing instead as 'soft, monstrous masses, in disorder—naked, with a frightening, obscene nakedness' (Sartre, 1963, p. 183). The world as it is experienced through nausea is not simply a place without purpose or function but a place where purpose and function are no longer conceivable.[4] A mood like this is, at the same time, a shift in the range of possible emotions. Sartrean nausea occurs only fleetingly in its full-blown form. But were such a mood to linger, one could no longer be excited, delighted, annoyed, or disappointed by worldly events, as one would no longer experience those events through concerns that such emotions presuppose.

Heidegger warns against philosophical perspectives that construe mood as 'an object swimming in the stream of consciousness' (1995, p. 90). A mood is not an internal mental state that we experience ourselves as having within a world. Neither is it an intentional state that has a substantial chunk of the world as its object. It is not 'an inner condition which then reaches forth in an enigmatical way and puts its mark on Things and persons' (Heidegger, 1962, p. 176). Rather, a mood is a background sense of belonging to a meaningful world, a condition of possibility for having intentional states: '*The mood has already disclosed, in every case, Being-in-the-world as a whole, and makes it possible first of all to direct oneself towards*

---

[3] Distinguishing and categorizing all the ways in which things and people are experienced as mattering to us and exploring how the various emotions depend upon them would be a huge undertaking. My aim here is to argue for the more general claim that emotion presupposes mattering and mattering depends upon mood.

[4] A strikingly similar experiential transformation is often reported by schizophrenic patients and is closely associated with changes in feeling (for further discussion, see, for example, Sass, 2003; Ratcliffe, 2008, ch. 7).

*something*' (1962, p. 176). Mood constitutes a phenomenological background in the context of which intentionally directed experience is possible.

A similar account of mood (*Stimmung*) is offered by Stephan Strasser (1977), who distinguishes moods from other kinds of emotional state by appealing to different *levels* of feeling. Like Heidegger, he claims that intentional states are structured by moods, which determine the range of ways in which things can be encountered (as threatening, inviting, etc.). A mood is thus deeper than an intentional state; it is 'the primordial phenomenological characteristic of self-experiencing life' (1977, p. 121), which 'precedes everything that has the character of an act' (1977, p. 182). The importance of mood is seldom appreciated and this, Strasser suggests, is because its depth serves to make it phenomenologically inconspicuous. A mood is not an object of experience but a space of possibilities in the context of which we experience other things. As he puts it:

> . . . precisely *those* attunements [*Stimmungen*] to which we pay no heed at all, the attunements we least observe, those attunements which attune us in such a way that we feel as though there is no attunement there are all, as though we were not attuned in any way at all—these attunements are the most powerful. (1977, p. 68)

So we should not confuse the intensity of an emotional state with its depth. A phenomenologically inconspicuous mood can be deeper than an intense emotion, as mood constitutes the kinds of concern in relation to which such emotions are intelligible. Emotions always occur in the context of moods. As Heidegger observes, we are always in a mood even when we don't realize it. Even the 'pallid, evenly balanced lack of mood (*Ungestimmtheit*), which is often persistent and which is not to be mistaken for a bad mood, is far from nothing at all' (1962, p. 173).

The difference between intensity and depth is made clear by Heidegger's (1995) lengthy phenomenological analysis of boredom (*Langeweile*), which distinguishes three kinds of boredom.[5] First of all, there are those occasions when we are 'bored by' something. Heidegger offers the example of waiting at a quiet, rural railway station for a train that is not due for another few hours. In such circumstances, we are very much aware of the situation *as* boring. Our surroundings appear boring; the station is experienced as something that 'does not yet offer us what it properly ought to' (1995, p. 103), as something that puts our projects on hold. We try to distract ourselves from the situation by walking up and down or drawing pictures in the sand with our fingers. Every so often, we look up at the clock and will the time to pass more quickly. In this case, our boredom is intense and, although its object is not neatly defined, it is still an intentional state directed at a particular situation.

---

[5] Heidegger's discussion places particular emphasis on the temporal structure of boredom. However, I do not discuss this aspect of his analysis, as it is not required in order to draw the distinction between intensity and depth.

Heidegger contrasts this with a second form of boredom; being 'bored with' a situation. He offers the example of attending a dinner and being struck, upon leaving, by the realization that one was bored all night. The odd thing though is that one was not aware of being bored at the time. The situation did not present itself as an object of experience, as something that was boring. In fact, one quite happily chatted away all night, expressed oneself with enthusiasm and more generally immersed oneself in the evening. Yet, Heidegger says, what we have here is actually a more 'profound' form of boredom than being bored by something. During occasions like the dinner, the boredom is not intense in the way that being bored by something is. But it is deeper all the same. We are aware of the station as boring because alternative possibilities present themselves; it stands in the way of projects and concerns that are not themselves experienced through the boredom. So boredom is experienced *within* a space of other possibilities. However, during the dinner, one experiences one's whole situation *through* the boredom. It no longer incorporates the possibility of one's not being bored and so there is no vantage point from which to resist the boredom: 'any seeking to be satisfied by beings is absent in advance' (1995, p. 117). Hence, in the case of the station, a particular thing fails to satisfy us, whereas, at the dinner, the possibility of anything satisfying us is absent from the experience; we are *in* the boredom. The latter is phenomenologically deeper as it is 'a preventing of' a 'seeking' that is still there when we find something intensely boring (1995, p. 117).

However, Heidegger indicates that there is an even deeper form of boredom. At the dinner, the boredom is *my* boredom, a realm where only I dwell. I can still conceive of other perspectives on this and other situations. Thus the space of possibilities that I currently inhabit does not exhaust my sense of what the world might have to offer. This is not so in the third form of boredom, being 'boring for one'. Here, the boredom is all-encompassing. A sense of there being any alternative to this way of finding oneself in the world for *anyone* is absent from experience; 'we find ourselves in the midst of beings as a whole, i.e., in the whole of this indiffer-ence' (1995, p. 138). All experience is structured by a space of possibilities that is quietly lacking. Things 'offer us no possibility of acting and no further possibility of our doing anything. There is a telling refusal on the part of beings as a whole with respect to these possibilities' (1995, p. 139). Certain possibilities that remain pre-supposed by the first and second forms are now absent. Hence the third form is the deepest, as it involves a loss of certain kinds of concern that the shallower forms of boredom continue to depend upon. While waiting at the station, things are experienced as 'refusing' possibilities (1995, p. 140). And, in the second form, not all situations offer the same possibilities as the dinner. In the third form, however, there is nothing left to refuse and no alternative on offer.

I suggest that we think of the distinction between emotions and deep moods in these terms. Emotions are, for the most part, intentional states, such as Heidegger's being 'bored by'. Moods, in contrast, are presupposed possibility spaces that we find ourselves in. As Heidegger notes, not all moods are equally *deep*. The second form of boredom is not as deep as the third. It is not experienced as encompassing the world for everyone, as a way of being in the world to which there is no alternative.

The kind of tripartite distinction proposed by Heidegger can be applied to a range of other emotional states too.[6] For example, Garrett (1994, pp. 73–4) distinguishes three kinds of despair. There is 'project-specific despair', which is an intentional state where one despairs about a specific state of affairs. There is also 'personal despair', where one despairs over one's entire life. And there is 'philosophical despair', which is despair over the meaninglessness of all lives.[7] Again, we have a specifically directed intentional state, a mood that shapes one's intentional states and a deeper mood that envelops all conceivable predicaments.[8]

What Garrett calls 'philosophical despair' is closely related to the experience of depression, and deep mood changes are vividly conveyed by numerous autobiographical descriptions of altered experience in depression. It is clear from such accounts that the experience of depression involves, amongst other things, a shift in the kinds of significant possibility that shape experience of self, other people, and the surrounding world. Many authors describe a loss of both practical connectedness with things and emotional connectedness with people. What is lost is not just experience of *actual* connections. Experience no longer incorporates the sense that such connections are possible. This is frequently communicated in terms of an invisible but impenetrable barrier or container that irrevocably separates the sufferer from things and people. For example, Andrew Solomon reports that 'I felt as if my head had been encaged in Lucite, like one of those butterflies trapped forever in the thick transparency of a paperweight' (2001, p. 66).[9] A sense of anything as offering potential pleasure is also gone. As William Styron (2001, p. 14) remarks, there was 'a sense that my thought processes were being engulfed by a toxic and unnameable tide that obliterated any enjoyable response to the living

---

[6] Although I distinguish moods from emotions, I use the term 'emotional state' in a more general way to refer to both.

[7] See Steinbock (2007) for a good discussion of the phenomenology of despair, which suggests that despair involves a loss of possibilities that various other emotional states, such as disappointment and desperation, continue to presuppose.

[8] However, I wonder whether the case of 'personal despair' suggests a fourth form of boredom, located between Heidegger's forms two and three. I can find myself in a boring situation or experience boredom as a space of possibilities in which we are all situated. But between the two is what one might call 'personal boredom', where one finds one's entire life irrevocably boring. This is more extreme than the case of the dinner, as it encompasses *every* possible situation one might find oneself in, rather than just the one situation. Yet it is still only *my* boredom and thus not as deep as form three.

[9] Solomon also recalls Sylvia Plath's metaphor of being stuck in the suffocating atmosphere of a chemical bell jar (Plath, 1966).

world'. And, as Andrew Solomon puts it, 'the first thing that goes is happiness. You cannot gain pleasure from anything. That's famously the cardinal symptom of major depression. But soon the other emotions follow happiness into oblivion' (2001, p. 19). It is not just that things no longer make one feel happy; a sense of their even having the potential to do so is gone. Also gone is the conceivability of any alternative to the depression. Almost all authors who offer detailed accounts of a major depressive episode state that, whilst suffering from depression, they could not contemplate the possibility of any alternative to the world of depression and therefore could not conceive of the possibility of recovery. For example, Styron states that 'all sense of hope had vanished' (2001, p. 58), and Sally Brampton, in a recent memoir, describes her predicament as follows:

It is the glass wall that separates us from life, from ourselves, that is so truly frightening in depression. It is a terrible sense of our own overwhelming reality, a reality that we know has nothing to do with the reality that we once knew. And from which we think we will never escape. It is like living in a parallel universe but a universe so devoid of familiar signs of life that we are adrift, lost. (2008, p. 171)

As her account illustrates, although we are often oblivious to deep moods, this is not always so. Changes in mood are phenomenologically conspicuous in depression partly because of the awareness that something has been lost. The sufferer knows all too well that the world used not to be like this, that something is missing from experience. However, to be aware in this way that things were once different is not to retain the kinds of possibility that previously characterized experience. The sufferer can remember that things used to be different but she cannot rekindle the experience of their being different; she can no longer feel the possibilities that were once there and that might one day return. Although she knows that something is gone and is able to speak of what has been lost, there remains something she cannot fully conceive of, an appreciation of things that none of her thoughts or words are able to evoke. It is the possibility of actually experiencing things as mattering in the ways that they once did which she cannot entertain. For example: 'What time is it? A little after ten in the morning. I try to remember what ten in the morning means, how it feels. But I cannot. Time means nothing to me any more' (Brampton, 2008, p. 29).

Depression thus involves a transformation of deep mood, a shift in the kinds of concern that structure experience of people, things, and also, of course, oneself. So there is a big difference between at least some of the emotional changes that occur in depression and an increase in the intensity of emotions like sadness. The sadness of severe depression is not adequately characterized as an intensification or generalization of some intentional state. The world is experienced through the sadness. It is how one finds oneself in the world rather than an emotion that one has within the world. One cannot see outside it, which is partly why telling people with depression to 'snap out of it' is notoriously ineffective.

The depth of depressed mood will of course vary from case to case. Like Heidegger's second form of boredom, it often seems to take the form of *my depression*, rather than *the world for all of us*, but more severe cases involve an inability to appreciate that there are alternative possibilities available to anyone. Depression is reality and any activities that seem incongruous with it appear as absurd rather than as pointing to possibilities beyond depression:

During my long morning walks I watched people hurrying along in suits and trainers. Where was it they were going, and why were they in such haste? I simply couldn't imagine feeling such urgency. I watched others throwing a ball for a dog, picking it up, and throwing it again. Why? Where was the sense in such repetition? (Brampton, 2008, p. 249)

Deep depression is not a complete absence of all forms of significance though. Many sufferers report intense feelings of fear, dread, isolation, and loneliness. They still relate to the world in some way, but in a way that is quite different from what most of us take for granted most of the time. Everyday world-meaning is replaced by a radically altered relationship with the world, characterized by irrevocable alienation, despair, futility, guilt, and the like, with no hope of reprieve. Sufferers often describe the change as akin to having died. They have lost the feeling of being alive, a sense of being practically entwined with the world and emotionally related to others that everyday experience obliviously takes for granted:

People talk about the way disembodied spirits roam the world with no place to park themselves, but all I can think is that I am a dispirited body, and I'm sure there are plenty of other human mollusc shells roaming around waiting for some soul to fill them up. [ . . . ] with every day that goes by, I feel myself becoming more and more invisible, getting covered over more thickly with darkness, coats and coats of darkness that are going to suffocate me in the sweltering heat of the summer sun that I can't even see anymore even though I can feel it burn. Imagine [ . . . ] only knowing that the sun is shining because you feel the ache of its awful heat and not because you know the joy of its light. Imagine always being in the dark. (Wurtzel, 1996, pp. 42–54)

It is not that one doesn't feel joy but that one cannot feel joy. The 'darkness' is a loss of certain possibilities, with the result that everything is experienced through a sense of insurmountable estrangement.[10]

Although I have focused on negative moods here, much the same point can be made, I think, by appealing to more 'positive' moods, such as feeling wholly at peace with the world, at one with things, and at least some instances of being *in* love. A love that is 'blind' is a love *through which* one experiences the world, a love in which one is oblivious to certain possibilities. And an all-encompassing, unchangeable mood of being completely at peace with the world would be one in which the possibilities of fear, worry, and the like were absent from experience. Moods thus open up certain kinds of possibility and close down others. This role is

---

[10] See Ratcliffe (2009) for a more detailed discussion of the phenomenology of depression.

not readily apparent unless we reflect upon various kinds of extreme alteration in mood.

It would therefore be quite wrong to conceive of deep mood as a subjective gloss, resting on top of a pre-understood objective world. A mood, as Heidegger points out, has neither an internal nor an external phenomenology: 'A mood assails us. It comes neither from "outside" nor from "inside", but arises out of Being-in-the-world, as a way of such Being' (1962, p. 176). When we experience something as a state of ourselves or as a state of the world, we are already *in* a mood. Hence it is a mistake to think that we can contemplate and describe the world in a neutral, detached fashion by simply discarding a subjective overlay. One's mood is not discarded; it is a context of intelligibility that continues to be presupposed by all experience and thought. In a world devoid of all significance, an objective account of the structure and origin of the universe could be of no more worth than a comprehensive account of the precise configurations of all the grains of sand in a bucket. There could be no motivation for formulating a scientific theory, no sense of it being of any potential interest or consequence. It is doubtful that scientific theories would even be intelligible to someone in such a mood. Without relevance, significance, purpose, without a sense of the world as a place that merits explora- tion and explanation, the possibility of seeking to understand anything would be absent. Indeed, it is arguable that a kind of seeking is inextricable from the process of understanding. Hence a sense of what it *is* to understand something would be gone. One would be presented with a series of hollow claims that one might indifferently assent to or deny but which one could not fully *grasp*. Just such a loss of intelligibility is often reported in severe depression. For example, Brampton remarks that she found herself unable to read: 'Words are no more than patterns on a page' (2008, p. 33). Background mood is not something that any experience, thought, or conceptualization can simply transcend. However, as the deeper moods are often phenomenologically inconspicuous, their role tends to be overlooked. Hence scientific and philosophical accounts of how we experience the world generally fail to incorporate a sense of being in the world that they obliviously take for granted. As Heidegger remarks, 'science becomes blind to what it must presuppose' (2001, p. 75) and 'one must see that science as such (i.e., all theoretical-scientific knowledge) is founded as a way of being-in-the-world—founded in the bodily having of a world' (2001, p. 94).[11]

A question still to be addressed is what moods actually consist of. Granted, we can describe them as playing a distinctive kind of phenomenological role but what kind of state could play that role? In the remainder of this chapter, I will suggest that moods are comprised of bodily feeling and that the apparent

---

[11] Similar statements can be found in other works by Heidegger (e.g. 1962, 1995).

implausibility of this view is symptomatic of a commonplace misconception of bodily feeling.[12]

# 15.4 Emotions and Bodily Feelings

The term 'feeling' is used in various different ways. We might speak of the feeling of being in love, the feeling that all is well, the feeling that something is not true, the feeling of being at the beach on a hot, sunny day or feeling like one is on a rollercoaster. One could maintain, as Nussbaum (2001, p. 60) does, that certain uses of the term 'feeling', including those associated with emotions and moods, are synonymous with 'judgement' or 'belief'. Thus, when we refer to a feeling that relates to states of affairs outside of the body, we are talking about something quite different from a 'bodily feeling'. Nussbaum is of course right that not all talk of feelings refers to bodily feelings. Nevertheless, it is a mistake to think of all bodily feelings as states that have an exclusively bodily phenomenology. The same feeling can be referred to as bodily in nature and also as a way of experiencing something other than the body.[13] We can talk about the same feeling in different ways, and what might appear to be different feelings are often one and the same.

We do not perceive our bodies in complete isolation from how we perceive everything else, and then link the two kinds of perception together by means of some subsequent mental process. Consider, for example, the sense of balance. Losing one's balance or feeling disorientated is not just a perception of one's body or of the world outside the body. It is a perception of the relationship between one's body and its surroundings.[14] A sense of bodily orientation is integral to world-experience; the perceived world is organized in terms of 'up', 'down', 'left', and 'right'. A *feeling* such as disorientation is a bodily feeling but it is not just an experience of the body. In fact, the term 'bodily feeling' is ambiguous. It could be understood as referring exclusively to feelings of the body, experiences where the body or a part of it is phenomenologically conspicuous in some way. This is consistent with the pervasive tendency to think of bodily feelings as having an

---

[12] Heidegger's view on this matter is not at all clear. He does not discuss the phenomenology of the body at all in *Being and Time*, but does later acknowledge that it needs to be addressed (e.g. 2001, p. 81). Strasser (1977, ch. 7) is not wholly clear on the relationship between bodily feeling and mood either, but does seem to acknowledge that the two are intimately related.

[13] For other recent approaches which challenge the assumption that bodily feelings have a wholly 'internal' phenomenology, see Goldie (2000, 2002, 2009), Stocker (2004), Greenspan (2004) and Drummond (2004).

[14] In Ratcliffe (2008, ch. 3) I make a similar point by discussing, at length, the phenomenology of tactile feelings.

exclusively internal phenomenology. However, bodily feelings can also be conceived of as experiences where the body *feels* something, and here there is no commitment to the assumption that they are experiences of *internal* states. I suggest that what applies to a feeling of disorientation also applies to many if not all of the bodily feelings that are implicated in emotional states. The feeling body is an aspect of the experience but it need not be the exclusive object of the experience. Indeed, it need not be an *object* of experience at all. A bodily feeling can be a way in which something other than the body is experienced. It can be that *through* which we experience something, an agent of perception rather than an object of perception.

This conception of bodily feeling follows naturally from the increasingly widespread recognition amongst phenomenologists and others that we do not experience and understand the world primarily as detached spectators but through our practical, purposive, bodily involvement with it. A background sense of interconnected bodily potentialities structures perception of one's surroundings:

The body is the vehicle of being in the world, and having a body is, for a living creature, to be intervolved with a definite environment, to identify oneself with certain projects and be continually committed to them. (Merleau-Ponty, 1962, p. 82)

The body is not simply an object of experience that one is intimately associated with or perhaps even identical with. Bodily dispositions to act, recoil, immerse oneself in activity, or withdraw from it are reflected in what things are perceived as offering. Hence perception of the body and perception of what is outside it cannot be disentangled. Much the same point is also made by J. J. Gibson:

Egoreception accompanies exteroception, like the other side of a coin. Perception has two poles, the subjective and the objective, and information is available to specify both. One perceives the environment and coperceives oneself. (1979, p. 126)

There is considerable current interest in 'enactive' approaches to perception, which develop the ideas of Gibson and others, in order to argue that perception of the world incorporates proprioception and also bodily activities embedded in particular kinds of environment. Accounts such as that of Noë (2004) maintain that salient possibilities for perception and action are reflected in how objects are experienced. For example, integral to experience of an object is the sense that it might be perceived from another angle, revealing its hidden aspects.[15] Although I endorse the view that we experience things in terms of significant possibilities (see, for example, Ratcliffe, 2008, ch. 4), I also think that enactive approaches generally fail to appreciate the wide range of different ways in which things and people are perceived as significant. Consider what Gibson (1979) calls 'affordances',

---

[15] So far as I know, the most sophisticated formulation of this kind of position is that of Husserl (e.g. 1973, 2001). See Ratcliffe (2008, ch. 4) for a discussion.

opportunities that things are perceived as offering. One can say that a fast-approaching and unavoidable avalanche affords curling up in a ball and waiting to die but this is uninformative. It needs to be acknowledged that many different kinds of significance relation feature in our experience, such as 'threatening and impossible to escape from', 'desirable but beyond one's grasp', 'interesting', 'easy to obtain', and so on. Different emotions depend upon different kinds of significance, different ways in which things matter to us.

Solomon's claim that some emotions incorporate kinaesthetic judgements is susceptible to much the same criticism. There is too much emphasis on bodily activity, on *'getting engaged in the world'* (2004a, p. 86), and insufficient acknowledgement of the *variety* of ways in which things are felt to matter. Once it is appreciated that feelings in general do not have an exclusively bodily phenomenology, that we do not experience our bodies as sealed containers with some experiences falling clearly on the inside and others wholly on the outside, it becomes clear that not all world-directed feelings are akin to the kinaesthetic judgements involved in catching a ball or running up the stairs. Bodily feelings can involve a sense of disengagement and passivity as much as they can engagement and activity.

All sorts of different experiences serve to illustrate the double-sidedness of feeling, how feelings can be both perceptions of self and at the same time perceptions of non-self.[16] Consider Sartre's description of experiencing eyestrain while reading:

... this pain can itself be indicated by objects of the world; i.e., by the book which I read. It is with more difficulty that the words are detached from the undifferentiated ground which they constitute; they may tremble, quiver; their meaning can be derived only with effort.... (1989, p. 332)

When one is concentrating on the words, the experience of eyestrain, the discomfort, is clearly there but it is experienced primarily as a way in which the words on the page appear. Then, as one attends to the experience, there is a phenomenological shift. One becomes aware of a pain around one's eyes and, in so doing, disengages from the text. The object of experience shifts but the discomfort, although not previously an object of experience, was surely not wholly absent from the experience. Strasser (1977, pp. 238–9) makes a complementary point in relation to the experience of tiredness:

I can simply live 'in' my tiredness. I intransitively 'feel', then, in the mode of attraction or mood. But I also transitively 'feel' my tiredness; then I examine it on the basis of a knowledge-intention and possibly identify sensations of pain in this or that group of muscles, organ-sensations, and so forth.

A feeling of tiredness need not be first and foremost a feeling of the body. We can inhabit our tiredness, experiencing the world through it rather than scrutinizing

---

[16] For detailed discussion of many such experiences, see Ratcliffe (2008).

the tiredness itself. It can happen that someone who is extremely tired, perhaps for a prolonged period, remains curiously unaware of it. Even though the tiredness is not itself conspicuous in a case like this, it might well be phenomenologically deep, a shape that all experience takes on rather than an inconvenience that one actively tries to shake off. We can thus distinguish between intentional bodily feelings like the eyestrain, which present the body or something else in some way, and 'pre-intentional' feelings, such as a background feeling of tiredness that shapes all experience and thought. As Strasser notes, 'governance by feeling operates partially on the preintentional level, partially on the intentional level' (1977, p. 229).

We are often oblivious to the role played by pre-intentional feeling. However, as Heidegger (1962, pp. 226–7) recognizes in his discussion of *Angst*, its role can become noticeable during extreme shifts in mood. In some such cases, what one previously took for granted becomes salient in its absence, as illustrated by everyday metaphors such as 'having the rug pulled out from under one's feet'. John Hull, in his autobiographical account of becoming blind and living with blindness, describes what I take to be a shift in pre-intentional feeling, an experience which he concedes is extremely difficult to express. He refers to the onset of depression and to a feeling much deeper than mundane feelings, which came to encompass all experience and thought: 'the deepest feelings go beyond feeling. One is numbed by the feeling; one does not experience the feeling' (1990, p. 168). It is not a localized experience but a way of being that transforms the range of possible emotional experience: 'The emotional life is no longer experienced as content (i.e., an emotion having the identifiable content of anger, sadness, and so on) but as a sort of numbness or recoil. I take refuge in sleep, or sleep seeks to inhabit me' (1990, p. 153). Numerous other reports of painful feeling in depression make clear that such feelings are neither directed at the body in isolation from the world nor vice versa. They are bodily feelings and, at the same time, ways of finding oneself in the world. For example, Tracy Thompson (1995, p. 73) describes the transition from grief to depression as follows: 'As the months went by, the breathtaking reality of my father's death became a physical hurt, a heaviness in my bones, a pervasive lethargy.' A world that is all too conspicuously empty of value, practical significance and potential communion with others is quite literally painful. As William Styron (2001, p. 49) remarks, 'the gray drizzle of horror induced by depression takes on the quality of physical pain' (Styron, 2001, p. 49).[17]

---

[17] As several authors have noted, the phenomenology of painful estrangement often reported in depression is characterized by a kind of unpleasant bodily conspicuousness. The body as a whole feels different, taking the form of an oddly conspicuous object of experience rather than a medium through which other things are experienced (e.g. Fuchs, 2003, p. 225). However, a contrast between the body that invisibly belongs and the body that is unpleasantly salient is, I think, an over-simplification. There are many different ways in which the body can be phenomenologically conspicuous, not all of which are unpleasant or alienating (Young, 2005, ch. 3; Ratcliffe, 2008, ch. 4).

Deep moods, I suggest, are pre-intentional feelings that remain consistent over fairly long periods of time. It follows from this that the role of constituting a space of significant possibilities is not performed solely by these moods. Sometimes, background feelings shift only momentarily. In other cases, these feelings might be so consistent and enduring that we refer to them as character or personality traits rather than moods. Hence the term 'mood', even when restricted to deep moods, is not wholly adequate. For this reason, I have recommended using the term 'existential feeling' instead (Ratcliffe, 2005, 2008). Whether sporadic, longer term or operative over a whole life, a feeling is 'existential' insofar as it constitutes a sense of belonging to a significant world. Even so, the term 'mood' does at least serve to capture many of the relevant predicaments. Furthermore, the distinction between *having* an emotion and being *in* a mood is a useful one.

It is important to recognize that, even though existential feelings (amongst which I include deep moods) and intentionally directed emotions play different phenomenological roles, the two aspects of experience are intimately related. Existential feelings and emotions are not wholly separate, static 'states' but inextricable aspects of experience that shape each other. For example, a sudden change in deep mood is often brought about by an intense emotion or series of interrelated emotions. These emotions, although intense, might at first be specifically focused and thus not very deep. However, such emotions often provoke reorientations of mood, a process that is referred to in some cases as something's 'sinking in'. Sue Cataldi (1993) describes the process by reflecting upon how she felt when attacked on the street. To begin with, there is a gradual realization of her situation, involving a loss of practical, bodily 'grip' or 'hold' on her surroundings. The initial disorientation gives way to an awareness of danger. As she is assaulted and a knife is revealed, the experience takes on the form of 'sheer terror', which is not a localized emotion but an all-encompassing way of being. The terror is not felt within a situation; it is the situation (p. 15). It is, as she says, 'deep', a deep emotion being something one is 'in' (p. 2).

When intense emotions culminate in deep mood changes, the process is essentially *bodily* in nature. For example, here is how the philosopher Havi Carel describes her experience of receiving a diagnosis of serious illness:

Pain and fear struck like a physical blow. It is difficult to describe the physicality of bad news. I remember looking at the room and feeling confused: it looked the same, while my life had been turned upside down. Make it stop, I thought. This is the wrong story. Someone come and fix it. Someone do something. The realization that everything was about to change, that a new era was about to begin, seared like burning oil on skin. It crushed me with invisible force. It is difficult to describe the pain and fear that descended on me at that moment. Now I cannot imagine my life without this pain and fear. (2008, p. 4)

What she conveys here is a way the body feels and, at the same time, a dramatic and ultimately enduring shift in the space of significant possibilities. How the body feels cannot be pulled apart from world-experience, and Carel herself explicitly rejects contrasts such as mental/physical and internal/external, which are engrained in so much of philosophical discourse (2008, p. 21).

Experiences like these do of course involve more than just alterations in intentional and pre-intentional bodily feelings.[18] There is also a conceptual understanding at play, and I think it likely that many of the experiences we refer to as 'emotions' are not comprised exclusively of bodily feelings. Emotions can be complicated, dynamic processes, which have an elaborate conceptual structure that often takes the form of an unfolding narrative. As Peter Goldie suggests, an emotion is:

... a relatively complex state, involving past and present episodes of thoughts, feelings, and bodily changes, dynamically related in a narrative of part of a person's life, together with dispositions to experience further emotional episodes, and to act out of the emotion and to express that emotion. (2000, p. 144)

However, I suggest that existential feelings, in contrast, are comprised wholly of pre-intentional, non-conceptual feeling. They can be influenced by emotions and thus by the conceptual appraisals that are integral to at least some emotions. But existential feelings are not themselves conceptual. They do not incorporate judgements or appraisals of *any* kind. By implication, they do not incorporate any conceptual content. An existential feeling is a space of possibilities within which we experience, think, and act, as opposed to being an experience or thought content. As these feelings are presupposed by conceptual judgements rather than being wholly separate from them, it would be better to call them 'pre-conceptual' than 'non-conceptual'.

It might be objected that non-conceptual feeling cannot amount to a sense of salient possibilities. Conceptual understanding is required for that. However, I doubt that this is so. Consider the experience of surprise. In order to be surprised, one need not have conceptualized expectations about a situation. Rather, the anticipation of what is likely to happen can take the form of an unthinking, habitual, bodily engagement with the world (Husserl, 1973, 2001). Expectations are often only conceptualized after one has met with the unexpected. I see no reason why the same point cannot be applied more generally—we anticipate salient possibilities through our feeling bodies.

One might also question the relationship between existential feeling and thought. I have argued that deep moods and other existential feelings structure experience by constituting spaces of possibility. But do they similarly structure

---

[18] Again, I should stress that, although I have chosen to focus upon negative emotions here, the process of reorientation does not always take the form of a negative event provoking intense and unpleasant emotions, which eventually tear one out of a realm of cosy belonging. For instance, the joy, delight, relief, gratitude, pride, or elation that follows very good news could equally provoke a change in mood.

thought? Of course, they have *effects* upon what we think and upon how well we think. But the relationship, it might be argued, is causal; background feelings do not make our thoughts intelligible. Unlike emotion, thought does not have a phenomenology that presupposes existential feeling, the reason being that thought does not have a phenomenology at all. However, this kind of view is, I suggest, mistaken. When a native speaker hears a sentence spoken in his or her own language, their experience is quite different from that of someone who hears the same sentence but does not speak the language. Drawing on such examples, Galen Strawson (e.g. 2004) suggests—quite rightly, in my view—that philosophers need to acknowledge the category of 'cognitive experience'. The view that conceptual understanding and, by implication, the process of thinking have a phenomenology can be further supported by a consideration of alterations in the experience of thinking that are reported in various psychiatric illnesses. If there were no phenomenology of thought, there could be no such changes. It also seems that these changes are, in every case, intimately associated with alterations in feeling. For example, people with schizophrenia may complain that their thoughts are not only fragmented but also strangely object-like. Louis Sass (e.g. 2003), amongst others, has argued at length that these alterations in the phenomenology of thought are inextricable from anomalous background feeling. Patients suffering from depersonalization likewise complain of changes in how their thoughts are experienced, which seem to be bound up with anomalous feeling. For example, Simeon and Abugel quote a patient as saying that 'thinking just *felt* different, as if coming from somewhere else' (2006, p. 26).

Hence I propose that experience and thought are both structured by a felt sense of belonging to a meaningful world, a world that *matters* in various different ways. This existential background, when it remains consistent over a period of time, is often referred to as a mood. Such moods, and existential feelings more generally, are responsible for what Solomon calls *the meaning of life*. But they are not judgements and they are not generalized emotions. Instead, they are bodily feelings and, at the same time, spaces of significant possibility.

## REFERENCES

BRAMPTON, S. (2008). *Shoot the Damn Dog: A Memoir of Depression*. London: Bloomsbury.

CAREL, H. (2008). *Illness: The Cry of the Flesh*. Stocksfield: Acumen.

CATALDI, S. (1993). *Emotion, Depth and Flesh: A Study of Sensitive Space*. Albany: State University of New York Press.

DAMASIO, A. (2004). Emotions and Feelings: A Neurobiological Perspective. In Manstead, S. R., Frijda, N., and Fischer, A. eds. *Feelings and Emotions: The Amsterdam Symposium*. Cambridge: Cambridge University Press: 49–57.

DRUMMOND, J. J. (2004). 'Cognitive Impenetrability' and the Complex Intentionality of the Emotions. *Journal of Consciousness Studies* 11 (10–11): 109–26.

FUCHS, T. (2003). The Phenomenology of Shame, Guilt and the Body in Body Dysmorphic Disorder and Depression. *Journal of Phenomenological Psychology* 33: 223–43.

GARRETT, R. (1994). The Problem of Despair. In Graham, G. and Stephens, G. L. eds. *Philosophical Psychopathology*. Cambridge, MA: MIT Press.

GIBSON, J. J. (1979). *The Ecological Approach to Visual Perception*. Hillsdale, NJ: Lawrence Erlbaum Associates.

GOLDIE, P. (2000). *The Emotions: A Philosophical Exploration*. Oxford: Clarendon Press.

—— (2002). Emotions, Feelings and Intentionality. *Phenomenology and the Cognitive Sciences* 1: 235–54.

—— (2009). Getting Feeling into Emotional Experience in the Right Way. *Emotion Review* 1: 232–9.

GORDON, R. (1987). *The Structure of Emotions*. Cambridge: Cambridge University Press.

GREENSPAN, P. (2004). Emotions, Rationality and Mind/Body. In Solomon, R. C. *Thinking about Feeling: Contemporary Philosophers on Emotions*. Oxford: Oxford University Press: 125–34.

HEIDEGGER, M. (1962). *Being and Time* (trans. Macquarrie, J. and Robinson, E.). Oxford: Blackwell.

—— (1995). *The Fundamental Concepts of Metaphysics*. Bloomington: Indiana University Press.

—— (2001). *Zollikon Seminars: Protocols—Conversations—Letters* (ed. Boss, M.; trans. Mayr, F. and Askay, R.). Evanston, IL: Northwestern University Press.

HULL, J. (1990). *Touching the Rock: An Experience of Blindness*. New York: Pantheon Books.

HUSSERL, E. (1973). *Experience and Judgment* (trans. Churchill, J. S. and Ameriks, K.). London: Routledge.

—— (2001). *Analyses concerning Passive and Active Synthesis: Lectures on Transcendental Logic* (trans. Steinbock, A. J.). Dordrecht: Kluwer.

LEDOUX, J. (1999). *The Emotional Brain: The Mysterious Underpinnings of Emotional Life*. London: Phoenix.

MERLEAU-PONTY, M. (1962). *Phenomenology of Perception* (trans. Smith, C.). London: Routledge.

NOË, A. (2004). *Action in Perception*. Cambridge, MA: MIT Press.

NUSSBAUM, M. (2001). *Upheavals of Thought: The Intelligence of Emotions*. Cambridge: Cambridge University Press.

PLATH, S. (1966). *The Bell Jar*. London: Faber & Faber.

RATCLIFFE, M. (2005). The Feeling of Being. *Journal of Consciousness Studies* 12 (8–10): 43–60.

—— (2008). *Feelings of Being: Phenomenology, Psychiatry and the Sense of Reality*. Oxford: Oxford University Press.

—— (2009). Understanding Existential Changes in Psychiatric Illness: The Indispensability of Phenomenology. In Broome, M. and Bortolotti, L. eds. *Psychiatry as Cognitive Neuroscience*. Oxford: Oxford University Press: 223–44.

ROBERTS, R. C. (2003). *Emotions: An Essay in Aid of Moral Psychology*. Cambridge: Cambridge University Press.

SARTRE, J. P. (1963). *Nausea* (trans. Baldick, R.). London: Penguin.

—— (1989). *Being and Nothingness* (trans. Barnes, H. E.). London: Routledge.

Sass, L. A. (2003). 'Negative Symptoms', Schizophrenia, and the Self. *International Journal of Psychology and Psychological Therapy* 3(2): 153–80.

Simeon, D. and Abugel, J. (2006). *Feeling Unreal: Depersonalization Disorder and the Loss of Self.* Oxford: Oxford University Press.

Solomon, A. (2001). *The Noonday Demon.* London: Chatto and Windus.

Solomon, R. C. (1993). *The Passions: Emotions and the Meaning of Life* (revised edition; originally published 1976). Cambridge: Hackett.

—— (2003). *Not Passion's Slave: Emotions and Choice.* Oxford: Oxford University Press.

—— (2004a). Emotions, Thoughts, and Feelings: Emotions as Engagements with the World. In Solomon, R. C. *Thinking about Feeling: Contemporary Philosophers on Emotions.* Oxford: Oxford University Press: 76–88.

—— (2004b). On the Passivity of the Passions. In Manstead, S. R., Frijda, N., and Fischer, A. eds. *Feelings and Emotions: The Amsterdam Symposium.* Cambridge: Cambridge University Press: 11–29.

Steinbock, A. J. (2007). The Phenomenology of Despair. *International Journal of Philosophical Studies* 15: 435–51.

Stocker, M. (2004). Some Considerations about Intellectual Desire and Emotions. In Solomon, R. C. *Thinking about Feeling: Contemporary Philosophers on Emotions.* Oxford: Oxford University Press: 135–48.

Strasser, S. (1977). *Phenomenology of Feeling: An Essay on the Phenomena of the Heart.* Pittsburgh, PA: Duquesne University Press.

Strawson, G. (2004). Real Intentionality. *Phenomenology and the Cognitive Sciences* 3: 287–313.

Styron, W. (2001). *Darkness Visible.* London: Vintage.

Thompson, T. (1995). *The Beast: A Reckoning with Depression.* New York: Putnam.

Wurtzel, E. (1996). *Prozac Nation: Young and Depressed in America.* London: Quartet Books.

Young, I. M. (2005). *On Female Bodily Experience: 'Throwing like a Girl' and other Essays.* Oxford: Oxford University Press.

# CHAPTER 16

·······································································

# SAYING IT

·······································································

## DAVID PUGMIRE

> You cannot draw the seed up out of the earth. All you can do is to give it
> warmth and moisture and light; then it must grow (You mustn't even
> *touch* it unless you use care.)—Wittgenstein
>
> . . . my thought processes were being engulfed by a toxic and unnameable
> tide . . . To most of those who have experienced it, the horror of depres-
> sion is so overwhelming as to be quite beyond expression.—William
> Styron

In the beginning feelings are opaque. Especially (but not only) when very young,
we can brim with feeling that is inchoate, in that we may be unclear why it has
arisen, or what it is directed at, and thus unclear quite what it is. Primordial
feelings graduate into fully formed emotions through an understanding of their
connections with the events out of which they emerge. Baffled consternation
becomes *bitterness* to one who can appreciate it as a response to wilful betrayal.
Experiences of emotion will typically have some perspicuous relation to relevant
paradigmatic circumstances (exemplars of, e.g., the funny, the menacing, the
outrageous, etc.). Perhaps it is even necessary that they should.

It does not, however, seem necessary for all episodes of emotion to be like this.
Emotion can sometimes flourish in minimally descriptive mediums. Consider an
example taken almost at random, the feeling in the poignant theme which opens
(and closes) Elgar's first symphony. It is strikingly abrupt, fully formed with scant
preparation. There is no context for it, no story, few illuminating references,
beyond being borne on a march-like beat. The feeling, however, is sharp and
clear; once had, never forgotten. But *what* is it? It is resonant and confident, it

seems to reach towards some distant good in a quiet, steady hope of eventual triumph, which seems finally at hand when the theme reappears in the finale. So the theme contains a joy that can move from the tentative to the realized.— Notice that such characterizations may be true, however detached they are from defining circumstance; but even then they only grope at and sketch what is *felt* perfectly clearly in this theme. This raises the question whether emotion (as well as some other kinds of experience) can ever, at least in part, elude description. This turns on a further question: is there anything that giving verbal form to experience, especially emotional experience, *does* to the nature of that experience? What happens to feeling when we put it into words? At an unpromising extreme, we might ask whether anything can be *ineffable*.

# 16.1 INEFFABILITY

It makes no difference to a table that we describe it. Nor does a table elude description. Does the same go for experiences? In particular, are emotions affected by being put into words? And can they elude that?

To begin at a very general level, consider a limit case, the idea of something's being *ineffable*. This might seem an obvious impossibility. For how could we ever recognize that something was ineffable if we could not specify what it was, thus achieving descriptive purchase on it? Wouldn't even that much confound our claim to find it ineffable? In any case, what could be the basis of such a claim? It is unsafe to infer that something is ineffable from the fact that it is hard to describe. For it might yield to someone more articulate than oneself (to whom one might exclaim, with a spasm of secret envy, "Exactly! *Just* what I wanted to say."); or it might yield to a more evolved conceptual system than we now possess. On the other hand, to insist that one or the other of these of these *must* be the case would be to treat the effability of all mental content as a priori; and that, too, might need defending.

We must concede from the outset that ineffability, if possible at all, will be a matter of degree rather than an either/or property. To speak of something of which we could say nothing whatsoever would be evidently paradoxical. Bare reference to any candidate for ineffability requires some semantic location, however crude. "The nameless dysphoria of dense depression", "an uncanny physical sensation", or "scene that beggars description" exemplify this kind of introductory description. And an "ineffable" theme may admit of yet further characterizations, perhaps of a quite searching order. That is, "ineffability" is actually compatible with there being something, even much, that we *could* say about its alleged theme; and it needs this.

What could be claimed impossible is conveying the *full* nature of this theme that we gesture at, invoking verbally its living presence.

Candidates for ineffability turn up in very different places. There are certainly aspects of the larger world, available theoretical descriptions of which have reasonably satisfiable truth-conditions but which we cannot represent outside of technical languages which we cannot make "comprehensible" to ourselves imaginatively. This is notably the case in higher reaches of geometry and mathematical physics (Bohr: "Anyone who isn't baffled by quantum theory doesn't understand it."). But however conceptually penetrable or impenetrable esoteric facts about the remoter physical reaches may prove, they are certainly not *manifest* to us. It is different with experience. If we turn from remote cosmic exotica to the contents of our experience as we receive it, perhaps no such problems arise or even could arise. For experience, it may seem, just *is* the display to us of what is happening and is the accessible par excellence. And it is easy to assume that what is on display is open to description or can express itself in ways that are open to description. Innocent common sense supposes that experience we are aware of is, trivially, open to us and can be conveyed perfectly satisfactorily in language that we and others understand. This optimism is shared by two of the major (and opposing) models of the mind. On the one hand, Cartesianism tried to conceive of the mind in terms of its subjectivity, in John McDowell's words, "a picture of subjectivity as a region of reality whose layout is transparent—accessible through and through—to the capacity for knowledge . . . there are no facts about the inner realm besides what is infallibly accessible to the newly recognized capacity to acquire knowledge".[1] On the other hand, many philosophers have subsequently come to accept the argument that to avert the absurdities of other minds scepticism, the images, ruminations, feelings, impulses, and the like, which Cartesians packed into the private receptacle of the soul, must be transparent publicly, at least in principle ("An inward state stands in need of an outward criterion."). On either view the mind displays itself, whether privately or publicly or both. And how could what is transparent elude description? Whether by saying or by showing, the mind must be conveyable. There may be secrets, but these are merely kept. They do not extend to the inexpressible.

I will suggest that such optimism about the descriptive availability of experience (verging on the a priori) is misguided. I will try to show that there can be aspects of experience that finally can evade our best efforts at formulating them. I do not urge this just out of theoretical interest, however. A further aim is to show that it has practical import. We may have weighty reasons for respecting this descriptive elusiveness of experience and for acceding to it. I will also suggest that the contrasting possibility also exists: we can sometimes have weighty reasons precisely for *giving* verbal shape to experience, reasons that go deeper than merely the need to communicate. Whether to "*say* it" can be an important choice.

---

[1] "Singular Thought and the Extent of Inner Space", in Philip Pettit and John McDowell (eds.), *Subject, Thought, and Context* (Oxford: Clarendon Press, 1986), 149–50.

## 16.2 REASONS FOR RETICENCE

At least three kinds of experiential content can resist verbalization. They are: affects, sensations, and aesthetic properties of things. Affects comprise emotions and desires, and here I will focus on these.

Of course, articulating an emotion may be easy and quite innocent ("I am so relieved you came."). In some cases, however, giving it verbal shape may be a less straightforward act and a less neutral one. Consider the person who is concerned to let an experience find its own form and keep that form (what exactly I really feel). This person may have an intuition shared by many from time to time: "Put words to this experience and you will lose it." Articulation somehow jeopardizes. The worry here is Orphic: turn to fix Eurydice in your sight and she will vanish. Such scruples needn't be groundless; indeed, there are three sorts of grounds that they may have. These are, in sum: (1) Adequacy. What one can say of the experience is not quite true of it, and therefore in saying this one is not being true *to* it. (2) Intervention. The experience itself is distorted by submitting it to description.—In short, description can be distorted or distorting. (3) Description can also be distancing, disengaging. What exactly are these risks?

(1) Adequacy. The cautionary intuition here is that an allurement, a germinating feeling, a subtle taste, may be violated by being forced into words. How? There are various possibilities. Formulation can harden what needs to be left supple and changeable. Or, a charm may rely on its being implicit rather than explicit; and words can have a forcing effect that profanes it. But perhaps the likeliest risk is of loss of distinctiveness, the loss of the integrity of the experience in its uniqueness, where that is something about it that matters (which it doesn't always). This risk of compromise by formulation is greatest where we rely on conventional language and the literal taxonomies. Public discourse needs and has language that can be understood by all, not just by Hamlet. Blunt instruments such as "fancies", "nice", "hothead", "flaky", "miffed", "chuffed", "yucky", "gutted", the standardized popular lingo of feeling, may suffice, perhaps all too well. Yet each common term sweeps together an assortment of hazily similar cases. Experience couched in popular idioms is absorbed into stereotypes and catchwords. Individuality is eclipsed. The most militant warnings against this taint of common coinage must be Nietzsche's:

The emergence of our experiences into our own consciousness, the ability to fix them and, as it were, exhibit them externally, increased proportionally with the need to communicate them to *others* by means of signs . . . given the best will in the world to understand ourselves as individually as possible, . . . each of us will always succeed in becoming conscious only of what is not individual but 'average'. Our thoughts are translated back into the perspective of the herd. Fundamentally, all our actions are altogether incomparably personal, unique, and infinitely individual; there is no doubt of that. But as soon as we translate them into consciousness *they no longer seem to be*... [T]he world of which we can become conscious is only a surface and sign world, a world that is made common and meaner...[2]

Fortunately, however, we need not be bullied by this into letting the dangers of absorption into the generic justify a blanket refusal to put words to experience. For there is always that further resource, figurative language, which precisely slips the traces of conventional usage. This offers to solve Nietzsche's problem at least (as his own writings regularly demonstrate). But even here, behind the triumphs, dangers lurk. Thus,

(2) Intervention. Were it ever true that being given verbal form *altered* experience, then *that* pre-verbalized experiential content would be logically unrepresentable, and the ineffable would indeed be no myth. It would follow from this that where one had reason to shield and preserve deliverances of feeling, desire, or imagination as they came, one would have good reason to hesitate putting them into words.

Has the intervention thesis any basis? Consider even our most sensitive linguistic resource for characterizing experience, figurative usage. Take as an example Sylvia Plath's use of the figure of the moon in her poem, 'The Rival'. Here, a word, "moon", is extracted from its conventional seating and used where there are no standing rules for its use, where, indeed, it should by rights lack meaningful use (women are incidental to planetary systems). An analogous attempt to cannibalize parts from one kind of precision machine for installation in another kind would court disaster. And indeed only certain of such semantic long shots themselves avoid senselessness. Yet there is such a thing as getting it right, although there are no rules for doing so. And the result can be uncannily illuminating. How in place out-of-place usage can be. In particular, these figures seem to capture a thing in its uniqueness. Ordinary predication is guided by similarities: *depressed, jealous, delectable, sinister,* and the rest of the taxonomy, are useful but rough-and-ready abstractions. They collect certain things into kinds (allowing us to relate them to others in mildly predictable ways). Figurative use, on the other hand, seems to present the thing as a particular instance of its kind. It inverts taxonomical discrimination. In this sense, figurative depiction is not really description. Thus, no one would suppose that Plath's use of the moon image works for every grim feeling towards every rival of every woman. It may (and need) work only *here*.

What does this familiar point show? Well, it might seem to weigh precisely *against* the claim that articulating experience alters it. Haven't I just admitted that figurative language, at any rate, does *not* "murder to abstract" but preserves the distinctiveness of what it illuminates?

---

[2] Friedrich Nietzsche, *The Gay Science*, ed. Bernard Williams (Cambridge: Cambridge University Press, 2001), 213.

This impression is misleading. To see why, compare figurative language to Gestalt perception. It could be tempting actually to identify the two. For very many figurative uses of words invoke visual images, images of physical things, in terms of which something may be seen (in an unfamiliar but resonant way), even something that is not physical (e.g., a belief as a *shield*). In both verbal figures and Gestalt figures a thing is presented in terms of an image brought from elsewhere. But how do verbal figures and perceptual Gestalts stand to the material on which they are brought to bear that gets configured by them? Very differently. On glimpsing the Necker cube we do not first take in an array of lines meeting in two dimensions and, finding this nothing much, then try configuring this array in three dimensions, to find that it emerges in three dimensions as any one of several cubical figures. Rather, the Necker cube looks cubical straightaway. It cannot but appear in Gestaltist form, since seeing that figure as an array of abutting lines in two dimensions is itself a Gestalt (one that is not easily achieved). In other words, there is as good as *no* Gestalt-independent content here. The wandering line that is the duck/rabbit, the porous splotch that is the young woman/old woman do not *already* have the character that the Gestalt serves to bring into view. If verbal figures were like this (perhaps as themselves Gestalt phenomena), the claim that their use alters what they are applied to would be wrong, because the antecedent content which they transfigure is insignificant. Despite the initial resemblance, verbal figures part company with perceptual Gestalts at just this point. A word used where it cannot be given its usual sense will not find a new one just anywhere. Success is highly context-dependent. Figurative language is not a free-for-all. To pick up sense, it relies on being able to find and convey character as distinct from conferring it, as Gestalt figures mainly do. To be sure, a perceptual Gestalt does depend to an extent on its antecedent sensory core: a sphere cannot be seen as cubical. But *this* antecedent content serves merely to *enable* the Gestalt. The Necker cube does not *do justice* to the lines out of which it is formed. In what it gets us to see (a cube), it does not bring out something in the drawing we might have missed, its third dimension; for it has no third dimension. The duck/rabbit doesn't take us insightfully to the heart of that winding line, to its lurking duckiness or bunniness. Verbal figures, by contrast, can and must depend on their "rightness".

Where a verbal figure secures purchase, then, there is an awaiting experiential content that is its subject. But we must now ask whether the use of the figure could depend on its rightness for that content whilst at the same time changing it? If we are able to tell whether a word, such as "blackness" in "blackness of heart", serves well to elicit a content that is independent of it, how could it be supposed simultaneously to rebound on that content and transform it? Here is how. The application of a verbal figure is not rule-guided. Nor does it trace to precise, specifiable points of attachment. There is an immediate grasp *that* the figure serves, but *how* is very elusive. The illuminative fertility of a good verbal figure is not delimitable in advance (one of its virtues). And like a refractive instrument, it may bring out aspects of the original that were not apparent before. This, however, ushers in a Wittgensteinian difficulty: there may be no way of settling whether *some* of what the figure plies me with is a revelation of the *original*, or an enticing artefact of the *figure* instead (as is a Gestalt effect). It can be unclear whether and where the figure is stealthily running away with me. Here, *is right* is hard to distinguish from *seems right*; and it is also hard to determine just *where* this problem arises. Once such language is at work, revelation cannot be safely and sharply distinguished from confabulation. Thus, in her sardonic invocation of the smiling moon, Sylvia Plath does designate certain points of significant attachment of this moon to the rival: "something beautiful but annihilating./Both of you are great light borrowers". And later: "The moon, too, abases her subjects." But these draw some of their force laterally from a wider field of unspoken meanings the moon carries into this context (no harvest moon, this), such as inaccessible isolation, barrenness, relentlessness, glare, and silence. This penumbra of flanking meanings gives the figure its rich allusiveness and tone. Delimiting these elements, much less separating them out singly or in subgroups to try their adequacy, is impossible.[3] So for some of what the original is made to seem by a telling verbal figure, there is effectively no difference between being right and seeming right, between being true and being captivating. Figurative language can create an evocative (and affective) momentum all of its own, and without our being able to tell just where. (Autobiographical poetry could be a treacherous undertaking.)

It is this problem that inevitably ramifies into the one we started with, the possibility of influence. For, how can the brilliant forcefulness of the figure of the moon, with its uncertain mixture of revelation and construction, actually avoid influencing the attitude it is being used to illuminate? Such a sophisticated and vivacious evocation compels to the point of acquiring a certain authority. How can this be reliably held at bay, safely apart from, in our example, the actual feeling towards the rival? After all, with the advent of the figure, much has happened to one's *view* of what one's feeling is about. May not some of what one feels about it not adjust accordingly, perhaps on the quiet? The point is that language could have this catalyzing power and that one cannot positively determine whether this might be happening, or where, or with what justice.

---

[3] Contrast with the case of seeing that a word is misspelled. In the first moment it just looks wrong, but one can then run through it letter by letter and separate out the misplaced letter from the others. The impinging meanings accompanying a figure cannot be broken down in such a precise manner.

Both the above levels of depiction, literal and figurative, raise the third problem with submitting experiences to formulation:

(3) Distancing. A person's experience is apt to matter to him primarily for how it is to *have* it. *Knowing* how it is to have this experience, in the sense of casting it descriptively, is a priority of his only in special cases. Being represented is, as such, no part of the constitutive concerns of melancholy or of longing, for instance. Hovering taxonomic curiosity is not normally a feature of immersion in experience. Indeed, a *description* of my attitude shifts me into a third-person perspective on my experience. To cast in words is to distance myself. For me to identify with a third person vantage point on myself (however true it might be) is for me to detach myself from my own natural vantage point, from the having of my attitudes and immersion in them. (That can sometimes have its uses, of course.) And even where I formulate myself in figurative language, with its accommodating subtleties, distancing still occurs. As we noted, the wit and the workings of figurative illumination are seductive in their own right and can occlude the original. I can become enrapt by the very image (and not necessarily because it is supposed to be of me). Aesthetic detachment is achieved.

In sum, there can be reasons for reticence, for jealously guarding some of one's mental life from the light of language, for recognizing leading edge of experience as ineffable and for accepting it as such. Scruples about this are not always dismissible as fear of exposure or fear of intimacy.

## 16.3 REASONS FOR GIVING VOICE

Curiously, however, there is another intuition about putting words to experience. It is the mirror image of the first. This is that taking the step of putting words to an attitude of mind hitherto harboured mutely, *augments* and *completes* it. The attitude is actually brought to fullness by being made explicit and proclaimed (even if only privately, to oneself). Formulation consolidates and even boosts; it is a vehicle of final emergence. This effect is not hard to notice but is hard to characterize. I will call this effect *Affirmation*. Affirmation would show that experiential content does allow of articulation and precisely *because* articulation changes it: it can come into its own precisely *though* formulation. In this sense, experience, except perhaps in primordial stages of formation, is *necessarily* effable.

Does Affirmation really exist? If so, what is it? Let us take a desire. Suppose a budding athlete was nurtured in older traditions of sportsmanship. Winning, he had learned to accept, is fine but takes its place alongside other aspects of playing. He is, however confronted daily with the fact that public acclaim, recognition, and money are increasingly focused exclusively on winners. And certainly victory—let's do call it that—*is* sweet. Over time this athlete grows inwardly restless. His susceptibilities strain against his values. Eventually it dawns on him that the craving for personal acclaim that he increasingly harbours isn't really just a foible, playing harmlessly around the edges of his desires. No, now it is what he is here for! He says to himself with fervour, "Yes that's it: what I really *want* is to win, to *WIN*, to be *A WINNER!*" This asseveration, with *that* word, is a personal watershed, like a conversion. (Compare "Oh, but that would be *theft!*" and note how the sheer utterance can consolidate the disincentive.)

Verbal avowal has a ritual quality that gives force to what is avowed, be this avowal public or private. Reciting the key words is more than just assenting to a description. In saying the Creed, declaring love, uttering sexual words during love-making, in vowing, and in oath-taking, Affirmation is at work. A negative example of it is found in Alban Berg's *Wozzeck* with Marie's stark declaration about herself, upon closing the Bible, which she has been reading in the wake of her adulterous betrayal of Wozzeck: "Ich bin ein *schlecht* Mensch!" (The words are made starker by being spoken rather than sung.) The effect I am calling Affirmation here is to be distinguished from the performative force, self-encouragement, or the social impacts that uttering the formulation may also, and relatedly, achieve. Again, Affirmation can be mimicked, self-deceptively, out of some need to see oneself in a given light; and it can fail. But it can also be real and none of these things, as in Marie's self-confession.

One way Affirmation might be thought an illusion is this. The impression that an attitude gains *through* being avowed might be a confusion of cart with horse. Maybe people give voice to attitudes of already mature power to which they just giving vent. Here, the robustness and finality of attitude issues in the avowal rather than issuing from it. This can undoubtedly happen, but the question for us is not what the articulation of experience might reflect but what, if anything, happens *through* it.

Just how could formulation achieve Affirmation? There are five possibilities. (1) *Identification*: so long as the attitude is left to itself to grow, change, or fade as it will, a certain detachment from it exists. Avowing it, claiming ownership over it, closes this gap. Thereby, I give myself over to it. (2) *Consolidation*: to settle on a state is to suspend openness to change and to ambivalence. I commit myself thereby and henceforth to orienting myself through it (e.g., in the alignment of other relevant attitudes). Accordingly, (3) *Reorientation*: upon identifying, this and nothing else as my attitude, I see myself as related to the world in the appropriate way. This could amount to a Gestalt switch. Suddenly things fall into place in a new way. And they emit a re-enforcing echo. And so, (4) *Initiation*: the label with which I now baptize myself is also like a key; with it I may join myself to a larger cultural system (which, in my avowing, I endorse), and this, as I do it, is exciting, for better or worse. Once I *say*, not just mutely recognize in my heart of hearts, "All right, then, I *am* JEALOUS", I find myself belonging to a world in which I may be what they once called a "cuckold" (a figure of pathos wearing horns that others can see), in which I deserve sympathy I may not get from anyone but myself, though it is a world in which I do have certain entitlements, such as tolerated ventings of bitterness, or dramatic and permissibly impetuous actions. (5) *Transfiguration*: Affirmation is at its most powerful when the labels of common language are avoided in favour of the figurative characterization of the object of the attitude. Love poetry and elegiac poetry are obvious examples. Affirmation here could be the feeling of the massive powers of evocation that language can release. My attitude seems reflected back, transformed in the captivating quality of the language. It becomes dazzling and achieves memorial form. Sappho wrote,

> As a whirlwind
> Swoops on an oak
> Love shakes my heart[4]

The very utterance of such lines could itself be a voice in that whirlwind.

Looking back, a certain picture emerges. It seems that there can be reasons *both* for putting words to experience *and* for forbearing to do this. The characteristics of avowal that seem to underwrite each of these conflicting approaches seem, however, to be much the same! As I said earlier, curious. There are no obvious general rules for deciding whether to articulate a feeling or to forbear. Many things will be relevant and will vary from case to case. But deliberation and judgement are apt to be rather lumbering here. It requires a knack for telling quickly what is called for, a knack that belongs to the art of living.[5]

---

[4] *Sappho: A New Translation* (Berkeley: University of California Press, 1958), 44.

[5] It is interesting to relate these two contrasting approaches to articulating feeling to *sincerity* as understood by Stuart Hampshire in his memorable paper, "Sincerity and Single Mindedness" (in Stuart Hampshire, *Freedom of the Individual* [London: Harper & Row, 1965]). For that relation is problematic. An attitude is sincere, according to Hampshire, when it engages the mind as a whole. It carries with it all other relevant attitudes, is held with all one's heart and soul, as the saying goes. Where an attitude is sincere, one's mind is not partially disengaged from it or engaged but troubled by reservation or contrary tendencies. This may be an aspect of depth in emotion (see D. Pugmire, *Sound Sentiments* [Oxford: Oxford University Press, 2005], Chapter 2]). Like most of us, Hampshire seems to regard sincerity as a virtue. In terms of the present discussion, however, it is Affirmation that most closely exemplifies Hampshirean sincerity. Thus, in Affirmation ownership of the emotion is claimed, and responsibility for it taken; and it is accorded connection with the attendant semantic and cultural systems. Reticence, on the other hand, seems precisely not to qualify. For it attends to, and tends, what is particular to the experience at hand, insulating it from ambient fields of concern. If there is ever a case for doing that along the lines sketched in this article, perhaps we must conclude that sincerity is not always a virtue after all. It may be that sometimes the whole mind should hesitate to rush in where angels fear to tread.

# 16.4 A Concluding Theoretical Perspective

The opposing approaches of Reticence and Affirmation reflect concerns for, respectively, the isolation of an experience in its singularity from the standing mass of one's intentional attitudes and its energizing integration into that. This is the contrast that has ineffability at one end of it. That is, isolation and integration form the limits on a scale, with ineffability lying at the former (never quite reached) end and explicitness (often reached) at the other. Now, the conceptual content of an experience can also be understood in terms of this contrast. So perhaps the ineffability of some emotional feeling, which Reticence wants to respect, can be understood in terms of unconceptualized content in experience. Ineffable experience would be experience that had some content that could not be specified conceptually. Tim Crane's treatment of the non-conceptual content of experience (in his paper of that name) allows us to see how this might be.

For a given intentional state to contain concepts, Crane argues, is for there to be other intentional states to which one is thereby committed, e.g., beliefs (the "holism of the intentional"). A concept carries, and is even defined by, a pattern of inferential commitments.[6] To possess the concept *cheese*, for example, is to believe cheese to be a foodstuff and that it is made of milk and offers one or another of a loosely grouped set of looks, fragrances, and tastes, for which it may be desired. Such a battery of intentional attitudes follows the concept wherever it is applied and constitutes its generality of sense. Those intentional attitudes that are composed of concepts are those containing the dispositions to make the relevant inferences (of the types mentioned that give the concept its content). Now this also tells us what it is for the content of an intentional state to be *non*-conceptual:

Since possessing a concept is being in intentional states whose contents are appropriately inferentially related, then a state without conceptual content is one whose contents are not so related. So in order to be in such a state, one does not have to be in other inferentially related states of the kind that give the contents of beliefs their conceptual structure.[7]

The awareness of something for its inferential relations requires focus on its generality, as distinct from its individuality (Socrates is a man and mortal). But if need be, the latter can often be categorized into the former reasonably innocuously. Thus, non-conceptualized experience is not the same as non-conceptualizable experience. It is normally possible to articulate "whole" experiences conceptually if need be.[8] But I suggest that an experience might be unconceptualizable at least temporarily if its contents were sufficiently novel or exotic (as in Crane's example

---

[6] Tim Crane, "The Nonconceptual Content of Experience", in Tim Crane (ed.), *The Contents of Experience* (Cambridge: Cambridge University Press, 1992), 12.

[7] Ibid., 14.    [8] Ibid., 11.

of a child's first sighting of a cathode ray tube), where one's grasp at the time did not extend much beyond "that thing". It would not (yet) elicit a wider field of inferential commitments. More radically, an experience could be unconceptualiz-able altogether, at least in parts, and there ineffable, to the extent that it just was not a token of an inferentially freighted type. This might apply to that in the content of an experience that is fresh. Clearly this will happen the more individuated and unprecedented the content of that experience is. Unconceptualizable does not mean opaque or even mute, however. We have seen that the individuating aspect of a thing can offer purchase (albeit sometimes uncertain purchase) to those uses of language that break their frame of semantic convention (comprising their defining inferential commitments) to show the content of experience rather than to say it.

Where does this leave us? Our position with regard to formulating our feelings verges on the paradoxical. Much can hang in particular cases on whether we allow the conceptualizing and integrative effects of Affirmation or hold these in suspen-sion.—And once released by Affirmation, the genie cannot be put back into the bottle. Whichever way we turn, this is definitely something we choose and do or let ourselves do: it does not just happen. And yet, it seems vital that this doing be spontaneous. It would be interesting to understand just how that is managed.

# CHAPTER 17

# EPISTEMIC EMOTIONS

## ADAM MORTON

I could have stopped there. I could have chosen ignorance, but I did what you would have done—what you've already done, if you've read this far. I chose knowledge instead. Most of us will. We'll choose knowledge no matter what, we'll maim ourselves in the process, we'll stick our hands in the flames for it if necessary. Curiosity is not our only motive: love or grief or despair or hatred is what drives us on.
Margaret Atwood *The Blind Assassin*

Emotions serve vital functions in human psychology. If we could not fear and hope we would not make plans, if we could not love we would not make deep long-lasting social bonds. What about thinking: do we need emotions for that? Most readers of this chapter will have heard of the neurological evidence, highlighted in Damasio's work, that people with damage to areas of the brain associated with emotions often have diminished capacities to exercise some kinds of judgement (see Damasio 1994). So it is not implausible that there are links in human constitution between emotion and thought. But that is a very weak point. Is it the emotions themselves whose absence derails these cognitive processes, or is there something about some neural circuits involved in some emotions that also makes them important in some aspects of decision-making? Is it conceivable that a person

This chapter benefited from my conversations with Stephanie Buri Choy, and my correspondence with Peter Goldie.

could be cured of her judgemental deficits but retain her emotional ones? The connections may be biologically important but conceptually incidental.

I suspect this is not the case, and at the end of this chapter I shall return to the issue. My focus, though, will be on one particular kind of thinking, the acquisition of beliefs. I will be asking whether there are emotions that play an important role in our attempts to acquire beliefs correctly, beliefs that we have reason to continue holding and which serve the purposes for which we acquired them. In this case, I shall argue, there are emotions that play an important and hard–to-replace role. They are conceptually vital. That is, I shall defend the existence of epistemic emotions. Moreover, I will suggest, there are emotions that are specifically directed at epistemic ends.

Some candidates come immediately to mind. Curiosity, intellectual courage, love of truth, wonder, meticulousness, excitement, humility. One might have doubts whether all or any of these are really essential to epistemic thought, rather than being often incidentally helpful. But before we grapple with that question there is the question of whether their relevance is as emotion, or as some other kind of state. In particular, these names can often denote virtues as much as emotions. So first we need to understand the difference between virtues and emotions.

## 17.1 Emotion, virtue, character

'Generosity' can refer to three subtly but importantly different things. A person with a generous character exhibits a particular pattern of activity. She is sensitive to the situations of others and will suppress her own benefit or glory for their sake. She is particularly aware of situations where her greater resources can benefit a less well endowed person, and can manage them to that person's benefit. Someone has intellectual generosity if she is more concerned that discoveries are made and issues clarified than that she get credit for it, and if she takes account of other people's needs to have their contributions recognized in various ways. The standard example is priority disputes: an intellectually generous person is not overly concerned that she rather than others is recorded as the first to have an idea. More directly epistemic is her tendency to solve problems with whatever method works best, including methods that stem from rival sources. (This is an epistemic virtue in the stricter sense of Hookway 2003, and not merely in the sense of some virtue epistemologists, according to which any epistemically useful capacity or skill is an epistemic virtue.) A person can have a generous character even if she gives too much to others, for example slowing down a research project by insisting on including the work of an incompetent colleague. In that case she is indulgent or soft-hearted. Such people do not have the virtue of generosity. Or, to put it differently, their generosity is not a virtue.

Contrasted with both the state of character and the virtue is the emotion. A person who has exhibited admirable generosity may say 'I didn't *feel* generous'. In crediting a rival view she took herself just to be functioning in her normal scientific mode. Her emotional experience lacked a characteristic sense of giving something for nothing. It would be too simple to identify the emotion with the presence of the feeling. But there are other reasons, as we will see, to take emotions to be separate from both virtues and traits of character.

Generosity is far from alone. Similar remarks could be made about courage, optimism, carefulness, humility, and many others. (Courage in particular functions rather differently as a character trait, a virtue, and an emotion. But courage is in some ways a misleading example of a virtue.) Even when we do not often think of an emotion corresponding to a character trait we can often on reflection find one. A responsible person will sometimes, not always, have a feeling of responsibility to the person, intellectual topic, or tradition, they are concerned with. A lazy person will sometimes feel lazy. Moreover a character trait can always be associated with a virtue, the virtue of exhibiting the relevant disposition at the right times to the right degree. Sometimes this will mean never: the character trait of cruelty is perhaps never appropriately indulged, so if we want to speak of a virtue of cruelty it would be the limit case of a virtue that consists in never unleashing the disposition. But there are many traits of character that are useful on particular occasions, even when it is not traditional to think of there being corresponding virtues. Thus we may talk of a virtue of (appropriate) anger, meaning the virtue of becoming angry when it serves a good purpose, to a degree that serves that purpose well. We might even speak of a virtue of panic, meaning a capacity to stop thinking and take instinctive evasive action *when required*. We could usefully speak of the virtue of appropriate intellectual sloppiness, meaning the capacity to cut corners when there are more important things to think about. We do not standardly include anger, panic, and sloppiness on our list of virtues because according to the folk wisdom that formed the list our need to learn not to give in to anger and panic or slide into sloppiness is greater than our need to learn to reveal them when needed. The folk wisdom may often be right, but we should not assume that it always is.

For any emotion we can define a corresponding character trait, namely the disposition to have that emotion readily. Generosity is showed by generous people, though people who are not generous by character can on occasion experience generosity. Confidence is shown by confident people, among others. And with a character trait we can associate the virtue of exhibiting it at the right times, though it may not be a virtue on traditional lists. There is the virtue of being fearful at the right times; it is a vivid form of prudence. There is the virtue of being confident at the right times, a form of self-respect.

So it is not surprising that the words often do triple duty. Character links to virtue links to emotion. Those links mask deeper differences, though. The three are very different kinds of states. A character trait is a report or a prediction. It says 'this is how this person acts'. Sometimes it says 'this is how this person thinks': the person may be careful or meticulous or imaginative. Virtues are normative concepts; they pick out dispositions to profitable, correct, or admirable patterns of action or thought. Both traits of character and virtues are long-term states; one cannot be honest for just a moment, though one can act honestly for once in one's life. Moreover they apply to people over longish stretches of time, so that a sleeping person can still be a restless character. Emotions on the other hand are ocurrent things; they happen at particular moments and through determinate stretches of time, during which they have causal influence on the person. As a result they can be associated with conscious affects as, potentially, any occurrent state can. So we can have feelings of being brave or considerate or careful, just as we can be consciously aware of a thought forming or a desire nagging. Most significantly, emotions are motives; they cause behaviour by making particular desires and beliefs salient. (For emotions as salience-making motives see de Sousa 1987 and Greenspan 1988. For emotions versus virtues see Morton 2002. For the possibility that the three-way contrast is not enough, and we need to distinguish emotion-like states that are neither emotions, virtues, nor character-traits, see Goldie 2006.)

Now we are in a position to see more clearly why the answer to our question 'are there epistemic emotions?' might not be any interesting form of 'Yes'. In order to acquire beliefs successfully people need to be careful, curious, imaginative, and responsible, all at the right moments and to the right degree. That much is fairly uncontroversial. It does not follow that people have to experience any emotion characteristic of care, curiosity, or the rest, though no doubt often they do. The virtue is what is required, not the emotion. There is plenty of room for emotion; since actions at particular times play a particular role in the nature of virtues: the appropriate degree of the disposition for a particular time. One can have a feeling at that crucial time, and it may be a feeling that is characteristic of a particular emotion. That does not mean that it is the emotion that is doing the epistemic work. It may not even mean that the whole emotion is present, whatever work it is doing, rather than a characteristic feeling at a moment crucial to a virtue which shares the emotion's name.

That is the sceptical possibility: there may be no essential epistemic emotions. Virtues may be the epistemically relevant states. The aim of the rest of this chapter is to make a dint in this possibility.

## 17.2 EPISTEMIC MOTIVATION

Imagine an extraordinarily well-trained and malleable young scientist. From early on in her career she has been mentored by older scientists who not only are top researchers in her field, but are also pedagogically sharp and sensitive. The result is that she has a superlative grasp of research techniques, is aware of the live problems at the cutting edge of her subject, and has the patience and intelligence to do very good work. There is one flaw, however. She does not care about the subject. She has no curiosity. She wants a career, and she knows that with her background she is more likely to succeed by pushing some lines of theory than others, so she is capable of a form of scientific partisanship. But she does not find herself wanting the truth to turn out one way rather than another in more than this instrumental way. She does not sometimes wonder whether lines of enquiry that are, with good reasons, disparaged by her research group might not in the end give important clues to the underlying processes she is investigating.

This scientist may well go on to do excellent work, and make significant discoveries. She may become eminent. But it is unlikely that she will lead her subject in radically new directions. Nor that she will be the one to find the new way ahead if current approaches stall, or to see deep subtle flaws in those current approaches, or willingly take her work in a direction that seems to her important but risks a lifetime of obscurity. She is rather like the child prodigy musician with rare skills and a marvellous technique, lacking only a love of music.

There are emotions she lacks, at any rate with respect to her chosen field. She does not feel wonder at the connections between facts that she can glimpse through the data. She does not feel curiosity about what scientists two hundred years later will have arrived at. Nor does she feel momentary scepticism—in everyday language a loaded attitude rather than a philosophical position—about whether current techniques can unlock the further secrets of the topic. These are rather grand emotions with rather grand objects. We could have brought them closer to the ground by choosing a research field for her and supplying some details. But they are emotions that people feel in everyday life when they care what the truth is about everyday topics. Good examples of dispassionate curiosity are provided by our reactions to mysteries about public figures publicized in the media. A film star is charged with murder: is he guilty? We may have no bias either way but the evidence pro and con is tantalizing. We hope that a new piece of evidence will settle the matter one way or another; we are upset when a promising lead proves to be a hoax. Our attitude to mysteries in history is similar. I have no preference between the various hypotheses about why the Viking settlements in Greenland died out, but I would like to know which of them is right. I may feel vaguely disconcerted when a promising explanation turns out to be impossible. We feel all these emotions with respect to even more familiar questions too. Who keeps leaving half-filled cups of coffee in the photocopier room?

These are clear cases of emotion, because they involve mental events that occur at particular times, activate deep instinctive routines, and motivate us to courses of action. They connect with both the limbic system and the frontal lobes. We can be conscious of many of them, and may express this by saying 'I feel', and the feelings can be intense—joyful, bitter, exhilarating—or nagging. In ascribing one of these states to a person we are providing material that could be used in causal explanations of her thoughts and actions: we are alluding not just to typical patterns of the person's behaviour but to events that can be part causes of particular items of behaviour.

Some of these emotions are linked to virtues—curiosity, originality, caution—but they are not redundant given the virtues. The connection here has to be stated carefully. After all, our almost-perfect scientist had a large clutch of epistemic virtues, enough to equip her to do well in her field and make real discoveries. Even her lack of curiosity is qualified; she wants to find out the answers to many questions, though she wants the answers for reasons that are not purely epistemic. And all scientists and all inquirers of any sort are like this. We are motivated, most of the time, by the need to solve particular problems, and by the need to get ahead with our occupations. If we are in knowledge-gathering occupations then the requirements of our jobs dominate our researches. And in our researches we show real epistemic virtues. So the scientist I described is not a monster. What she is lacking is subtle, and will show up only in particular circumstances. (Cases like this are discussed in Stocker 2004.)

The normal connections are these. We have instrumentally epistemic emotions: we are curious about the answers to questions of practical importance to us. To satisfy our curiosity we can inquire, of course; we can exercise our epistemic virtues in the required ways. We can also become curious about the truth of various propositions that arise in the course of the enquiry. But, we can investigate these without being curious about them, since we can be guided just by our need to know the answers to the main question, and our curiosity about that is generated by the practical problem that made it important. Most people, in fact, in most inquiries, do become curious about some of the questions that arise in the course of a practically motivated enquiry. Never about all of them. And most enquiry can proceed without these secondary curiosities.

Two additional factors complicate the picture. First there is curiosity not generated by any practical concern. It isn't always a noble thing. For example people are often very nosy about other people's lives: they feel frustrated if they cannot discover interesting facts about others' emotions and habits, and they feel disappointed if the facts they discover are too ordinary and unremarkable. (We are all like this to some extent, though it can become pathological.) But people are also commonly interested in political, religious, historical, or scientific questions quite independently of any practical needs. Different people have different amounts of curiosity for different topics, of course.

Related to this is the second complicating factor, the peculiar occupation of professional knower: detectives, scientists, scholars, fortune-tellers. People with such occupations are employed to discover truths about particular topics. Usually someone employs them and there are some kinds of information that they are expected to come up with. However, often in such an occupation people are motivated to discover truths about particular topics, not because they will lead to solutions of practical problems for the researchers themselves, but because it is part of the job description to do so. The truths they discover may be of practical importance to other people. The motivation of professional enquirers is often practical in an indirect way: they want to come up with answers in order to further their careers or satisfy their employers.

One connection between disinterested curiosity and professional enquiry is that some professional inquirers think of themselves as primarily motivated by disinterested curiosity. Physics is 'natural philosophy', a special kind of love of wisdom, taking wisdom to consist in the possession of important truths about nature. No doubt there is a wide range of motivations here, between pure love of wisdom and calculated professional advancement. No doubt enquirers have self-images that can deviate from the actual facts about their motivation, in either direction. And some forms of enquiry require and generate epistemic virtues that are linked to disinterested curiosity. For example, when in the course of an investigation into whether some theory is true an interesting possibility arises, whose truth is not obviously relevant to the theory, a good scientist will be interested in whether the possibility is true. (But, life and resources being short, a good scientist will also be careful not to let the main investigation get side-tracked by such things.)

The aim of this section has been to show how epistemic emotions such as curiosity, intellectual disappointment, and fascination can serve to motivate aspects of many enquiries. From what we have seen so far, though, they do not seem to be essential for many of these aspects. A person utterly devoid of curiosity would need to be strongly motivated in non-epistemic ways in order to function well as an enquirer, but such strong motivation does not seem to be impossible. Such a person might be blocked from the most creative and far-reaching aspects of enquiry, but for most everyday purposes—as far as we have seen already—the absence of epistemic emotion seems to make things harder rather than impossible. Probing a little deeper into the nature of enquiry may clarify the picture further.

## 17.3  KNOWLEDGE: RELEVANT ALTERNATIVES

When you are curious about something you want to know the truth about it. You don't just want to have a belief, and perhaps even not just a belief that happens to be true. Large amounts of philosophy have been directed at the question of what is special about knowledge, and why we should value it (Sosa 2007). My aim here is to draw connections between the concept of knowledge and core epistemic emotions.

One obvious connection is that knowledge is what slakes curiosity. Imagine a situation in which conclusive evidence is hard to come by. For example you want to know whether a particular coin is biased. It was supplied by a gambler you do not trust, whose character you are curious about in any case. You flip the coin seven times and it comes down H,H,T,H,T,T,T, which is well within the expected range for seven tosses of a fair coin. But there is a very slight preponderance of tails, so you do not rule out completely the possibility that the coin is biased to tails. You are offered a bet on the coin and you choose heads. For the amount you are betting it seems to you that you are sure enough that the coin is at any rate not biased towards tails. But you wouldn't say you knew this. To take yourself as knowing it you would have to toss the coin more times, or check into its history. Doing this will take time, or expense, and you may be willing to pay this price—not in order to be in a reasonable position to place a small bet but in order to slake your curiosity. For many practical purposes probability is enough, but our curiosity is not satisfied until we take ourselves to know.

There are many accounts of knowledge current in epistemology. One of them, the relevant alternatives theory, provides a frame on which many contemporary ideas about knowledge can be presented. According to this account when a person forms a belief there are various possibilities which have to be excluded if the belief is to count as knowledge. For example to know that my bicycle is in the shed I may have to rule out the possibility that the friend who borrowed it yesterday did not return it as promised, or that it has been stolen. Without some assurance on these points my belief is naive complacency or wishful thinking rather than knowledge. On almost all accounts I do not have to exclude the possibility that the bike was stolen by aliens, or even that it has been confiscated by my bank. These are not relevant alternatives in my situation, or at any rate they are not unless my situation has some bizarre elements. Exactly what makes an alternative relevant in a given situation is a subtle issue that divides various approaches (Dretske 2000; Lewis 1996.)

Sometimes the fact that an alternative ought to be excluded is a mechanical matter, a matter of good epistemic training. Sometimes, though, it requires that a person be subtly in tune with the demands of the situation. Suppose for example that you are in charge of a project to establish whether the chemicals used in the manufacture of a brand of babies' bottles are carcinogenic. You are supervising a team of researchers who have to analyse the plastics that result from the manufacturing process, test them in cell culture models, test them on animals, investigate breakdown paths for them in terms of chemical theory, construct computer models for their interaction with various enzymes, and more. The aim is to be able to say that you know that the chemical is or is not safe. You clearly have to check such things as that the composition of the bottles really is what it is claimed to be, and whether familiar digestive enzymes degrade the plastics into well-known carcinogens. But there are many other things you may have to investigate. Suppose that preliminary results suggest that the plastics interact with mild acids to produce a family of chemicals that are not thought to be harmful but which have been very little studied since they are rarely associated with food. Should you get into issues about the basic chemistry of this family? Suppose that the results for one kind of enzyme are different for those for others: should you check whether the person charged with doing that set of experiments is less thorough than the rest of your team?

You will have difficult decisions to make about which possibilities to investigate. You are likely to *worry* about some of them; you will *be haunted* by the thought that some subtle interaction may have gone unnoticed. You will feel *responsible* for the accuracy of your results and the performance of your team; you will be *concerned* about anomalies for which you have no good explanation. You will be *fascinated* by preliminary results that suggest that the picture is not what you originally thought, though you may also be worried by them. You will be *attracted to* lines of investigation that might settle questions that arise during the project, and *wary* of others because of their potentiality to distract your attention or waste your time. You will be *satisfied* that you have ruled out some worrying possibilities, and *unsatisfied* with respect to your investigation of others.

Worry (haunting, obsession), concern (responsibility), interest (fascination, attraction, wariness), (dis)satisfaction. These are epistemic emotions that are linked to a common theme. That is the situation of a person facing a large network of possible topics to investigate. The topics branch into subtopics, possibly endlessly. She has questions that she wants the answers to, and usually reasons why she wants them, and needs to define and carry out a strategy for getting to a satisfying answer in a limited time given limited resources. So she has to look ahead, and at suitable times take stock. When looking ahead she will fasten herself on some lines of investigation, to the exclusion of others; and when taking stock she will consider whether she has fastened on and excluded the right ones. It is like any other complex project requiring a large personal investment: there are delicate questions of emphasis and strategy, and some of them require long-term attention and mobilization of resources. We could not manage such projects without emotions of self-management.

The question that haunts this chapter is still with us. Grant that when people undertake serious epistemic projects they experience emotions such as those I have listed. Grant even that unless they experienced these emotions they could not carry out these projects as intended: they would not end up with knowledge. Does it follow that it is the emotions as emotions that are essential, rather than the associated epistemic virtues? The emotions might just be side-effects. (The same questions can arise with morally as well as epistemically relevant emotions.) I think we can put this worry to rest in the case of emotions associated with finding and eliminating relevant alternatives.

Consider epistemic worry. The scientist of a few paragraphs back, investigating possible carcinogens in baby bottles, may early in her investigation have considered the possibility that a well-established carcinogen is produced by interaction of the plastic with normal food acidity or with digestive enzymes. She may have investigated the obvious pathways by which it might be produced and have satisfied herself that they do not lead to it. But that does not show that it does not result from some unobvious pathway. To deal with that, she will remain alert for chemical processes involving the carcinogen and its precursors. She will notice them when they arise in the course of other considerations, and she will try to imagine possible such processes. Most likely this alertness and this imagination cannot be carried out at one moment and separately from other investigations: they have to be a constant background theme, ready to surface at opportune moments. That is to say, they have to *worry* the person, haunt her in fact. It is not just that the person has to have the epistemic virtue of worrying about the right possibilities at the right moments and to the right degree. The worry has to work on her as epistemic motive. It has to nag.

Worry gives a model for the operation of other epistemic concerns, such as standing curiosity or concern. Suppose that in the course of investigating the possible carcinogenicity of the bottles, our chemist discovers that an enzyme that should be disintegrating a certain protein is not. This fact seems irrelevant to the problem at hand, but it is intriguing. It would be wrong to divert the investigation to it, but it is too interesting to ignore. So she remains vigilant, hoping that something the research team discovers will give a clue to the anomaly. Her vigilance is driven by curiosity about the anomaly, and hope that they will come across something relevant to it. The curiosity is not a side-effect of the epistemic virtue but a factor intrinsic to its operation. And it operates through a pressure on the person's patterns of awareness, what she notices and ignores, so that it comes with a characteristic feeling.

Knowledge requires exploration of a maze of possibilities, some consistent with the fact that is known, and some incompatible with it. Some of this exploration is impossible for us unless we are prompted, pushed, and goaded by epistemic emotions such a worry, fascination, and curiosity. The relation between the emotions and the virtues here is not unique to the epistemic domain. The normal human operation of many virtues involves the activation of emotions that move the agent to the required pattern of action. Kindness for example usually involves the sentiment of affection; fair-mindedness often involves the sense of injustice; courage that of outrage. In none of these cases is the emotion always required for the operation of the virtue, but normal human beings would find it hard to sustain the virtue if they were not capable of the emotion. So too with knowledge. There are many circumstances where unmotivated epistemic virtues need not be driven by epistemic emotions, but where a subtle or complex network of alternative possibilities needs to be explored, creatures at all like us will need to care about what facts they hope to discover.

# 17.4 RESPONSIBILITY

In the case of the chemist the investigation was not driven by pure scientific curiosity. A carcinogen in baby bottles is a deadly threat, and if the scientist has ignored some factor that later proves to have awful consequences she is likely to feel a kind of epistemic guilt. She will feel that she ought to have known better (see Buri Choy 2008). We usually have a practical reason for enquiry, and very often this reason involves the welfare of others. We are then responsible for finding out truths relevant to their concerns, and we will be concerned not to fail in this responsibility. Again there is a distinction between virtues and emotions. One can exercise the virtue of epistemic responsibility without experiencing any emotion. The emotion I shall focus on here is that of anticipated remorse: one feels a foretaste of the regretful feelings consequent on not living up to one's responsibility, which spurs on one's diligence. Since the concern is with epistemic responsibility, the remorse in question is that of not having carried out an enquiry as one should have.

The responsibility for an object of concern, typically another person, can be separated from the responsibility for an aspect of the enquiry. Consider a baby-sitter. He is spending the evening in the house of a small child, and his core responsibility is to ensure that the child survives the evening unharmed. There are things that he needs to be informed of in order to do this, such as whether the child is awake or asleep, whether the child's breathing and temperature are normal, whether the house is on fire. Most of these are easy to ascertain, but the babysitter is adolescent and easily distracted, particularly by the presence of his girlfriend who drops around, against the wishes of the child's parents, for an evening of smooching and television watching. Suppose that during a two-hour stretch the babysitter does not check on the child's well-being or pay attention to the condition of the house. The babysitter is acting irresponsibly. Since he has not yet developed habits of responsible action the easiest way for him to act responsibly would be to feel concerned about the child's welfare in a quasi-parental way. He would then have a crude emotion of responsibility which would generate a rudimentary virtue.

If the babysitter had felt responsible for the child's well-being, he would have paid less attention to his girlfriend and more to the state of the child and the house. He would have taken on a responsibility to stay informed about the child and the house. In this way the emotion of moral responsibility, with a particular person and situation as its objects, generates an emotion of epistemic responsibility, with the gathering of information as its objects. Like other epistemic emotions, the feeling of responsibility can instigate open-ended projects with unspecific aims: the babysitter may become curious about where the fire extinguisher and the first aid kit are and whether they have been well maintained.

The emotion of responsibility is associated with epistemic worry. If you feel responsible for knowing something you worry about possible leads you have not explored and possibilities you have not excluded. These may nag at you, leading to scrupulous or obsessive investigation, checking, and imagination. You need to set your mind at rest. Sometimes the result is desirable, in that the person proceeds in an epistemically responsible way. Sometimes it is an obsessive distraction from more important things. But whether or not it is functioning as an epistemic virtue, it is an epistemic emotion.

## 17.5 EPISTEMIC CONSEQUENCES OF NON-EPISTEMIC EMOTIONS

Most emotions are non-epistemic. Fear, anger, or sadness, for example, are not usually directed at knowing or believing but at the threatening, offending, or disappointing thing or situation. But most emotions also generate an interest in knowing. If you are afraid you want to know how to get away, and if you are angry you want to know how to hurt. Very often this interest in knowing generates an epistemic emotion. If you are afraid of something you may have a very live curiosity about ways of avoiding it, which may direct your intellectual energies in the typical way of epistemic emotions. This may become obsessive, and may spread to an interest in everything about the feared object; it is not unusual for people to have an abnormally intense interest in things they fear or hate. There is a natural rationale for this: if something is dangerous then any information about it might be useful. Of course for finite creatures like us the time and effort expended on gathering not obviously useful information about dangerous things should be proportionate to how dangerous they are. Very often the focus on the object of the emotion is disproportionate. Then the epistemic emotion is irrational, but it is still an epistemic emotion. All the more reason for distinguishing between emotions and virtues.

Emotions are complex states combining cognitive and affective elements in ways that are discussed by Deigh's and Roberts' chapters in this book. An emotion nearly always has an associated cognitive aspect: a collection of beliefs and desires concerning the object of the emotion with themes characteristic of the emotion. In crude stereotype if you fear something you believe it is dangerous and want to get away from it, and if you hate something you believe it is bad and want to hurt it. As many writers (for example Goldie 2000) have pointed out, these formulas are often too crude. A person can have a fear of a particular spider even though they believe that it is completely harmless. And their desire to get away may be motivated more by the unpleasantness of the sensation of fear than by any intrinsic benefit of distance from the tiny harmless creature; in fact, the person may say that they do not want to avoid the spider though they find themselves tending to move away. In many such cases what we have instead of full-blown cognitive states are cognitive tendencies: the person afraid of the tiny spider will be more receptive to evidence that it is poisonous than if she was not afraid, and will be more interested in random facts about it. These are likely to be manifested in epistemic emotions. The arachnophobe will look frequently at the spider, notice when and where it moves, and will go out of her way to open a book entitled *One Hundred Small but Deadly Spiders*. These are epistemic strategies, the strategies that would result from epistemic emotions of interest and curiosity about the spider.

Often an emotion has no conscious affect. This is most likely when we do not want to know that we are subject to it, as when we dislike a person that we ought to love. Quite often when this is the case the unconscious emotion will generate an epistemic emotion of which the person is conscious, and this will be a clue for the person about the existence of the primary emotion. The person who does not know that they have come to dislike their spouse may find that they are fascinated by divorce advice stories in popular magazines, find themselves trying to remember the plot of the old Marcello Mastroianni film *Divorzio all'italiana*, and listen very patiently to friends' stories of the escapades that led to the end of their marriages. In typical Freudian style this may generalize into an interest in escape in general, so that facts and stories about getaways become more interesting to the person. Someone who does not know that she is afraid of men may ask herself why her career as a biologist is driven by an enquiry into the hypothesis that groups of females need to incorporate males as a protection against other groups of females armed with males. The epistemic emotion is often easier to detect than the underlying hatred or fear because our patterns of enquiry cannot function without a lot of conscious input, so that we are often aware of their general direction. Of course the inferences from the epistemic strategy first to the epistemic emotion and then to the underlying emotion are dangerous and fallible. We are often wrong about what we feel, especially when we are driven by theories about ourselves. And of course many epistemic motions are not generated in anything like this way.

# 17.6 CONCLUSION: THE PERSISTENCE
## OF CURIOSITY

The aim of this chapter has been to defend the existence and necessity of epistemic emotions. At the beginning I referred to the fact that deficits in the capacity to feel emotions are often linked to cognitive deficits. But I warned that this may not tell us much about whether we need emotions in order to think, in particular to acquire accurate beliefs. An alternative hypothesis is that human beings happen to be wired up in a way that means that damage to the capacity to experience emotions tends to involve damage that interferes with the workings of some epistemic virtues.

I have presented some reasons for thinking that epistemic emotions play a more essential role than this hypothesis would suggest. Enquiry based on emotion-less virtues would tend to be shallower and less disinterested than much of our enquiry is. Much enquiry is shaped by the ambition to acquire knowledge rather than simple evidenced belief, which is closely linked to alternative-elimination procedures which easily exploit emotions of exploration and persistence. One theme that has run through these and other considerations has been the need for persistent motivation impelling us to follow up lines of enquiry to their ends and develop new lines when the ones we have followed have got to unsatisfying ends.

It is appealing to describe this motivation in biological terms, as following up scents, foraging, and exploring. A domestic rabbit, for example, put in a new environment, will explore it thoroughly, frequently rehearsing the routes that return to a safe location. A dog in a park will take stock of all the old and new dog smells, updating its database of who is in the neighbourhood. These are forms of curiosity, as basic an emotion as fear, anger, and affection. The most important feature of curiosity, for our purposes, is its persistent, hard-to-satisfy, quality. You may have acquired a perfectly serviceable belief, but curiosity drives you on to find a better one, or to check out the remote likelihood that it is mistaken. You may have explored all the lines of enquiry into a topic that you can think of, but in the middle of the night you find yourself toying with far-fetched ways of getting more information or applying different kinds of consideration. These are signs of curiosity, intrigue, and fascination. It is worth noting though, since the readership of this Handbook is largely scholars, students, and others whose lives are dominated by enquiry, how narrow the divide is between these emotions and other less admirable ones: obsession, compulsion, nosiness, fixation.

# REFERENCES

Buri Choy, Stephanie (2008). *When We Should Know Better: Investigative Virtues and Moral Blameworthiness for Ignorance* (MA Dissertation, University of Alberta).

Damasio, Antonio (1994). *Descartes' Error: Emotion, Reason, and the Human Brain* (New York: Quill).

De Sousa, Ronald (1987). *The Rationality of Emotion* (Cambridge MA: MIT Press).

Dretske, Fred (2000). 'Epistemic Operators', in *Perception, Knowledge and Belief* (New York: Cambridge University Press), pp. 30–47.

Goldie, Peter (2000). *The Emotions: A Philosophical Exploration* (Oxford: Oxford University Press).

——(2006). 'Wollheim on emotion and imagination', *Philosophical Studies* 127, pp. 1–17.

Greenspan, Patricia (1988). *Emotions and Reasons* (New York: Routledge).

Hookway, Christopher (2003). 'How to be a virtue epistemologist', in L. Zagzebski and M. De Paul, eds. *Intellectual Virtue: Perspectives from Ethics and Epistemology* (New York: Oxford University Press).

Lewis, David (1996). 'Elusive knowledge', *Australasian Journal of Philosophy* 74, pp. 549–67.

Morton, Adam (2002). 'Beware stories: emotions and virtues', in Peter Goldie, ed. *Understanding Emotions* (Aldershot: Ashgate), pp 55–63.

Sosa, Ernest (2007). *A Virtue Epistemology* (Oxford: Clarendon Press; New York: Oxford University Press).

Stocker, Michael (2004). 'Some considerations about intellectual desire and emotions', in Robert Solomon, ed. *Thinking about feeling* (New York: Oxford University Press), pp. 130–50.

# CHAPTER 18

## INTELLECTUAL AND OTHER NONSTANDARD EMOTIONS

### MICHAEL STOCKER

THIS work is mainly about intellectual emotions—briefly, emotions about intellectual matters. It is also about some other *nonstandard* emotions, to rely on William James' categorization of emotions in his 'What is an Emotion?'[1]

We philosophers are familiar with intellectual emotions—perhaps as familiar and familiar in the same, even if unknowing, ways, that M. Jourdain in Molière's *Le Bourgeois Gentilhomme* was familiar with prose. It is only a bit of an exaggeration to say that we talk about these emotions all the time (even if we do not talk about them under the rubric of 'intellectual emotions') and have done so from our earliest writings. To remind ourselves of this, we could start by considering the etymology of 'philosophy' itself, followed by reading the description of Socrates' life and works in the *Phaedo* and throughout many other dialogues; the discussion in the *Republic* of the methods, contents, and goals of the guardians' education; the steps on and ultimate goal of the ascent to love of wisdom and goodness in the *Symposium*. So too, we could read Aristotle about contemplation and the pleasures of inquiry and of knowing (discussed below); and Aquinas about these, especially when turned to

---

[1] *Mind*, 9, 1884, 188–205; widely reprinted.

God; Hume on how philosophy and hunting have much the same pleasures and emotions; Mill on the value, the need for, intellectual culture; and so on.

Nonetheless, some thirty years ago, some of us complained, I think with complete justification, that our philosophical contemporaries often denied, explicitly, or implicitly by ignoring them, the importance or even the existence of intellectual emotions.[2] And often enough, I still am asked whatever could I have in mind by 'intellectual emotions', how could there be emotions where intellect is concerned? (Sometimes I am asked whether I am concerned with the cognitive content of emotions—e.g., that fear of F requires thoughts or beliefs that F is dangerous. This is not my present concern.) I mention this to make a point about the history, especially the recent history, of our subject: what needs to be explained is how and why, during (roughly) the first part of the twentieth century, a major concern of earlier philosophers came to be forgotten. As shown by other chapters in this work, and by some of the theorists I discuss below, intellectual emotions are no longer forgotten.

To help characterize these various emotions—both intellectual and other nonstandard ones—and to set the stage for my discussion of them, it may help to mention some contrasts used by philosophers and other theorists in their discussions of emotions. The contrasts are doing and thinking; body and mind; activity and passivity; practical and theoretical; personal and interpersonal. These are important contrasts, but like many other contrasts—e.g., reason and emotion, a contrast I will not examine—they have often been misused in ways that hinder our understanding of emotions.

I want now to present several somewhat long passages of texts important for this work, presented in chronological order: the first by Aristotle, the second by William James, the third by Théodule Ribot, the fourth by two psychologists, both theorists of emotions, Nico H. Frijda and Louise Sundararajan. The main goals here are to show that intellectual and other nonstandard emotions are well known in our tradition; to show some of the variety they come in; and to begin to answer some questions and issues they raise.

# 18.1 Aristotle

In Book X of the *Nicomachean Ethics*, Aristotle writes, that 'complete happiness is a contemplative activity... the activity of God, which surpasses all others in

---

[2] See, for example, Israel Scheffler, Chapters 3–17. 'In Praise of the Cognitive Emotions', in *In Praise of the Cognitive Emotions and Other Essays in the Philosophy of Education* (New York: Routledge, 1991), originally published in *Teachers College Record*, 72, 1977, 171–86; and Michael Stocker, 'Intellectual Desire, Emotion, and Action', in *Explaining Emotions*, Amélie O. Rorty, ed. (Berkeley: University of California Press, 1980) pp. 323–38.

blessedness, must be contemplative; and of human activities, therefore, that which is most akin to this must be most of the nature of happiness'. And also

So if among excellent actions political and military actions are distinguished by nobility and greatness, and these are unleisurely and aim at an end and are not desirable for their own sake, but the activity of intellect, which is contemplative, seems both to be superior in worth and to aim at no end beyond itself, and to have its pleasure proper to itself (and this augments the activity), and the self-sufficiency, leisureliness, unweariedness (so far as this is possible for man), and all the other attributes ascribed to the blessed man are evidently those connected with this activity, it follows that this will be the complete happiness of man, if it be allowed a complete term of life (for none of the attributes of happiness is incomplete). (Nicomachean Ethics, X, 7, 1177b7–1177b26.)

I suggest that we take what Aristotle says about contemplation to show the value he attaches to intellectual activity and emotions. To be sure, what we mean by 'contemplation' is different enough from what Aristotle means by (what is here translated as) 'contemplation', namely, *'theoria'.* Nonetheless, I use this passage from Aristotle to show that he, too, recognizes the existence and, more importantly, the high value of thinking that is not a constituent of action.[3] I recognize that, here and elsewhere, Aristotle does count thinking as activity, as in 'the activity of intellect' in the passage just quoted. So I should have said that Aristotle recognizes the high value of thinking that is not a constituent of action, *as 'action' is often understood,* e.g., in our contrasting pairs *thought and action* or *thinking and doing.* Further complicating my use of this contrast, I continue to hold what I have long argued for, e.g., in 'Intellectual Desire, Emotion, and Action', that thinking can be an action, a doing. Thinking is, after all, part of our job description, part of what we are hired to do.

It should, further, be noted that contemplation as understood in this passage from Aristotle almost certainly does not involve emotions. When they are contemplating, his gods and the men of perfect or best *eudaimonia* may well not be excited, interested, enthralled by, curious about, in awe, and so on. Aristotle considers contemplation to be an example of perfect or total activity, and thus no passivity, no *pathē,* and thus no emotions, although, as just seen, he does allow for contemplation and other acts of thinking to be pleasurable. In these ways, it might seem misleading to use Aristotle on contemplation to introduce intellectual emotions.

However, to be a useful introduction, there need not be the sorts of similarities that, as just suggested, our contemplation and thinking do *not* have with contemplation as understood by Aristotle. I suggest that if we think about what Aristotle is saying, we can be (and I was) naturally, even though not necessarily, led to thinking about our intellectual activities, including at least some instances of what we call contemplation, that do or can involve emotions.

In Book X we also read, 'Now the activity of the *practical* excellences is exhibited in *political* or *military* affairs.' This quote in conjunction with the earlier quote from

---

[3] For a similar use of 'contemplation' and a defense of using it this way, see Peter Goldie, 'Virtues of Art', *Proceedings of the Aristotelian Society, Supplementary Volume,* 82, 2008, 179–95.

Book X might suggest that, on Aristotle's view, intellectual activity is to be divided exclusively and without remainder between practical thinking and contemplation. But this suggestion is clearly mistaken. In the *Metaphysics*, Aristotle writes,

All men by nature desire to know. An indication of this is the delight we take in our senses; for even apart from their usefulness they are loved for themselves; and above all others the sense of sight. For not only with a view to action, but even when we are not going to do anything, we prefer sight to almost everything else. The reason is that this, most of all the senses, makes us know and brings to light many differences between things. Metaphysics, I, 1, 980a28–980b24.

And in Book X of the *Nicomachean Ethics*, 'those who know will pass their time more pleasantly than those who inquire', suggesting once again that inquiring can be pleasurable.

It must also be remembered that Aristotle was keenly interested in gaining, deploying, and contemplating knowledge about all sorts of matters, and that many of these matters allowed for intellectual delight even though they are not the subject matter of contemplation nor are they for the sake of the political or military action. Biology and the constitutions of various city states come immediately to mind.

There would be a further problem in delimiting practical thought that is 'exhibited in political or military affairs' so that practical thought—even when limited to those affairs—does not allow for intellectual emotions. One very ruthlessly constraining way to try to do this would limit the practical thinking or its emotional uptake to what goes into and is essential for the practical activity. To this end, it might be held that the only emotions about an episode of military strategizing would be about its effectiveness and efficiency in producing the activity or its goal, e.g., winning. This would be to hold that the cleverness of the strategizing, its profundity, its fiendishness, its beauty, . . . could not be sources of delight or upset; nor even could the thought that it succeeded against all odds; nor could there be awe at its audacity, delight in what the victory will allow, and so on—unless these in turn are understood just in terms of effectiveness and efficiency. This would allow no room for anything like the emotional refinement and savoring discussed by Frijda and Sundarajan below, nor, of course, for pleasures of philosophizing about the nature of military courage as in the *Laches* or in the *Nicomachean Ethics*—unless, of course, these are understood simply as bearing on efficiency and effectiveness. I think such excessive practical mindedness is a caricature even of Spartans. It would be more than simply strange to apply it to Aristotle.

# 18.2 WILLIAM JAMES

For a use of the contrast between mind and body as that is relevant to emotions, we could hardly do better than quote at length from James' 'What Is An Emotion?'

I should say first of all that the only emotions I propose expressly to consider here are those that have a distinct bodily expression. That there are feelings of pleasure and displeasure, of interest and excitement, bound up with mental operations, but having no obvious bodily expression for their consequence, would, I suppose, be held true by most readers. Certain arrangements of sounds, of lines, of colours, are agreeable, and others the reverse, without the degree of the feeling being sufficient to quicken the pulse or breathing, or to prompt to movements of either the body or the face. Certain sequences of ideas charm us as much as others tire us. It is a real intellectual delight to get a problem solved, and a real intellectual torment to have to leave it unfinished. The first set of examples, the sounds, lines, and colours, are either bodily sensations, or the images of such. The second set seem to depend on processes in the ideational centres exclusively. Taken together, they appear to prove that there are pleasures and pains inherent in certain forms of nerve-action as such, wherever that action occur. The case of these feelings we will at present leave entirely aside, and confine our attention to the more complicated cases in which a wave of bodily disturbance of some kind accompanies the perception of the interesting sights or sounds, or the passage of the exciting train of ideas. Surprise, curiosity, rapture, fear, anger, lust, greed, and the like, become then the names of the mental states with which the person is possessed. The bodily disturbances are said to be the 'manifestation' of these several emotions, their 'expression' or 'natural language'; and these emotions themselves, being so strongly characterized both from within and without, may be called the standard emotions.

Our natural way of thinking about these standard emotions is that the mental perception of some fact excites the mental affection called the emotion, and that this latter state of mind gives rise to the bodily expression. My thesis on the contrary is that the bodily changes follow directly the PERCEPTION of the exciting fact, and that our feeling of the same changes as they occur IS the emotion. Common sense says, we lose our fortune, are sorry and weep; we meet a bear, are frightened and run; we are insulted by a rival, are angry and strike. The hypothesis here to be defended says that this order of sequence is incorrect, that the one mental state is not immediately induced by the other, that the bodily manifestations must first be interposed between, and that the more rational statement is that we feel sorry because we cry, angry because we strike, afraid because we tremble, and not that we cry, strike, or tremble, because we are sorry, angry, or fearful, as the case may be. Without the bodily states following on the perception, the latter would be purely cognitive in form, pale, colourless, destitute of emotional warmth. We might then see the bear, and judge it best to run, receive the insult and deem it right to strike, but we could not actually feel afraid or angry. ('What is an Emotion', 189–90, his emphases)

Many, if not most, commentators take James to be claiming an identity between feelings of bodily changes and emotions—that's what emotions are. It is generally thought that this identification is obviously wrong, indeed wrong headed because it fails to recognize, and even denies, that emotions involve cognitive content, not just feelings of bodily changes; and more particularly that it fails to recognize and even denies that emotions are to be characterized, and to be differentiated from other emotions, in terms of such content, not or not just these feelings of bodily changes.

But there is another way to understand James' claim. This is to follow an interpretation offered by Charles Young.[4] Young suggests that James does not identify emotions and those feelings, and that he does recognize that emotions have cognitive content including thoughts, desires, and values. Young suggests that James holds that these feelings are, indeed, a differentiating feature of emotions: perhaps serving to differentiate emotions from other emotions, but far more importantly, serving to differentiate an emotion from its own constituent thoughts, desires, and values. As just read, James holds that, without the bodily feelings, those other constituents are 'pale, colourless, destitute of emotional warmth'. This is to take James as holding that these feelings of bodily changes are what make emotions emotional. These feelings are what make for affectivity.

I agree with James that emotions require affectivity and on the need to differentiate affectivity from the other constituent elements of emotions. However, I do not agree that affectivity can be characterized in terms of feeling of bodily changes.[5] In the passage just quoted, James suggests that while the emotionality of the standard emotions is to be understood in terms of bodily feelings, the emotionality of nonstandard emotions is not. As will be discussed below, somewhat later in 'What is an Emotion?' James significantly modifies this view about the nonbodily nature of the emotionality of nonstandard emotions.

A further point against taking James to *identify* emotions or emotionality with feelings of bodily changes—and, not incidentally, against the charge of failing to see that thoughts, desires, and values are constituents of emotions—is found in his holding, for there to be an emotion, these feelings of bodily changes must be '*interposed* between' mental states. If both the bodily feelings and the mental states are constituents of the emotion, emotions cannot be just the feelings. The feelings cannot be the emotion—i.e., the whole of the emotion.

If, on the other hand, those mental states are not constituents of the emotion, but only important, even essential, elements of a series—mental states, feelings of bodily changes, mental states—the consensus view that James identifies emotions with bodily feelings turns out to be almost merely terminological, turning on the question of whether in fact or on James' view, the term 'emotion' applies to the *whole* series or just *part* of it. I say *almost* entirely because, as just said, James holds that the feelings are needed to make the second lot of mental states emotional, rather than 'pale, colourless, destitute of emotional warmth'.

[4] In his review of Sarah Broadie's *Ethics With Aristotle*, *The Journal of the History of Philosophy*, 31, 1993, 625–7, 625. Young's suggestion is discussed briefly in my and Elizabeth Hegeman's *Valuing Emotions* (Cambridge: Cambridge University Press, 1996) at pages 25–6.

[5] See *Valuing Emotions* and my 'Psychic Feelings: Their Importance and Irreducibility', *Australasian Journal of Philosophy*, 61, 1983, 5–26.

The eminent contemporary theorist of emotions, the psychologist James Averill puts these points well.[6] He says, correctly in my view, that James defined emotions, not as identical to bodily feeling but rather as 'subjective experience dependent upon bodily change' (216).[7]

What is perhaps of most importance in this passage from James' 'What is an Emotion?' for present concerns is that he restricts his discussion of these issues about bodily feelings to what he calls the *standard* emotions. As we read, he states that he does not intend it to apply—indeed, that he intends it not to apply—to some other emotions. I will call these *non*standard emotions—a term I do not think he uses. He includes among these nonstandard emotions, first, some intellectual emotions; second, some other nonbodily emotions; and, I think, third, some other emotions that do involve the body but are not, primarily, bodily, and do not involve, are not manifested by, bodily disturbances. (Whether or not he had Darwin in mind in making these suggestions about nonstandard emotions, James might be read as supplementing and perhaps correcting Darwin's very brief comment on intellectual activity: that it is often expressed by a frown and downcast eyes.[8] James says that he was concerned to supplement and perhaps correct Darwin on standard emotions: 'But not even a Darwin has exhaustively enumerated all the bodily affections characteristic of any one of the standard emotions' [191].)

James characterizes these nonstandard emotions by means of briefly sketched examples with some very brief commentary. On intellectual emotions, he writes, 'It is a real intellectual delight to get a problem solved, and a real intellectual torment to have to leave it unfinished' and gives examples that, he says, 'seem to depend on processes in the ideational centres exclusively'. For other nonstandard emotions that do not involve feelings of bodily changes, he writes, 'Certain arrangements of sounds, of lines, of colours, are agreeable, and others the reverse, without the degree of the feeling being sufficient to quicken the pulse or breathing, or to prompt movements of either the body or the face'. (These, of course, are also some of the objects of pure pleasures in Plato's *Philebus*, 51b ff.)

Although he does not say this, I take the last quoted passage to suggest that James holds that there is a third group of nonstandard emotions. These involve still

---

[6] 'Analysis of psychophysiological symbolism', in *The Emotions: Social, Cultural and Biological Dimensions*, eds. Rom Harré and W. Gerrod Parrott (London: Sage, 1996), pp. 204–228, from which the following is taken, originally in *The Journal for the Theory of Social Behavior*, 4, 1974, 147–90.

[7] Averill notes that Carl Lange, also a nineteenth-century emotion theorist, in work originally published in 1885, did *identify* emotions with bodily changes or bodily events. James' theory and Lange's theory were often paired—perhaps conflated—giving us what is now called the 'James–Lange Theory', not the 'James and Lange Theor*ies*'. This pairing might be explained by James and Lange being listed as co-authors of the still well known book, *The Emotions*, which includes both Lange's 1885 work and James' 'What is an Emotion?'—e.g., the 1922 edition (Baltimore: Williams and Wilkins).

[8] Darwin, *The Expression of the Emotions in Man and Animals* (New York: Appleton, 1898), 222.

other arrangements of sounds, lines, and colors that (perhaps in addition to be being agreeable or otherwise) do have a degree of feeling that is sufficient to quicken the pulse or breathing, or to prompt movements of the body or face. The second and perhaps also the third set of examples are 'either bodily sensations or the images of such'. (These, too, are discussed in the *Philebus*, a bit earlier.) Nonetheless, bodily feelings that may be associated with these are not said to be what makes these emotions emotional. Rather, it is strongly suggested that these feelings, if any, are not what makes these emotions emotional.

In another of his articles, aptly named 'Intellectual Emotions', Averill suggests that *hope* is an intellectual emotion.[9] As I understand Averill and James, hope does not fit completely well into any of James' categories of nonstandard emotions. It seems most like James' second (and perhaps also the third) nonstandard emotion, not his first, which he calls intellectual.

But it is of only terminological interest whether Averill uses the very same categories James does. James uses only a few examples with very brief commentary—in my view, too few examples and far too little commentary—to tell us what he will *not* be concerned with. He did not give, and did not set out to give, a complete typology of what he was not concerned with. I wholeheartedly endorse Averill's closing claim that what is important is that there are any number of different emotions and different sorts of emotions:

Most contemporary theories do not recognize hope and other 'intellectual emotions' as true emotions. I believe this says more about the nature of our theories than about the nature of hope.

For the most part, our theories of emotion have been erected on a very narrow base. Fear, anger, and to a lesser extent, love and grief have been the primary emotions investigated. Yet, literally hundreds of emotions are recognized in ordinary language. [36]

As just noted, James gives hardly any attention to the nonstandard emotions—at least in the passages just quoted—but only the brief examples and commentary just quoted. His own lack of discussion may help explain why these emotions, or even the fact that James thinks there are such emotions, are absent from at least many of the commentaries on him or on 'What is an Emotion?'

I want to make two very brief comments about James on these nonstandard emotions. First, as he recognizes, they are a heterodox lot, with few, if any, common features—other than the negative one of *not* being a standard emotion. In these passages, he further suggests that there need be no feelings of bodily changes in intellectual emotions or in emotions of the second group of nonstandard emotions; nor is their emotionality, their affectivity, to be explained in terms of such

---

[9] *The Emotions: Social, Cultural and Biological Dimensions*, eds. Rom Harré and W. Gerrod Parrott (London: Sage, 1996); originally in C. D. Spielberger et al., eds., *Stress and Anxiety* (Washington: Hemisphere, 14, 1991).

feelings. The third sort of nonstandard emotions may well involve such feelings, but their being emotional is said not to depend on that. Nonetheless, there is no suggestion here that any of the emotions of these three nonstandard sorts is 'pale, colourless, destitute of emotional warmth'. Indeed, to the contrary. (These last characterizations will be questioned below.)

Second, James gives every indication of seeing nothing strange or problematic or unusual about these nonstandard emotions. He gives every indication of confidently expecting his readers to recognize what he is talking about and to be able to distinguish between standard and nonstandard emotions and among the various sorts of nonstandard emotions. (This is taken up below, in the discussions of Ribot and of Frijda and Sundarajan.)

What I have reported as James' views about nonstandard emotions is, I think, accurate to what he says in the early part of 'What is an Emotion? ' But he later adds to that view, changing it significantly: holding that without bodily feelings, there are no intellectual and other nonstandard emotions but only judgments that are not emotional but rather dry, pale, and lacking all glow.[10] He writes,

Rapture, love, ambition, indignation, and pride, considered as feelings, are fruits of the same soil with the grossest bodily sensations of pleasure and of pain. But it was said at the outset that this would be affirmed only of what we then agreed to call the 'standard' emotions; and that those inward sensibilities that appeared devoid at first sight of bodily results should be left out of our account. We had better, before closing, say a word or two about these latter feelings. They are, the reader will remember, the moral, intellectual, and aesthetic feelings. Concords of sounds, of colours, of lines, logical consistencies, teleological fitnesses, affect us with a pleasure that seems ingrained in the very form of the representation itself, and to borrow nothing from any reverberation surging up from the parts below the brain.... We have then, or some of us seem to have, genuinely cerebral forms of pleasure and displeasure, apparently not agreeing in their mode of production with the so-called 'standard' emotions we have been analysing.... Unless in them [i.e., cases of pure cerebral emotion] there actually be coupled with the intellectual feeling a bodily reverberation of some kind, unless we actually laugh at the neatness of the mechanical device, thrill at the justice of the act, or tingle at the perfection of the musical form, our mental condition is more allied to a judgment of right than to anything else. And such a judgment is rather to be classed among awarenesses of truth: it is a cognitive act. But as a matter of fact the intellectual feeling hardly ever does exist thus unaccompanied. The bodily sounding-board is at work, as careful introspection will show, far more than we usually suppose. Still, where long familiarity with a certain class of effects has blunted emotional sensibility thereto as much as it has sharpened the taste and judgment, we do get the intellectual emotion, if such it can be called, pure and undefiled. And the dryness of it, the paleness, the absence of all glow, as it may exist in a thoroughly expert critic's mind, not only shows us what an altogether different thing it is from the 'standard' emotions we considered first, but makes us suspect that almost the entire difference lies in the fact that the bodily sounding-board, vibrating in the one case, is in the other mute. [201–2]

---

[10] My thanks are owed to Peter Goldie for urging me to pursue this.

So, James now says that the nonstandard emotions, along with the standard ones, involve and depend on bodily feelings: that without bodily feelings, there is no emotionality in either the standard or the nonstandard emotions.

I see various interpretive possibilities here: first, James no longer distinguishes between standard and nonstandard emotions—perhaps, he now holds that, although many theorists and others do claim there is a difference in kind, they are mistaken. Second, he holds that all emotions involve bodily feelings, but that there are differences of strength or kind between those feelings the standard emotions involve and those the nonstandard ones do. (This probably should be that there are such differences between the two classes of emotions: between [most] every standard emotion and [most] every nonstandard one.) Third, he sees the difference in terms of what the emotions are about—e.g., an onrushing bear, a neat argument. Fourth, he holds that the bodily feelings are 'manifestations', 'expressions', 'natural language' of only the standard emotions, and not also of the nonstandard ones.

A full study of James' ultimate view on intellectual and other nonstandard emotions would require determining which, if any, of these interpretations is right. Emotion theorists have given extensive consideration to the third and fourth possibilities. I think we have already profited enough from these brief comments on James not to pursue these issues or that full study.

To conclude my study of James, I will simply make a suggestion about how I see some contemporary studies of emotions. It is that few, if any, contemporary emotion theorists accept the details of James' account of emotions, standard or nonstandard. However, some theorists, including the groundbreaking researcher Antonio Damasio, do praise James and say they are inspired by his work.[11] And many do retain what to my mind is the 'flavor' of James, at least to the extent that they divide up the emotions in ways that, again to my mind, suggest James. We have already seen this in Averill's criticism of his fellow emotion theorists, for using 'a very narrow base' composed mainly of 'fear, anger, and to a lesser extent, love and grief'. (Frijda and Sundarajan will be seen to make a similar criticism.)

I am also reminded of James—in particular of his reliance on the body and biology in his account of emotions and his bifurcation of emotions—by the work of many who look to neurobiology for help with their accounts of emotions. At least roughly, where James talked of bodily feelings, they talk of neurobiological structures and happenings. As just indicated, I am thinking here of Damasio—and his distinction between primary and nonprimary emotions. I am also thinking of Paul Griffiths' *What Emotions Really Are*,[12] especially his distinction between basic emotions and higher cognitive emotions. As Jason Clark writes,

---

[11] *Descartes' Error* (New York: Putnam, 1994), pp. 129–31.
[12] Chicago: University of Chicago Press, 1997.

According to Griffiths, basic emotions are evolutionarily old sets of stimulus-detection mechanisms and stereotyped physiological and behavioral response patterns rooted in dedicated neural circuits, with a genetic basis that has evolved in response to recurrent evolutionary challenges, and which we share with nonhuman mammals. These patterns are capable of being activated by unconditioned stimuli and lead to unconditioned, involuntary responses . . . [13]

# 18.3 THÉODULE RIBOT

That these emotions, or at least the intellectual ones, were seen as everyday, ordinary emotions—even if also seen as nonstandard emotions—around this time can also be seen in *The Psychology of the Emotions* written by the French psychologist, Théodule Ribot.[14] The following passage from Ribot was written within a decade or so of James' work, to which he refers. Ribot writes,

I shall be very brief in treating of intellectual emotion, since it is rare, and usually temperate in character; however, . . . [it can spring] up with the true characteristics of intense emotion. . . . Most human beings are not passionately eager for the search after or the discovery of pure truth, any more than they are afflicted by privation of it; but those possessed by this demon are given up to him, body and soul. . . . The biographies of learned men furnish us with innumerable examples: the perpetual physical sufferings of Pascal, Malebranche nearly suffocated by the palpitations of his heart when reading Descartes, Humphrey Davy dancing in his laboratory after having made the discovery of potassium, Hamilton suddenly feeling something 'like the closing of a galvanic circuit' at the moment of discovering the method of quaternions, etc. There is no need to extend our search so far; everyday life provides us moment by moment with examples which, though prosaic, are none the less valuable as proofs. The instinct of curiosity is at the root of all intellectual emotion, whether lofty or commonplace. Does not the man who perpetually watches his neighbour's conduct and the thousand petty details of his life, feel when his puerile curiosity is baffled, all the physical anguish of unsatisfied desire? [101]

I offered this passage simply to give evidence that talk of intellectual emotions was accepted as entirely ordinary. I will not discuss it further, except to note that, as they are put, the claims about the bodily feelings, e.g., physical anguish, do not make it clear whether Ribot accepts James' later, modified account or Lange's or some other account of the relations between bodily feelings and emotions.

---

[13] My thanks are owed to Clark for help here. The quotation is from an unpublished work of his.
[14] New York: Scribners, 1897.

# 18.4 Nico H. Frijda and Louise Sundararajan

I turn now to Frijda and Sundararajan's fascinating and illuminating 'Emotion Refinement: A Theory Inspired by Chinese Poetics'.[15] This work includes an extensive bibliography of works on emotions, mainly psychological, some philosophical, and some on Chinese aesthetics. Works of particular note for us include N. Frijda, *The Emotions* (Cambridge: Cambridge University Press, 1986); R. Lazarus, *Emotion and Adaptation* (New York: Oxford University Press, 1991); K. Oatley, *Best Laid Schemes: The Psychology of Emotions* (Cambridge: Cambridge University Press, 1992); D. Keltner and J. Haidt, 'Approaching Awe, a Moral, Spiritual, and Aesthetic Emotion', *Cognition and Emotion*, 17, 2003, 297–314; M. Kubovy, 'On the Pleasures of the Mind', in D. Kahneman, E. Diener, and N. Schwarz, eds., *Foundations of Hedonic Psychology: Scientific Perspectives on Enjoyment and Suffering*, (New York: Russell Sage, 1999); L. Sundararajan, 'Religious Awe: Potential Contributions of Negative Theology to Psychology, "Positive" or Otherwise', *Journal of Theoretical and Philosophical Psychology*, 22, 2002, 174–97. Frijda and Sundarajan write,

William James made a distinction between coarse and noncoarse emotions. In the present article, we explore the nature of such noncoarse emotions, which we designate as emotions with refinement. We take our cue from the treatment of refined emotions in Chinese poetics and philosophy. The theory and description of savoring (in Chinese, *pin-wei*) points to several features of emotion experiences and behavior that are usually absent in direct emotional responses of emotional events, such as self reflexivity and higher level second-order awareness, detachment, and restraint. Emotions with those features can be found outside savoring and aesthetic contexts, for instance while dealing with actual life events.... Coarse emotions [James' standard emotions] are characterized by distinct bodily upset, overt behavior manifestations with brisk time courses, and relatively simple event–emotion relationships. They are more or less paradigmatic and are the main subject of psychological studies of emotion (e.g., Frijda, 1986; Lazarus, 1991; Oatley, 1992).

They are best illustrated by an emotion-arousing event like meeting a bear in the woods. Coarse emotions differ from emotions that are more felt than acted upon, and thus do not obviously manifest themselves in overt behaviors like attack, embrace, or flight; may not show very pronounced physiological upset; are often about complex events or subtle event aspects; and are not easily done justice by common emotion labels. We will refer to noncoarse emotions collectively as...refined emotions.... We hold that they do not form a subset of emotions. It is not that anger would be considered as a coarse emotion and that love would be considered as a refined emotion. Rather, refinement represents a mode of perhaps all emotions that language or emotion taxonomy could distinguish. There exist refined anger, love, and sexual ecstasy, as well as coarse, straightforward anger, love, or

---

[15] *Perspectives on Psychological Science*, 2, 2007, 227–41.

sexual ecstasy. We think it worthwhile to examine emotion refinement to benefit emotion theory by shedding some light on the relationship between refined and coarse emotions, on emotions that are not done justice by simple emotion labels, and on emotions aroused by perceiving objects of art, often called aesthetic emotions, which pose unresolved problems for theories of emotion.

Our analysis will show how refined is an appropriate designation for emotions that show few outward signs but still involve strong feelings and that share the following features: They occur under attitudes of detachment and restraint, their experience involves reflexive second order awareness, they result from and contain extensive elaboration of appraisal of the eliciting events that may invest the events with meanings far beyond their immediately given aspects, and they include virtual states of action readiness rather than states that manifest in overt acts or suppressed action impulses. [227]

Again, we get a division of emotions. And again, one sort, coarse emotions, is characterized largely in terms of coarse bodily feelings and reactions. In terms of James' categories of nonstandard emotions, refined emotions fit most easily into the first sort, intellectual emotions. But not all intellectual emotions, as discussed ever so briefly by James, fit easily into the category of refined emotions. Again, this is only of the barest, merely terminological importance. The refined emotions are of obvious importance, both to our emotional lives, how we live, and also to our accounts of emotions. Once we are—now that we have been—introduced to them by name and description, we see that we have known them and their importance well, even if we were rarely if ever aware that we knew them. So far as theories and accounts of emotions are concerned, we are brought once again to wonder how it was possible to be satisfied with coarse emotions, with James' standard emotions— as the major emotional elements of our lives or of our accounts of emotions. Perhaps this is to be explained in terms of coarse thinking. As I said at the outset, Frijda and Sundarajan present us with a fascinating and wonderfully illuminating work.

This concludes my showing that we, joined by many of our philosophical predecessors, know full well that there are intellectual emotions. I now want to turn to two general issues about intellectual emotions. These issues deserve far more time than I can give them here. But I hope that what I say will make a good start on them. These issues are, in turn: first, are some or all of the intellectual emotions the same emotions as found elsewhere? Are some or all of the non-intellectual emotions found in intellectual emotions? And, second, how, if at all, are emotions, especially intellectual emotions, needed for successful action, especially intellectual action?

Are some or all of the intellectual emotions the same emotions as found elsewhere? Are some or all of the nonintellectual emotions found in intellectual emotions? One way to start on answering these questions is by noting that emotions of the same name occur in both. There are any number of lists of emotions that bear this out. Consider, for example, the chapter headings of David Konstan's deeply informative *The Emotions of the Ancient Greeks*:[16] anger, satisfaction, shame, envy and indignation, fear, gratitude, love, hatred, pity, jealousy. It is, I think, obvious that all of these can be about intellectual issues or exercises of the intellect and in other sorts of nonstandard, mental, perhaps refined, nonbodily emotions. Let us consider, even if very briefly, only the first and the last, anger and jealousy.

I can be angered by a belittling review. So too, I can be angry at my own stupidity for continuing down what I should have seen was a dead end. (Anger in the last sentence moves away from Aristotle's requirement of insult for anger where 'anger' is used to translate *orgē* as discussed by Aristotle in *Rhetoric* II, 2, which in turn is discussed at length in *Valuing Emotions*.[17] It moves away from this to our contemporary and more capacious notion of anger.) Now jealousy: I can be jealous about my reputation: I am consumed by fear that I will lose my reputation or that it will be stolen from me (perhaps by the person who made the belittling remark, who, I now surmise, made the remark to steal my thunder).

I recognize that having the same name, e.g., 'anger', is compatible with the emotions being different, at best only analogically similar. This, however, involves a very general issue, not just between standard emotions, taken as a unified group, and nonstandard ones, taken as another unified group.

Suppose I am asked whether intellectual courage—willingness to risk ridicule, loss of job or freedom, loss of reputation to think along certain lines or to publish my conclusions—involves the same sort of courage as courage understood as a standard emotion. Is this question different from a question we might ask about courage as treated by Aristotle: are his paradigm and nonparadigm 'sorts' of courage—courage in battle and courage in facing dangerous and painful medical conditions—really different sorts of courage? Or are they only different sorts of objects or occasions for the selfsame emotion? Returning to intellectual emotions, we might ask whether courage in pursuing one's research—facing the danger and pain of challenging one's own or one's society's deeply held beliefs—is yet another sort of courage or only a different occasion for the selfsame courage as found in military or medical situations.

These questions about sameness can, also, be asked about courage in battle. So, we might ask whether courage in facing a cavalry charge is the same courage as courage in facing missiles; or about courage in facing a cavalry charge when you know that your army is about to be routed and when you know that the opposing army is about to be routed; and so on.

My point here is not that I think these questions and their answers are silly or pointless. It is, rather, that, first, I think that questions and answers about sameness and difference can come up all over the place. (Here we might turn to the *Philebus* around 18a and Socrates' warnings about going haywire about the one and the

---

[16] University of Toronto Press: Toronto, 2006 and 2007.
[17] See footnote 4.

many.) Second, I think these questions are the same questions whether they are about just one intellectual emotion or just one nonintellectual emotion, or about pairs consisting of one of each, or about suitably chosen groups of each taken severally or jointly. I would put these two together to suggest, third, that differing answers to the original question—'Are some or all intellectual emotions the same emotions as found in or about nonintellectual objects and situations?'—are perhaps disguised applications of differing accounts or theories of emotion identity and individuation. (So too, of course, for holding that these are or are not the same questions.) And I would suggest, fourth, that even if it can be done, we have no present need to sort out and evaluate these different accounts and theories. All this may be little more than showing that I don't embrace realism about emotion individuation and identification.

I want now to consider some very general questions of how, if at all, are emotions, especially intellectual emotions, needed for successful action, especially intellectual action. For example, is interest, engagement, or love of truth needed for good intellectual activity or even just any intellectual activity. If it is, how and why is it needed? I have just suggested that the same emotions are found in both standard and nonstandard cases. So, I will start on these questions by following up a theme from Aristotle's discussion of courageous action. He holds that courageous action requires, inter alia, facing the dangers of battle with or from the right emotions, including not too much and not too little, but rather a mean amount of, fear, and also with or from the right sorts and amount of concerns, such as an ultimate desire to do what is good, e.g., save one's fellows and one's city. Winning in battle is a goal of such action. (We need not be concerned here with whether winning is only *a* goal or *the* goal; nor with what winning is, e.g., wounding, killing, driving off the enemy, . . . ) The best men will, if the situation arises, act courageously. But, on Aristotle's view, the best men may well not be the best at winning. A mercenary—who fights for money rather than for the good— might be better at this; and he might be better because he has less fear, perhaps because he has less to fear, less to lose, than a good man would.

I use this—whether or not I agree with it—to illustrate a way that emotions can be essential to an act's being a given sort of act and, indeed, for being a good and successful instance of such an act.

Aristotle's understanding of courage as differentiated from being a good soldier is, of course, tied up with his concern with virtue and his rejection of what is often seen as a utilitarian account of virtue, in terms of doing good things, getting good things done. On such a view, a good person, a person of virtue, is a person who succeeds at doing or bringing about what is good. Perhaps we should not call this *the* utilitarian view, but *a* utilitarian view. For some utilitarians reject that view and agree with Aristotle. I have particularly in mind Mill's claims in *On Liberty* and elsewhere that we should be concerned 'not only [with] what men do, but also what manner of men they are that do it'. I have mentioned this, not because I am concerned with the adequacy or otherwise of utilitarianism, but, rather, because I am concerned with showing that in some cases at least, the answer to whether emotions are or are not required by various acts and conditions can have to do with the moral views involved with the relevant understanding of those acts and conditions.

Identifying the relevant understandings (or arguing for or against particular understandings) will be difficult and perhaps controversial. Nonetheless, let us start by considering what professors, lecturers and other teachers, and students of philosophy are expected to do. (I do not assume, one way or the other, whether other disciplines are the same.) Let us start by asking what is required of professors giving lectures on, say, moral realism or physics to other equally advanced professors.

Suppose we hold that they have succeeded if they present the relevant theories and accounts adequately and that they have done this if (but certainly not, only if) their lecture is pretty much like the pages of a good text book—perhaps they are reading out loud the page proofs of their most recent book. What need, it might be asked, is there for intellectual (or other) emotions in those giving the lectures or in those listening to them? Some might think it obvious that there is no need and perhaps even no room. But there is some controversy here, which I will only mention, not try to adjudicate. One strand of this controversy concerns the question of whether we can understand a particular philosopher's position without a deep understanding of the philosopher, where that requires something like a deep psychological understanding of the philosopher, the philosopher's temperament, emotional makeup, and the like. (Iris Murdoch suggests something like this in *Metaphysics as a Guide to Morals*.)

Another strand of the controversy concerns the very nature of understanding and whether to be understandable a position, claim, or whatever must answer to our interests; or must be capable of engendering *feelings of certainty* (for or against) or of *uncertainty*; or requires some form of commitment. (I think suggestions favoring something along one or other of these lines are found in writings of Hilary Putnam, Jurgen Habermas, *Knowledge and Human Interests*,[18] and Bas Fraassen, *The Empirical Stance*.[19])

Further, some have held that at least at the highest level, large-scale claims and theories—at least in the pure sciences and perhaps also in philosophy—are to be evaluated in terms of simplicity, elegance, and power and (other) pragmatic considerations. These claims are sometimes put as being about the content of the theories, what they are about; and sometimes as being about theory acceptance and reception. It would go considerably too far afield to enter into these debates.[20] So

[18]  Boston: Beacon Press, 1971.
[19]  New Haven: Yale University Press, 2002.
[20]  For a useful and compelling discussion, see David Owens, *Reason without Freedom* (New York: Routledge, 2000); see also Habermas and van Fraassen, as above.

too, it would go too far afield to explore the relations between emotions and simplicity, elegance, power, and pragmatic considerations.

But two points can be made: first, even if understanding itself, or simplicity, say, are ultimately to be understood as involving emotions, that, by itself, does not show that a theorist who aims to be understood or for simplicity or judges work in terms of understandability or simplicity has those emotions. (The point is at least somewhat like this one: a theorist may use procedures that have been developed in light of certain mathematical proofs without being able to do those proofs or, indeed, without even knowing about their existence.) This may be to say little more than that the needed emotions and proofs need not be in these theorists' heads or minds. It will be sufficient, I think, if the discipline itself incorporates those goals— if, for example, they are part of the relevant research programs.

Second, having certain emotions may certainly be useful for those theorists. So for example, without his interest in moral realism, a given member of the audience might not have the energy or commitment to keep his attention focused on the lecture. This, of course, can be true of some members of the audience but not others. These others might 'just see' what the lecturer is on about. For a parallel, some people 'just see' that the butler committed the murder, while others have to struggle with the clues, which only those deeply interested by such mysteries would do.

Let us turn briefly to lower level lecturers. Judging from the evaluation forms for teachers that I have seen, securing students' understanding of the subject is the bare minimum. It is expected, even required, that enthusiasm or at least interest in the subject be engendered. In part, this is for budgetary reasons, where a university department receives funds in proportion to the number of students in their classes; and one important factor in taking a class is interest in the subject. (It is obviously not the only factor; classes that satisfy prerequisites for further study may be uninteresting, even boring or worse.)

There are also other reasons for engendering interest. One such reason is (the view) that part of what it is to be well educated, to be a person of even moderate culture, to be well rounded, a good citizen, even . . . is to be interested in some intellectual disciplines or at least to find them interesting: perhaps poetry or music, or perhaps one or more sciences or a social science or . . .

Teachers of all ranks are evaluated not only in terms of the interest they engender in their students and colleagues but also in terms of the interest they have and show. To be judged 'not interested in the subject' is a matter of some considerable concern—for retention, promotion, and the like. In part, I think, this has to do with (thoughts about) effectiveness in teaching and research. It is often thought, correctly or not, that teachers who do not evince interest do not engender interest. Theories and anecdotes about emotional 'contagion' are often cited here. So too, it may be that students are unlikely to be interested or sustain interest in a subject unless the teachers show that they consider it important, and it may also be that showing interest is one of the best ways, perhaps even a needed way, to show that. (Only the greatest actor, it might be thought, is able to be successful in simulating or faking such interest.)

These instrumental needs for interest are important. But I think there may be more to say. Some comments on interpersonal relations and group dynamics should help fill this out. Most of us know how unwelcome hostility and divisiveness are in a department (and, of course, elsewhere). For similar reasons, not being interested in the subject is also unwelcome. Here we should think of what it is like for others in a department to have one or more colleagues who have suffered burn-out, who have lost commitment and interest, whose hearts are no longer in it. We should also think of what this may be like for the people who have lost interest.

This has been to speak about the roles of certain intellectual emotions—mainly interest in philosophy—in a highly particular, nonuniversal 'setting': a contemporary philosophy department, in universities like ours, in societies like ours, with social needs and possibilities like ours, with students like ours, staffed with people like us, with experiences, psychologies, expectations, . . . like ours, and so on.

Some changes in such settings may make emotions, sometimes including intellectual and other nonstandard emotions, more important or less important. Here, instead of focusing on a philosophy lecture, we could consider other 'talks': e.g., a sermon intended to rally the faithful; a keynote address at a political meeting; heartening troops about to enter battle; a declaration of love; soothing an angry customer; and so on. It would misunderstand these talks to hold that, to be successful, they do not need to engender emotionally laden assent but will be counted successful if they engender only the emotionless assent or understanding of the sorts I suggested are all that is required by the advanced philosophy lectures.

I want now to turn to a somewhat different issue. It is obvious enough that intellectual emotions can be useful. A moment's thought should be sufficient to see that they can also be harmful for intellectual activity. Consider savoring, as discussed by Frijda and Sundarajan. It is often good to stop to smell the roses. But there are times when this is inappropriate, dangerous, wasteful of time, and so on. There are some people who are too eager to get things done, too fixated on doing and achieving (as these are commonly understood—doing as contrasted with thinking), who are unwilling to spend time thinking out and reconsidering what is to be done, and so on. So too, there are some who are too willing to stop, to digress, to be distracted from the tasks at hand, to rethink over and over, who are unable to commit themselves to action, and so on—who do not get beyond thinking to doing. Some people are too enthusiastic, with never a moment of repose and stillness; they enthuse over and get caught up in every new fad or theory. Some are never enthusiastic enough. These can be character flaws or problems that arise only occasionally or even just this once. Much the same holds for reflection and theorizing. There are times and places for engaging in these and times and places where to engage in them would endanger the very activity reflected on.

All this is obvious enough. But it leaves open the question of how, if at all, intellectual emotions are important, perhaps even essential, for good intellectual work. I do agree that many of our intellectual heroes were deeply interested in what they thought and did. Ribot's pantheon of Pascal, Malebranche, Davy, and Hamilton make this clear, as do the intellectual biographies of Einstein and of Watson and Crick, and so many others.

But perhaps on the other side, there is Fleming's just happening to notice the precursor of penicillin. As the story goes, his noticing what he did was more attributable to his attentiveness to anomalies in his surroundings than it was to his engagement. As well, we have to deal with science and other intellectual inquiry done by teams of researchers, technicians, and other workers. Here what is important for success may be more tied to their taking part in progressive research programs (to use Lakatos' terms) with a good division of labor, good leadership, and the like than to interest, fascination, curiosity, and other intellectual emotions.

As I see matters, we are here confronted by at least two very difficult, if not intractable, problems. The first has to do with the relative importance of individuals and of groups, and their interrelations, in accounts of intellectual (and other) work. As this might be put, are we to look more to psychology and or to sociology and social theory for these accounts? Emphasis on intellectual emotions seems to suggest concern with individuals. (Of course, it need not. It can allow for group psychology and it can see individuals as being shaped by, as expressing the concerns of, groups.) These very difficult issues have been discussed at length, and, I think, inconclusively in the subdiscipline of the philosophy of history, under the rubric of the role of the hero, the great man or woman, in history.

I intend to avoid any explicit concern with these issues and to turn to an issue, perhaps to be located in moral psychology, about intellectual and other *interest*. At issue is the likelihood of significant intellectual work being done by an individual or a group without intellectual interest and without excitement about the subject, even without interest in or love for the subject.

To put this, I will sketch how I imagine medieval scribes copying documents—an activity of incalculably immense intellectual worth. (Those bothered by my deficient imagination are invited to think of members of a contemporary research team.) I imagine that one lot of scribes found the documents themselves, or copying them exactly, deeply engaging. A second lot, however, found the copying just a job of work, even drudgery. They were told by their superiors to copy carefully and exactly, which they did because they were told to. A third lot did it out of a sense of duty or a religious or a professional calling.

Were these last two sorts of scribes *interested* in what they were doing? We might conclude that they were not interested in the copying as such. But it might be replied that the second lot must have been interested in having and keeping a job, despite the drudgery; and the third lot must have been interested in fulfilling their duty or their calling.

The reply about these people, especially the second lot, is useful as a way to put my worry about interest. I do see how it can be said that these people were, must have been, interested in having and keeping the job. (I am imagining that they were not forced, as prison inmates might be, to do the copying.) But—and this is my worry—the considerations leading us to hold that they were interested in having and keeping their jobs are pretty much the same considerations that could lead us (and have led some) to say that those considerations show that they *wanted* to have and keep the job. Why else would they do it? The reply might be 'to earn a salary to pay for their keep'. The reply, in turn, to this is that this shows that they were *interested* in earning a salary to earn their keep; and similarly for *wanting* to earn a salary to earn their keep.

I agree that there is a case for saying that they were *interested* in something—much like the case for saying that they *wanted* something. Some might say that this uses a discredited, over stretched sense of 'wanting'. But I think this is a legitimate use of 'wanting', even though it comes to little more than acting intentionally, intending or trying to achieve what the person is said to want. I think 'interest' in these last cases is understood similarly: what in this sense interests people is whatever they are intending or trying to achieve; whatever, from their point of view, is the point of what they are doing.

This, or a similar, understanding of 'interest'—interest understood simply in terms of acting intentionally with a goal—is of importance for us in at least two ways. First, some such interest of these last two sorts of scribes is not *intellectual* interest in the copying. So, intellectual interest in copying is not needed for good copying, even if some other interest is needed. Second, this sort of interest may well not be (part of) an emotion. So, the claim that good intellectual work requires an intellectual emotion of interest is doubly wrong.

My second point relies on the more general claim that acting intentionally toward a goal is possible even if one does not act with or from an emotion: intentional action need not involve any emotion. If this is right, we should examine whether intellectual interest must involve the intellectual *emotion* of interest or any other intellectual emotion. If it need not, then the claim that good intellectual work requires the emotion of intellectual interest or some other intellectual emotions will be wrong in three ways.

This in turn raises questions about the role and nature of intellectual interest vis-à-vis being a person of intellect, in common parlance an intellectual. An intellectual, as I understand this notion, is a person who is interested in intellectual matters, who has intellectual interests, and is admirable as a person in light of having such interests. I think intellectual *emotions* are also needed. It thus seems that, in these regards, an intellectual vis-à-vis intellectual emotions is like Aristotle's good man vis-à-vis the emotion(s) of courage. In both cases, having the emotion(s) is needed.

Aristotle's courageous person and an intellectual may also be similar in the following way: Aristotle holds that courage is not needed to be the best and most successful soldier; a mercenary can be a better soldier than a courageous man. I suggested above that having intellectual emotions, not just intellectual interests, may be necessary for being an intellectual. But someone who is *merely* intelligent, careful, attentive to details, and the like may well be a better intellectual worker, producing more and better intellectual products. (The issues surrounding whether we should hire and admire the best intellectual worker or the best intellectual raise similar issues about being red vs. expert, as discussed and fought over in China in the middle decades of the twentieth century, or about being a loyal party member vs. a skilled technocrat, as raised in examinations of the 'spoils system' entrenched in American governmental practices.)

I think these issues quickly lead to very large and difficult issues, some of which were mentioned earlier and most of which are too large and too difficult to do more now than simply announce them. I do not think we know—I know that I do not know—enough about the general, panhuman roles of intellectual emotions in the production of good intellectual work. I am unable to declare on the possibilities of intellectual success in a society or organization where intellectual workers—most, many, a significant number, . . . of them—do not have intellectual emotions, much like some of the scribes mentioned above. I think that in some cases at least, other interests, other incentives, could achieve what, in other cases, intellectual emotions would.

This last claim might seem to go against what I said earlier about the roles of intellectual emotions in teaching and learning. If it does, I should have been more specific. I said something like 'good teachers of philosophy to undergraduates need to engender intellectual emotions, at least curiosity about, perhaps even a love of, philosophy'. I may not have made it clear enough that I was talking about how I think matters now stand with the students we now have. I am thinking not of all students but those who will not pursue studies that do not interest them, that do not engender and sustain interest and other (positive) intellectual emotions. I include under the term 'studies' those as large scale as, say, physical sciences; or, somewhat smaller, philosophy; or still smaller, a particular course offered by a particular teacher.

There is, of course, controversy whether students' following their interests is good or bad. So too, there is controversy over whether students' following their interests marks a significant change in student behavior. I do not know if it is; nor, if it is, how much of a change there has been in, say, the last hundred years; nor, again if it is, how to explain it.

I have been concerned with the question of how important intellectual emotions are for good intellectual work. My comments about students following their interests and scribes doing what they are told to do or acting from a calling or duty raise two interrelated questions about these different motivations. One concerns the issue of how likely it is that the different motivations could have the same results. How likely is it that both finding the copying interesting and feeling a calling or duty could result in equally good intellectual work, perhaps even the same intellectual work? The other concerns the relative importance in people's psychic economies—their organization and budget of motives—of pursuing what one finds interesting, on the one hand, and following a calling or the call of duty, on the other. I think it clear that there are some people in whom one predominates and others in whom the other does: so, in order to get good copying done, it may well be sufficient to have some scribes who find this of interest or some others who feel called or duty bound to do this (or, of course, some mixture of both).

I will consider both of these by examining Adam Morton's comments on his powerful example of

an extraordinarily well-trained and malleable young scientist.... [with] a superlative grasp of research techniques, . . . [who has] one flaw, however. She does not care about the subject. She has no curiosity.... she does not find herself wanting the truth to turn out one way rather than another in more than . . . [a career enhancing] instrumental way. She does not sometimes wonder whether lines of inquiry that are, with good reasons, disparaged by her research group might not in the end give important clues to the underlying processes she is investigating. This scientist may well go on to do excellent work, and make significant discoveries. She may become eminent. But it is unlikely that she will lead her subject in radically new directions. Nor that she will be the one to find the new way ahead if current approaches stall, or to see deep subtle flaws in those current approaches, or willingly take her work in a direction that seems to her important but risks a lifetime of obscurity. She is rather like the child prodigy musician with rare skills and a marvellous technique, lacking only a love of music.[21]

I agree with what is implicit in Morton's example: that a person with those skills and training who also cares about her subject is likely enough—or as likely as anyone can be—to be curious, to wonder about disparaged lines of inquiry, to start radically new directions of research, to be alive to subtle flaws, and so on. What I am unconvinced of, however, is that such caring about the subject is necessary for any or all of these. As suggested about the scribes—and earlier, in a related way, about the advanced lecture on moral realism or physics to other equally advanced professors in the field—I think she could do any or all of these things without the intellectual emotion of caring for the subject. It would be sufficient, I think, if her team leader gave her well articulated directions: 'look into lines we disparage; make bold conjectures; get your colleagues and students to follow these out; check for subtle or other flaws'; and so on. So too, I think it would be sufficient if she had a sense of calling or duty.

This is to agree with Morton that something more than abilities, skills, and training is needed to make those accomplishments realistically likely. They are,

[21] From a draft of his 'Epistemic Emotions' for this volume.

after all, above and beyond the ordinary. It is also to agree with him that care for the subject might supply this something. But, now disagreeing with him, it is also to suggest that other conditions—other motivations or incentives—can also supply that something.

My general point here is that as useful as intellectual emotions are for good intellectual work, they are not part of or essential to that work, as work is understood in the relevant text or field, e.g., a philosophy article, a physics lecture. In this, such work differs from music as depicted by Morton. (All I will say on Morton's claim about music is that it is controversial, as are other, similar views that great art requires emotions in some or all of these ways: the artist's having them, transmitting them, and the audience receiving and experiencing them.)

I have said that it seems to me that Morton's researcher does not need the intellectual emotion of caring for her subject to achieve those great intellectual goods. But, for reasons given above, I am not entirely confident that this is right. So even at the end of my inquiry, I am unable to declare with certainty on whether— and if so, how—good intellectual work requires intellectual emotions.

This is to understand any such need *factually*—e.g., in terms of the psychic economy of different motivations and whether the same work could be done from other motivations or incentives. However, I am confident about at least some of the *evaluative* needs of the one for the other. Here I take my lead from Aristotle's discussion of how the value of courage differs from the value of winning and how what makes for the one value differs from what makes for the other.

I have given the materials for my evaluative comments throughout this work and elsewhere.[22] So, I will be very brief here. Intellectual emotions are instrumentally valuable, whether or not necessary, for good intellectual work and good intellectual workers. Intellectual emotions are also intrinsically valuable—as constituents of good societies or good aspects of societies, and also as constituent values of good lives and good aspects of lives. For both instrumental and intrinsic, constitutive reasons, then, intellectual emotions are to be recognized, respected, encouraged, and sustained. It is in part due to these emotions that philosophy and philosophers (both in and outside the academy) are valuable—indeed, valuable enough to merit social support and personal commitment. These emotions can be, and often are, central to the self conception and positive self appraisal of intellectuals, people who pursue and even love what is so valuable. Having those emotions is not just a job description, it is also a matter of accomplishment, pride, and value.

Recognizing the value and the different ways intellectual emotions are valuable is, I think, at least as important as being able to determine the extent to which good intellectual work requires those emotions.

---

[22] For example, in 'The Schizophrenia of Modern Ethical Theories', *The Journal of Philosophy*, 73, 1976, 453–66, 'Values and Purposes', *The Journal of Philosophy*, 78, 1981, 747–65, and *Valuing Emotions*.

# CHAPTER 19

....................................................................

# A PLEA FOR
# AMBIVALENCE

....................................................................

## AMELIE RORTY

# I

....................................................................

Perhaps purity of heart is, as Kierkegaard said, to will one thing. Perhaps, as Harry Frankfurt has suggested, the capacity for wholehearted commitment is an indication of responsible persons.[1]

But as these philosophers—call them purists—are the first to testify, ambivalence seems our natural condition. We are rarely wholehearted. We are ambivalent—multivalent—about most of the salient and important features of our lives, our relatives and colleagues, our occupations and projects, even about our hopes and ambitions.[2] Our motives and emotions are overdetermined; our maxims are ambiguous; their

For stimulating and helpful discussions, I am grateful to Jonathan Adler, MindaRae Amiran, Melissa Barry, Matthew Carmody, Jennifer Church, Joseph Cruz, Felmon Davis, Fred Dretsky, Catherine Elgin, Ronald de Sousa, Steven Gerrard, Aryeh Kosman, Genevieve Lloyd, Jonathan Malino, Susan Russinoff, Stephen Salkever, Susanna Siegel, David Wong; and audiences at colloquia at Harvard, Williams College, Union College, North Carolina State University, the National Humanities Center, and Bogazici University in Istanbul.

[1] See Harry Frankfurt, *The Importance of What We Care About* (Cambridge: Cambridge University Press, 1988).

[2] I take ambivalence to encompass a wide range of contrary cognitively laden attitudes: beliefs, emotions, doubts, commitments, evaluations, motives. For the sake of brevity and convenience, I shall speak of these as *attitudes* throughout. Love and hate, belief and doubt, prizing and despising, confirming and denying are contrary attitudes to a specific intentional content. I shall argue that a person can sometimes be justified in maintaining such contrary attitudes.

priorities are indeterminate; and we often take dim views of our ideals. We frequently waver between affirming our immediate desires and denying them in favor of (what we take to be) our more enlightened interests. We have different priorities in different contexts, without having criteria for distinguishing contexts, let alone well-formed principles for ranking compartmentalized preferences.

More suspect perhaps, but also widely acknowledged, is our ambivalence about moral righteousness, a moral stance so confident in what it conceives as right that it only acknowledges its fallibility in ritual general terms. We both envy and fear a species of righteousness that is so gripped by its convictions that it takes disagreement as a threat or a sign of culpable error. Such rectitude is on guard against acceding to dissenting views without first reinterpreting them to conform to its own pre-conceived judgment. While we hope that morality forms a coherent and unified structure, we are some- times also ambivalent about the kind of morality—and it is common—that is imperi- ous in theory as well as in practice, set to deny its own ambivalence.[3]

Purists typically see ambivalence as a barrier to the high road of rational or prudent action. It threatens to endanger steadfast and reliable commitments. Purists with a moral agenda see it as an impediment to wholeheartedness or to an unqualifiedly good will. It appears to signal a failure of personal integrity. More practically, it involves erratically shifting priorities, competing attitudes, conflicting emotions, and wavering commitments that can readily present problems for the specification of choice and action. Actions prompted from multi-valent attitudes tend to undermine one another's projects. Ambivalence is unsettling because it endangers the kind of confident and well-directed action that is taken to be a sign of moral assurance and integrity that is supposed to support moral efficacy. You don't have to be a purist to be suspicious of ambivalence. It may be a sign of intellectual or moral laziness, masking vague or ambiguous judgments, a disinclination to press for clarity and precision in one's attitudes, values, and commitments.

Yet even the most earnest moralist acknowledges that we are often conflicted about how to assign priorities among our multiple wholehearted commitments. Most canonic moral theorists—utilitarians, Kantians, virtue theorists and contem- porary moralists like Charles Taylor and Harry Frankfurt—implicitly offer second order counsel. "Don't dither. Pull up your socks and get over ambivalence. Work to formulate clear order of context-sensitive priorities about your commit- ments to what is important, to your integrity and identity. If you can't find such an order, choose or construct one, and—until you find commanding reason to elaborate or modify it—remain steadfast. If you do, you may find that the very act of deciding realigns your attitudes."[4] Typically, such moral theorists offer

---

    [3] See Susan Wolf, "Moral Saints", *Journal of Philosophy*, 1982, 410–39; "Above and Below the Line of Duty", *Philosophical Topics*, 1986, 131–48.

    [4] I am grateful to Jonathan Adler for this point. See Bas van Fraassen, "Value and the Heart's Command", *Journal of Philosophy* 70 (1973), 5–19 and his "The Peculiar Effects of Love and Desire", in

criteria for achieving moral clarity in perception and wholehearted integrity in action, guidelines for overcoming ambivalence by determining or evaluating priorities among moral principles/aims/virtues.

Why—considering the discomforts of ambivalence and the many counsels for overcoming it—is it nevertheless so prevalent and obdurate? The exuberant diversity of cultures in a genuinely pluralistic society allows us to absorb and internalize the mentality of a wide variety of modes of life, whose organizing values and perceptual saliences are sometimes incompatible and incommensurable. We are all (in one way or another) Algerian-American-academic-entrepreneurial-jazz-musician-parents. Ambivalence is one of the costs of the latent tensions among the competing priorities of our multiple allegiances.[5] The vicissitudes of psychodynamic development charted by Freud and Melanie Klein—the layered and continued identification and rejection of primary figures—provides another source of ambivalence.[6] Ambivalence is also sometimes the countercurrent of our experiences of change. Bewildering rapid and dramatic shifts in circumstances are enough to prompt us to attempt to find ways to retain the various terms that create apparent tensions among the directions of our various intellectual and emotional habits. Increasingly finding ourselves in novel and unfamiliar situations, we are presented with options that challenge deep-seated habits of perceptual salience, emotional reactions, and value commitments.[7] Ambivalence is sometimes an expression of our attempts to preserve long-standing, well-tested habits while also responding to novel situations that elicit radically different—and sometimes incompatible— attitudes.[8] We have good reason to retain entrenched patterns of salient responses; and yet at the same time we have good reason to adopt radically innovative attitudes. We want—and do not want—to revise our habits of perception and interpretation. We do—and do not—preserve our evaluative attitudes. In maintaining our multiple attitudes, we make ourselves vulnerable to the kind of confusion that attends ambivalence. But honest confusion may be preferable to righteous but self-deceptive closure.

I want to persuade you that high-minded purism needs to be modified and supplemented. Despite its uncomfortable shortcomings, despite the fact that it can

*Perspectives on Self-Deception*, eds. Brian MacLaughlin and Amelie Rorty (University of California Press, 1988), 123–56.

[5] See Amelie Rorty and David Wong, "Aspects of Identity and Agency", in *Identity, Character and Morality*, eds. Owen Flanagan and Amelie Rorty (Cambridge: MIT Press, 1990), 19–36.

[6] See Melanie Klein, *Narrative of a Child Analysis; Love, Guilt and Reparation* (London: Virago, 1989).

[7] For the sake of convenience, I shall concentrate on options for intentional action, but as—it will shortly become clear—I intend to refer to options more broadly, to include those of extending or narrowing the scope or focus of intentions and actions.

[8] See Albert Hirschman, *The Passions and the Interests* (Princeton: Princeton University Press, 1977), *passim*, and J.B. Schneewind, "Moral Problems and Moral Philosophy in the Victorian Period", presented to English Institute, New York, September 1964, *Victorian Studies*, Supplement, September 1965, 29–46, reprinted in *English Literature and British Philosophy*, ed. S.P. Rosenbaum (Chicago, 1971).

sometimes block reasonable and effective action, at least some forms of ambivalence are appropriate, and sometimes also morally and politically constructive, worth preserving.[9] Since ambivalence seems as inescapable as the experience of conflict, what matters in finding ourselves ambivalent is what we do with it, what we do about it. When certain types of ambivalence are unresolvable, when there is reason and justice on both sides, it is appropriate to retain the force of their terms and reasons, affirming them without self-deceptively denying their conflicts or moving to an nth-level of justification or, failing that, to self-identification ("Here I stand. I can do no other."). Even when choice seems inescapable, the considerations for the rejected alternatives should remain active in the space of the person's reasons and values. They can affect the thick description of actions, the manner in which they are performed.

I want to explore the skills and strategies that enable us to use appropriate ambivalence constructively, validating and preserving the multiple terms of psychological and moral conflict.[10] Understanding these strategies brings surprising insights into the constitutive function of imaginative thinking in substantively well-formed robust practical reasoning. They highlight the need for norms of epistemic responsibility. Analyzing techniques for preserving appropriate ambivalence may also help chart the ways that reflective equilibrium can be maintained and constructed. The strategies of constructive ambivalence provide models for addressing conflicts in the public sphere: while they cannot ensure morality, they are among the civic virtues.[11]

# II

It's high time to give a rough initial characterization of ordinary ambivalence. Having classified ambivalence as a species of conflict, Frederic Schick offers this pre-philosophic folk-psychological account: "A person is ambivalent towards y if she wants y and also does not want y and thinks these are incompatible."[12] But ambivalence is not limited to preferences or to courses of action. Even when there is no desire in the offing, we can be ambivalent about how to perceive or describe what

[9] See Bernard Williams, "Ethical Consistency", *Problems of the Self* (Cambridge University press, 1973, 166–86); Stuart Hampshire, *Justice is Conflict* (Princeton, 2000); Michael Walzer, "The Problem of Dirty Hands", *Philosophy and Phenomenological Affairs*, vol. 2, 1973, 160–80.

[10] "The Desirability of Creating Moral Conflict", *Proceedings of the Philosophy of Education Society*, 1996.

[11] I shall speak interchangeably of strategies, skills, methods, and techniques for addressing appropriate ambivalence. Roughly speaking, a strategy is a heuristic formulation of a method, skill, or technique. As I use them, these active procedures may, but need not be, consciously applied; and, as I shall argue, their use can become habitual.

is most salient about a person or situation, even about judgments about the past or works of fiction. As a wife can be ambivalent about her husband's ambitions, an historian can be ambivalent about whether she thinks, all things considered, it was a fault in Caesar that he was ambitious; and a literary critic can be ambivalent about whether Nabokov's *Pale Fire* is, all things considered, a tedious flop or a brilliant tour de force. It is of course not surprising—even to be expected—that we might have different and even opposed attitudes in different contexts, or under different descriptions. There is no ambivalence in changing one's mind, in finding that yesterday's political enemy has become today's political ally. But being simultaneously of two minds about the proper criteria for enmity and friendship—about whether to give precedence to political over military alliances in a specific context—seems to undermine acting effectively from resolved judgment.[13]

Attributions of ambivalence are notoriously slippery. We sometimes attribute it to a person only if she experiences herself as having unresolvable tensions in her attitudes to a specific object. But we are also prepared to attribute it to someone who self-deceptively denies that her attitudes conflict. Like most attributions of intentional attitudes in opaque contexts, the attribution of ambivalence is subject to the ambiguity and fluidity of identifying the context and boundaries of intentional attitudes. Locating their proper objects—and thus the focus of a person's attitudes, their intentional objects—is sensitive to the ways that the boundaries and contexts are defined. Because the specification of the focus and boundaries of the intentional objects of attitudes affect the scope of considerations relevant to their evaluation, they are subject to normative epistemic considerations, some but not all of which may be moral.

We need an example. Natasha, chair of the philosophy department in a small liberal arts college, is conflicted about which of two candidates she thinks would best serve the interests of the department.[14] The department needs another logician; and it also needs someone—a "generalist"—who can convey the attractions of philosophy in introductory courses. One of the candidates—call her Andrea Keen—is a brilliant, highly focused productive scholar who has already published influential papers in . . . let's call it "the decision semantics of mathematical logic". The other, call him Max Saftig, has wide interests in aesthetics, Sino-Russian art history, and the psychology of perception. He is apparently an excellent colleague and teacher; he is, however, slow to publish and the department might eventually have difficulty tenuring him. Natasha wants to appoint Keen and does not want

[12] Frederic Schick, *Making Choices* (Cambridge: Cambridge University Press, 1997), 59–60 and *Ambiguity and Logic* (Cambridge: Cambridge University Press, 2003).

[13] I distinguish ambivalence from indecision, uncertainty, and vacillation in Section VII.

[14] I'll initially use examples of individual ambivalence, but a community can, and sometimes should, be appropriately ambivalent. Because individuals are as pluralistically divided as the communities that form them, it is by reflecting on the appropriateness of community ambivalence that we can gain insight into its constructive function for individual persons.

to appoint her (because she also wants to appoint Saftig and thinks she cannot appoint both Keen and Saftig). Similarly she wants to appoint Saftig and does not want to appoint him (because she also wants to appoint Keen and thinks she cannot appoint them both).[15] Like Natasha, the other members of the department are of divided mind about the candidates: roughly half marginally favor Andrea while the other half lean towards Max. Because they agree that, *ceteris paribus*, Andrea and Max are—by some measure—equally "intelligently strong" of their kind, the source of their ambivalence about Keen and Saftig—the proper focus of their contradictory attitudes—is an ambivalence about the *sort* of philosopher they want, an ambivalence about the criteria they should use in making the appointment. Because they are conflicted about the appropriate focus and contextual boundaries of their choice, they are ambivalent about the relevant criteria for evaluating their candidates. They think they should appoint the person with the highest professional reputation; and they think they have equally strong grounds for not appointing that person. They think they should appoint the person who is likely to have the greatest outreach influence on their students; and they think they have equally strong grounds for not appointing that person. Their commitments are contradictory as well as conflicted.

Let's call "appoint the person with the most established reputation" and "appoint the person with the widest intellectual scope" the *thin descriptions* of the department's options; and let's call their conflict about these two options a case of thin *ambivalence*. As I shall use these terms, *thin descriptions* of options are, roughly speaking, identified by a set of semantically conventional descriptions of action-types as they might be externally or extensionally identified by non-partisan native speakers.[16] The thin descriptions of standard action-types tend to carry implicit cultural assumptions about agent intentions, but even in ordinary unambivalent choice, action options are intentionally identified by the perceptions and interpretive descriptions that set their evaluative salience for a specific agent.[17] The thin descriptions of actions do not specify their temporal scope, the agent's intentions or reasons, or ways they are performed (e.g. "She greeted him." "She ignored him."). The *thicker descriptions* of these actions include their adverbial and

---

[15] Without committing myself to the view that the cognitive content of desires form propositions with determinate satisfaction conditions, I shall—for the sake of convenience—speak of desires as judgments about satisfaction conditions.

[16] See Clifford Geertz, "Thick Description: Towards an Interpretation of Culture", in *The Interpretation of Culture* (New York: Basic Books, 1973), 3–32. Bernard William uses the contrast between thin and thick concepts for a somewhat different purpose. See *Ethics and the Limits of Philosophy* (Cambridge, MA, Harvard University Press, 1985).

[17] See Paul Grice, "Utterer's Meaning, Sentence Meaning and Word Meaning", "Utterer's Meaning and Intentions," *Studies in the Way of Words* (Cambridge, MA: Harvard University Press: 1989), passim. For instance, "going to the bank", "going to the post office" carry cultural assumptions about agent intentions. But these can be overridden in individual cases: "going to the post office to apply for a passport".

temporal scope (e.g. "She greeted him warmly/coldly." "She always pointedly ignored him."). Still thicker descriptions include the person's evaluative intentions or rationale (e.g. "Vengefully, she snubbed him."). As we shall see, such action modifiers and specifications enable a person to express both terms of an ambivalence: performing the thin action-type acknowledges one side, tempering its thickened token performance expresses the other side (e.g. "Standing dutifully in the wedding reception line, the bride's brother greeted her guests coldly and sardonically.").

In being conflicted about the candidates for the appointment, Natasha is expressing ambivalence about the criteria she thinks are relevant to the decision, an ambivalence about where she thinks she *should* focus in making this decision. The *thick* detailed descriptions of Natasha's ambivalence includes the intentional description of what is salient in her perceptions of the alternatives, as indicating the way she envisages their respective connection to her long range preferences and values. Natasha's ambivalence has a bite—it is troubling to her—because she thinks normative considerations should not only guide her vote on the appointment but also the focus and salience of her perception of these candidates and the way she should characterize the scope and boundaries of her choice. Ambivalence about desires or courses of action tends to be regressive: it has its sources in a species of cognitive dissonance about what should be salient about them once a context is specified. It extends to a conflict about how to characterize what might be relevant to choice.[18] Let's call cases of regressive ambivalence that include the thick descriptions of the focus of thin ambivalence, cases of *thick ambivalence*. Strictly speaking, thick ambivalence moves from ambivalence about options to further ambivalence about what is relevant or salient about them, to ambivalence about normative conceptions of the relevant boundaries and criteria for choice in the context at issue.

But is Natasha—as we've described her—genuinely ambivalent? There is no contradiction in Natasha seeing Andrea under one description and Max under another, thinking of each as strengthening the department in a different way. Ambivalence seems problematic only when it involves cognitive dissonance that preserves *object constancy* and violates *belief consistency*. As she was originally described, Natasha does not have conflicting attitudes towards the *same* object, to the *same* contextually located object or state of affairs. She perceives the strength of each candidate differently. For her to be ambivalent, she would have to see Andrea's focused hard-edged talents a both as counting in favor of the appointment *and* as counting against it. Similarly, the scope of Max's interests would have to be seen as a liability *and* as an advantage.

[18] See Leon Festinger, *A Theory of Cognitive Dissonance* (Evanston, Ill.: Row, Paterson, 1957); E. Aaronson, "The Theory of Cognitive Dissonance", in *Advances in Experimental Social Psychology*, vol. 4, ed. L. Berkowitz (New York: Academic Press, 1969).

Ambivalence is often disguised by laziness or self-deception. Natasha might have sneaky ways of avoiding facing the discomforting work of addressing her ambivalence about the role she thinks philosophy should play in an undergraduate college. She could, for instance, use an accordion principle, thinly describing the criteria for the appointment so as to disguise the tensions that might emerge if she troubled to develop a thicker description of her choice. Rather than thinking about the various ways that the appointment might have long-range effects on the future of the department, she could self-deceptively avoid recognizing her ambivalence by narrowing or fragmenting the focus of the decision so as to shirk the work of forming an all-things-considered judgment about how she thinks philosophy should be taught to undergraduates.[19]

Ambiguity and vagueness are often both a source and a disguise of ambivalence.[20] Recognizing them can also dissipate its appearance. Unaware of what she is doing, Natasha might waffle between three senses of "philosophy" as designating: (1) a professionally self-defined and self-accrediting discipline, (2) a reflective mode of thought about a range of topics (morality, life and death, right and wrong, reality and appearance), (3) a normative conception of a method and set of topics that are a subset of professionally accredited topics or questions. (This last sense is most often used to discredit a specific approach or questions, as in "That's not philosophy!" or "That's not really philosophy!") When Natasha faces a choice between her conflicting conceptions of the department as preparing students for graduate work in professional philosophy and as performing a more general cultural and intellectual function, she may come to realize that this conflict not only reveals an ambivalence about the rationale of the appointment but also an ambivalence about philosophy itself. She may in fact have a normative conception of philosophy (3) that would support her appointing only one of the candidates, while using the professionally defined frame of (1) to narrow the short list. In such a case, she may be confused without being ambivalent. As long as she recognizes the ambiguity and compartmentalizes the thin description of her attitudes, she simply has a difficult, perhaps even conflicted choice. Her conflict only emerges as a case of thick or regressive ambivalence when she attempts to unite the object of her attitudes to form a unified single conception of philosophy. Taking such epistemic responsibility might move her first to acknowledge and then to address her ambivalence.

---

[19] As we shall see, narrowing the boundaries of action descriptions can, as it did in Eichmann's case, also affect the allocation of responsibility. ("I was only doing my official duty.") Less dramatically, a person could disclaim responsibility for causing pain to a subject in a psychological experiment by arguing that (although she knew that she produced a shock by flipping a switch) she only intended to follow the experimenter's directions.

[20] I am grateful to David Wong for this point.

# III

With the example of Natasha in hand, we are now ready to extend Schick's initial folk-psychological characterization of ambivalence.

Roughly, a person $p$ is *ambivalent* when:

(1) under a particular description $d$ of a contextually located object or state of affairs $s$, $p$ takes a specific attitude $a$ towards it; under a different description $d'$ of what she believes is extensionally the *same* object or state of affairs, $p$ either takes a different attitude $b$, or rejects attitude $a$; and

(2) $p$ believes that the two attitudes are incompatible; and

(3) $p$ thinks some resolution is required; she believes that she should accord salient priority to either $d$ or $d'$ in that context; and

(4) $p$ is unable to accord either of the two descriptions or attitudes a ranked priority of context-based appropriateness; *or p* has conflicting beliefs/attitudes about the norms for the appropriate description of the contextually based scope and focus of her choice.

Before showing that Natasha's ambivalence can sometimes be appropriate and constructive, we need to show how persistent it is. Like all attitudes, those that form Natasha's ambivalence have a latently wide scope. They are embedded and entrenched in her practices; they ramify in ways that affect the field of her perceptions and values. The considerations that formed her ambivalence are also reflected in her tastes and her choice of friends; they affect the tenor and manner of a wide range of her actions and preferences. Because the terms of her original ambivalence ramify widely, their residue would remain no matter who had been appointed. Natasha might well have regretted having lost Saftig if Keen were appointed, and vice versa. Although she has resolved one ambivalence, she has not—or anyway not yet—become an entirely different person. The repressed returns and ambivalence pursues her. Integrity and the harmonious integration of a person's attitudes may sometimes pull in opposite directions. A person of integrity acknowledges the range of her values and attitudes even when they conflict, while a person is integrated when her attitudes are unconflicted, harmoniously.[21]

We are now in a position to characterize appropriate ambivalence. Natasha's continued ambivalence will be *appropriate* when both of her conflicting thick intentional descriptions of her situation are reasonably well grounded; and although she thinks that she should preserve both of her conflicting attitudes, she reasonably does not presently see how she can do so.

---

[21] (Contrary to Plato), a person of integrity may fail to be integrated; and a well-integrated tyrant may fail to have integrity. See Amelie Rorty, "The Hidden Politics of Integrity", in *Integrity in the Private and Public Domains* eds. Alan Montefiore and David Vines (London: Rontledge, 1998), 108–20.

Roughly, a person *p* is *appropriately ambivalent* when

(1) *p* believes that both of at least two apparently conflicting thick descriptions, *d* and *d'*, of her situation are well grounded or well founded in context *s*; and

(2) they are reasonably well-grounded and well founded; and

(3) *p* is ambivalent about which descriptions should be salient in dominating her attention in *s*; and

(4) *p* reasonably believes that she cannot—and should not—discard or eradicate her perceptions of her options; she believes that the considerations that support them should remain in the space of her reasons.

The criteria for "reasonably" in conditions 2 and 4 do some heavy lifting. Natasha's beliefs about her ambivalence are reasonable when her implicit reasons for holding them conform to the dominant epistemic norms of intersubjective confirmation in her culture. This condition combines subjective and objective perspectives: (1) relative to her position (i.e. level of education, intelligence, scope of experience, access to information and reliable authority), she has good grounds for her beliefs and attitudes *and* (2) she has been a responsible epistemic agent. (As we would have it, she been open to evidence and arguments, has engaged in reflective equilibrium about her values and attitudes). There are two perspectives for identifying cases of appropriate ambivalence. Given the context of her situated epistemic standards, a person might be judged appropriately ambivalent about a specific practice—say that of colonial taxation— yet also be judged inappropriately ambivalent about them, all things considered. Appropriate ambivalence is context- and perspective-dependent; its several grounds may be incommensurable, without a determinate dominance in one context, but not in another. Because moral responsibility typically depends on (but is not ensured by) epistemic responsibility, responsible agents are accountable for framing the contextual boundaries of their intentions, choices, and actions appropriately.

It might at first seem as if appropriate ambivalence should present no threat to Natasha's integrity and peace of mind. Her ambivalence—and her regret—should have no sting if she thinks that the various descriptions of her options are appropriately germane and that all her options are permissible and constructive. In this case, she might think that the interests of the department would be equally though quite differently well served by Keen and by Saftig. But while this reflection may preserve her sense of integrity, she is likely to find attempting to maintain wholeheartedness difficult, unending, and unsatisfying work. In such circumstances, regret may be the only available homage to integrity.[22] Even though she might judge Andrea to be a strongly contributing member of the department, she may nevertheless continue to regard her manner and her highly focused philosophic interest with some distaste. To the extent that she fears that students

---

[22] See "Agent Regret", *Explaining Emotions* (Berkeley and Los Angeles: University of California Press, 1976), 489–506.

may come to resemble Keen, she retains remnants of her original ambivalent perceptions. While all things considered, she does not regret her choice, she may nevertheless also find that the project of wholeheartedness exacts what she perceives as an unacceptable cost. It prevents her from accepting the multiple potentially conflicting perspectives to which she is committed. Ironically, even austere moral purists who think that morality forms a strictly consistent system may become ambivalent about wholeheartedness.[23]

In searching for ways to address what has become a deep and apparently intractable second level ambivalence about wholeheartedness, Natasha surprisingly finds that the inventive methods and imaginative skills of Thomistic and Talmudic disputation can provide some guidance.

A typical Article of the *Summa* begins with a question or a problem, for example, "Is choice only concerned with means, or are ends also sometimes chosen?"[24] Citing Scripture and the authority of other commentators, Aquinas proceeds to outline a *thin* description of one position on the question (choice is only of means) followed by a thin description of an apparently inconsistent view (ends can also be chosen). In the next step, he speaks in his own voice, reconciling the two by introducing a distinction between intermediate and final ends that provides a *thick* description of each of the initial responses: intermediate but not final ends can be chosen. The Article concludes with Aquinas replying to both of the initial thinly described positions, showing in what sense—or in what context—they are partially correct but limited or misleading when abstracted from their thick specification. In one sense the opposition set by the initial thin responses to the question has been preserved; but their appropriately expanded thick descriptions have transformed the original opposition. It remains an open question—one which would engage an interpretation of much of the *Summa*— whether it is philosophically appropriate to preserve the thin descriptions of the oppositions in their original forms.

Although it differs from a typical Thomistic Article, Talmudic reasoning resembles its structure. A practical problem is posed or an ambiguous text is presented for interpretation. Various rabbis propose different and apparently competing ways of interpreting and addressing the issue, each citing a respected authority or a proof text for confirmation. As the discussion proceeds, the formulation of an initial problem is increasingly expanded by a set of distinctions and qualifications. In the next round, one rabbi claims that the conflicting views have been reconciled by the redescription of the relevant issues. Others—also citing respected authorities— maintain that the expanded description only complicates, but does not resolve, the problem. Clarifying distinctions and ingenious arguments have been offered at each stage of the discussion. Thomistic Articles end with a definitive resolution that

---

[23] See "The Many Faces of Morality", *Midwest Studies in Philosophy* 20, 1996, 67–82.
[24] *Summa Theologica*, Article 3 of Q. 13 in prima secudae.

resolves the apparent conflict while also preserving the insights of both views. Talmudic discussions are implicitly left open: there is no consensus about whether the discussion can be considered definitively settled. The disputation is reported, printed on a page whose margins present conflicting views of later commentators about whether a resolution was reached. Contemporary scholars argue that, although each position remains contentious and contended, it presents a view that is meant to be preserved, maintained in the field of reasons and values.

Both Thomistic and Talmudic methods of conflict resolution enable apparently incompatible positions to stand together, while nevertheless also retaining and developing what is distinctive—and apparently opposed—about them. By conserving what seem to be mutually exclusive positions, Talmudic strategies preserve the possibility of continued deliberation in potentially divided communities. As Aquinas and the rabbis reinterpreted and restructured the competing views of respected authorities, so too an appropriately ambivalent person can attempt to reinterpret and restructure the terms of her original apparently incompatible options. And as Talmudic discussions leave the question of whether the disputation has been resolved open for further disputation, so too some attempts to resolve ambivalence may appropriately reintroduce it on another level.

# IV

Natasha and her colleagues can attempt to preserve her apparently conflicting perceptions by transforming their options in a variety of ways. The strategy of *compartmentalizing* preserves the original perception of the incompatibility of various options while creating a buffer to prevent their coming into direct conflict. (For instance, the administration could create a new interdisciplinary program in linguistics, mathematics, and philosophy to house Keen, enabling the philosophy department to hire a generalist.) The strategy of *compromising* and *compensating* would involve attempting to preserve both options by revising their descriptions or conditions[25] (e.g. the department could try to persuade both Keen and Saftig to accept a three-quarter time position with special privileges and research leaves). *Reframing* would involve revising the aims and contextual boundaries of choice and changing the criteria for options that might be relevant to it (e.g. the department might treat the appointment as an experiment in revising their curriculum; or they might decide it doesn't matter whom they appoint because they would make something worthwhile of the new position in either case).

---

[25] See Avishai Margalit, *Rotten Compromise and Honorable Peace* (Tanner Lectures, 2005).

*Reconciling* and *integrating* would involve reconceptualizing intentional descriptions of the valences of options so as to overcome their apparent opposition.[26] (For instance, instead of thinking of focused and latitudinarian philosophy as incompatible, Natasha might come to think of philosophy as well formed only when it combines focused precision with robust fertility. As a result of integrating the terms of their original ambivalence, the department might decide to hire neither Keen nor Saftig and to reformulate the description of their position.)

While these strategies are by no means mutually exclusive or exhaustive, each exploits the advantages of the fluidity of the focus and boundaries of choices and actions. As they stand, they are morally neutral: they can be used for good or ill. Each imaginatively attempts to combine the thin descriptions of intentions and actions within a thicker description that extends the boundary and context of the agent's intentional description of her action. These strategies can take a Thomistic or neo-Hegelian form of reconciliation in which the compounded layers of the thick descriptions of the choice are seen as compatible, even as mutually supportive within an enhanced frame. In such cases, ambivalence has—for the time being—been temporarily overcome. But they can also take a more Talmudic form, preserving the tensions among the layers of their thick descriptions. The first is more comfortable; the second can be more searching and far-reaching. Instead of addressing her ambivalence by discarding or eliminating some of its terms—a species of lobotomy that often prompts the return of the repressed—attempting to preserve her ambivalence can, with luck, make Natasha more ingeniously effective in all her projects. Using these strategies she has in a sense "resolved" her ambivalence. But since she has preserved both attitudes, their implications remain subject to a regressive return in another context. When the struggles of ambivalence seem inescapable, what matters is the robust fertility and subtlety of temporary resolutions.

# V

It's all very well to claim that appropriate ambivalence can be adapted, constructively preserved by a set of imaginative strategies. The question still remains:

---

[26] See Erving Goffman, *Frame Analysis* (Cambridge: Harvard University Press, 1979); J. A. Fodor, *The Modularity of Mind* (Cambridge: MIT Press, 1983); Z. W. Pylyshyn, ed. *The Robot's Dilemma: The Frame Problem in Artificial Intelligence* (Norwood, N.J.: Ablex, 1987); D. Sperber and D. Wilson, *Relevance* (Cambridge: Blackwell, 1995); Avishai Margalit, "Ideals and Second Bests", *Philosophy for Education*, ed. Seymour Fox (Jerusalem: van Leer Institute, 1983).

how are these improvisations constructed? While it is tempting to postulate and reify a special faculty, "the imagination" as the source of inventive thinking, the skills exercised in compartmentalizing, compromising, reframing, and integrating actually comprise a diverse set of heterogeneous cognitive and rhetorical activities. Our brief sketch of strategies for preserving the terms of ambivalence suggests a rough list of the activities engaged in practical imaginative thinking. They are of course neither exhaustive nor mutually exclusive. Needless to say, all these modes of imaginative thinking are morally neutral. They can be used well or ill, beneficently or harmfully.

- generating or enlarging alternative options of action
- generating or enlarging unconventional conceptions of the affordances of objects and situations (e.g. treating an academic appointment as an experimental adventure)[27]
- specifying the sensory and phenomenological details of options[28]
- shifting perspectives on a situation
- revising descriptions and interpretations of perceptions (e.g. seeing a person as eager rather than aggressive, ingenious rather than cunning, collaborative rather than manipulative)[29]
- developing and specifying the implications of analogies (e.g. working through the details of historical analogies: "Remember Munich" or "Remember Vietnam")
- tracing the ramifications of competing policies (e.g. tracking the long-range consequences of the consequences of redistricting voting eligibility)
- varying some of the variables that define or compose situations or contexts (e.g. rearranging the seats of an inner-city classroom to change the dynamics of student interactions)
- specifying the details of hypothetical thought experiments (e.g. Parfit's accounts of mind–body switches, Thomson's Trolley Problem, Hardin's Life Boat Ethics)[30]
- role-playing, modeling, pretending, simulating[31]
- applying a general principle or maxim to new or hypothetical cases (e.g.

---

[27] See J. J. Gibson, *The Senses Considered as Perceptual Systems* (Boston: Houghton Mifflin, 1966).

[28] Merleau-Ponty, "Interrogation and Intuition", in *The Visible and Invisible* (Evanston, Ill.: Northwestern University Press, 1964), 105–26; see the essays in Ned Block, *Imagery* (MIT Press, 1984); E. Casey, *Imagining: A Phenomenological Study* (Bloomington: Indiana University Press, 1976); J.-P. Sartre, *The Psychology of the Imagination* (NY: Washington Square Press, 1966).

[29] Iris Murdoch, "The Idea of Perfection", in *The Sovereignty of Good* (London: Routledge, 1970), 1–45.

[30] See Derek Parfit, *Reasons and Persons* (Oxford: Oxford University Press, 1984), Judith Thomson, "A Defense of Abortion", in *Philosophy and Public Affairs*, 1971, 47–66; Garrett Hardin, *Morality within the Limits of Reason* (Chicago: University of Chicago Press, 1988); Roy Sorenson, *Thought Experiments* (New York: Oxford University Press, 1992); Martin Bunzl, "The Logic of Thought Experiments", *Synthèse* 106(2), 1966.

[31] See Colin McGinn, *Mindsight* (Cambridge: Harvard, 2004); Shaun Nichols and Stephen Stich, *Mindreading* (Oxford: Oxford University Press, 2004); Kendall Walton, *Mimesis as Make Believe* (Cambridge, MA: Harvard University Press, 1990); Alvin Goldman, *Simulating Minds* (New York: Oxford University Press, 2006) Ch. 11.

applying the doctrine "men are created equal and with inalienable rights" to Iraqi prisoners of war)

- reframing, extending, or narrowing contexts
- reframing and revising criteria for relevance in decision-making (e.g. introducing new conditions for college admissions)[32]
- introducing distinctions to bypass the force of polarized options (e.g. innate vs. acquired, good vs. evil)[33]
- constructing idealized models of explanation[34]
- sympathetic and empathic projection.[35]

Like the strategies used in basketball and chess, all of these imaginative skills can be acquired: they can be taught, they can be imitated; they can be practiced. Brilliant and resourceful kindergarten teachers convey the techniques, strategies, and habits of imaginative practical reason. Without marking them as Moral Education, they engage children in activities common to all successful practical enterprises: role-playing; asking questions to elicit suggestions for unconventional uses of ordinary objects (how many things can you do with a brick?); considering the consequences of hypothetical situations (how would things be different if our playground had been on the shore of a lake?; how would home life be different for you if you had ten sisters and brothers?; how would home life be different for your parents if they'd had ten children?). This sort of education does not stop with kindergarten. Courses in medical ethics can raise questions that enable physicians to develop the capacities of imaginative thinking about the needs and fears of indigent undocumented immigrant patients; courses in business ethics can raise questions that enable employers to think imaginatively about how to address the concerns of their employees; courses in international economics can raise questions about the consequences and ramifications of outsourcing. Even—perhaps especially—those engaged in training military personnel can try to develop the improvisatory skills involved in

---

[32] See Avishai Margalit, "Ideals and Second Bests"; Sabina Lovibond, *Realism and Imagination in Ethics* (Minneapolis: University of Minnesota Press, 1983) pp. 194 ff.

[33] See Jonathan Adler, "Distortion and Excluded Middles" and "Refute or Accept", unpublished manuscripts.

[34] See Gerald Holton, *The Scientific Imagination: Case Studies* (Cambridge University Press, 1987); Ulrich Neisser, "Perceiving, Anticipating, Imagining", *Minnesota Studies in the Philosophy of Science*; Nancy Nersessian, *Creating Scientific Concepts* (MIT Press, 2008); Nancy Nersessian, "Interpreting Scientific and Engineering Practices: Integrating the Cognitive, Social, and Cultural Dimensions", in *Scientific and Technological Thinking*, M. Gorman, R. Tweney, and D. Gooding, eds. (Hillsdale, N.J.: Lawrence Erlbaum, 2005), pp. 17–56; Christopher Hill, "Modality, Modal Epistemology and the Metaphysics of Consciousness", in *The Architecture of the Imagination*, ed. Shaun Nichols (Oxford University Press, 2006), 205–35; Tamara Szabo Gendler and John Hawthorne, eds. *Conceivability and Possibility* (Oxford University Press, 2002).

[35] See Carol Gilligan, *In a Different Voice* (Cambridge: Harvard, 1993); Nel Noddings, *Caring* (Berkeley: University of California Press, 2003). For a refined discussion of the moral force of empathy, see Stephen Darwall, "Empathy, Sympathy, Care", in *Philosophical Studies*, 89, 1998 261–82.

situations of great danger and uncertainty. Rather than offering appeals to the imagination conceived as a distinct generative and somewhat mysterious poetic faculty, we need to integrate these sorts of skills, strategies, and habits *within* our textbooks and courses on critical thinking, *within* philosophic treatises on moral education, *within* our educational practices, *within* our ordinary interactions with one another. The skills and techniques of imaginative thinking should become a constitutive part of a person's second nature in thought. Resourceful and improvisatory thinking should be effortless, integrated within perceptions and experience, without needing to be summoned in situations of difficult or conflicted choice.

It should by now be obvious—or at least clearly plausible—that all practical reasoning and, for that matter, all inquiry and justification engage the varied cognitive activities conventionally encompassed and reified as "imaginative". Every step of critical thinking, of practical deliberation, of demonstration and persuasive justification involves working through hypothetical counter-factual inferences. When it is radically constructive, such thinking can realign and revise conventional classifications and fundamental categories.[36] The strategies of imaginative thinking are not just stylistic ornaments in otherwise rigorous linear Bauhaus thinking. They are essential to any kind of robust reasoning, whether practical or theoretical, exploratory or demonstrative, morally dubious or morally responsible. They are engaged in hypothetical reasoning, theory construction, even in ordinary explanation. An historian may revert to some of the strategies of imaginative thinking in order to explore the rationale of Caesar's decision to cross the Rubicon; an economist's attempt to understand and predict consumer behavior typically requires imaginative thinking. Rather than appealing to the imagination conceived as a distinctive and somewhat mysterious creative or poetic faculty, we need to integrate its skills and strategies—its habits of improvisation—within our ordinary cognitive practices. The modes and techniques of imaginative thinking should become constitutive, part of a person's second nature, exercised without having to be summoned.

You might object that, as I have described it, imaginative thinking has been made to encompass all thinking, including what was, in OldSpeak, called rational inference. You might be concerned that the strategies of imaginative thinking cannot be ensured to be self-corrective, constructive, or productive. They can be wild, wooly, and distracting, indeed sometimes epistemologically and prudentially dangerous. Poetic imagination needs no justification, no criteria of responsibility. But when thinking has an aim, its activities need to be checked by considerations of plausible relevance. In attempting to preserve appropriate ambivalence, imaginative thinking needs the constraints of epistemic relevance and responsibility.

---

[36] See Daniel Kahneman and Dale Miller, "Norm Theory: Comparing Reality to Its Alternatives", *Psychological Review* 93, 1986, 136–53.

Rationality without imaginative thinking is empty and sterile; imaginative thinking without rationality is chaotic.

We can sketch some initial provisional conditions for epistemic responsibility in preserving ambivalence.[37]

Roughly, a person $p$'s *ambivalence is epistemically responsible* in situation $s$ when:

(1)  $p$ is appropriately ambivalent about $s$, that is, both sides of her ambivalence are well grounded;

(2)  $p$ is aware of the implications of the conventional descriptions of $s$ and of the standard norms governing its descriptions; and

(3)  $p$ has imaginatively found ways to preserve the terms of her ambivalence; and

(4)  $p$'s imaginative thinking has remained within the bounds of plausible and practicable relevant alternatives; that is, the range of alternative descriptions she considers acceptable would not require massive further revisions in the space of her reasons and values.

While a person cannot be morally responsible without being epistemically responsible, someone might be epistemically responsible without being morally responsible. J. Robert Oppenheimer[38] might have been epistemically responsible in thinking about the presuppositions and ramifications of his work in Los Alamos without taking its moral consequences into account. A medical researcher might be epistemically responsible about her work without thinking about its moral implications. When morally responsible agents extend and thicken the frame and context of their action descriptions to include their morally relevant features, they may find themselves appropriately ambivalent about what they do. Yet a person may sometimes overcome her ambivalence when further reflection reveals her commitment to overriding moral considerations. If—despite her commitment to the dominant moral principle—she continues her practice, she might be akratic, or even an akratic believer, but her ambivalence would typically dissipate. She might be regretful, but no longer ambivalent.[39]

# VI

When it is epistemically responsible as well as ingenious, preserving appropriate ambivalence can be highly constructive. Instead of addressing ambivalence by

[37]  See Dan Sperber and Deirdre Wilson, *Relevance*; Paul Grice, "Utterer's Meaning"; Fred Dretsky, "Epistemic Operators", *Journal of Philosophy*, 1970, 1007–23; David Hitchcock, "Relevance", *Argumentation*, 1992, 251–70.

[38]  See Amelie Rorty, "Questioning Moral Theories", forthcoming.

[39]  I am grateful to Catherine Elgin for calling my attention to the complexities of some of these cases.

discarding or eliminating some of its terms—a species of lobotomy that often prompts the return of the repressed—attempting to preserve ambivalence can, with luck, make a person more ingeniously effective; it can enlarge and enrich the scope of her activity.

A person has been *constructively* as well as responsibly ambivalent when she has imaginatively and responsibly thickened and restructured the thick descriptions of her options, finding ways to preserve the apparently opposed value perceptions that make her various options salient to her.

Roughly, a person *p* is *constructively ambivalent* when

(1)  *p*'s ambivalence is appropriate; and
(2)  *p* has preserved both of the thin descriptions of her apparently incompatible perceptions of her options within a thick description that compartmentalizes, compromises, reframes, or embeds them, while also recognizing that—taken in isolation, out of context—the thin descriptions of her alternatives may remain apparently incompatible; and
(3)  *p* has been epistemically responsible; and
(4)  given the total economy of her priorities, *p* has the energy and resourcefulness to engage in the work of preserving the terms of her ambivalence.

# VII

Let's suppose that you've now been convinced that appropriate ambivalence can sometimes be constructive, and that imaginative thinking is essential to its proper preservation. You might still have some objections and questions. Let me just touch on these briefly.

*First*, you might wonder how preserving ambivalence differs from the kind of tolerant fallibilism advocated by Mill and Dewey. Far-sighted fallibilism argues for retaining dissenting views in the space of reasons; sound prudence argues for their inclusion in community deliberation. Mill argues in favor of intellectual and political tolerance for the expression of dissent because he thinks that open discussion in the marketplace of ideas conduces to clarity and precision, to appropriate self-criticism. But although he acknowledges that there is a wide range of morally permissible values and attitudes, he thinks that the core system of true beliefs and moral evaluations is coherently unified. By contrast, preserving constructive ambivalence goes beyond open-minded tolerance and support for diversity: it remains agnostic about Mill's conviction that imaginative and critical deliberation ultimately converges in a consensus about a unified and justified moral system.

*Secondly,* you may wonder how ambivalence differs from indecision, uncertainty, and rapid vacillation. These conditions are often attributed interchangeably in ordinary speech; and they are not distinguished by their intensity or degree of discomfort.[40] They can nevertheless be usefully, if artificially distinguished by the strategy that is best suited to address them. If Natasha is *uncertain* about which candidate to favor, she is in a neither/nor epistemic condition, not confident that she knows enough about the skills and abilities of either candidate to determine which would best suit the needs of the department. Since she doesn't have sufficient evidence in the matter, she should adopt a position of epistemic modesty and attempt to discover more about whether the candidates have hidden strengths that have not appeared in their conventional job applications. If Natasha is *indecisive,* she is not prepared to support either candidate because she has not determined which considerations she thinks should serve as criteria for the decision, and believes she should be able to rank their relative importance or relevance. Her best policy is to engage in the method of reflective equilibrium, subjecting both her particular intuitions and her general principles to mutual critical evaluation, hoping to arrive at guiding criteria for a responsible choice. If Natasha is *appropriately ambivalent* about her decision, she has sound but incommensurable reasons for both of her commitments. She is in a both/and epistemic condition. A persistent, imaginative, and responsible attempt to find ways of preserving the terms of her ambivalence is her best epistemic policy. Natasha *vacillates* among her preferences when she wholeheartedly endorses one at time t and wholeheartedly endorses an incompatible preference at time t+1. Ambivalence has sometimes been redescribed, reconstructed, and deconstructed, as involving rapid *vacillation* between genuine but incompatible attitudes or commitments.[41] But vacillation presents the same problems for well-constructed judgment and choice that ambivalence does. If consistency—and by extension, appropriate stability in perspective—are virtues, they are required over a reasonable period of time as well as at a time-slice. In any case, at least some vacillation is prompted and explained by ambivalence rather than the other way around.

*Finally,* you may wonder why it is desirable to develop the abilities exercised in preserving the terms of ambivalence when doing so evidently often generates yet more ambivalence. A true but unhelpful reply is that we have no other option. Since ambivalence is prevalent and intractable we might as well attempt to find its benefits and attempt to cultivate the skills that best address its inevitability. More significantly, the imaginative skills exercised in preserving appropriate ambivalence are precisely those that are also needed to resolve tensions within a community. The skills and ingenuity exercised in compartmentalizing, compromising, reframing,

---

[40] I am grateful to Elliot Sober for insisting on this point.

[41] See Patricia Greenspan, "A Case of Mixed Feelings: Ambivalence and the Logic of Emotion", *Explaining Emotions,* ed. Amelie Rorty (Berkeley: University of California Press, 1980), 223–50.

and embedding the terms of an individual's ambivalence are also those that are engaged in addressing public dissent and conflict. They involve describing and constructing public policies in terms that succeed in preserving and coordinating apparently incompatible perspectives and attitudes. As citizens in a pluralistic democracy, notionally committed to acknowledging and respecting a wide range of occasionally conflicting value preferences, the abilities involved in addressing appropriate ambivalence are among the civic virtues. Like other civic virtues, they encompass perceptual, imaginative, rhetorical, and conceptual skills. And like other civic virtues—courage, moderation, resourcefulness, fortitude, clarity of mind—they can be misused. In any case, there may be situations in which other considerations—epistemic, prudential, or moral—should take precedence over even the most soundly imaginative, responsible, and constructive ambivalence.

We can now see that both pessimists and optimists can support our plea for ambivalence. The pessimist says: "See? We'll never escape ambivalence." The optimist says: "Rejoice in the ambivalence that avoids the boredom of stupefying wholeheartedness." The despairing pessimist adds: "The virtues you propose can serve the unjust as well as the just." The sanguine realist responds: "That's how it is with all the virtues: Taken individually, their skills are not automatically self-corrective."

I want to end with a Yiddish story about ambivalence. A very wise and famous rabbi was asked to settle a long-standing dispute between two philosophers. He listened intently as the first philosopher presented his case, and, after reflecting carefully, he said, "You're right." After hearing the second philosopher's brilliant and ingenious refutation, the rabbi said, "You're right." Somewhat confused by this performance, his wife complained: "You told both philosophers that they were right, but their arguments were totally contradictory. They can't both be right." The rabbi replied, "You know something? You're also right."

# CHAPTER 20

# EMOTION, SELF-/OTHER-AWARENESS, AND AUTISM: A DEVELOPMENTAL PERSPECTIVE

R. PETER HOBSON

## 20.1 INTRODUCTION

If humans were to lack psychological concepts to serve as the vehicles of thought about mental life, we should be hard-pressed to disembed ourselves from what Hutto (2006) has called 'unprincipled engagements' with the world. Through the related abilities to symbolize and abstract this or that aspect of experience and/or behaviour from the hurly-burly of our transactions with the social and non-social environment, we acquire the ability to articulate thoughts about our own and others' psychological relations with people, objects, and events.

Yet the processes that give structure to thought may also introduce distortion in our vision of the way things are. As Wittgenstein (1958) illustrated so vividly, our concepts can lead us into disguised nonsense. For example, the act of abstracting this from that may trap us into supposing there is some essential rightness about how we have drawn our distinction, or lead us to think that our concepts identify particulars in the world that can be separated from each other. Such convictions may not be justified. In particular, we are inclined to think in terms of affective, cognitive, and motivational components of mental functioning; we draw a marked distinction between perceiving bodies and understanding minds; we consider thinking to be an activity accomplished by individuals, rather than an emergent property of social-relational systems; and we suppose that we understand other people by some form of cognitively elaborated role-taking, often expressed as 'putting oneself in the other's shoes'. Of course, not all people think in these ways; nor, for some intents and purposes, is it inappropriate to do so. Yet the distinctions we draw can beguile us into misconceiving the nature of what we are describing.

In addressing these matters, it may be helpful to adopt a developmental perspective. If we can discern how adult-style capacities to think and feel and be aware of oneself have developed, then this may contribute to our view of how feeling is related to thought, how motivation enters or leaves the picture, and what is and what is not 'social' about self-awareness. To this we can add another perspective, and explore whether developmental *disorders* might change our view of how thinking, feeling, and willing, and with these, self-awareness, are structured. Such viewpoints may prompt us to reconfigure our thinking about emotions, and in particular, those emotions that are intimately involved with our experience of persons, if we are to achieve a more adequate perspective on the nature and development of human psychology.

My approach is heavily influenced by two rather different strands of theoretical and empirical work within developmental psychology. The first is that founded by Jean Piaget (e.g. 1972), namely genetic epistemology. As Hamlyn (1978) has argued, genetic epistemology is, or should be, the study of the conditions that make certain forms of knowledge possible. In the present context, I shall focus upon the role of emotional experience in underpinning our knowledge of persons-with-minds, and our concepts of self and other. In addition, I shall offer some observations on the structure of 'social emotions'. Yet there are other, even more basic issues in genetic epistemology to which I shall refer by way of introduction, in particular the relation between feeling and thought.

The second strand of work is that of developmental psychopathology. Developmental psychopathology is the study of typical and atypical child development in relation to one another. The aims are to elucidate the course of psychopathological development through the study of typically developing children, and to further our understanding of the processes of typical development through the study of atypical cases. One of the strengths of this approach is that it may reveal how aspects of typical children's psychological functioning that seem to develop in tandem are potentially dissociable, and how disparate aspects of children's functioning are more intimately intertwined than had seemed to be the case. In this way, findings from developmental psychopathology may provide empirical grounds for re-examining the concepts in terms of which we characterize the workings of the mind. Here I shall focus on the condition of early childhood autism.

## 20.2 THE PLACE OF EMOTION

When, in the seventeenth century, the distinction between knowledge and desire was elaborated into a threefold division of mental activity involving cognition, conation, and affect, we gained powerful conceptual tools to think about the mind. Yet those very tools may be appropriate and effective for some purposes but inadequate for others. For example, are thinking, willing, and feeling separate throughout development, even in human infancy, or is there a developmental story to tell about whatever separateness is achieved? From a complementary viewpoint, are there different species of thinking and feeling, for instance in relation to the social vis-à-vis the non-social world, or is each domain relatively coherent?

These are hot topics within psychology. One might imagine that, this being so, the psychological literature would be characterized by flexibility and innovation when it comes to fashioning the terms in which our theories of thinking and emotion are framed. Yet we find two symptoms of intellectual malaise in unconvincing accounts of the cognitive nature of emotions (e.g. contributions to Scherer & Ekman, 1984), and unenlightening rhetoric to the effect that 'everyone knows' how cognition and emotion are not completely separable. We seem a long way from devising a satisfactory theoretical scheme to encompass and contextualize human emotions. The problem becomes acute when one considers how the very concepts of 'emotion', 'thinking', and 'willing' differ when they are applied to infants, on the one hand, and to toddlers (never mind adults), on the other.

Here is a distillation of some of the psychological-cum-philosophical points for which I shall be arguing:

(i) The relative separation of feeling, thinking, and willing is a developmental achievement. Or to express this differently, there is little justification for supposing that concepts of 'emotions', 'thoughts', and 'motives' characterize *components* of infant mental life, even though there are circumstances in which they do so (more or less) when characterizing adult mental functioning. Instead, it is sometimes justifiable and worthwhile to highlight emotional, cognitive, and conative *aspects* of the relations between infants and the social and non-social world (Hobson, 2008).

Indeed, these aspects of relatedness are critically important for what become relatively differentiated components later in development.

I shall dwell upon an emotional-cum-cognitive-cum-motivational process that has special importance for human social experience, especially in structuring intersubjective linkage and differentiation, namely that of *identifying with* the attitudes of other people. The thesis I shall present is that identification determines the character of some, but only some, emotions that are directed towards other people. These emotions have what psychoanalysts call an 'object-relational' (effectively, person-related or part-person-related) structure.

(ii)  The emotional aspects of infants' interpersonal relations are critical for what become older children's abilities to think. This fact of development (if fact it is) has implications for our concept of what thinking is. Two especially important considerations were stressed by the Russian developmental psychologist Lev Vygotsky. Firstly, Vygotsky (1962, p. 8) envisaged how thinking is forever bound up with feeling, in that he posited 'the existence of a dynamic system of meaning in which the affective and the intellectual unite. It shows that every idea contains a transmuted affective attitude toward the bit of reality to which it refers.' Why *every* idea? The reason, I take it, is that thinking is derived from person-world relations that have affective aspects.

Secondly, Vygotsky (e.g. 1978) proposed that higher cognitive functions arise through the interiorization of interpersonal processes. If such processes are structured by mechanisms that implicate emotions, as I shall argue, then this is another reason why emotions are foundational for thinking.

(iii) Affectively configured personal relatedness provides the grounding for our understanding of persons-with-minds. We do not have a 'theory of mind', because there is almost nothing theory-driven about the way we derive our concepts concerning people's mental life. I shall stress two points here (having discussed others in Hobson, 1990, 1991, 1993a,b). Firstly, our concepts of mind require symbolic mediation. Symbolic thinking is not only a developmental achievement grounded in specific forms of interpersonal relatedness but also (I argue) an ability that recruits a person's understanding of what he or she is doing in symbolizing (Hobson, 2000). If this is so, then certain forms of symbolizing require self-awareness, just as certain forms of self-awareness require one to symbolize. As G. H. Mead (1934) suggested, there are essential links among Mind, Self, and Society.

Secondly, the contents of our concepts of mind draw upon our experience of relating with feelings to other embodied persons. Hamlyn (1974, 1978) argues that, in order to know about a given object of thought, one needs to stand in relation to that object in ways that are fitting for the object in question. In the case of knowing about human beings, one would not know what a person is unless one could experience, or could have experienced, mutual interpersonal relations involving feelings. A corollary is that, if a child were limited in the potential to engage in and experience appropriately patterned social–emotional relations, then that child would also be limited in his or her understanding of what a person is.

Moreover, to conceptualize persons is part and parcel of conceptualizing mental states such as feelings, thoughts, or beliefs, for the reason that these states are ascribed to persons who are also selves. Therefore any account of the acquisition of mental state concepts entails an account of understanding self and other. From an empirical standpoint, there appear to be several separate strands of experience that contribute to concepts of oneself and others. Correspondingly, there are several separate components (not merely aspects) to self- and other-awareness. Some, but only some, of these components are *inter*personal in nature. It follows that, if a child were limited in the ability to engage in affectively co-ordinated mutual engagement with others, then that child might acquire partial concepts of self and other, and with this, partial concepts of what it means to have mental states.

(iv) Current theories about the development and structure of 'complex' social emotions such as guilt and concern overestimate the role of self-*concepts* in providing a cognitive architecture for such feelings. There are grounds for thinking that some descriptively complex emotions are developmentally and phenomeno- logically primitive social-relational/emotional states. They do not depend on the prior development of thinking regarding oneself and others. On the contrary, such states contribute to the conditions that lead to the emergence of concepts of self and others around the middle of the second year of life, as well as to the contents of these concepts. A complication is that not all supposedly complex social emotions occupy a common developmental line: for example, jealousy contrasts with some other social emotions in its origins and nature.

These four themes may prompt us to reconsider how far and in which respects certain emotions are *essentially* social.

## 20.3 SOME DEVELOPMENTAL OBSERVATIONS

For the present purposes, I shall distil some observations of typically developing infants at three phases of life: when infants are approximately two months of age, then towards the end of their first year, and finally when they reach the middle of the second year of life.

One classic study of early infancy was that conducted by Brazelton et al. (1974), who filmed infants from four weeks old under two conditions; firstly, as they related to an object (a small fuzzy monkey suspended on a string) which was brought towards the infant's 'reach space' and then withdrawn again; and secondly, as the infants interacted with their mothers in relaxed face-to-face contact. The authors reflected on their observations as follows: 'We felt that we could look at any segment of the infant's body and detect whether he was watching an object or interacting with his mother—so different was his attention, vocalizing, smiling, and motor behavior with the inanimate stimulus as opposed to the mother' (Brazelton et al., 1974, p. 53). The object would hook the attention of infants and prompt them to make jerky movements accompanied by mouth-opening. When the infant was interacting with his mother, on the other hand, there seemed to be patterns of interpersonally regulated affective attention, with smoother movements and shorter spans of attentiveness and looking away. It is also the case that young infants react to perturbations in such natural, co-ordinated interpersonal exchanges. Cohn and Tronick (1983) instructed mothers of three-month-old infants to interact with depressed expressions during three-minute periods of face-to-face interaction. The effect was that the infants became negative and showed protest and wariness. Murray and Trevarthen (1985) sat individual two- and three-month-old infants before a television monitor which showed the mother's live face, looking towards the infant. Mother and baby were able to engage with each other via television in a surprisingly natural and fluent way—except when the researchers desynchronized the exchange by introducing a delay of 30 seconds in the time when the mother's responses were relayed to the baby over the TV link. The effect was considerable infant distress, with the infants turning away from and darting brief looks back towards the mother's image, a qualitatively different set of reactions than occurred when the mother merely looked away.

Then somewhat later in development, towards the end of the first year in what Trevarthen and Hubley (1978) call the stage of secondary intersubjectivity, infants relate to others' relations to a shared world. For example, in episodes of joint attention, infants may bring objects to show to someone else, apparently with the aim of sharing experiences (Bretherton et al., 1981; Carpenter et al., 1998). In instances of social referencing, where an infant is confronted with an emotionally ambiguous object or event, the infant looks and then responds to the affective expression of a parent, as this has directedness to the object or event in question. In one well-known early study (Sorce et al., 1985), for example, what seemed like a 'cliff' prevented the child reaching a goal, and the majority of 12-month-olds who perceived that their mothers were looking to the cliff with smiles tentatively proceeded towards their goal, whereas none of those who witnessed their mothers showing fear towards the cliff did so.

Subsequently, in the middle of the second year of life, as a child moves out of infancy, he or she comes to conceptualize self and other as separate individuals who have their own takes on the world. At this age, toddlers come to make self-descriptive utterances such as 'my book' or 'Mary eat' (Kagan, 1982), they show abilities to comply and co-operate with others, and they engage in co-ordinated role-responsive interactions (e.g. Kaler & Kopp, 1990). Hoffman (1984) tells the story of how Marcy, a girl of 20 months, drew her sister away from playing with a toy she wanted by climbing up on her sister's favourite horse and crying: 'Nice horsey! Nice horsey!'. Such more or less explicit forms of emotional understanding, role-taking, and self-reflective awareness (Zahn-Waxler et al., 1992), together with a capacity to symbolize in play (Hobson, 2000; Lewis & Ramsay, 2004), appear to emerge hand in hand from around the middle of the second year of life.

How might these developmental observations influence how we conceptualize emotion, thinking, willing, and self-/other-awareness? I shall select a few points for consideration.

## 20.4 Interpersonal engagement

### 20.4.1 Primary intersubjectivity

From the early months of life, we can distinguish among different modes of relatedness between an infant and the world. Of special importance for the present purposes is the distinction between I-Thou and I-It relations (Buber, 1937/1958). Here there is a complication in interpreting the evidence, insofar as it is not necessary that 'personal relatedness' is always manifest in an infant's relation to persons, since at times infants (like adults) may appear to interact with non-personal objects or animals as if they were persons. There is a further difficulty in specifying what features of relatedness are necessary and/or sufficient for a given mode of relatedness to be identified as 'personal'. Notwithstanding these caveats, it appears that, at least by two months of age, infants engage in co-ordinated exchanges with people that differ in certain important respects from their relations with things.

The claim here is not that, by two months of age, infants have refined sensitivity nor responsiveness to everything that can be expressed by someone else. Rather, they appear to have the capacity to engage with other people with feeling and something akin to communication—at the same time as 'social smiles' appear around eight weeks, they also make effortful vocalizations that appear to be directed to another person with whom they are engaged—and more than this, they are perturbed if the other person does not co-ordinate his or her behaviour accordingly. Importantly, the adult's experience in such exchanges is of making rewarding emotional contact with the baby, and of sharing the experience of the exchanges.

It is difficult to see why one should dissect these kinds of infant-other relations into cognitive/perceptual, affective, and motivational components that need to be assembled in order for such relatedness to occur. Although the infant appears to distinguish people from things (a cognitive accomplishment), shows affects that appear to be organized in relation to others, and is motivated to engage in special ways, each of these descriptions captures *aspects* of the observed personal related-ness. Insofar as the infant engages differently with persons and things, this is manifest in patterns of relatedness in which, at least on the face of it, feeling and motivation are inextricably linked.

In perceiving another embodied person, then, infants are drawn into emotional relations with that person; as Buber (1937/1958, p. 18) put it, 'In the beginning is relation'. Infants do not distinguish between bodies and minds because they relate to what we call persons; and, to begin with, what they experience in their relations with persons is, in effect, the kind of 'understanding-in-relation' that they have of persons. Just as the person is a more fundamental concept than those of the human body, on the one hand, and the human mind, on the other (Strawson, 1959), so, too, prior to the advent of conceptual understanding of what a person is, relations with embodied persons are foundational for such understanding. What infants apprehend *through* perceiving a person's expressive body, and what they experience as they respond in mutually co-ordinated affective exchanges with other embodied persons, constitute Buber's I-Thou relation.

These features of interpersonal engagement with others have significance throughout life. This is more than a matter of developmental precedence. It is also a matter of genetic epistemology, in that experience of personal relations continues to ground understanding of persons as persons. As Wittgenstein (1980, vol. II, p. 100e) wrote: 'We do not see facial contortions and *make the inference* that he is feeling joy, grief, boredom. We describe a face immediately as sad, radiant, bored, even when we are unable to give any other description of the features.'

## 20.4.2 Secondary intersubjectivity

I have implied that, from two months of age at least, infants register the otherness of a person with whom they are involved in face-to-face exchanges—a point to which I shall return. However, other-centredness as a feature that determines the character of social experience becomes unmistakeable only with the advent of what Trevarthen and Hubley (1978) called secondary intersubjectivity towards the end of the first year of life.

How are we to interpret a 12-month-old's ability to learn about the environment through his or her (emotional) responsiveness to the attitudes of someone else? One might suppose that this could be much like discovering things for oneself. Such appears to be the case in instances of social referencing among non-human primates, who also monitor and make adjustments in accord with conspecifics' behaviour in relation to the world. Yet where human infants differ from non-human primates is in their propensity to show things to people, dwelling on the other people's reactions. Here infants appear to be powerfully engaged with the other person. This other person is not merely a way-station to learning about the world but instead is a pivot in 'triadic' person–person–world relatedness. The infant has a focus upon, and at times is moved by, the attitudes of the other as 'other'.

In the case of identifying with the (perceptible, bodily expressed, emotionally toned) stance of the other towards the world in episodes of joint attention or social referencing, I suggest, an infant has a kind of 'double take' on the object or event at the focus of attention. He or she both has an initial way of apprehending the object or event, and then in addition, he or she responds to, assimilates, and (potentially) adopts the attitude of the other. The critical element in this suggestion—and one for which direct evidence is hard to come by—is that, in the child's own experience, the otherness of the other-person-anchored attitude is registered, even in infancy. Although not conceptualized at this stage of life, the structure of such co-orientation in relation to a given object or event is such as to establish the possibility of the infant coming to differentiate how two person-anchored attitudes can be brought to bear on the same object or event in the environment. As Campbell (2002) argues, in joint attention it is constitutive of your experience that the other is, with you, attending to something.

According to this perspective, it is not merely that there is something cognitively styled (one might say) about an individual's way of relating to another person as another person, or relating to objects and events with meanings that may shift in accordance with another person's attitude. More than this, the infant is responding to and with affective expressions and relatedness, and is motivated both to engage with the other person and to alter in attitude towards the world related-to by the other. If the notion of 'being moved' is appropriate here, this is because it captures something of the motivational and emotional as well as cognitive aspects of what social referencing entails. So once again, we might apply the concept 'cognition' in relation to one aspect of a process that has indissolubly conative and affective aspects as well. The cognitive part is that one comes to construe something in a new way, and that new way entails tendencies to action and feeling.

As a bridge to the next part of the argument, it may be worth illustrating how this kind of developmental perspective, with its focus upon infants' and toddlers' experience alongside that of adults, might alter how we characterize emotion. I shall select the writings of Goldie (2000) for comment, for the reason that Goldie's critique of the over-intellectualization of emotion and his advocacy of the concept of 'feeling towards' are very much in keeping with the position outlined here. If Goldie can be taken to task for importing too much cognition into his account of emotions, certainly he is not alone in this respect. Goldie (2000, p. 19) states that 'Feeling towards is *thinking of* with feeling, so that your emotional feelings are directed towards the object of your thought.' Although it is possible to apply the expression 'thinking of' to infants, this carries risk—a risk that might still be present, but obscured, when applying the terms to adults. The reason is that one might presume 'thinking of' means thinking with concepts, or perhaps refers to thinking that is 'with feeling' in the sense of being alongside rather than integral to the feeling. An alternative way of putting the matter is to suggest that infants relate to the world with attitudes that we might choose to describe according to their cognitive and emotional and motivational *aspects,* whilst not yet wishing to characterize these relations as involving 'thinking of'. Or again, Goldie (p. 193) considers a situation in which one person shares emotion about a scene or speech with an audience, and states: 'my sharing of it with another in no way serves to *explain* my understanding of what it is about—either in myself or in the other members of the audience or crowd; rather, my realization that the object of emotion is shared *requires* my understanding of what the emotion—mine and theirs—is about'. This may be so in some circumstances, but it is still possible to claim (as I do) that an infant's sharing of experiences of objects and events situated in a world common to both parties does *not* require understanding (except in a very minimal sense that is not in question here), and also that such non-inferential sharing is a critical part of the developmental story of how conceptual understanding of person–world relatedness is acquired. When Goldie (p. 181) argues that to understand and explain another person's emotion, '*it does not require that any emotion be felt by the interpreter*' (author's italics), this may not apply to an account of how a child's understanding of a person's emotion develops in the first place.


## 20.5 SYMBOLIC THINKING AND THE CONSTRUCTION OF CONCEPTS OF SELF AND OTHER

My claim is that movements in affective stance through responsiveness to the attitudes of others establish a framework within which a child can, between about nine and 18 months of age, come to conceptualize—that is, think about—how different persons have different takes on the same shared world. One contribution to this development is that the infant begins to adopt the stance of the other towards his or her own attitudes, which as Mead (1934) described, is important for at least some forms of reflective self-awareness. The reversibility of communication—that what X means when you use it to communicate something to me is what X means when I use it to communicate to you—and the emancipation of meanings (anchored in symbols) from the objects in which those meanings inhere amount to the dawning of symbolic thinking.

Through identifying with the attitudes of others towards a shared world, then, infants come to grasp the distinction between person-anchored attitudes and the objects and events that are at the focus of those attitudes; that is, more or less, they acquire the ability to differentiate between thoughts and things. Through communication shaped by identification, they also learn about the nature of predication in which a topic is distinguished from whatever is said about it.

## 20.6 IDENTIFYING WITH THE ATTITUDES OF OTHERS

The observations and reflections offered thus far beg a series of theoretical as well as empirical questions about the nature of interpersonal engagement. In particular, how are we to characterize those forms of face-to-face sharing experience in the first year of life that are special to humans? What might give differentiation to experience such that, even in infancy, a baby has some experiences that include another special kind of 'thing' (what we adults recognize as a person) as participating in the experiencing? How is it that, around the end of the first year, human infants but not non-human primates show things or point things out to other people in 'sharing' acts of joint attention? And how is it that very young children are not only moved to adopt the orientation of others towards a shared world (which, in one sense, non-human primates are, too) but also come to be able to relate to their own relations to that world around the middle of the second year, as in choosing to make one thing stand for another in symbolic play, or in conceptualizing their own and others' feelings and preferences?

A tradition of thinking about modes of sympathy, relatedness, and primary communication that may be traced through writings in philosophy (e.g. MacMurray, 1961; Merleau-Ponty, 1964) and psychoanalysis (e.g. Winnicott, 1958) to contemporary psychology (e.g. Bråten, 1998; Decety & Chaminade, 2003; Meltzoff, 2002; Trevarthen, 1979) posits that a basic unit of study is self in relation to other. For example, Neisser (1988) describes an embodied direct perception that occurs when the self is engaged in immediate, unreflective social interaction with another person. If we can characterize the structure of infant 'feeling perception' that gives rise to experiences of self-in-relation-to others, then we may be in a position to account for the development of increasingly explicit forms of self–other differentiation and, in due course, conceptual understanding of what it means to be a self.

We may come close to achieving this characterization by following Freud (1921/1955) in positing a biologically based, quintessentially human propensity to identify with others. The definition of identification provided by Laplanche and Pontalis (1973, p. 205) is a good place to start: 'Psychological process whereby the subject assimilates an aspect, property or attribute of the other and is transformed, wholly or partially, after the model the other provides.' Through the process of identifying with others' bodily expressed emotional attitudes, for example, an individual perceives and assimilates the attitudes as other-person-centred, in such a way that they become possibilities for the person's own relations with the world, including the individual's relations towards him- or herself.

There is a complication here, namely that the very nature of identification changes with development. Although Freud (1921/1955) illustrated his notion with a cognitively elaborated instance, namely a boy's wish to be like his father, he concluded a brief essay on identification with a footnote in which he made the following claim: 'A path leads from identification by way of imitation to empathy, that is, to the comprehension of the mechanism by means of which we are enabled to take up any attitude at all towards another mental life' (p. 110). Clearly this refers to a much more basic level of identifying-with, but one for which it remains true that 'identification is not simple imitation but *assimilation*' (Freud, 1900/1953, p. 150, author's italics). Indeed, the developmental evidence already cited may indicate that the kinds of sharing that occur between much younger infants and other people *also* entail both connectedness with and differentiation from the other's state. The critical requirement is that the infant registers the otherness of the embodied, expressive other as part and parcel of this species of experience. However, if experience with this structure is already present well before the middle of the first year of life and lays the ground for identification proper, it would not necessarily involve the kind of non-inferential role-taking that characterizes paradigmatic instances of identifying-with.

The capacity to share experiences is only one kind of interpersonal engagement that requires something like identification. When one is frightened of another person's anger, one may experience (in the one experience) conflicting attitudes of fear-towards-an-angry-other-person. The partitioning implicit in such seemingly unified states becomes evident in other settings, for example in the play that one observes in young children who re-enact troubling encounters from the perspectives of *both* protagonists in the exchanges. Goldie (2000, p. 191) is surely correct that 'where one's interaction with another person is of such a nature—confrontational for example—that one can very clearly recognize another's emotion, [yet] it would be absurd to presume that one *has* the same emotion as the other person'. However, this does not mean that the emotion one has lacks any contribution derived from one's registering the other's feeling within oneself, through identification. Rather, it leads us to consider whether we need a more complex and refined specification of what is entailed in feeling 'fear' and other emotions in different settings, one that is in keeping with Goldie's own approach to thinking of sympathy as a 'sort of emotion' (p. 9).

It is worth stressing that an infant can identify with someone else's attitudes prior to conceptualizing another person as a person. The experience of otherness as one aspect of infants' interpersonal experience is a vital part of what enables growth towards understanding persons-with-minds. Once developed, conceptual understanding never completely replaces the more intuitive and unconceptualized modes of identification on which it is founded. It is also worth restating that the process of identification is not merely cognitive in nature. It is also a motivational and paradigmatically emotional process. We are *drawn to* and *moved by* our affective engagements with other people. In virtue of the structure of identification, we are also moved towards assuming, as well as relating to, the psychological stances and perspectives of others.

If this account of identification is preliminary and in many ways question-begging, we may achieve a better grasp of what the process entails by considering the case of children who seem to be limited in experiencing and conceptualizing other people *as* persons-with-minds, namely those with early childhood autism.

## 20.7 THE CASE OF AUTISM

Autism is a syndrome, which means a constellation of clinical features that happen to co-occur (Kanner, 1943). Central among the features of autism are impairments in social relations, deficits in creative flexible thinking and language, and the presence of unusual mannerisms and/or preoccupations. Classic descriptions from Kanner (1943) and Bosch (1970) convey something of the children's strikingly unusual relatedness towards others. For example, Kanner wrote the following about five-year-old Paul (case 4, p. 228): 'He never looked up at people's faces. When he had any dealings with persons at all, he treated them, or rather parts of them, as if they were objects.' As Bosch (1970) recorded of one individual with autism: 'We never noticed that his gaze merged in mutual understanding with that of another' (p. 8).

One of the most influential theories about autism attributes a range of the children's difficulties to their limitations in what has been called (regrettably, in my view) their 'theory of mind', that is, in their ability to conceptualize certain mental states including those of believing. 'Theory of mind' theorists characterize this as a cognitive deficit because it amounts to a limitation in thinking about people's minds. Yet is it *merely* cognitive, either in its origins or in its manifestations among individuals with autism?

### 20.6.1 Interpersonal relations and identification

A first step in addressing this question is to note how deficits in 'theory of mind' among children with autism are situated within a broader range of social-relational as well as cognitive limitations. For example, there is substantial evidence (reviewed in Hobson, 2005) that affected children have impairments in recognizing and responding to other people's emotional states, not merely in understanding some mental state terms. Many studies (e.g. Charman et al., 1997) have documented the onset of their limitations in joint attention and other kinds of person-with-person engagement well before they could be expected to conceptualize minds. Perhaps most relevant for the present purposes, they are atypical in their relative lack of engaging in sharing forms of joint attention and in social referencing. For example, Sigman et al. (1992) videotaped 30 young children with autism who had a mean age of under four years, together with matched children without autism, in the presence of an adult who appeared to hurt herself by hitting her finger with a hammer, simulated fear towards a remote-controlled robot, and pretended to be ill by lying down on a couch for a minute, feigning discomfort (and see Charman et al., 1997, for similar events involving 20-month-olds). In each of these situations, children with autism were unusual in rarely looking at or relating to the adult, and seldom being affected by the adults' attitudes to the robot. When the adult pretended to be hurt, for example, children with autism often appeared unconcerned and continued to play with toys. These observations confirm the relative lack of emotional con-nectedness between young children with autism and other people, and illustrate the children's lack of engagement with other people's attitudes towards a shared world—a world that, amongst other things, contains themselves. These areas of impairment appear to involve more than limited attentiveness or even affective responsiveness to other people. There is also a lack of sharing of the kind that entails a partial *movement into* or assimilation of the stance, the attitude, or the communi-cative intention of the other (Hobson, 1993a, 2002).

One might enquire how the actions and gestures of others are perceived by individuals with autism. In particular, is their capacity for 'feeling perception' compromised? Colleagues and myself have addressed this question in a series of studies (summarized in Hobson, 2005), of which the following by Moore et al. (1997) is an example. We assessed how children and adolescents experience and describe a person presented through moving pin-points of light, created by attach-ing reflective patches to the limbs and torso of a person, against a dark background. The point-light person enacted gestures of surprise, sadness, anger, fear, and happiness which were later displayed as brief video vignettes to the participants. In the anger sequence, for example, the point-light person gestured in an irritated manner with his arms while stamping his feet forcefully. Although participants with and without autism noticed and commented on the actions, the groups were markedly different in referring to the subjective experiences of the person. Where a participant without autism would be likely to describe angry feelings, participants with autism would be likely to say, 'dancing to some music'. The point-light person had meaning for the participants with autism, but it was meaning as viewed from the outside, so to speak. Often these children failed to get beneath the skin of the person they observed. Another instance of this from a later part of the study is that, whereas children without autism described how a point-light-person display was 'itchy', a typical description from children with autism was 'scratching'.

In a paper entitled 'Imitation and identification in autism', Hobson & Lee (1999) tested groups of children with and without autism, matched according to verbal ability and chronological age, for their ability to imitate a person demonstrating four novel goal-directed actions on objects in two contrasting 'styles', most often (but not exclusively) either harshly or gently. Despite almost all participants' ability to copy the goal-directed aspect of the actions, the children with autism were less likely to copy the styles with which the actions were demonstrated. Moreover, the majority of participants without autism copied the 'self-orientation' with which one action was demonstrated, imitating how the experimenter positioned an object against *his* shoulder by positioning the object against *their own* shoulder. This pattern of responding was rare among the participants with autism, most of whom laid the object on the table in front of them.

In our view, these results were not merely an index of imitative styles that *followed* perception; rather, they rendered explicit what the perception entailed in terms of registering and assimilating the stance of the person demonstrating the actions. Indeed, we interpreted the findings as reflecting how children with autism have a relative ability to copy (as well as perceive) simple goal-directed actions on objects, but a reduced propensity to *identify with* the person whose actions those were. Once again, children with autism seemed to view the actions from the outside, rather than getting beneath the skin of the person they observed.

A study of what this can mean for communication was conducted by Hobson & Meyer (2005). We presented a 'sticker test' in which children needed to communicate to another person where on her body she should place her sticker-badge. The majority of children without autism pointed to a site on their own bodies to indicate the tester's body, that is, anticipating that the other person would identify with their act of identifying with her body. The children with autism rarely communicated in this way; instead, most pointed to the body of the investigator to indicate where the sticker should be placed. Although it is possible that this style of flexible self–other communication depends upon thinking or understanding other people's minds, we consider it more likely that such seemingly effortless and natural stance-shifting reflects a more basic form of self–other connectedness and differentiation that has a cognitive aspect, but motivational aspects too.

Affective aspects of such communication were brought out in a further study. Hobson et al. (2007) created a setting in which participants had the task of observing an investigator who demonstrated an action, and then communicating to another tester who only subsequently entered the room that he should complete the same action. There were six actions demonstrated and, for each in turn, the demonstrator's instruction was: 'Get Pete to do this'. Three actions involved goal-directed use of objects (e.g. using a mechanical arm to place a cloth frog into a waste-bin), two were non-goal-directed involving the body (e.g. raising hands above head), and three included a form of expressive style (e.g. placing hands on hips in proud, assertive stance). As predicted, the results were that participants with autism contrasted with matched participants without autism in showing lesser degrees of (a) emotional engagement with the testers, (b) forms of joint attention that implicate sharing of experiences, (c) communication of styles of action, and (d) role-shifting from that of the learner to that of the teacher. When these measures were combined in a composite index of identifying with someone else, the two groups were almost completely distinct: apart from a single individual with autism who achieved a score equal to the lowest-scoring three participants without autism, there was complete separation of the two groups.

We have conducted one further study to test whether, in one-to-one interpersonal communicative exchanges—the kinds of exchange familiar between typically developing young infants and their caregivers—the structure of communication is shaped by processes of identification. Hobson & Hobson (2007) invited independent raters to watch videotapes of participants interacting (one at a time) with an adult whose actions they had been asked to imitate, and to judge the quality of each look they made to the adult's face. The actions could be imitated either as seen from the participant's point of view, or as adopted from the point of view of the demonstrator (Meyer & Hobson, 2004). There was a significant group difference, in that participants with autism were less likely to adopt the tester's orientation-to-herself as an orientation-to-themselves. For example, if they saw the tester rolling a wheel far-from-herself and close-to-participant, they were less likely than participants without autism to roll the wheel far-from-themselves and close-to-tester. More important for the issue of sharing was that those participants who imitated the tester's self-/other-orientation (a relatively rare event among those with autism) *also* tended to be those most likely to manifest 'sharing looks' towards the tester in the imitation task itself. This relation did not hold for looks in which participants were judged to be checking out or responding to prompts from the tester. The result applied within each group of participants, and had been predicted on the basis that *both* the imitation of self-/other-orientation *and* qualities of person-with-person engagement reflected in sharing looks are structured by processes of identification.

Therefore aspects of social engagement that might appear to be quite distinct—forms of sharing experience, as reflected in sharing looks, and the adoption of other-centred-stances when imitating—turned out to be intimately related to one another. The results suggest that the mode of social perception that involves sharing looks is the very same mode of social perception that gives rise to self/other transpositions in imitation. Moreover, it is this mode of social perception—one that we believe implicates the process of identifying with someone else—that is especially impaired among many individuals with autism. We also believe that prototypically, such perception is also feeling perception. In the 'Get Pete to . . .'

study, for example, children's limited abilities to share and to imitate styles of action were also related to lack of emotional engagement and role-taking. These results add force to the suggestion that, in each case, what one observes is a quality of intersubjective engagement that implicates a degree of identification with the person related-to.

One point in citing these studies is to highlight that to think about other human beings' states of mind and to adjust communication in relation to those states implicates feelings in relation to those others, and it is also to be motivated ('moved') to act and communicate accordingly. A failure to grasp this fact is apparent within the literature on autism, where researchers question whether the children suffer limitations in understanding *or* affect *or* motivation. The following quotation from an able adolescent with autism (described by Cohen, 1980, p. 388) captures how it is not possible to separate the nature of understanding persons-with-minds from affective and motivational engagement with embodied persons: 'I really didn't know there were people until I was seven years old. I then suddenly realized there were people. But not like you do. I still have to remind myself that there are people.'

## 20.6.2 Symbolic thinking

Perhaps it is obvious that the arguments I have been outlining have relevance for *all* symbolic/conceptual thinking, not only thinking that applies to persons-with-minds. The central idea is that what become the relatively, but never wholly, separate components of thinking, feeling, and willing have their origins as aspects of relatedness between a human being and the personal and non-personal world. It is this that accounts for the connectedness between thoughts and what those thoughts are about. To paraphrase the quotation from Vygotsky cited earlier, thoughts are distilled out of relations with the world that are affectively configured. Moreover, the story I have sketched about young children's conceptual development in differentiating between self and other with their distinct and yet connected attitudes to a shared world is also a story about growth in infants' understanding of the differentiation between people's takes and attitudes towards objects or events, and those objects or events at the focus of such attitudes. When around the middle of the second year of life in typical development, children achieve the insight that they, as persons, can adopt different (originally person-centred) takes on given objects and events, and that such meanings can be anchored in what we adults call symbols—an insight for which experience of communication with others is critical—then we see the dawn of conceptual and symbolic thinking (Hobson, 2000). In accordance with the ideas of Mead (1934) as well as Werner and Kaplan (1963), the achievement of self-reflective awareness and the ability to think about self and other appears to be one side of a coin, of which the other face is the ability to grasp how symbols can function as the means to thought. One could not think about self and other without symbols, but one could not achieve the requisite ability to use symbols without the appropriate kind of differentiation between symbolic vehicles and their referents. Each entails a grasp of what it means to take alternative person-anchored perspectives on a shared world.

An important caveat here is that there appear to be alternative forms of symbolizing, some of which do not require the kinds of intersubjective engagement I have described. Moreover, there may be alternative routes to acquiring some ability to employ those forms of symbolizing that *typically* entail relating to and identifying with the attitudes of others. Here is a final illustration from children with autism.

Symbolic play is an especially clear manifestation of children's ability knowingly to apply alternative meanings to materials that do not usually have these meanings. There is substantial evidence that children with autism are limited in their creative representational play, especially in their spontaneous play (e.g. Lewis & Boucher, 1988; Wing et al., 1977). On the other hand, many children with autism do achieve some ability to make one thing stand for another, so it is difficult to argue that, as a group, they completely lack the ability to 'represent representations'. The really important question here is whether the developmental underpinnings of the play they achieve, and therefore the qualities and creativity of this play, are the same as in the case of typically developing children.

Again we encounter a debate in the literature (Jarrold et al., 1993), whether the children have limited potential to engage in symbolic play, or whether they are less motivated to do so. In the view of colleagues and myself, the reason they are less motivated is the same reason that their ability to engage in symbolic play is restricted: lacking the usual interpersonal sources of symbolic functioning, they also lack the kinds of motivation and investment that come with engaging with other people's stances. Just as they are limited in their propensity to be moved among alternative person-anchored perspectives, so, too, they are limited in the spontaneous impetus to move among alternative symbolic meanings.

We have recently completed a study in which we compared two matched groups of children, one with and one without autism, for their ability to engage in symbolic play (Hobson et al., 2009). As it turned out, these two groups were similar in the mechanics of play, that is, on ratings of whether they were able to make one thing stand for another, or represent absent properties, or pretend that something was present when it was not. Yet there were significant group differences insofar as the children with autism were rated as less invested in the new meanings of the play, and less aware of themselves as initiators of the new meanings. Also, they showed less creativity and fun. One option is to interpret these results as demonstrating that the children with autism were perfectly able to symbolize in play, but, as a separate matter, they showed little affective and motivational investment. In our view, by contrast, these very qualities of affective and motivational investment betrayed what it meant for the children *without* autism to symbolize. The investment and fun that accompanied their play was intrinsic to their symbolic thinking, and reflected the interpersonal transactions from which this form of thinking was derived. If this is so, then at least some of the lack of creativity and flexibility in thinking that characterizes autism might derive from social-emotional deficits.

Although there is more to consider about the ways in which children with autism are limited and yet often surprisingly proficient in some domains of symbolic thinking, and, in particular, more to be done in delineating their strengths and weaknesses in using language (where they have particular difficulties with pragmatics), the example of symbolic thinking in play serves to illustrate how once again, thinking is intricately linked with affect and motivation. More than this, forms of thinking achieved by individual human beings may be acquired through affective-cum-motivated communicative transactions that are inter-individual in nature, as Vygotsky (1978) proposed long ago.

## 20.6.3 Self- and other-awareness

At this point I shall narrow the focus to features of emotional life that are widely acknowledged to entail self-other awareness. How, if at all, is other-person-centred intersubjective engagement (structured by identification) needed for 'self-conscious emotions'?

Colleagues and myself (Hobson et al., 2006) devised a situation that would prompt self-conscious feelings of coyness and embarrassment among school-aged children. There were 12 children with autism and 12 children without autism who each met with a familiar female tester. The tester introduced the children to a cuddly stuffed dog ('Doggie'), and began by nuzzling the dog against the face of a toy, saying: 'Doggie likes . . .' with a rising intonation, until the child had made verbal or non-verbal reference to the toy. Next, the tester nuzzled the dog against the side of her own face and tilted her head affectionately, repeating 'Doggie likes . . .' until the child made verbal or non-verbal reference to the tester. Finally, the tester playfully stated, 'And Doggie likes . . .' while inching Doggie towards the child, and then nuzzling it against the side of the child's face until the child referred to himself or herself.

Although there were group differences in ratings of overall coyness, in that 12 of 19 participants without autism but only 7 of 20 with autism were rated as clearly showing coyness, the most striking finding was in the patterning of response to this situation. Children were very similar in showing self-conscious smiling and squirmy movements. Roughly half of the children in each group showed both these manifestations of self-consciousness. Yet around two-thirds of the children without autism, but not a single child with autism, showed a re-engagement to the tester immediately following the experience. Here we find that what one might consider to be a coherent set of phenomena of 'self-consciousness' separates out into at least two different forms, only one of which appears to require the kind of other-person-centredness that typifies identifying with someone else's attitudes, in this case towards oneself.

In this same series of studies, we conducted a semi-structured interview with parents of children with autism, and children without autism of similar age (6–13 years) and verbal mental age (3.5–9 years). Most of the questions concerned whether the children showed social emotions such as jealousy, guilt, and concern. We enquired after specific instances of each emotion. For example, the question about jealousy was: 'Have you observed jealousy in your child—that is, resenting the attention you or someone else is giving to other individuals?'

Parents of both groups of children reported that their offspring showed feelings such as happiness, distress, and anger (although we did not enquire closely on the person-directedness of the anger). They also reported that their children were affected by the moods of other people, and here it was clearly *not* the case that the children with autism were globally unresponsive. Nor was it the case that all forms of differentiated relatedness were absent. In particular, the groups were almost identical insofar as the majority of children with as well as without autism showed clear signs of jealousy. Indeed, of the only two parents who thought that their children with autism did not show jealousy, one was our only poor respondent, and the other was far from confident about the matter. Here are examples of what parents said about their children with autism:

H: 'Yes, she's very possessive towards her nanny and her mum. She just blocks others out. She loves spending time with them.'

I: 'He doesn't like S (partner) and me hugging or holding hands sometimes... When he was very tiny, like two, he was very jealous of us I think. He didn't like us sitting next to each other or hugging. I remember one occasion when he actually led you [to partner] to the door and shut the door.'

On the other hand, when parents were asked about their children's emotions of pity, concern, and guilt, there were marked group differences. A majority of children without autism were said to show clear manifestations of these feelings. In the case of the children with autism, a majority showed *possible* or *atypical* signs of pity and concern, but only one was reported to show clear instances of these feelings. In the case of guilt, moreover, seven out of ten of the children with autism, but not a single one of those without autism, were said not to show guilt at all.

How are we to interpret this pattern of results? It is relevant to note that children with autism form attachments (e.g. Shapiro et al., 1987; Sigman & Ungerer, 1984). Therefore, although there is ample evidence that the children are atypical in the patterns of their social relat*edness*, as for example manifest in their greetings and farewells (Hobson & Lee, 1998) as well as affective engagement (Garcia-Perez et al., 2007), aspects of their relation*ships* are relatively typical in at least certain respects. It seems that the biologically based processes that underlie human and probably non-human animals' propensities to form attachments and to manifest jealousy are dissociable from other processes that lead humans to experience and respond to—and, in due course, think about—other-person-centred emotional states. To be more specific, attachments and jealousy may not require a human to have much by way of intersubjective engagement or identification with other persons. On the other hand, emotions such as pity, concern, and guilt, at least when fully organized and differentiated, do depend on the capacity to identify with the emotions of others *as* the states of other people with whom one is emotionally connected and from whom one is differentiated. The evidence from autism highlights how, among children without autism, emotional experience and behaviour is organized in a particular way that yields the capacity to feel *for* someone else.

Therefore an important part of what it means to identify with someone else is that one apprehends and responds to the other-person-centred source of attitudes. The evidence on autism thus far points to a specific impairment not only in the children's ability to think about other people's emotional states, but also to feel for and relate to the people whose states they are. As Wittgenstein (1958, Section 286) observed, 'if someone has a pain in his hand . . . one does not comfort the hand, but the sufferer: one looks into his face'. Here we can see that what it means to understand minds involves more than thought. Feelings are constitutive of the kinds of thought that really make a difference to social relations.

If children with autism tend to show less concern than children without autism, then does this amount to more than a failure to perceive and/or respond to expressions of pain? According to the present account it reflects a more far-reaching limitation in the children's propensity to experience and orientate to other persons as centres of subjectivity. In a recent study (Hobson et al., 2008), we tested 16 school-age children with autism and 16 children without autism of similar age and verbal ability for showing concern towards another person whose drawing was torn by a second tester. The children were between the ages of eight and 16 years, with a mean verbal mental age of about seven years. In this study, the tester whose drawing was torn did not show any overt emotional reaction to the event although she did witness its occurrence. Therefore it could not be the case that her 'observable emotional display' played a role in triggering participants' responses.

Two testers invited each child individually to play a game. The child was seated beside one tester and across from the other. Everyone drew an animal. The tester seated beside the child ascertained that the child knew who drew the turtle (the tester seated across) and then proceeded to tear this drawing in two. Both testers maintained a neutral facial expression. On another day, six months later, a similar scenario was repeated with the exception that the drawing torn was a blank note card.

Videotapes of the episodes were given to two blind raters who were asked to find each look to the tester whose drawing was torn, and then evaluate which of those looks expressed concern. These were looks in which the child appeared to become involved with the tester whose drawing was torn, apparently taking on her psychological stance (becoming upset on her behalf), experiencing concern for her feelings, or showing a sense of discomfort about her position (e.g. through nervous laughter). The raters had excellent agreement on the quality of such looks. The results were that when the blank index card was torn, the children rarely looked at the tester seated across the table. When it was the tester's drawing that was torn, however, some of the children with autism but especially those without autism looked at her during or *immediately* after the event. More importantly, while on the 'blank drawing' condition only one child (a child without autism) ever showed a concerned look—and only once—on the 'tear drawing' condition, ten out of 16 children without autism showed between one and six concerned looks, while only three out of 16 children with autism *ever* showed a concerned look. Any interpretation of the results needs to account for the speed with which, as well as the feeling with which, participants without autism looked to the tester whose drawing was torn. This synopsis of the findings fails to convey how charged an atmosphere was generated by the procedure—albeit not for the participants with autism—nor how swiftly many children without autism cast concerned looks to the injured party.

# 20.8 CONCLUSIONS

It remains to reflect on the ways in which studies in developmental psychopathology may influence our thinking about emotions.

Again I begin by taking Goldie's (2000) admirable work as a target for comment, this time in relation to feeling concern for others. Goldie (p. 214) states: 'It is entirely mistaken to assume that in addition to this recognition of, feeling towards, and response to another's difficulties, sympathy also involves undergoing difficulties and having feelings *of the same sort* as the other person's...your feelings involve *caring* about the other's suffering, not *sharing* them.' There is an important point here, but also a lingering question: is it 'entirely mistaken', when considered in developmental perspective? Or when Goldie (pp. 177–8) writes that 'our abilities to empathize, to imagine ourselves in another person's shoes, and to sympathize themselves *presuppose* some degree of understanding', is this true of the kind of concern that may be structured by processes of identification which require little by way of understanding? In other respects, too, one might join Goldie's project to criticize over-intellectual thinking about emotion and take things one step further.

For example, do we need to follow Goldie in supposing that jealousy requires imagination, or that envy necessarily includes 'the thought that . . .'? Identifying-with might shape a substantial part of phenomenology with relatively little need for thinking, understanding, or imagination.

It is especially challenging when evidence emerges that the coherence among different forms of emotion is not what theories had seemed to dictate. For example, Lewis (2003) has argued that social emotions, including jealousy, require that an individual has a self-concept, and therefore that such emotions are not possible for an infant prior to the acquisition of such a concept around the middle of the second year of life. The evidence from autism suggests that jealousy is distinct from other supposedly 'self-conscious emotions' such as embarrassment or guilt, and appears to be present in children who have very limited self-concepts. On the other hand, it would seem that even when children with autism acquire some (albeit limited) concepts of self and other—as would have been true for many of the children we tested—this does not appear to be sufficient for the emergence of feelings of embarrassment or guilt.

What might lead us to suppose that it is with the advent of concepts of self and other that children come to feel jealousy, concern, guilt, and so on? Where is the phenomenology of these feelings supposed to come from? There appears to be no *logical* reason why states for which we need complex descriptions, such as those of jealousy or envy or guilt (and, of course, in infancy these need not be and will not be exactly like cognitively elaborated, more sophisticated versions of the feelings in question), should not be phenomenologically primitive and early in onset. On the other hand, a constraint on *certain* of these feelings appears to be an infant's ability to identify with others, and this is a very different kind of constraint than that favoured by social-cognitive theorists. Moreover if the process of identification is critical for a range of social emotions, then there need to be sufficiently diverse feelings with which infants can identify, as a precondition for infants to experience the movements in stance through others that are critical for the development of concepts of self and other in the first place.

Secondly, atypical development may suggest how we should conceptualize the relations among emotion, cognition, and motivation. Earlier I stated, but did not explain, how one might be justified in contrasting emotional, cognitive, and motiva-tional components of mental life in adults, even though I had contested such an approach to characterizing the psychology of infancy. The reason is that if symbolic thinking emerges through a complex social process in which thought is, as it were, distilled out of infant–world relations involving attitudes, then this very process is critical for the emancipation of thought from action and attitude. In the case of propositional attitudes, it is through a developmental process of the kind I have indicated that 'propositions' as relatively detached descriptions of states of affairs can be instated as a part of a human being's mental economy. It is only through an individual's intersubjective experience of co-ordinated person-centred attitudes and takes on the world that he or she comes to think or desire or believe that such-and-such. As Vygotsky argued, the separation of thought from feeling is never complete, but nevertheless we adults can have very different feelings and motivations in relation to given thoughts, just as different thoughts can serve to express or modify given feelings or motives. All this is relevant to philosophical discussions concerning the connectedness between thoughts and the objects of thought.

Thirdly, autism may tell us something about the inter-relations among communication, self-awareness, and symbolizing, as well as about the emotional contribution to each. Vital aspects of psychological development occur through the interiorization of interpersonal transactions, as long argued by psychoanalysts and developmentalists in the tradition of Vygotsky. The notion of identification has promise for solving the conundrum as to how the individual constructs the social, where what is social then makes a pivotal contribution to the individual's development. In virtue of identification, certain emotions entail an expectation and/or experience of otherness, and have what psychoanalysts call an 'object-relational' structure (where 'object' means either a person or a part or even function of a person). The simplest example of what identification can yield is that of sharing experiences, where to have the experience of sharing is to register another person as experiencing alongside and in relation to one's own experiencing (albeit in the case of infants, with neither party conceptualized as such). In other instances, one's interpersonal experience may encompass a registration of the other's attitude, for example of anger, alongside a complementary feeling of a different kind, say of fear. In yet other cases, where one might identify with attitudes directed elsewhere than towards oneself, the other's attitude may be registered with relative equanimity. In each instance, there is a special structure and phenomenology to such experiences, one that entails that one registers the distinctiveness of whatever is experienced as originating in the other.

Perhaps it is appropriate to conclude with some final reflections on where the present account is situated within current philosophical debate on the nature of and basis for interpersonal understanding. It diverges in very many respects from 'theory theory' attempts to explain *basic* mechanisms of interpersonal understanding (e.g. Hobson, 1993*b*). This is notwithstanding my acknowledgement that mental concepts and self-reflective forms of role-taking feature in developmentally elaborated forms of mind-reading. Perhaps the most important point is that quintessentially (although not exclusively), early forms of identifying-with are perceptually grounded emotional processes that are necessary for, rather than dependent upon, the acquisition of concepts of persons-with-minds.

The present approach also eschews ideas that appear in versions of simulation theory. For example, identifying-with does not work from an egocentric stance. Rather, it is a process that structures interpersonal engagement. Self-/other-awareness and understanding is constructed on the basis of emotionally configured intersubjective experience. Therefore it is *not* the case that, in the early phases of life, a child uses him- or herself as a model for understanding someone else. Simulationist accounts tend to underestimate how much development in self-awareness and conceptual ability needs to have taken place before a child *could* use 'him-/herself' as a model for anything. Secondly, identifying-with does not depend upon imagination, in any of the usual senses of that term. On the contrary, imaginative role-taking becomes possible on the basis of infants experiencing specific forms of interpersonally grounded shift in attitude towards the world though their affectively configured perception of and alignment with the attitudes of others.

I should add that an account in terms of identifying-with alters the prominence given to a range of self–other and person–world relations in our explanation of what it means to understand oneself and others, and how we come to such understanding. For example, consider a very young child's ability to perceive and respond to what one might call a possessive or acquisitive attitude in someone else. Is not this a candidate for an emotional attitude that one can perceive and identify-with, without having much by way of conceptual understanding? And is not this, too, of great significance for our grasp of what it means to be a self with a set of person-anchored desires towards and beliefs about the world?

To wrap up: through developmental psychopathology, and specifically the case of autism, we may be able to trace the developmental implications when, from very early in life, children suffer a (relative) lack of a distinctive organizational principle of social-emotional life. The study of autism helps us to see how emotions are structured, and to appreciate how interpersonally situated emotions lift the child out of an egocentric, one-track take on the environment. Through identifying with the attitudes of others, the child is drawn into a world that is not only shared with others, but also a world that is at the focus of multiple orientations and a topic of diverse communicative exchanges—even within the child's own mind. The case of autism helps us to appreciate the deeply social-relational nature of human cognitive as well as emotional life.

# REFERENCES

Bosch, G. (1970). *Infantile autism* (translated by D. Jordan & I. Jordan). New York: Springer Verlag.

Bråten, S. (1998). Infant learning by altercentric participation: The reverse of egocentric observation in autism. In S. Bråten (ed.) *Intersubjective communication and emotion in early ontogeny*, pp. 105–24. Cambridge: Cambridge University Press.

Brazelton, T.B., Koslowski B., & Main, M. (1974). The origins of reciprocity: The early mother-infant interaction. In M. Lewis & L. A. Rosenblum (eds.), *The effect of the infant on its caregiver*, pp. 49–76. New York: Wiley.

Bretherton, I., McNew, S., & Beeghly-Smith, M. (1981). Early person knowledge as expressed in gestural and verbal communication: When do infants acquire a 'theory of mind'? In M. E. Lamb & L. H. Sherrod (eds.), *Infant social cognition: Empirical and theoretical considerations*, pp. 333–73. Hillsdale, NJ: Erlbaum.

Buber, M. (1937/1958). *I and Thou*, 2nd edn. (trans. R. G. Smith.) Edinburgh: Clark.

Campbell, J. (2002). *Reference and consciousness*. Oxford: Oxford University Press.

Carpenter, M., Nagell, K., & Tomasello, M. (1998). Social cognition, joint attention, and communicative competence from 9 to 15 months of age. *Monographs of the Society for Research in Child Development*, *63*.

Charman, T., Swettenham, J., Baron-Cohen, S., Cox, A., Baird, G., & Drew, A. (1997). Infants with autism: An investigation of empathy, pretend play, joint attention, and imitation. *Developmental Psychology*, *33*, 781–9.

Cohen, D. J. (1980). The pathology of the self in primary childhood autism and Gilles de la Tourette syndrome. *Psychiatric Clinics of North America*, *3*, 383–402.

Cohn, J. F. & Tronick, E. Z. (1983). Three-month-old infants' reaction to simulated maternal depression. *Child Development*, *54*, 185–93.

Decety, J. & Chaminade, T. (2003). When self represents the other: A new cognitive neuroscience view on psychological identification. *Consciousness and Cognition*, *12*, 577–96.

Freud, S. (1900/1953). The interpretation of dreams. In J. Strachey (ed.), *The standard edition of the complete psychological works of Sigmund Freud*, Vols. iv and v. London: Hogarth.

—— (1921/1955). Identification. In J. Strachey (ed.), *The standard edition of the complete psychological works of Sigmund Freud*, Vol. xviii, pp. 105–10. London: Hogarth.

García-Pérez, R. M., Lee, A., & Hobson, R. P. (2007). On intersubjective engagement in autism: A controlled study of nonverbal aspects of conversation. *Journal of Autism and Developmental Disorders*, *37*, 1310–22.

Goldie, P. (2000). *The emotions: A philosophical exploration*. Oxford: Clarendon.

Hamlyn, D. W. (1974). Person-perception and our understanding of others. In T. Mischel (ed.), *Understanding other persons*, pp. 1–36. Oxford: Basil Blackwell.

—— (1978). *Experience and the growth of understanding*. London: Routledge & Kegan Paul.

Hobson, J. A., Harris, R., García-Pérez, R., & Hobson, R. P. (2009). Anticipatory concern: A study in autism. *Developmental Science*, *12*, 249–63.

—— & Hobson, R. P. (2007). Identification: The missing link between imitation and joint attention? *Development and Psychopathology*, *19*, 411–31.

Hobson, R. P. (1990). On acquiring knowledge about people and the capacity to pretend: Response to Leslie. *Psychological Review*, *97*, 114–21.

—— (1991). Against the theory of 'Theory of Mind'. *British Journal of Developmental Psychology*, *9*, 33–51.

—— (1993a). *Autism and the development of mind*. Hove: Erlbaum.

—— (1993b). The emotional origins of social understanding. *Philosophical Psychology*, *6*, 227–49.

—— (2000). The grounding of symbols: A social-developmental account. In P. Mitchell & K. J. Riggs (eds.), *Reasoning and the mind*, pp. 11–35. Hove: Psychology Press.

—— (2002). *The cradle of thought*. London: Macmillan (and 2004, New York: Oxford University Press).

—— (2005). Autism and emotion. In F. Volkmar, A. Klin, & R. Paul (eds.), *Handbook of autism and developmental disorders*, pp. 406–22. New York: Wiley.

—— (2008). Interpersonally situated cognition. *International Journal of Philosophical Studies*, *6*, 377–97.

——, Chidambi, G., Lee, A., & Meyer, J. (2006). Foundations for self-awareness: An exploration through autism. *Monographs of the Society for Research in Child Development*, Serial no. 284, 71.

—— & Lee, A. (1998). Hello and goodbye: A study of social engagement in autism. *Journal of Autism and Developmental Disorders*, 28, 117–26.

—— & —— (1999). Imitation and identification in autism. *Journal of Child Psychology and Psychiatry*, 40, 649–59.

——, ——, & Hobson, J. A. (2007). Only connect? Communication, identification, and autism. *Social Neuroscience*, 2, 320–35.

——, ——, & —— (2009). Qualities of symbolic play among children with autism: A social-developmental perspective. *Journal of Autism and Developmental Disorders*, 39, 12–22.

—— & Meyer, J. A. (2005). Foundations for self and other: A study in autism. *Developmental Science*, 8, 481–91.

Hoffman, M. L. (1984). Interaction of affect and cognition in empathy. In C. E. Izard, J. Kagan, & R. B. Zajonc (eds.), *Emotions, cognition and behaviour*, pp. 103–31. Cambridge: Cambridge University Press.

Hutto, D. D. (2006). Unprincipled engagements. In Menary, R. (ed.), *Radical enactivism*, pp. 13–38. Amsterdam: Benjamins.

Jarrold, C., Boucher, J., & Smith, P. (1993). Symbolic play in autism: A review. *Journal of Autism and Developmental Disorders*, 23, 281–307.

Kagan, J. (1982). The emergence of self. *Journal of Child Psychology and Psychiatry*, 23, 363–81.

Kaler, S. R. & Kopp, C. B. (1990). Compliance and comprehension in very young toddlers. *Child Development*, 61, 1997–2003.

Kanner, L. (1943). Autistic disturbances of affective contact. *Nervous Child*, 2, 217–50.

Laplanche, J. & Pontalis, J.-B. (1973). *The language of psychoanalysis*. London: Hogarth.

Lewis, M. (2003). The development of self-consciousness. In J. Roessler and N. Eilan (eds.), *Agency and self-awareness*, pp. 275–95. Oxford: Clarendon.

—— & Ramsay, D. (2004). Development of self-recognition, personal pronoun use, and pretend play during the 2nd year. *Child Development*, 75, 1821–31.

Lewis, V. & Boucher, J. (1988). Spontaneous, instructed and elicited play in relatively able autistic children. *British Journal of Developmental Psychology*, 6, 325–39.

MacMurray, J. (1961). *Persons in relation*. London: Faber & Faber.

Mead, G. H. (1934). *Mind, self, and society*. (C. W. Morris, ed.). Chicago: University of Chicago Press.

Meltzoff, A. N. (2002). Elements of a developmental theory of imitation. In A. N. Meltzoff & W. Prinz (eds.), *The imitative mind: Development, evolution, and brain bases*, pp. 19–41. Cambridge: Cambridge University Press.

Merleau-Ponty, M. (1964). The child's relations with others (trans. W. Cobb). In M. Merleau-Ponty, *The primacy of perception*, pp. 96–155. Evanston, IL: Northwestern University Press.

Meyer, J. A. & Hobson, R. P. (2004). Orientation in relation to self and other: The case of autism. *Interaction Studies*, 5, 221–44.

Moore, D., Hobson, R. P., & Lee, A. (1997). Components of person perception: An investigation with autistic, nonautistic retarded and normal children and adolescents. *British Journal of Developmental Psychology*, 15, 401–23.

MURRAY, L. & TREVARTHEN, C. (1985). Emotional regulation of interactions between two-month-olds and their mothers. In T. M. Field & N. A. Fox (eds.), *Social perception in infants*, pp. 177 97. Norwood, NJ: Ablex.

NEISSER, U. (1988). Five kinds of self-knowledge. *Philosophical Psychology, 1*, 35–59.

PIAGET, J. (1972). *The principles of genetic epistemology*. London: Routledge & Kegan Paul.

SCHERER, K. R. & EKMAN, P. (eds.) (1984). *Approaches to emotion*. Hillsdale, NJ: Erlbaum.

SHAPIRO, T., SHERMAN, M., CALAMARI G., & KOCH, D. (1987). Attachment in autism and other developmental disorders. *Journal of the American Academy of Child and Adolescent Psychiatry, 26*, 485–90.

SIGMAN, M. D., KASARI, C., KWON, J. H., & YIRMIYA, N. (1992). Responses to the negative emotions of others by autistic, mentally retarded, and normal children. *Child Development, 63*, 796–807.

SIGMAN M. & UNGERER, J. A. (1984). Attachment behaviors in autistic children. *Journal of Autism and Developmental Disorders, 14*, 231–43.

SORCE, J. F., EMDE, R. N., CAMPOS, J., & KLINNERT, M. D. (1985). Maternal emotional signaling: Its effect on the visual cliff behavior of 1-year-olds. *Developmental Psychology, 21*, 195–200.

STRAWSON, P. F. (1959). *Individuals*. London: Methuen.

TREVARTHEN, C. (1979). *Communication and cooperation in early infancy: A description of primary intersubjectivity*. In M. Bullova (ed.), *Before speech: The beginning of human communication*, pp. 321–47. London: Cambridge University Press.

—— & HUBLEY, P. (1978). Secondary intersubjectivity: Confidence, confiding and acts of meaning in the first year. In A. Lock (ed.), *Action, gesture and symbol: The emergence of language*, pp. 183–229. London: Academic Press.

VYGOTSKY, L. S. (1962). *Thought and language* (trans. E. Hanfmann & G. Vaker). Cambridge, MA: MIT Press.

—— (1978). Internalization of higher psychological functions. In M. Cole, V. John-Steiner, S. Scribner, and E. Souberman (eds.), *Mind in Society: The development of higher psychological processes*. Cambridge, MA: Harvard University Press.

WERNER, H. & KAPLAN, B. (1963/1984). *Symbol formation*. Hillsdale, NJ: Lawrence Erlbaum.

WING, L., GOULD, J., YEATES, S. R., & BRIERLY, L. M. (1977). Symbolic play in severely mentally retarded and in autistic children. *Journal of Child Psychology and Psychiatry, 18*, 167–78.

WINNICOTT, D. W. (1958). *Collected papers: Through paediatrics to psycho-analysis*. Oxford: Basic Books.

WITTGENSTEIN, L. (1958). *Philosophical investigations* (trans. G. E. M. Anscombe). Oxford: Blackwell.

—— (1980). In G. H. von Wright & H. Nyman (eds.), *Remarks on the philosophy of psychology*, Vols. 1 and 2 (trans. C. G. Luckhardt & M. A. E. Aue). Oxford: Blackwell.

ZAHN-WAXLER, C., RADKE-YARROW, M., WAGNER, E., & CHAPMAN, M. (1992). Development of concern for others. *Developmental Psychology, 28*, 126–36.

# PART V

EMOTION, VALUE,
AND MORALITY

CHAPTER 21

...........................................................................................

# EMOTIONS AND VALUES

...........................................................................................

## KEVIN MULLIGAN

## 21.1 INTRODUCTION

...........................................................................................

The philosophy and psychology of emotions pays little attention to the philosophy of value and the latter pays only a little more attention to the former. This is surprising. For according to many philosophies and psychologies of the emotions appraisals, evaluations, assessments, valuing, and impressions of value and importance are essential to our emotional lives. And according to many philosophies value is to be understood in terms of emotions. Three families of questions which can only be answered by combining accounts of emotions and of value may be distinguished.

First, what role do values and value-properties play in triggering emotions? What role do values play in the "intentionality" or "aboutness" of emotions? One type of intentionality is that peculiar to knowledge. Can emotions ever provide us with knowledge of value? If not, what is the relation between our impressions of value and emotions? Secondly, is it possible to understand value in terms of emotions, for example in terms of emotional dispositions or in terms of certain types of emotion, correct or appropriate emotions? Finally, do emotions themselves exemplify value-properties?

Work on this chapter was supported by the Swiss NCCR on affective science. Thanks for their help to Otto Bruun, Richard Davies, Julien Deonna, Olivier Massin, Wlodek Rabinowicz, Toni Rønnow-Rasmussen, Fabrice Teroni, Cain Todd, and the Editor.

In order to introduce and evaluate some answers to these questions by drawing on accounts of emotions and of values some assumptions must be made.

## 21.2 EMOTION AND VALUE

In what follows I shall assume that a particular account of emotions—(E)—and a particular account of value—(V)—are true.

(E) Emotions enjoy the property of intentionality, of being "directed towards" objects. Emotions are not to be understood in terms of other intentional acts or states, for example, in terms of beliefs and desires. Emotions are relatively transient affective episodes which differ in kind from other affective phenomena such as bodily feelings (localized pain sensations or feelings), moods (despair, felicity), sentiments (love, hate, reverence, belief in something or someone), emotion dispositions (shame-proneness), passions and preferences. Emotions are ascribed by instances of "x emotes y"—for example, "Sam admires Maria"—and by instances of "x emotes that p"—for example, "Sam regrets that he went to the cinema". An emotion consists of two parts or aspects. First, its basis or presupposition—a perception, an expectation, a memory, a belief, a judgement, or some other act or state of that ilk. Second, an affective colouring. The relation between the two aspects is that the affective colouring colours and depends on its basis.

(E), then, does not claim that bodily feelings, expression, behaviour, or behaviour tendencies are essential to emotions.

(V) There are many different value-properties. There is the thin positive property of being valuable and the thick positive property of being sublime. There is the thin negative property of being disvaluable and the thick negative property of being unjust. There are also thin value relations such as being valuable for someone, being more valuable than and being more valuable for—than for–. And thick value relations such as being more unjust than and being more shameful than. Objects (persons, animals, trees, mountains, psychological and biological states) exemplify value-properties and stand in value relations. Situations, facts and states of affairs also exemplify value-properties and stand in axiological relations. Value properties and relations are not natural properties and relations. Thick value-properties and relations are not combinations of thin value-properties and relations together with natural properties and relations. To be dumpy is not just to be disvaluable and to have a certain shape.

There is a difference between values and value-properties. Mountains and symphonies exemplify the property of being sublime. But the sublime *is* a value, a positive value. Values stand in relations of height (rank, greater or lesser importance) to each other: the value of justice is higher than that of the pleasant. Values are referred to in two quite different ways. In expressions such as "the value of beauty" or "the disvalue of injustice" the definite description functions appositively—beauty *is* a value and injustice a disvalue. But expressions such as "the value of pleasure" or "the value of knowledge" do not function in the same way. Pleasure is not a value, it exemplifies a value-property, the property of being pleasant. Similarly, knowledge is valuable but is not a value. And—*pace* some neo-Kantians—truth is not a value but is valuable. But in what follows I usually ignore the difference between values and value-properties.

How many families of thick value-properties are there? There are the *aesthetic* properties of being beautiful, elegant, or sublime. There are the *cognitive* value-properties of which clarity, distinctness, illusion, error, knowledge, truth and falsity are the bearers and the property of being foolish. There are the *ethical* properties of being evil and good, and the properties corresponding to different ethical virtues and vices, for example, the property of being a coward. There are the properties of being right, just and unjust. There are the *religious* properties of being holy or sacred and profane. There are the *vital* value-properties of which health, life, and illness are the bearers. And the *sensory* value-properties of being pleasant and unpleasant. Within each of these families further value-properties can be found. Thus within each family there are more or less determinate value-properties, for example different ways of being beautiful or foolish.[1]

The value-properties mentioned in the last paragraph are properties objects and facts exemplify or fail to exemplify intrinsically. If something is intrinsically valuable or intrinsically unjust, it is not valuable or unjust in virtue of some other object or in virtue of the properties of some other object. The relational expression "–is valuable to/for–" is often used to ascribe extrinsic value, as when we say that a tool or other good is of great value to someone. The value of the tool derives from the value of some action or goal. But the relational expression "–is valuable to/for–" is also used to ascribe intrinsic value: a loved one is intrinsically valuable for a lover, a state is intrinsically valuable for a (conservative) citizen or subject.[2] Loved ones and states are also, sometimes, extrinsically valuable for lovers and citizens respectively.

(V) is a variety of *naive realism* about values. In section 21.5 we shall consider a less naive variety of realism. According to (V) value is predicable and so value is not always attributive. According to attributivism value is always attributive: to be good

---

[1] On determinate value-properties, cf. Johnston, M. 2001. The taxonomy of thick value-properties in this paragraph resembles that given in Scheler 1973, 81–110. More modest taxonomies, which allow only for a handful of value-properties, are to be found in the writings of Moore and Ross. Kraft (1981, ch. 2§2) allows only thin values. Perhaps the most florid taxonomy is that to be found in Hartmann 1932, Vol. II. The distinction between thin and thick ethical concepts was introduced by Williams (1985, 129–30, 140–2). Evil and its opposite, ethical goodness, are often classified, with goodness and badness, as thin. Perhaps because ethical goodness is thought to be simple.

[2] Within the theory of value, intrinsic value is sometimes distinguished from an object's being valuable as an end or for its own sake, cf. Rabinowicz & Rønnow-Rasmussen 2000. Similarly, the three value relations mentioned here, being more intrinsically valuable than, being intrinsically valuable for someone, being extrinsically valuable for someone, are only the tip of an iceberg.

or valuable is to be a good or valuable F. From the fact that something is a good F it does not follow that it is good, that goodness can be predicated of it.[3] (V) is incompatible with two more economic views—the claim that only facts are valuable,[4] and the claim that only objects are valuable. Attributivism, for example, has to deny that facts can be good or bad since a good fact is just a fact which is good. (V) takes the distinction between

(1) Disvaluable/bad/ugly (x)

and

(2) It is disvaluable/bad/shameful/unjust that p

to correspond to a real difference. In instances of (1) value-expressions occur as predicates, in instances of (2) as functors. One distinctive feature of value-functors is that they are factive. If it is disvaluable/shameful/bad that p, then p.

## 21.3 VALUE AND THE INTENTIONALITY OF EMOTIONS

Emotions, like beliefs and desires, are "directed" towards objects, they possess the property of "intentionality". It is often claimed that emotions have "formal objects" and that these formal objects are just values. Thus the formal objects of emotions such as fear, shame and guilt are, respectively, danger, shamefulness and (objective) guilt. Similarly, the formal object of a combination of astonishment or reverence and awe is the sublime, and of pleasure the pleasant. If emotions have formal objects, it is perhaps also plausible to ascribe formal objects to affective phenomena other than emotions: the formal object of hate is an enemy who is evil;[5] the formal object of a preference for y over z is the greater value of y with respect to z. And to non-affective mental episodes and states: judgements and beliefs have formal objects—the truth of truth-bearers or the obtaining of states of affairs. Desires, it may also be thought, have formal objects—the *oughtness* of particular actions. Perhaps, too, some actions and behavioural reactions have formal objects. The formal object of irony, we might think, is foolishness, of many types of laughter the comic.

However appealing such claims may appear to be at first sight they are obscure and, on some natural readings, false. First, if Sam is afraid of a dog, the object of his fear is

---

[3] Cf. Geach 1957, Thompson 1992.

[4] Lemos 1994. Moore may have thought that goodness is primarily a property of states of affairs—cf. Moore 1903/1966, 183, but contrast Moore 1903/1966, 27. On this interpretation cf. Baldwin 1990, 73 ff. For criticisms of the view that facts can be valuable cf. Hall 1952, ch. 4.

[5] Kolnai 1998.

the dog. Second, the dangerousness of the dog for Sam is a value relation. In fact, all the formal "objects" of affective phenomena referred to in the last paragraph are properties or relations. Third, the distinction between the objects of emotions ascribed by instances of "x emotes y" and their value-properties has to be modified when we consider the emotions ascribed by instances of "x emotes that p". If Sam regrets that he behaved in a certain way, he is not the object of his regret. The formal object of his regret is the disvalue of the fact that he behaved the way he did. Finally, in some of the emotions ascribed by instances of "x emotes y" the formal object of the emotion is not a value-property of y. If Sam is jealous of Erna (a friend of his mistress, Maria), then the formal object of his jealousy is not simply some disvalue which Erna has for Sam but the disvalue of the fact that Maria's affections have turned towards Erna. If Sam envies Sally, the formal object of his envy is the disvalue of the fact that she possesses some goods he would prefer her not to have.

If we consider the simplest sort of case, we may say that the object *proper* (the material object) of Sam's fear is the dog, and the *improper* object (the formal object) of his fear is the dangerousness of the dog; that the proper object of Sam's admiration is Maria and its improper object her elegance. What, then, is the relation between an emotion and its improper object? Does some feature of an emotion present or represent value? If the basis of an emotion is a non-conceptual visual content, then *it* cannot present or represent value. It might nevertheless be the case that the affective dimension of an emotion presents or represents value, just as predicates or concepts (are said to) represent properties and visual contents (are said to) present colours. This is tantamount to claiming that the intentionality of an emotion is not exhausted by the intentionality of its basis, that the intentionality of an emotion is not simply inherited from the intentionality of its basis.[6]

One constraint on the relations of presentation and representation is that whereas many different (re)presentations may (re)present the same object, one and the same (re)presentation cannot (re)present different objects. Some emotions behave in a way compatible with this constraint. The affective colourings of fear and shame, we might think, (re)present danger and shamefulness respectively. But this view presupposes that negative affective colourings are qualitatively distinct. Even if we accept the qualitative heterogeneity of the affective dimensions of emotions, there is good reason to think that some emotions cannot (re)present their formal objects. Consider admiration. The formal object of Sam's admiration of Maria may be her elegance, her charm, her courage, or her gentleness among many other things. (Is admirability the formal object of admiration? No. First, "admirable", like, e.g., "regrettable" is incomplete. To be admirable is to be ad-mirable in virtue of, in the first instance, a particular value-property: Maria is

---

[6] Tye (2008) argues that emotional experiences represent objects as having evaluative features.

admirable because she is elegant, charming etc. Secondly, if "admirable" means: may or ought to be or is to be admired, then it is a deontic property not a value-property). But one and the same affective colouring cannot (re)present different value-properties.[7] If there are emotions which are such that neither their affective colouring nor their bases (re)present values, it is hard to see how *any* of these emotions, as a whole, might (re)present value. Two interesting recent suggestions challenge the foregoing. The first concerns the nature of the formal objects of emotions, the second the nature of the relation of (re)presentation.

De Sousa says that "each emotion has its own specific formal object . . . [The formal objects] of our emotions are multifarious, as our emotions themselves".[8] This, he argues, is due to the fact that each emotion plays a different role in our lives and has its own history. According to (V) there are objects which exemplify intrinsic value and objects which are intrinsically valuable for one person but not for another and there may be intrinsic thick values which are values for different persons. For example, specific types of generosity. The claim that thick values can be very specific is most familiar in aesthetics: the comic in Dickens is not the comic in Wodehouse, the sublimity of Mont Blanc differs from that of a symphony. As Moore says, "different emotions are appropriate to different kinds of beauty".[9] De Sousa's suggestion is not just that there are multifarious specific, thick values but that this specificity is relative to emotions and their bearers. His view relies on the claim that emotions and their history constitute value. That is incompatible with the naive realism of (V).

Prinz argues that what was called above the relation of (re)presentation between the affective dimension of an emotion and value is in fact a relation between (a) emotions, which are identified with states which perceive, register, and track bodily changes, and (b) "core relational themes" such as "danger, threats, losses, or other matters of concern". This relation is a product of two relations: the perception of bodily changes and reliable co-occurrence between tokens of a type of bodily change and tokens of a type of organism–environment relation.[10] Emotions, we might say, flag or signal the exemplification of value.

Emotions do flag value.[11] But is the intentionality of emotion best understood as the relation of signalling? And does the view work for all types of emotion, for example for aesthetic emotions?[12] Many objections have been raised against the

---

[7] On the relation between "the multiplicity of" values and the multiplicity "of the emotions that present them" cf. Meinong 1968, 279.

[8] de Sousa 2007, 328, cf. de Sousa 2002.

[9] Moore 1903/1966, ch. VI 190.

[10] Prinz 2004, 69, cf. ch. 10.

[11] "In feelings of fatigue there is a warning that may be expressed in the language of common sense as 'stop working' . . . The vertigo we experience when we stand before an abyss urges us to 'step back' . . . Fear, which indicates a possible damage to life as a 'danger'; . . . appetite and disgust in which the use or harm of food . . . are emotionally represented for us" (Scheler 1992, 82; translation modified).

[12] Cf. Robinson 2005.

view that the intentionality of perception, belief, or thought should be understood in terms of signalling, in particular its inability to give an account of error and illusion.[13] But perhaps not all of these objections apply to the claim that emotions represent values by flagging them.[14] In any case, in section 21.4 we shall examine two philosophies of our grasp of value which do not identify the intentionality of such a grasp with signalling.[15]

Suppose that emotions do not (re)present value. What, then, could it mean to say that emotions have formal objects which are values? One answer has it that value occurs in the "correctness" or "rightness" conditions of emotions. Fear is correct iff what is feared is dangerous. A combination of astonishment or reverence and awe is correct iff the proper object of the emotion is sublime. One obstacle to generalizing such claims is the phenomenon already encountered of one–many emotion–value correlations (for example, admiration–generosity/elegance/charm . . . ) and the phenomenon of many–one emotion–value correlations (admiration/pleasure in/liking/enjoying–elegance). Perhaps only a necessary condition for the correctness of an emotion can be given—that its object exemplifies either the thin property of being (dis)valuable or stands in a thin value relation. Alternatively, moving closer to de Sousa's suggestion, we might say that particular emotions have correctness conditions but not or not wholly in virtue of the type which they instantiate.

The view that every emotion has a correctness condition may be taken to form part of an account of the "intentionality" of emotions, a concept which is anyway rather vague. It can be compared with the claim that other types of mental states and acts which have formal objects also have correctness conditions in which these formal objects figure. Thus a preference for y over z is correct if y is of greater value (better) than z. One who prefers that p rather than q prefers correctly iff it is more valuable that p than that q. Judgement or belief that p is correct if the proposition that p is true or the state of affairs that p obtains. A desire to F is correct if the desirer ought to F.[16]

---

[13] Cf. Crane 1995, ch. 5.

[14] Cf. Bridges 2006.

[15] For the view that bodily feelings present and do not merely indicate value, cf. Stein 1970, 141–6, Deonna & Teroni 2008, 77–82. Stein, unlike Prinz and Deonna & Teroni, distinguishes between bodily feelings (or perceptions thereof) and emotions: bodily feelings, she argues in 1922, disclose value, emotions react to values.

[16] The view that many mental states and acts have correctness conditions, that to specify these is to specify in part the intentionality peculiar to such acts and states and that formal objects ("correlates" or "improper" objects) as well as the proper objects of such acts and states occur in these conditions goes back to Husserl and other phenomenologists. Related views are to be found in analytic philosophy. Thus Kenny (1963, ch. 9) distinguishes between the formal and material objects of emotions, desires, and other mental attitudes as well as actions. Findlay writes: "It is *sub specie provocationis* that objects anger us or annoy us . . . " (Findlay 1954, 152). And de Sousa says: "*good* is the formal object of wanting, as *true* is the formal object of believing . . . [T]ruth and good are the *targets* of belief and want" (de Sousa 1974, 538). For a critical discussion of claims about the formal objects of emotions see Lyons 1980, 49ff., ch. 6.

But, as we have set it out, the view that emotions have correctness conditions is mute about whether the person who undergoes an emotion thereby stands in some intentional relation to value. A woman's emotions might be correct even if she enjoyed no (re)presentations of the value-properties ascribed in the correctness conditions for her emotions. In the next section we look at two views about the relation between emotions and values according to which there is an affective grasp of value.

## 21.4 AFFECTIVE KNOWLEDGE OF VALUE

Ever since the beginning of the twentieth century philosophers have been tempted by the view that in certain optimal circumstances emotions can constitute or help to constitute knowledge of value, knowledge that something exemplifies value or knowledge of (acquaintance with) the value of objects. This view is a variant of the idea that there is an intuitive awareness of value. But unlike the more familiar cold-blooded variants of this idea it tells us that this awareness is emotional. A modest version of this view has it that the perceptual capacities of one who has suitable affective dispositions include being able to see what is the kind thing to do, that this or that is the kind thing to do; the awareness of value is then not any type of emotion but depends on emotions and affective dispositions.[17] Stronger versions of the view have it that emotions themselves may amount to a perception of value and that this perceptual knowledge of value includes both acquaintance with value and knowledge that something is valuable.

Christine Tappolet writes:

The different analogies between emotions and perceptual experiences suggest that emotions are perceptions of value. Emotions, like perceptual experiences, have correctness conditions. Thus both have a certain type of content. It is therefore possible to maintain that emotions allow us in certain cases to be aware of values. Whether or not representation is a matter of causal correlation emotions represent values. It is important to note that, unlike axiological beliefs or judgements, these representations are non-conceptual . . .[18]

Similarly, according to Mark Johnston, affects (which he distinguishes from emotions) may disclose value:[19]

---

[17] Cf. Goldie 2007, Kraft 1981.
[18] Tappolet 2000, 191–2.
[19] Johnston 2001, 182 n.1, 182, 183 n.2, 189–90, 204, 206, 213.

Seeing the utterly specific ways in which a situation, animal or person is *appealing* or *repellent* requires an appropriate affective engagement with the situation, animal or person. Absence of appropriate affect makes us aspect-blind.[20]

If one has never been moved or *affected* by the determinate ways in which things are beautiful or charming or erotic or banal or sublime or horrific or appealing, then one is ignorant of the relevant determinate values.[21]

Two pupils of Brentano who defend the view that emotions may disclose value are (late) Meinong and Husserl. According to the former:

If O is the [non-formal] object of a value experience [emotion] which has O′ as its proper object [formal object, a value], then that O exemplifies O′ is either true or false. If it is true and hence the judgement that "O is O′" right, then one who connects to O the value experience which has as its proper object O′ is in the right, and the value experience itself may count as right...[22]

Similarly, Husserl argues for a type of "fulfilment" (knowledge) which is emotional. Emotions are what he calls "valuings". Valuing "does not see, does not understand...does not predicate".[23] But valuing may be "not only right but completely grounded and grounding here means... affective grounding [*Gemütsbegründung*]".[24] What does this involve? The proper objects of valuings may "have...certain inner or relative predicates which are...valuable and make their subjects have value".[25] If this is the case and the basis of the valuing is knowledge of these predicates, then the valuing is not only correct but also a piece of knowledge.[26]

Another example of the view that emotions can provide knowledge of value is due to Fabrice Teroni and exploits some suggestions made by Peter Goldie. Suppose Sam has behaved in a shameful way, that he is ashamed of his deed, and that the various non-axiological features of his behaviour that make his behaviour shameful are presented or represented in the basis of his shame. Then Sam's shame constitutes knowledge of the shamefulness of his deed. As Teroni puts it, "when one feels fear as a result of seeing a facial expression, it is only insofar as one feels fear that one apprehends danger".[27]

---

[20] Johnston 2001, 181.

[21] Johnston 2001, 183.

[22] Meinong 1968, 643. Meinong, it should be noted, calls what I have called the formal or improper object of an emotion its "proper" object.

[23] Husserl 1988, 69.

[24] Husserl 1988, 241, cf. 278ff., 322–5, 342–3. A third pupil of Brentano's also puts forward a similar view: Marty 1908, 232–7, 370–1, 427–31. According to Carnap different types of emotion "constitute" different types of value (Carnap 1974, §152).

[25] Husserl 1988, 256, cf. 255

[26] Husserl 1988, 343–4, cf. 323.

[27] Cf. Teroni 2007, 413, Goldie 2004, 2007. Teroni's paper is an acute discussion of many of the points raised in this section. On emotional perception of value, see also de Sousa 2002, Zagzebski 2004, Deonna 2006, Döring 2007, Achtenberg 2002.

Graham Oddie argues that, whether or not emotions are experiences of value, there are good reasons for thinking that desires can play this role with respect to the value of states of affairs and are in fact the best candidate for this role. In optimal circumstances such experiences constitute knowledge by acquaintance of the value of states of affairs.[28]

Claims to the effect that emotions can constitute cases of axiological knowledge are not always very explicit about whether the knowledge in question is knowledge that p (or coming to know that p) or knowledge by acquaintance (or coming to be acquainted with something). It is perhaps natural to think that if the emotion or desire which is to be a case of axiological knowledge is propositional (desire, regret, being afraid that) or non-propositional (fear of, admiration), then this will determine whether the relevant type of axiological knowledge is knowledge that or acquaintance. But Oddie's theory, for example, is incompatible with this suggestion since it claims that desire, a propositional attitude, can provide knowledge by acquaintance of value. The importance of the distinction between the two types of knowledge can be brought out by considering a theory of perceptual knowledge which makes claims like the following: "If Sam sees that Maria is sad and what justifies Sam's experience is his grasp of those features of Maria which necessitate or constitute her sadness, then his knowledge *that* Maria is sad is as close as he can get, epistemically speaking, to her sadness. In particular, there is no such thing as acquaintance with Maria's sadness, no simple seeing of her sadness".[29]

Can emotions constitute knowledge of value? One objection to many versions of the view is that, as already noted, emotions and values do not always seem to match up in the right way. Perhaps shame can constitute a grasp of shamefulness. But can admiration of a gesture which is elegant constitute knowledge of elegance and admiration of a person who is charming constitute knowledge of charm? Similarly, whether or not a desire that p may constitute knowledge of the value of the state of affairs that p, it is difficult to see how desires, which vary only in intensity, in urgency, and in their objects (and perhaps also in being positive or negative), could begin to constitute knowledge of different thick values—of the shamefulness, funniness, or tragic nature of different states of affairs. A further objection to Oddie's view is that it is incompatible with the claim that the formal object of desire differs in type from the formal object of emotions. It is, for example, incompatible with the view, already mentioned, that the desire to F is correct only if one ought to F.

---

[28] Oddie 2005, 41–2, 77, 180, 236–9. Although the philosophies of value and of emotion pay little attention to each other, this is not true of the relation between the philosophies of desire and value thanks to Oddie's remarkable investigations.

[29] It is not always clear whether claims that emotions can constitute cases of axiological knowledge are committed to the view that emotions, whether correct or not, present value-properties. Thus Husserl says: "Something appears in the valuing acts . . . not merely the objects which have value but the values as such." But he also rejects such claims (Husserl 1988, 323, 339).

Another objection to the very idea of emotional axiological knowledge begins with the observation that if emotions are to furnish knowledge of value, then such knowledge of value is to be understood as emotions qualified in certain ways. One of these qualifications is that the emotion be correct, another that it be justified. Thus the notion of knowledge employed is analogous to that to be found in views of intellectual knowledge which have it that knowledge is a type of belief which has certain properties, the properties of being true and justified. If one thinks that intellectual knowledge is or involves a relation to facts and is not any type of belief,[30] one will be inclined to look for an alternative to the view that knowledge of value is a type of emotion (desire)—correct emotion (desire) plus, for example, a grasp of whatever non-axiological properties make the object of the emotion valuable.

Emotions are above all reactions or responses—they are for or against something. But knowledge is not any sort of response. It is a discovery or the result of a discovery. So no emotion can be knowledge. We can always ask someone why he feels the way he does. We do not ask someone why he knows that p or perceives something. We ask him *how* he knows that p. If some emotion of Sam were a disclosure of value, we ought not to be able to ask him why he feels the way he does.

Not only are emotions responses or reactions, they are responses or reactions to what is known or to what seems to be known. Ascriptions of emotions and of their formal objects are typically of the form:

x emotes y because of the (dis)value of z
Sam admires Maria because she is generous
Sam despises the EU because of its illegitimacy
Sam is ashamed of himself because his behaviour yesterday was shameful.

In this respect, reasons to feel (emote) behave just like reasons to desire, to act, and to believe. In the most basic cases, emotions neither present nor represent value. Rather, they are reactions to a grasp or apparent grasp of value. The emotions we feel and undergo are felt and undergone on the basis of this (apparent) grasp of value. The formal object of an emotion is the material object of whatever mental act or state presents or represents what a person affectively responds to.

In some non-basic cases a value-property *is* indeed the material or proper object of an emotion:

Sam despises Giorgio's elegance because it is effeminate
Sam admires Maria's occasional dishonesty because it makes life easier for her husband.

But if the material object of Sam's scorn (admiration) is Giorgio's elegance (Maria's dishonesty), the formal object of his scorn (admiration) is the effeminacy of Giorgio's elegance (the non-intrinsic value of the consequences of Maria's dishonesty).

---

[30] Cf. Williamson 2002; Hossack 2007; Mulligan 2007.

Considerations like these led a handful of the early realist phenomenologists to reject the view that emotions can furnish affective knowledge of value and to propose a little-known alternative: the most basic type of acquaintance with value occurs when we feel the elegance of a gesture, the ugliness of an utterance, the injustice of a situation. There is a sense of "feel" according to which to feel is not to emote nor to feel an emotion or a pain. Our emotions are responses to the values and disvalues of objects and situations, values and disvalues we feel or seem to feel. As the most eloquent proponent of the view puts it:

I see in the street how a child is being mistreated and a terrible indignation wells up in me. I am indignant about the vileness and brutality of this behaviour. This indignation is clearly a response ... to these qualities, qualities with which I am already acquainted ... [31]

To come to be acquainted with value is to feel value. The inability to feel values of a certain type is, von Hildebrand notes, the most basic type of value-blindness. It differs from that type of value-blindness which consists in an inability to employ a value-concept properly. Since acquaintance is not any type of propositional knowledge or belief, the values and disvalues a person is sensitive to may fail to match his evaluative beliefs.[32]

This view places our grasp of value, in the simplest cases, "outside" emotions. The formal object of an emotion is ascribed in the clause that follows "because" in explanations and justifications of emotions: Maria is afraid of Sam because he is dangerous; Sam is incandescent because of the injustice of this or that situation. Sam is pleased that the sun is shining because of the value (to him) of this state of affairs.

Contrast this with the two views which place Maria's relation to danger and Sam's relation to injustice "inside" their emotions. On one of these two views, Maria's fear (re)presents danger and Sam's indignation (re)presents injustice. But we have seen that there are reasons to reject such claims. On the other view, the basis of Maria's fear contains the concept of danger and the basis of Sam's indignation contains the concept of injustice. But the presentations and representations which constitute the bases of emotions are typically presentations and representations of the proper objects of these emotions, of their features and of the relations they stand in. The presentations and representations which constitute the bases of emotions are not (re)presentations of what these emotions respond to.

Suppose Maria is afraid of Sam. What is her intentional relation to danger? According to the early realist phenomenologists she feels or seems to feel the danger of the situation. Similarly, if Sam is indignant because of the injustice of a situation, then he feels the injustice of the situation. Although knowledge or apparent knowledge of value is not a constitutive feature of emotions on this view, emotions do depend on such knowledge or apparent knowledge. If feeling

---

[31]  von Hildebrand 1916, 137; cf. Scheler 1973, 35 ff., 68 ff., 96 ff. Against the view cf. Jury 1937, 177 ff.
[32]  Hildebrand 1916, 202 ff., 1922, 467 ff.

value and seeming to feel value are appraisals, then emotions depend on appraisals but appraisals do not go to make up emotions.[33]

Is there such a thing as feeling (dis)value? A natural suspicion is that the philosophers who took this idea seriously are making a theoretical mountain out of a mole-hill, a handful of locutions in English, French, and German.[34] But is there really any such thing as feeling value (*Wertfühlen*) as opposed to emoting?

Consider what happens when one finds a situation or a joke funny. Laughter and mirth or amusement may result. But is it not possible to be struck by the comic nature of a situation or joke without reacting affectively? Or without laughing? Mechanical laughter at what one finds funny in the absence of any affective response seems to be a common phenomenon. Or consider exclamations. Some exclamations, such as

> How unhappy/sad/ashamed/wretched I am!

express emotions. If sincere, the speaker is reacting affectively to something. Some exclamations are dominated by axiological predicates:

> How tragic/funny/unjust/shameful/lovely/vulgar!
> What a fool I am/he is/you are!

Do such exclamations not often express the speaker's felt awareness of the tragedy, funniness, injustice, or foolishness of some object or situation? Then there is the case where Sam suddenly becomes aware of the generosity of Hans, an enemy he hates. Can Sam only be struck by Hans' generosity if his otherwise unwavering hatred of Hans is fleetingly interrupted by admiration of his generosity? Finally, is affective acquaintance with the values of objects and persons which are important to us, for example models and counter-models, not something which remains constant across considerable variations in our affective reactions to these persons and objects?[35]

If we reject the view that emotions can furnish knowledge of value and the view that value can be felt, we should not reject the latter view's starting point.

---

[33] The "appraisal" theory of emotions in psychology sometimes asserts that emotions are episodes which are triggered by appraisals and sometimes that such appraisals are constitutive of emotions. Frijda 2007, ch. 4. distinguishes appraisals as antecedents of emotions and as components of emotions. Ellsworth & Scherer 2003 argue that appraisals are constitutive of emotions. The view that the intentionality of many emotions is to be understood in terms of reasons to feel has also been put forward by linguists. Thus Norris argues that the structure of "a disgusts b" is: *b is disgusted because of a* (Norris 1978, 65–73, cf. Postal 1971). But it is difficult to see how this suggestion could be generalized, e.g. to "a admires b".—The first and indeed classic formulation and theoretical defence of "the causal-evaluative theory" of emotions is Lyons 1980. Lyons surveys the history of the "causal-evaluative (cognitive)" account of emotional states in Lyons 1999.

[34] In *Mansfield Park* we learn that there "was a charm, perhaps, in [Edmund's] sincerity, his steadiness, his integrity, which Miss Crawford might be able to feel, though not equal to discuss with herself" (ch. 7). Stendhal writes that the citizen of New York has no time to "sentir le beau" and distinguishes between "sentir le beau inculte et terrible" of the Colosseum and feeling "le beau joli et arrangé" (of the Vatican) (*Promenades dans Rome*).

[35] On the last two examples, cf. Scheler 1973, 173.

Knowledge or apparent knowledge of value is not a constitutive feature of emotions. Rather, such knowledge or apparent knowledge is what triggers emotions and what emotions respond to. Similarly, the reasons on the basis of which we act are not parts of our actions, the reasons on the basis of which we desire are not parts of our desires.

A full evaluation of the view that emotions can furnish knowledge of value and the view that emotions are responses to felt value would have to consider the relation between emotions and longer-lasting affective phenomena. Sentiments and value-preferences, for example, may be understood in terms of emotions, for example, emotion dispositions. But there is also the diametrically opposed view that emotions are typically justified and explained by reference to enduring sentiments, beliefs in this or that, and value-preferences.[36] On such a view it is plausible to think that the formal objects of emotions are in part inherited from and determined by the objects of enduring affective states. Thus the formal object of fear, danger, is normally inseparable from a lasting concern for the value of one's life and physical integrity and perhaps for the value of life. Similarly, the formal objects of many of the emotions, positive and negative, of the devout Pentecostalist or Muslim will be determined by the objects of his enduring attitudes of reverence and belief in. His preference for the holy over other values and for what he takes to exemplify the former over what he takes to exemplify the latter will play a similar role. A third example is provided by the formal objects of those emotions of politicians and journalists which are in part determined by their opposed preferences with respect to the values of national security and of truth. If sentiments and value-preferences do determine the formal objects of emotions, the relation between such sentiments and preferences and grasp of value becomes more important than the relation between emotions and grasp of value.

## 21.5 VALUE AS APPROPRIATE EMOTION

As already noted, three of Brentano's pupils—Husserl, Meinong, and Marty—argued for the view that emotions provide us with our most basic cognitive access to values; one of Husserl's students, Edith Stein, argued that bodily feelings disclose value; other phenomenologists argued that it is rather a *sui generis* type of feeling which provides us with such knowledge. Brentano himself came to think that all such views are quite incredible. As he says in a letter to Marty in 1909:

---

[36] Cf. Shand 1914/1926; Scheler 1973; Frijda et al. 1991; Goldie 2002, ch. 6. On "background evaluations" understood dispositionally, see Lyons 1980, 86–7.

What you seek to gain here with your belief in the obtaining [*Bestehen*] of goodness, to which the emotions are supposed to be found to be adequate, is incomprehensible to me. Do you really believe that this existence of goodness is accessible to you via perception just as mental emotional activities are, and that you then recognize by comparing what you perceive inwardly with what you perceive externally their agreement and thus that your emotion is correct? I should think that the mere formulation of such a question would suffice to make it apparent to anyone that it cannot possibly be answered affirmatively.[37]

Brentano's alternative is the view that certain intentional affective phenomena, for example a pro-attitude towards love, enjoy a species of self-evident correctness and present themselves to us as having this feature. Brentano's predecessors include James Martineau, Herbart and some of his followers (and perhaps Mill and Sidgwick). Herbart took himself to be developing ideas of Adam Smith and, like Smith and Brentano, was familiar with ancient discussions of correct, seemly, fitting, and inappropriate emotions.

Brentano's view combines an epistemological and an ontological claim. The latter tells us that the value of love consists in the fact that a pro-attitude towards love is correct. Throughout the twentieth century philosophers have defended similar views. These views—sometimes referred to as "buck-passing" (Scanlon) theories or "neo-sentimentalism"—belong to the family of what Meinong called "recessive analyses". They vary with respect to, first, the deontic concepts employed and, secondly, the status and scope of the analyses proposed.

Thus the buck-passer's analysans of value-ascriptions sometimes refers not to *correctness* or *rightness* but to what there is *reason* to feel, or to what *a subject has reason* to feel, or to what it is *appropriate* or *fitting* to feel, or to *justified* (defeasibly or non-defeasibly justified) emotions, or to what one *ought* to feel or *may* feel, or to the feelings an object *merits* or *deserves*, or to *worthy* feelings,[38]

By no means all buck-passers take themselves to be providing analyses, as opposed to, say, elucidations of value or to be providing a metaphysics of value. Similarly, not all accounts of value in terms of deontically qualified emotions (are intended to) deal with the same types of value. Some concentrate on thin value, some on particular thick values, such as ethical goodness and evil—thus Broad[39] claims that many ethical terms can be analysed in terms of other ethical notions

---

[37] Brentano 1952, 207–8. A just man, Brentano found equally incredible the remarkable naturalist and dispositionalist theories of values of his students, the early Meinong and Ehrenfels (cf. Eaton 1930). On Brentano's philosophy of emotions and values cf. Chisholm 1986, Kraus 1937, 165–200, Zimmerman 1980.

[38] Variants of the buck-passing account are given by: Eaton 1930, ch. 3; Broad 1930/1934 281 ff., 1934, 1944–5, 1985, 266; Osborne 1933, chs. 5, 11, 12; Kraus 1937; Brandt 1946; Ewing 1947, 1953/1964 104; Hall 1952, ch. 5; Mandelbaum 1955, ch. 3; McDowell 1985; Wiggins 1991; Gaus 1990, ch. 4; Gibbard 1990, 1998; Anderson 1993; Lemos 1994; Scanlon 1998, 2002; Mulligan 1998; Parfit 2001; Stratton Lake 2002; Skorupski 2007*a*,. For criticisms see: Scheler 1973, 181–2; Strawson 1949*a*, 1949*b*; Tappolet 2000; D'Arms & Jacobson 2000*a*, 2000*b*; Rabinowicz & Rønnow-Rasmussen 2004, 2006; Dancy 2005; Crisp 2005.

[39] Broad 1938, 659.

such as "right", "ought", "fitting". Some concentrate mainly on monadic value. A good example of what the buck-passing theory is capable of is provided by Rønnow-Rasmussen's analysis of what it is for something to be valuable for someone: x is valuable for y iff there is reason to favour x for y's sake.[40]

One challenge to accounts of value in terms of deontically qualified emotions stems from the observation that, even if it is possible to isolate the right deontic qualification, each such qualification turns out to comprehend many sub-kinds. Thus suppose that for an action to be shameful is for shame about oneself and the action to be appropriate. Appropriateness may be understood prudentially, socially, ethically, in moral and many other terms. Thus shame might be counter-productive or socially frowned on or morally retrograde. If shame is to be understood in the way the account wants to understand it, then the account has to tell us what the appropriate type of appropriateness is and, if possible, do this without distinguishing senses of "appropriate", "ought", etc.[41] Another challenge stems from the phenomenon already noted that it is often not possible to pair up emotions and values in the neat way illustrated by the shame–shameful couple.[42]

Meinong noted that analyses of value in terms of justified or correct emotions avoid circularity only if justification and correctness are deontic properties and if deontic properties and axiological properties are different types of property. He accepted both claims and took deontic properties and value-properties to be the formal objects of desire and of emotions, respectively.[43] But then such analyses seem to be committed to the claim that one type of deontic fact, appropriateness, is either not grounded in any axiological fact or, if it is grounded in an axiological fact, then this in its turn requires an analysis in deontic terms. Similarly, that some appropriate emotion occurs is presumably a good thing. But then the buck-passer has to say that the value of this fact is something that must be analysed in terms of appropriate emotions.

With the exception of Brentano and his immediate followers, buck-passers seem to have provided next to no account of what it is to come to know that some object is valuable or to come to be acquainted with the value of an object. Certainly no epistemology can be inferred from an account of what the exemplification of value consists in. But it may be noted that, although it is doubtless possible to find out *that* some emotion is appropriate to some object or situation, this sort of discovery appears to be very different from the sort of quasi-perceptual discovery of the

[40] Rønnow-Rasmussen 2007. On "for its own sake" cf. the reference in Note 2. Against *value for someone*, cf. Moore, 1903/1966, 150. In favour of both the *in itself valuable for someone* and *the in itself valuable* and on how to combine *value-individualism* and *value-universalism* cf. Scheler 1973 490–2.

[41] Cf. D'Arms & Jacobson 2000*a*; Rabinowicz & Rønnow-Rasmussen 2004, 2006; Skorupski 2007*b*, Louise 2009.

[42] Mulligan 1998, 174–5; Crisp 2005, 82; Reisner 2009.

[43] Meinong 1968, 644.

elegance of a gesture or the injustice of a situation on which the two theories discussed in section 21.4 lay so much weight.

The reasons to feel (emote) which are central to buck-passing theories are either defeasible or non-defeasible. In the most basic cases, these reasons are supposed to be provided by non-axiological, in particular, natural properties of the proper (material) object of the relevant emotion or of objects suitably related to this object. Reasons to emote may be merely reasons which speak in favour of or against, for example, admiring or being afraid of something. A reason may also be a motive: a reason on the basis of which one emotes. One widely accepted constraint on motives is that they be available to the subject for whom they are reasons. Natural properties are the properties which make scientific theories true as well as, say, the spatial and colour properties of everyday life. But, as has often been pointed out, the properties which loom largest in everyday life (the world of common sense, of the natural world-view, the *Lebenswelt*) are typically axiological properties of one sort or another. We are surrounded by criminals, cynics, friends, foes, fools, heroes, hunks, liars, oppressors, sentimentalists, traitors, victims, whores, models, and counter-models; as well as by goods, artefacts, and products which are more or less useful, elegant, well-made or ugly.[44] It is thus not clear where the buck-passer is to find the natural, non-axiological properties which could furnish motives for feeling (emoting) as opposed to reasons which speak in favour of or against feeling. Complex distributions of colour and spatial properties, it is true, provide both mere reasons to emote and motives and thus may yield some very simple value-properties, for example, the beauty and ugliness of ornaments.

If there are natural properties which make an object valuable, then these provide non-defeasible reasons for favouring the object. Other natural properties, for example those which contribute to making an object valuable, provide defeasible reasons to favour the object. But in everyday life one is frequently incapable of identifying or ascribing the natural properties which lead one to find a person charming, a crook, evil or a fool, or to find a gesture generous or elegant. Thus the buck-passing account of the nature of value-exemplification seems to be obliged to appeal to reasons which are not available to the subject. The buck-passer may insist that the emotings and reasons which constitute value are to be found, along with the subjects who emote and have these reasons, in very distant possible worlds. This may seem to preclude the buck-passer from giving an account of knowledge of value in the actual world. (The same holds for the views mentioned in section 21.4 which, although they do not analyse value in terms of reasons

---

[44] The "entanglement" of thick value-properties and natural properties can be understood in a variety of ways. There is the view that even the properties which are isolated by the sciences are inseparably bound up with value-properties (cf. Putnam 2002). Then there is the view that such entanglement holds within the world of common sense. The weak view relied on here is that we often find it difficult to disentangle value-properties and other properties in everyday life.

to emote, do claim that emotions and grasp of the non-axiological properties which make an object valuable can together yield knowledge of the object's value.) But if there is acquaintance with the exemplifications of (dis)value which make true the correctness conditions of different emotions, then non-defeasible justifications for emoting are available which are not natural facts but axiological facts.

## 21.6 VALENCE AND THE VALUES OF EMOTIONS

Emotions are among the least controversial candidates for the role of what has positive and negative value. Hedonisms and egoisms of many stripes tell us that pleasure and happiness are good things, that suffering is a bad thing and common sense agrees. Affective phenomena other than emotions also have positive and negative value—pain sensations are disvaluable and love is a good thing. Mental phenomena, whether affective or not, as well as vital phenomena have seemed to many philosophers to provide the most plausible candidates for what is intrinsically valuable—knowledge is valuable and true belief is more valuable than false belief. Indeed Brentano thought that every mental presentation or idea has positive value. Psychologists and philosophers often say that all or at least most emotions are positive or negative, that is, have positive or negative valence. Is valence value?

The claim that pleasure is valuable can mean many different things. This is true of both the referring part and the predicative part of the claim. If an object pleases or displeases Sam or if the fact that p (dis)pleases him, then he undergoes an emotion.[45] But the pain sensation or feeling in Sam's left foot, like the pleasurable sensation or frisson he feels in his neck, is no emotion according to (E). An emotion of pleasure has a basis—for example, a perception or a belief, for example, that one has won a race. And there is a third type of pleasure which is not obviously either an emotion or a sensation—pleasure in activity, for example, the pleasure one takes in running or skiing.[46]

If all value is thin, then there is no axiological difference between the value of knowledge, the value of pleasure, and the value of other affective phenomena such as love. The value of knowledge is surely of a different type than the value of pleasure. But what might the value of pleasure be?

---

[45] On the propositional attitude of taking pleasure in cf. Feldman 2004.

[46] On pleasure in activity cf. Johansson 2001. Rachels 2004 argues persuasively that where "pleasure" refers to a feeling its antonym is "unpleasure" (cf. the German couple "Lust-Unlust").

The most plausible candidate is one already mentioned—the value of pleasantness. Pleasure is pleasant, displeasure unpleasant. Pains sensations are unpleasant,
pleasure sensations are pleasant. Moore and Broad, however, seem to have thought
that pleasantness is a psychological and not a value-property.[47] But what is pleasant
may not please and what is unpleasant may not displease. According to one view of
the phenomenon of pain asymbolia,[48] a subject may be aware of a pain in his foot
and of its unpleasantness without being displeased, without disliking it or suffering.

If the pleasantness of pleasure *is* a value, is it the same value as the pleasantness of
champagne and oysters? Non-psychological objects are perhaps pleasant in virtue of
the pleasantness of our interactions with them. But there remains the possibility that
there are at least three distinct types of pleasantness, the pleasantness of sensations, of
the emotion of pleasure and of activity. Pleasantnesses, we may say, are hedonic values.

If the affective colourings of all emotions were simply the affective colourings of
pleasure and displeasure, then the hedonic values of all emotions would be the
values we have just identified. But suppose affective colourings come in many
different colours, that the affective dimensions of admiration, gladness, relief,
enjoyment and happiness differ qualitatively. On one version of this view, pleasure
and displeasure are aspects or components of all emotions and the different
pleasures are all of a kind as are the displeasures. On another version, the pleasure
which goes to make up happiness differs in kind from the pleasure which goes to
make up enjoyment. Similarly, what holds of emotions holds of other affective
phenomena—the pleasure of love differs from the pleasure of skiing, the displeasure of despair differs from that of sadness.[49] Such a view may be thought to have as
a consequence that the variety of pleasantness and unpleasantness is very great.
Different types of emotion and other affective phenomena are pleasant in different
ways just as different symphonies and buildings are sublime in different ways.

Psychologists and philosophers often claim not only that all or most emotions
are either positive or negative but also that all or most emotions exhibit positive or
negative "valence". Thus it is often argued that surprise is no emotion because it is
hedonically neutral;[50] there are pleasant surprises, unpleasant surprises, and surprises which are neither pleasant nor unpleasant. A weaker claim is that although
particular emotions or affects have valence instances of a type of emotion or affect
typically do not or need not have the same valence.[51]

---

[47] Broad 1930/1934, 229ff., 1942, 57–67; Moore 1942/1968, 587. Prinz (2004, 167) even says that
"'pleasant'and 'unpleasant' are words that describe conscious feelings"; for the view that pleasantness
is a value, cf. von Wright 1968, 64ff. Mendola 1990; Scheler 1973, 105–6.

[48] On pain asymbolia cf. Grahek 2007.

[49] The view that there are many distinct psychological types of pleasure has led some to define
pleasure as the object of certain types of attitudes. On this view cf. Feldman 1997.

[50] On this view cf. Reisenzein 2008.

[51] Charland 2005*a*, 2005*b*.

"Valence" means different things to different psychologists. Thus in addition to emotion valence and affect valence psychologists often refer to object valence, behaviour valence, the valence of expression, and evaluation valence.[52] It may seem tempting to identify the valence of emotions with the intrinsic values of pleasantness and unpleasantness. But this answer is by no means a popular one. Thus Prinz writes: "Positive emotions are ones we want to sustain, and negative emotions are ones we want to get rid of."[53] This and other "teleological" or functional views which characterize the valence of emotions in terms of goals, effects, or functions[54] are, of course, compatible with the claim that the valence of emotions is a matter of their value. But only with the claim that the type of value involved is extrinsic. The identification of the positive valence of an emotion with the desire to sustain it invites the question: Why do we want to sustain some emotions and not others? And one answer to that question is: because of their intrinsic value.

It is not, however, difficult to see why such an answer is unpopular. First, as we have seen, there is the difficulty of specifying the bearer of such values. Secondly, the difficulty of specifying the relevant type of intrinsic value—how many types of pleasantness should we countenance? Thirdly, it is arguably no part of the nature of psychological episodes to be intrinsically valuable or disvaluable. Finally, even if emotions of one type are necessarily valuable and emotions of another type necessarily disvaluable, and if these are non-natural facts, has an empirical science of the mind any right to refer to such non-natural facts?[55]

If emotions and other affective phenomena *are* intrinsically valuable or disvaluable, this has a number of consequences for the views about the relations between emotions and value described above and for some theories of emotion. One group of consequences concerns buck-passing accounts of value; another the view that there is affective knowledge of value; a third concerns the view that emotions are perceptions of bodily feelings.

Suppose that emotions are perceivings or registerings of bodily changes (cf. the theory of Prinz described in section 21.3 above). These states or activities are not intrinsically pleasant or unpleasant. Perceptual and intellectual states and acts—inner perception, judging, memory, retention—may be intrinsically valuable but they do not exemplify any hedonic values. They are neither positive nor negative. If the valence of an emotion is its intrinsic (un)pleasantness and if emotions are

---

[52] Colombetti 2005*a*, 2005*b*.

[53] Prinz 2004, 174.

[54] Cf. Colombetti 2005, 111 ff., Goldstein 1989, 260 ff.

[55] For the view that, although it is no part of the nature of emotions to exemplify value, natural facts, for example natural psychological facts nevertheless *normatively necessitate* the exemplification of value, see Fine 2005; Mulligan 2009. Goldstein (2000) argues that what makes a quale pleasure is just its intrinsic goodness.

perceivings or registerings, then emotions have no valence and are neither positive nor negative.

Suppose, now, that the buck-passing account of the exemplification of value is correct. Then the various emotions referred to in accounts of the exemplification of value will themselves be pleasant or unpleasant. If we say that the danger of a situation consists in the rightness or appropriateness of fear, we must add that any such fear is itself unpleasant. The buck-passer must then accept that his account of danger requires him to give an account of the unpleasantness of fear and then of the disvalue of whatever emotion he appeals to in giving an account of the disvalue of fear. And so on.

We noted above that one account of betterness or comparative value open to the buck-passer understands these in terms of correct or appropriate preference. Preferences of all types, object-preferences as well as preferences which range over options and states of affairs, are not emotions. Preferences typically last or endure and so are not episodes. But they are arguably affective phenomena. However, they have no valence. They are neither positive nor negative, they are neither pleasant nor unpleasant, although they are preferences *for* something *over* something else. The buck-passer may, then, be advised to accept this account of comparative value, an account which does not require him to account for the value of any emotion. The attraction of such an account would increase if it could be shown that monadic value can be defined in terms of comparative value.

If there are emotions and other affective phenomena which are intrinsically valuable or disvaluable, then the two accounts of affective knowledge of value described above should apply. Suppose that the most basic type of knowledge of value is provided by emotions, appropriate or correct emotions. Then if Sam is happy, his knowledge by acquaintance with the pleasantness of his happiness will take the form of an emotion the object of which is the pleasantness of his happiness. A slightly more plausible alternative is that Sam's knowledge of the pleasantness of his happiness consists simply in the fact that he feels the value of his happiness. Perhaps one of the many phenomena which are ascribed by instances of "x feels y" is our affective grasp of the value of the emotions we undergo.

One task for a theory of the (dis)value of emotions is to give some account of the intuition that it is better—non-hedonically better—to have appropriate emotions than inappropriate emotions. What might it mean to say that admiration of what is valuable is better than admiration of what is disvaluable, that the pleasure proper to a worthy activity is good, and that proper to an unworthy activity bad?[56]

Suppose Sam prefers that his emotions be correct rather than incorrect. This is doubtless an admirable state of affairs. He might also prefer that emotions in general be correct rather than incorrect. Another possibility is that he prefers that emotions be

---

[56] Cf. Aristotle, *Nicomachean Ethics* 1175b 27, 1101b; Zimmerman 1980.

responses to knowledge of what makes true the correctness conditions of these emotions rather than not. This is surely also an admirable state of affairs. But what is the relation between the objects of Sam's last two preferences? One tempting answer is that emotions which are responses to knowledge of value are better than emotions which are merely correct. Such an answer is analogous to the claim that desires which are responses to knowledge of what one ought to do are more valuable than desires which are merely correct. And to the claim that knowledge is more valuable than true belief. In the latter case it is natural to say that the relevant type of comparative value is comparative cognitive value: knowledge is *cognitively* better than mere true belief. Perhaps, too, emotions which are responses to knowledge of value are cognitively better than emotions which are merely correct. Not because emotions could be pieces of knowledge but because they can be responses to known value and so to value. Another (not incompatible) possibility is that the person who prefers that desires and affective responses be responses to knowledge of the way things axiologically are rather than not is concerned to avoid a type of injustice.

# REFERENCES

ACHTENBERG, D. (2002). *Cognition of Value in Aristotle's Ethics: Promise of Enrichment, Threat of Destruction*, Albany, NY: SUNY Press.

ANDERSON, E. (1993). *Value in Ethics and Economics*, Cambridge, MA: Harvard University Press.

BALDWIN, T. (1990). *G. E. Moore*, London, New York: Routledge.

BRIDGES, J. (2006). "Does Informational Semantics Commit Euthyphro's Fallacy?", *Noûs*, 60, 522–47.

BRANDT, R. B. (1941/2). "An Emotional Theory of the Judgement of Moral Worth", *Ethics*, 52, 41–79.

—— (1946). "Moral Valuation", *Ethics*, 56, 106–21.

BRENTANO, F. (1952). *Die Abkehr vom Nichtrealen*, Hamburg: Felix Meiner Verlag.

BROAD, C. D. (1930/1934). *Five Types of Ethical Theory*, London: Kegan Paul.

—— (1934). "Is 'Goodness' a Name of a Simple Non-natural Quality?", *Proceedings of the Aristotelian Society*, 34, 249–68 (reprinted in Broad [1971] *Critical Essays in Moral Philosophy*, London: Allen & Unwin, 106–23).

—— (1938). *Examination of McTaggarts' Philosophy*, Vol. II, Part II, Cambridge.

—— (1942/1968). "Certain Features in Moore's Ethical Doctrines", *The Philosophy of G. E. Moore*, ed. P. Schilpp, Open Court: La Salle, IL, 41–68.

—— (1985). *Lectures on Ethics*, ed. C. Lewy, Dordrecht: M. Nijhoff.

CARNAP, R. (1974). *Der logische Aufbau der Welt*, Frankfurt am Main: Ullstein.

CHARLAND, LOUIS C. (2005a). "Emotion Experience and the Indeterminacy of Valence", in *Emotion and Consciousness*, eds. Lisa Feldman-Barrett, Paula Niedenthal, & Piotr Winkielman, New York: Guilford Press, 231–334.

—— (2005*b*). "The Heat of Emotion. Valence and the Demarcation Problem", *Journal of Consciousness Studies*, 12 (8–10), 82–102.

CHISHOLM, R. (1986). *Brentano and Intrinsic Value*, Cambridge: Cambridge University Press.

CRANE, T. (1995). *The Mechanical Mind: A Philosophical Introduction to Minds, Machines and Mental Representation*, London: Penguin Books.

CRISP, Roger, (2005). "Value, Reasons, and the Structure of Justification: How to Avoid Passing the Buck", *Analysis* 65, 80–5.

DANCY, J. (2005). "Should we Pass the Buck?", in *Recent Work on Intrinsic Value*, eds. T. Rønnow-Rasmussen & M. J. Zimmerman, Berlin: Springer, 33–44.

D'ARMS, J. & JACOBSON, D. (2000*a*). "The Moralistic Fallacy: On the 'Appropriateness' of Emotions", *Philosophy and Phenomenological research*, 61 (1), 65–90.

—— (2000*b*). "Sentiment and Value", *Ethics*, 110, 722–48.

DEONNA, J. (2006). "Emotion, Perception and Perspective", *Dialectica*, 60 (1), 29–46.

—— & Teroni, F. (2008). *Qu'est-ce qu'une émotion?*, Paris: Vrin.

DE SOUSA, R. (1974). "The Good and the True", *Mind*, 83, 534–51.

—— (2002). "Emotional Truth", *Proceedings of the Aristotelian Society*, Supp. Vol. 76, 247–63.

—— (2007). "Truth, Authenticity, and Rationality", *Dialectica*, 61 (3), 323–45.

DÖRING, S. (2007). "Seeing What to Do: Affective Perception and Rational Motivation", *Dialectica*, 61 (3), 363–94.

EATON, H. O. (1930). *The Austrian Philosophy of Values*, Norman: The University of Oklahama Press.

ELLSWORTH, Ph. & SCHERER, K. (2003). "Appraisal Processes in Emotion", *Handbook of the Affective Sciences*, eds. R. J. Davidson, H. H. Goldsmith, & K. R. Scherer, New York: Oxford University Press, 572–95.

EWING, A. C. (1947). *The Definition of Good*, New York: Macmillan; London: Routledge & Kegan Paul.

—— (1953/1964) *Ethics*, London: The English Universities Press.

Feldman, F. (1997). "On the Intrinsic Value of Pleasure", *Ethics*, 107, 448–66.

—— (2004). *Pleasure and the Good Life: Concerning the Nature, Varieties, and Plausibility of Hedonism*, Oxford: Clarendon Press.

FINDLAY, J. N. (1954). "The Justification of Attitudes", *Mind*, 63, 250, 145–61.

FINE, K. (2005). "The Varieties of Necessity", in *Modality and Tense. Philosophical Papers*, Oxford: Clarendon Press, 235–60.

FRIJDA, N., MESQUITA, B., SONNEMANS, J. & VAN GOOZEN, S. (1991). "The Duration of Affective Phenomena or Emotions, Sentiments and Passions, *International Review of Studies on Emotion*, Vol. 1, ed. K. T. Strongman, New York: John Wiley & Sons, 187–225.

—— (2007). *The Laws of Emotions*, Mahwah, NJ, and London: Lawrence Erlbaum Associates.

GEACH, P. T. (1956). "Good and Evil", *Analysis*, 17, 33–42.

GIBBARD, A. (1990). *Wise Choices, Apt Feelings*, Oxford: Clarendon Press.

—— (1998). "Preference and Preferability", eds. C. Fehige & U. Wessels, *Preferences*, Berlin: de Gruyter, 239–59.

GOLDIE, P. (2002). *The Emotions. A Philosophical Exploration*, Oxford: Clarendon Press.

—— (2004). "Emotion, Feeling, and Knowledge of the World", in *Thinking about Feeling: Contemporary Philosophers on Emotions*, ed. R. C. Solomon, New York: Oxford University Press, 91–106.

GOLDIE, P. (2007). "Seeing What is the Kind Thing to Do: Perception and Emotion in Morality", *Dialectica*, 61 (3), 347–61.

GOLDSTEIN, I. (1989). "Pleasure and Pain: Unconditional, Intrinsic Values", *Philosophy and Phenomenological Research*, 50, 255–76.

—— (2000). "Intersubjective Properties by Which We specify Pain, Pleasure and Other Kinds of Mental States", *Philosophy*, 75, 89–104.

GRAHEK, N. (2007). *Feeling Pain and Being in Pain*, Cambridge, MA: MIT Press.

HALL, E. W. (1952). *What is Value? An Essay in Philosophical Analysis*, London: Routledge & Kegan Paul.

HARTMANN, N. (1932). *Ethics*, tr. by S. Coit, London: George Allen & Unwin, 3 Vols, I: *Moral phenomena*; II: *Moral values* (Reprint: New Brunswick, Transaction Publishers, 2002–2004).

HILDEBRAND, D. VON (1916). "Die Idee der sittlichen Handlung", *Jahrbuch für Philosophie und phänomenologische Forschung*, III, 126–251; Sonderdruck, Halle: Niemeyer (1930).

—— (1922). "Sittlichkeit und ethische Werturteile", *Jahrbuch für Philosophie und phänomenologische Forschung*, V, 463–602.

HUSSERL (1988). *Vorlesungen über Ethik und Wertlehre 1908–1914*, Husserliana XXVIII, Dordrecht: Kluwer.

JOHANSSON, I. (2001). "Species and Dimensions of Pleasure", *Metaphysica*, 2, 39–71.

JOHNSTON, M. (2001). "The Authority of Affect", *Philosophy and Phenomenological Research*, 63 (I), July, 181–214.

JURY, G. S. (1937). *Value and Ethical Objectivity. A Study in Ethical Objectivity and the Objectivity of Value*, London: Allen & Unwin.

KENNY, A. (1963). *Action, Emotion and Will*, London: Routledge.

KOLNAI, A. (1998). "The Standard Modes of Aversion: Fear, Disgust and Hatred", *Mind*, 107, 427, 581–94.

KRAFT, V. (1981). *Foundations for a Scientific Analysis of Value*, Vienna Circle Collection, Vol. 15, ed. H. Mulder, Dordrecht: D. Reidel.

KRAUS, O. (1937). *Die Werttheorien. Geschichte und Kritik*, Brünn, Vienna, and Leipzig: Verlag Rudolf M. Röhrer.

LEMOS, N. M., 1994, *Intrinsic Value: Concept and Warrant*, Cambridge Studies in Philosophy, Cambridge: Cambridge University Press.

LOUISE, J. (2009). "Correct Responses and the Priority of the Normative", *Ethical Theory and Moral Practice*, special number ed. by K. Mulligan & W. Rabinowicz, forthcoming.

LYONS, W. (1980). *Emotion*, Cambridge: Cambridge University Press.

—— (1999). "The Philosophy of Cognition and Emotion", in *Handbook of Cognition and Emotion*, eds. T. Dalgleish & M. Power, Chichester, UK, and New York: John Wiley & Sons Ltd., 21–44.

MANDELBAUM, M. (1955). *The Phenomenology of Moral Experience*, Glencoe, IL: The Free Press.

MARTY, A. (1908). *Untersuchungen zur Grundlegung der allgemeinen Grammatik und Sprachphilosophie*, Halle: Max Niemeyer.

McDOWELL, J. (1985). "Values and Secondary Qualities", in *Morality and Objectivity*, ed. T. Honderich, London: Routledge, 110–29.

—— (1994). *Mind and World*, Cambridge, MA and London: Harvard University Press.

MEINONG, A. (1968). *Abhandlungen zur Werttheorie*, Gesamtausgabe, Vol. 3, Graz: Akademische Druck-u. Verlagsanstalt.

MENDOLA, J. (1990). "Value and Subjective States", *Philosophy and Phenomenological Research*, 50 (4), 695–713.

MOORE, G. E. (1903/1966). *Principia Ethica*, Cambridge: Cambridge University Press.

—— (1968, 1942). "The Philosopher Replies", in *The Philosophy of G. E. Moore*, ed. P. Schilpp, Open Court: La Salle, IL, 533–688.

MULLIGAN, K. (1998). "From Appropriate Emotions to Values", in *Secondary Qualities Generalized*, ed. P. Menzies, *The Monist*, January 84 (1), 161–88.

—— (2007). "Intentionality, Knowledge and Formal Objects", *Disputatio*, 2 (23), 154–75.

—— (2009). "Values", *Routledge Companion to Metaphysics*, eds. R. Poidevin, P. Simons, A. McGonigal & R. Cameron, London: Routledge, forthcoming.

NORRICK, N. R. (1978). *Factive Adjectives and the Theory of Factivity*, Tübingen: Niemeyer.

ODDIE, GRAHAM (2005). *Value, Desire and Reality*, Oxford: Clarendon Press.

OSBORNE, H. (1933). *Foundations of the Theory of Value. An Examination of Value and Value Theories*, Cambridge: Cambridge University Press.

POSTAL, P. M. (1971). *Cross-Over Phenomena*, New York: Holt, Rinehart & Winston.

PRINZ, J. (2004). *Gut Reactions. A Perceptual Theory of Emotion*, New York: Oxford University Press.

PUTNAM, H. (2002). *The Collapse of the Fact/Value Dichotomy*, Cambridge, MA: Harvard University Press.

RABINOWICZ, W. and RØNNOW-RASMUSSEN, T. (2000). "A Distinction in Value: Intrinsic and for its Own Sake", *Proceedings of the Aristotelian Society*, 100 (1), 33–51.

—— (2004). 'The Strike of the Demon: On Fitting Pro-attitudes and Value,' *Ethics*, 114, 391–424.

—— (2006). 'Buck-Passing and the Right Kind of Reasons', *Philosophical Quarterly*, 56, 222, 114–20.

RACHELS, S. (2004). "Six Theses about Pleasure", *Philosophical Perspectives*, 18, *Ethics*, 247–67.

REISENZEIN, R. (2009). "Surprise", in *Oxford Companion to Affective Science*, eds. D. Sanders & K. Scherer, Oxford: Oxford University Press.

REISNER, A. (2009). "Abandoning the Buck-Passing Analysis of Final Value", *Ethical Theory and Moral Practice*, special number ed. by K. Mulligan and W. Rabinowicz, forthcoming.

RØNNOW-RASMUSSEN, T. (2007). "Analysing Personal Values" 2(4), *Journal of Ethics*, 2(4), 405–35.

SCANLON, T. M. (1998). *What We Owe to Each Other*, Cambridge, MA: Harvard University Press.

SCHELER, M. (1973, 1913–1916). *Formalism in Ethics and Non-formal Ethics of Values*, trans. M. S. Frings & R. L. Funk, Evanston, IL: Northwestern University Press.

—— (1992). *On Feeling, Knowing and Valuing*, Chicago and London: University of Chicago Press.

SHAND, A. (1914/1926). *The Foundations of Character*, London: Macmillan and Co.

SKORUPSKI, J. (2007a). "What is Normativity?", *Disputatio*, II, 23, 247–68.

—— (2007b). "Buckpassing about goodness", in *Hommage à Wlodek. Philosophical Papers Dedicated to Wlodek Rabinowicz*, ed. T. Rønnow-Rasmussen, B. Petersson, J. Josefsson, & D. Egonsson, <http://www.fil.lu.se/hommageawlodek/site/papper/Skorupski:John/pdf>.

SOLOMON, ROBERT C. and LORI D. STONE (2002). 'On "positive" and "negative" emotions', *Journal for the Theory of Social Behavior*, 32, 417–36.

STEIN, E. (1970). *Beiträge zur philosophischen Begründung der Psychologie. Eine Untersuchung über den Staat*, Tübingen: Max Niemeyer.

STRATTON-LAKE, P. (2002). "Introduction", in *Ethical Intuitionism*, ed. P. Stratton-Lake, Oxford: Clarendon Press.

STRAWSON, P. (1949a). "Critical Notice of Ewing", The Definition of Good, *Mind*, 58, 84–94.

—— (1949b). "Ethical Intuitionism", *Philosophy*, 24, 23–33.

TAPPOLET, Ch. (2000). *Emotions et valeurs*, Paris: Presses Universitaires de France.

THOMSON, J. J. (1992). "Goodness and Utilitarianism", *Proceedings and Address of the Eighty-ninth Annual Eastern Division Meeting of the American Philosophical Association in Washington*, 67, 145–59.

TYE, M. (2008). "The Experience of Emotion: An Intentionalist Theory", *Revue internationale de philosophie*, special number ed. J. Proust, 243, 25–50.

WIGGINS, D. (1991). *Needs, Values, Truth. Essays in the Philosophy of Value*, Aristotelian Society Series, Vol. 6, Oxford: Blackwell.

WILLIAMS, B. (1985). *Ethics and the Limits of Philosophy*, London: Fontana.

WRIGHT, G. H. von (1968). *The Variety of Goodness*, London: Routledge & Kegan Paul.

ZAGZEBSKI, L. T. (2004). *Divine Motivation Theory*, Cambridge: Cambridge University Press.

ZIMMERMAN, M. J. (1980). "On the Intrinsic Value of States of Pleasure", *Philosophy and Phenomenological Research*, 41 (1/2), 26–45.

# CHAPTER 22

# AN ETHICS OF EMOTION?

## JEROME NEU

The scripture for today is:

Matthew 5: 43–8: Ye have heard that it hath been said, Thou shalt love thy neighbour, and hate thine enemy. But I say unto you, Love your enemies, bless them that curse you, do good to them that hate you, and pray for them which despitefully use you, and persecute you; That ye may be the children of your Father which is in heaven: for he maketh his sun to rise on the evil and on the good, and sendeth rain on the just and on the unjust. For if ye love them which love you, what reward have ye? do not even the publicans the same? And if ye salute your brethren only, what do ye more than others? do not even the publicans so? Be ye therefore perfect, even as your Father which is in heaven is perfect.

Christ's message is that, despite its difficulty, loving one's enemy is valuable; indeed, that the value is evidenced by the difficulty. One might well wonder why difficulty should be thought valuable—is there something morally defective about living in undemanding temperate climes, such as California's, where one does not need to shovel winter snow? But aside from the question of the nature and evidences of moral value, there is an issue of psychological possibility. Freud, in *Civilization and Its Discontents* (1930a, 109–12, 142–3), famously ridicules Christ's commandment of universal love. His complaint is that loving one's enemy is not merely difficult but psychologically impossible, and perhaps even morally dubious. After all, what has one's enemy done to deserve one's love, and, assuming that love affects what one actually does, doesn't it have costs in terms of the favor or preferential treatment that one owes and will have to deny to those who have loved one and treated one well? He suggests impartiality in love may be a kind of injustice. Crucially, for Freud, the special psychological difficulty in loving one's enemies is connected with natural human aggression. Its objects, like the objects of love, would seem fixed in human nature. You can't overcome hatred simply because society or religion tells you that you ought to; you can't make yourself love someone because you think you should. Freud quotes Heine's humorous take on the matter:

Mine is a most peaceable disposition. My wishes are: a humble cottage with a thatched roof, but a good bed, good food, the freshest milk and butter, flowers before my window, and a few fine trees before my door; and if God wants to make my happiness complete, he will grant me the joy of seeing some six or seven of my enemies hanging from those trees. Before their death I shall, moved in my heart, forgive them all the wrong they did me in their lifetime. One must, it is true, forgive one's enemies—but not before they have been hanged.

(Freud 1930a, 110n.1; Heine, *Gedanken und Einfälle*, Section I)

What kind of a moral imperative is it that ignores the facts of human psychology? What is the point of telling people they ought to do something that they, psychologically, cannot? Kant would doubtless respond to Freud that he is misunderstanding the nature of moral imperatives. They are addressed to the pure, not the empirical, will. He writes in the *Grundlegung*,

Undoubtedly in this way also are to be understood those passages of Scripture which command us to love our neighbor and even our enemy. For love as an inclination cannot be commanded; but beneficence from duty, when no inclination impels us and even when a natural and unconquerable aversion opposes such beneficence, is practical, and not pathological, love. Such love resides in the will and not in the propensities of feeling, in principles of action and not in tender sympathy; and only this practical love can be commanded.

(Kant 1785/1993 Ak. 399)

Emotions, Kant would apparently agree with Freud, are not in our control. Moral commands are restricted to what is in one's control. The moral will, which for Kant is the only unconditionally good thing in the world or out of it, is what matters. Moral worth depends on acting from duty, from respect for law in accordance with the Categorical Imperative. Our "principles of action"—what we try to do—are supposed to be for us to determine, even when "tender sympathy" is beyond our powers.

But can we really make sense of respect for the moral law apart from our understanding of the empirical world of so-called "pathological" emotions? What, in the end, is "respect"? Is it too an emotion? Certainly, like emotions in general, it functions in Kant's account as an attitude and a motive. Kant himself acknowledges it is a feeling, but insists it must be distinguished from the ordinary run of feelings that can be reduced to inclination or fear, are linked to self-love, and are not purely rational (Kant 1785/1993, Ak. 401n.14). It is supposed to be the effect on us of recognition of the majesty of the law. We are to act from duty. The dutiful "principles of action" or maxims of our conduct are what Kant equates with the "practical love" that he thinks can be commanded. But can we choose our motives? Do we determine the reasons that move us?

## 22.1 WHAT MOVES US

Bishop Butler prefaces both of his seminal sermons on forgiveness ("Upon Resentment" and "Upon Forgiveness of Injuries") with the first words of the passage from Matthew quoted above (1726/1970, 72, 80). He interprets Christ's command to love our enemies as a call for forgiveness (84), where forgiveness is at the least a foreswearing of revenge (as Charles Griswold argues—2007, 19–37), but may also involve a more inner transformation, a foreswearing of resentment itself (as on Jeffrie Murphy's early formulation—1982, 504). Butler starts with a general obligation of benevolence or good-will towards mankind—what amounts to a Kantian respect for the fundamental humanity even of evildoers. He adds to it a belief that self-love and partiality regularly lead us to take more offense than is proper and a further belief that we are all sinners and that a forgiving spirit is necessary if we are to hope for pardon of our own sins. So our own need for forgiveness, the tendencies to excess in personal resentments (especially when the harms we suffer are considered from more realistic and impartial perspectives), and the wrongness of demonizing those who injure us together make forgiveness compelling. Forgiveness is a virtue.

The objects of the Christian duty to love (if we may call it that) may be unusually extensive on Butler's account. Butler insists: "It is not man's being a social creature, much less his being a moral agent, from whence *alone* our obligations to good-will towards him arise. There is an obligation to it prior to either of these, arising from his being a sensible creature; that is, capable of happiness or misery" (1726/1970, 84). This shifts the basis of a duty of respect for humanity—of treating as ends never merely as means—from a shared rationality to a shared sensibility. This making of a Benthamite sensibility rather than a Kantian rationality central to our distinctively moral humanity may also require a broadening of the obligations of respect, good-will, and love to other creatures. Whether these broadened obligations can be met without control of "pathological" feelings remains to be seen. For now, it should perhaps be noted that Christian love would seem to need to be more robust than simply a universal good-will towards all, at least if it is to enable us to overcome intemperate desires for revenge while still leaving a passion for justice, as Bishop Butler would have it.

As one would expect on an Aristotelian understanding of virtue, forgiveness lies at a mean between an excess and a deficiency: it lies between slavishness and servility on the one side, and an unyielding hard-heartedness and vengefulness on the other. Its benefits may be many: self-healing from consuming anger, restraint of cruelty, and restoration of relationships. Moral humility and the recognition that we may all need at times to be forgiven, and that the ability to forgive is essential to maintaining intimate relationships, to having friends and lovers, make forgiveness a virtue—even if it is an "imperfect duty" in that, at a given time, no one may be entitled to be forgiven. But there is a further Aristotelian point to be borne in mind. Aristotle teaches that virtue is a mean, but also that one must act well out of the right motive. If it is to be a virtue, forgiveness must be given for the right reasons, the right moral reasons.

It should be understood that one of the grounds for respecting resentment (and holding on to it) is that, unlike simple anger, it always claims to rest on moral principle. Resentment presumes a certain sort of justification not required by anger (at least by anger caused by simple frustration of desire). It is, as Bishop Butler argues, "settled and deliberate" (1726/1970, 73–6). Of course resentment may, like anger, on occasion be unjustified (the beliefs involved may not be true). But resentment, unlike anger, typically asserts a moral claim, as John Rawls explains: "A person without a sense of justice may be enraged at someone who fails to act fairly. But anger and annoyance are distinct from indignation and resentment; they are not, as the latter are, moral emotions" (Rawls 1971, 488). Rawls distinguishes the moral emotions, including resentment and indignation, on the basis of the type of explanation required for a feeling to count as a particular emotion. Rawls writes, "In general, it is a necessary feature of moral feelings, and part of what distinguishes them from the natural attitudes, that the person's explanation of his experience invokes a moral concept and its associated principles. His account of his feeling makes reference to an acknowledged right or wrong" (1971, 481). As Murphy argues, the value of resentment lies in its ties to "self-respect, self-defense, and respect for the moral order" (2003, 19). Where resentment is justified, there must be good reasons for giving it up.

Forgiveness involves an interplay of attitudes. The forgiver foreswears resentment, but the evildoer, to be morally deserving of that effort, must acknowledge his wrong and repent, or in some other way suitably distance himself from his wrong and the message of disrespect so often tied to it. Only then does the forgiver have the sort of moral reasons needed to make his or her act of forgiveness the manifestation of a virtue.

And here we must be wary. Kant himself points out that there is room for ambiguity, confusion, and uncertainty in our knowledge of our own motives. (This is apart from questions concerning choice, that is, limits on our control over our own motives—questions to which we will be coming shortly.) Even when we do the right thing, we may not be certain that we are doing it for the right reasons (on Kant's view, reasons of duty), for our motives may be mixed—including perhaps simple inclination or self-interest—and sometimes hidden. Kant writes, "We like to flatter ourselves with the false claim to a more noble motive, but in fact we can never, even by the strictest examination, completely plumb the depths of the secret incentives of our actions" (Kant, 1785/1993, Ak. 407, cf. 397ff., 419). And similar problems may arise concerning feeling the right thing. When we think our resentment, for example, is tied to concern for justice and the moral order, we may be self-deceived. Both the individual state of mind and the punitive social practices that it supports may have darker forces behind them—as, indeed, may apparently more forgiving and loving states of mind and practices.

In addition to Freud's critique of Christ's injunction to love our enemies, we should recall Nietzsche's suspicion that the Christian call to love one's enemies is fueled by impotent hate, by *ressentiment*. Nietzsche declares (in the voice of his interlocutor):

Weakness is being lied into something *meritorious*, no doubt of it . . . and impotence which does not requite into 'goodness of heart' . . . [The weak man's] inability for revenge is called unwillingness to revenge, perhaps even forgiveness ('for *they* know not what they do—we alone know what *they* do!'). They also speak of 'loving one's enemies'—and sweat as they do so.

(Nietzsche 1887/1969, First Essay §14)

There is a related risk that Nietzschean *ressentiment*—what Murphy describes as "an ugly emotional brew of malice, spite, envy, and cruelty" (2006, 57; cf. 1999 and 2003, 14)—may also lie behind retributivist justifications of punishment. Nietzsche continues:

These cellar rodents full of vengefulness and hatred—what have they made of revenge and hatred? Have you heard these words uttered? If you trusted simply to their words, would you suspect you were among men of *ressentiment*? . . . [And his interlocutor responds] I understand; I'll open my ears again (oh! oh! oh! and *close* my nose). Now I can really hear what they have been saying all along: 'We good men—*we are the just*'—what they desire they call, not retaliation, but 'the triumph of *justice*'; what they hate is not their enemy, no! they hate 'injustice,' they hate 'godlessness'. . .

(Nietzsche 1887/1969, First Essay §14)

We should be wary that what lies behind retributive urges to punish is less respectable resentment than self-deceptive *ressentiment*—and *ressentiment* (unlike rational and well-founded resentment) has no redeeming features. Freud, that other great questioner of consciousness, of commonsense self-understanding, has a similar suspicion that it is envy and reaction-formation that lie at the root of calls for justice (1921c, 119–21; see also Forrester 1996). That is to say, there may be motives that we should mistrust lying behind what presents itself as calls for loving fellow-feeling and for equality, as demands for everyone to get respect and their just deserts.

The Nietzschean suspicion that cruelty may lie behind Christian calls for universal love and retributive calls for justice presupposes both the power of self-deception and our lack of power to choose our motives, including our emotional impulses. Both contribute to the uncertainty, remarked by Kant and felt by all, in knowing what moved us on a particular occasion. Self-deception may involve a choice, at some level, of what motives to admit to and self-ascribe, but it does not change the facts about what, in reality, moves us. So are resentment and forgiveness, the foreswearing of resentment, up to us? Are these things about which we have a choice and matters on which reason can move? (See Neu 2008, Ch. 10: "To Understand All Is to Forgive All—Or Is It?") And what of other claims about what we ought (or ought not) to feel?

## 22.2 WHAT WE "OUGHT" TO FEEL

Quite apart from the question of specifically moral emotions in the embodiment and enforcement of ethics—emotions such as guilt, shame, resentment, indignation, regret, remorse, sympathy, and perhaps Kantian "respect"—I want to ask whether there is an "Ethics of Emotion" that extends to the full gamut of emotions (see also Neu 2002). Should we love our enemies? More generally, apart from Christ's injunction, there are any number of things that it is said one ought, or ought not, to feel. Traditionally, it has been held a sin (indeed, a "deadly" sin) to feel envy, pride, or anger. And there are other emotions, such as *Schadenfreude*, that are equally frowned upon. Just as envy, pain at the success of others, is supposed to be wrong, *Schadenfreude*, its inverse, pleasure at the pain of others, is supposed to be a sign of bad character. Good character is supposed to exclude certain structures of emotional response.

Once more, are there things that we ought or ought not to feel, and how are we to go about meeting our obligations (if there are any) in this sphere? Certainly there are disreputable emotions, such as the envy and Schadenfreude I just mentioned. Ought we not to feel them? Do we have grounds to disapprove of those who nonetheless do? Is it wrong to be amused by racist or sexist jokes? Ronald de Sousa tells us that, when it is the matter rather than the manner (the content rather than the envelope) of the joke that amuses us, it is the non-hypothetical attitudes revealed that are subject to criticism. Racist and sexist acts are doubtless immoral. What of racist and sexist attitudes? Does it matter where they came from and whether they are in our control? (see de Sousa 1987, Ch. 11: "When Is It Wrong to Laugh?"; Neu 2008, Ch. 9: "Insult Humor"; and Smith 2005). What of jealousy? Ought we strive to eliminate it? How? (see Neu 2000, Ch. 3: "Jealous Thoughts" and Ch. 4: "Jealous Afterthoughts"). There have been changing attitudes towards such emotions, maybe even moral progress. (Some of the field of history of the emotions tracks changes in social attitudes towards such things over time—e.g., Stearns 1989.) For a long time many felt it was wrong to have hostile feelings towards people we supposedly love, that it somehow belies the love. Freud's Rat Man suffered from a host of neurotic symptoms because of his repressed rage (Freud 1909*d*). He could not face his unconscious hatred for his deceased father (who had in certain ways interfered with his love life) and his lady love (who had rejected his proposals). But through Freud's efforts to make the unconscious conscious, the Rat Man overcame his obsessive-compulsive symptoms, and it is arguable that through Freud's efforts society has come to accept ambivalence as natural, so that we can face the mixed feelings we all (arguably, inevitably) have towards our beloveds. (Indeed, we now tend to suspect any love that professes to be too pure, too unmixed.) It can even be argued that the recognition and acceptance of emotional ambivalence is a kind of moral progress, part of a larger trend towards self-acceptance and rejection of psychologically impossible ideals.

But still, are there some things that we *ought* to feel? Camus' *Stranger* was doubtless a criminal, but he appears particularly heartless in his failure to feel grief at the death of his mother (Camus 1946). Is the failure to feel grief proof of an absence of love? Might there be other explanations for the failure to feel grief? (see Deutsch 1937.) One might also wonder in this connection whether there is a way to cultivate grief (the inner state, not the mere outward behavior) independent of cultivating love. The potential significance of the link is enough at least to suggest that the norms involved are not merely statistical or social expectations but a matter of patterned relations among emotions, such that the value we attach to one may come to inform our attitudes towards another. There may also be norms internal to an emotion, as with the notion that genuine grief should not be gotten over too quickly. (Remember Hamlet's complaint about his mother Gertrude's too speedy remarriage: "The funeral bak'd meats / Did coldly furnish forth the marriage tables" *Hamlet* 1.2.180–1.) And there may be other norms that demand expression in emotion. Elizabeth Spelman (1989) and other feminists, for example, have argued that sometimes one ought to be angry. Failure to be angry or to express anger might involve subservience or insufficient self-respect, or even self-deception—though we should remember that the failure in particular to *express* an emotion might sometimes have an alternative explanation in the costs of such expression or its simple pointlessness. At least since Aristotle, philosophers have proposed ideals of right feeling as part of the good, the virtuous, life. There are issues about the mean (when, why, and with whom to get angry to what degree) and the extremes that moderate living would have us avoid. Some Stoic sages would have us feel virtually nothing at all, thinking that ideals of self-sufficiency should put us above the reach of that which we cannot control. Spinoza, perhaps the sagest of all, would have us aim at the maximum level of activity in our mental life, including our emotional life, that the limitations of our condition allow. What are those limits? Surely they must depend on what emotions are and what they are connected with.

Certainly there is an ethics of action, views about what one ought and ought not to do. Those ideals might well extend to the realm of emotional expression, which includes behavior and dispositions to behavior (some voluntary and some perhaps involuntary but controllable). More dubiously, some think there is an ethics of belief, but most often this refers to a kind of hygiene of belief—what investigations one should embark on, what evidence one should insist on, before committing oneself to a belief. Less often, it involves notions such as that one ought to believe one's lover faithful or one's business partner honest—a "benefit of the doubt" presumption in social relations. Still, in the law the notion that a person is presumed innocent actually requires no one to believe anything (surely prosecutors do not, or at any rate should not, prosecute unless they believe the accused guilty, indeed, provably guilty). The presumption is simply a matter of who has the burden of proof. And in the social sphere, whatever principles of charity or optimism one might prefer, and whatever principles of restraint in action in the absence of certainty, surely no one can insist on a duty of self-deception.

Given the situations in relation to action and belief, it becomes compelling to consider whether there is or ought to be a more direct "Ethics of Emotion", specifying things that one ought or ought not to feel. How might such an ethics be possible? People are quite commonly enjoined to feel certain things or to not feel certain things. At the same time, however, it is commonly thought that emotions are not in our control, that we cannot simply choose what to feel. How is one to reconcile the existence of widespread expectations about how one ought to feel or ought not to feel with the notion that morality can command only that which is in one's control? An ethics of action is confronted by its own dilemmas of determinism. Are these the same dilemmas faced by emotional norms? Are they open to the same solutions (Kantian two-worlds, Humean compatibalism, a resigned fatalism . . . )? In any event, only a fuller understanding of the character of emotions and of the nature and implications of the expectations that we have in relation to them can clarify the place of emotions in moral character (the moral character that we praise and criticize in others and aspire to for ourselves).

Given the modern dominance of cognitive views of the emotions, the prominence given to beliefs and other cognitive states in constituting emotions, we will have to consider the issue of the relation of belief to the will. Can we choose our thoughts and beliefs? To approach the matter, we will return once more to the question of loving our enemies, to resentment and forgiveness. But there is another aspect of the problem we should turn to first, to get clearer about the sorts of norms that are being invoked, and consideration of anger may help give us a way into that.

## 22.3 "APPROPRIATE" FEELINGS

There is, we have seen, an apparent tension between the widespread belief that there are norms governing how we ought (or ought not) to feel and the equally widespread belief that we cannot control how we feel. The place to begin in understanding that tension is with some scrutiny of the nature of the relevant "norms" and of the forms and limits of any needed "control". First norms.

Let us go back to Aristotle. Aristotle certainly thought anger, to take a prominent example, has its proper place. He speaks of those who fail to be angry enough:

> The deficiency, whether it is a sort of inirascibility or whatever it is, is blamed. For those who are not angry at the things they should be are thought to be fools, and so are those who are not angry in the right way, at the right time, or with the right persons; for such a man is thought not to feel things nor to be pained by them, and, since he does not get angry, he is thought unlikely to defend himself; and to endure being insulted and to put up with insults to one's friends is slavish.

> (Aristotle 1984, 1126a)

And certain modern feminists follow Aristotle in calling on women to be angry at their subordination. This call has various aspects. Certainly feeling angry when one is treated unjustly is *appropriate*. One cannot be faulted for having an emotion with an incoherent object or an object unsuited to the conceptual constraints on that type of feeling. One might even say such a feeling in such a context is *justified*. It might be argued that feeling anger (and variants such as resentment and indignation) when appropriate may be a condition of self-respect, and so failure to feel appropriate anger may be a sign of insufficient concern for one's rights and dignity, insufficient self-respect (see Hill 1973, Murphy 1982, and Spelman 1989). This begins to move towards the clearly moral question of whether one *should* feel angry, at least if one makes the common assumption that psychological character-istics may constitute virtues or vices, which is to say, moral strengths or moral flaws. Certainly that was Aristotle's view and is the view of modern virtue ethics.

But two further questions remain. One is whether one should act on one's feelings of outrage. Here even feminists who urge anger and insubordination, assertion of one's rightful place and one's legitimate demands, recognize that there can be danger and costs in acting on the outrage one feels. Feeling an emotion and expressing it are two different things (unless one follows William James and those who would collapse an emotion into what is normally thought of as its expression, so that one is afraid because one runs, sad because one cries, and—in general—does not experience an emotion unless one is aware of, that is feels, what is normally thought of as its visceral or outward expression). Whether one should express one's feelings is a part of the ordinary ethics of action. In the case of the relatively powerless, expressing their anger to those with power who oppress them may be a step towards liberation, but it also runs the risk of bringing down fearsome retaliation. Whether one should express one's anger is a moral and political and strategic question. Our question, whether one should feel anger (whether or not one chooses to express it), remains. On this Spelman and others hesitate. While she argues that "in certain circumstances people perhaps ought to be angry" and that "good clear thinking on the part of people in subordinate positions is likely to make such people angry", she recognizes there are issues about what one "ought" to believe and that (whatever the relation of belief and the will) feeling angry is more than just forming a belief (Spelman 1989, 266–71). The question of what is within our power becomes pressing. Certainly one should try not to feel inappropriate emotions. That is a point about rationality (see de Sousa 1987; Elster 1999). But while one should certainly try to feel only appropriate emotions, should one try to feel *all* emotions that it might be appropriate to feel in the circumstances? If not all, which? Why? And can one? (And when we speak of "circumstances" is it only the immediate circumstances and occurrent emotions that are at issue, or is there a call for long-standing emotions in the face of long-standing situations such as political oppression or unforgivable atrocities, even if they are long past?)

Let's focus for a moment on "appropriateness". This notion may appeal to normativity in at least three different senses. It is, of course, "natural" to feel grief at loss and fear of danger. This could point to simple regularities in the order of nature. (Given a Humean understanding of emotion, founded on mechanisms of association between impressions and ideas, that is all it *could* mean.) When people lose a loved one to death they naturally, normally, usually feel grief. When people face a physical threat that might lead to their own death they naturally, normally, usually feel fear. Of course, some are less fearful than others and some less prone to grief than others, but a failure to feel fear or grief, however unusual or even abnormal, need not involve a violation of an exception-less law of nature. Nor need it be irrational, which is the second sense of "appropriateness" sometimes at issue in the evaluation of emotions. This is a conceptual form of normativity. That is, there would be something irrational at feeling grief at the finding of a loved one that had been presumed lost or fear on being rescued from danger. Loss is the notional object of grief as danger is the notional object of fear. There may be complex situations in which the recovery of a loved one involves grief at some hidden object (say, at the lost freedom to become involved with others) or mixed feelings of a variety of sorts (relief can be accompanied by anxiety etc.). That is, in the absence of the notional object, some special explanation must be provided for the presence of the associated feeling, at least if that feeling is to make sense. How could one even begin to recognize a felt unease in the presence of, say, an ashtray as "shame" in the absence of some story that filled in the needed conceptual relations? If one were, let us imagine, an ashtray manufacturer, one might feel ashamed at the inferior quality of one's product, of the fragility or planned obsolescence built-in out of hope of economic gain. The story need not be true (and such delusions might introduce irrationality of a different kind), but at least the conceptual requirement of belief in violation of some standard that is requisite for shame would be met. There are conceptual constraints on particular emotions that make identifying a feeling as a particular emotion subject to normative evaluation as irrational, and so inappropriate in that sense. Natural history may sometimes feed into conceptual conditions, forming a criterion. As Wittgenstein asked, "Why does it sound queer to say: 'For a second he felt deep grief'? Only because it so seldom happens?" (1953, II.174). But the norms of the causal order or of the conceptual order are to be distinguished from the norms of the moral order. That brings us to the third sense in which emotions might be held to be appropriate or inappropriate, the sense which is our primary concern in this discussion. Different moral theories (whether Aristotelian, Kantian, Benthamite, or of other forms and traditions) might fill in the criteria of such appropriateness in different ways.

So leaving open the nature of ethics (I believe the problems arise on any conception), and having left aside questions about guilt, shame, remorse, "respect", and other emotions often thought to be specifically "moral" (that is, to play a role in constituting and giving life to morality), we can turn now to issues of control, central on any account to our budget of problems around the question of whether there is (and if there is how it is that there can be) an "Ethics of Emotion".

## 22.4 "Control" over Feelings Psychological and Moral Possibility

Murphy and Griswold insist that genuine forgiveness, if it is to be a moral virtue, must be based on moral reasons—and so, it would seem, it must be a matter of choice. And yet, most of the time, we believe that we cannot choose what we feel— at least not directly, and perhaps not even indirectly. We cannot make ourselves love someone because we think we ought. Can we make ourselves forgive someone because we think they (having repented or met other of the moral conditions Murphy, Griswold, and others spell out) have separated themselves from their wrongful deed and its implications and that we *ought* to forgive—both for their sakes and for our own, so that we do not become cold unrelenting judgers unable to have ongoing relationships? (It would be an odd virtue that one ought never to practice or that it was merely permissible to indulge.) What is needed to have a change of heart? Is it up to us? These are serious issues for moral judgment, for therapeutic aspirations, and for educational and would-be reforming institutions (prisons, after all, used to be referred to as "penitentiaries").

Certainly we can try, but trying (unlike wishing) is limited by belief in the possibility of success. (What would constitute "trying" to leap over the Empire State Building if one believed the mission impossible?) What would count as success in the dynamic described above? Not just the disappearance and non-recurrence of the feelings of resentment that we are trying to foreswear. Simple forgetting or perhaps even drugs might yield that result. As a virtue, forgiveness would seem to require that the inner shift be brought about for the right reasons. (Recall that for Kant acting on maxims or principles of duty is essential to moral worth, just as for Aristotle doing the right thing for the right reason is essential to virtue. And even on a utilitarian approach, the proper description of an action and the calculation of its consequences may well turn on the underlying motives.) Whether the motive needs to involve repentance on the part of the wrongdoer or might simply be a desire to be perfect on the part of the forgiver ("Be ye therefore perfect" being the conclusion of Christ's admonition in the passage from Matthew) is open to argument. The argument might bring us back to a contrast between notions of forgiveness as a free gift and as conditioned on reasons, such as repentance. It is difficult to see how an easy, unconditional, forgiveness could maintain respect for self, for others, and for the moral order (again, the central arguments in support of a sometimes persisting resentment). It is difficult to see how such a forgiveness could be a virtue. It is also difficult to see how difficulty alone could make something a perfection. In addition, it should be noted that it is dubious that mere desire for psychological ease or "closure" could provide the sort of moral motivation that forgiveness as a virtue requires. Surely it runs the risk of excusing or condoning (and thus perhaps encouraging) wrongdoing, and it is questionable that psychological self-interest is itself properly "moral" (not that it is wrong, but does it merit moral praise?).

There are limits on choosing our emotions and motives. Murphy usefully notes: "Of course forgiveness is not always in my power. I can resolve and try the best I can to overcome resentment, but I will sometimes fail" (1982, 516 n22). And Griswold apparently concurs: "[B]ecause the sentiments are not wholly at the command of the will, the forswearing of resentment cannot be obligatory let alone subject to coercion" (2007, 68; though there may be issues of entitlement raised by Griswold's claims about "lack of warrant" for or "inappropriateness" of persisting resentment in the light of what is "due" a properly repentant offender—2007, 43, 69–70, 117–19, 183). The persistence of passions may have many explanations. Some of the difficulties may lie within the very nature of emotions. Once one accepts the centrality of cognitive states in constituting emotions, some of the limits on choosing our emotions may be understood in terms of limits on our control over our thoughts and beliefs. Those who follow Descartes in thinking that belief is directly subject to the will, such as Sartre, tend to believe that we can choose our emotions. Sartre in particular thinks passions are actions, that we are responsible for them, that they are attempts (typically magical and so perhaps ineffectual attempts) to change the world (Sartre 1948; cf. Solomon 2003 and Elster 1999, 306–12). So what we ought to feel is as much an issue as what we ought to do. Those who follow Spinoza in thinking that there is no separate process of assenting to a proposition once one has recognized the evidence as evidence (seeing is believing, so to speak) will tend to think that we must always, to some degree, be the passive subjects of our emotions. It is a matter of degree, along multiple dimensions. I myself would be of that school.

But once one accepts a degree of passivity, lack of control, it does not follow that ethical judgments are out of place—despite Kantian presumptions to the contrary. After all, Bernard Williams's truck driver who, without fault, hits a child who runs out in front of his truck, is right to feel what Williams calls "agent-regret", and we might regard him as morally deficient if he failed to feel it (Williams 1981). What we cause matters, even if we are not at fault. The actual may be a part of who we are, even if we did not choose it and we were not negligent in its coming to be. And a person who wishes another dead may appropriately feel guilty at the thought, even in the absence of a deed, in the absence of a choice. (Freud denied that responsibility for such wishes could be removed by tracing their infantile origins—1909d, 185 n2. Angela M. Smith, 2005, usefully explores the tension in our views on responsibility for thoughts and failures to think, contrasting volitional and rational relations accounts of responsibility. See also Oakley 1992.) Indeed, issues of choice and control may arise at multiple points in time, with significant consequences for responsibility. Aristotle makes the argument in terms of earlier choices determining later outcomes (and so sometimes obviating excuses) as well as in terms of our responsibility for the formation of our own character (which, once formed, may perhaps unalterably determine our behavior): "[W]e punish a man for his very ignorance, if he is thought responsible for the ignorance, as when penalties are doubled in the case of drunkenness... since he had the power of not getting drunk and his getting drunk was the cause of his ignorance... So, too, to the unjust and to the self-indulgent man it was open at the beginning not to become men of this kind, and so they are such voluntarily; but now that they have become so it is not possible for them not to be so" (Aristotle 1984, 1113b, 1114a). The causal story and the developmental story may matter, even if there is no choice in the end.

But if we cannot simply and directly will our anger and resentment away, steps can be taken, and perhaps sometimes ought to be taken. Therapy depends upon the hope that attitudes can be changed—if not by a direct act of will, by a variety of techniques (some involving appeals to reason and some not). Education depends on similar hopes. We regularly try to shape moral character. Take gratitude, which, like forgiveness, is supposed to be a virtue (or at least an imperfect duty). We teach children to say "thank you" (and also to apologize, even when they may not yet feel sorry). We suppose that with the ritual may come the feeling. New reasons can become operative. Aristotle has much to say about the shaping of the dispositions that make up character, about how we become the kind of person who perceives certain aspects of the world and is responsive to them. And Spinoza has much to say about the improvement of the understanding and correcting beliefs in connection with overcoming passive emotions, about increasing freedom through reflection on the causes of emotions, thereby transforming them.

But then, we should be alert to the possibility that therapy and education can lapse into distasteful manipulation. We should remember that advertising too assumes attitudes are subject to change. And torture can transform. Remember that, at the end of George Orwell's *1984*, the rebel Winston Smith, through the hard (or should we say, "difficult"?) path of "Room 101", has been driven to the point where "He loved Big Brother" (Orwell 1949). Is a love with a causal history of this sort still "love"? The techniques of transformation are in need of scrutiny.

There is a psychological literature of "emotion regulation" (e.g., Philippot and Feldman 2004; Gross 2007) as well as volumes that explore historically shifting emotional norms. I would look to all these resources to better understand the history of changing attitudes towards various emotions and the techniques that have helped produce changes—though I would emphasize the need to attend to the distinction between changes in the expression of feelings and in the occurrence of the feelings themselves, a distinction too often neglected in social science approaches, as well as to the distinction between social change and individual change.

Psychologists of emotion regulation focus on processes of situation selection, situation modification, attention deployment, and cognitive change—as well as response or behavior modulation (Gross and Thompson 2007, 9–16). These processes, both automatic and deliberate, have been studied in adults, developmentally, and cross-culturally, and as applied both internally and externally, that is, where aimed at producing change in the self or in others. Historians of emotion such as Peter N. Stearns and historical sociologists such as Cas Wouters trace interesting patterns and tell the tale of shifting standards and efforts at their enforcement. For example, in *American Cool: Constructing a Twentieth-Century Emotional Style* (1994), Stearns describes the rising consensus against intense or strong emotions, whether negative and uncomfortable, like anger and grief, or potentially positive, like love. The advice varied for particular emotions, but management and restraint marked the move from Victorian middle-class standards to a new emotional culture in the twentieth century. The mechanisms of management are what is of particular interest in relation to our issue of the possibilities of control. Interestingly, he tells us,

Victorian standards had also urged management, as in controlling the use of fear and anger, but they had also recognized certain emotional areas in which regulation was not necessary, either because individuals were not considered to have certain emotions (as in the case of women and anger) or because restraint was not appropriate (as in spiritualized love). Twentieth-century culture, on the other hand, called for management across the board; no emotion should gain control over one's thought processes. (Stearns 1994, 184)

"Cool" for Stearns marks emotion rules that call for restraint in emotional expression (1994, 2). ("Feeling rules" are "the recommended norms by which people are supposed to shape their emotional expressions and react to the expressions of others".) The norm is one of disengagement and nonchalance. There is a serious question of whether rules for controlling expression are rules requiring control of the emotions themselves, the emotions being expressed (or not). Of course, one way to inhibit expression is to suppress the emotion itself—leaving nothing pressing for expression. Sociology would then recapitulate psychology. But that level of control, control of inner state rather than outward behavior, seems to call for forms of self-command deeper and more complex than direct willing.

Controlling what we do is one thing. Controlling what we feel is another. Stanislavski-type method acting brings the two together, but as Diderot argued in *The Paradox of Acting*, what matters in the theater is the outward performance, and for that to be effective, the inner state need not match. (See Neu 2000, Ch. 2: "A Tear Is an Intellectual Thing".) In the theater as elsewhere, pretense does not require authenticity—it would indeed be most peculiar if it did. But the effects may work backwards, that is, from standards of external behavior to the shape of internal life: "[E]motionological change also affects social interactions and elements of emotional life itself . . . Emotional culture forms the basis for constructing reactions to one's own emotions, and in some respects the emotions themselves" (Stearns 1994, 2–3). Norbert Elias's story of the civilization of manners over the centuries, *The Civilizing Process: Sociogenetic and Psychogenetic Investigations* (1939/2000), is also a story of growing emotional self-control. Cas Wouters (2007) tells a somewhat different story.

There certainly is a place for discussion of the value of retaining or overcoming certain passions, whether resentment and anger or jealousy and pride, or any number of other emotions (see Neu 2000 and 2008). But in these discussions, the separation between fact and value should not be taken as wider than it is. In addition, ideals of "authenticity" (as discussed, for example, by Lionel Trilling in *Sincerity and Authenticity*) need to be considered in conjunction with the complex of particular norms governing what one ought to feel.

Murphy, in the concluding remarks of *Getting Even* (2003, 115), contrasts the difficulties of forgiveness conceived of as *psychological* (it can be hard to control strong passions) and as *moral* (it can be hard to avoid compromise of important values of self-respect, self-defense, and respect for the demands of morality). My argument here is that these matters may be more entwined and the distinction between the psychological and moral (fact/value) more questionable than might at first appear. Some of the psychological obstacles to loving forgiveness (especially as detailed by Freud and Nietzsche) may bespeak moral difficulties. And some of the moral obstacles to too-hasty forgiveness (especially as detailed by Bishop Butler, Murphy, and Griswold) may give grounds for caution in connection with the ambitions of certain psychological therapies. And the problem of choosing one's inner attitude (whether we think of it as feeling, emotion, motive, maxim, principle, reason, or under some other heading) is both pervasive and inextricably psychological *and* moral.

## References

ARISTOTLE (1984). *Nicomachean Ethics*, trans. W. D. Ross and J. O. Urmson. In *The Complete Works of Aristotle*, vol. 2, ed. Jonathan Barnes (Princeton University Press).

BUTLER, BISHOP JOSEPH (1726/1970). *Butler's Fifteen Sermons*, ed. T. A. Roberts (London: SPCK).

CAMUS, ALBERT (1946). *The Stranger*, trans. Stuart Gilbert (New York: Alfred A. Knopf).

DE SOUSA, RONALD (1987). *The Rationality of Emotion* (Cambridge, MA: MIT Press).

DEUTSCH, HELENE (1937). "Absence of Grief", *Psychoanalytic Quarterly* 6, pp. 12–22.

ELIAS, NORBERT (1939/2000). *The Civilizing Process: Sociogenetic and Psychogenetic Investigations* (Oxford: Blackwell, Revised Edition).

ELSTER, JON (1999). *Alchemies of the Mind: Rationality and the Emotions* (Cambridge University Press).

FORRESTER, JOHN (1996). "Psychoanalysis and the History of the Passions: The Strange Destiny of Envy", in John O'Neill, ed., *Freud and the Passions* (Pennsylvania State University Press), pp. 127–49.

FREUD, SIGMUND (1909d). "Notes Upon a Case of Obsessional Neurosis". *Standard Edition of the Complete Psychological Works of Sigmund Freud (SE)*, ed. James Strachey (London: Hogarth, 1953–74), 10.

—— (1921c). *Group Psychology and the Analysis of the Ego. Standard Edition*, vol. 18.

—— (1930a). *Civilization and Its Discontents. Standard Edition*, vol. 21.

GRISWOLD, CHARLES L. (2007). *Forgiveness: A Philosophical Exploration* (Cambridge University Press).

GROSS, JAMES J., ed. (2007). *Handbook of Emotion Regulation* (New York: The Guilford Press).

—— and Ross A. THOMPSON (2007). "Emotion Regulation: Conceptual Foundations", in J. J. Gross, ed., *Handbook of Emotion Regulation* (New York: The Guilford Press), pp. 3–24.

HILL, THOMAS E. Jr (1973). "Servility and Self-Respect", *The Monist* 57, pp. 87–104.

KANT, IMMANUEL (1785/1993). *Grounding for the Metaphysics of Morals*, trans. James W. Ellington, 3rd edn. (Indianapolis: Hackett Publishing Company).

MURPHY, JEFFRIE G (1982). "'Forgiveness and Resentment", *Midwest Studies in Philosophy* 7, pp. 503–16.

—— (1999). "Moral Epistemology, the Retributive Emotions, and the 'Clumsy Moral Philosophy' of Jesus Christ", in Susan A. Bandes, ed., *The Passions of Law* (New York University Press), pp. 149–67.

—— (2003). *Getting Even: Forgiveness and Its Limits* (Oxford University Press).

—— (2006). "Legal Moralism and Retribution Revisited", Presidential Address, *Proceedings and Addresses of the American Philosophical Association*, 80 (2), pp. 45–62.

NEU, JEROME (1977). *Emotion, Thought, and Therapy* (London: Routledge & Kegan Paul; Berkeley: University of California Press).

—— (2000). *A Tear Is an Intellectual Thing: The Meanings of Emotion* (Oxford University Press).

—— (2002). "An Ethics of Fantasy?", *Journal of Theoretical and Philosophical Psychology*, 22(2), pp. 133–57.

—— (2008). *Sticks and Stones: The Philosophy of Insults* (Oxford University Press).

NIETZSCHE, FRIEDRICH (1969 [1887]). *On the Genealogy of Morals*, trans. W. Kaufmann and R. J. Hollingdale (New York: Vintage Books).

OAKLEY, JUSTIN (1992). *Morality and the Emotions* (London: Routledge).

ORWELL, GEORGE (1949). *1984* (London: Secker & Warburg).

PHILIPPOT, PIERRE and ROBERT S. FELDMAN, eds. (2004). *The Regulation of Emotion* (Mahwah, NJ: Lawrence Erlbaum Associates).

RAWLS, JOHN (1971). *A Theory of Justice* (Harvard University Press).

SARTRE, J.-P. (1948). *The Emotions: Outline of a Theory*, trans. B. Frechtman (New York: Philosophical Library).

SHAKESPEARE, WILLIAM (1969). *The Complete Pelican Shakespeare*, ed. Alfred Harbage (New York: Viking Penguin).

SMITH, ANGELA M. (2005). "Responsibility for Attitudes: Activity and Passivity in Mental Life", *Ethics*, 115(2), pp. 236–71.

SOLOMON, ROBERT C. (2003). *Not Passion's Slave: Emotions and Choice* (Oxford University Press).

SPELMAN, ELIZABETH V. (1989). "Anger and Insubordination", in Ann Garry and Marilyn Pearsall, eds., *Women, Knowledge and Reality: Explorations in Feminist Philosophy* (Boston: Unwin Hyman), pp. 263–73.

SPINOZA, BARUCH DE (1677/1985). *Ethics*, in *The Collected Works of Spinoza*, vol. 1., trans. E. Curley (Princeton University Press).

STEARNS, PETER N. (1989). *Jealousy: The Evolution of an Emotion in American History* (New York University Press).

—— (1994). *American Cool: Constructing a Twentieth-Century Emotional Style* (New York University Press).

TRILLING, LIONEL (1971). *Sincerity and Authenticity* (Harvard University Press).

WILLIAMS, BERNARD (1981). "Moral Luck", in *Moral Luck* (Cambridge University Press), pp. 20–39.

WITTGENSTEIN, LUDWIG (1953). *Philosophical Investigations*, trans. G. E. M. Anscombe (Oxford: Basil Blackwell).

WOUTERS, CAS (2007). *Informalization: Manners and Emotions Since 1890* (London: Sage Publications Ltd.).

# CHAPTER 23

························································

# THE MORAL
# EMOTIONS

························································

## JESSE J. PRINZ

EMOTIONS play many roles in human psychology. Fear alerts us to dangers, surprise registers novelty, and disgust helps us avoid potential sources of contamination. Many of these functions unite us with simpler creatures, and are, in that sense, among our more primitive or ancient psychological capacities. But emotions also play a role in the most sophisticated aspects of human mental life: they play a role in forming enduring social bonds to individuals and large groups, they give us pleasure in the arts, and they make fundamental contributions to human morality. It is this latter vocation that we will explore here. Three questions will be addressed: what roles do emotions play in morality? Which emotions play those roles? And are the emotions that play these roles distinctively moral? To forecast my response to this last question, I will argue that the emotions involved in morality actually serve non-moral functions as well or derive from non-moral emotions; if taken to designate a proprietary class, the term "moral emotions" is something of a misnomer.

I am grateful to Peter Goldie for comments that helped me think more deeply about issues in this chapter.

## 23.1 THE ROLES OF EMOTION IN MORALITY

There is an old philosophical tradition according to which emotions are an impediment to rational and noble behavior. On this view, emotions reflect our most primitive, animalistic nature, and should be repressed wherever possible. This perspective is sometimes expressed in moral philosophy, where emotions are seen as an impediment to good conduct rather than a facilitator. This kind of approach is sometimes attributed to Kant, who insists that morality cannot be based on mere sentiments or inclinations. This may be a cartoon version of Kant's actual view, since he places emphasis on respect, and he says we have a duty to be sympathetic. Kant also says that human beings have a "susceptibility to feel pleasure or displeasure merely from being aware that our actions are consistent with or contrary to the law of duty" (Kant, 1885/1996: 160). Kant even goes so far as to say that "any consciousness of obligation" depends on these feelings. Thus, the textbook claim that Kant wants to exorcize the emotions is inaccurate, even if he does not think emotions are the source of moral laws. In any case, Kant's project is normative in nature—it is a characterization of how we should make moral decisions, not how we actually do. It is uncontroversial to claim that, as a matter of fact, emotions play a significant role in moral psychology. Or rather, *several* significant roles. Before offering a taxonomy of which emotions contribute to morality, it is important to gain some clarity on how emotions contribute. Two major contributions can be distinguished.

First of all, emotions play an important role in motivating moral behavior. We want to be good, and we find good behavior rewarding. Bad behavior is, in contrast, emotionally costly. And we are motivated to help others, in part, because we feel affection for them, affinity, or compassion. The nature of prosocial motivation is hotly debated: do we help out of self-interest or out of genuine and fundamental concern for others' welfare? But, whether motivation is egoistic or genuinely altruistic, emotions seem to matter. Egoists credit self-love and altruists credit love of others. Emotions also motivate us to punish and seek revenge, which are both moralistic behaviors. One might be able to ascertain that a person violated a norm without emotion, and one might be able to ascertain that punishment would be appropriate (e.g., that it would serve as a deterrent), but the motivation to punish is often retributive in nature, and when it is, emotions are actively involved.

Second, emotions play a role in moral epistemology. Moral evaluation is sometimes compared to perception: we see things as good or as bad. This capacity is widely believed to have an emotional basis. Something strikes us as good or bad in virtue of the emotional response it elicits. By comparison, a food might strike us as delicious because of the gustatory pleasure it produces, and a joke might strike us as funny because of its tendency to amuse. As we will see, different emotions may contribute to moral evaluation in different ways.

The issue of moral evaluation raises an important question that is beyond the scope of this chapter: can one judge that something is morally good or bad in the absence of emotion? Or is evaluation essentially affective? The answer depends on the most fundamental question in metaethics: what is the ultimate basis of morality? If moral judgments refer to a class of facts whose essence does not involve the emotions, then the answer would seem to be yes. Suppose, for example, that a morally good action is one which maximizes happiness (Mill). Or suppose a bad action is that which we cannot, on pain of practical irrationality, will as a universal law (Kant). One could ascertain that a given action is good or bad in either of these senses without having any emotional response. One can ascertain that action produces happiness without being happy. So these leading normative theories open the possibility for a dispassionate moral epistemology. Still, one might believe that these ethical theories are right, while allowing that emotions, as a matter of fact, play a role in moral epistemology. Properly trained, emotions might come to register cases where utility is increased or moral duties are violated. Emotions could serve as rough-and-ready tools for perceiving moral facts, in much the way that fear alerts us to dangers. Danger is not itself an emotional thing, but fear serves as a danger detector. Likewise, emotions could alert us to the presence of morally significant events. A sympathetic response to a victim of cruelty might help us perceive that the act is not conducive to happiness. One could discover that without emotions, but emotions surely help.

Other ethical theories entail that emotions are essential. Consider emotivism, which says that moral statements of the form "$\phi$-ing is morally bad" or "$\phi$-ing is morally good" are not statements of fact but expressions of feeling. On this view, the analogy between moral epistemology and perception breaks down. There are no moral facts out there to be perceived. Morality is more like a projection of feelings onto the world (see Chapter 26, this volume). But emotivism is not the only option for those who think emotions are components of moral judgments. An alternative would be to adopt a form of subjectivism, according to which the statement "$\phi$-ing is morally bad" is true just in case "$\phi$-ing is disposed to cause a certain negative emotional response in the person making that statement, under certain conditions. Subjectivist theories come in many variants (see McDowell, 1985; Wiggins, 1987; Prinz, 2007), but the basic idea is that moral statements express facts whose existence depends on the response of evaluators. Defenders of these views sometimes compare moral facts to facts about properties such as funniness, scariness, or deliciousness, all of which are arguably subjective as well. The tradition also draws inspiration from John Locke's account of "secondary qualities". For Locke, certain perceivable properties, including colors, can be characterized in terms of the responses that certain objects cause in observers: for example, red can be characterized as the power that red objects have to cause a red experience in observers under adequate lighting conditions. If morality is like this, the analogy to perception is fairly straightforward. Red is perceivable and out there on the surface of objects, even though it depends on us. Likewise moral badness is out there, even though it depends on our responses, and we pick up badness through our emotions.

Both of these approaches face serious challenges. Emotivists must explain why moral statements appear to be assertoric if they are merely expressive, and subjectivists must overcome charges of vicious circularity and must characterize ideal observation conditions (or some alternative). Both approaches also face difficulties relating to moral disagreement and relativism: moral debates look like genuine disagreements, but, if emotivists and subjectivists are right, there may be no single set of moral facts that could adjudicate a debate between two people with opposing moral values.

This is not the place to address such concerns. I mention emotivism and subjectivism to illustrate the role that emotions play in some accounts of moral epistemology. Whether or not some version of these views can be defended, there is wide agreement that moral judgments often occur with emotions. Some will say those emotions cause moral judgments, some will say they are components, and some will say they are effects. These debates need not concern us here. What matters is that, when we come to regard something as morally good or bad, we have characteristic emotional reactions. Surprisingly, this widespread observation is often made without careful discussion of what these characteristic reactions are. That will be one of the main tasks in what follows. We will see that different emotions arise in the context of different kinds of evaluations.

In summary, emotions are said to play different roles in morality, and chief among these are roles in moral motivation and moral evaluation. In discussing the moral emotions, it will be useful to bear these two roles in mind. I will begin by surveying emotions that play a role in evaluation, and then move on to motivation. Some emotions, we will see, play both roles, and others may not. Each moral emotion makes a distinctive contribution to moral psychology.

One final note is necessary before we begin our survey. Throughout this discussion, I will try to be neutral about the nature of emotions. On some theories, emotions are cognitive in nature: they are or contain judgments. On other theories, emotions are non-cognitive; for example, they are feelings. But this classic debate in emotion theory can be bypassed by finding some common ground. Both cognitivists and non-cognitivists typically assume that emotions have characteristic eliciting conditions; for example, fear occurs in response to (real or anticipated) danger, and sadness occurs in context of loss. Both sides also agree that emotions typically promote different patterns of behavior, and that behaviors require bodily changes that can be experienced as conscious feelings. So, in what follows, I will characterize emotions by their eliciting conditions and action tendencies. In so doing, I will try to avoid begging any questions against cognitivists or non-cognitivists.

## 23.2 Evaluative Emotions

### 23.2.1 Emotions of Blame

There are many different kinds or moral evaluations: we might describe some behavior as morally permissible, impermissible, or compulsory. We might describe an action as cruel, or kind, or forgivable. We might say a choice is the right thing to do or the wrong thing to do. We might describe a person as vicious or virtuous. But we also have a kind of evaluation that is simpler and, arguably, more fundamental. We judge that certain things are morally good or bad (moral or immoral). We apply these assessments to actions, events, persons, political regimes, and so on. Williams (1985) says that judgments of goodness and badness are thin, as opposed to thick, because, unlike "cruel" or "kind", they have no overt descriptive content, demarcating the kind of thing being evaluated. I will focus on these thin concepts here, because the fact that they lack overt descriptive content means they are useful for discussing the psychology of evaluation as opposed to description. Judgments of moral goodness and badness can be characterized as purely evaluative. They also seem to be characteristically associated with emotions. As we will see, however, the emotions used in pure evaluation may smuggle in constraints on content akin to Williams' thick concepts. If so, the idea that we ever make an evaluation that is truly thin might be called into question. I return to this issue at the end of this section.

Pure evaluations come in two flavors: good and bad. Let us begin with the bad. The emotions that play a role in negative evaluations are, presumably, negative, but which ones? We have some negative emotions, such as fear and loneliness, that are not characteristically deployed in moral evaluation. But others, such as anger and guilt, are frequent players in morality. To demarcate the difference between negative emotions that are important for evaluations of moral badness and those that are not, we might say that the former are emotions of blame. Morality is a domain of blame. If someone does something bad or has bad character, we blame that person. We don't necessarily conclude that the person acted intentionally or with freewill, but we regard them with blame, in some broad sense: we regard them as morally faulty. It is difficult to characterize the notion of blame in a non-circular way, but one salient feature is that when we blame someone, we typically think they should be punished. Emotions of blame are typically associated with a desire to punish, and, as we will see, they may even exert an influence on the kind of punishment we come to desire.

Within emotions of blame, there is another broad distinction: some are self-directed and some are directed at others. Let's begin with other-directed moral emotions. One of these was already mentioned: anger. When we evaluate something as bad, we sometimes feel angry. Anger can be characterized by its eliciting conditions and action tendencies. Anger is typically elicited when one person does something harmful to another, especially when the harm is intentional or negligent. The harm can be symbolic, as in the case of an insult; indirect, as in the case of property damage or harm to a loved one; or direct, as in the case of physical assault. Anger is associated with physical aggression. When we get angry, blood flows to our extremities, heart rate increases, we make facial expressions that communicate potential attack (such as glaring or baring teeth), we raise our voices, and fists may clench.

As a moral emotion, then, anger can be associated with a specific kind of transgression: crimes against persons. A crime against a person is a behavior that harms or threatens to harm an individual. In a study by Rozin et al. (1999), subjects were presented with a list of moral transgressions, and they were asked to select which emotion they would feel for each. Some of these were crimes against persons (what Rozin et al. call violations of Autonomy norms). The cases included scolding, beating, embezzling, line-cutting, stealing, and so on. Anger was overwhelmingly and systematically chosen for these. Anger can also be associated with a specific kind of moral behavior: harmful punishment. When a harm occurs, and we get angry, we often desire that perpetrators be harmed by taking their property, depriving them of liberty, or making them experience physical pain or even death. Lerner et al. (1998) showed that desire for punishment is increased by anger induction, even when the anger is introduced independently of the behavior being punished. Fehr and Gächter (2002) showed that anger correlates with the desire to punish defectors in economic games. Parrott and Zeichner (2002) showed that men who are more angry in temperament administer more intense and longer electric shocks in a competitive task with another player.

The term "anger" can be regarded as an umbrella term for a range of more specific emotions that share the same broad category of elicitors and action tendencies. Anger varies in degrees and includes mild emotions such as irritation and intense emotions such as rage. Presumably, intensity will vary, in part, with the severity of the harm. If a man leaves the toilet seat up, his female roommate might be irritated, and, if someone commits and act of willful murder, the emotion might be rage. Intensity will also vary with proximity to the victim: if I am harmed I will normally feel more anger than if a stranger is harmed. We also have terms for specific species of anger that vary as a function of the kind of harm that has been perpetrated. The term "indignation" is often reserved for cases where the harm is a case of unfairness, such as an inequitable distribution, and the term "exasperated" usually refers to repeated mild offenses.

Contemporary moral philosophers tend to focus on harm, and, as a result, they might tend to think that anger is the primary (or perhaps even only) other-directed emotion of moral blame. But there may be other kinds of moral norms that don't primarily involve harming an individual. In some societies, victimless crimes are central to morality. For example, consider societies that condemn various victimless sexual behaviors, such masturbation or homosexual intercourse. Liberal

Western societies continue to enforce many such norms; we have rules against bestiality (assuming the animals don't mind), necrophilia, plural marriage, and consensual incest between adults. In some of these cases, a party may be harmed, but it is easy to imagine cases where no one is harmed and where there is nevertheless a tendency to find the behavior morally suspect or reprehensible. Sometimes, the person who judges such behavior to be wrong may experience anger. This will happen when the act is perceived as a potential threat (for example, homosexuality is sometimes portrayed as a threat to the fabric of society). But, in cases where there is no perceived threat (such as bestiality), the emotion experienced will be different: it will usually be disgust (Rozin et al., 1999). Gutierrez and Giner-Sorolla (2007) showed that in cases of taboo violation, anger occurs when there is a presumption of harm, and disgust occurs otherwise.

Outside the moral domain, disgust is a response to contamination (decay, rot, sickness, deformity). In this respect, it has much to do with the body. It protects the body of the disgusted by causing it to avoid contact with the object of disgust. Predictably, therefore, moral disgust arises most typically in the case of norms that involve bodily contact and bodily fluids—potentially sources of contamination. Sexual norms are the most obvious cases. We call these unnatural acts or crimes against nature, and we see violators as impure. Moral disgust also arises in cases of norms that have to do with animals or animality, since animals are a potential source of contamination. This includes bestiality, but also dietary norms pertaining to animals, which can be found in some cultures, such as kosher rules or rules against eating human flesh (even if the people died of natural causes). If disgust deals with the body, then moral disgust should also arise in cases where a transgression causes salient bodily damage, as in the case of mutilation or genocide (because it draws attention to masses of dead bodies). In these cases, anger may also be experienced because harm is involved. We may also extend disgust to cases of "moral deformity" or "moral sickness": a racist or someone who shows egregious moral indifference might be regarded as aberrant and repulsive.

Disgust has action tendencies. Contamination leads to expulsion and avoidance. We want to distance ourselves from the things that disgust us. We pull away and shield ourselves from disgusting things. We close our eyes and mouths, and we wrinkle our noses (to reduce inhalation). This action pattern also carries with it a tendency towards magical thinking. Since disgust protects us from contamination, and contaminants are often invisible, we avoid things that have come into contact with something that is visibly disgusting. This is true even if the object is known to be harmless. For example, we won't drink from a cup that has been used to transport a urine sample, even if we know it has been sterilized (Rozin et al., 1986). The fact that knowledge does not eliminate disgust suggests that disgust is not elicited by explicit beliefs about contamination but is rather an evolved response that uses simple heuristics, such as contact with bodily fluids and rot, to keep track of potential sources of contamination. In the moral case, the same principles operate. People refuse to put on a sweater if they believe it was worn by Hitler (Rozin et al., 1994).

The contrast between disgust and anger is striking, because disgust promotes withdrawal and anger promotes approach behavior (aggression). This may have an impact on such things as how we treat criminals: you might prefer to live next to a convicted thief than a convicted pedophile, even if you have no children. The emotions also seem to govern significantly different domains. Nevertheless, both might be used in the context of evaluating something as morally bad. For example, someone might feel disgust when they judge that it's "morally bad" to derive sexual pleasure from a pet cat and "morally bad" to steal money from the Oxfam donation jar, even though the underlying emotions differ. Distinguishing moral emotions can help us distinguish kinds of moral badness.

Disgust and anger are certainly among the most prominent emotions of other-directed blame, but they are not the only ones. Another important moral emotion is contempt. Rozin et al. (1999) show that disgust is the dominant response for "crimes against community". These include cases of disrespect to parents and authorities, cases where a wealthy person shows bias against a worker, and cases of flag burning. In some of these cases, individuals are harmed (e.g., if a teen is rude to her parents, they may become upset), but the salient focus of these violations is that the perpetrator has failed to appreciate a person's rightful place in society. In this sense, society itself is a kind of victim. Contempt also arises in cases where public trust or public property is destroyed.

Contempt may be a blend of other emotions, especially anger and disgust (Prinz, 2004). This makes sense on the proposal that contempt occurs in response to crimes against community, because the community can be construed as the natural order of persons, so a crime against community is both a crime against persons and an unnatural act. Contempt also exhibits a kind of directionality. We look down on those for whom we have contempt. This suggests that contempt may also be related to emotions that regulate social status hierarchies in mammals. Perhaps there are feelings associated with dominance that come out in contempt. Those feelings may also be components of related emotions such as derision and smugness, which are not fundamentally moral emotions (they do not involve blame).

It is not obvious what the action tendencies are when we experience contempt. If contempt blends anger and disgust, the action tendencies should be practically inconsistent: contempt should promote both approach and withdrawal. This may in fact be the case. Consider a politician who violates public trust. We may be angry and crave punishment, but we will also say that the public office has been defiled, and we may be literally repelled when we see the politician's image in the newspaper.

Another emotion of blame is disappointment. Disappointment occurs when we had high expectations for someone and the expectations were not met. In the moral case, it arises when we expect someone to be morally good and they are not. This is most likely to be true for people we like and care about, such as loved ones. If your child is caught cheating in school, you may be disappointed rather than angry. The action tendency may not be aggressive or punishment-focused. You may sulk or feel a general reduction in motivation—a feeling of hopelessness or defeat.

These emotions (anger, disgust, contempt, and disappointment) may not be the only emotions of other-directed blame, but they are certainly the most prevalent. Each one arises under somewhat different conditions, and each results in somewhat different behavioral dispositions. In addition to these other-directed emotions of blame, there are self-directed emotions of blame. Two such emotions are especially common: guilt and shame.

Guilt and shame are sometimes treated as if they are the same, but they are actually quite different (see, e.g., Tangney, 1996). Guilt arises when a person does something that harms another person, most typically someone they regard as part of their in-group. It is most intense when the victim is a loved one (or when the harm is egregious). Because it is harm-related, guilt is an analogue of anger. The harm dimension also means that guilt arises when a person has performed an action that can threaten an attachment relationship with another individual (Baumeister et al., 1994). If I harm my friend, I may lose my friend's affection. So guilt carries with it a threat of loss. It is not surprising then that the primary action tendencies associated with guilt are reparative in nature. We try to either apologize, confess, or make amends. When people feel guilty, they are more likely to be helpful, as if being helpful can compensate for the harm they have done. Carlsmith and Gross (1969) showed that people are more likely to volunteer for a charity after they have been asked to administer electric shocks to a stranger. Such acts can even the moral score card and reduce feelings of guilt. Guilt can also be reduced when an apology is accepted. That informs the perpetrator that the threatened attachment relationship has been restored.

Shame differs from guilt in its elicitation conditions and action tendencies. Shame arises when one performs an action that is perceived as being likely to bring about unwelcome attention from others. Unwelcome attention isn't just anger or, say, amusement. Shame is particularly likely when one fears that one will be viewed as a defective person. It is said that guilt is act-focused (I did something bad), and shame is person-focused (I am a bad person). Consequently shame is likely to arise when an action is seen as rendering one's self impure, corrupt, or contaminated. It is, thus, an analogue of disgust. We feel ashamed when we violate sexual norms, or if we cause harms that might be viewed as monstrous. Like disgust, shame is associated with magical thinking. My shame can contaminate others. My shameful acts can bring shame to my family.

Simple reparative behaviors, such as confession or apology, cannot alleviate shame very effectively because these behaviors cannot eliminate feelings of contamination. Instead, shame is associated with concealment. People lower their heads in shame (Fessler, 2004) or try to hide. Tangney et al. (1996) shows that guilt increases social health, whereas shame tends not to because it does not promote reparation. Shame may be related to embarrassment, but it is more aversive and harder to "save face". Confession can help with embarrassment (a blush reveals that I know I did something inappropriate), but a blush will not suffice for shame. In extreme cases, shame may promote suicidal behavior, because the ashamed person feels so corrupted that death in the only option. This has even been culturally ritualized, as with *seppuku* in feudal Japan. A person who brings shame may also be killed, as in the case on honor-killing.

Though incomplete, this survey of blame emotions is sufficient for illustrating how important it is to treat moral emotions differentially. They play different functional roles. This is true even when the emotions belong to the same broad category, such as emotions of blame. It is plausible that people experience such emotions when they use so-called thin moral concepts, *immoral* or *morally bad* (Williams, 1985). But on each use of the concept *morally bad*, a different emotion might occur depending on what kind of transgression has been committed and the identity of the perpetrator. Thus "morally bad" can express different emotions on different occasions.

This discovery suggests that we should be somewhat cautious about embracing Williams' idea that there are thin moral concepts. Admittedly, the *word* "immoral" conveys very little about what kind of norm violation has occurred, in comparison to words such as "cruel" or "cowardly". But when someone sincerely describes an action as immoral, there may be an emotion of blame that arises, and the emotion may serve to identify or delimit the kind of norm violation that has occurred (Was someone harmed? Am I the culprit?). There is a thorny issue here about whether concepts should be identified with linguistic items and their referents or inferential roles in language, or with the underlying psychology states that occur when linguistic items are used. If the concept *immoral* is identified by its linguistic role, then it may qualify as thin, because it is used in so many contexts that there is little by way of a descriptive common denominator uniting the cases to which is applies (in sharp contrast to "cruel"). But if the concept *immoral* is a psychological state, then individual tokens of that concept may in fact be thick: they may have content that covers specific kinds of cases and not others. Put differently, there may be a family of different concepts that we express with the word "immoral" and these may have contents that could best be expressed using some of the kinds of descriptive information that Williams associates with thick concepts. A token of the concept *immoral* that is realized by feelings of disgust will represent crimes against the body, and a token that is realized by *anger* will represent crimes against the autonomy of persons. Now I am not suggesting that these differences are reflected in mental descriptions (it's rare to explicitly think, "there has been a crime against the body!"). Rather, each emotion has the function of occurring in response to different kinds of crimes, and, consequently, they represent different things. Thus, tokens of these moral concepts may be structurally simple but semantically rich, and each token has a distinctive motivating feeling and a circumscribed class of transgressions to which it refers. If this picture is right, then, when we use words that seem thin, such as "immoral", we may actually be expressing psychological states that are both affective and referentially restrictive. In this respect, the psychological states function more like Williams' thick concepts, even if the vocabulary used conceals this fact.

## 23.2.2 Emotions of Praise

I have been focusing on emotions of blame. These are emotions that arise when we judge something to be bad or immoral. But there are also emotions of praise, which arise when we judge and action to be good or moral. Sometimes, a good action is just an action that it would have been bad not to do. In that case, moral praise involves withholding negative emotions. But sometimes good actions are supererogatory: they go beyond the call of duty. In these cases, we may experience emotions that reflect positive attitudes towards the do-gooder. Comparatively little research has been done on these emotions of praise, but I will offer some brief speculations (see also Prinz, 2007).

It does not seem that we experience different emotions of praise for different praiseworthy actions. For example, it is far from obvious that acts of charity elicit different emotions than acts of praiseworthy sexual conduct (imagine a society where pre-marital abstinence is regarded as a rare and morally praiseworthy achievement). On the other hand, it does seem to be the case that emotions of praise vary as a function of who performs the good deed or who receives the benefit. For example, if someone gives generously to a worthy cause, we might experience admiration. If someone gives generously to me when I am in need, I will feel gratitude. If I give generously to a worthy cause, I might feel pride.

These emotions may also be associated with different action tendencies. When we admire someone, we bestow praise, when we are grateful we express thanks or reciprocate, and when we feel pride, we may take the opportunity to do ourselves a good turn or we might even boast or advertise our good conduct. These behaviors have not been well studied, but certainly warrant investigation.

One interesting fact about moral praise is that we tend not to praise people for simply conforming to moral norms. Decent behavior is usually expected and goes uncongratulated. Thus, emotions of praise are typically reserved for cases of extreme goodness. This suggests that they may be less important than emotions of blame. Social stability depends on people conforming to norms, not on performing remarkable acts of charity. A stable moral society can exist without heroes or saints. But we are grateful for our saints, and we like to promote good deeds, thus we do express positive emotions when people act nobly. This is even true when the noble act is small or symbolic. For example, if someone allows me to walk through a doorway first, I will express thanks. We praise common courtesy. A society without common courtesy might be stable but it would be less pleasant. Perhaps the main function of positive moral emotions is to safeguard against adversity. If things get bad, we depend on the charity of others. By praising acts of supererogatory goodness, we make it rewarding to help those in need. If conditions worsen suddenly (as when natural disasters strike), we benefit from the kindness of those who have been less badly affected, and moral praise may play a role in recognizing and promoting such kindness.

I say "recognizing and promoting" because emotions of praise may serve a dual function. They are first and foremost epistemic: they occur in response to some real or imagined events and they serve to acknowledge that something good has been done. But they also serve to promote prosocial behavior. The same is true of emotions of blame. I turn to prosocial emotions now.

# 23.3  PROSOCIAL EMOTIONS

## 23.3.1  Blame and Praise Again

Why do we behave morally? One answer is that we are epistemically sensitive to norms. In many contexts there is a gulf between knowledge and action. One can *know* that there is a rule in place (such as a rule against jay-walking) and not be remotely tempted to follow it. But the moral emotions of praise and blame close the gap between knowledge and action.

Consider blame first. If you have an emotion of moral blame, it serves as a way of recognizing that something was bad. But it can also serve as a cause of good behavior. This can happen in at least three ways. First, emotions of blame can motivate punishment, and punishment can promote good behavior by deterrence. Second, emotions of blame can contribute to moral education. We shape children's behavior when we get angry or disgusted with them because they desire our affection. Children are also great imitators and they can catch our negative attitudes and thereby internalize our norms. Finally, emotions of blame can help us avoid the temptation to be bad. If contemplating an action makes you anticipate guilt or shame, you may resist that action, even if carries some obvious rewards.

Emotions of praise are similarly conducive to moral behavior. Receiving praise or thanks feels good, and positive emotions are behavioral reinforcers. Actions that elicit social praise are likely to be repeated. Pride also feels good, and actions that make us proud are rewarding. It feels good to eat a candy bar, but it may feel even better and last longer to give to charity. Anticipating and experiencing moral pride can increase the probability of moral conduct.

It follows from this that an emotionally grounded recognition of moral goodness or moral badness can, in and of itself, promote good behavior. Emotions of praise and blame serve both epistemic and motivational functions. From a philosophical perspective that is interesting because of a long-standing debate about the relationship between moral judgment and moral motivation. Motivational internalists argue that when we make moral judgments, we are thereby motivated to act in accordance with moral rules. Motivational externalists argue that we can make moral judgments without being the least bit motivated. If emotions of praise and blame are morally motivating, then the debate between externalists and internalists may hinge on whether moral judgments have an emotional component. Emotions of praise and blame could serve the role that internalist theories require, so internalists would do well to argue that emotions are intrinsic to moral judgment.

## 23.3.2 Sympathy, Empathy, and Concern

Emotions of praise and blame are moral emotions in two senses: they play epistemic and motivational roles. But sometimes we have emotional states that are motivationally moral but not epistemically moral. That is, they motivate us to do good things even if they do not constitute recognition of something as morally significant. The dissociation is important because it leaves room for the possibility that one might be motivated to do the good without doing it because it's good. Indeed, sometimes morality demands that we act this way. If all one's acts of charity were motivated by a desire to be moral, they might seem less noble than acts of charity performed out of a desire to help someone in need, regardless of the moral significance. Sometimes it is best to help someone because they need help rather than to help someone because of the fact that helping behavior is morally praiseworthy. This is particularly true in light of my discussion of emotions of praise. Emotions of praise feel good when they are received. So if one helps someone simply because doing do is praiseworthy, then there is a sense in which one's behavior may be motivated by reward. Such behavior may be self-serving. But sometimes we may help because we are moved by the anguish of others, and helping in these cases seems more genuinely altruistic. In this section, I want to consider altruistic emotional responses, which can be collectively described as fellow-feelings.

Consider, first, empathy. "Empathy" can be defined in a number of different ways, but I will use it narrowly to refer to cases where a person experiences an emotion that another person experiences (or is thought to experience) as a result of recognizing that emotion. If I see that you are afraid and feel fear as a result, that is empathy. Empathy is a vicarious emotional response. Empathy is not itself an emotion but is rather a way that some emotions come about. Empathetic fear is fear brought on by recognizing or imagining the fear of another person. In some cases, empathetic emotions might be brought about automatically, in a bottom-up way by emotional contagion (Hatfield et al., 1994). Simply seeing fear can cause fear. This contagion processes is believed to be underwritten by mirror-neurons: neurons that are activated both when something is observed in another and when it is experienced in the observer (Adolphs, 2002). In other cases, empathy might be driven top-down by cognitive processes. Reflecting on the situation of rescue workers, I might realize that they are in danger, and I might come to experience fear as a result, even if I haven't seen their expressions of fear.

Empathetic emotions are moral emotions insofar as they motivate morally praiseworthy behavior. It is easy to see why they might contribute in this way. Suppose you are in danger, and I feel fear as a result. In effect, I feel your fear. This may alert me to your situation in a very visceral way, and I might form the desire to help you overcome your fear. Or, if you are outraged about the way someone has treated you, I may become outraged too, and be motivated to help you respond to the person who has done you harm. If emotions help a victim cope with bad circumstances, vicarious emotions may help observers cope as well, by alerting them to the hardship, making the hardship of another aversive to the self, and motivating intervention. In some cases, empathy may lead us to catch others' emotions of moral praise and blame, but empathy can also lead us to catch emotions of hardship, and, in these cases, we may become motivated to help even if we have not judged that helping would be a morally praiseworthy thing to do.

Empathy, as defined here, was once called "sympathy" (compare Hume, 1739/1978; Smith, 1759/2000), but it is now customary to distinguish these two (see, e.g., Darwall, 1998). One way to draw the distinction is to say that empathy refers to any vicarious emotion and sympathy refers to negative emotions felt on someone else's behalf. Three differences should be emphasized here. First, one can feel empathetic joy, but not sympathetic joy, because sympathy is always negative. Second, sympathy is kind of feeling-for someone, whereas empathy is feeling-because (it is causally linked to the emotion of the person for whom one is empathetic, not semantically linked). If I am sad that you are sad, then that's sympathy. Third, sympathetic emotions need not be the same as the emotions experienced by the people for whom we sympathize; I may feel sad that you are angry or afraid, for example. But like empathy, sympathy involves having a feeling as a result of someone else's feeling. And like empathy, sympathy is not itself an emotion but a process by which emotions are brought about and directed. Sympathetic emotions are characteristically elicited by real or imagined emotions in others and they are directed at those emotions.

Sympathy may be even more intimately tied to prosocial behavior than empathy. Empathetic emotions can be alleviated by taking actions directed towards the self. If I catch your fear by emotion contagion, I can rid myself of fear by ignoring you or leaving the scene. But if my fear is directed towards your fear, as with sympathy, then leaving the scene won't necessarily help. As long as I know you are afraid, and as long as my fear is about that fact, then my fear will last. Helping you escape from the frightening situation may be the best cure. Sympathy is more overtly other-related than empathy, and, consequently, it may lead more reliably to other-directed behaviors. Moreover, empathy can lead to a breakdown in helping behavior because the emotions we catch empathetically can interrupt motivation. If I am scared as a result of your fear, I may flee, since fear motivates flight. But suppose I have a sympathetic anger response because I know someone has frightened you. I may elect to intervene rather than flee. When we acquire emotions sympathetically, the resulting emotions may be more helpful than the emotions towards which they are directed.

Empathy and sympathy can both be contrasted with a third kind of fellow-feeling, concern. Some authors treat "empathy" and "concern" as synonyms. Peter Goldie had drawn my attention to one clear and egregious example of this; Dan Batson, who has done some of the most important empirical work in this area, tells us that, "empathic concern includes feelings of sympathy, compassion, tenderness, and the like" (Batson et al., 2007: 65). I think it is helpful to treat concern and empathy separately. One can define concern as a negative emotion that arises when one thinks or perceives that another person is in a bad situation. There are three points of contrast to emphasize. First, concern in an emotion—it may be thought of as a kind of worry or anxiety about another's well-being. Second, the party for whom one is concerned need not be experiencing any negative emotions. One can be concerned for someone who doesn't realize that danger in immanent, for example. So concern isn't necessarily a matter of feeling-with someone. Its focus need not be the emotion of another person but rather the predicament one takes another to be in.

Concern may be especially conducive to prosocial behavior. If you are worried about another person, you will be thereby motivated to act on their behalf. This is true even if the person does not realize there is any threat to her well-being. Concern motivates helpfulness even when the victims don't realize they are victims. Also, sympathy is a just matter of feeling badly for someone, and bad feelings don't always help. If I am sad about your pain, I may withdraw or sulk. If I say, "You have my sympathy", I express that I am sorry that you are suffering, not that I intend to do anything about it. But if I am concerned I am more likely to intervene. If I say, "I am concerned about you", that implies that I want to actively find a way to help you.

In the empirical literature, these different responses are not always distinguished, and that makes empirical research on fellow-feelings difficult to interpret. For example, Neuberg et al., (1997) use a meta-analysis to show that empathy is not especially motivating. It leads to moderate prosocial behavior only when there is little cost. But this conclusion may apply to some forms of fellow-feeling and not others. Empathy may be relatively weak as a moral motivator (Prinz, forthcoming), and concern may be relatively powerful. In the developmental literature, there is evidence that concerned attention, but not shared emotion, predicts prosocial behavior (Eisenberg et al., 1989). This suggests that empathy is not a major motivator in children. Indeed, empathy may normally depend on concern if it is to promote prosocial behavior only when coupled with concern (or at least sympathy). If I catch your misery, I need to be concerned about you and not preoccupied with my own well-being if my empathy is going to motivate me to help you rather than myself.

All forms of fellow-feeling are subject to bias. We feel more fellow-feeling for those who are perceived to be similar to ourselves (Batson et al., 2005), and fellow-feeling can lead to preferential treatment (Batson et al., 1995). But fellow-feeling is important from a moral perspective because its existence suggests that we can be motivated to help someone even if we have not made the moral judgment that helping is good. In the case of concern and sympathy, the helpful behavior is not driven by self-interest. Batson (1987) has shown that, when people are given an opportunity to alleviate their own negative feelings of sympathy and concern by simply escaping an uncomfortable situation, they often won't take that easy self-serving way out. They will instead help the person whose well-being is threatened. On this basis, Batson concludes that human beings have genuinely altruistic motivations and are not driven solely by self-interest.

Fellow-feelings may even be part of our biological make-up. There is evidence that other creatures find suffering of conspecifics aversive. In some cases, this may merely be empathetic distress. For example, rats show distress when they experience the suffering of other rats (Rice and Gainer, 1962), but they may not be concerned for other rats (Rice, 1964). Evidence for concern is easier to demonstrate in primates. Great apes can be extremely selfish and ungenerous (Silk et al., 2005), but they also engage in conciliation behavior (de Waal, 1989) and helping (Warneken et al., 2007). And monkeys will starve themselves to relieve the agony of another (Masserman et al., 1964).

Such findings do not entail that non-human animals have a moral sense. Recall that fellow-feeling can be independent of moral evaluation. Animals may help each other out of concern, not out of a desire to do what morality requires. Thus animals may do things that are morally praiseworthy even if they never engage in moral praise or moral evaluation. In this respect, moral goodness may precede the capacity to recognize the morally good. Moral motivation may precede moral epistemology.

# 23.4 ARE THERE DISTINCTIVELY MORAL EMOTIONS?

I have been arguing that the term "moral emotion" is ambiguous: it can refer to emotions that are involved in making moral judgments or to emotions that are involved in motivating morally praiseworthy behavior. I have surveyed some of the main emotions that play these two roles. But this survey leaves us with one final question: Are any of these emotions distinctively moral? That is, are there moral emotions that are dedicated to morality (either moral conduct or moral judgment) and do not serve important functions outside the moral domain? And if there are some distinctively moral emotions, are these biologically based, or do they derive from emotions that are not distinctively moral?

This question can be addressed by reviewing the emotions and emotional processes that we have been considering. Let's begin with anger. It is sometimes suggested that anger depends on the judgment that there has been a moral offense (cf. Solomon, 1976). But I think it is plausible that anger has non-moral analogues. Some things irritate us without being regarded as morally wrong. A sound can be irritating as can a difficult and recalcitrant task. Sometimes we experience an aggressive response without judging that we've been wronged. This can happen spontaneously if someone glares at you, or it can be built up intentionally as when athletes compete against an opposing team. I think these are cases of non-moral anger, which may be an evolutionary ancient emotional state that is the basis of moral anger. Moral anger can be described as a kind of aggressive irritation that occurs when a moral norm has been violated, especially a norm pertaining to harm.

Disgust is an even more obvious case. As mentioned, disgust can occur as a response to contamination and, in this context, it isn't moral. Arguably moral disgust is just physical disgust as it arises in response to moral norm violations, especially norms conceptualized as pertaining to the purity of the body.

Above I suggested that contempt might be a blend of anger and disgust, and perhaps feelings of dominance. All these component emotions are not distinctively or originally moral. Moreover, contempt itself has non-moral applications. The rich feel contempt for the poor, and the poor feel contempt for the rich, but these attitudes do not always connote any kind of moral assessment.

Disappointment, of course, is just a form of sadness. We can be disappointed about any event that does not live up to our expectations. These cases are only moral when the expectation involves conformity to a moral norm.

Guilt and shame appear to be distinctively moral emotions, because we tend not to talk about them outside of the moral domain. But here too an argument can be made that these moral emotions derive from emotions that are not moral in nature. I said earlier that shame might be an aversive form of embarrassment. Guilt may be linked to sadness. We feel sad about harming people in our in-group because doing so threatens attachment relationships. Guilt may also occasionally encompass anxiety because loss of attachment and punishment often follow when we cause harm. So guilt may be an anxious sadness elicited by the harms we have caused (Prinz, 2004). If guilt and shame derive from non-moral sources, we might expect them to crop up in non-moral contexts from time to time, and indeed they do. Survivor guilt occurs when a person is among the few to survive a calamity that killed members of the in-group. In some societies shame arises in the presence of people who have higher social station (Fessler, 2004). In both these cases, the emotions may be genuine even if no moral judgment has been made.

Fellow-feelings, I have argued, can occur in the absence of moral judgments, and are thus not moral emotions in one meaning of the word. They can arise in creatures that make no moral judgment. From the perspective of such creatures, the role of fellow-feelings is not to motivate morally good behavior. These emotions only qualify as moral because we praise the behaviors they bring about. But they may also promote behavior that is not especially praiseworthy, such as preferential treatment of the in-group. Indeed, in non-human animals fellow-feelings are best demonstrated where there are kinship relations or direct reciprocity. Animals are concerned about their family members and members of their cooperative groups. Caring for your family is not exactly a morally praiseworthy act; it's just something we are expected to do. If I do something good for a relative, it's nepotism, not charity. So fellow-feelings may originate in contexts that we wouldn't even characterize in moralistic terms. In human beings, the umbrella of fellow-feelings broadens, and they become unambiguous as moral motivators, but it would be misleading to call such feelings distinctively moral.

This discussion has been very brief, but the considerations brought to bear should at least raise the possibility that there are no distinctively moral emotions. Moral emotions seem either to serve additional functions that are not moral or derive from emotions that are not moral. If this is right, there are two important implications. First, from an evolutionary and developmental perspective, it may suggest that morality emerges out of more general psychological resources (Prinz, 2008). This could mean that morality is not innate or not modular or not vulnerable to selective deficits.

Second, if no emotions are distinctively moral, this raises a philosophical question about the very category under consideration. What makes an emotion moral if it is not intrinsically linked to morality? One possibility is that moral emotions are either ones that occur as a result of moral judgments or ones towards which our judgments of moral praise are directed. But this kind of answer implies that we have some purchase on what moral judgments are independent of moral emotions.

Many philosophers would be happy with that assessment, but some think that moral judgments must be defined in terms of moral emotions rather than the other way around. This introduces a threat of circularity. There may be ways to get out of the circle, or at least to show that it isn't vicious (see Prinz, 2007; Wiggins, 1987). For example, one can define a moral rule as one that is underwritten by a disposition to experience emotions of both self-directed and other-directed blame (depending on the protagonist). One can identify these emotions by appeal to the non-moral emotions from which they derive, while also saying that they become moral when they converge together to form such dispositions. The conspiracy of self-directed and other-directed emotions of blame is what makes the resulting attitude qualify as a moral norm, and its status as a moral norm is what makes these emotions of blame qualify as moral. Whether such a proposal can work is beyond the scope of this chapter. I hope we have seen, however, that we can do a reasonably good job of identifying moral emotions, even if there remain philosophical puzzles and controversies about how to circumscribe the category.

## REFERENCES

ADOLPHS, R. (2002). Recognizing emotion from facial expressions: Psychological and neurological mechanisms. *Behavioral and Cognitive Neuroscience Reviews*, 1, 21–62.

BATSON, C. D. (1987). Pro-social motivation: Is it ever truly altruistic? *Advances in Experimental Social Psychology*, 20, 65–122.

—— HÅKANSSON, H. J., CHERMOK, V. L., HOYT, J. L., and ORTIZ, B. G. (2007). An additional antecedent of empathic concern: Valuing the welfare of the person in need. *Journal of Personality and Social Psychology*, 93, 65–74.

—— KLEIN, T. R., HIGHBERGER, L., SHAW, L. L. (1995). Immorality from empathy-induced altruism: When compassion and justice conflict. *Journal of Personality and Social Psychology*, 68, 1042–54.

—— LISHNER, D. A., COOK, J., and SAWYER, S. (2005). Similarity and nurturance: Two possible sources of empathy for strangers. *Basic and Applied Social Psychology*, 27, 15–25.

BAUMEISTER, R. F., STILLWELL, A. M., HEATHERTON, T. F. (1994). Guilt: An interpersonal approach. *Psychological Bulletin*, 115, 243–67.

CARLSMITH, J. M., and GROSS, A. E. (1969). Some effects of guilt on compliance. *Journal of Personality and Social Psychology*, 1969, 11, 232–9.

DARWALL, S. (1998). Empathy, sympathy, care. *Philosophical Studies*, 89, 261–82.

DE WAAL, F. B. M. (1989) *Peacemaking among primates*. Cambridge, MA: Harvard University Press.

EISENBERG, N., FABES, R. A., MILLER, P. A., FULTZ, J., SHELL, R., MATHY, R. M., and RENO, R. R. (1989). Relation of sympathy and personal distress to prosocial behavior: A multimethod study. *Journal of Personality and Social Psychology*, 57, 55–66.

FEHR, E. and GÄCHTER, S. (2002). Altruistic punishment in humans. *Nature*, 415, 137–40.

FESSLER, D. M. T. (2004). Shame in two cultures: Implications for evolutionary approaches. *Journal of Cognition and Culture*, 4, 207–62.

GUTIERREZ, R. and GINER-SOROLLA, R. (2007). Anger, disgust, and presumption of harm as reactions to taboo-breaking behaviors. *Emotion*, 7, 853–68.

HATELD, E., CACIOPPO, J. T., and RAPSON, R. L. (1994). *Emotional contagion*. New York: Cambridge University Press.

HUME, D. (1739/1978). *A treatise of human nature*. P. H. Nidditch (ed.). Oxford: Oxford University Press.

KANT, I. (1885/1996). *The metaphysics of morals*. M. J. Gregor (Trans.). Cambridge: Cambridge University Press

LERNER, J., GOLDBERG, J., and TETLOCK, P. E. (1998). Sober second thought: The effects of accountability, anger, and authoritarianism on attributions of responsibility. *Personality and Social Psychology Bulletin*, 24, 563–74.

McDowell, J. (1985). Values and secondary qualities. In T. Honderich (ed.), *Morality and objectivity* (110–29). London: Routledge & Kegan Paul.

Masserman, J. H., Wechkin, S., and Terris, W. (1964) "Altruistic" behavior in rhesus monkeys. *American Journal of Psychiatry*, 121, 584–5.

Nemeroff, C. and Rozin, (1992). Sympathetic magical beliefs and kosher dietary practice: The interaction of rules and feelings. *Ethos*, 20, 96–115.

Neuberg, S. L., Cialdini, R. B., Brown, S. L., Luce, C., Sagarin, B. J., and Lewis, B. P. (1997). Does empathy lead to anything more than superficial helping? Comment on Batson et al. (1997). *Journal of Personality and Social Psychology*, 73, 510–16.

Parrott, D. J. and Zeichner, A. (2002). Effects of alcohol and trait anger on physical aggression in men. *Journal of Studies on Alcohol*, 63, 196–204.

Prinz, J. J. (2004). *Gut reactions: A perceptual theory of emotion*. New York: Oxford University Press.

—— (2007). *The emotional construction of morals*. Oxford: Oxford University Press.

—— (2008). Is morality innate? In W. Sinnott-Armstrong (ed.), *Moral Psychology, Vol. 1: The Evolution of Morality: Adaptations and Innateness* (367–406). Cambridge, MA: MIT Press.

—— (forthcoming). Is empathy necessary for morality? In P. Goldie and A. Coplan (eds.), *Empathy: Philosophical and Psychological Perspectives*. Oxford University Press.

Rice, G. E. J. (1964). Aiding behavior vs. fear in the albino rat. *Psychological Record*, 14, 165–70.

Rice, G. E. J. and Gainer, P. (1962). "Altruism" in the albino rat. *Journal of Comparative and & Physiological Psychology*, 55, 123–5.

Rozin, P., Lowery, L., Imada, S., and Haidt, J. (1999). The CAD triad hypothesis: A mapping between three moral emotions (contempt, anger, disgust) and three moral codes (community, autonomy, divinity). *Journal of Personality and Social Psychology*, 76, 574–86.

——, Markwith, M., and McCauley, C. R. (1994). The nature of aversion to indirect contacts with other persons: AIDS aversion as a composite of aversion to strangers, infection, moral taint, and misfortune. *Journal of Abnormal Psychology*, 103, 495–504.

——, Millman, L., and Nemeroff, C. (1986). Operation of the laws of sympathetic magic in disgust and other domains. *Journal of Personality and Social Psychology*, 50, 703–12.

Silk, J. B., Brosnan, S. F., Vonk, J., Henrich, J., Povinelli, D. J., Richardson, A. S., Lambeth, S. P., Mascaro, J., and Shapiro, S. J. (2005). Chimpanzees are indifferent to the welfare of unrelated group members. *Nature*, 437, 1357–9.

Smith, A. (1759/2000). *The theory of moral sentiments*. Amherst, NY: Prometheus Books.

Solomon, R. C. (1976). *The passions*. New York, NY: Doubleday.

Tangney, J. P. (1996). Conceptual and methodological issues in the assessment of shame and guilt. *Behaviour Research and Therapy*, 34, 741–54.

——, Wagner, P. E, Hill-Barlow, D., Marschall, D. E., and Gramzow, R. (1996). Relation of shame and guilt to constructive versus destructive responses to anger across the lifespan. *Journal of Personality and Social Psychology*, 70, 797–809.

Warneken, F., Hare, B., Melis, A. P., Hanus, D., and Tomasello, M. (2007). Spontaneous altruism by chimpanzees and young children. *PLoS Biology*, 5, 1414–20.

Wiggins D. (1987). A sensible subjectivism. In *Needs, values, truth: Essays in the philosophy of value* (185–214). Oxford: Blackwell.

Williams, B. (1985). *Ethics and the limits of philosophy*. Cambridge, MA: Harvard University Press.

# CHAPTER 24

································································

# LEARNING EMOTIONS AND ETHICS

································································

## PATRICIA GREENSPAN

EVOLUTIONARY psychologists and others thinking in scientific terms about the sources of morality sometimes hark back to eighteenth-century British moral philosophy, which works from a conception of innate human nature. Darwin himself (see 1871/1981, ch. 3) followed eighteenth-century models such as Hume 1739–40/1978 and Adam Smith 1759/1982 in basing morality on the social emotions. Recent arguments for an innate basis of ethics often take for granted some sort of explanation in terms of cross-cultural commonalities in emotion (see, e.g., Wilson 1993, Pinker 1997).

However, contemporary moral philosophers would question whether attempts to capture the origins of our moral responses can reveal appropriate bases for moral judgment. Explanation is one thing, justification another, and a central point of philosophic inquiry is to get beyond our emotional reactions to results

I owe thanks to Stephen Leighton for comments on a very early draft of this chapter. A poster based largely on Section 24.1 was presented to the meetings of the International Society for Research on Emotion in 2002. Later versions of this interdisciplinary part of the chapter were presented at meetings of the U.K. Arts and Humanities Research Board project on "Innateness and the Structure of the Mind" in 2002–2003 and at Ege University's Cultural Studies Seminar in Izmir, Turkey, along with a philosophy colloquium at Bosphorus University in Istanbul in 2003; it appears along with other contributions to the CSS conference in Isci et al. 2005, pp. 17–31. Let me also thank members of these audiences for helpful reactions. Section 24.2 was written for the present volume.

of rational reflection. Even Hume held that genuine moral sentiments emerge only after we eliminate the distortions of natural sympathy – to the point where moral judgments on his emotion-based account need not involve feeling.

Some of the contemporary literature specifically on emotions feeds into a tendency to see them as irrelevant to moral judgment by linking the claim of innateness to a view of emotions as feelings or physiological responses lacking any complex cognitive content. I think it should be possible, though, to find a reasonable spot in between the polarities in recent debate that gives the full range of emotional sources of ethics its due and thereby allows a role for emotions in developed moral judgment. The view I favor recognizes innate emotional sources of ethics but lets emotions incorporate cognitive elements of a sort susceptible to cultural influence but compatible with objectivist ethics.

At one point not too long ago work on emotions in psychology and the social sciences was divided into opposing camps on the issue of innate emotions. Theories of basic emotion in psychology (see, e.g., Ekman 1971, Izard 1977) were opposed by a "social constructivist" position favored by anthropologists (cf. Averill 1980, Lutz 1986), which in extreme form holds that all emotion types are variable inventions of culture. But there is room for a less extreme version of both this and the "nativist" approach, which need only hold that some original subset of emotions precedes social influence.

In philosophy a version of the social constructivist position appears in Armon-Jones 1991. By contrast, Griffiths 1997 defends basic emotions as evolutionary "affect-programs", clusters of responses to selected classes of stimuli – physiological and behavioral as well as affective responses – that might be said to be programmed into us by evolution. They are found in all cultures, though without the sort of fixity or unchangeability by either culture or further development that the term "innate" is often taken to imply.

Griffiths acknowledges responses resembling emotions that are set up entirely by culture, but he thinks of these as "social pretenses" of emotion that should be dealt with in a separate category (see esp. pp. 140ff.; but cf. Greenspan 2004). He also raises questions about whether the full range of states that seem offhand to be genuine emotions can be explained in terms of the basic set – whether we can "get there from here", as it were, with "there" taken as covering what he calls "the higher cognitive emotions". Though not himself concerned with moral emotions, Griffiths's discussion of attempts to "get there from here" by appeal to evolution deals with authors such as economist Frank (1988) who do assign a central role to moral (and other social) emotions.

This chapter explores how we might at least move *toward* moral emotions, and thence to moral judgment, from a fairly minimal innate basis in emotion – along with whatever learning mechanisms and other conceptual equipment we also possess innately. Despite its ambiguities, which lead Griffiths to reject the term, I use "innate" to mean roughly what Griffiths has in mind when he speaks of evolutionary "programs": unlearned responses or response tendencies, emerging (sometimes well after birth) as a consequence of genetic endowment – but also subject to serious cultural modification, in ways that are particularly significant in the moral sphere.

Although I think it is plausible to suppose that there is an innate basis of morality, understood in such terms, this should not be equated, as it often is, with the eighteenth-century notion of a universal "moral sense". Among other things, there is more learning in this area than meets the eye – particularly an inexplicit (and initially undifferentiated) kind of moral learning that rests on educating the emotions. I later provide some examples of how an innate emotional basis of ethics might be modified in essential ways by adult interaction with pre-linguistic children.

At various points in my argument I also indicate how an emotional basis may be further altered and expanded through language-encoded cognitive elements of emotion at more advanced stages. I use some neuroscientific evidence to suggest that we can break down basic emotions into even more basic components *of* emotion that can combine with cognitive components to generate the full set of developed human emotions. On the sort of account I favor, emotions can thereby incorporate an element of evaluative thought that is capable of taking on sophisticated content.

My discussion will draw attention to a factor that often seems to be overlooked in the literature on innate emotions: besides innate emotion *types*, we also have some general *mechanisms* whereby infants and children pick up reactions from others. These include the tendency of an infant to follow a caretaker's gaze (to look where the caretaker looks) and to imitate facial expressions or other behavior, including behavior that evokes emotions. An everyday illustration will suffice to show how these learning mechanisms allow for the social transfer and modification of emotions. So even if the mechanisms are themselves innate, as I assume in what follows, they serve to provide support for emotional learning.

The initial aim of my discussion here is to bring together diverse lines of inquiry into emotions and the origins of ethics in support of a moderate view on innate-ness Section 24.1 attempts a rough overview of the earlier literature in psychology on basic emotions, along with some more recent neuroscientific results indicating how basic emotions might be broken down further, with a source of cultural plasticity supplied by innate learning mechanisms. I also indicate how such materials might give rise to specifically moral emotions, with room for increasing cognitive complexity and a further source of cultural variability as emotions come to incorporate linguistic influence. Then, in Section 24.2, I focus more narrowly on my own area, moral philosophy, to defend moral learning in conjunction with emotion as an influence on moral judgment that need not undermine objectivity. In particular, I use the treatment of moral development in Rawls 1998 to supply the structure for an alternative to the Humean sentimentalist picture of the derivation of ethics from emotion.

# 24.1 CONSTRUCTING MORAL EMOTIONS

The evidence for basic emotions in psychology concerns the ability to identify emotion types cross-culturally, in the first instance by facial expression (following Darwin 1965). Exactly which emotions are included in the basic set is a matter of dispute, but familiar states like fear and anger are on everyone's list and also are commonly attributed to animals, so that the view feeds into an evolutionary perspective. On the other hand, disgust is also on everyone's list, though disgust (as distinct from taste aversion) is thought to be distinctively human (see Miller 1997, esp. p. 12; cf. Rozin and Fallon 1987). The application to animals also involves appeal to other bodily signs of emotion besides facial expression, along with confirming evidence from physiology and neuroscience.

Psychologists' work on basic emotions thus suggests an evolutionary approach to emotions, but it does not connect in a clear way to evolutionary accounts of morality. Positive or altruistic social emotions such as love and gratitude do not appear on the standard lists of basic emotions. Agreed items on the list include anger, disgust, fear, happiness, sadness, and surprise. Contempt was added to Ekman's initial list in Ekman and Friesen 1986 but remains controversial. There is also disagreement about whether to include shame and guilt, which require broadening the criterion for inclusion to features of bodily posture rather than simply facial expression (cf. Izard 1977, esp. pp. 83–92). This area is still in flux, then, but there is evidence from other fields for attributing some social emotions, or at any rate evolutionary predecessors of social emotions, to animals.

Recent work on brain circuits by neuroscientist Joseph LeDoux (1996) indicates that even standard entries on the list of basic emotions such as fear fall into two different "tracks" of neural response, some involving the cerebral cortex and some – a behavioral "freezing" response to a loud sound, say (LeDoux's measure of fear in rats) – only the amygdala. But the second, more primitive, track might also be taken to cover elements of the social emotions. For instance, physiological psychologist Jaak Panksepp (1998, ch. 13) discusses maternal love in rats in terms of the secretion of oxytocin – not itself an emotion, but apparently an element of love and related emotions such as trust (cf. Grimes 2003).

This suggests a way of breaking down basic emotions so that cortical involvement might allow for more fundamental modification of the basic set than we get on a model of derivation of emotions that is essentially inherited from seventeenth-century philosophy. Descartes (1970, pp. 331–99), most notably, understands "the passions of the soul" as derived from a list of "primary" emotions – analogous to primary colors in that more complex cases can be explained as blends of several primaries, which are not themselves subject to a similar explanation. But the more advanced forms of emotion need not be seen as combinations of states that are already fully constituted as emotions. Instead, we might expect the more primitive neural elements of emotion to take on more of the features of full-fledged human emotion when the link is made to the cerebral cortex.

Now, even relatively primitive emotions can be said to possess a kind of evaluative content: to the extent that affective states are motivationally rewarding or aversive, they "say" something positive or negative about the objects they are directed toward, as worth seeking or avoiding (cf. Greenspan 2003). Fear, for instance, says that its object is to be avoided as a threat. But once this element of content, whether itself learned or innate, comes to be cortically mediated, it is subject to modification on the basis of cultural influence – and, for that matter, individual reflection. Sometimes it may be modified in ways that influence how a given emotion feels. Consider some of the variants of love: possessive, devoted, or dependent, wild or subdued, depending in part on how we are taught to conceptualize the love object.

For some purposes, of course, one might want to exclude the more primitive, pre-intentional states – "objectless" anxiety, for instance, as a state that persists into adult human life – from the category of genuine emotions. In my own work the aim of such line-drawing has not been to establish the uniqueness of human emotional response (cf. de Sousa 1987, ch. 4), but instead to bring out the role of emotions in the justification of action (Greenspan 1988, p. 50), a distinctively human concern. Which states we should treat as paradigm cases of emotion, the more primitive or the more developed and cognitively complex, will vary with our theoretical purposes, normative or scientific.

Might there be a theoretically principled reason for drawing the line differently for different types of emotion? Some would be inclined to deny genuine love to nonhuman animals while readily granting them fear. Apart from the moral or religious significance assigned to love, one possible reason for love's exclusion from the list of basic emotions has to do with variable cultural influences on expression. If expressions of love or other of the more developed social emotions in humans are more subject to cultural influence, then they will not form the same relatively stable clusters of response that we get with fear, anger, and similar entries on the standard list.

Unlike psychologists' work on basic emotions, the treatment of emotions in terms of brain circuits would not put any special emphasis on facial expression; nor would it even imply stable clusters of bodily response perceptible to the agent and others. However, according to common evolutionary arguments, emotion types that originally evolved as mechanisms promoting behavioral readiness – "fight-or-flight" in the case of fear – later came to be selected for their communicative function. The central role of facial expression in humans essentially serves to concentrate this secondary function of emotions into an area that facilitates social transfer. In the first instance, transfer of emotions from caretakers is accomplished by patterns of shared attention, or "gaze-following", along with the tendency of the human infant to imitate facial expression (see, e.g., the discussion in Bloom 2000, pp. 62–4; for relevant work more specifically on emotions see Witherington et al. 2002 and the evidence cited in Hobson [this volume]; cf. also de Sousa 1987, p. 183). These are social mechanisms below the level of culture but capable of conveying cultural influence, even if themselves innate.

The innate emotional basis of ethics thus need not be limited to a set of discrete emotion types, or basic emotions, but also would seem to include general mechanisms of emotional learning capable of modifying and expanding the basic set. Hoffman 1982 appeals particularly to the mechanism of emotional empathy, originating in the tendency exhibited by newborns to cry at the sound of other newborns' cries, as a basis for guilt, a distinctively human emotion involving empathy with a victim of one's own harmful behavior. On this sort of account there is no implication of a culturally invariant "moral sense" as a feature of human nature.

The universal element of morality lies more importantly in its application *to* everyone, regardless of culture or some narrower set of personal affiliations. Universality in this sense – as in Hume 1978 on the correction of sympathetic emotions to eliminate distortions of personal standpoint – is a question of the content or scope of morality. This does seem to require cognitive advancement beyond animals, specifically the development of language, as needed to generate the full range of objects of moral response. But it also would seem to be facilitated by cross-culturally recognizable basic emotions, just insofar as they enable us to learn moral responses *from* anyone, regardless of culture. I think this is the real point of basic emotions in relation to ethics: they essentially allow for extension of a particular group's social contract.

At the same time, though, social influence introduces variations in the circumstances thought to justify a given emotion – what counts as an appropriate object of guilt or shame, say, in a given culture. For that matter, morality enlists competing emotional mechanisms – empathy or sympathy, but also the retributive tendencies encoded in resentment, indignation, and the like – that might be mixed or balanced differently in different cultures or even by different personality types. So there is ample room for divergent moralities or patterns of moral behavior or moral codes – for another point of contrast with the "moral sense" tradition.

What we seem to have, then, as innate bases of ethics are, first, a set of primitive states or elements of emotion, some but not all of which we are willing to count as full-fledged emotions, at any rate at earlier stages of development or in nonhuman animals, and, secondly, a set of mechanisms for emotional learning, or social transfer of emotions. What we do not have is either the seventeenth-century notion of emotional primaries whose combination yields the full range of human emotions or the eighteenth-century idea of an innate "moral sense" grounded in human nature.

Note that my discussion so far concerns innate *emotional* bases of ethics, albeit not limited to innate moral emotions – emotions with a specifically moral content, such as shame or guilt. Though animals might be said to have rudimentary social emotions – or even the rudiments of moral emotions, as in philosopher Allan Gibbard's explanation of guilt in terms of the submissive posture in animals (see Gibbard 1990, ch. 7) – full-fledged moral emotions are usually placed solidly in the "higher cognitive" category. Hauser 2000, for instance, denies nonhuman animals genuinely moral emotions (and genuine empathy) on the grounds that they lack self-awareness (p. 224): awareness of themselves (and also of others) as bearers of the intentional states to which moral behavior in humans responds, such as beliefs, desires, and needs (see pp. 250ff.; but cf. Waal, e.g. 1998).

It is still possible, of course, that moral and other cognitively complex reactions are innate in humans – in a sense compatible with emerging well after infancy and requiring certain conditions to emerge, on the model of the capacity to learn a language. But this cannot be established just by appeal to psychologists' evidence for basic emotions. While brain studies supply further evidence (see, e.g., Rolls 1999), some current authors instead put forth arguments for innateness based on Chomskian "poverty of stimulus" arguments in linguistics, appealing to the paucity of explicit moral teaching to account for cross-cultural commonalities in moral judgment (see Dwyer 1999; cf. Hauser 2006).

However, we should note that moral teaching takes many forms apart from explicit instruction. We educate the moral emotions in children, for instance, by reacting to characters in the stories we tell them in a way that encourages shared emotional response. Chomskian nativists appeal to results on the order of psychologist Elliot Turiel's (1983) finding of a distinction made cross-culturally by preschool children between moral and merely conventional rule infractions (but cf. Haidt et al. 1993 for anthropologists' criticism of Turiel's research). However, whether we express indignation or rather amusement at a certain character's exploits in a story can convey the idea that harm or a slight to another is of serious moral concern in a way that mere flouting of conventional rules is not.

There is also an abundant supply of implicit moral instruction that only much later gets pulled apart from the other purposes of our use of emotional display to train children. Just saying "no" in an emphatic or warning tone counts as moral instruction in this not-yet-differentiated sense, which does not distinguish wrong from discourteous or dangerous action. Moreover, even if "poverty of stimulus" arguments based on Turiel's results favor innate origins of the *concept* of morality, this should not be confused with an innate basis of *morality*, in the sense of moral motivation and behavior – which can precede thought *about* morality, or reflective moral judgment deploying the concept.

Some of the ways we teach moral motivation via emotion in advance of the development of moral thought – and also without reliance on specifically moral emotions – can be seen by looking at our play rituals with prelinguistic children. A child thrusts one of its toys at us and we respond by elaborately portraying surprise and gratitude. The point is not just to teach the phrase "thank you", or conventions of politeness, but rather to convey and heighten joy at social exchange. We give the toy back, are handed it again with an expectant look and repeat the emotional display. Our feelings, or pretended feelings, are contagious – not as gratitude per se, at this stage, but rather as a combination of simpler positive responses to giving and taking: excitement, delight, and amusement. The elements of affectionate interest and attention involved in caregiving and general play begin to get transferred by these means to other forms of social exchange and sharing.

This is a kind of early moral learning, though it has not yet been put to an explicitly moral use. When we include such interactions, though, the stimulus for moral learning can be seen to be quite rich, even if susceptible to further development by way of its pairing with language. At this stage we are not (or not merely) teaching language but rather are using language as one vehicle of emotional expression in an effort to shape social emotions in children.

A more specifically moral example involves encouraging sympathy: a child kicks its mother and the mother exaggerates her expression of pain and hurt feelings, conveying the sadness and resentment of a victim that becomes moral guilt. We also may discourage certain emotions, or in the first instance overt expression of them – by not making too prolonged a fuss, say, about a child's own minor hurts and pains. Clearly all of this is subject to the influence of cultural or other local norms, even if it presupposes some innate emotions, along with innate mechanisms of social transfer of emotions, possibly along with some innate conceptual categories or structures of moral thought, of the sort that Chomskian nativists have in mind. Ekman 1971 used the term "display rules" to explain Japanese subjects' denial of negative emotions in the presence of authority figures; the term was meant to represent such rules as extrinsic to the content of emotions, but on an account like the one I favor they can come to be incorporated into emotional content. Whose pain counts, how you should feel about causing it, and whether and when you may express or acknowledge those feelings, even to yourself, are questions that can be answered differently at an early enough stage of social learning to influence what people feel.

There are also, at least arguably, other concerns of morality besides harm or pain that can be emphasized and interpreted differently by different cultures. Disgust is one of the entries on the standard list of basic emotions, and it is put to use particularly by moralities that depend on a concept of moral sin (see, e.g., Shweder et al. 1997). But it also is one of the emotions expressed in our own, primarily guilt-based, morality in response to behavior seen as "beneath" a scrupulous moral agent. While the emotion itself is found in all cultures, apparently there is not much cultural uniformity in its specific objects – in which food sources evoke disgust, and which acts seem morally repugnant.

A different sort of example in support of cultural shaping of emotions is provided by feelings of respect or deference. These are essential to the workings of social hierarchy – and arguably, in a different way, to social equality – but it is not obvious how they could be derived from entries on the standard list of basic emotions. They seem to lack any tight connection to fear, for instance. Perhaps they might be understood as originating in reactions *to* certain basic emotions in others – submissively accepting the anger of caretakers when one disobeys them, say, as an instance of Gibbard's understanding of guilt (1990, ch. 7; cf. Blackburn 1998, ch. 1, sec. 3). But coming to distinguish among sources of anger, assigning rightful authority only to some of them, involves augmenting the set of basic emotions with further materials provided by cognition and social interaction.

Some might be inclined to say that feelings like respect that do not constitute relatively stereotyped sets of responses like the items on the list of basic emotions do not really count as distinct emotions. But note, for instance, that gratitude is subject to similar questions, though it is an entry on standard lists of *non*basic emotions that plays a crucial role in evolutionary accounts of morality, as what motivates reciprocal altruism. Both of these emotions, respect and gratitude, might be thought of as originally special forms of love – one a response to general dependency, the other to a particular helpful act. We would be missing much of relevance to moral and practical life if we confined attention to "affect-programs", or even to standard emotion categories, in discussing the role of emotions.

If we do not thus restrict the range of emotions, the role of language as the ultimate vehicle of cognitive content makes the number and variety of emotions potentially limitless. An affective element – not necessarily a whole affect-program – just needs to be brought into connection with an evaluative thought or cognition. This might be a complex thought *about* emotions, as suggested by Gibbard's account of moral judgment – accepting someone else's anger toward oneself as warranted, in the case of guilt – but in the simplest cases, cognition and affect just need to register a corresponding kind of significance of the situation for the organism, on the model of threat in the case of fear. Specifically moral emotions result from having the linguistic resources to capture social norms, plus some way (whether evolutionary or social) of acquiring an aversive reaction to a norm violation.

What rough picture emerges if we combine Gibbard's interpretation of moral judgments with Hoffman's account of the guilt response as based on emotional empathy? Though it begins just as sympathetic distress, guilt picks up its characteristic moral content when objects of childhood dependency identify with a victim of the child's harmful actions, conveying a sense of social censure and rejection in response to a misdeed. A display of corresponding self-directed affect then becomes part of the child's submissive routine for assuaging such reactions on the part of others. Where an innate concept of morality might play a role is in determining how the reaction eventually generalizes – extending beyond caretakers' concerns to a certain class of concerns of people generally, ultimately giving rise to the sense of respect for persons as such.

What the child absorbs, though, is initially just a view of others' negative reactions as warranted in response to certain behavior on its part, specified in accordance with variable social norms. Concern for a younger sibling, say, might be something for which society exacts guilt for failure or instead treats as someone else's responsibility. Once language is learned, such norms can be spelled out explicitly and modified on the basis of explicit criticism.

This is not to deny that evolutionary responses have a kind of primacy (cf. D'Arms and Jacobson 2003); nor is it just to say that innate and cultural factors interact somehow in generating moral emotions. Rather, the suggestion is that the innate factors *include* the very mechanisms whereby emotions incorporate cultural influence of the sort requisite for moral emotions. The Chomskian distinction between principles and parameters – the former innate, the latter set differently by different cultures – might be useful as a way of summing this up, were it not for a tendency to take the relevant "principles" in this area as very general moral principles (cf., e.g., Hauser 2006, pp. 44ff.). Even where moral principles are shared cross-culturally, they need not be innate, but instead might be explained as responses to common features of life in a social group.

Incidentally, guilt was not a recognized emotion category until relatively recently: the noun as used in English to name an emotion was apparently the result of linguistic error in the period of the Protestant Reformation, with its stress on emotions of religious despair and self-accusation (see my account in Greenspan 1995, ch. 4). The possibility of reconstructing emotional guilt in terms of items on the list of basic emotions – variants of sadness or anger, conveyed by the mechanism of emotional empathy – may explain why the word seems to name something that was there all along, but it is something that not all societies put to a moral use (cf., e.g., Benedict 1946 and Doi 1973 on Japan as a "shame culture"; cf. Williams 1993 on the Homeric Greeks).

Gibbard explains the distinction between guilt and shame by pairing them with different emotions on the part of others: guilt involves submitting to others' anger, whereas shame involves accepting their contempt. This explanation may make appeal to others' basic emotions (at least if contempt is allowed on the list), but it does not obviously derive guilt and shame from specific basic emotions in the individual's own repertoire – from her own anger or contempt, considered as a particular cluster of expressive and physiological responses.

There is no requirement, of course, that the higher cognitive emotions fall into categories that correlate one-one with sources in the basic set, even if they are derived from basic emotions. But moral emotions also seem to have a basis in caretakers' and others' behavioral responses to the child – incidents of social rejection in an overall situation of acceptance and trust – that may not evoke standard emotion types but rather just generalized discomfort or unease. This acquires a cognitive content when the child comes to view others' responses, or some of them, as appropriate or warranted. The resulting picture accords with the cognitivist or appraisal-based approach to emotions in twentieth-century philosophy and psychology (see esp. Bedford 1957 and Solomon 1976 in philosophy, and Arnold 1960 and Frijda 1987 in psychology), but as limited to fully developed human emotions. Emotions as such also involve noncognitive states of feeling or affect (cf., e.g., Robinson 1995), both as their initial source and as a motivationally important component, albeit often present only in modified or attenuated form.

## 24.2 MORAL OBJECTIVITY AND EMOTION

An account that connects cognitive and affective components of emotion in the way I have suggested might seem to bear only on psychological questions about the origins of moral thought and behavior, not more strictly philosophic questions about what moral judgments or norms we ought to accept. It might even seem to undermine the aims of philosophic justification, if a basis in emotions influences the developed content of moral norms in a way that reflects variable cultural sources. In fact, Gibbard, the philosopher whose interpretation of guilt I have used as illustration, is a noncognitivist on the issue of how to interpret a moral judgment: rather than amounting to a cognitive state of belief, a moral judgment on his account simply expresses acceptance of a norm for assessing moral emotions.

Gibbard's theory is in the tradition of both mid-twentieth-century emotivism and a common (though now disputed) reading of Hume in the eighteenth century as a skeptic about the foundations of ethics (cf. Mackie 1995, ch. 9). In fact, it is often assumed that the only possibilities for linking ethics and emotion are the eighteenth-century alternatives of Kantian rationalism and Humean sentimentalism: either disallowing emotion any role in grounding moral judgment or understanding moral judgment entirely in terms of emotion. This reason-versus-emotion dichotomy underlies recent work in the social sciences by Haidt et al. 1993 (cf. Haidt 2001) on "dumbfounding," which takes the finding that people stick to their gut feelings on moral taboos such as incest as evidence against philosophers' emphasis on rational argument in ethics.

However, I think we can extract an intermediate view from Rawls 1998, which includes an account of emotions underlying the sense of justice (see ch. 8) in support of principles derived from considerations of rational choice. Rawls essentially interprets emotional guilt as developing in stages into a full-blown moral emotion on the basis of increasing cognitive sophistication in an environment of love and trust that promotes self-esteem. Chomskian nativists often quote from Rawls's general theoretical discussion (see pp. 41–2) an analogy he briefly draws between the complex principles of justice his view ascribes to us and the principles of grammar we employ without awareness in making ordinary judgments of grammaticalness on a Chomskian account. However, Rawls's use of the language analogy has no direct bearing on questions of innateness – its point is just that we can act on principles we could not make explicit – though he later indicates affinity for views of the moral sentiments that assign us an innate psychological proclivity toward morality rather than treating it as an alien social imposition (cf. pp. 401ff.). In any case, very little attention is paid to Rawls's account of the moral sentiments. Hauser 2006, which treats a "Rawlsian creature" as a creature with "moral instincts" insofar as it relies on unconscious principles (p. 42), works from a contrast between principles and feelings as embodying opposite sources of moral motivation. Let me try to correct things a bit by spending some time on Rawls's account of how we learn moral emotions.

In part, my aim will be to detach the general bearing of Rawls's account on the issues under discussion here from some of the particulars of his theory of justice. While moral emotions do not play a central role in his theory of justice, he does ascribe an important role to them – or to moral sentiments, conceived as the general dispositions they manifest – in moral motivation. His developmental account comes up in defense of the stability of the "well-ordered society", a society arranged in accordance with principles of justice. Stability amounts to the tendency of a set of social arrangements to give rise to sentiments that support rather than undermining it, such as a desire to act in accordance with its principles and a tendency to feel guilt if one violates them. Rawls essentially argues that his two principles of justice yield enough stability to make a society founded on them viable – more so than the principles proposed by competing theories such as utilitarianism.

Rawls's account of the development of moral emotions, and ultimately of the sense of justice, thus proceeds from the assumption of just institutions. Besides understanding the well-ordered society as arranged in accordance with the principles of justice, it presupposes supportive families and peer and other cooperative groups that operate fairly. He takes this to distinguish his account from work in scientific psychology, which is supposed to be value-free. Since the elements of his developmental account are often described in terms of features of his overall theory of justice, it will take some work to detach just those elements of it that are relevant here; for a detailed scholarly treatment of Rawls's moral psychology and its role in the theory – a theory he ultimately saw as political rather than moral – see Baldwin 2008.

Guilt comes up in Rawls's account because infractions of principles of justice are bound to occur even in a well-ordered society. The emotion serves as a force tending to bring behavior back into line with the principles. A version of guilt is said to correspond to each of his three developmental stages, or in his terms "moralities": the morality of authority, of association, and of principles. At each stage a corresponding type of guilt arises from what amounts to a variant of love, assuming an appropriate element of reciprocity in feeling and behavior. Its initial basis is love and trust directed toward childhood caretakers whose behavior exhibits similar feelings toward us and thereby tends to instill in us a sense of our own self-worth, so that we essentially come to imitate their reactions to our misdeeds. Later, in the various groups we come to be involved in – from the family, through associations formed in play and education, to the larger society – guilt gets linked to fellow feeling toward others seen as well-disposed toward us and as doing their part in a cooperative arrangement. Finally, the sense of justice effectively adds to this a kind of gratitude toward the principles of justice themselves, as underlying social arrangements seen to benefit us and those we care for, though a given application of them may instead advance the interests of others outside our circle of personal affiliations.

Rawls speaks of commonsense morality, and of moral guilt and other moral feelings, in his account of the second stage, which turns on the development of various cognitive skills, especially the ability to take the perspectives of others and to appreciate their contributions to an overall cooperative enterprise. Though he suggests at one point that we do not have guilt "in the strict sense" (p. 415) until the third stage, when we see ourselves in relation to principles, I take him to mean that, understood strictly, guilt is based on an abstract judgment that one has committed a moral wrong, irrespective of any personal attachment to those who suffer it. He distinguishes guilt from shame in that guilt involves the idea of right, whereas shame rests on the broader notion of good (pp. 422–3), which extends beyond moral good.

With the interpretation of Rawls's principles of justice as political rather than moral, which emerged more clearly in his later work (see esp. Rawls 1993), we also apparently need to recognize as part of the third stage of moral development a commitment to general *moral* principles, distinct from those governing basic social arrangements, but more abstract and systematically organized than the norms of commonsense morality. Here is where one sort or element of an innate concept of morality might be said to kick in – morality in contrast, not just to mere convention, but also to merely personal considerations.

While Rawls's political principles allow for various different moral views as reasonable alternatives, his own views favor a Kantian ethic of respect for persons. However, what I want to take from him here is limited to two main structural features of the role he assigns emotions in defense of a normative view, whether moral or political. First, the role is evidently justificatory, even if secondary to the argument already presented for the two principles of justice. Insofar as his developmental account is needed to establish the stability of a society ordered in accordance with the principles, it provides essential support for them, without which they would not be worth instituting. He at one point denies the account justificatory status (see, e.g., p. 439), but I take that to mean that he understands his argument for the principles as complete without it, as required by its reliance on institutions determined to be just by some independent measure.

Second, and crucially, Rawls sees the role he assigns to emotion in support of normative principles as compatible with the assignment of objective status to them. The claim of objectivity comes out explicitly in his later writings on Kantian constructivism in metaethics (see esp. Rawls 1980), but as interpreted in a sense distinct from factual truth, with Rawls's principles of justice seen as limited to a certain cultural setting, namely democratic pluralist society. The contractual basis of Rawls's theory – in the rational choice of principles in an "original position" characterized by individuals' ignorance of their particularizing features – is understood as a reasonable procedure under these circumstances for constructing principles of justice. The principles therefore count as objective, without any claim of correspondence to an independent order of moral facts. It is their basis in a reasonable decision procedure that confers objectivity.

Let me now pull away sharply from the particulars of Rawls's theory, while making use of its basic structural features, in order to ask what it is that emotions might add to the backing for a moral code. When Rawls himself turns to arguing that his principles would promote greater stability than competitors, he does not extend his comments on guilt and other moral emotions but focuses instead on self-esteem, as a product of the same developmental process. However, I want to suggest that the role of emotions in early moral teaching itself promotes something analogous to stability – understood, not as a feature of political systems set up in accordance with one or another philosophical theory, but instead as a feature of commonsense moral codes, diverging across different cultures.

In Greenspan 1995 (ch. 6) I treat this question under the heading of "viability": whether a given moral code is up to the task of sustaining a society based on it. As with stability, all that is really needed for viability is to pass a certain threshold, not to outdo competitors, though in the contemporary situation of global communication and mobility, competition for members (or for their adherence to the local code) may push some otherwise viable codes below the threshold. Cross-cultural divergence in moral norms may well be compatible, then, with moral objectivity in Rawls's sense – and also, I would add, with truth (on a less metaphysically demanding conception than Rawls sets up for contrast to objectivity in his sense). Many variations in codes will of course just be due to differing circumstances – including historical circumstances, such as acceptance of different customs or conventions – but, additionally, there may be more than one way of arranging cooperative social life that counts as reasonable in its distribution of benefits and burdens. So objectivity on this conception is compatible with a degree of cultural relativity – though we also would expect to find certain cross-cultural constants, given uniformities in both the cooperative aims of social life and the innate basis for moral learning provided by human emotions.

What my account of emotions adds to Rawls's basic structure is an interpretation in terms of emotion of the motivational force that authors following Hume 1978 make out as essential to morality. In a nutshell: I take the viability of a moral code to depend on how well suited it is to being learned at an early stage on the basis of our innate stock of emotions and mechanisms of emotional transfer.

In the first instance, this is meant to allow for an intuitively satisfying answer to the question in contemporary moral philosophy of whether motivational force is internal to the very meaning of a moral judgment – what is summed up as (motivational or judgment-) internalism. Early teaching in conjunction with emotions would invest moral judgments with motivational force, not necessarily in every case, but as a function of the meaning of moral language (see Greenspan 1995, ch. 3; cf. also Greenspan 1998 and Blackburn 1998) – so that it would make sense, but at the same time be linguistically odd as well as psychologically abnormal, for someone (an "amoralist") to claim to be completely unmotivated by a moral judgment she accepts.

Moreover, the account of how emotions supply morality's motivational aspect makes them out as reinforcing the status of moral judgments as reasons for action in a way that supports the viability of a moral code. It is important to the account that moral language is taught to us in childhood more or less simultaneously with moral emotions and simple moral rules, as illustrated by the cases in Section 24.1. Moral reasons and moral reactions are thus developmentally intertwined. Guilt, for instance, becomes a distinctively moral emotion in Rawls's "strict" sense once innate responses like empathetic sadness get refined to incorporate a notion of wrong that is conveyed to a child initially just by inducing those simpler emotions in reaction to various rule violations. So even emotions with a distinctive moral content do not simply incorporate pre-existing moral judgments. Philosophers may tend to reconstruct the relevant relations in more systematic terms, with moral language taught first, providing the basis for a set of judgments expressed in terms of it, and certain emotions then rendered moral when annexed to those judgments to enforce moral behavior. But while this picture may afford a clearer explanation of how a philosophic theory of wrong might come to be endowed with motivational force – as in the account of "internal sanctions" of utilitarian morality in Mill 2001 (ch. 3) – it does not help explain how we actually manage to get commonsense morality off the ground. Nor is the only alternative to it a developmental picture running in reverse, with distinctively moral emotions such as guilt seen as available early on to provide an independent foundation for moral judgment (cf., e.g., Nichols 2008).

Instead, we learn moral emotions and judgments in the same breath. Even if the rough-and-ready rules we learn in childhood ultimately give way to more complex principles, the way they develop initially in conjunction with emotions thus tends to leave us with a tendency toward emotional discomfort at rule violation. It therefore erects a barrier to the inclination in adult life to discount moral requirements as reasons for action. While an agent can legitimately discount some reasons – set them aside as motivational influences, perhaps by appeal to higher-order considerations on the order of personal priorities – reasons of the sort that ground moral requirements are not supposed to be subject to discounting insofar as they incorporate criticism from other agents' standpoints, standpoints an individual agent lacks authority to discount (see Greenspan 2007 and Greenspan forthcoming-*a*). In practice, though, we sometimes do set moral reasons aside when they compete with our personal aims. But the fact that moral language typically retains a penumbra of feeling from the process by which it was learned gives us a reason against discounting that at least makes it harder to manage, given that emotional reactions are not normally malleable case-by-case on the basis of rational reflection. They are subject to alteration, of course, but on the basis of the long-term cultivation of new reactive habits that is familiar from Aristotle 2002. The upshot is that emotions function as barriers to rational discounting and are useful to us morally because they do.

Emotional learning may be seen as a way of building social norms into individual practical reasoning and motivation. I argue in Greenspan 1988 (ch. 6; cf. Frank 1988) for a sense in which emotions serve to undercut weakness of will. In prudential reasoning, they bring the future to bear on the present standpoint – reflecting envisioned consequences of action in more or less immediate emotional comfort or discomfort. In relation to ethics, they reflect the social in the individual standpoint, bringing home to an agent the consequences of her action for others. I see them as reinforcing moral reasons with further practical reasons in the agent's interests: reasons for sustaining or minimizing emotional affect. That I might feel guilty if I did something, for instance, is a reason for me to avoid doing it, given that guilt is an unpleasant feeling I have reason to avoid undergoing. Thus understood, emotions do not function merely as blind psychological forces acting upon us (cf. Greenspan 2009). Instead, in adult life they play a kind of back-up role within practical reasoning (see Greenspan 1988, ch. 6, and Greenspan 2004; I also plan to extend and clarify this argument in light of later work on reasons in Greenspan forthcoming-*b*). Of course, explicit appeal to how we feel would keep us from acting for exclusively moral reasons in the way favored by a Kantian approach. But what is normally in question in adult life is just the availability of emotions as reinforcement for moral reasons that we otherwise might be inclined to discount. At the childhood stage at which emotions launch awareness of moral reasons, moreover, purity of moral motivation is hardly a reasonable concern. Moral reasons have not yet begun to be distinguished as such at that stage, and this initial blurring of boundaries is part of what supports moral learning.

I should note that I do not see guilt and similar emotions simply, or even primarily, as serving to bring agents back into line after a norm violation. In anticipatory form – when brought to bear on the thought of a possible future norm violation – what amount to self-punitive responses to moral wrong also motivate adherence to the norms and thus tend to minimize violations. So a moral code that was not learned in conjunction with emotions would be at a serious disadvantage with respect to viability. "Wrong" and similar moral terms and concepts would carry no more motivational force than, say, "out-of-bounds", in a game that any particular agent might be disinclined to play.

Emotions constrain the content of a moral code, then, insofar as norms based on considerations too remote from ordinary human concerns or too complex to be teachable in the way indicated would not be viable. However, the important point for the question of objectivity is that contemporaneous emotions do not supply the content of ethics on this account. Instead, certain emotions in adult life have come to incorporate moral reasons that by that stage are capable of independent formulation. The moral reason for feeling guilty – that the act one is contemplating would harm someone, say, or that it therefore would be wrong – supplies the content of the emotion. Despite having developed in conjunction with the element of emotional affect, with motivational force that depends on that history, it can be fine-tuned separately at a more advanced stage. In effect, emotions involve *two* layers of reasons, corresponding to the affective and evaluative components defended in Section 24.1. At the advanced stage we can pull apart the element of affect from a moral reason stemming initially from the simple precepts of care-takers, but ultimately, as Rawls allows, capable of reflecting principles too complex to be accessible to ordinary moral consciousness. Whatever objectivity applies to moral reasons derived from these sources – possibly interpreted in realist rather than Rawlsian constructivist terms – will not be undermined by their also having a motivational basis in emotion.

Now, besides being motivators, emotions on an evaluative account also come to have an *epistemic* function. Often our readiest means of access to the norms we accept, sometimes apparently our only means of access, is to ask ourselves how we feel about some proposed course of action. Emotions have even been said to amount to perceptions of value (see esp. de Sousa 1987). But we need to understand any perceptual role in light of the ability of emotions to incorporate content from an independent source subject to philosophic refinement and grounding.

We can all think of cases where our emotions incorporate values taught to us as children but now superseded, so that they turn out to be *illusory* perceptions of value. A similar point applies to cross-cultural variation: different moral codes can be learned in conjunction with emotions, but some of them, maybe all of them, will turn out to get things wrong in some way or other, perhaps even systematically. This is compatible with a claim of objectivity that is meant to apply just to some unspecified moral code, possibly one that has not yet been realized or even conceived.

What if it were suggested, though, that in the process of working toward the right or most reasonable system of moral norms, the role of emotion would eventually be superseded? Given the tendency of emotions to resist revision, as just noted, along with other well-known pitfalls of emotional response, freeing morality of emotional influence is a tempting ideal for philosophers and others. Sometimes this ideal is summed up in the image of the "Star Trek" character "Mr. Spock" (though Mr. Spock did show signs of compassion). More realistically, we often manage to satisfy moral demands just on the basis of habit, without occurrent emotion. Moreover, reflecting critically on the moral reactions instilled in us as children can depend on setting emotions aside. For that matter, we have to be able to override various emotions (including even some moral emotions) when they undermine moral resolve. So emotions might be depicted as a ladder to adult morality that we really ought to kick away once we get there.

Alternatively, one might grant that moral action in adult life sometimes has to rely on emotions, but only as "heuristics": mental short-cuts, or rough aids to decision-making that sometimes misfire and yield the wrong answer (cf., e.g., Kahneman et al. 1982; for a more recent approach, stressing the benefits of heuristics, cf. Gigerenzer et al. 1999 and Gigerenzer and Selten 2002). Note, however, that the heuristic role of emotion is in the first instance epistemic: emotions aid us – most of the time, though not always – in quickly forming a correct moral judgment (cf. the treatment of "snap" evaluations in Greenspan 1988, ch. 2). Whether we act on a moral judgment once we have formed it is another matter, however, and that is what my argument here concerns. On my account, emotions serve in part to constitute morality as such by endowing moral judgments with motivational force. The heuristics suggestion is helpful in capturing the role of emotions as an adaptive resource, but only if we resist the conclusion that unlimited time to access and apply an independently worked-out moral system would let us dispense with emotions in moral life.

This is not to say that it would be impossible to act morally at an advanced stage solely on the basis of intellectual apprehension of moral reasons, at any rate some of the time. I do not endorse the Humean claim that reason without emotion is necessarily inert; I mean just to question how reliable a motive that would be in a creature with other, possibly conflicting motives, and thus how viable a moral code could be that relied solely upon it.

The image of the ladder that eventually is kicked away also raises a different question: could the right moral system, once it is elaborated, turn out to be one that fails to elicit any of the emotional responses that figured in moral development? Giving the system motivational force might then seem just to require annexing it to some *new* motives – in the simplest terms, a desire to achieve some social end on the order of group flourishing or some other conception of the total good. On a certain reading of Mill 2001 (ch. 4), we need only engineer that social end into individual motivation.

We had better start early, though – and where else could we start *from* than our stock of innate emotional responses and mechanisms of social influence? The engineering would consist in rearranging the circumstances that elicit emotional response, more or less as Mill's account suggests. Moreover, any later transitions to a motivationally effective replacement code would have to rely on continuity with our responses as so far constituted. Without that, as far as I can see, we would just be replacing morality with something else: a nonmoral system of behavioral rules aimed toward achieving a social end that might or might not mean anything to a particular agent. The replacement might improve our theoretical decisions on cases considered from a removed standpoint but still be a very bad bet for influencing individual practical reasoning. An attempt to "program in" the social end at a later stage of development could succeed only if we are at that point still able to modify our emotional responses in the way needed to back it up. But that, once again, would mean learning emotions and ethics in the same breath.

# References

ARISTOTLE (2002). *Nicomachean Ethics*, trans. by C. Rowe. Oxford: Oxford University Press.

ARMON-JONES, C. (1991). *Varieties of Affect*. Hertfordshire, England: Harvester.

ARNOLD, M. (1960). *Emotion and Personality*. New York: Academic Press.

AVERILL, J. R. (1980). "A Social Constructivist View of Emotion", in R. Plutchik and H. Kellerman (eds.), *Emotion: Theory Research and Experience*, vol. 1. New York: Academic Press.

BALDWIN, T. (2008). "Rawls and Moral Psychology", in R. Shafer-Landau, *Oxford Studies in Metaethics*, vol. 3. New York: Oxford University Press.

BEDFORD, E. (1957). "Emotions," *Proceedings of the Aristotelian Society*, 57, 281–304.

BENEDICT, R. (1946). *The Chrysanthemum and the Sword: Patterns of Japanese Culture*. Boston: Houghton Mifflin.

BLACKBURN, S. (1998). *Ruling Passions*. Oxford: Clarendon Press.

BLOOM, P. (2000). *How Children Learn the Meanings of Words*. Cambridge, Mass.: M.I.T. Press.

D'ARMS, J. and JACOBSON, D. (2003). "The Significance of Recalcitrant Emotion (Or: Anti-Quasijudgmentalism)", in A. Hatzimoysis (ed.), *Philosophy and the Emotions: Royal Institute of Philosophy Supplement 52*, pp. c-45.

DARWIN, C. (1872/1965). *The Expression of the Emotions in Man and Animals*. Chicago: University of Chicago Press.

—— (1871/1981). *The Descent of Man, and Selection in Relation to Sex*. Princeton, N.J.: Princeton University Press.

DESCARTES, R. (1970). "The Passions of the Soul", in *The Philosophical Works of Descartes*, Vol. I, trans. by E. S. Haldane and G. R. T. Ross. Cambridge: Cambridge University Press.

DE SOUSA, R. (1987). *The Rationality of Emotions* Cambridge, Mass.: M.I.T. Press.

DOI, T. (1973). *The Anatomy of Dependence*. Tokyo: Kodansha International.

DWYER, S. (1999). "Moral Competence", in K. Murasugi and R. Stainton (eds.), *Philosophy and Linguistics*. Boulder, Col.: Westview.

EKMAN, P. (1971). "Universals and Cultural Differences in Facial Expressions of Emotion", in J. K. Cole (ed.), *Nebraska Symposium on Motivation*, vol. 19. Lincoln: University of Nebraska Press.

—— and FRIESEN, W. V. (1986). "A New Pan-Cultural Facial Expression of Emotion", *Motivation and Emotion*, 159–68.

FRANK, R. H. (1988). *Passions Within Reason: The Strategic Role of the Emotions*. New York: Norton.

FRIJDA, N. H. (1987). *The Emotions*. Cambridge: Cambridge University Press.

GIBBARD, A. (1990). *Wise Choices, Apt Feelings: A Theory of Normative Judgment*. Cambridge, Mass.: Harvard University Press.

GIGERENZER, G. and SELTEN, R. (2002). *Bounded Rationality: The Adaptive Toolbox*. Cambridge, Mass.: M.I.T. Press.

——— TODD, P., and the ABC Research Group. (1999). *Simple Heuristics that Make us Smart*. Oxford: Oxford University Press.

GREENSPAN, P. S. (1988). *Emotions and Reasons: An Inquiry into Emotional Justification*. New York: Routledge, Chapman and Hall.

——— (1995). *Practical Guilt: Moral Dilemmas, Emotions, and Social Norms*. New York: Oxford University Press.

——— (1998). "Moral Responses and Moral Theory: Socially Based Externalist Ethics", *Journal of Ethics*, 2, 103–22.

——— (2003). "Emotions, Rationality, and Mind/Body", in A. Hatzimoysis (ed.), *Philosophy and the Emotions: Royal Institute of Philosophy Supplement 52*, pp. 113–25.

——— (2004). "Practical Reasoning and Emotion", in A. Mele and P. Rawlings, *Handbook of Rationality*. Oxford: Oxford University Press.

——— (2007). "Practical Reasons and Moral 'Ought'", in R. Shafer-Landau (ed.), *Oxford Studies in Metaethics*, vol. II. Oxford: Oxford University Press.

——— (2009). Interview, in J. H. Aguilar and A. A. Buckareff (eds.), *Philosophy of Action: 5 Questions*. London: Automatic Press/VIP.

——— forthcoming-*a*. "Moral Reasons, Imperfect Duties, and Choice", *Social Philosophy and Policy*.

——— forthcoming-*b*. "Craving the Right: Emotions and Moral Reasons", in C. Bagnoli (ed.), *Morality and the Emotions*. Oxford: Oxford University Press.

GRIFTHS, P. E. (1997). *What Emotions Really Are: The Problem of Psychological Categories*. Chicago: University of Chicago Press.

GRIMES, K. (2003). "To trust is human". *New Scientist*, 178, 32–37.

HAIDT, J. (2001). "The Emotional Dog and Its Rational Tail: A Social Intuitionist Approach to Moral Judgment", *Psychological Review*, 108, 814–34.

———, KOLLER, S. H., and DIAS, M. G. (1993). "Affect, Culture, and Morality, or Is It Wrong to Eat Your Dog?" *Journal of Personality and Social Psychology*, 65, 613–28.

HAUSER, M. D. (2000). *Wild Minds: What Animals Really Think*. New York: Henry Holt.

——— (2006). *Moral Minds: How Nature Designed Our Universal Sense of Right and Wrong*. New York: HarperCollins.

HOFFMAN, M. L. (1982). "Development of Prosocial Motivation: Empathy and Guilt", in N. Eisenberg-Berg (ed.), *Development of Prosocial Behavior*. New York: Academic Press.

HUME, D. (1739–40/1978). *A Treatise of Human Nature*. Oxford: Clarendon Press.

ISCI, G. S., DIRENC, D., and OKTEM, Z. C. (2005). *Inside Outside In: Emotions, Body and Society*. Izmir, Turkey: Ege University Press.

IZARD, C. E. (1977). *Human Emotions*. New York: Plenum.

KAHNEMAN, D., SLOVIC, P., and TVERSKY, A. (eds.) (1982). *Judgment under Uncertainty: Heuristics and Biases*. Cambridge: Cambridge University Press.

KANT, I. (1993). *Grounding for the Metaphysics of Morals*. Indianapolis, Ind.: Hackett.

LeDOUX, J. (1996). *The Emotional Brain: The Mysterious Underpinnings of Emotional Life*. New York: Simon & Schuster.

LUTZ, C. (1986). "The Domains of Emotion Words on Ifaluk", in R. Harré (ed.), *The Social Construction of Emotions*. London: Oxford University Press.

MACKIE, J. L. (1995). *Persons and Values: Selected Papers*, Vol. II. Oxford: Clarendon Press.

MILL, J. S. (2001). *Utilitarianism*, 2nd ed. Indianapolis: Hackett.

MILLER, W. I. (1997). *The Anatomy of Disgust*. Cambridge, Mass.: Harvard University Press.

NICHOLS, S. (2008). "Sentimentalism Naturalized", in W. Sinnott-Armstrong (ed.), *The Psychology and Biology of Morality*. Cambridge, Mass.: MIT Press.

PANKSEPP, J. (1998). *Affective Neuroscience: The Foundations of Human and Animal Emotions*. New York: Oxford University Press.

PINKER, S. (1997). *How the Mind Works*. New York: W. W. Norton.

——. (2002). *The Blank Slate: The Modern Denial of Human Nature*. New York: Viking.

RAWLS, J. (1980). "Kantian Constructivism in Moral Theory", *Journal of Philosophy*, 77, 515–72.

—— (1993). *Political Liberalism*. New York: Columbia University Press.

—— (1998). *A Theory of Justice*, rev. ed. Cambridge, Mass.: Harvard University Press.

ROBINSON, J. (1995). "Startle", *Journal of Philosophy*, 92, 53–74.

ROLLS, E.T. (1999). *The Brain and Emotion*. Oxford: Oxford University Press.

ROZIN, P. and Fallon, A. E. (1987). "A Perspective on Disgust", *Psychological Review*, 23–41.

SHWEDER, R. A., MULCH, N.C., MAHAPATRA, M., and PARK, L. (1997). "The 'Big Three' of Morality (Autonomy, Community, and Divinity), and the 'Big Three' Explanations of Suffering", in A. Brandt and P. Rozin (eds.), *Morality and Health*. New York: Routledge.

SMITH, A. (1759/1982). *A Theory of the Moral Sentiments*. Indianapolis: Liberty Fund.

SOLOMON, R. C. (1976). *The Passions*. New York: Doubleday.

SRIPADA, C. and STICH, S. (unpublished). "Explaining Social Norms: Psychological and Evolutionary Foundations".

TURIEL, E. (1983). *The Development of Social Knowledge: Morality and Convention*. Cambridge: Cambridge University Press.

WAAL, F. DE (1998). *Chimpanzee Politics: Power and Sex among Apes*. Baltimore: Johns Hopkins University Press.

WILLIAMS, B. (1993). *Shame and Necessity*. Berkeley: University of California Press.

WILSON, J. Q. (1993). *The Moral Sense*. New York: The Free Press.

WITHERINGTON, D. C., CAMPOS, J. J., and MATTHEW J. HERTENSTEIN, M. J. (2002). "Principles of Emotion and its Development in Infancy", in G. Bremner and A. Fogel (eds.), *Handbook of Infant Development*. Oxford: Blackwell.

# CHAPTER 25

# EMOTIONS AND THE CANONS OF EVALUATION

## ROBERT C. ROBERTS

## 25.1 INTRODUCTION

Emotions have long been suspected of having something important to do with evaluation. If we rejoice over some event, we see it as good, and if we grieve over it, we see it as bad. But how does a further explanation go? Do we rejoice over the good event because it is good, or is the event good because we rejoice over it?

Plato thought that the human power of loving could be cultivated, by a good upbringing and philosophy, to become *accurate* in its evaluations—to respond to what is genuinely good with emotional pleasure, and to what is genuinely bad with displeasure (see *Republic*, Books III and VII; *Symposium*). He supposed that goodness and badness were objective qualities, and that emotion could therefore be an epistemic power, or at any rate an aspect of such. It is true that the same event (say, a victory in the athletic games) may occasion rejoicing in some people and grieving in others, but this is due to a lack of perspective on the part of the two groups of perceivers—to the fact that such people are not epistemically and morally mature, or to the fact that they are not expressing the best part of themselves at the moment.

Some of the most influential philosophers in the eighteenth century were of an opposite mind to Plato. They wanted to humanize our view of all things, among others the phenomena of value. These philosophers therefore tried to develop a theory according to which values derive from emotions. The qualities of good and bad are produced by human emotions and are not there, independently of our emotions, in the things we have emotions about. Among the values they were trying to explain were the moral ones, especially concepts of virtue and vice. Thus, David Hume:

The distinction of moral good and evil is founded on the pleasure and pain, which results from the view of any sentiment or character; and as that pleasure or pain cannot be unknown to the person who feels it, it follows, that there is just so much vice or virtue in any character, as everyone places in it, and that it is impossible in this particular that we can ever be mistaken.[1]

But objectivity has a way of sneaking back, and Hume is aware that vice is sometimes met with a pleasing sentiment of approbation, and virtue with repugnance or indifference. The intelligence and self-possession of a man's rival for a lady's hand may strike the man as repugnant, but they are not vice, for all that. So Hume says that the pleasure or uneasiness in question is "of a particular kind" (p. 471) and he lays down some restrictions on the sentiments that reliably determine values. Notably, the character has to be "considered in general, without reference to our particular interest" (p. 472): an emotional response to the character of a rival for a lady's hand will be a reliable index of the rival's virtue only if he is contemplated *disinterestedly*.[2] The discriminating person will no doubt have "interested" emotions, but will trust only the disinterested ones in matters of serious evaluation.

But failure of emotion to get moral objects right does not always stem from partiality or egoism. It may come from moral insensitivity or immaturity. A person may fail to recognize an injustice with indignation, not because he is in prospect of some personal gain from the injustice but because of a simple insensitivity to justice issues. Perhaps he has lived a sheltered life, or had poor moral training, or is simply too young. In general, virtues like compassion, truthfulness, and a sense of duty sensitize us emotionally to moral objects, and the lack of any of them leaves us morally obtuse. Hume is quite aware that moral character is unequally distributed in the population, so that not everyone's emotions—even if disinterested—sight moral objects with equal depth and precision. But Hume aside, the ability to adopt the point of view of an impartial, but morally committed, spectator in situations where one has powerful self-interests is itself a somewhat rare achievement of moral character. Needed to ensure that one's emotions discriminate virtue and vice is not a mental technique of adopting an impartial view, but a range of sensitivities

---

[1] *A Treatise of Human Nature*, ed. L. A. Selby-Bigge (Oxford: Oxford University Press, 1896), pp. 546–7.

[2] Adam Smith's version of this idea is that to be a reliable indicator of moral value an emotion must be one with which an "impartial spectator" can sympathize. See *The Theory of Moral Sentiments*, ed. E.G. West (Indianapolis: Liberty Classics, 1969), pp. 139–42 *et passim*.

borne along with virtue. Perhaps it is not sentiment *as such* that determines moral distinctions but the very special sentiments of the morally refined person, one who is *therefore* able to take a disinterested perspective.

But then the question arises, which *kind* of morally refined person? Even the sages of the world sometimes contradict one another in their moral sentiments. In "The Standard of Taste" [3] Hume points out that "the sage ULYSSES in the GREEK poet seems to delight in lies and fictions, and often employs them without any necessity or even advantage" (p. 228). Mohammed, in the Qur'an, "bestows praise on such instances of treachery, inhumanity, cruelty, revenge, bigotry, as are utterly incompatible with civilized society" (p. 229). In the second *Enquiry*, Hume remarks with evident disapproval that "EPICTETUS has scarcely ever mentioned the sentiment of humanity and compassion, but in order to put his disciples on their guard against it".[4] Hume would no doubt be equally repelled by the moral approvals and disgusts of Nietzsche's sage Zarathustra, or Dostoevski's warm appreciation of some of the more "monkish" traits of Alyosha Karamazov (humility, devotion to God; see *Enquiry*, pp. 73ff.).

The tone of Hume's remarks suggests he is not a relativist; in fact, he seems to take all the above-mentioned "sages" to be in serious error about values. So it seems that, if the distinctions on which correct moral judgments turn are created by emotions, they are not created by just any emotions. But if they are created by some special set of morally qualified emotions, or the emotions of some specially qualified person(s), one is left with the question, *Which* set? The emotions of *which kind* of sage? Emotions are themselves subject to moral formation, discrimination, and critique. *Within* a tradition—say, Stoicism or Christianity or Aristotle's or Nietzsche's ethics or Humean humanism—we find standards of correct and incorrect emotional response, and these may be applied, in part, by having a wise representative of the moral tradition in question consult and report his or her emotions in response to whatever is being morally adjudicated, including emotions. But behind these adjudicatory emotional responses are *conceptions* of right and wrong, of good and evil, of virtue and vice, moral *practices*, and differing understandings of human nature and of the nature of the universe in which we find ourselves.

The problem faced by the "sentimentalist" tradition, both in its eighteenth- and its twentieth- and twenty-first-century incarnations, is how to derive morality from emotions without putting morality into the emotions first. Or, how can we derive morality from human sentiments regarded as purely "natural" phenomena, that is, as having nothing properly moral already "in" them?

---

[3] In *Essays Moral Political and Literary*, edited by Eugene F. Miller (Indianapolis: Liberty Classics, 1985), pp. 226–49.

[4] *An Enquiry Concerning the Principles of Morals*, edited with an introduction by J. B. Schneewind (Indianapolis: Hackett, 1983), p. 103.

## 25.2 EMOTIONS IN MORALITY

Let us begin at a frankly moral level, and see whether we can work our way down to something like what the sentimentalists are seeking. I'll begin by sketching a person of moral character, and then propose some observations about the evaluation of emotions, using this person's emotions as a standard. Note that I use "moral" in a broad, somewhat older sense familiar from British early modern philosophy and translations of Aristotle in which any virtues other than the intellectual ones are "moral".[5] By the order in which I mention the virtues, I do not mean to suggest an order of importance.

This person will be truthful. He will seek to do and contribute significantly to justice in the institutions and relationships on which he has influence. He will be generous with his possessions and time, compassionate toward those who are suffering, not given to inordinate anger, or to vanity, arrogance, or an urge to dominate others just for the sake of dominating them. He will be grateful to those who have been generous with him. He will respect and value every other human being simply as such, independently of the other's wealth, education, ethnicity, good looks, and so forth; but he will also have appreciation for human accomplishments and other special excellences. He will have a sense of humor about himself, and will be open to admitting his errors as they come to light. He will have a sense of duty, and will not be easily frightened away from worthy undertakings, nor quickly discouraged by difficulties, but still will be neither reckless of risk nor stolidly persistent in hopeless enterprises. He will have a moderate and well-ordered inclination to indulge his appetites for food, sex, and the acquisition of wealth and prominence; large among his reasons for moderation of such appetites will be the effects of their expression on other people. He will be disinclined to bear grudges against those who have offended him, but will quietly make healthy and proper demands for respect from others. He will give a certain priority to some people who are "special" to his life, in concentric circles of mostly diminishing priority—of family, friends, colleagues, fellow citizens, and so forth. Where he is required to choose among courses of action suggested by more than one of the above traits, he will choose with intelligent sensitivity to the particulars of the situation, while realizing, with regret, that some situations call for hard and even "tragic" choices.

I intend this as a sketch of a morally mature person. I suppose it is a moral ideal. It is perhaps a synthesis (maybe an uneasy one) of classical, Christian, and liberal elements; it is not the whole of the ideal that I would endorse, but if I added more elements I would garner less agreement. It is not uncontroversial even

---

[5] Not "moral" in contrast with "ethical". See Bernard Williams, *Ethics and the Limits of Philosophy* (Cambridge, MA: Harvard University Press, 1985), Chapter 10.

as it stands; Aristotle and Nietzsche will disagree with some elements of it, as will Stoics and Kantians.

I think that each of the traits of this ideal person has something or other to do with emotions. The traits have different kinds of things to do with emotions. Some of them are dispositions to have emotions (as well as to perform actions) of certain types in certain types of situations (justice, compassion); others are dispositions to overcome or master emotions of certain types in certain types of situations (courage, perseverance); some seem to be dispositions *not* to have emotions of certain types in certain types of situations (see "not given to inordinate anger, or to vanity, and so forth"). Let us consider some possible evaluations of instances of emotions, in the light of this moral ideal.

Take anger. We sometimes criticize a person's anger by saying, "You shouldn't be angry with him; he did no harm." Or: "Don't be angry with him; he's not to blame for the harm he did." Criticisms of this sort have seemed to many philosophers and psychologists, including me, to suggest that anger is itself a kind of assessment or appraisal of the situation it is about. It is as though the state of anger itself attributes agency of harm and blameworthiness to the person at whom the anger is directed. So when we criticize a person's anger by denying the reality of the harm, the agency of harm, or the blameworthiness of the agent, we are evaluating an evaluation, appraising an appraisal, and finding it wanting.

How is it wanting? My descriptions of the criticism so far suggest that it is wanting as a representation: in the first case, the anger represents an agent as causing some kind of harm (it could be "psychological", like an insult or a slight) where in fact he caused no such harm; in the second case, the anger represents the agent as blameworthy for the harm, where in fact he isn't. But the criticism isn't just epistemological: "You made such-and-such cognitive mistake." The criticisms of the anger as a representation are intended as moral criticisms. In both cases, we might also say, "Your anger is unfair." Accuracy of evaluative attribution seems to be one of the conditions of justice; as just, a person's anger-episodes will be aimed at the right persons, for the right reasons. They will rightly represent people's offenses against oneself and what one cares about. And it seems that the morality of anger is entangled with its evaluative fittingness because anger itself, as an emotion type, makes moral kinds of attributions: agency and blame.

Consider another emotion type: joy. We sometimes criticize people's joy (or lack of it) for being vicious. We say, "You take the wrong kind of joy in people's expressions of gratitude to you. They gratify your sense of power as the Big Donor." Or we criticize their want of joy: "How wonderful that your mother has recovered from her illness; but it doesn't seem to matter to you." These evaluations of joy or its lack, like those of anger, also seem to turn on whether the emotion fits its object. The good thing about people's expressions of gratitude is not that they indicate your importance, but (among other things) that they express appreciation of the benefit and your benevolence. But the good that *your* joy attributes to them is that of making you important; therefore your joy is morally sub-par. Or: Your mother's recovery is a very good thing, but your lack of joy over it seems to indicate that you're missing this fact; so something seems to be morally wrong with you. In both cases, the moral value of the joy seems to turn on its accuracy as an evaluation of the situation; and the criticism is thus that the evaluation is errant.

But again, the errors are not on all fours with mere factual mistakes. They are specifically errors of evaluation, misattributions of value; and if we were to ask *how* they are erroneous in just this way, part of the story that my moral outlook would tell would be that they bespeak bad (dysfunctional, inappropriate, unhealthy) *personal relationships* (with the recipients of one's generosity, and with one's mother).[6] To the extent that these emotional misrelationships go back to emotional dispositions, they also express imperfections of character, because they express a deficiency of concern for something important, or positive concern for something that does not merit it. The one person would be deficient in the virtue of generosity (because too concerned with his own importance), the other in filial attachment.

An emotion type that is morally interesting in a different way is envy. In the moral outlook represented by the character ideal I sketched, the evaluation of envy is a universal thumbs-down. Anger and joy have both vicious and virtuous instances, but envy is pure vice, at least for the major type of envy, which we might call "invidious envy" (as opposed to "friendly envy"). When we explain why envy comes in for blanket moral rejection, we mention the following: to envy someone is to see the other as a rival for personal value or status, and to see oneself as losing in the rivalry. The personal value or status is so conceived that the more of it the other has, the less one has oneself, and the less of it the other has, the more one has. Because one's value or status is inversely proportional to that of the envied other, envy's impulse is to put the other down, to belittle him (in the eyes of others and in one's own eyes), to wish him bad luck. So envy is a kind of malice. It is seeing the other's superiority as a bad thing, and his potential for inferiority and failure as a good thing.

The negative evaluation of envy seems to show the same pattern that we have noted for the other emotion types. Partisans of the moral ideal I sketched will point out that in a couple of profound ways envy is a misrepresentation of its objects. It represents personal value or status as negatively correlated with that of the envied other; but personal value is not like that: my excellence does not depend on someone else's inferiority, nor does someone else's excellence imply my inferiority. And it represents the envied quality of the other (money, good looks, intelligence, education, etc.) as the proper measure of a person's value; but it isn't. The difference between envy and the other two emotion types we have considered is that the false appraisal is built into envy as a *type* of emotion, whereas joy and anger admit only of false *instances*. On this moral understanding, the morally ideal

---

[6] I have explored the constitutive role of emotions in personal relationships in "Emotional Consciousness and Personal Relationships", *The Emotion Review* I(3) (2009): 279–86.

person will never feel envy. And again, the error that envy commits is not just a factual error but one that stems from human concerns and is bad from the point of view of human concerns.

Finally, consider the emotion (or quasi-emotion) of amusement at things that are funny (jokes, cartoons, situations, narratives, turns of phrase, etc.). People are sometimes morally criticized for finding things funny. The response of the critic to the laughter of the morally immature is, "That's not funny." The amused person "sees something funny" in the joke or the situation, and the critic denies the veracity of the amused person's perception. When someone morally criticizes your envy of another's intelligence, the critic is not denying that intelligence is a good thing, or that it would be a good thing for you to have more of it (and is therefore "enviable"). Similarly, when your amusement is criticized for finding something funny that isn't funny, the critic is not denying that some of the elements of the funny are there. For example, he is not denying that you are seeing a genuine incongruity in the situation. But amusement is more than just noticing incongruities; it is finding them pleasurable in a special way. So, for example, if someone who stutters comes out with a particularly embarrassing combination of sounds, and then, because he is so flustered, comes out with another embarrassing combination in rapid succession, you might find this a pleasant incongruity and laugh. And your moral critic might say, "Sorry, that's not funny." He means that it is not a pleasant thing to see, because there's something pitiable in this situation that would, for the compassionate person, be salient enough to cancel any pleasure that the incongruity might otherwise evoke. Once again, the moral point of view makes a claim about what kind of thing fits, or fails to fit, the emotion type. If one asks a conceptually adept adherent of this moral point of view to explain why cases like that of the flustered stutterer are not funny, he will point to the kind of appraisal that amusement is and the kind of situation that the case of the stutterer is, and the misrepresentation that the one therefore is of the other. (In an analytic mood he might admit that the case of the stutterer *would* be funny if it were not so painful for the stutterer. In the above example, I assume that the stutterer is painfully humiliated, and not heartily laughing along with the other.)

## 25.3 PROSPECTS FOR SENTIMENTALISM

This account of the nature of moral appraisals of emotions encourages sentimentalism in one way, and in another way discourages it. It suggests that emotions are highly subject to moral appraisal because they are themselves appraisals in moral or potentially moral terms. Anger attributes responsibility and blame; joy attributes goodness; envy attributes negative self-value. We could go on: pride attributes positive self-value; fear attributes threat; compassion attributes suffering; grief attributes loss; guilt attributes guilt; shame attributes contemptibleness to oneself; contempt attributes contemptibleness to another; and so forth. In morality, all of these concepts come to take on moral import, and so in making the kind of attributions that emotions make, they are wide open to moral evaluation. They are susceptible to moral evaluation because they are moral evaluations (in a broad sense of "moral"). Emotions' affinity with morality encourages the thought that maybe morality can be explained in terms of the emotions.

But the nature of sentimentalism as a moral theory will not allow us to make the transition from the emotions to morality so easily. Sentimentalism is an ambitious naturalistic explanatory project; it aims to explain moral evaluation from something other than moral evaluation, something more "natural". The problem with deriving morality from the kind of emotions that we have been discussing so far is that they are already regulated with respect to moral concepts; the fact that we've been talking about an ideal of personal moral maturity as a base from which to appraise emotional appraisals vitiates the sentimentalist project by making the proposed explanation circular. The sentimentalist project must therefore posit, and find, a very special set of emotions that make something like moral appraisals and thus have the susceptibility to moral appraisal that we have seen in the everyday emotions that we've been considering, but do not originate in any morally circumscribed or trained organism. For example, babies seem to get angry long before they have mastered the language and concepts of agency- and blame-attribution, long before they know anything about the practices of morality. So baby anger, but not adult anger, might be an emotion from which a sentimentalist explanation of (part of) morality could proceed. The idea would be that aspects of morality are somehow pre-figured in this primitive, natural, non-conceptual anger, without having been put there by training in the terms of some moral tradition.

In a series of articles in the last few years, Justin D'Arms and Daniel Jacobson have worked to identify the concept of emotion that the sentimentalist theory requires, and to determine whether there are some such emotions. The needed concept, they argue, must be of emotions that are not imbued with judgment, thought, or belief, since presumably the judgments or thoughts involved in the emotions would include the kind that we have found in the anger, joy, envy, and amusement that we discussed above. Thus judgmentalist theories like those of Robert Solomon and Martha Nussbaum, which make judgments essential to, or even completely constitutive of emotions, are of no use to sentimentalists. Even a "quasijudgmentalist" theory like that of Patricia Greenspan, that takes thoughts to be essential to emotions, though without the thoughts' needing to rise to the status of judgments, will not do. Yet despite the stricture that these emotions must lack judgmental or thought content, they have to be the sort of thing that can be evaluated in terms of thought so that moral evaluation can apply to them and in some sense arise out of them. Emotions cannot *contain* judgments because, if they do, the sentimentalist explanation is circular; but they must be *potential* judgments or *susceptible to* evaluative judgments because, if they aren't, the sentimentalist explanation (of morality in terms of emotions) is deprived of its essential characteristic, the derivation of norms from emotions.

The case of "recalcitrant" emotions seems to D'Arms and Jacobson an important clue. An example is phobic fear. Someone with a phobia of riding in airplanes may judge with full conviction that air travel is one of the safest kinds around—much safer than biking or driving, which the phobic may do without anxiety. The knowing phobic's emotion is significantly disconnected from—indeed, at odds with—his beliefs, concepts, and judgments. Yet for most people, information about the relative safety of air travel does calm their fears, at least somewhat. Thus it looks as though the kind of emotion that phobic fear is occupies just the right place on a cognitivity scale: it's not completely unsusceptible of cognitive influence, but it's not fully cognitive either. D'Arms and Jacobson chide other theorists, like Allan Gibbard and John Deigh, for making emotions *too* noncognitive. They quote Deigh's comment that

What makes the [phobic] fear unreasonable is not that it contains a faulty belief but rather that it is felt despite a sound belief that should have immunized its subject from feeling this fear. What makes it unreasonable, that is, is not faulty reasoning resulting in false thoughts, but rather the persistence of a tropism that should have yielded to sound reasoning and firm belief.[7]

A tropism is an involuntary reorientation by an organism or one of its parts that is a positive (seeking) or negative (avoiding) response to a stimulus. An example is the sunflower's turning to receive the sun's rays more directly. D'Arms and Jacobson seem to accept Deigh's description of the phobic's fear as a tropism, but point out that this description leaves something important unexplained.

If fear is indeed a tropism—an involuntary, reflexive reaction—in what sense is it *unreasonable* when one knows one isn't in danger? If fear need not involve the thought that one is in danger, then why should it yield to the judgment that one is *not* actually in danger, as Deigh suggests?[8]

Good question. D'Arms and Jacobson offer the following sketch of an answer. The various emotion types (anger, fear, shame, etc.) are "special purpose mechanisms of the mind" that involve both feeling and behaving in characteristic ways in kinds of situations. For example, fear is a protective mechanism that involves emitting defensive behavior—say, fleeing or freezing in place—in situations that involve

---

[7] The quotation is from "Cognitivism in the Theory of Emotions", *Ethics* 104 (1994): 824–54; pp. 850–1.

[8] "The Significance of Recalcitrant Emotion (Or, Anti-Quasijudgmentalism)", in Anthony Hatzimoysis, ed., *Philosophy and the Emotions* (Cambridge: Cambridge University Press, 2003), pp. 127–45. Italics original.

threats to the organism. But particular implementations of these mechanisms may be "mistaken" in the sense that the situation to which the mechanism is responding in its characteristic way is not of the kind that fits it. This susceptibility to error occasions one kind of place for critical reflection: Is the situation really of the right kind? Is there really a threat in the environment? In more complicated organisms, strategic considerations will also become the matter of critical reflection: even if the situation is of the kind that "fits" the particular mechanism (say, the situation is dangerous and the mechanism is fear), it may be counterproductive for the mechanism to kick in. Maybe fear makes the situation even more dangerous. These features of the mechanism–situation relation thus make practical rational evaluation of emotions imperative, and so give rise to canons of evaluation. Some of these canons bear on "fit", others on strategic considerations.

If this is generally the right kind of story to tell about rational evaluations of emotions, then the account I gave in the second section of this chapter is otiose and too "cognitive", at least for the emotions that are at the foundation of our canons of evaluation. That account had it that the canons of evaluation for the emotions pick up on logical features of the emotions themselves—that anger attributes agency, fear threat, joy goodness, and so forth. But if the emotion types are really just tropisms, then they do not contain any such conceptual content. Thus D'Arms and Jacobson criticize my "defining propositions methodology" for individuating emotion types, and lump the account of emotions that I have given over the past 25 years together with "judgmentalist" and "quasijudgmentalist" accounts that make emotions into highly discursive, generically rational, language-dependent, sophisticated cognitive states that are far beyond the reach of many of the creatures to which we attribute emotions, such as non-linguistic mammals and infant children—and also beg the sentimentalist question.

I think this particular lumping of my construal account is a mistake, but it is easy to see how a reader would make it. The defining propositions methodology is exemplified *in excelsis* in Chapter 3 of *Emotions,*[9] where I offer more than fifty defining propositions for various emotion types. Here are four examples.

> **Fear:** *X presents an aversive possibility of a significant degree of probability; may X or its aversive consequences be avoided.*
>
> **Anger:** *S has culpably offended in the important matter of X (action or omission), and is bad (is to some extent an enemy of what is good); I am in a moral position to condemn; S deserves (ought) to be hurt for X; may S be hurt for X.*
>
> **Envy:** *It is important for me to have the personal worth that would be established by my being or appearing to be equal or superior to R in respect X; however, I am or appear to be inferior to R in respect X; may R be or appear to be degraded in respect X.*

---

[9] *Emotions: An Essay in Aid of Moral Psychology* (Cambridge: Cambridge University Press, 2003).

**Shame:** *I am or appear unrespectable (unworthy, disgraced) in some way that it is very important to be or appear respectable (worthy); may I be or appear more respectable.*[10]

These "propositions" are of course really propositional schemata, as is suggested by the variable terms that occur in many of them. They thus correspond to emotion *types* in a way that is supposed to follow roughly the typology of English emotion vocabulary. They are schemata for the actual propositional form possessed by instances of the type. For example, an instance of anger might have the form, *Joe intentionally hurt my sister's reputation, the bastard, and ought to have his teeth kicked in for doing so; yes, by golly, I'm in a position to judge.*

Despite the defining propositions approach to emotion type individuation, the view of emotions that I have proposed since the early 1980s[11] is not that emotions are judgments or discursive thoughts or quasijudgments (whatever that might be), nor that they necessarily involve such thinking, but that they are a kind of structured *perception* that I call concern-based construals. D'Arms and Jacobson seem to be half persuaded of this view, despite rejecting the construal view as a version of quasijudgmentalism. They say, "we think it has not yet been adequately explained just what is meant by a construal or perception of danger",[12] yet they exploit the idea when they say,

The unstable position of feeling an emotion while resisting its evaluative presentation is like being aware of perceiving an optical illusion. The famous Müller-Lyer lines continue to appear unequal in length, despite our knowledge to the contrary; similarly, anger that is acknowledged to be groundless continues to make an evaluative presentation.[13]

They point out that two significant disanalogies of emotions with sense perceptions are "the lack of dedicated emotional organs, and the fact that one need not be in the presence of the object of one's occurrent emotions".[14] But some significant analogies with sense perception are that (1) emotions *present* the situation in their

[10] These formulas are found on pp. 195, 204, 262, and 230. There they are preceded by discussions in the light of which they are to be understood.

[11] The earliest publication in which this view appeared was *Spirituality and Human Emotion* (Grand Rapids, MT: Wm. B. Eerdmans, 1982). It underwent further development in "Solomon on the Control of Emotions", *Philosophy and Phenomenological Research* 44 (1984): 395–403 and "What An Emotion Is: A Sketch", *The Philosophical Review* 97 (1988): 183–209. I applied it to the emotions of non-linguistic animals in "Propositions and Animal Emotion", *Philosophy* 71 (1996): 147–56.

[12] "Significance", p. 130. But see my rather extensive discussion of the nature of construals at *Emotions*, pp. 69–83.

[13] "The Moralistic Fallacy", *Philosophy and Phenomenological Research* 61 (2000): 65–90; p. 67.

[14] Ibid., footnote 5. The point about dedicated organs is true only if we restrict "organs" to the outer surface of the body, as common sense might restrict the organs of sense perception. But in truth the visual apparatus is not limited to eyes; vision is accomplished partly by dedicated parts of the brain. And the neuroscience of emotions is showing more and more that parts of the brain are analogously dedicated to emotion-production, and even more narrowly to the production of particular emotion types. For the anatomical story about an emotion type that we might call "fright", see Joseph LeDoux, *The Emotional Brain* (New York: Simon and Schuster, 1996).

characteristic ways (contrast mere judgment, which need not involve any "impression"), (2) emotions have structure (similarly, sense perceptions are always more than sense "data"; otherwise, they could not present states of affairs), (3) they present "information" (like sense perceptions, emotions can be propositionally characterized: if fear of a dog presents "the dog is dangerous", it seems analogous to the "message" I get from my eyes, "the sparrow is on the reed"), and (4) emotions can "fit" or not "fit" the situations they present. In all of these interlocking ways, emotions—even when experienced by (at least some) non-human animals—are like perceptions and go beyond being mere tropisms.[15]

So what about my claim that emotions have a propositional structure and so can be type-individuated by defining propositions? How can a propositional analysis apply to emotions that are so "basic" as to be experienced by dogs, babies, and other beings that lack language? I distinguish three ways in which a mental state can be propositional.[16] In the strongest sense, a mental state is propositional if it has explicit propositions (sentences, occurrent thoughts) as its content. This possibility is most likely to be instantiated when the state is brought on by "utterances", oral, written, or thought-discursive. Thus if I get angry as a result of somebody's telling me what some offender did, or if I read the story about his action, or if I come to construct it by reflectively putting together various pieces of evidence, my anger will have excellent prospects of being propositional in the first, strongest, sense. A mental state will be propositional in a second degree if its intentional object is such as can be accessed only by someone who has had a certain conceptual/propositional training, one involving discourse, even if the present accessing of it involves no actual use of language or discursive thought. So when a microscopist trained in tissue pathology (with lectures, reading, and discussion as required background) sees basal cell cancer on a slide, she is seeing something that could not be seen by someone who lacks her conceptual/propositional training, and so her perception is propositional even if she does no discursive reasoning as a direct lead-up to seeing the cancer. Emotions can be propositional in this way as well. For example, I may become alarmed upon seeing the oil light on my dashboard light up as I cruise down the highway, and do so without processing any discursive propositions. But my emotion may still depend on my having the relevant information about automobiles' need for oil pressure and the significance of the red light. We might say that emotions of this kind are indirectly propositional. The propositional form of the construal will come out when the subject or someone else—say, his therapist—explains his emotion.

[15] I discuss the emotions of nonhuman animals in "The Sophistication of Non-Human Emotion", in Robert W. Lurz, ed., *Philosophy of Animal Minds* (Cambridge University Press, forthcoming 2009).

[16] These distinctions were first proposed in "Propositions and Animal Emotion", but elaborated more definitely in *Emotions*, pp. 106–12.

The third and weakest sense in which emotions are propositional is that they are susceptible of reasonably accurate propositional characterization. This is the sense in which I claim that the vast majority of emotions are propositional, whether their subjects are cultured adult human beings, six-month-old infants, or giraffes or chipmunks. In a sense a chipmunk has the concept of a threat; that is, it sees certain configurations of things (that is, situations) in its environment in a way strongly analogous to the construal of situations that we linguistic animals would characterize with the word "threatening". It does not see everything in this way; it picks out only certain configurations of things in this characteristic concern-based way. For example, it does not always see major predators this way, but only ones that are in a position (proper distance, not behind an effective barrier, etc.) to constitute a threat.[17] This power of significant object-in-situation discrimination is our reason for thinking the chipmunk has a concept. It picks out other things as rivals or as offenders or as sex partners, and these too are types of objects of its concerns, with different kinds of situation-relative significance for it. It does all this probably without having any vocabulary for it.[18] But as long as it sees the various situations in distinct ways that are strongly analogous to the ways of concern-based situational seeing that we would call fear, jealousy, and anger, we are warranted in calling the mental state propositional in the third and weakest sense.

I wrote "reasonably accurate propositional characterization" above because of course we don't think that our concept of *threat* is exactly right for the way chipmunks see things when they are frightened. "Threat" has special associations for us human beings that chipmunks have no way of making. But then, "threat" has associations for one human individual that it doesn't have for another, or for members of one culture or generation that it doesn't have for another. It's a somewhat vague concept, but that doesn't keep us from thinking that it characterizes pretty well the way people see things when they are afraid.

One of the advantages of a perceptual view of emotions over judgmentalist or quasijudgmentalist views is that it makes better room for the whole range of beings that are capable of having emotions, and makes it possible for us to see emotional similarities at a wider variety of places on the phylogenetic ladder. A related advantage for the sentimentalist is that the third sense of "propositional" gives the sentimentalist just the paradoxical properties he needs emotions to have if his theory is to have even a prayer of success. If emotions are just tropisms, sentimentalism seems doomed because nothing even remotely like rational canons of evaluation could be grounded in them. If emotions are full-fledged evaluative

---

[17] I give examples and develop the idea that animals perceive not just things but situations, and thus have perceptions that have a propositional structure, in "The Sophistication of Non-Human Emotions".

[18] But see the fascinating studies of prairie dog signaling, for example, C.N. Slobodchikoff, C. Kiriazis, C.Fisher, and E. Creef, "Semantic Information Distinguishing Individual Predators in the Alarm Calls of Gunnison's Prairie Dogs", *Animal Behavior* 42 (1991): 713–19.

judgments, then any extraction of the canons from them would be circular. But if emotions can be construals that are propositional, but propositional in no stronger sense than the third one, then emotions have at least a long shot of serving the sentimentalist purpose. Some of them have not yet been infected with the moral qualities that the sentimentalist wants to ground in them, but they are still something more "cognitive" than tropisms.

# 25.4 Two Proposals for Individuating Emotion Types

D'Arms and Jacobson resist the construal view because of misgivings about its commitments to propositional structure and the applicability of the idea of perception. But they have their own quasi-cognitive concept of emotions, specially designed for sentimentalist use. For them, too, emotions are not merely tropisms: "we hold that emotions involve evaluative presentations".[19] They make much of the fact that English has nominalizations that correspond to some of the main emotion types and whose surface grammar seems to suggest that instances of these types attribute type-fixed properties to situations that they may thereby either fit or fail to fit. Thus amusement attributes *the funny*, fear *the fearsome*, guilt *guilt*, and shame *the shameful*. D'Arms and Jacobson think this conceptualization superior to the defining propositions methodology (dpm) because it does more credit to the theoretical requirement that emotions be somehow "noncognitive", and thus provides a possible non-question-begging source for the canons of evaluation. In their view, such canons will be in the first and most basic place norms for the fittingness of the attributions that the emotion types involve; and then, perhaps, other (strategic and moral) norms governing whether to feel the emotions. The norms of fittingness will be conceptual, propositional, reflective, and discursive; but the emotion types from which they arise will be possessors of properties that do not yet have this "rational" character.

Thus, according to D'Arms and Jacobson, people who think that emotions already have the kind of cognitive structure that is suggested by words like "judgment" and "thought", as well as by the defining propositions methodology, have things back-wards. The most basic emotions don't *have* this structure, but at most *suggest* it. The norms that we impose for the fittingness of emotions create, by a kind of retrospect, the *illusion* that they are speaking to a structure that was already in the emotions.

---

[19] "The Moralistic Fallacy", p. 67.

What shall we say about this alternative to the defining propositions methodology? (Let us call it the formal property methodology, fpm for short.)

I would note that defining propositions provide the same kind of criterion as the formal properties purport to supply for whether an emotion fits a situation, but instead of saying that a fear-token fits its situation only if the situation is fearsome, we analyze the fearsome, so to speak. If one of the elements of the defining proposition is missing from a situation to which the emotion is directed, then the emotion does not fit the situation. Thus (following my defining proposition for fear) if a situation to which fear is directed does not actually include a significant probability of the attributed aversive possibility, then the fear is misplaced. But it looks to me as though the dpm does a better criteriological job than the fpm.

First, note that while we can formulate a defining proposition for any emotion type we know of, only some of the emotion types have the nominalizations on which the fpm trades. Some of the major categories of emotions seem to lack the needed nominalization. What is the property that corresponds to anger?—The angering? The offensive? The first seems contrived, and the second seems to carry too broad a concept. What about joy?—The enjoyable? The joyworthy? The good? Or grief—the grievable, the griefworthy, the grievous? Other emotion types do have corresponding nominalizations, but the latter do not denote the property attributed by the emotion type. The intentional object of outrage is not the outrageous, nor is the intentional object of envy the enviable.

This last example is instructive. In distinguishing an emotion's fit from other kinds of appropriateness D'Arms says, "it might be inappropriate, because mean-spirited, to envy your friend's well-deserved success. But to think so is surely not yet to deny that the success is enviable."[20] It would be easy to be misled here by the surface of the language. "Enviable" ought, one might think, to denote the property that makes situations fit the emotion of envy. But it doesn't.[21] To call your friend's well-deserved success "enviable" means something like "it's worth having" or "it's worth having for me". And that is *one* of the conditions for envy, as an emotion, to "fit" what it is about. But this is hardly the whole story about what envy attributes to the situation. Envy has been thought universally unfitting because it involves evaluating a situation as *bad because someone else has some kind of excellence*, or evaluating someone's having something good as *bad because it diminishes one's own status*. Being "enviable" in the sense that is the property that envy, the emotion, attributes to situations, is a complex relational property that requires something like a defining proposition to lay out. It requires analysis that is beyond the power of any current English nominalization to convey. The formal property methodology is thus a blunt and awkward tool by comparison with the defining propositions methodology.

---

[20] "Two Arguments for Sentimentalism", *Philosophical Issues* 15 (2005), *Normativity*, 1–21, p. 3.
[21] D'Arms and Jacobson note this fact at "The Moralistic Fallacy", p. 71, footnote 14.

Because it is analytical, the dpm makes it clear where counterexamples might get a foothold against any defining proposition that might be proposed, and thus has the potential to be more rigorous, because more carefully testable, than the fpm. D'Arms and Jacobson take this very openness to counterexample to be a weakness of the dpm. They say,

Understood as an account of the thoughts necessary to have a given emotion, even the best glosses either are subject to counterexample, or else succeed only because the relevant thought can be attributed to an agent simply because he is feeling the emotion.[22]

Their idea here is that to be a good testing tool, counterexamples need, not only to eliminate inept formulas but to sort toward formulas that are counterexample-free; but the dpm is such that plausible counterexamples to any defining proposition can *always* be found. As an example of the vulnerability to counterexample they take Philippa Foot's claim that pride requires that the subject see what he is proud of as "in some way splendid and in some way his own".[23] But their interpretation of her formula is uncharitable. They take it as implying that for someone to feel proud of a team's win, the proud person must construe the win as "his own doing", that he is "himself responsible for the triumph", that he had "extravagant thoughts about his own role in the outcome" (ibid.). But Foot didn't say this, and has no reason to accept the implication. She only says that the proud person must see the win as "in some way his own". Typical cases would be those in which the team belongs to the proud person's school, town, or region. The team may even have been "elected" one's own, as in my 8th grade classroom in north Wichita, Kansas in the 1950s where it was *de rigueur* to align oneself either with the New York Yankees or the Brooklyn Dodgers during the World Series. "Who are you for?" we would ask one another. And the team you were "for" would be your team. If we had not aligned ourselves in any way with one of the teams, it would make no sense for one of us to feel proud if, say, the Yankees won the Series.

As to the second part of the objection: It is true that once an analyst is satisfied that a clause in a defining proposition expresses a necessary condition, she will attribute the corresponding "thought" to the subject of an emotion of that type, and look for ways that the subject can be said to have the "thought". She will respond to proffered counterexamples by devices for saving the analysis. Then the question will be, "Is the device a legitimate way to handle counterexamples of this kind?" and the device will be assessed for its merits. The device I just used to save Foot's analysis of pride was an interpretation of the clause "in some way his own". Another device I deploy in this chapter is to think of emotions as a kind of perception rather than as a judgment or

---

[22] "Significance", p. 135.

[23] Ibid. The quotation is from Foot's "Hume on Moral Judgement" in her *Virtues and Vices* (Berkeley: University of California Press, 1978), p. 113. Foot makes the condition a matter of the subject's belief; I have phrased it as a matter of construal.

linguistically discursive thought. The battle against the defining propositions methodology needs to be fought on such fronts as these.

The formal (noncognitive) property methodology seems to suppose that the
properties in question (*the fearsome, the shameful, the funny, the enviable*, etc.) are
simple and unanalyzable. If they are not simple and unanalyzable, they threaten to fail
the purposes of sentimentalism by being too conceptual. But if they are simple and
unanalyzable, then we would like to know how the defining propositions have even
the degree of plausibility that D'Arms and Jacobson admit they have. For they say,

...the obvious plausibility of Foot's gloss, and some others like it, seems to demand
explanation. We will suggest that what these glosses capture must be reinterpreted, not as
a logical requirement for what to count as pride, but as circumscribing the conditions
under which that feeling is fitting.[24]

So it's not the emotion that has the analyzable complexity, but the norm that applies to
the emotion. But this explanation just shifts the locus of mystery from the emotion to
the norm. How does the norm get to have the conceptual structure that it has, if what it
is supposed to apply to has no such structure? For example, if the norm is,

*Thou shalt feel no pride in what is not thine,*

how does the concept of *thine* come to govern this feeling that in itself makes no
claim that the thing in which I take pride is *mine*? I find the idea that an emotion is
a simple impression opaque, whereas it seems fairly clear that if an emotion is a
perception that is structured in such a way as to be analyzable, as to type, in a
defining proposition, then a norm that utilizes the concepts on which the defining
proposition turns would naturally apply to it. Further, it seems that we can know
that a norm for pride applies to a particular emotion episode only if we know what
type of emotion it is; but how we can know this if we are effectively mute with
respect to the analysis of the emotion is beyond me.

D'Arms and Jacobson do not say that there is no use for the formulas that cognitively
oriented emotion theorists offer as defining propositions; they just say that these
formulas are actually norms for the fittingness of the emotion type rather than defining
propositions. But if defining propositions are infinitely vulnerable to counterexample,
why wouldn't the norms that have the same form suffer the same debility?

D'Arms and Jacobson object that the defining propositions methodology is too
fine-grained:

Our worry is...with the possibility of infinitesimal division between cognate emotions.
This threatens to turn seemingly genuine disputes over the nature of an emotion into
merely terminological quarrels.

The judgmentalist methodology seems to license exceedingly fine-grained distinctions
between emotions, which can obscure their fundamental similarities. The usefulness of

---

[24] Ibid., p. 136.

Roberts' distinction between friendly and invidious envy, for instance, can easily be doubted. This distinction, which is motivated by a desire to differentiate morally permissible envy from more vicious strains, does so by assimilating the benign form with mere longing.[25]

T'ain't so. Is this a case in which the fpm obscures difference by discouraging analysis? In mere longing (say, wishing I were smarter) no rival is in the picture, but in friendly envy, the good that is envied is seen in terms of a rival who has the good (say, my smart sister; I've always competed with her, but I also adore her). The main difference between friendly envy and invidious envy is the nature of the rivalry. The rivalry with my sister is playful and does not entail malice, any more than the rivalry in a game of Scrabble implies malice toward the opponent. Because my emotion about my sister's smarts is a rivalry it will, however, imply a feeling of triumph (friendly triumph, no doubt) when on occasion I solve a puzzle faster than she.

Contemporary sentimentalism is not foundational*ist* in quite the way early modern versions were; in particular, it does not seriously expect to achieve the social firmness of universal assent. As a theoretical program, however, contemporary sentimentalism is seeking a foundation and a way to attach norms firmly to that foundation. It therefore has a stake in there being a fixed set of stable, culturally non-negotiable (or extremely widespread) basic human emotion types. This is the idea of a class of humanly primitive emotions that have not been infected with cognition, worldview, beliefs, or moral or other evaluative tradition. The fpm as a methodology corresponds to such a program; the dpm is anathema because the list of emotion types it generates is not sufficiently secure against contamination by tradition, and therefore is too long, too fine-grained, and too diverse. In particular, if *moral* canons are to be somehow derived from the emotions, there must be a class of emotion types that are free of moral taint, yet beguiling of morality. Is there such a set of emotions?

## 25.5 ARE THERE NATURAL EMOTIONS?

D'Arms and Jacobson admit that many emotions fail to satisfy these requirements. In attempting to determine "the order of priority between emotions and evaluative judgments",[26] they distinguish basic human emotions or natural emotion kinds, from what they call "cognitively sharpened" ones. The former

---

[25]  Ibid., pp. 133–4.
[26]  "Significance", p. 143.

are prior to, and partially fix the content of, the concepts used to regulate them. An experience of shame or fear involves a distinctive sort of emotional evaluation, and the judgment that something is shameful or fearsome must be understood in terms of such appraisals. But the critics of sentimentalism were not entirely wrong. There *also* exist a wide range of states, which we have called cognitive sharpenings, that are best understood as involving beliefs or thoughts. These states are not amenable to sentimentalism precisely because they are compatible with a judgmentalist account.[27]

It is questionable whether, on their noncognitive view of the evaluations that the basic emotions make, D'Arms and Jacobson can legitimately talk about "the terms" of those evaluations. But if we employ the dpm, we can make sense of the idea. Let us assume that the main concepts expressed in the defining propositions for the natural emotion types identify the "terms" in which the appraisals embodied in their tokens are to be understood. For example, in the defining proposition for shame, the concept of *unworthy of respect* is one central "term" in shame; and another is *way in which it is important to be or appear worthy of respect*. Thus when a person feels shame over some quality or action or relation of his, he construes himself as being or appearing, on its account, unworthy of respect in a way that it is important for him to be or appear worthy of respect. This evaluation is subject to evaluation in its turn: does the existence or appearance of the quality, action, or relation in question *actually* make a person unworthy of respect?; and, is it really important to be or appear worthy of respect in this way? For example, does having a mother who speaks with a Dutch accent make a person unworthy of respect? Is it really important to appear to others to be a non-immigrant? If the answer to both of these questions is "yes", the shame fits the situation; if not, it doesn't. On the dpm, then, we have a reasonably clear account of what it is for the natural emotions "partially [to] fix the content" of their evaluative norms. The norms evaluate the natural emotions for whether the situation to which the emotion is directed is properly read as having the evaluative features that the emotion "claims" the situation to have.

Sentimentalism aspires to give an account of the origin of the norms that govern the natural emotions. Let us consider first a case that is simple in a certain respect. Envy (that is, invidious envy) bids fair to be a natural emotion. It seems to be pan-cultural, at least. According to the defining proposition above, in envy a person ascribes to himself a potential personal worth that depends on his being or appearing equal or superior to a rival in a certain respect (for example, beauty or intelligence). The Christian tradition has regarded this kind of envy as one of the capital vices, and I have suggested that one reason is that this attribution is false: this kind of personal worth does not exist. If this is right, then the norm for envy is a simple rule:

*Envy is out.*

---

[27]  Ibid., pp. 143–4; italics added.

This rule is not found in the defining proposition, but it does depend on the structure identified in the defining proposition; envy would not be so simply "out" if the properties that envy attributes to situations were ever instantiated. Any answer to the question where this norm came from will have to make reference to the nature of envy's attribution, but clearly the norm does not come from the internal structure of envy. Where does it come from?

A variety of answers are possible. Christians may say that the rule comes from revelation: a story that gives God's view of the worth of persons. Kant will say that the rule comes from practical reason; somehow reason tells us that we have intrinsic dignity and thus don't get our worth by equaling or besting others. Utilitarianism will tell us that the project of getting personal worth the way envy would prescribe is counterproductive of happiness. If sentimentalism is to have its own distinctive story to tell, it will need to explain the proscription of envy by reference somehow to the nature of emotions. If envy has no good instances, the emotional basis of the norm for envy will have to come from *other* basic emotions. Which others might these be?

Most other natural emotions contrast with envy in having some good instances. Consider anger and shame. Many situations in which people get angry or feel ashamed do not call for anger or shame, but presumably some do. So the norms for the fit of these emotions are more complicated than the norm for envy. It would be a daunting task to try to specify them in detail, and one is tempted to fall back, with Aristotle, on the notion of the person of practical wisdom. No doubt the person of practical wisdom will be a pretty reliable judge of the fittingness of emotions, and there is little doubt, as well, that his judgments about emotions will themselves have an emotional character: he will have a certain repugnance for unfitting shame and anger, for example. Or he may feel ashamed of his envy, or angry or contemptuous about the envy of others. But these observations will be of little comfort to the sentimentalist, because the emotions by which the person of practical wisdom judges emotions will be "cognitively sharpened" ones, and therefore not fit for use in the sentimentalist theory of norms. So if we try to derive the prohibition against one natural emotion (envy) from other natural emotions, we don't get the result that sentimentalists want; we get that result only if we use "non-natural", morally qualified, anger and shame. But then we have fallen back into the circle that sentimentalism needs to avoid.

But even if we could get a canon for the proscription of one natural emotion from other natural emotions, the question would arise why we should not run the argument the other way. Even if natural anger and shame rule out natural envy, by what canon do we take our bearings from this anger and shame? Why not take our bearings from envy and deny the reliability of this anger and shame?

So far in this section I have been granting that several emotion types might be natural or basic emotions. But we might wonder whether the notion of a basic emotion, as required by sentimentalism, is a mere theoretical abstraction or a fiction. D'Arms and Jacobson give a provisional list: "amusement, anger, contempt, disgust, embarrassment, envy, fear, guilt, jealousy, joy, pity, pride, shame, and sorrow".[28] The idea of a basic emotion, as it arises in sentimentalism, is the idea of an emotion prior to its subjection to norms for its fittingness. But the list of emotion type names that I have just quoted is not limited to emotions that are basic in this sense. The emotion dispositions of the morally well-formed person whose character I sketched at the beginning of this chapter will include most of the emotions in this list. But the very idea that this person is emotionally well formed is that his emotions are more or less automatically regulated according to the norms of fittingness. As Aristotle would say, this person's fears, angers, prides, joys, and sorrows are felt on the *right* occasions, for the *right* reasons, and so forth. So this person's fears and shames are not basic but "cognitively sharpened". Now we might ask about the people who are less well formed. From the fact that they are less well formed than the moral paradigm, it does not follow that they are not formed at all. In fact, it seems plausible that D'Arms and Jacobson's list of basic emotions, as found in any human being over the age of three, will have been socially conditioned. That is, they will spring in part from the inculcation of principles as to what are appropriate objects of fear, anger, shame, sorrow, etc.

People feel shame according to their concept of what makes them unworthy of respect. But to have a concept of what makes a person unworthy of respect is just what it is to have a norm for the fittingness of shame. Shame is probably pan-cultural, all right; and that is why it might be thought to be a basic or natural emotion. That is, it is pan-cultural *as a type*. The defining proposition is an attempt to analyze that pan-cultural concept—to abstract from the *particular kinds* of things that people are ashamed of. But people are ashamed of many different kinds of things: having thin hair, being unable to keep up in a graduate philosophy seminar, being naked at the beach, having parents who speak with a Dutch accent, being crippled, being homosexual, being a religious believer, being an atheist, making less than $150,000 a year, making more than $150,000 a year, masturbating in public, being a coward, having spent too much time in one's early philosophical career fixing up old houses, spending money needlessly on oneself while neglecting those in need around one, making fun of cripples, laughing at stutterers, and so forth. The reader will probably think that some of the things in this list are proper occasions for shame, while others are not. So it's not just shame *as such* that should appear in a list of natural emotions but a particular *kind* of shame that will suggest the proper norm for shame-fit (but without actually having that norm). I have no idea where to find such an emotion type.

Some of the "basic" emotions in D'Arms and Jacobson's list have distinct facial expressions and other physiological markers; in the ideal case, then, every instance

---

[28] "Significance", p. 138.

of a basic emotion type will carry the markers of the type. But this kind of universality does not get us anything like universal standards of fittingness for the type. The fact that joy is correlated reliably with a certain facial expression and other physiological markers does not tell us what particular kinds of situations are going to evoke joy in any individual; that will be controlled by the person's values, by her internalized norms for joy, her character. It is hard to see how the really basic instances of the type, such as infantile anger—that is, the instances that are not shaped by an already in-place system for evaluating their fit—are going to yield anything like the definite canons of evaluation that sentimentalism wants to explain by them or ground in them. And so forth for all of the so-called basic emotions in the list.

D'Arms and Jacobson object to the fineness of grain afforded by the dpm, because it threatens to undermine the case for basic emotions. But this objection is poorly targeted. It is not defining propositions that undermine the case for basic emotions but what appear to be the empirical data: the ubiquity, in human life, of standards, good or bad, rational or irrational, for the more particular situation-types that evoke the common emotions. Perhaps all anger attributes agency and blame and offense, and perhaps it is pan-cultural; but this formal similarity and universality are compatible with quite various standards for what counts as an offense, and therefore for what counts as fitting anger. It is the work of the moral psychologist or virtue ethicist to discuss these varieties of standards as they are embodied in the human virtues and vices. The defining propositions methodology is important to this work, not just in identifying a few universal emotion types but in distinguishing virtuous sub-types from vicious or morally indifferent ones. The joy in the grateful response, for example, that is characteristic of generosity is *not* a joy in the submissiveness of the grantee but a joy in the grantee's conscious-ness of wellbeing and in the reciprocal goodwill of grantor and grantee. Without some such distinction among joys, all of which have a common defining proposi-tion, the philosopher could not get to the heart of generosity.

Emotions that have not undergone cognitive sharpening via normative shaping are very hard to find in human life. We can no doubt find some in earliest infancy, though we will probably not find representatives of all the types in D'Arms and Jacobson's list (for example, envy, contempt, embarrassment, guilt). Similarly, we can find some in the animal world. The farther down the phylogenetic scale we go, the more "basic" will the emotions be. But these will hardly serve the purposes of sentimentalism, which seeks to ground fairly sophisticated canons of human evaluation in the formal structure of emotion types. The old problem persists: we can't derive canons of evaluation from emotions that already embody such canons without falling into a circle, and we can't derive such canons from emotions that don't embody such canons, because there is no guarantee that the evaluations they embody are reliable or, if they are reliable (say, for survival purposes), that they are the kind of canons (say, moral or aesthetic) that we are seeking.

## 25.6  CONCLUSION

Sentimentalism needs something like the construal view of emotions. The construal view ascribes to emotions just the right kind of "cognitivity"—at the minimal end of the continuum, "propositional" content in an attenuated sense, but nevertheless in a sense that allows, in its defining propositions methodology, for greater analytical precision than the formal property methodology allows; and at the maximal end of the continuum, explicit propositional involvement in the structure of emotions. Thus the construal view makes more promising the sentimentalist project of deriving explicit rational norms from "basic" (non-rational) emotions. Nevertheless, the project seems to be without hope of realization, because emotions that are rich enough in normative content to yield the kind of norms that sentimentalism intends to explain already presuppose the norms; and ones that do not contain the norms are too poor in normative content to yield norms.

CHAPTER 26

........................

# DEMYSTIFYING SENSIBILITIES: SENTIMENTAL VALUES AND THE INSTABILITY OF AFFECT

........................

JUSTIN D'ARMS AND
DANIEL JACOBSON

## 26.1 THE STABILITY OF SENTIMENTAL VALUES
........................

Sentimentalist theories hold, of some target value, that it essentially "depends on some internal sense or feeling, which nature has made universal in the species" (Hume 1975: 173). We shall term Hume's universal feelings—these days commonly called basic or pan-cultural emotions, which are part of normal human nature—

We are grateful to Peter Goldie, Geoff Sayre-McCord, Michael Weber, and audiences at Bowling Green and The Inter-University Center in Dubrovnik for helpful comments on earlier drafts of this chapter.

the *sentiments*.[1] As a matter of terminology, we propose to adopt a broad conception of the emotions, so as to include disparate states, some of which are culturally constructed rather than anthropologically universal, while understanding the sentiments in a narrower and more technical sense, as a term of art. In this chapter we will simply assert that the class of sentiments includes amusement, anger, contempt, disgust, fear, guilt, pride, and shame. The important point is that sentiments are (nearly) universal human responses, not that humans alone are capable of them. This universality ensures that, although we may disagree profoundly over what is funny, shameful, or worthy of pride, our distinct perspectives on such questions concern a common subject matter, founded in our shared sentiments.

Sentimentalist theories are thus response-dependent, in that they explain some set of values in terms of associated sentiments, as the funny might be explained by way of amusement. By contrast, the leading response-independent theory of humor, the *incongruity theory*, holds (roughly) that the funny is the incongruous.[2] Some of the attraction of sentimentalism arises from the obvious inadequacy of alternative accounts of what is at issue in disputes over such values as the funny. These disagreements clearly seem to involve differences in sense of humor that cannot be settled by appeal to some response-independent conception of incongruity. Hence, in order for the incongruity theory even to be plausible, it must become tacitly response-dependent. As Roger Scruton (1987: 162) puts it, "To know what is meant by 'incongruous' you would have to consult, not some independent conception, but the range of objects at which we laugh." We prefer to phrase Scruton's trenchant observation this way: to know what is meant by incongruous, you would have to consult your sense of humor.[3] One problem with simply consulting dispositions to laughter (or amusement) is that this threatens to undermine the possibility of criticizing people's tastes and responses. The funny is a normative concept, not simply a dispositional one, so it must be possible to insist that something granted to amuse most people (or even oneself) nevertheless fails to be funny. Idiosyncratic senses of humor are not guaranteed to be false

---

[1] It is an empirical question whether there are any such sentiments, just how many exist, and which of the states commonly called emotions count as sentiments (D'Arms and Jacobson 2003). This terminology makes sensibility theory a relative, rather than a version of, sentimentalism. This is a semantic issue, but we're now inclined to distinguish views such as ours that claim priority for the sentiments from those of McDowell (1985, 1987, 1996) and Wiggins (1987), on which there is no priority, in either direction, between value property and evaluative response.

[2] See Jacobson (1997) for discussion of the insights and inadequacies of response-independent theories of humor.

[3] There are three reasons to prefer our formulation, though we do not mean to be charging Scruton with error; we put these forward as friendly amendments to his view. (1) Laughter doesn't always express amusement, but it's only relevant when it does—nervous laughter doesn't count. (2) Not everything that in fact amuses us is funny, even by our own lights; sometimes we're in a silly mood or sleep-deprived. (3) Not everything that amuses some (or even most) people is funny, according to us. Elitism and idiosyncrasy must not be rendered incoherent or necessarily false.

simply because they are unusual; on the contrary, some people might be better judges of what is and isn't funny. Whereas the simplest form of sentimentalism would analyze the funny as whatever amuses, it is more promising for a sentimentalist theory of humor to hold that what it is for something to be funny is for amusement at it to be *fitting* (or, equivalently, for it to merit amusement).[4]

Hence the most tenable form of sentimentalism, in our view, is a version of the fitting attitude theory of value, where the relevant attitudes are the sentiments and the values targeted are limited to those directly associated with some particular sentiment. This theory, which we call *rational sentimentalism*, explains the shameful in terms of fitting shame, the funny in terms of fitting amusement, and so forth. Although this theory does not aspire to give an all-encompassing theory of value or an account of generic goodness, some psychologically important but philosophically neglected values are particularly amenable to this treatment. These are what we'll call *sentimental values*, whose conceptual connection to independently identifiable sentiments seems especially clear: values such as the funny, shameful, fearsome, disgusting, enviable, pride-worthy, and the befitting of anger.[5] Response-independent accounts of any of these values founder for the same reason the incongruity theory of humor is untenable: either they fail to capture what is at stake in the attribution of the value, or they tacitly rely on our senses of disgust, shame, and so forth in order to determine when the putatively response-independent characteristic obtains. Thus some sort of sentimentalist account of such values seems unavoidable—as we will henceforth assume. Even with respect to these most amenable values, however, sentimentalism faces an important problem, which we'll refer to as the *instability of affect*.

The challenge posed by the instability of affect can be illustrated with the example of amusement and the funny. Funniness seems a relatively stable property of good jokes, comic situations, and witty remarks. When amused by a joke, one ordinarily judges it funny and acts accordingly—perhaps by retelling it when opportunity arises. While we may differ about what things are funny, each of us takes it that whatever is funny remains so over (some period of) time and in various circumstances. Common sense thus presupposes that funniness belongs to the joke, so to speak, in that it will be there to be appreciated when the joke is repeated to a new audience.

There are admittedly some complications concerning performance: the effects of delivery, context of telling, and the like. Furthermore, it can be less the joke than the situation as a whole that is funny; as it's said, sometimes "you had to be there"

---

[4] See D'Arms and Jacobson (2000*a*, 2000*b*) for discussion of the distinction between endorsements of emotions as fitting versus other forms of endorsement of them.

[5] We consider it unimportant that the primary sense of some of these terms deviates from our usage. We focus on their evaluative sense: by "disgusting" we mean what merits disgust, by "enviable" what merits envy, and so forth.

in order to see what was funny about it. Even then a good recording of the scene ought to capture the humor, though, or else one begins to suspect that the situation wasn't so funny after all. Perhaps other factors, social or chemical, were more responsible for the amusement than was the material. These complications do not undermine the claim that some jokes are stably funny, because a good joke counts as funny despite being ruined on an occasion by a bad performance or inappropriate circumstances. Similarly, a mediocre joke that amuses due to adventitious factors doesn't thereby become funny—it does not even come to reflect one's comic taste (i.e., sense of humor). Rather, one is then amused by something that isn't funny even by one's own lights. Observations such as these will be at the heart of our argument in this chapter. The present claim is merely that the commonsense view of comic value, reflected in ordinary thought and practice, takes it to be relatively stable across contexts. We will therefore focus primarily on jokes whose funniness depends largely on their content rather than essentially involving the circumstances of their telling. The instability problem infects even these paradigmatically funny jokes.

Although senses of humor purport to track stable evaluative properties of their objects, emotional responses themselves are notoriously fickle. This disparity creates the problem. Elijah Millgram expresses the challenge for sentimentalism clearly, while arguing against modern forms of the view that compare values with colors and other secondary qualities in order to vindicate them as real despite their admitted anthropocentrism. As Millgram (1999: 253) notes, "the scarf still looks red the hundredth time you see it, whereas the joke no longer gets a laugh the hundredth (or usually even the second) time through". This is just one example of a general phenomenon. In various ways, our dispositions to amusement, shame, disgust, and other sentiments are prone to vicissitudes that challenge the purported stability of sentimental values.

The instability problem arises from an apparent tension between three propositions that seem irresistible to sentimentalists, each of which we have now canvassed. The first is the response-dependency thesis: the claim that sentimental values depend essentially on their associated evaluative responses, the sentiments.[6] Hence it is inevitable and unobjectionable that people ordinarily rely on the responses generated by their senses of humor, honor, and the like, when they take things to be funny or shameful. The second thesis concerns the stability of sentimental value. Our concepts of these values take them to be relatively stable features of the objects to which they are properly attributed. Yet these claims are in tension with the obvious instability of sentimental response. Sentimentalists must acknowledge that actual patterns of amusement and other sentiments are fickle in ways that seem ill-suited for tracking a stable value.

---

[6] Thus the sentiments are not merely sensitivities to some independently existing value, in this view; amusement in not just our primary epistemic route to the funny, though it is that too.

So framed, the instability problem arises not only as a problem for how to locate what is genuinely funny, shameful, and so on, but even for identifying an individual's perspective on such questions. Most of the considerable literature on response dependency has focused on the first of these issues, but when the discussion moves from secondary qualities to value, the second issue becomes highly significant. Sentimental responses are far more disparate than color experience. Color blindness and other pathologies notwithstanding, people don't have different "senses" of color as they have different senses of humor. Under the same conditions, people with similar organs of perception but disparate tastes can be expected to agree about what is red but much less about what is funny (or shameful, outrageous, etc.). Obviously the role of culture and learning is far greater when it comes to value than color. There is so much variation among people that any attempt to settle what is funny or shameful must adjudicate between different patterns of reaction and correspondingly different views about sentimental value. To anticipate our leading thought, this variation motivates our posit of disparate sensibilities to explain people's differing evaluative perspectives, as well as to make sense of disagreement and change of mind.

We do not aspire to adjudicate such disputes here; our goal is considerably more modest. We seek to understand the contours of different people's senses of humor, honor, purity, and the like, such that these can be understood as constituting relatively stable and coherent perspectives on these values. We see this enterprise as a necessary precursor to the larger task of adjudicating evaluative disputes. The best prospect for any such adjudication or reconciliation involves first locating and understanding distinct evaluative perspectives, and then seeking resources either to reconcile them or to vindicate some at the expense of others. Perhaps the issue of realism about comic value—whether certain things are *really* funny and others not—hangs on whether people's senses of humor would converge under some ideal conditions of inquiry.[7] Our discussion does not presuppose any robust form of realism about these values, though, nor does it presume that there are intersubjectively available standards for sentimental value. In fact, we're optimistic about the existence of such standards, at least in certain cases and to some extent, but the significance of identifying distinct senses of humor and other perspectives on sentimental value does not hang on the prospects for realism. Sentimental values play a crucial role in the human mental economy which, we contend, renders skepticism about them moot; one might say that human nature forces us to take them seriously.

People care deeply and (we think) ineliminably about what is shameful, disgusting, or worthy of pride. We cannot do without these evaluative concepts, because of the universality of the sentiments and our common need to regulate them with

---

[7] See Smith (1994) and Railton (1997) for two different sorts of suggestion along these lines.

standards. Of course individuals and societies differ vastly in their senses of humor, honor, purity, and the like. But the standards these values impose are profoundly important to us all, in deciding how to live. Doubts about their metaphysical status do not loosen their hold on our moral psychology. The sentimental values can, quite literally, be matters of life and death. Not infrequently people kill and die over matters of honor, for instance; and those stranded in the wilderness have been known to starve to death rather than engage in the disgusting and, to many, shameful practice of cannibalism. When reading about these ordeals, it's easy to think that those who died of starvation rather than even attempt to eat human flesh overestimated the importance of avoiding intercourse with the disgusting, and that there's nothing shameful about eating the dead when it's necessary to stay alive—but the vitality of such disagreement makes our point. The goal of this discussion is not to eliminate differences over sentimental value but to reveal them, in order to locate the fundamental evaluative disagreements that arise from conflicts in sensibility.

## 26.2 How Sensibilities Solve the Instability Problem

Two obvious avenues of response to the instability problem present themselves, but each involves serious revision of how people actually treat sentimental values. We will consider these two inadequate approaches before suggesting a less obvious response that better captures the phenomena both in the specific case and, more importantly, in general. First, one might claim that the reason the joke ceases to amuse is that it's no longer funny: its humor grows stale after a few hearings. (Notice that this seems just the right thing to say about a formerly delicious cake that grows stale after a few days.) This approach denies the proposition that the funny, unlike the delicious, is a relatively stable property of objects, supposing instead that the funny is a matter of whatever amuses at the moment.[8] It then seems forced toward radical subjectivism by the fact that the same joke will predictably amuse others who haven't heard it before—which is precisely why we endeavor to remember and retell good jokes. The most you would be justified in

---

[8] Although this suggestion amounts to abandoning one of the three propositions leading to the problem, both of the other two approaches attempt to accommodate all three claims. In this chapter we take the response-dependency of sentimental values as a given, for reasons already explained; and the instability of sentimental response seems an indisputable psychological fact.

saying, when a joke grows stale, is that it is no longer funny *for you*, where this means no more than "it no longer amuses me".

Moreover, such relativism would not solve the instability problem for long, because the joke will likely become funny-for-you again after you've forgotten about it for a while. We therefore find it strange that Millgram (1999: 254) embraces this approach: "When the joke is told again and again, we cease laughing; because the pattern of reaction gives its shape to the secondary quality, we say the joke isn't funny anymore." Although people sometimes do speak this way, this manner of speech is misleading, because to say the joke isn't funny implies more than that it doesn't amuse the speaker (anymore, for now). It suggests that amusement is not fitting. Nonetheless, Millgram's supposition that *the pattern of reaction shapes the property* aptly characterizes this first avenue of response, which treats sentimental values as secondary qualities, whose contours are fixed entirely by our actual dispositions to respond. Although this approach might be adequate for genuine secondary qualities such as color, which are response-dependent but not evaluative, it is widely held to founder with the funny and other sentimental values.[9] Even when you are no longer amused by a joke because you've heard it too often, you typically will not change your judgment of its comic value, Millgram's suggestion to the contrary notwithstanding. Thus the first answer to the instability problem, which in effect locates the instability in the value of the objects themselves, fails to capture ordinary evaluative judgments. The underlying stability that we take such values to have also strongly suggests that senses of humor should not be modeled directly on patterns of response. You repeat a "stale" joke to friends who haven't heard it because, though it no longer amuses you, it still accords with your sense of humor. But you wouldn't serve your friends stale cake just because it used to taste delicious. Our sense of humor assigns a temporal stability to the funniness of jokes that our sense of gustatory taste does not assign to the deliciousness of cakes.[10]

The second obvious answer to the instability problem is more promising but ultimately unsatisfactory. This strategy identifies our sense of humor not directly with our pattern of response, like the first solution, but with our sincere comic

[9] As John McDowell (1985: 207) noted in his seminal paper "Values and Secondary Qualities", there is a crucial disanalogy between the two sorts of concept: unlike redness and red appearances, the funny does not merely cause but *merits* amusement. Sentimentalist theories have largely adopted this merit schema, which makes them versions of the fitting attitude theory of value. Thus, insofar as Millgram is arguing against the claim that sentimental values are secondary qualities, we agree with him—but so do his foils, McDowell and Wiggins.

[10] Although we reject this simple dispositionalism, on which the actual pattern of response "shapes" the property, we grant that other dispositions—such as the tendency to retell the joke—can be revelatory of our underlying sense of humor. Moreover, repetition can affect our response to food by making us tire of even delicious things. This fits the story we want to tell, on which overexposure obscures our tastes, at least in the short run, even if habituation changes them over the long term. We are grateful to Peter Goldie and Michael Weber on these points.

judgments.[11] It can thus recognize that the stale joke we still deem funny, even though it no longer amuses us, continues to be endorsed by our sense of humor. In order to explicate this strategy, we will need to introduce a technical sense of judgment, which contrasts with a belief of the same content. Clearly your sense of humor is not simply a matter of what you believe to be funny, since you can believe something to be funny without deploying your sense of humor, for instance on the basis of testimony. Hence we will stipulate that *judgments* of sentimental value are beliefs somehow grounded in one's responses.[12] In order to make a judgment about the funny, the shameful, the fearsome, and so forth, you must have responded to the object with amusement, shame, fear, or whatever the relevant response, and come to an evaluative belief on that basis; similarly, judgments that something is not funny or shameful must be grounded in one's lack of response.[13] This stipulation mirrors Kant's claim that judgments of taste must be based on aesthetic pleasure taken in an object by the judge.

According to the second answer to the instability problem, then, although our sentimental responses are in various respects unstable, our sense of humor is constituted by our sincere judgments about what is funny (and the like), which are relatively stable. This improves on the first answer and adequately handles the case of funny jokes that grow stale with repetition, but it will not do as a general solution. One problem is that judgments too tend toward instability, when based on unstable responses. This point can be explicated by differentiating between what we'll call transparent, translucent, and opaque factors that generate instabilities of affect. A transparent factor is one so obvious that you account for it in judgment without second thought, like the good joke rendered tedious (to you, for now) by overexposure. Since the first answer founders on such transparent factors, it gets our judgments wrong. Translucent factors can affect judgment, but self-awareness and consideration of consistency pressure often suffice to reveal that your initial

[11] We have a modest notion of sincerity as a form of honesty, on which one makes a judgment sincerely simply by believing one believes it (on the right grounds). We do not require self-awareness or single-mindedness for sincerity, although, when one is aware of being conflicted, sincerity requires one to admit it. However, it will prove crucial that one can fail to be aware of one's own sensibility, and that one important way in which people are not single-minded is that their evaluative beliefs conflict with their sensibility. But these circumstances must be sharply differentiated from another important case, where one (to a greater or lesser extent) dissembles about or deliberately ignores one's own sensibility—and we use "sincerity" to mark these failures. On this point we are grateful to Nicole Smith and Peter Goldie.

[12] Or equivalently, judgments are beliefs that are *based upon* emotional responses. These locutions are of course difficult to analyze, for reasons familiar from their other applications. We do not propose to say anything novel about what grounding or taking as a basis are here. We will assume, however, that beliefs formed on the basis of responses still count as judgments if they persist when one is no longer having the response. This parallels analogous claims about beliefs based on perception.

[13] Unless the non-response arises in a situation where we would expect to respond to the relevant value, we do not even make judgments on the basis of failing to respond. Judgments are only grounded in non-responses in those conditions where we would expect to respond.

judgment was mistaken even by your own lights. Suppose that, feeling somewhat depressed, you go to a comedy to try to improve your mood. But the movie doesn't amuse you, and you leave the theater thinking it just wasn't funny. If you later talk to a friend with a sense of humor similar to yours and hear that she found it hilarious, you might well conclude that you didn't give it a fair chance and therefore withdraw your previous judgment. Of course, whether such a factor is transparent or translucent has no sharp boundary. One person might withhold judgment while another needs some additional reason to doubt before doing so. Later we will consider opaque factors, which cannot be recognized by the agent, but the problem with the second answer already arises in the translucent cases. Were you to judge based on a lack of response to the movie that was actually caused by your bad mood, then your sincere judgment would not reflect your underlying sense of humor. Hence the existence of translucent instability demonstrates the inadequacy of constructing a sense of humor directly from one's comic judgments.

The problem with the second approach, in short, is that since not all instabilities of response are obvious, not all our judgments take account of them. In order to solve the instability problem, sentimentalism must posit the existence of an underlying *sensibility* that may or may not be manifested in any particular response or judgment, but which ultimately explains what an agent finds shameful, disgusting, or funny—when other factors don't interfere with his judgment or response. We have previously invoked the commonsense notion of a sense of humor as a model for the comic sensibility; other instances include an esteem sensibility connected to such sentiments as pride, shame, and contempt, and a purity sensibility connected to disgust. We propose to posit such sensibilities in order to explain the coherent patterns of reaction to which people are prone, in virtue of which they can be understood as having a distinctive perspective on various sentimental values, rather than just a welter of emotional responses. Then we go on to explaining a fundamental form of disagreement as difference in sensibility, and change of mind in terms of its alteration over time.

The sensibility theories advanced by John McDowell (1998), David Wiggins (1987), and David McNaughton (1988) appeal to the idea that evaluative thought and judgment rest on an inculcated sensibility—what McDowell (1996: 196–7), following Aristotle, calls a "second nature".[14] The leading thought of sensibility theory is that the sensitivity to values is at once a (cognitive) way of seeing features of the world and a (conative) way of caring about them. Possession of a sensibility is supposed to make possible the perception of values that would be unavailable to someone who lacked it, while also explaining the internal connection between evaluation and motivation. But many philosophers have found the notion of a sensibility obscure and this central claim on their behalf mysterious. We aspire to

---

[14] The helpful term "sensibility theory" is due to Darwall et al. (1992).

demystify sensibilities by connecting them to familiar psychological states and processes. So clarified, a more modest and psychologically realistic version of the sensibility theorists' central thesis becomes plausible—though we do not take it to have the metaethical consequences claimed for it, whether realist (McNaughton 1988) or "anti-anti-realist" (McDowell 1998: viii), for reasons explained in D'Arms and Jacobson (2006a). Our own view of sensibilities and their role in evaluative thought deviates from that of the sensibility theorists, in this and several other crucial respects.

Consider the claim that in order to see an object as having certain evaluative features, it is (or may be) necessary to feel some way about it. As a matter of phenomenology, it seems right that one often takes oneself to "see" the funniness of a joke, the disgustingness of a scene, or the contemptible nature of a person, precisely by feeling some way about it. Such talk should not be taken over-literally, however, as the essence of the perceptual metaphor is simply that our emotional experience presents us with a non-inferential basis for evaluative judgment.[15] For each of us, there are recurring themes in what appears to have those features and what does not, in virtue of which one person has a dark sense of humor, and another is squeamish about raw meat. But these themes are typically not matters of theoretical conviction, and someone who does not see what is funny in dark humor will be a poor predictor of which macabre jokes will be found funny and which merely tasteless, say. Even those who possess the relevant sensibility often cannot articulate precisely what makes something funny, disgusting, or even contemptible. And even when they can cite the factor to which they're responding, in virtue of which they take something to be valuable or disvaluable in one of these ways, there are other cases where that feature does not seem to have the same force. Then people are prone to fall back upon the claim directly to perceive, with their feelings, the beauty, humor, disgustingness, or shamefulness of this but not that object. Whether or not we agree with their verdicts, we must recognize the ways in which the idiosyncrasies in their own patterns of response generate a distinctive perspective on these values.

The metaphorical nature of this perceptual talk is significant because, as Hume suggests, the similarity in how beautiful things look is to be found in how they make us feel. Even if I am acquainted with delicious and beautiful things, the only sense in which I can confidently anticipate the experience of something on the basis of a purely evaluative characterization of it—for instance as delicious or beautiful—concerns how I can expect to feel about it. I will be *pleased* by the taste of the wine, the look of the face, the sound of the tune. Thus the phenomenological claim is grist for the sentimentalist mill. As for the idea that it might be necessary to have the right emotional responses to an object in order to perceive it as having

---

[15] This classically sentimentalist thought can be buttressed with evidence drawn from recent empirical moral psychology. See Haidt (2001) for details and bibliography.

certain evaluative features, the sentimentalist understanding of this claim renders it more modest and plausible than some other formulations.

The Humean point is not that actually having a response in a given case makes one especially likely to get it right. Someone with a good sense of humor can be expected to make better comic judgments—even about jokes that have grown stale to her—than will someone with a juvenile sense of humor. Rather, the point is that possession of an evaluative perspective requires one to find certain things funny or shameful through one's feelings of amusement or shame. Thus imaginatively simulating a response (as it's said, "off-line") is often crucial to appreciating what will be considered insulting, rather than funny, by someone else's lights. What funny jokes have in common is an essentially response-dependent appearance of incongruity, and what pride-worthy achievements share is a response-dependent notion of what is "splendid and mine" (or so we will contend). Although it is not strictly necessary to respond with amusement or pride in order to register the fittingness of those responses, such sentiments serve to make salient the putative grounds for the relevant judgments. Thus the difficulty of imaginatively placing ourselves in another's position explains why we often fail to perceive values the way they do: for instance, we may not anticipate the umbrage that someone takes at a remark we thought innocent. Sometimes that failure can be explained by one's ignorance of the other's circumstances, but at other times the best explanation will adduce the failure to be able to take up her sensibility imaginatively.

Our way of drawing the distinction between someone's sensibility and her evaluative judgments (grounded in affect) makes our view diverge from that of sensibility theorists in at least two respects other than metaethics. First, McDowell and Wiggins conceive sensibilities as indefinitely malleable through critical reflection. Refinements in one's theoretical convictions about value alter one's sensibilities in part by altering the very affective responses to which the sensibilities give rise.[16] Our view of the sentiments as natural psychological kinds common to human nature suggests a contrasting position, according to which variation in comic or esteem sensibility is limited by what kinds of things can elicit these specific responses, the nature of which is not determined by critical reflection. Indeed, we will argue that a person's evaluative sensibilities are often at odds with his reflective verdicts.

---

[16] In this picture, coming to regard one's ancestry as too far removed from one's agency to be a suitable target of shame or pride could lead to a communal refinement of these attitudes that tied them conceptually to what is under a person's control. This possibility seems to be a consequence of sensibility theory's insistence that the character of our emotional responses is not prior to the values to which they respond; instead the responses themselves undergo refinement along with the evaluative concepts with which they are paired (McDowell 1985; Wiggins 1987). We dispute this claim with respect to the sentiments, and hold that the character of shame and pride cannot be so thoroughly revised by reflection or even socialization.

Furthermore, McDowell (1979: 53) holds that practical wisdom (or virtue) functions as a kind of master sensibility that affords its possessor a unified perspective on value, allowing her to mediate among values without internal conflict. Instead she simply sees the demands that a particular situation imposes upon action and feels no pull from considerations contrary to the demands of virtue. Such countermanding and overridden considerations are, in McDowell's famous term, *silenced*. We offer an alternative account of the phenomenon of silencing, which interprets it not as the product of an integrated sensitivity to what matters most (such as generic practical wisdom) but as a frequent effect of conflict between distinct sensibilities and sentiments. In the first place, we are impressed by the extent to which even the most admirable people are prone to be emotionally torn by conflicts of value and obligation. So we think silencing is less common than McDowell seems to suggest, and we are less impressed by single-mindedness even as an ideal. We think it more psychologically realistic to see such single-mindedness as people can muster, in the face of conflicting values, as due to the propensity to have certain evaluative sensibilities short-circuited or over-whelmed by others—for better or worse. Thus even *less weighty* factors that arouse sentiments such as anger will often make a perceived slight more salient than other considerations. Since the weaker reason can silence the stronger one, silencing is not unique to the virtuous psychology; and even when virtuous it can involve insensitivity to value. For instance, the offense I take at the put-down of my friend can prevent my sense of humor from registering its funniness. In such cases the joke may accord with my own sense of humor, though its comic merits were silenced by the feelings aroused due to allegiance to my friend. This interference may be for the best, but only because one cannot always pay one's emotional respects to every value present.

What, then, is a sensibility? A person's discrete sensibilities consist in facts about him (some idiosyncratic, some common to most human beings) that underlie and explain many of his dispositions to specific sentiments—though not all such dispositions, as we shall see. Sensibilities issue in affective responses, in the first place, and it is by looking at the right responses that they are most clearly revealed. In the most straightforward sort of case, these responses provide a basis for evaluative judgments. So ordinarily one's evaluative judgments arise out of one's sensibility by way of sentimental response. However, not all such responses, let alone failures to respond, arise from the relevant sensibility. The simple cases we have discussed so far, based on repetition and mood effects, illustrate this point. In what follows we will argue that the posit of more or less coherent sensibilities is necessary to solve the instability problem, while also allowing for a moral psychology that makes better sense of internal conflict, fundamental evaluative disagreement, and change of mind.

Consider the sense of humor as a model. In the standard case, one's sense of humor issues in amusement at a joke or it does not; it thereby serves as the basis for many of our comic judgments. But the tendency of amusement (and other emotions) to fade with repetition, for example, is not itself an expression of the sense of humor (or other sensibilities) but a feature of our dispositions that does not reveal anything about our values. This point is tacitly acknowledged by common sense when we do not treat our failure to be amused, on the tenth hearing, as grounds for doubting that the joke that amused us the first nine times is funny. We can grow desensitized to other sentimental values too upon overexposure. When we become used to even outrageous behavior, it gradually ceases actually to outrage us. No doubt this tendency has useful consequences, since perpetual outrage, amusement, disgust, or fear quickly grows counterproductive. In such cases, where one's dispositions to amusement stop reflecting one's sense of humor due to overexposure to the object, we can say that repetition is an *obscuring factor* with respect to a joke's funniness: it affects one's response without revealing one's underlying sensibility. Although you cease to be amused by the joke, it thus remains funny by your own lights; it continues to reflect your sense of humor. Indeed, ordinarily you will still believe, based on your previous amusement, that the joke is funny.

Two important caveats need to be emphasized here. First, we do not claim that repetition always figures as an obscuring factor, even when it alters response. Especially with objects more complex than jokes, you might gradually come to appreciate features of the object that weren't evident on initial exposure. Then repetition reveals rather than obscures sensibility, although still more repetition may lead to overexposure and thereby become obscuring. This complication doesn't much apply to jokes due to their simplicity—generally one merely needs to "get" a joke in order to appreciate what is there to be appreciated—but it does apply to comedy more generally. Second, we certainly do not mean to imply that sensibilities are static. One's sense of humor (and other sensibilities) change over time, especially early in life, and an important factor in their development is exposure and habituation. Over the long term, then, repetition—especially when combined with social influence and reflection—can alter one's sensibilities. Hence, when we say that repetition is a common obscuring factor we mean this as a generalization with at least these two important qualifications. Although the question of when someone's sensibility has changed, and when it is in flux, may have no neat answer, many cases clearly fall on one side or the other. In Millgram's example, for instance, we should not say that your sense of humor changed on second (or even tenth) hearing of the joke; rather, it grew stale to you.

It is a commonplace of folk psychology that we possess such sensibilities, which constitute what are sometimes called our "senses" of humor, shame, honor, and the like. The most philosophically influential notion in this area is of course the moral sense; but the suggestion that morality is grounded in sensibility is, we think, the most problematic case, and we will not tackle it here. No part of our argument in this Chapter requires vindicating a moral sense or representing right and wrong as sentimental values, though morality will play a leading role in our conclusion, as a potentially obscuring factor in much evaluative judgment. Rather, our primary thesis is that sentimentalism can best accommodate the instability of affect and the opacity of judgment by positing sensibilities that underlie many of our judgments and constitute our affective take on sentimental values such as the funny. These evaluative sensibilities are distinct both from our dispositions to respond and from our sincere judgments. In what follows we develop this alternative approach to the instability problem, as a way of avoiding the implausibility of the more obvious proposals. But our interest in sensibilities goes well beyond finding a solution to the instability problem. In fact, we think this notion an important and under-explored element in human moral psychology. In the final section of this chapter we will address some respects in which identifying and distinguishing separate evaluative sensibilities is necessary to an adequate understanding of evaluative conflict and disagreement.

Specifically, we will argue that a previously underappreciated form of intra-psychic conflict between one's sensibilities explains an otherwise puzzling way in which one can be a stranger to oneself. We contend that people often falsely believe that judgments about what is funny, shameful, or disgusting are based upon the deliverances of the relevant evaluative sensibility. Yet they can be mistaken when factors unknown to them, and adventitious to the values at issue, affect their responses. Self-esteem and moral qualms, in particular, can muddle our evaluative judgments in ways that are opaque to us, undermining their warrant even by our own lights—that is, without considering whether or not our sensibility tracks evaluative facts (or even if such facts exist). Thus even some *sincere* judgments about what is or isn't funny, shameful, or disgusting are revealed as, in a deep sense, spurious.

## 26.3 OBSCURING FACTORS

We now turn to considering various *obscuring factors*, which generate or suppress emotional responses in ways that do not reveal the agent's underlying sensibility. In section 26.2 we considered desensitization through repetition as such a factor. Enough repetition of even a funny joke renders it no longer amusing, as a purely dispositional matter, yet the joke is still funny by the agent's lights: it still accords with his sense of humor despite no longer causing amusement. Since most people are familiar with the desensitizing effects of repetition when it comes to jokes, they typically continue to believe that the stale joke is funny; and since this belief is based on their previous amusement, it still counts as a comic judgment in our technical sense. Notice, though, that if someone changed her comic judgment, deciding that the joke isn't really funny because it no longer amuses her, she would be making a mistake. It's not that she would necessarily be making a mistake about the funny, since the joke might not have been funny in the first place—in which case she would accidentally be coming to a true belief. Even so, she would be getting herself wrong, in that her sincere comic judgments would not accurately reflect her sense of humor. Moreover, other obscuring factors are much less obvious than is repetition, and therefore are less likely to be accounted for in an agent's judgments. These cases illustrate the need to posit a sensibility distinct not only from the agent's dispositions to respond affectively, and his beliefs about the relevant value that are not grounded in sentiment, but even from those beliefs that *are* so grounded.

The following discussion of obscuring factors does not aspire to be exhaustive. The factors discussed here are chosen because they are pervasive and help illustrate our larger argument for the importance of sensibilities as a theoretical posit. Recall too that the goal is not to find conditions under which a person's responses to a value are correct, merely those that reveal his own perspective. The differences that remain between individuals will then be genuine differences in evaluative perspective, which this Chapter aspires to locate, not to resolve. Thus the conditions we seek by removing obscuring factors are not exactly those Philip Pettit (1999: 137) refers to as "favorable for detection"; they might rather be called those "favorable for revelation"—that is, for revealing the contours of agents' evaluative sensibilities. Our primary example remains the sense of humor, but this serves as only one model for a more general inquiry, and throughout this discussion we will be noting ways in which each of the factors discussed can obscure other sensibilities as well.

Some of the least controversially obscuring factors are mood effects. When someone is sad or angry, for instance, this tends to suppress amusement quite generally, flattening the distinction between what is and isn't funny (by the agent's lights). While people are often aware of these effects and reserve judgment accordingly, mood effects can sometimes lead to false negative judgments—that the comedy wasn't funny, say—when an agent either lacks the self-awareness necessary to recognize her mood, or gives too much credence to her lack of response. Similarly, sadness and other moods (as well as bouts of sentiment) can prevent someone from taking pride in an accomplishment that she genuinely deems prideworthy. Mood effects can be translucent, but when one suspects that a mood caused a response—that one would have responded differently if not depressed or excited, say—then one does not judge on its basis. In order to understand people as having a relatively stable sense of what is funny and worthy of pride, common sense therefore treats the presence of mood effects as obscuring the contours of their underlying sensibilities.[17]

---

[17] This is not to deny that long-term depression can affect a person in systematic ways that can alter the contours of his sense of humor. But there is a difference between something temporarily interfering with one's sense of humor and changing it.

This commonsense argument that mood effects obscure our sensibilities can be bolstered by a psychological explanation invoking the interference of other emotions. A familiar fact about the emotions is that they can be mutually incompatible: fear tends to drive out contrary emotions such as amusement or pride. These incompatibilities may sometimes be due to the different physiological responses that are part of the syndrome of distinct sentiments—the increased arousal characteristic of fear and anger inhibits amusement, for instance. But they are sometimes caused simply by the fact that emotions direct our attention to certain features of objects rather than others. If you are fixated on the danger of a precipice it will be more difficult to feel proud of the feat of having just climbed it, despite the fact that these two evaluations are not at all in tension: part of what merits pride is the danger of the accomplishment. In these cases emotional responses that reveal our sensibility with respect to one aspect of a situation divert us from having another response to a different aspect of it. Such diversions involve one sensibility obscuring another. More generally, the presence of some psychologically incompatible affect should be taken as an obscuring factor, which suggests that a failure to respond (with amusement, pride, or whatever) does not reveal a negative verdict (of lack of funniness or pride-worthiness) from the sensibility subject to interference.

In light of these familiar limitations on our emotional capacities, it should not be surprising that the failure to feel an emotion may not reveal that this emotion is unfitting but merely that one's affective resources are otherwise deployed. Thus the fact that one was not amused by something isn't always a negative verdict of one's sense of humor, and in general many dispositions to lack of response obscure rather than reveal one's sensibilities. But although factors suppressing response are more common, some other factors initiate or amplify responses in ways that obscure the relevant sensibility. Two clear examples are *contagion* and *social ingratiation*. When surrounded by people laughing, it is not uncommon to find yourself becoming amused as well.[18] You may then fix on whatever the environment offers as a potential object of amusement, and think yourself amused by it. In such cases, the object you fix upon may not really be funny even by your lights. Suppose that the same joke told under normal circumstances would not amuse you. Then this joke is not a match for your sense of humor; rather, the contagion effect has obscured your underlying sensibility. Contagion counts as a generically obscuring factor, whenever it generates or amplifies such emotions as sadness, anger, and fear.

Social ingratiation offers another, less transparent example of a factor that can affect response without revealing anything about the relevant sensibility. Certain social circumstances affect a person's propensities to amusement in ways that

---

[18] For a survey of some psychological studies of emotional contagion, see McIntosh et al. (1994).

primarily reflect how useful it is for him to respond.[19] For example, often people are disproportionately amused by their boss's jokes, or the stories of their attractive date. If the same joke would not elicit amusement were it told equally well by a friend, then the social ingratiation effect has obscured the agent's sense of humor. While sometimes these reactions are merely feigned or exaggerated, often this is not the case. It would be a mistake to overestimate the degree to which we humans have conscious awareness of even our quite observable psychological tendencies. In fact, many of these phenomena work best precisely when the agent is unaware of them. Then one will be inclined to judge sincerely but erroneously on the basis of one's responses. It might be objected that these effects, far from being adventitious to amusement, are central to its function as a form of social bonding. Though we accept this claim about the role of amusement in the human mental economy, we think this no objection to our view. Rather, what it shows is that not all causes of amusement count as funny-makers. This is borne out by the fact that one would not cite such factors as justifying one's responses as fitting (though we might find them convenient). It seems undeniable that what was funny about the remark is *not* that I'm more likely to be promoted if I laugh at it. Thus people do not treat social ingratiation effects as comically relevant, even though they are undoubtedly important factors in explaining our dispositions to amusement—and even some of our comic judgments.

A similarly obscuring feature has the opposite tendency. It seems obvious that one's antipathy to the teller tends to suppress one's amusement at the joke, whether or not it accords with one's sense of humor. The instability here arises from the fact that the same joke, told by someone else, would have a different effect. (For it to be the same joke, its content cannot rest in any essential way on the identity of the teller.) It would be peculiar to interpret someone's sense of humor as ratifying jokes on the basis of who tells them, rather than explaining away the inconsistency in response on this basis. Again the more charitable interpretation draws support from an obvious explanatory hypothesis. Hostility can generate feelings of antagonism, or simply momentary flashes of negative affect, which inhibit or prevent amusement; and this tends to focus one's attention on features of the teller, in ways that divert one's attention from the object's comic value.

Hostility can obscure other sensibilities as well, such as the sense of honor and esteem, which are revealed by certain dispositions to shame, contempt, and pride. Insofar as your generic hostility toward someone contributes to your contempt at his lousy dancing, say, this may obscure rather than reveal your esteem sensibility

---

[19] This is one instance of what Paul Griffiths (2003) has termed "Machiavellian emotions": a tendency of emotional responses to arise because they are useful in ways insensitive to their fittingness. Another example is that how angry people actually get at various slights and infractions—not just how angry they act in response to them—is influenced by how likely it seems that the perpetrator will react to their anger in ways beneficial to them (Stein and Trabasso 1993).

with respect to whether the inability to dance is contemptible. The instability emerges here if you don't feel contempt at other lousy dancers. This is not to deny that hostilities and anxieties often play a significant role in *shaping* a person's sensibilities, as well as in obscuring them, and hence that some reaction initially caused by hostility might become integrated into one's sensibility. When it does, the instability will go away, however, since one will then have acquired a general tendency to feel such contempt. Despite the role of hostility in the development of one's sensibilities, those instabilities explained by hostility toward the object of one's contempt are best interpreted as obscuring factors.

We expect our next claim to be more controversial. It's hard to deny that your hostility toward the teller of a joke, when it explains your lack of amusement, obscures your sense of humor. This seems obvious in part because the explanation of your response, or rather lack thereof, cannot be offered as a justification of the right kind for it.[20] Yet an analogous argument supports a more surprising conclusion. Suppose you find a joke at the expense of someone you dislike very funny, but would not be amused by the same joke when a stranger is the butt.[21] These different responses to the same joke constitute an instability. The interpretive question, then, is how to make your sense of humor coherent in the face of this inconsistency in your disposition to amusement. An explanation of the tension isn't hard to find. People use humor not only to strengthen social bonds but to do so specifically by excluding others; this is the core truth revealed (and exaggerated) by the *superiority theory* of humor, and by the observation that so many jokes have butts. Nevertheless, although this explains why people are so often amused by jokes at the expense of those they dislike or resent, it does not justify them as funny. "I hate the guy being ridiculed" is a wrong kind of reason to claim amusement fitting, though it's often the best explanation for why one is amused. Of course people may seek a reason of the right kind in the neighborhood, such as that the butt of the joke is pompous and self-important. But the less they are in fact amused by isomorphic jokes at equally pompous but less antipathetic targets, the less well this reason reconciles the instability. Hence, to the extent that your amusement or failure to be amused is caused by hostility or affinity toward the butt of the joke, we claim this to be an obscuring factor that does not reveal your sense of humor.

The previous argument suggests a similar treatment of other sensitivities that frequently prevent people from being amused by comedy that comes at their own expense, or at the expense of others with whom they sympathize. Obviously, people

---

[20] This is not to say that it cannot be offered as a justification of any sort, since one could give "I don't want to give him the satisfaction" as a reason for not laughing, which might be a fine justification but is a wrong kind of reason: it does not speak to the fittingness of amusement and, hence, is irrelevant to the funniness of the joke.

[21] Note again that the claim that the two jokes are isomorphic is not always a simple matter. In many cases, however, the identity claim is extremely hard to deny. Our arguments should be understood as appealing to such cases.

are often defended against such humor, especially when it concerns aspects of themselves about which they're particularly touchy: things that register with their esteem sensibility. Yet if the same joke told at another's expense would have amused the agent, then this is an instability that must be reconciled in order to reveal a coherent sense of humor. The materials are ready to hand for an explanation that undermines our response (or rather lack of response) to jokes at the expense of those we care about. When jokes anger or shame us, or make us anxious, these competing affective responses often prevent amusement by creating incompatible psychological states, or merely by directing our attention away from what is funny about the joke. Here too the deliverances of one sensibility divert another, preventing it from registering its distinctive response.

This conclusion is admittedly somewhat revisionist of common sense. People do say that someone "has no sense of humor" about some area to which he is sensitive, or that he is "blind to" the funniness of jokes at his own expense. Of course, as Millgram notes, people also say "that joke isn't funny anymore" after they have been overexposed to it—even, we think, when they don't really make that judgment. In the case at hand, it seems much more likely that those who aren't amused make such judgments literally and sincerely; they aren't just reporting their lack of amusement. Nevertheless, we favor an analogous conclusion. Considerations of interpretive charity, and the plausibility of diversion and interference as explanations for the failure to respond, suggest that these responses often obscure rather than reveal a person's sensibility. In some cases, one sensibility can obscure another. Thus someone's self-esteem, wounded by a joke that ridicules her in some sensitive way, can preempt the deployment of her sense of humor. Our approach is novel for its suggestion that such jokes might nevertheless accord with her comic sensibility —or whatever the relevant sensibility is—despite conflicting with some other sensibility, which diverts her emotional resources and attention in ways that obscure the value at issue. In that case the joke is funny by her own lights, though she does not realize it; in fact, she sincerely judges to the contrary. If this conclusion still seems strange, consider that our examples have somewhat exaggerated the phenomena for purposes of illustration. Most of us are capable of laughing at ourselves when the conditions are right. Were the offending joke told in other circumstances, by someone whose good will we trust, we could laugh at it. In such cases it seems hard to deny that the joke matches our sense of humor, although social sensitivity and other psychological defenses can get in the way of our amusement at it, thereby obscuring the expression of our underlying sensibility.

Certain background beliefs and values can also affect an agent's dispositions to have a sentimental response without thereby revealing his sensibility. These commitments are in the background because they are not part of the sensibility itself, unlike other beliefs and values which require deployment of the sensibility—as you need a sense of humor in order to see what is incongruous in the relevant, funny-making respect. Whereas disagreement about such incongruity often reflects a genuine difference in sensibility, disagreements about background beliefs can play an obscuring role by creating specious evaluative disagreement. Let's start with an obvious case: a Latin pun. You can't "get" the joke without having at least the relevant bit of Latin, in that it's impossible to identify (let alone appreciate) what is funny about it. Suppose though that were you to understand the pun, you would be amused and judge it funny. It should be uncontroversial that the pun always reflected your sense of humor, though your ignorance of Latin obscured this fact.[22] Notice that our claim that ignorance of some fact is an obscuring factor, with respect to one's sense of humor, does *not* imply that the fact isn't part of what's funny about the joke. Perhaps it would properly be cited in support of one's comic judgment. Differences in background belief also affect other emotional dispositions without reflecting anything about the underlying sensibilities. If the only reason I am not afraid is that I have no idea what that gauge in the cockpit means, then giving me an additional bit of information will frighten me without changing anything about my fear sensibility.

Now consider the evaluative judgment that someone is self-righteous or a hypocrite. These are judgments people frequently disagree about, which can be made sense of and engaged in without any reference to the funny. These disagreements are moral or political, not comic. We don't use our sense of humor to detect self-righteousness the way we use it to determine what counts as (in the relevant respect) incongruous. Nevertheless, self-righteousness and hypocrisy are among the most easily and effectively ridiculed traits. Although it's not impossible to be amused by the lampooning of someone's character when you don't think he deserves it, it's much easier when (you think) the target really has the traits for which he's being ridiculed. Hence one's judgment about people's viciousness will help predict how amused one will be by certain jokes at their expense. People's dispositions to amusement will thus vary with their judgments in ways that reflect their values but not specifically their sense of humor. I might think the joke isn't funny because it presupposes a proposition I don't believe, while you think it funny partly because you do believe it. Moreover, the truth or falsity of the proposition will often be relevant to the joke's comic value.[23] Nevertheless, although both our moral and our comic judgments differ in this case, our senses of humor might be identical.

---

[22] Admittedly, sometimes an inability to get jokes is taken as marking a bad sense of humor. This may be apposite, when the inability seems to reflect a perceptual weakness; for instance, when someone (who knows the language) doesn't readily pick up on double meanings in witticisms. But when the inability is based on ignorance that could easily be fixed, then surely this additional piece of information did not change the agent's sense of humor. Rather, this cognitive limitation does not reflect badly on the agent's sensibility, despite affecting his dispositions to amusement and thus his comic judgment.

[23] This is not to endorse the theory that truth is always a funny-maker, or even that falsity can never be one; sometimes a malicious half-truth does the trick.

For a non-comic example, consider the question of how difficult is some accomplishment. That question doesn't seem to require an esteem sensibility to answer, and it would be odd to claim to perceive difficulty via sensibility. Yet how difficult one takes some accomplishment to be makes a great difference to how worthy of pride one considers it. Hence judgments of difficulty alter our dispositions to pride, despite not issuing from our esteem sensibility. In contrast, compare the judgment of whether some accomplishment counts as mine. According to Philippa Foot (1963: 76), in order for someone to be proud of something, he must believe it to be "in some way splendid and in some way [his] own". Now consider a dispute between a philosopher and a football fan over whether he can be proud of "his team's" triumphs. You might think that what is and isn't yours does not involve any judgment requiring sensibility—indeed, perhaps not even an evaluative judgment but a matter of fact. But closer examination reveals that disagreements over whether or not something is your own in the relevant sense are located in our sensibilities. To paraphrase Scruton, in order to know what is meant by "mine" (or even by "splendid"), you would have to consult, not some independent conception, but your esteem sensibility.[24]

This discussion of factors that obscure rather than reveal one's sensibility aims to draw two distinctions. First, we illustrated circumstances in which one's sentimental responses might predictably vary in ways that do not reveal one's underlying sensibility. Second, we argued that one's judgments do not always reflect one's sensibility, when such obscuring factors are present and fail to be transparent to the agent. In such circumstances he will typically judge on the basis of his response (or lack thereof), despite the fact that his response is caused by other, adventitious factors. In the final section of this chapter we argue that sensibilities are central to understanding fundamental disagreement over sentimental values, and we begin to explore their distinctive role in the epistemology of value.

# 26.4 Sensibilities and Fundamental Evaluative Dispute

The discussion of obscuring factors showed that our actual responses reflect our evaluative perspective less often than might be supposed. Unfortunately for our

---

[24] This claim is argued in more detail in (D'Arms and Jacobson 2003). Note that this is a hypothetical dispute. We are not attributing the philosopher's view to Foot in either essay. The point is rather that Scruton's objection to the incongruity theory of humor also tells against Foot's putatively response-independent gloss of pride.

self-understanding, the nature of emotional experience does not ensure that people can tell by introspection which of their reactions issue from their sensibilities and which from the various obscuring factors, several of which are opaque or at least translucent. Recall our technical notion of judgment as those evaluative beliefs formed on the basis of the agent's emotional responses to an object. The discussion of obscuring factors implies that some of the judgments people make about sentimental value will lack the backing of their own sensibility. They conclude that something is very funny because they were so amused, or that something isn't contemptible because they don't feel contemptuous of it; but in fact they are wrong about this *by their own lights*—for instance because the influence of contagion in the one case, or pity in the other, has obscured their underlying sense of humor or honor. Such judgments are alienated, in that they conflict with the agent's own sensibility. In this concluding section we will suggest that alienated judgments are often defective, and that disagreements in which they figure are, in a sense, spurious. This will help secure our claim that it's an agent's sensibility, rather than his responses or even his judgments, that normally constitutes his perspective on some sentimental value.

We will begin by arguing that an especially important form of dispute, worthy of the name *fundamental evaluative disagreement*, occurs only when the disputants differ specifically in the relevant sensibility. A. J. Ayer (1952: 102 et seq.) noted that some disagreements expressed in evaluative language are not really evaluative disagreements, because they rest on prior disagreement over matters of prosaic fact or meaning.[25] If the disputants agreed on the meaning of their terms and on the relevant matters of fact, then their apparent evaluative disagreement would disappear. Such disagreements do not really concern what they purport to be about; they are in that crucial respect spurious. A disagreement over some politically contentious matter of fact between two people with similar senses of humor, for instance, might explain their different responses to a joke that presupposes the fact. The disputants think that their disagreement essentially concerns the question of the joke's funniness, and they make conflicting judgments on that score. Nevertheless, their dispute is not *fundamentally* evaluative because it would be resolved, we are supposing, were they to agree about the prosaic facts.

We want to extend Ayer's insight to reflect that even some genuinely evaluative disagreements are spurious, because they are not grounded in the sensibility specifically relevant to the evaluative question at stake. This was demonstrated by the case of a disagreement, putatively about funniness, that is really over hypocrisy. Of course it can be disputed whether or not someone is hypocritical, and to what

---

[25] We borrow the term "prosaic fact" from Gibbard (2003), using it, as he does, to refer to facts that are universally recognized as such even by those who harbor doubts about whether the *evaluative* status of objects is likewise factual. We do not here deny that value claims are factual, nor do we affirm it.

extent. However such a dispute is to be resolved, though, it is surely not by utilizing one's sense of humor; and whatever reasons can be given on either side, they are not considerations about funniness. Hence, when a joke trading on the hypocrisy of some figure amuses one person but not another because they differ over whether the butt of the joke really is a hypocrite, and they would feel similarly were they in agreement on this aretaic question, their dispute does not reflect a difference in their sense of humor. Moreover, there is then an important respect in which the disagreement does not really concern the funny at all, even though they have different beliefs and make different judgments about the joke's funniness. Yet the responses on which those judgments are founded would be similar, if they could reconcile their prior disagreement. In our terms, they actually share a comic sensibility. This example thus helps illustrate why the underlying sensibility better reflects their intuitive, pre-theoretic sense of humor than do their actual responses, beliefs, or even comic judgments.

Now consider what we'll call *alienated* judgments, where someone makes claims that lack the support of his own sensibility. There are several kinds of defect commonly attending such judgments, and at least two distinct problems with the disputes to which they give rise. First, because obscuring factors can be opaque, people often falsely think that they are judging on the basis of their own sensibilities. Thus alienated judgments commonly manifest a failure of self-understanding by lacking the grounding in the agent's sensibility that he takes them to possess. Second, alienated judgments often issue in pronouncements that mislead others, because the agent's failure to understand himself leads him to misrepresent his evaluative claims.

Suppose, for instance, that someone reports that a film isn't funny on the basis of her own experience: she was not at all amused by it. But suppose also that she was depressed and agitated about work when she saw it, and that, were it not for these mood effects, the film would have amused her. While she may sincerely believe that the film isn't funny, her judgment to this effect is defective because her lack of amusement is not a deliverance of her sense of humor. Moreover, her verdict inadvertently misleads those who infer, incorrectly, that the movie does not jibe with her sense of humor. Were she more self-aware, she should have given a different verdict. In order to avoid such misunderstanding and any misleading implications, she should have said something like "I wasn't in a good position to judge", or at any rate, "I wasn't amused by it, but maybe I didn't give it a fair chance." This is what people say when they are aware of potentially obscuring factors at play—but, as we've seen, in many cases such factors are translucent or even opaque.

These observations cohere nicely with Kant's insistence that judgments of beauty must be based upon one's taking pleasure (of the right sort) in the object judged. Furthermore, they show that judgments of sentimental value require more than a basis in affective response. Even when our judgments are sincere and grounded in our own responses, they can still be alienated from our sensibility; and when this is so, they cannot be avowed without qualification, because such pronouncements are supposed to express the agent's own evaluative perspective. These claims are buttressed by familiar, if often tacit, norms governing evaluative discourse. It is normally expected that such discourse will express one's own take on the value in question. If what you offer instead is someone else's verdict, or a judgment based on a response caused by an obscuring factor, then you are expected to acknowledge that the belief expressed is not in fact a deliverance of your own sensibility, for instance because it is based on testimony. That explains why it would be an embarrassment to be exposed as not having seen a film that you have pronounced funny, without making the proper qualifications, no matter how authoritative the testimony on which you rely.

The cases we have considered so far are those where it is likely that, if aware of the obscuring factor, an agent would withhold judgment about the sentimental value. In such cases our insistence on identifying *this person's* evaluative perspective with his sensibility seems undeniable, because his beliefs defer to his sensibility once its deliverances become apparent. But the most complex and interesting cases are those where someone knows her avowed position conflicts with her sensibility but endorses it nevertheless, on the basis of reasons she thinks decisive. In such circumstances, we suggest, she is at odds with herself. Her avowals are belied by her own evaluative perspective, or perhaps she lacks a coherent perspective. Moreover, we contend that there is something wrong with such alienated judgments—or beliefs lacking the grounding in response necessary for judgment—beyond the fact that they do not express a coherent evaluative perspective. There are reasons to doubt that they are really responsive to the nature of the value at issue.

Consider one final case of alienated evaluation, where our insistence on the priority of sensibility may seem especially difficult to maintain. Suppose that Christian (hereafter, Chris) thinks that various physical deformities and intellectual incapacities are not shameful, because they are not under the agent's control. Friedrich (Fred) holds, to the contrary, that although people may be admirable in various ways despite these traits, nonetheless the traits themselves are shameful: shame on the part of their possessors, and contempt from others, is fitting.[26] Suppose further that this disagreement would not be resolved by settling some non-evaluative dispute between the parties. Then their disagreement apparently concerns what sort of traits are shameful; specifically, whether features that are not your fault can nevertheless be shameful.

---

[26] We take it that "shameful" and "admirable" attach to persons, but they need not be all-in evaluations—they apply to a person for some specific trait or traits, and he may have other traits to which other and opposite evaluations apply. Someone can be shamefully lazy and admirably talented, or admirably industrious and shamefully stupid.

In order for this example to test our claims about alienated evaluations, we must suppose that Chris's own sensibility is at odds with his view. He is in fact disposed to be ashamed of some qualities that are not his own fault, and often feels contemptuous of such things as stupidity and clumsiness in others. Such conflicts between endorsed and felt values are quite common, and people often fail to recognize them. If that were the situation, and yet Chris asserted without qualification that there is nothing shameful about blameless stupidity, then his dispute with Fred would be problematic for reasons already discussed: he would be espousing values he had not himself internalized, without recognizing or acknowledging this fact. He thereby misleads others about his reasons, and perhaps deceives himself, even if his beliefs are sincerely avowed.

Suppose that Chris is more self-aware than most people, however, and recognizes that he is prone to feelings at odds with his considered opinion. Moreover, he believes (correctly) that these reactions are not obscuring factors but reveal his own evaluative sensibility. He does not base his views about the shameful on his sentimental responses when they reflect his sensibility. Indeed, he has to admit that when his actual responses do line up with his considered view, and he feels no contempt for someone's stupid mistake, there is often an obscuring factor present—such as friendship, or perhaps desensitization. He thus recognizes that stupidity is contemptible by the lights of his sensibility, and that in the absence of these obscuring factors, he would have been contemptuous. But Chris finds this objectionable. Since shame and contempt are powerful negative responses, he thinks it mistaken to direct them at aspects of a person that the person can't reasonably be expected to control. Thus Chris considers his sensibility pervasively in error for finding things shameful that, on reflection, he believes are not. He acknowledges his affective shortcomings forthrightly in his dispute with Fred and thereby avoids misleading him, by expressly canceling the ordinary implication that his claims about the shameful have the backing of his esteem sensibility.

Chris's verdict is not a judgment, in our sense of the term, because it is not grounded in his affective responses. His reflective position is in tension with his own sensibility, and in this respect it remains conflicted. Such cases are rare, we think, because people are seldom so clear about ways in which the actual contours of their own sensibilities are at odds with their theoretically motivated position. But in such a case, we will not insist that Chris's evaluative perspective goes with his sensibility. Perhaps the truth is that he has no coherent evaluative perspective on the shameful. There is a rational tension in his view of the matter that would have to be resolved in order for him to have a coherent take. His way of seeing a portion of the evaluative landscape, informed by his responses, cannot be brought into accord with his theory of that value. Until he revises his theory or reforms his sensibility, there is simply no good answer to the question of what is shameful by Chris's lights.

But there is more to be said about such situations. While we cannot adjudicate every possible conflict between rational norms and sensibilities, we can make two final, generic complaints against alienated beliefs about sentimental value that cannot be made against sensibilities. We submit that there are still important defects in Chris's sincere evaluative beliefs, even if they turn out to get the right answer. Chris lacks reason to believe that his alienated standards can serve the essential function of sentimental value concepts, and also lacks grounds for confidence that the standards he finds intuitively compelling are apt for the particular values to which he would apply them.

Our argument for these claims depends upon views we can here only assert programmatically, concerning the nature of sentimental values.[27] Sentimental value concepts arise from our need for a set of standards for regulating specific sentiments. In order to serve this function effectively, these standards must be attuned to the nature of the responses in question. Forward-looking pragmatic or moral considerations are widely acknowledged to be wrong kinds of reason: they cannot be used to govern our emotional responses, because they are not relevant to the value at issue.[28] People cannot regulate their admiration or contempt with incentives to admire or contemn someone, and such incentives seem irrelevant to whether he is admirable or contemptible. Moreover, we have argued elsewhere that moral reasons for having or not having emotions are likewise of the wrong kind: they too do not bear on the question of whether the emotion is fitting.[29] In order for some consideration to be eligible as a funny-maker, for instance, it must be the case that someone with a normal human psychology could be responsive to this consideration in coming to be amused, or not. Incentives (that is, rewards and punishments) will not do; at most they can motivate you to take steps to ensure that you will or won't be amused by something. This constraint illustrates what is ultimately so absurd about the most extreme stoic claims, such as that the loss of a child gives one no grounds for sorrow, and an important blunder no grounds for regret.[30]

These considerations provide additional support for favoring the deliverances of sensibility over the verdicts of dispassionate theory, when it comes to sentimental values. Judgments grounded in the relevant sensibility have something going for

---

[27] Some of these claims are developed and defended in D'Arms and Jacobson (2006b).

[28] See D'Arms and Jacobson (2000b) and Rabinowitz and Rønnow-Rassmussen (2004).

[29] See D'Arms and Jacobson (2000a).

[30] This is not a complaint against the pragmatic argument that sorrow and regret don't help (as in, "Don't cry over spilt milk"), but against the claim that the objects of these responses are mere "indifferents" of no real value. We object to the pragmatic argument too, but on pragmatic grounds: in most cases trying to extirpate the passions seems not just impossible but counterproductive. A more realistic approach seeks to diminish them in size and duration rather than extinguish them altogether; but this approach implicitly *grants* the badness of losses and blunders rather than denying it.

them that mere reflective endorsement does not: they constitute evidence that the supposedly decisive reason can in fact govern human responses in this domain. Chris's view about the shameful may not be one that people can internalize in sensibilities that govern human patterns of shame and contempt. In fact, we doubt that it is. But whether or not we are correct about this empirical claim, Chris is not in position to defend his theoretically motivated norm as a tenable claim about a sentimental value, because he has not succeeded in internalizing it. Thus even if we are mistaken about what can be shameful, his view is defective as it stands, because he lacks grounds for thinking this norm can successfully regulate his shame and contempt.

In contrast, sensibilities possess a guaranteed connection to the value they purport to detect. Recall our earlier point that response-independent characterizations of these values do not suffice to capture their particular character. The incongruity theory gets it roughly right about what is and isn't funny—but only roughly. Similarly, one can gloss shamefulness as being concerned with inabilities that reflect badly on their possessor, and this gets it roughly right. But such glosses can only be rough-and-ready, because shame and contempt take the offending trait to reflect badly on its possessor in a specific way, which cannot be fully articulated despite the fact that we are all familiar with it in virtue of being subject to these sentiments. Our esteem sensibility is concerned with this particular way of being bad, because the kind of disvalue in question is fixed by the way in which, in feeling shame or contempt, one takes the trait and its possessor. Theoretical convictions about what can really reflect badly on someone run the risk of being grounded in considerations that are not actually pertinent to the particular kind of badness relevant to shame and contempt. This is our diagnosis of Chris's norm. He fixes on considerations that demonstrate that stupidity and clumsiness are not bad in one way: they don't show you to be a bad person. But he supposes this to show that such traits do not reflect badly upon you in the distinctive way that shamefulness or contemptibility do. We suspect that the considerations he finds persuasive speak to a subtly different question regarding the moral propriety of feeling shame or contempt over blameless faults. But this moral claim, even if true, does not show that such traits aren't shameful.

We are not claiming that sensibilities are guaranteed to get matters right, or even that they are statistically more likely to be correct than are sincere evaluative beliefs. Our point is rather that they have internal connections to sentimental values which theoretical reflection does not. This fact renders such reflection prone to forms of error and confusion from which sensibilities are immune. Human sensibilities are our most important and systematic connection to the sentimental values which occupy a central place in our lives. This chapter has argued that, despite the vicissitudes of affective response and the inconsistencies in judgment to which these give rise, most people are properly interpreted as having relatively coherent and stable perspectives on sentimental values. The best way to understand the contours of these perspectives requires positing discrete emotional sensibilities, and identifying other familiar psychological forces that interfere with these sensibilities. Such posits are confirmed to the extent that our explanations of various patterns of affect, evaluative judgment, and discourse about sentimental values have been compelling. We contend that an adequate philosophical understanding of these crucial domains of human value, and of disagreement within these domains, requires a theory of sensibilities.

# REFERENCES

AYER, A. J. (1952). *Language, Truth and Logic*. New York: Dover.

D'ARMS, JUSTIN and DANIEL JACOBSON (2000a). "The Moralistic Fallacy: On the 'Appropriateness', of Emotions". *Philosophy and Phenomenological Research* 61: 65–90.

—— and —— (2000b). "Sentiment and Value". *Ethics* 110: 722–48.

—— and —— (2003). "The Significance of Recalcitrant Emotion (or, Anti-Quasijudgmentalism)". Reprinted in *Philosophy and the Emotions*, ed. Anthony Hatzimoysis. Cambridge: Cambridge University Press, 2003.

—— and —— (2006a). "Sensibility Theory and Projectivism". In *The Oxford Handbook of Ethical Theory*, ed. David Copp. Oxford: Oxford University Press, 2006.

—— and —— (2006b). "Anthropocentric Constraints on Human Value". *Oxford Studies in Metaethics* 1: 99–126.

DARWALL, STEPHEN, ALLAN GIBBARD, and PETER RAILTON (1992). "Toward *Fin de siècle* Ethics: Some Trends". *The Philosophical Review* 101: 115–89.

FOOT, PHILIPPA (1963). "Hume on Moral Beliefs". Reprinted in Foot, *Virtues and Vices*. Berkeley: University of California Press, 1978.

GIBBARD, ALLAN (1990). *Wise Choices, Apt Feelings: A Theory of Normative Judgment*. Cambridge, Mass.: Harvard University Press.

—— (2003). *Thinking How to Live*. Cambridge, Mass.: Harvard University Press.

GRIFFITHS, PAUL (2003). "Basic Emotions, Complex Emotions, Machiavellian Emotions". In Anthony Hatzimoysis, ed. *Philosophy and the Emotions*. Cambridge: Cambridge University Press.

HAIDT, JONATHAN (2001). "The Emotional Dog and Its Rational Tail: A Social Intuitionist Approach to Moral Judgment". *Psychological Review* 108: 814–34.

HUME, DAVID (1975). *Enquiries Concerning Human Understanding and Concerning the Principles of Morals*, ed. L. A. Selby-Bigge and P. H. Nidditch. 3rd edition. Oxford: Clarendon Press.

JACOBSON, DANIEL (1997). "In Praise of Immoral Art". *Philosophical Topics* 25: 155–99.

McDOWELL, JOHN (1979). "Virtue and Reason". Reprinted in McDowell (1998).

—— (1985). "Values and Secondary Qualities". Reprinted in McDowell (1998).

—— (1987). "Projection and Truth in Ethics". Reprinted in McDowell (1998).

—— (1996). "Two Sorts of Naturalism". Reprinted in McDowell (1998).

—— (1998). *Mind, Value, and Reality*. Cambridge, Mass.: Harvard University Press.

McIntosh, D., D. Druckman, and R. B. Zajonc (1994). "Socially Induced Affect". In *Learning, Remembering, Believing: Enhancing Human Performance*, eds. D. Druckman and R. A. Bjork. Washington DC: National Academy Press.

McNaughton, David (1988). *Moral Vision*. Oxford: Blackwell Publishing.

Millgram, Elijah (1999). "Moral Values and Secondary Qualities". *American Philosophical Quarterly* 36: 253–5.

Pettit, Philip (1999). "A Theory of Normal and Ideal Conditions". Reprinted in Pettit, P. *Rules, Reasons, and Norms*. Oxford: Oxford University Press, 2002.

Railton, Peter (1997). "Aesthetic Value, Moral Value, and the Ambitions of Naturalism". Reprinted in Railton, *Facts, Value, and Norms*. Cambridge: Cambridge University Press, 2003.

Rabinowitz, Wlodek and Toni Rønnow-Rasmussen (2004). "The Strike of the Demon: On Fitting Pro-attitudes and Value". *Ethics* 114: 391–423.

Scruton, Roger (1987). "Laughter". In *The Philosophy of Laughter and Humor*, ed. John Morreall. Albany: SUNY Press, 1987.

Smith, Michael (1994). *The Moral Problem*. Oxford: Basil Blackwell.

Stein, N. L., T. Trabasso, et al. (1993). "The Representation and Organization of Emotional Experience: Unfolding the Emotion Episode". In *Handbook of Emotions*. M. Lewis and J. M. Haviland, eds. New York, Guilford Press.

Wiggins, David (1987). "A Sensible Subjectivism?" In Wiggins, *Needs, Values, Truth*. Oxford: Basil Blackwell, 1987.

# PART VI

EMOTION, ART,
AND AESTHETICS

# CHAPTER 27

...............................................................................

# EXPRESSION IN
# THE ARTS

...............................................................................

## DEREK MATRAVERS

THERE are many different relations the emotions bear to the arts. In this contribution I am going to focus on the ways in which emotions are manifest in the arts. According to some philosophers, it is of the essence of art that it manifests emotion – that, indeed, is art's defining feature (Collingwood 1945). Although I shall not discuss Collingwood's theory, I shall discuss the concept that is central to it: namely, the expression of emotion in the arts. There is a great deal of published work on the expression of emotion in music; there is significantly less on the expression of emotion in the other art forms. In this chapter, I shall discuss the expression of emotion in music and then the expression of emotion in paintings. In the course of doing so, I will discuss some other ways in which the emotions can be manifest in the arts.

First, I shall say something about what I take the problem of expression to be, as it is not clear what we mean when we claim that works of art express certain emotions. I shall assume that the reason we want to clarify the nature of expression, is that we can throw light on what it is to understand a work of art; that is, there is something to understanding a work qua art. I shall assume that, primarily, what there is to be understood is capable of being accessed by an ideal spectator of the work through their experience of it. I say 'primarily' as there are properties of a work, relevant to understanding, which are not accessible through the experience.

I am grateful to Peter Goldie and to Jenefer Robinson for a number of extremely helpful suggestions for improvement on an earlier draft of this chapter.

Examples of such properties might be whether the work was original or derivative, whether it was a precursor of some later artistic movement, and so on. The properties that cause the spectator's experience of a work can be divided into two sorts: those of which the spectator is aware and those of which he or she is not aware. The muted tones of the picture cause me to see it as melancholy, and it is the muted tones that I see as melancholy. However, there may be other properties of the picture (the size of pupils in the model's eyes, to take one famous example) that influence my experience of the picture but of which I am unaware. We do not experience the model's pupils as being (in this case) indicative of sexual attraction. The division I have made is compatible with some properties bringing about a certain experience, and then, through reflection, our coming to be aware that those properties are the focus of our experience. For example, some of Rothko's canvasses have an immediate expressive impact. On reflection, we become aware of which properties cause that impact and begin to see those properties as expressive; that is, they become present in our experience. Of the properties present in our experience, it is only those of which we are aware that are relevant to our understanding, and hence relevant to expression.

This enables us to distinguish two questions. The first, which properly belongs to empirical psychology, attempts to find the properties of a work of art that cause us to experience it as expressive. Unless those are properties of which are aware, they are not relevant to our discussion as I have outlined it in the previous paragraph. Thus, we can put to one side those parts of the literature that attempt to answer this psychological question. The second question is the constitutive – and philosophical – question: can we clarify the nature of expression in such a way that it illuminates our understanding of art? That is what I shall discuss in this chapter.

In his account of musical expressiveness, Jerrold Levinson lists several desiderata that any theory should try to meet. Amongst these is what he terms 'the analogy requirement':

Musical expressiveness should be seen as parallel or closely analogous to expression in its most literal sense, that is, the manifesting of psychological states through outward signs, most notably behaviour. (Levinson 1996: 91)

This suggests that we should begin our discussion by looking at expression 'in its most literal sense', that is, in the central, non-artistic cases. Here, however, one encounters a problem. We do not seem to mark, in ordinary speech, the distinctions that have been indicated by some philosophers. For example, one might begin by distinguishing between betraying an emotion (where one's appearance and behaviour are unmediated effects of a felt emotional state) and expressing an emotion (which involves some sort of work of clarification) (Collingwood 1945). This raises at least two issues. First, if we take tears as the paradigm instance of betraying an emotion, we get the counter-intuitive consequence that the tears pouring down my face do not express my sadness (Davies 1994: 173–5). Second, we might wonder how much of our behaviour is an unmediated effect of a felt emotional state. Consider what might seem to be a paradigm example: I stub my toe, and shout 'ouch!' However, even this seems to involve some degree of choice: 'ouch!' would be an odd thing to shout if one were the victim of torture. Hence, what seems natural can in fact be subject to (fairly minimal) intentional input (Davies 1986: 150).[1]

As there is no settled ordinary language distinction, any definition will have an air of stipulation. The following definitions (to which I shall, at least provisionally adhere) have the virtue of clarifying some of the arguments over expression in the arts: I *betray* an emotion when either I manifest my emotion in an unmediated or, at most, a minimally intentional way and I *express* an emotion when I intend to communicate that I feel an emotion by virtue of manifesting signs associated with the betrayal of that emotion. In both cases 'intend' is to be read very weakly, so as not to imply 'deliberately intend' or even 'consciously intend'. In addition I shall add a third relation which I shall call 'exhibiting an emotional aspect' (or 'exhibiting'). The difference between exhibiting, on the one hand, and betraying and expressing emotion, on the other, is that, in the case of exhibiting, there is no emotion to be made available to onlookers. Rather, the person 'has an air' of a certain emotion about them (to pick up on a delightful chapter title from a book by Dominic Lopes [Lopes 2005: Ch. 2]). That is, someone who wears the appearance of an emotion and this appearance is not caused by any actual feeling of emotion. It is tempting to maintain that what it is to exhibit an emotion is, without any intention being involved, to appear as one would appear if one were betraying an emotion. What it is to have a sad face is to have a face that looks as it would look were sadness being betrayed. Rather than being over-hasty, I shall leave the question hanging as to whether such a reduction is possible.

So far, I have interpreted Levinson's desideratum as concerning the emotions. However, what he says is broader than that: he talks of 'the manifesting of *psychological states* through outward signs'. This could cover a variety of phenomena, including manifesting a belief through speech (we do talk of 'expressing an opinion'). I shall follow Richard Wollheim in restricting talk of expression to the emotions and closely related phenomena (what used to be meant by 'the passions') (Wollheim 1968: 84–5). Of these related phenomena, it is helpful to distinguish one that is important: a mood. The following loose definition of emotion is taken from Peter Goldie's perspicuous comparison between the two states:

An emotion . . . is a relatively complex state, involving past and present episodes of thoughts, feelings, and bodily changes, dynamically related to a narrative part of a person's

---

[1]  I am grateful to Rob Hopkins for bringing this to my attention.

life, together with dispositions to experience further emotional episodes, and to act out of the emotion and to express that emotion. (Goldie 2000: 144)

A mood is distinguished by 'the degree of specificity of their objects': that is, a mood has a less specific object (Goldie 2000: 145). Being anxious, irritated, nervous, jumpy or depressed would usually be classed as moods, while fear, hatred, and joy would usually be classed as emotions. The difference is one of degree, and mood and emotion cannot always be distinguished. To return to the distinctions above, moods can be betrayed, expressed, or exhibited. That is, none of those seems ruled out by their having a non-specific object. Indeed, exhibiting a psychological state is more closely linked to mood than emotion. If a look is not caused by any such state, we will generally not experience it as the manifestation of a state with a specific object. That is, we generally experience someone exhibiting (for example) sadness as looking sad, rather than looking sad about anything. However, it is not impossible to exhibit an emotion (rather than a mood): we might experience someone we know is at ease with themselves as looking scared of the assembled company. In what follows I will not, unless it matters, distinguish between emotions and moods, but use 'emotion' to cover both.

What these distinctions are intended to clarify is the confusion engendered by some philosophers taking the broad view that 'expression' covers a wide range of relations between art and the emotions, and others taking the narrow view that it covers a specific relation between art and the emotions: namely, a relation modelled on the central case phenomenon picked out by the definition of 'expression' given above. This is particularly apparent in the work on expression in music. This distinction (between philosophers who take the narrow and those that take the broad view of expression) cuts across another way of classifying the theories: into those that take the experience of expression in music to be some kind of imagined content, those that take the experience to be some kind of perceived resemblance, and those that take the experience to involve some kind of aroused feeling. I shall consider each of these latter three approaches in turn.

Jerrold Levinson takes the narrow view of expression, and believes that the experience of expression is some kind of imagined content. Indeed, he makes a case for the second following from the first. Taking expression in music to correspond to the narrow sense of expression in the central case suggests that when we say 'we experience the music as the expression of sadness' what we mean is something akin to 'we experience the music as being the externalisation of sadness by someone'. That is, we experience the music as the intentional communication of an emotion by virtue of manifesting signs associated with the betrayal of that emotion. Clearly we cannot do this literally, as we do not experience instrumental music as sounding anything like the sounds associated with the betrayal of human emotion. Although we cannot literally experience the music like that, we can *imagine* of the music that it is the expression of emotion. That is, we imagine the music is the externalization of some inner psychological state by some indefinite fictional agent, whose only role is to be that of which we hear the music as an externalization (Levinson calls this agent 'the persona'). More formally, Levinson's theory is as follows:

A passage of music P is expressive of an emotion E if and only if P, in context, is readily heard, by a listener experienced in the genre in question, as an expression of E... To hear music as such and such is, perhaps, to imagine *that* the music is such and such, and more specifically, to imagine *of* the music, *as* you are hearing it, that it is such and such. (Levinson 2005*b*: 193–5)

We could hear the music as (to return to an earlier distinction) expressing either an emotion or a mood. That is, we might hear the music as the expression of a specific object, even if the nature of that object is not part of the experience. We hear the persona as externalizing something in particular (whatever it might be). As he has taken the narrow view of expression, Levinson would claim to have accounted for the relation to the emotions of such works as the Adagio of Mozart's *Gran Partita*, or the first movement of Beethoven's Fifth. It is no part of this claim that this is the only relation between music and the emotions. For example, consider the emotional quality of Satie's *Gymnépodies*, or Schubert's Piano Sonata D. 960. These have an emotional quality, but they do not *express* emotions; rather, they are akin to the central case relation of *exhibiting* an emotion, or rather, being more precise, as exhibiting a mood (cf. Robinson 2005).

A second account that takes the content of the expressive experience as some kind of imagined state is due to Kendall Walton.

I propose that, although music does not in general call for imaginative hearing or imaginative perceiving, it often does call for imaginative *introspecting*. We mentioned the possibility that music is expressive by virtue of imitating behavioural expressions of feeling. Sometimes this is so, and sometimes a passage imitates or portrays vocal expressions of feelings. When it does, listeners probably imagine (not necessarily consciously and certainly not deliberately) themselves hearing someone's vocal expressions. But in other cases they may instead imagine themselves introspecting, being aware of, their own feelings. (Walton 1988: 359)

In a later paper, he elucidates this a little:

Anguished or agitated or exuberant music not only induces one to imagine feeling anguished or agitated or exuberant, it also induces one to imagine of one's auditory experience that *it* is an experience of anguish or agitation or exuberance. (Walton 1994: 55)

This imaginative endeavour is, for Walton, constitutive of the work sounding a certain way to us.

Levinson criticizes Walton's account for failing to match the desiderata given to any account of expression by taking the narrow reading of expression in the central case. That is, 'it casts the activity of experiencing musical expressiveness in too egocentric a light' – expression 'is something we encounter as residing fundamentally "out there"' (Levinson 1996: 94). The lesson here, which Levinson is happy to admit, is that Walton and Levinson have different targets: Walton is illuminating one connection between music and the emotions (akin to 'exhibiting an emotion') and Levinson another (expression, narrowly construed).

Both Levinson and Walton might take this attempt to dissolve the debate between them as too irenic. Levinson maintains that the primary case of expression in music is that of hearing the music as the expression of emotion by an imagined other. Walton's account – at least, the account to which he devotes most attention – construes expression as a matter of the music (to use a metaphor) speaking the emotions of the listener. It is difficult to see how this particular debate could be resolved. Indeed, the prevalence of this kind of disagreement is one of the unresolved peculiarities of work on expression in music.

One might criticize accounts that make use of the imagination as simply taking the description of the experience we find problematic (we experience the music as the expression of emotion), putting it within the scope of the imagination, and maintaining it is not problematic. This suspicion is lent force by the fact that there is no robust, background account of the imagination to which people such as Levinson and Walton can appeal that will give an independent grasp of its scope and explanatory power. However, they have a number of considerations on their side. First, we are not starting from nothing; we begin with an experience familiar to all of us. If the description provided by an account of the experience of expressive music appears accurate to people familiar with the experience, that is a point in its favour. Second, considerations can be brought forward to mitigate the concerns that we do not fully understand the content of the imagined state. Levinson says that musical expressing is music 'heard as doing something like what humans do in manifesting emotions... ones analogous to human gesturing and vocalizing and expressive movement, in all its forms, including dancing, but going beyond them' (Levinson 1996: 115). Walton points to various similarities between sounds and our feelings, such as that we 'reify or objectify sounds'; we think of them as having an existence in our experience rather than (like sights) existing 'out there' (Walton 1994: 57). Such similarities make it easier for us to accept that we can imagine of our experience of one that it is an experience of another.

Worries remain, however. The accounts attempt to provide the content of an imagined state that captures precisely the phenomenology of expressive music. How, therefore, can we adjudicate which of any competing accounts of the content of the imagined state is correct? Each account will claim that what it is like to be in the state is precisely what it is like to experience expressive music. This leads to two problems. First, it is not clear that the additional argumentative resources marshalled in the above paragraph will be sufficient to enable us to distinguish between accounts. Second, is it not clear what reply can be given to the person who claims that what it is like for him or her to experience music as expressive is *not* captured by the proffered account. Despite the contributors to the debate being qualified and experienced listeners to music, there is much disagreement as to what the phenomenology is. This does lead, sometimes, to a philosophical stand-off. Levinson, for example, wants to model his account of aesthetics properties on the basic equation for colour (Levinson 2005a). That is:

What it is for an object to be red is for it to cause, in the right sort of person in the right sort of circumstances, an experience of kind K (where 'an experience of kind K' is the experience of 'phenomenal red').

What it is for a piece of music to be sad is for it to cause, in the right sort of person in the right sort of circumstances, an experience of kind L (where 'an experience of kind L' is to hear the music as the expression of emotion by a persona).

The problem is that while we only have one route to experiences of kind K – it is the experience we get when looking at objects such as fire engines – we have two routes to experiences of kind L: it is the experience we get when we listen to pieces of music such as the second movement of Beethoven's Third Symphony and via Levinson's description. However attenuated, there is enough in Levinson's description to open up a gap for his critics to claim that two routes do not have the same destination. In other words, for them an experience of L is not an experience of the expression of emotion by a persona. It is not clear to what Levinson would appeal to answer such critics.

The second group of theories attempts to illuminate the connection between music and emotion, not by imagining of the experience of music that it is some kind of central case experience, but by experiencing the similarities between the experience of music and the central case experience. That is, the music appears to us a certain way, and the way it appears is similar to the appearance worn by people expressing their emotion. Stephen Davies (the most prominent proponent of this theory) disagrees with Levinson as to the phenomenology of expressive music. As we have seen, Levinson's account in based in expression being construed narrowly. Davies, instead, denies that music expresses emotions in this sense; rather 'it presents emotion characteristics in appearances' (Davies 1994: 261). We shall return to this disagreement shortly.

Davies' claim is that there are certain type appearances, linked to the emotions although not necessarily caused by a felt emotion. For example, some people have a sad face: that is, a face that looks as if it is expressing sadness, even if it is not. This type appearance can be tokened in places where talk of such inner states is not appropriate. For example, we can say of the St Bernard dog that it has 'a sad face'. Davies claim is that this appearance can be tokened in certain pieces of music: when this happens we have an instance of 'sad music'. We perceive this directly, as we do the sadness on the face of the St Bernard. Davies says, 'the expressiveness of music depends mainly on a resemblance we perceive between the dynamic character of music and human movement, gait, bearing, or carriage' (Davies 1994: 229). This is also one way of interpreting the view put forward by Peter Kivy (Kivy 1989).

Clearly, there are many things (including pieces of music) that are candidates for our experiencing them as tokening this appearance. In any particular case, whether we actually do so is a matter for psychology (Davies 1994: 228). There are two issues, however, where Davies theory looks vulnerable. The first is whether the explanation in terms of cross-modal type appearances is actually illuminating. There is a type of taste that is the taste of strawberries, which can be tokened in other things I can taste (for example, milkshakes and ice-cream) but there is nothing that is the sight or sound of the taste of strawberries. What sense can we attach to experiencing the sound of music as tokening a type, where that type is specified in terms of how something looks? Davies' reply to this is that there are certain properties – particularly those of movement – that can be tokened either in sight or in sound: both people and music can move slowly. However, such a reply faces an obvious problem: to be a literal case of movement, there must be a continuous existent that changes location over time. This is true in the case of people moving, but false in the case of our experience of music. The property underpinning the resemblance claim is not the same in both cases: we are comparing literal movement to metaphorical movement. Davies reply to this is to deny that the literal sense of 'movement' is restricted to the physical paradigm. He points out that movement vocabulary is not only virtually universal in describing music but also in many other non-musical mundane scenarios: stock-exchange indices shift up and down, and political parties lurch to the right (Davies 1994: 230–8). The second problem is whether there are things that we experience as tokening the relevant type appearance which we do not experience as cases of expression. It is difficult to adjudicate on this question. As we saw above, Davies and his critics differ as to the nature of the phenomenon they are attempting to explain. Levinson holds that the experience of musical expression is parallel to the narrow sense of expression in the central case. For Davies, the parallel is to the central case phenomenon of exhibiting an emotion – or, more precisely, a mood (as it is moods rather than emotions that – generally – are exhibited). Here, there is a mis-match between that which these two philosophers are attempting to describe. Davies is the broader of the two, but Levinson would argue that Davies misses the distinctive nature of the paradigm cases of expression.

The third group of theories construe expression as a matter of an aroused feeling. The crude version of the theory has some intuitive appeal: a piece of music expresses an emotion if it arouses that emotion in careful listeners. There are many objections to the account in the literature, and although several of these can be answered some serious difficulties remain (Matravers 1998). First, however, we need to put the account in a more plausible form: a piece of music expresses an emotion E if, amongst the mental states it arouses, is some non-cognitive state that is appropriately related to the experience of E in the central case. Much here rests on the nature of 'the appropriate relation'. A plausible candidate would be that the non-cognitive state is phenomenologically similar to the feeling component of an emotion. This presupposes that emotions consist of an amalgam of different states: traditionally, a cognitive state, some phenomenological state (the 'feeling component'), and some physiological changes. The claim is that if, amongst the mental states aroused by a piece of music, there is one that is phenomenologically similar to the feeling component of some particular emotion, then the music expresses that emotion (cf. Matravers 1998: 146).

One difficulty with this is that the emotion ends up in the wrong place. It is generally agreed that, when we experience music as expressing an emotion, we hear the expression as a feature of the music. The 'arousal theory' claims that our experience is a conjunction of two components: the music and some non-cognitive state. However, this simply does not seem accurate: our experience of the music as sad does not consist of our expression-free experience of the music plus the experience of sadness.

There is another possible model of the arousal theory that might escape this problem (I owe this suggestion to Malcolm Budd). Consider the case in which we 'catch' a feeling or emotion. For example, being in a room with someone who is nervous might make us nervous in turn. Kendall Walton has written in detail about this phenomenon, in an account of musical tension.

it is the music that I experience as infecting me with nervousness. Let this count as a kind of projection of my nervousness onto the music. It explains, in any case, the naturalness of describing the music as nervous, and it makes recognizing 'nervousness' in music very much like recognizing nervousness in people . . . The projection is technically in error; the music is not literally nervous, as I am, and to say that it is would be a category mistake. But of course in describing it as nervous, we don't mean, literally, that it possesses the mental state of being nervous. The property we do attribute seriously to the music is something like the property of being apt to produce in listeners an experience as of there being someone or something who is infectiously nervous. (Walton 1999: 432)

Walton himself does not take the step, but an arousal theorist could claim that there are cases in which a similar sort of emotion (or feeling associated with an emotion) is aroused. The property we would attribute to the music in such a case would be something like the property of being apt to produce in listeners an experience of there being someone or something who is infectiously (for example) sad. It is not obvious that this model would face the same problem as the previous model, for it is *the music* which is experienced as infecting me with sadness. We are not left with the problem of having to get the sadness out of the listener's head, and back into the music.

I have, so far, outlined three accounts of the relation between music and the emotions: as involving some kind of imagined state, the perception of resemblance and of aroused feeling. I have suggested that their range of application might be limited, but have not found decisive arguments to dismiss any of them. I shall return to consider the implications of this, after discussing one more account: that of Malcolm Budd. Budd puts forward his view as follows:

The basic and minimal concept of the musical expression of emotion comes to this: when you hear music as being expressive of emotion E – when you hear E in the music – you hear the music as sounding like the way E feels; the music is expressive of E if it is correct to hear it in this fashion or a full appreciation of the music requires the listener to hear it in this way. So the sense in which you hear the emotion in the music – the sense in which it is an audible property of the music – is that you perceive a likeness between the music and the experience of the emotion. (Budd 1995: 137)

Budd gives an extensive list of the resources in virtue of which music is able to mirror those aspects of feeling available to it. These include tension and relaxation, difference in upwards or downwards direction, magnitude, speed and rhythm of felt movement, and levels of felt energy. These points of resemblance may lie either above or below the levels of consciousness (Budd 1995: 142). If they are part of our conscious experience, we can defend particular judgements with respect to them. If they are not, then (I assume) we are left with an experience of similarity but, to defend our judgement, we shall have to appeal to 'a community of response' (ibid.).

The claim that music is expressive if it sounds the way our emotion feels is rather opaque. The claim is not the claim that music actually resembles our emotions; it is difficult to see how we could specify the relata in a way in which the claim would make sense. It is rather that music sounding the way our emotions feel is the most perspicuous description of our experience of expressive music; it captures what the experience is like in an enlightening way. Even if one granted the first part of this (it does seem to capture what our experience is like) one might have doubts about the second (how enlightening is the claim?). It is not clear we have a sufficiently robust grasp of the way the properties apparently common to both are manifested in either, to make the resemblance claim very enlightening. However, as a phenomenological description, it might be the best that is available to us.

Having argued for this concept of expression, Budd claims (presumably on the basis of reflecting on his experience of music) that 'there are other conceptions of expressive perception and the musical expression of emotion [which] exploit the accretions that the mere perception of alikeness between music and feeling is liable to attract' (Budd 1995: 147). The three main 'accretions' Budd lists correspond roughly to the arousal theory, to Walton's theory, and Levinson's theory (although there are important differences in nuance in all of the accounts). Finally, Budd allows that our conception of expressiveness can be broadened 'by dropping the demand that the imagining must be done in virtue of a perceived similarity between the music and the feeling imagined and allowing that the imagining can legitimately be controlled by the music in other ways' (Budd 1995: 152).

Budd's generous pluralism is justified, if at all, by reflecting on our experience of music and on the nature of our judgements on music. If one or both of those cannot all be fitted under a single account, then we have reason to allow accounts that do seem descriptively accurate to take their place along side each other (it is noteworthy that Budd claimed that an adequate theory of music would not be 'monolithic' in his first published work on the subject (Budd 1985: 176)). Although few are explicit as Budd, as noted above, both Levinson and Walton allow that there are conceptions of expression besides that on which their accounts focus. The arguments below – made with respect to paintings – also, I think, provide arguments for a more pluralist conception.

Above, I quoted Levinson's analogy requirement: the claim that any adequate theory of expression should relate expression in the arts to expression in the central case. In another of his desiderata ('the extendability requirement') he claims that whatever is said about expression in music should be generalizable to expression in the other arts.

> Musical expressiveness should be seen to be related intelligibly to expressiveness in other arts, either by being transparently a species of expressiveness in arts generally, according to some plausible account of that, or else a close relative of expressiveness as exhibited in other arts, where the divergence is explicable in terms of salient differences in the media involved. (Levinson 1996: 91)

As we have seen, there is a good deal of philosophical work that attempts to elucidate expression as it applies to pieces of music. There is significantly less writing on expressiveness in painting than there is in expressiveness in music. Exceptions are Richard Wollheim and Dominic Lopes (Wollheim 1987; Lopes 2005).

There are three contrasts between expression in painting and expression in music. First, expression is something that characteristically, if not necessarily, unfolds across time. That music is a temporal art is one reason that we are able to imagine, of the music, that it is an act of expression. Painting is not a temporal art in that sense (Lopes 2005: 63). Rather, when we look at an expressive painting, we do not look at the act of expression but rather at the result of an expressive act. Second, as we have seen above in the theory of Jerrold Levinson, we do not hear music as the 'natural' expression of emotion; rather, our hearing is imaginative: we hear it as the musical expression of emotion. However, we can see pictures as the natural expression of emotion. We see the paint as the product of the actions of (for example) an anguished person. There is an analogy with music here, which is related to the third contrast. There are two different objects that could be the vehicles of emotion in the performance of a piece of music: that way the piece is played, and the piece itself. We can hear a piece of music as having been performed resolutely, wistfully, or angrily. This is independent of the expressive qualities of the piece, as (obviously) a sad piece of music could be performed in all of those ways (it could even be produced in a happy manner, although this might be a bit bizarre). With the type of painting we are considering, we see the painting as the result of an action performed in a certain manner. In this respect there is an analogy with music. However, unlike music, the painting inherits its expressive qualities from the way we see it as having been produced. There is no distinction between performance and piece.

Lopes makes some useful distinctions between 'figure expression' (attributable to a figure depicted in the painting), 'scene expression' (attributable to the depicted scene and not any depicted figure), and 'design expression' (attributed to the picture's designed surface, and not to any figure or scene) (Lopes 2005: 50–7; Davies 1986). An example of figure expression would be Honoré Daumier's *Fatherly Discipline* (1851–2; The Art Institute of Chicago) and an example of scene expression would be Théodore Géricault's *The Raft of the Medusa* (1818–19; The Louvre, Paris). Lopes does not claim that these modes of expression are exclusive: a single picture might manifest all, some, or none of them. The problem, as Lopes sees it, is to account for 'the missing person problem'. This arises for both scene and design expression: '[how can there] be expression in the absence of being to whom the expressed emotion is attributable' (Lopes 2005: 58)?

One option is to attribute the expressed emotion to the maker of the picture. As mentioned above, there do seem to be instances of this. That is, there are paintings we experience as the expression of emotion: namely, as the manifestation of an inner state. As we see painting as an artefact, the product of a process of manufacture, we can notice the way in which the artefact was produced. For example, the brushwork in van Gogh's *Wheat Field with Crows* or de Kooning's *Women III* looks as if it was produced by someone externalizing an emotional state. Indeed, as it looks uncontrolled, it is experienced more as the betrayal rather than the expression of an emotion. Nonetheless, it is common parlance to describe such paintings as 'expressive' for just this reason. In the sense we are considering, expression in painting is broadly unproblematic. That is, we do not need to imagine of the agitated brushstrokes that they are something else. Rather, we see them as what they are: the externalization of some inner state. We do not have to believe that we are looking at the externalization of the inner state of the actual artist (although often we do). An artist might assume a personality when painting a picture: that is, they may paint as if they are anguished or agitated. Alternatively, we might simply hypothesize that the artist painted in this way. This, however, does not affect the way we experience the paint. We do not have to imagine, of the paint, that it is something different to what it in fact is.

Cases such as van Gogh and de Kooning fall under the narrow sense of expression, and would thus seem to be in line with both Levinson's analogy and extendibility requirement. That is, it is modelled on (indeed, it is a case of) expression in the central case, and parallels the account Levinson gives of expression in music. Experiencing paint as the externalization of some inner state is not, however, the principal way in which we experience paintings as connected to the emotions. Instead, we see paintings (to borrow the title of Lopes' chapter) as 'having the air' of an emotion. That is, we do not see them as expressing or betraying emotion but rather as simply exhibiting emotion (or, more precisely, a mood). Lopes has a general term to capture this: they exhibit an 'expression look' (Lopes 2005: 70).

This is the curiosity: it seems that Levinson's extendibility requirement is wide of the mark. Expressiveness in music and the usual case of expressiveness in pictures do not seem to have much in common (Lopes 2005: 50). The principal reason for this, I suggest, is that expression (as I have defined it) is something that characteristically, if not essentially, unfolds across time. That music is a temporal art is one reason that we are able to imagine, of the music, that it is an act of expression. Painting is not a temporal art in that sense (Lopes 2005: 63). Hence, putting aside the type of case considered above, whatever 'expression' is used to refer to in painting, it will be different from its use in music. The claim that we experience expressive pictures as the expression of emotion, by a persona, in a sui generis pictorial manner does not seem a good place to start in thinking about expression in pictures (Lopes 2005: 63–5). Levinson himself draws back from the extendibility requirement, maintaining that 'expressiveness in the arts is not necessarily a univocal notion' (even citing differences between temporal and non-temporal arts as a possible reason) (Levinson 1996: 124). The exhibiting of emotion (or more particularly, of mood) does not unfold across time. Hence, the extendibility requirement fails for Levinson because the manifesting of emotion is not analogous to the exhibition of mood. For those, such as Davies, who construe music as the exhibiting of mood, there will not be this reason for thinking expression in music and painting will be discontinuous. This depends on whether an account such as that of Davies can be given for painting, to which we will now turn.

How, then, to solve the 'missing person problem' in those cases where works exhibit rather than express emotion? The obvious place to look is the second group of theories considered above: those that turn on the experience of resemblance. Lopes holds that they are committed to two claims: (1) that the pictures exhibit an 'expression look' and (2) that this expression look is explained by resemblance (Lopes 2005: 70–1). It is not clear that the best construal of the theory would involve the second of these claims. For reasons analogous to those discussed at the beginning of this entry, the resemblance theorist might not want to make the causal claim. Instead, they might construe that second claim as a constitutive account of the expressive look: that is, (2*) what it is to experience the picture as exhibiting the expression look of (for example) sadness is to experience it as resembling the expression of sadness. Lopes refers to theories committed to (1) and (2) as 'robust contour theories' and to those committed to only (1) as 'minimal contour theories'. Let us refer to those committed to (1) and (2*) as 'constitutive contour theories'.

The constitutive contour theory does not look to be a good candidate for solving the missing person problem. Consider Rothko's *Red on Maroon* (1959, Tate Gallery, London) which Richard Wollheim claims expresses 'a form of suffering and of sorrow... barely or fragilely contained' (Wollheim 1970: 128). The constitutive contour theory would have to specify the property in virtue of which a resemblance was perceived between this picture and the expression of emotion in the central case. The properties that Davies relies on in the case of music ('human movement, gait, bearing or carriage') do not look likely candidates. Even if some such property can be found in particular cases, the claim that such a property can be found in every case is without foundation.

Lopes argues that we need only commit ourselves to the minimal contour theories, for the reasons given in the discussion of expression in music above. That is, no philosophical account needs to be committed to any particular causal mechanism for bringing about the experience of expression. Instead, he commits himself the following:

[The] contour theory of pictorial expression: the physical configuration of a picture's design or the figure or scene a picture depicts expresses E if and only if (1) it is an expression-look that (2) has the function, in the circumstances, of indicating E. (Lopes 2005: 78)

Lopes makes a virtue of this version of (2) being a weak claim. That is, the minimal contour theory 'does not even acknowledge' the task of specifying the mechanism through which a picture comes to have a certain expression look (Lopes 2005: 78). The requirement is only that the expression look in some way 'indicates' the emotion. Lopes has this clause as a way of satisfying the following condition:

[The] connection condition: an expression is not merely a physical configuration; it is a physical configuration connected to an emotion. (Lopes 2005: 57)

It is not clear, however, that having the function of 'indicating the emotion' is the only way in which the connection condition could be satisfied.

Richard Wollheim's account does not rely on our experiencing the picture as an expression look that indicates an emotion. Wollheim's view took slight different forms in different places, and is not easy to condense into summary. I shall base my account on the version given in 'Correspondence, Projective Properties and Expression' (Wollheim 1991). To understand the view, one first needs a grasp of projection. Wollheim distinguishes two sorts of projection: simple projection and complex projection. The first is the most familiar from the psychoanalytic literature: a person cannot tolerate their melancholy (for example) so they project it onto another person in their environment. This has two consequences. Their feeling of melancholy is lessened, and they come to believe the person on whom they have projected their inner state is melancholic. Complex projection occurs when an inner state is projected onto the environment. Once again, the melancholy is lessened. However, the person does not come to believe the environment possesses some psychological property; clearly, as the environment does not possess a mind, that would be a bizarre belief. Instead, he or she comes 'to look upon, or respond to, some part of the environment as melancholy' (Wollheim 1991: 151).

Expression occurs as follows. A piece of nature has a certain kind of appearance that makes it particularly suitable as the recipient of the projection of our mental state. We project our mental state and, once this is done, the piece of nature takes on a certain visual appearance to us: we do not believe that it literally possesses this mental state; rather we see it as being 'of a piece' with our emotions. However, this cannot be the standard account of expressive properties in nature, as it would require that someone could only see nature as (for example) melancholy after a particular episode of projection. That simply seems far-fetched – we do not need to be in a heightened emotional state to experience the world as expressive. Hence, Wollheim claims that we recognize a piece of nature as one 'on which we might have, or could have, projected this or that kind of feeling' (Wollheim 1991: 153–4). This state intimates its own history: that is, intimates its origins in the kind of experience it is – an experience of the projection of an inner state onto nature. This, in itself, is sufficient to bring about the change in appearance, and imbue the piece of nature with projective properties.

If Wollheim is right, then the attempt to reduce exhibiting an emotion to the appearance of betraying emotion – which I mooted above – will be unsuccessful. There is no reason, on Wollheim's account, to think that some part of the world which has the expressive property of melancholy will resemble the appearance of someone who is betraying their melancholy.

The move from expression in nature to expression in art can be accomplished quickly. It is a difference in what the spectator needs to know in order to see the painting as being one 'on which we might have, or could have projected this or that kind of feeling'.

The difference is that, in the case of art, the experience that is evidential for the projective property is based on a larger body of background knowledge, a larger cognitive stock that is required for the perception of correspondence in nature. The background knowledge must include beliefs about a work's history of production and the specific processes of art that went into its making. (Wollheim 1991: 156)

There is a concealed complexity in Wollheim's view, however. From this discussion it looks as if the mechanism is the same in nature as it is in art. The difference is only that, in the latter case, we engage more of our background knowledge in sensitizing ourselves to whether or not the object is an appropriate one on which to project our mental states. However, this sits ill with Wollheim's general view of understanding paintings: that it is a matter of our retrieving the creative process that went into its making (Wollheim 1980). For the process of retrieval suggests that it is not only that the spectator experiences the picture as having expressive properties but that they retrieve the projection that was part of the process of making. Wollheim puts this view forward in his essay 'The Sheep and the Ceremony' (Wollheim 1979: 11–12). In a rather obscure passage, Wollheim talks about 'the expressive value' of a painting resting in part on the quality of the psychological process that went into its making. That is, if, in the process of creating the painting, the painter deviated from a process that involves self-knowledge, the expressive value of the painting is diminished. In short, the expressive value of a painting has two sources: the finding of expressive properties (which has its origins in the spectator's capacity for projection) and the evaluation of the quality of the retrieved creative process by which the work came about.

Wollheim's view falls short of the strong contour theory as there is no claim that either expressive perception or the expressive value accruing to the retrieved creative process is grounded in resemblance. Whether it would count as a minimal contour theory, according to Lopes, is a moot point. Let us consider each of Wollheim's two accounts separately. The account in terms of expressive properties agrees with Lopes in that it attributes to paintings 'an expressive look'. This look is 'corresponds to' or is 'of a piece with' our emotions. The painting is deliberately made by the painter in order to engage the spectator in the mechanism Wollheim describes, so that the painting takes on the right expressive properties in the spectator's perception of it. To debate whether or not this accords with Lopes' claim that the expression look 'has the function of indicating [the emotion] E' would perhaps be to impute to this claim a precision that it could not be expected to bear. However, at the very least, the connection between Wollheim's expressive properties and the emotion is not accidental, which is perhaps all Lopes needs. The account in terms of the quality of the retrieved creative process is less obviously a minimal contour theory for the simple reason that it fails the first clause of the definition: the expressive value does not rest on an expression look but on a judgement as to whether the creative process was or was not a contribution to self-knowledge.

The conclusion I want to draw from this is that philosophy has provided some rich accounts of the relation between art and the emotions, which go under the broad heading of 'expression'. I have argued above that we need not choose between them but instead embrace a generous pluralism. However, there is one reason to be suspicious of such generosity. That is, there is reason for thinking that there is a single account that covers all cases. Any philosophical account should give us the content of claims such as 'the work is sad' or 'the work expresses sadness'. Whether or not the meaning of each of these sentences is invariant across the artistic media (that is, it means the same in talking about music as it does in talking about paintings), it certainly looks plausible that it is invariant within a single medium: the meaning of 'this passage of music is sad' does not vary depending on the nature of the experience that underpins it. Hence, if the meaning is tied to the nature of the experience (something on which all sides agree) then sameness of meaning would imply sameness of experience. This might seem to demand a single account of the experience, at least within an artistic medium.

Here, however, we can draw on the spirit of Lopes' minimal account. What it is for a work to express (in the broad sense) a particular emotion is for it to manifest an appearance, which appearance is broadly connected to the emotion. That is, that there is some such appearance is constant, and the nature of the connection to the emotion will vary between cases. Different connections will occur in different media and some (for example, in being experienced as the expression of the emotion by a persona) may very well occur in only one medium. This would not capture the thought that part of the expressive value of a picture comes through our judgement on the retrieved creative process of the artist. However, we could argue that this was only derivatively a case of expression: what we are judging is the quality of the experience of expression of someone else.

If this is right, we should be less sanguine about having general desiderata for any account of expression. We have met several such: the 'analogy requirement' (that expression in the arts should be rooted in expression in the central case); the 'extendibility requirement' (that an account of expression should apply across the expressive media); and the claim that the experience of expression draws on links between the works of art and an expressive appearance. There is no obvious reason why Wollheim should worry about not conforming to the analogy requirement, and even Levinson and the resemblance theorists fulfil that in very different ways. We have seen that Lopes rejects the extendibility requirement; he also (largely) rejects that analogy requirement (in that he thinks that some expressive looks are sui generis to the arts). We need not even worry if the causal story behind expression draws links with the expressive appearance (Kivy, Davies, and – to an extent – Lopes worry, Levinson and Wollheim do not). The moral of the story, at least with respect to this chapter on the nature of expression, is that the reason the problem has seemed so difficult to solve is that there was no single problem to be solved in the first place.

# References

Budd, M. (1985). *Music and the Emotions*. London: Routledge and Kegan Paul.

—— (1995). *Values of Art: Pictures, Poetry, Music*. Harmondsworth: Penguin.

Collingwood, R. G. (1945). *The Principles of Art*. Oxford: Clarendon Press.

Davies, S. (1986). 'The Expression Theory Again'. *Theoria* 52(3): 146–67.

—— (1994). *Musical Meaning and Expression*. Ithaca: Cornell University Press.

Goldie, P. (2000). *The Emotions*. Oxford: Clarendon Press.

Kivy, P. (1989). *Sound Sentiment: An Essay on the Musical Emotions*. Philadelphia: Temple University Press.

Levinson, J. (1996). 'Musical Expressiveness'. *The Pleasures of Aesthetics*. Ithaca: Cornell University Press: 90–125.

—— (2005a). 'Aesthetic Properties'. *Supplementary Proceedings of the Aristotelian Society* 79: 211–27.

—— (2005b). 'Musical Expressiveness as Hearability as Expression'. *Contemporary Debates in Aesthetics and the Philosophy of Art*. Ed. M. Kieran. Oxford: Blackwell: 192–204.

Lopes, D. M. (2005). *Sight and Sensibility: Evaluating Pictures*. Oxford: Oxford University Press.

Matravers, D. (1998). *Art and Emotion*. Oxford: Oxford University Press.

ROBINSON, J. (2005). *Deeper than Reason: Emotion and its Role in Literature, Music and Art.* Oxford: Clarendon Press.

WALTON, K. (1988). 'What is Abstract about the Art of Music?' *Journal of Aesthetics and Art Criticism* 46(3): 351–64.

—— (1994). 'Listening with Imagination: Is Music Representational?' *Journal of Aesthetics and Art Criticism* 52(1): 47–62.

—— (1999). 'Projectivism, Empathy, and Musical Tension'. *Philosophical Topics* 26(1 & 2): 407–40.

WOLLHEIM, R. (1968). 'Expression'. *On Art and the Mind.* London: Allen Lane, 1973: 84–100.

—— (1970). 'The Work of Art as Object'. *On Art and the Mind.* Repr. London: Allen Lane, 1973: 112–29.

—— (1979). 'The Sheep and the Ceremony'. *The Mind and Its Depths.* Repr. Cambridge, Mass.: Harvard University Press, 1993: 1–21.

—— (1980). 'Criticism as Retrieval'. *Art and Its Objects.* Repr. Cambridge: Cambridge University Press: 185–204.

—— (1987). *Painting as an Art.* Repr. London: Thames and Hudson.

—— (1991). 'Correspondence, Projective Properties and Expression in the Arts'. *The Mind and Its Depths.* Repr. Cambridge, Mass.: Harvard University Press, 1993: 144–58.

CHAPTER 28

.................................................

# AFFECTS IN APPRECIATION

.................................................

## SUSAN L. FEAGIN

THE affective responses to art that have been the main topic of discussion in the philosophical literature are emotions, identified by terms that have a fairly well-entrenched usage in our ordinary, everyday language, such as 'fear' and 'anger', and that are assumed to have fairly specifically delineable cognitive components in the form of beliefs, thoughts, or imaginings (and perhaps also desires). I am here concerned with a different subset of affective phenomena that I shall refer to as, for lack of a better term, 'feelings'. Feelings, as I shall understand them, are of relatively short duration, are sometimes thought of as pure affect, and are, in any case, more vague and inchoate than the 'garden-variety' emotions described above (for which I reserve use of the term 'emotions'). Examples of such feelings are harder to provide, in part because there is no systematic vocabulary for identifying them and in part because short-term feelings morph into longer-term moods (and vice versa); there is certainly an overlap in vocabulary. Some possibilities for everyday feelings are anxiety, awkwardness, feelings of alienation, and nostalgia.

I am concerned here with a particular variety of feelings that occur as part of appreciating literary works of art, paradigmatically novels. The lack of an adequate vocabulary is even more pronounced with such feelings, in part because they are typically closely associated with the character and content of the writing that is responsible for them. For example, I feel an awkwardness in the way an outside culture tugs at tradition in Chinua Achebe's *Things Fall Apart*, especially in the way characters use the language of that culture, which is not their own. I am slightly sickened by the Prince's sense of entitlement when Henry James tells us, at the beginning of *The Golden Bowl*, that he 'had always liked his London'. I feel a shiver when I read 'So it goes', in Kurt Vonnegut's *Slaughterhouse-Five*, just after being told the cab driver's mother was incinerated in the Dresden firestorm. I feel uneasy with and somewhat puzzled by the attitude it expresses. The next time the phrase is used my uneasiness intensifies, reinforced by the memory that the phrase has been used before, and some of the puzzlement is washed away as I recognize that it is likely part of a pattern. By the third time it appears, I am comfortably alienated from the attitude it expresses.

Such feelings are not mere reactions or relatively superficial responses to novels: they are deep and subtle, and of a sort that are commonly thought of as revealing something profound about ourselves as human beings. This is despite the fact that they are difficult if not impossible to describe, and that our attempts to articulate what is going on with them often changes how we feel or even drains away the feelings entirely. In addition, their closeness to—perhaps essential connection with—the written passages that give rise to them threatens the possibility of explaining why they are appropriate or relevant to appreciation in a noncircular way. It is puzzling how something so amorphous can be credited with such importance, and it is no surprise that attempts to do so are easily ridiculed as overly romanticized or even mystical.

My focus here is on such feelings in relation to a particular argument, the complexity argument, that states, crudely, that literary works of art are so complex that responding with feeling to what one reads *during the process of reading* risks taking attention away from what one ought to be attending to in the work: such things as the character of the writing, the structure of the plot, the subtle handling of themes, the vividness and intricacy of its detail. The ideal of appreciation that underwrites the complexity argument is a deep and subtle understanding *without* feelings, moods, or emotions; I call this view 'intellectualism' or the 'intellectual-ized view of appreciation', certainly not in order to malign it but to foreground its commitment to apprehending all the relevant artistic *properties* of a work. To be clear, I am not concerned here with the viability of intellectualism per se but only with the complexity argument that may be offered in support of it, the argument that, to maximize a certain *type* of appreciation, we should eschew affective responses, including feelings. Intellectualism may be proposed as only *one* way, not the only way, of appreciating a work; whatever the merits and defects of the complexity argument, they should not be affected by the acceptance or rejection of pluralism.

There is literature whose appreciation does not seem to involve—much less require—feelings or emotions in any essential way. A plausible example is the stories of Jorge Luis Borges, which are typically highly conceptual and take little interest in character or plot. On the other end of the spectrum, some novels are supposed to, as part of their mission, produce feeling, and the intellectualist model would not be a good appreciative option for them, any more than an 'arousalist' model, as it is sometimes called, would be appropriate for 'conceptual' literature such as stories by Borges. Jenefer Robinson, for example, has argued that a number of realist novels from the nineteenth century have as part of their mission to evoke various kinds of feelings in various ways: having the feelings is part of the goal and one's appreciation is defective if one doesn't have them, an interpretation that is consistent with recognizing that there may be passages where emotions and feelings are either optional or irrelevant. Presumably, in such cases, even *if* the appropriate emotions to certain passages get in the way of apprehending some of the work's artistic features, it would presumably be worth the risk.

It is safe to assume, however, that a large number of novels and short stories (as well as literary nonfiction) may fruitfully be read in a variety of ways, ways that are governed by different appreciative goals and reading strategies, and that realize different values of a work. With respect to this range of works, the complexity argument might seem quite reasonable, founded on the idea that a subtle and deep appreciation *without* feelings is a way of maximizing appreciation of a work's intricacy and subtlety.

In Section 28.1, I explain the complexity argument as offered by Peter Kivy (1997, 2006a, 2006b) in relation to absolute music, and why I find it to be compelling, even as it is applied to literature. I believe that there is a great deal to be learned from his exposition and use of the argument in relation to how it may be applied to appreciating literature. As will become clear, however, I am less interested in Kivy's formulation and use of the argument than how it might be defended in general, so I shall say little about the peculiarities of his own views here. In Section 28.2, I look at a particular criticism of the complexity argument: that feelings often alert us to what is important in one's current environment (for these purposes, what is important in the work one is reading) in a way that cannot be accomplished by reason or cognition, 'intellectual' activity, or even by affectless perception. Such a view of feelings in general currently enjoys substantial popularity among a variety of psychologists and philosophers, and, though it has its merits and focuses rightly, I believe, on the temporal character of the reading process, there is something important about that process and the feelings involved in it that this view leaves out. If one wishes to account for the subtle and sophisticated feelings described in the examples above, the story is going to have to be more complicated than this.

In Section 28.3, I present one intellectualist model for appreciation, courtesy of Kurt Vonnegut's *Slaughterhouse-Five*: the Tralfamadorean view, which connects the *absence* of time from the reading process, and from the process of living one's life, with the *absence* of feelings that reflect the human capacity for agency. Section 28.4 explores how feelings reflect intricacies and complexities in the work one is reading that are fundamental to our human (rather than our animal) nature. Such feelings do not signal something of temporary importance to me now, and are certainly not pure affect. They are a mode of apprehending a work, and, conceived as such, they not only undermine the first premise of the complexity argument but also help to explain several other puzzling features of feelings: why they are so difficult to describe; their malleability when one attempts to articulate them; why attempting to articulate them is nevertheless a valuable thing to do; and even why we are justified in taking such feelings as somehow revealing the core of our humanity.

## 28.1 THE COMPLEXITY ARGUMENT

Peter Kivy defends the view that one canonical way of listening to absolute music in the Western tradition involves *perceiving* expressive properties *in* the music *without* having or experiencing 'the garden-variety emotions or moods the music is expressive of' (2007: 312). Kivy calls this mode of listening 'enhanced formalism': 'enhanced' because it is cognitively informed by relevant musical traditions and is sensitive to *expressive* properties of music; but yet 'formalism' because it eschews garden-variety emotions and moods, along with whatever thoughts or ideas that may be essential to them, as irrelevant to appreciation.

The strongest application of the complexity argument is to the appreciation of instrumental or absolute music, precisely because (by definition) such music lacks the conceptual or cognitive content, whether believed or imagined, that is typically taken to be an essential component of emotions, and sometimes also of moods. The argument is also compelling when applied to *feelings*, however, and it is in that guise that I pursue it here. Further, considering it specifically in relation to feelings, whether or not one takes feelings to involve any cognitive components, bypasses concerns about whether one's affective responses involve irrelevant beliefs or thoughts and concentrates on other ways one may fail to appreciate a work's important properties. The argument runs as follows. The great, and even very good musical works from the Western tradition of absolute music are demanding, and it is difficult to hear their 'intricacy, subtlety, and complexity'. Having feelings makes a difficult task even harder because the feelings tend to divert one's attention away from the music. Furthermore, since feelings can get in the way of a sophisticated hearing of the music, they are likely to retard or damage the development of good listening habits (Kivy 2007: 317). Thus, to maximize one's enhanced formalist appreciation—one's perception of structural and expressive properties of a work—one should listen without feelings to absolute music.

The first premise of the complexity argument as just presented is the claim that *having* feelings tends to interfere with appreciation, though Kivy sometimes claims that it is *attending to* one's feelings that creates the interference. The latter claim makes the argument stronger, since, in such cases, there is clearly a shift of attention from the work to one's own mental states. But if one limits the first premise to attending to one's feelings, the argument has a narrower application that seems contrary to the spirit in which it is offered, and is of less interest, so I consider it here in its more full-bodied form. In addition, to admit feelings but not reflection on them might not only seem a bit arbitrary but also to absolve readers from the responsibility of reflecting on their mental states or activities.

Though the complexity argument has its strongest application to the appreciation of absolute music in the Western tradition, it has a compelling analogue to the appreciation of literature. Literature is no less intricate, subtle, and complex than music; in fact, it is arguable that because one must appreciate both, crudely put, the content and the form of the writing, there is even *more* danger that feelings would distract attention from what is artistically valuable about a great novel. Now even Kivy, the *uber*-formalist, grants the occasional appropriateness of garden-variety emotions and moods in response to narratives and the characters that appear in them because literature, unlike absolute music, has content. But his admission is somewhat grudging and he downplays their role in appreciation, cautioning readers that emotions and moods can have a tendency to distract attention from the conceptual power and formal and expressive properties of a work.

(There is evidence in Kivy's *The Performance of Reading* that he would deny that great literature is more or even equally intricate, subtle, and complex in comparison with great absolute music. Indeed, such a supposition is manifest in his argument that it is possible to 'perform' literature with a high degree of skill in a first reading where this is not possible with music. But we need not saddle the complexity argument with this or other peculiarities of Kivy's view.)

The complexity argument applies only to feelings that occur *during the process* of reading. It notably does not entail that, in pursuit of the intellectualist ideal, one should never feel *anything* in response to what one hears or reads. It is part of Kivy's credo that music can be deeply moving, that it arouses deep 'emotion', in scare quotes, denoting a special use of 'emotion' to refer to a range of phenomena other than garden-variety emotions and moods (2007: 312). For example, one may feel 'upbeat, ecstatic, exalted', to use Kivy's own words (2007: 314); one can be pleased by, excited about, and amazed at the quality of the writing and cleverness of the plot (to use mine). Moreover, he points out that such feelings, whether in response to absolute music or literature, are *not devoid of cognition*. Reading, like listening, is affected by one's knowledge of genre and context, and such knowledge is arguably *required* for any deep or subtle appreciation of a work (in any medium). Further, as a society, we may want to educate and encourage people to be able to appreciate music and literature so that they have such feelings, which would make it more likely that the institutions and practices that support the creation of literature will continue to exist and, more importantly, to flourish.

One initial retort to the application of the complexity argument from music to literature appeals to differences between listening and reading as human activities. Even though musical performances do not stop while one wanders comfortably through the snug and cozy foothills of human feeling (to adapt a phrase from Clive Bell), when affected with feeling when reading a given passage of a novel one can stop reading and take the time to reflect on one's feelings and what gives rise to them. This point has merit, but I would not want to rely too heavily on it precisely because it *concedes* that, in order to avoid missing anything, one must *stop reading*, and stopping reading to reflect on one's feelings, so the argument might go, would be a classic case of how one's attention can be diverted from the work. One could also interrupt the playing of a recording of a performance, but the advocate of the complexity argument might well respond that, even though such actions may be desirable as a *means* to appreciation, they hardly constitute the ideal. The ideal is to hear the complexity *without* having to stop the music, and one might say the same of reading.

The appropriateness of reflection cannot be so easily discarded, however, with respect to literature, in part because reflection on what has gone on in the novel, on how it is written, on why a certain image recurs, and so on, are on virtually every view of appreciation very important to the reading process. Kivy addresses this fact in his own theory of literature as developed in *The Performance of Reading*. He points out that the length of novels is typically sufficient to justify one's not reading the entire novel in a single sitting, and one will therefore have time between reading sessions to reflect on what one has read, making the subsequent period of reading more rewarding because, in this way, cognitively more enriched. Lengthy novels may well need to steep.

It is crucial that the feelings whose occurrence Kivy does allow, even in response to music—excitement, feeling upbeat or ecstatic—are not bound to some point or other *during* the listening or reading process. In fact, we might encourage short-sightedness if we were to judge a work's character too quickly before we see how it concludes. The complexity argument prohibits only feelings that occur during the process of reading. It is quite compatible with the view that feelings may be appropriate during a break between reading sessions or after one has finished the entire book. As one reflects, during breaks, on the character and actions of its protagonists and antagonists, one may well *then* have feelings or garden-variety emotional responses to what one has read.

Nevertheless, it does not seem right to have to 'save' one's concern for a character, dismay at his behavior, or admiration for his heroism until you stop reading for the day, much less until you finish the whole book, and the same could be said of feelings, such as the chill or emptiness one experiences when reading the mantra from *Slaughterhouse-Five*, 'So it goes'. It would certainly be desirable to find a way of understanding feelings so that they can be integrated into the process of reading *without* their getting in the way of apprehending the subtle, deep, and complex properties of a work.

Some recent theories about the nature of emotions and feelings incorporate the idea that they have a special function in the lives of human beings that is not cognitively replaceable, in particular, the function of indicating that something is important to a particular individual at a particular point in time. On this view, far from getting in the way of apprehending a work's artistic qualities, they would make us more effective at accomplishing this task, for at least some passages in a novel. In the following section, I look briefly at this rejoinder to the two premises of the complexity argument.

## 28.2 A FUNCTION OF FEELINGS

A number of psychologists have proposed that feelings are quick-and-dirty mechanisms that serve to alert one to what is important in one's environment at the time one has them. Such mechanisms are useful, it is argued, even though they tend to generate false positives, since the advantages of immediate action typically outweigh the disadvantages when such actions turn out not to be necessary or appropriate. Evolutionary, neurological, cross-cultural and intra-cultural psychological studies have all been recruited to demonstrate the temporal embeddedness of feelings in this way and its essential connection to any assessment of their value. There are variations among such views, but what they share is a commitment to the idea that some type of evaluative or evaluation-like event occurs before cognition (at least cognition in any remotely sophisticated sense). I describe three versions of this view and, why, despite its merits, it leaves the large and important class of feelings that concern me here unaccounted for.

The core idea of the view appears in its most concentrated form in Annette Baier's account of emotions (2004). She points to the human rapid-response mechanisms that serve to alert a person's attention to what is important to that person *now*, at that specific point in time. Indeed, she takes the feelings of heightened attention and readiness to action to be of sufficient importance to be identified, generically, as a *type* of feeling with a name of its own. Her suggestion is the ingenious 'chalance', which, though she does not pursue the point, as the unmarked counterpart of 'nonchalance', helps to reinforce its status as the norm rather than as an exception needing special justification.

James Laird's view of feelings (2007) is a direct descendant of William James's in that having a feeling (which he understands broadly to include emotions and other affective phenomena) is taken to begin with a pattern of physiological arousal that is first experienced as a feeling and cognitively assessed only later—though sometimes 'later' is measurable in mere milliseconds. Wisely, Laird explicitly excludes what he calls 'aesthetic emotions' from the domain of his analysis. And though many of us are leery of the term 'aesthetic emotion' because of its implication that all appreciative responses to art are alike, the exclusion acknowledges that feelings as they arise in appreciating literature, for example, may be sensitive to writing style, genre, themes, plots, character development, *and* their relationships to the history of the literary arts in ways that are not germane to feelings and emotions as they arise in the course of ordinary life. These are the intricacies and complexities that *feelings*, according to the complexity argument, will tend to obscure.

Jenefer Robinson's work on the startle response was groundbreaking (1995) and presents a slightly different paradigm for this sort of view. In *Deeper Than Reason* (2005) she works out its application to many forms of art, including music and literature (and includes useful summaries of much relevant psychological research on the topic). Robinson posits that there is a crude, immediate affective 'categorization', a 'non-cognitive appraisal', of the phenomenon one encounters at a given point in time (2005, see especially Chapter 2). She stresses the quick-and-dirty character of how our emotions are initiated and why it is important to respond before we have cognitively processed the significance of the situation in a more considered way. On her view, emotions are processes that begin with a non-cognitive appraisal of the situation, an appraisal that is re-evaluated at a later stage in the process. When reading literature, for example, emotions can *help us focus* or concentrate on what turn out to be important connections among various passages in a novel by heightening our awareness of them, making them more salient in our consciousness, and our dispositions to notice and be affected by what is important down the line. Authors drop hints. Repetitions of a phrase or type of imagery signal its importance—as do, we might point out, regularities in nature—and constitute one way that authors can lead readers mentally in the right direction. We may not know how an image or phrase will be important; its status and significance as a symbol may not be clear at the time, but, through their connections in the limbic system, like Baier's chalance, feelings can serve to keep the image or phrase, the source of the feeling, more accessible in the vast warehouse of the mind, so as to magnify appropriately the role of, say, a related image later on.

I do not want to deny that such processes ever occur, or that they occur in normal or average readers. But I still find the point compelling that a knowledgeable and sophisticated reader, like the knowledgeable and sophisticated listener to absolute music, may, at least on any given occasion, notice an image, apprehend the complexity, the rhythms, the hints and allusions in a novel without necessarily having to *feel* something in the bargain. Feelings may do something reason can't do, but it doesn't follow that they do something perception (or 'apprehending' what one reads) can't do—especially when the time between the initial affective appraisal and the later cognitive assessment is measured in milliseconds. 'Ready, Shoot, Aim', as the saying goes, may have been a useful sequence during the Pleistocene, but it hardly seems to display any advantage over 'Ready, Aim, Maybe not Shoot

After All' when it comes to appreciating literature. I suppose that I am not convinced that feelings provide an acuity that cannot be achieved otherwise, and without the risk of distraction—at least I can't hold it against the intellectualist for not being so convinced.

The emphasis on reflection as part of the process after the feeling occurs undermines the conviction that the feeling is useful in itself. It seems to be the reverse of how one wants the temporal character of reading to sort out. Further, the cognitive subtlety and intricacy of literature would, as the complexity argument states, tend to undermine the value of quick-and-dirty responses and heighten the need for a more knowledgeable apprehension of a work. The types of feelings I am concerned with contrast with those that are explicable and defensible in terms of an evolutionary residue of our success at survival, and whose paradigm instances are on the order of startle, surprise, attraction, and disgust.

The challenge is to explain how these 'deep and important' human feelings are involved in appreciation in ways that do not take attention away from the work. To do so, I shift perspectives from feelings as bestowing an animalistic advantage to their being deeply and distinctively human, exploring the way temporality is central to human agency. In the following section, I examine a version of intellectualism that eliminates the temporality of both the process of reading and the activity of living, a model provided courtesy of the Tralfamadoreans in Kurt Vonnegut's *Slaughterhouse-Five*. This model links the absence of living in time to the absence of feelings and to the denial of human agency (or 'free will', as it is characterized in the novel). Their absence is de-humanizing: it signals the withdrawal of meaning from human life.

# 28.3 The Tralfamadorean Version of Intellectualism

The title page of Kurt Vonnegut's *Slaughterhouse-Five* tells us that what we are about to read is 'somewhat in the telegraphic schizophrenic manner of tales of the planet Tralfamadore, where the flying saucers come from'. Eighty-some pages later, we learn that Tralfamadoreans do not experience the world in three dimensions through time but in four dimensions 'all at once'. Everything exists, as it were, at the same time—the past, the present, the future. There is therefore no role for emotions, no reason to take *pleasure* in someone's being alive or to *bemoan* anyone's death, since no one is any more alive than dead or any more dead than alive.

Since the Tralfamadoreans experience 'past', 'present', and 'future' at the same time, they have no temporally extended forms of art. They 'read' (if that is the right word) the components of their novels not in succession but all at once, and, as they explain to Billy Pilgrim, the novel's protagonist, 'when seen all at once, they produce an image of life that is beautiful and surprising and deep. There is no beginning, no middle, no end, no suspense, no moral, no causes, no effects. What we love in our books are the depths of many marvelous moments seen all at one time' (Vonnegut 1969: 88). Perhaps such literary productions are not novels at all but 'word pictures', or perhaps the prose analogue of imagist poetry that is, unlike typical novels, short enough to be appreciated in this way, all at once, by human beings. (Interestingly, there is no mention of whether there is Tralfamadorean music, and the cognitive contemporaneity of their 'reading' of novels seems somehow easier to imagine than the sonic contemporaneity of 'hearing' a piece of music.)

The implications of the Tralfamadorean mode of being are central to the theme of the novel, for Billy Pilgrim becomes quasi-Tralfamadorean, an ultimately inef-fectual way his psyche attempts to cope with the horror of what he has been through. Billy becomes 'unstuck in time', which washes away feeling along with any sense of the significance of anything he might do, or try to do or not to do, any and all potential desires, plans, hopes, and values. That his attempt at 'coping' is a failure is insinuated early on in the novel, on page 2, where we are told that the mother of his cab driver was incinerated in the Dresden firestorm: the novel's mantra, 'So it goes', the affectless acceptance of what will be will be, appears there for the first time, and is repeated without fail after every mention of disaster and death.

The connection between events so horrific that we think of them as incompre-hensible or 'unspeakable', being or becoming unstuck in time, and their relation to feeling is something of a literary theme. In Martin Amis's *Time's Arrow*, for example, a man tells the story of his life, in the first person, as if he were living it backwards (or, as if living it backwards were living it forwards). The ordinary direction of cause and effect, and how they are embedded in descriptions of actions and events, is reversed. The narrator is a doctor and, for example, patients leave the emergency room in worse shape than they go in. It is of course important to figure out why the author has chosen to present the narrative, if it is a narrative, in this way, something I leave as an exercise for the reader. Amis's writing is virtuosic, and the basic idea is anticipated by a brief passage in *Slaughterhouse-Five* that describes what Billy sees when watching a war movie on TV 'backwards' (Vonnegut 1969: 74–5).

Treatments of the theme are not confined to fiction. *While They Slept: An Inquiry Into the Murder of a Family* is the story of a woman who, as a child, survived her brother's clubbing to death their parents and younger sister while she was in the house, knowing that she was up next. Robert Pinsky, in his review of the book, writes thoughtfully about the paradox of needing to write about what is 'unspeak-able', what he describes as 'the violations that destroy human lives' (2008: 1).

He writes, 'Those of us who insist on speaking what's often called unspeakable discover there's no tone reserved for unnatural disasters, and so we don't use any. We're flat-affect; we report just the facts.' He adds, wryly, 'this alienates our audience' (2008: 10).

Pinsky describes how this kind of writing (whether fiction or nonfiction) can be part of a process of 'reconstruction' of one's self, a process that appears to be instrumental in regaining one's sense of agency and one's sense of self. (Interestingly, there is typically a significant time delay between the end of the horror and having or acquiring the ability to start writing about it.) Luca Pocci has argued that the major theme of *Slaughterhouse-Five* is the contrast between the struggle of the author-narrator to make sense of his experience in relation to who he is (or who he is now, at the time of his writing), and Billy Pilgrim's being buffeted around by circumstances beyond his control and being 'incapable of feeling any significant and firm connection with the past' (2005: 13). Indeed, Billy not only *feels* no significant connection with the past; he *has* no significant connection with the past, and is unable to recover his sense of agency. He is as helpless as the Maori prisoner-of-war who, at the end of the novel, after descending into the hole of slaughterhouse number five to retrieve the rotting and liquefying bodies there, cannot stop throwing up because of the smell. The Maori dies ('he tore himself to pieces' [Vonnegut 1969: 214]), and in a way, Billy Pilgrim dies, too. His mind keeps vomiting up vignettes of the 'past present future' without meaningful succession or relationships.

Tralfamadoreans may experience everything at once, but, back here on Earth, novels are a temporal art form: the canonical mode of access is temporally sequential, and though there are (experimental or nontraditional) novels for which no specific sequence is canonical, they *are* the exception. The modernist novel has made disconnects between the sequence of the telling and the sequence of what happens within the story told significant and familiar to us all, disconnects and ruptures that are often used to express or show something about the nature of human experience. Such ruptures exist with a vengeance in *Slaughterhouse-Five*, which, as the title page points out, is only *somewhat* like a Tralfamadorean novel.

There are more Earth-friendly variants of the Tralfamadorean view, such as what I call the Leibnizian version, where one's goal (as an admittedly unattainable ideal) is to experience every portion of an artwork as reflecting the entire work from its own point of view. But I sidestep these possibilities in order to focus on relationships between living in time and human agency, and in particular the connection between a lack of agency and a lack of feeling.

According to some theorists, the connection between living in time and agency is provided by the (alleged) fact that there is a causal connection between our mental acts and our overt behavior. On this view, a person's beliefs and desires play a role in causing one to act (or not act) in a given way, and causal processes exist in time because causes always precede their effects. The absence of a causal connection between Billy's mental states that should affect his actions but don't compromises his capacity to act as an agent and hence should affect our assessments of his rationality. For example, his Tralfamadorean perspective enables him to know that the plane he is about to board will crash, and that he will be the only survivor, but it doesn't prevent him from boarding the plane.

But the temporal implications of Billy's taking the Tralfamadorean perspective are more extensive and deeper than the appeal to causes is, in itself, able to handle. His problems are not merely a collection of momentary lapses of rationality, or even the occasional fantasy (for example, the events involving Montana Wildhack) that is experienced as if real. They rather have to do with longer-term inabilities. For example, consider that it would be only after the plane crash that he could experience himself as knowing, prior to the crash, that it will occur. We are to interpret Billy as mentally disturbed, of course, not as clairvoyant. His memories are not experienced as memories but as current events: he cannot, or does not, put them in anywhere near their proper places in past time. He is unable to make plans or choices for the future: the future is experienced contemporaneously with the present, invading the present, making the very idea of a plan for the future incoherent. A human agent is more than an individual who performs a number of rational actions at particular points in time; it is someone who lives in and through an extended period of time.

Michael Bratman's account of agency captures the deep temporality of human agency by requiring agents to have mental states and activities that have what he calls 'cross-temporal reference' (2000). We don't merely have wishes and desires, we make *plans* for the future and adopt *policies* to carry out those plans, and we do this in light of our knowledge, including memories of one's past (of successes and failures, sometimes in the very remote past), as well as in light of new information about oneself and the world, making changes in plans and policies that the new information necessitates. As Bratman says, the primary role of plans and policies is 'to support the coordination of actions by way of supporting connections and continuities which . . . help constitute the identity of the agent over time' (2000: 45–6). Thus, one's 'present intentional act may involve an intention that refers to a larger plan or policy in which it is embedded. Indeed, this is part of what plans and policies are for' (2000: 47). When acting as an agent, one's actions have embedded within them cross-temporal references of this more extended variety, references that are partly constitutive of the very nature or identity of the actions we perform. For one who is 'unstuck in time', cross-temporal references are dislodged and the identity of the actions one performs is subverted; they are not the same actions one would otherwise think they are, and can hardly be said to be actions at all. Billy Pilgrim's psyche loses its cross-temporal references to his past (or any past), and hence loses his ability to act as a human agent. He has no plans or hopes or dreams—no motives, no intentions, and no policies to help carry out his plans even if he were to have any.

## 28.4  FROM AGENCY TO FEELINGS

It may be in principle possible to separate cognitions from affects in any particular instance, so I shall not argue that there is a *necessary* connection between being an agent and having feelings, or between understanding what one does as an agent and having feelings, or between understanding another agent and having feelings, or between understanding characters in literature and having feelings. Indeed, the problem at issue is not whether feelings are necessary for appreciation but whether they tend to interfere with or distract from one's apprehension of the subtle and complex properties of a work, and to encourage bad reading habits. I propose instead that feelings of the sort under consideration here, far from potentially interfering with apprehending a novel's subtlety and complexity, are a manifestation of one's apprehension of it—as much as one's feeling upbeat and ecstatic, in Kivy's words, may be a manifestation of one's apprehending the greatness of a work of absolute music. Put another way, a way that addresses the second premise of the complexity argument, one does not show oneself to be a more responsible, or observant, reader when reading without feeling than one does reading with feeling. Indeed, the ability to read with feeling but without getting 'carried away', that is, without getting distracted from the work, is just as important as the ability to apprehend a work's important artistic features *simpliciter*.

The reading process is itself a temporally extended activity that requires integrating what one reads earlier in the process to what one reads later. This involves apprehending both such things as the unfolding structure of the novel and plot, and the cross-temporal references involved in the actions of the characters. In addition, these apprehensions will frequently be contextualized in relation to one's knowledge of relevant similarities and contrasts with various literary forms and in relation to facts about the world. The key is to understand feelings as a way of apprehending a work: not an effect of it, and not merely a signal or symptom of something's importance to me now, but a mental event or activity whose identity is structured in an important way by what one reads. Reading with feeling is analogous to perceiving in general, as not a phenomenological effect of certain mental processes but a relation between the perceiver and the object perceived. Feelings are not pure affects—not even affects conjoined with a set of thoughts— any more than an action is a simple combination of a thought with a bit of overt behavior. Rather, I suggest that, like our actions, they have embedded within them a complicated network of psychological connections with cross-temporal references. The character of the feelings, like the character of our actions, is informed or structured by a psychological network of cross-temporal reference. Thus, just as I resist the idea that actions are movements that occur as a consequence or result of a set of thoughts that constitute their causes, I also resist the idea that feelings are affective effects or consequences of a complex psychological network of activity.

It is typical to find the philosophical problem that I have been addressing here as concerning emotional *responses* to literature. For example, in *Reading with Feeling*, I referred to portions of a text that *elicit* affective responses, and proposed the main distinction to be between what in the text elicits a response and past experience, including what one has just been reading in the same work, that serves to affect or 'condition' how one responds to what one reads next. I thus distinguished responses to a work from mere reactions to it. Accounts of emotions as processes, such as those described in Section 28.2, represent them as *mental* processes that are *initiated by* or *stimulated by* an encounter with something in the world. For example, the self-perception model that James Laird develops and defends in his recent book *Feelings* takes the process to begin with an 'eliciting event' and takes the 'feeling' to be the result of the perception of bodily changes (including actions, autonomic arousal, and expressive behavior) that the event elicits (even though he clearly eschews the dualism that such a view seems to imply).

For many purposes, talk of causes and effects is innocuous enough—a kind of placeholder for whatever the relationships among mental states, behavior, and the world turn out to be. However, the cause-and-effect story of how feelings are generated encourages thinking of them as pure affect occurring after and as a consequence of a set of physiological or cognitive states or processes that function as causes. The cause-and-effect story thus inhibits the development of an adequate response to the complexity argument, which sees feelings or affects as separable from one's cognitive activity and both as taking up additional time and as a potential distraction from what is important in the work. (It seems to me that Kivy's term 'arousalist formalism' has this tendency.) Reading *with* feeling, just like acting with thought, is an ability, manifesting a kind of power and control. Intellectualism, which applauds reading *without* feeling, is also an ability, an ability that may be desirable, but not because feelings tend to distract us from the work or because *allowing* them ('indulging' them) risks developing bad reading habits.

This view that feelings are a way of apprehending a work coheres nicely with a variety of characteristics of this class of feelings. First, the *absence of a systematically developed vocabulary* to identify feelings is explicable not because they are 'pure phenomenology' (whatever that might be), whose varieties are hard to capture in a systematic way, but because of the variability and complexity of the cognitions, perceptions, and apprehensions that are embedded within them. Garden-variety emotions such as fear, anger, and disgust are conceptually relatively easy to deal with, since they involve relatively specific cognitive components (and, at least as argued by numerous psychologists, rather distinctive physiological and/or neuro-logical patterns). Perceiving a situation as dangerous is part of what it is to be afraid; perceiving or apprehending a character's getting into a dangerous situation is part of what it is to fear (sympathetically) for that character or (empathetically) with that character. But feelings tend to fluctuate with many more alterations in their cognitive components, as illustrated by the changes in readings of subsequent uses of 'So it goes'.

Second, feelings are *difficult to describe*. Again, this is not because they are independent of cognition but because there is so much cognition, and so much that functions largely underground, as with actions, within an elaborate psychological matrix. Further, feelings tend to fluctuate once one starts describing them, and we sometimes lose our grasp on what the feeling was to begin with (something that is often well lost). Accepting the changes is part of taking responsibility for oneself as an appreciator: a willingness to grow through, in part, the effort of articulation.

Third, if feelings are informed by a rich and variable network of thoughts (plans and policies, with cross-temporal reference) and tend to morph as aspects of this network change (or change in salience) as one articulates its components, these features would account for why it is so *difficult to explain what justifies, or warrants, them* as ways of apprehending or experiencing a work, and why a variety of feelings might be appropriate.

And, finally, many authors—not the least poets and artists of many stripes—have held that feelings are *at the core of our humanity*, that they reveal something deep and important about us as human beings. I suspect some apologists for feeling would be appalled at how cognitive, even intellectualized, I see the constituents and structure of feelings to be. Nevertheless, if cross-temporal references are embedded within them similar to the way they are embedded in human actions, we have good reason for thinking that the feelings people have are special in this way. And when they are removed, so are such feelings: the 'unnatural disasters' that destroyed Billy Pilgrim's life robbed him of his feelings precisely because they ripped him apart from his past and his future.

In sum, the complexity argument proposes that feelings take readers' attention away from a literary work. One way of countering this claim is to argue that feelings alert us to significant features of a work more quickly than, or with more salience than, reason or cognition would. However, I have proposed that many feelings involved in appreciation are more significant than such views accommodate. Their significance is due to their being structured by cross-temporal psychological connections, similar to the way the actions of human agents and our understanding of them are structured. Far from taking our attention away from a work, they reveal its complexity. In this sense, even attending to one's feelings, which the complexity argument contrasts with attending to the work, provides an opportunity to tease out at least some of the subtle and intricate features of characters and their stories that would otherwise lie, psychologically, largely underground. Our efforts to identify them despite the absence of a systematic way to think about them, to describe them despite their being vague and inchoate, to justify them despite the seeming circularity of that process, are efforts that draw us back into the literary and psychological intricacy and depth of a work, rather than diverting our attention from it.

## REFERENCES

ACHEBE, C. (1959), *Things Fall Apart* (New York: Anchor Books).

AMIS, M. (1991), *Time's Arrow, or, The Nature of the Offense* (New York: Vintage International).

BAIER, A. (2004), 'Feelings That Matter', in R. Solomon (ed.), *Thinking About Feeling: Contemporary Philosophers on Emotions* (Oxford: Oxford University Press).

BRATMAN, M. (2000), 'Reflection, Planning, and Temporally Extended Agency', *Philosophical Review* 109: 35–61.

KIVY, P. (1997), *Philosophies of Arts: An Essay in Differences* (Cambridge: Cambridge University Press).

—— (2006a), 'Mood and Music: Some Reflections for Noël Carroll', *The Journal of Aesthetics and Art Criticism* 64: 271–81.

—— (2006b), *The Performance of Reading: An Essay in the Philosophy of Literature* (Malden, MA: Blackwell).

—— (2007), 'Moodology: A Response to Laura Sizer', *The Journal of Aesthetics and Art Criticism*, 65: 312–18.

LAIRD, J. D. (2007), *Feelings: The Perception of Self* (Oxford: Oxford University Press).

PINSKY, R. (2008), 'Speaking the Unspeakable', review of K. Harrison, *While They Slept: An Inquiry Into the Murder of a Family*, in *New York Times Book Review*, June 8, 2008: 1, 10.

POCCI, L. (2005), 'Literary Themes and Cognition', from the conference, 'Art and Cognition', Erfurt University, June 9–11, 2005.

ROBINSON, J. (1995), 'Startle', *Journal of Philosophy* 92: 53–74.

—— (2005), *Deeper than Reason: Emotion and its Role in Literature, Music, and Art* (Oxford: Clarendon).

VONNEGUT, K. (1969), *Slaughterhouse-Five or The Children's Crusade: A Duty-Dance with Death* (New York: Dell).

# CHAPTER 29

# EMOTIONAL RESPONSES TO MUSIC: WHAT ARE THEY? HOW DO THEY WORK? AND ARE THEY RELEVANT TO AESTHETIC APPRECIATION?

JENEFER ROBINSON

## 29.1 THE PUZZLE OF MUSICAL EMOTIONS

It is widely agreed nowadays that emotions are set off by an *appraisal* of a situation. Many theorists think that each so-called basic emotion has its own type of appraisal corresponding to a particular "adaptational encounter" or "core relational theme", losses, offences, threats, and so on. A cognitive appraisal that a "demeaning offence" has been committed against me or one of "my own" is what sets off an angry emotional response.[1] Sadness is initiated by the apprehension of some kind of loss, fear by an appraisal that one is under threat, and so on. Alternatively, the appraisals that trigger emotions may be less specific to particular emotions and better analysed in terms of their various dimensions such as pleasantness or familiarity.[2] Whatever the details of their proposals, however, almost everyone agrees that these appraisals are, broadly speaking, *cognitive*, requiring some sort of interpretation of a situation in terms of its significance to the survival and/or well-being of me or mine. Emotional responses are evoked when the situation is cognitively appraised as one in which something is *at stake* for me or mine.[3]

There is another tradition in emotion theory, however, stemming from William James, which places more emphasis on the bodily components in emotion. In a famous passage from *The Principles of Psychology*, James (1981, p. 1065) claimed that when, for example, I face a threat or suffer a loss, "*bodily changes follow directly the perception of the exciting fact, and . . . our feeling of the same changes as they occur IS the emotion*". James's theory initiated over a century of work in psychology on the physiological and behavioural aspects of the emotions, including autonomic and hormonal activity, facial and vocal expressions, and action tendencies, which characterize episodes of sadness, anger, fear, and so on. What is sometimes ignored, however, is that James too seems to have thought that an "appraisal" of some sort is necessary to emotion. He linked the emotions to the instincts and argued that emotional responses are responses by "the bodily sounding board", reacting instinctively to events in the environment that are significant to the organism.[4] Following this suggestion, I have argued that emotions are information-processing systems that "register in the body" information that is important to the survival and/or well-being of the person or animal (Robinson 1995, 2005). Fear does not require a high-level cognitive appraisal but can be induced automatically by certain triggers such as a sudden loud sound, an object hurtling towards the eyes, or a large, threatening, hairy mammal with big teeth and claws. Even "high level" fears — of my boss's bad temper or the state of the markets — require registration in the

---

[1] Richard Lazarus (1991) introduced the term "core relational themes". He describes the core relational theme for anger as "a demeaning offense against me and mine" (1991, p. 122). LeDoux (1996) prefers the term "adaptational encounters".

[2] See, for example, Russell (2003) and Feldman Barrett (2006).

[3] Philosophers who defend some variety of cognitivism include Ben-Ze'ev (2000), Gordon (1987), Lyons (1980), Nussbaum (2001), and Solomon (1976, 1988). The cognitivists among psychologists include Ortony et al. (1988), Lazarus (1991), Phoebe Ellsworth, Ira Roseman, Klaus Scherer, and Craig Smith, all represented by articles in Scherer et al. (2001).

[4] If this is true, then James was exaggerating when he said that emotions simply *are* feelings of bodily change. It is pretty clear that when James is being careful, he claims that feelings of bodily change are necessary for emotion rather than both necessary and sufficient. See Ellsworth (1994).

body if they are to count as genuine emotional states.[5] Jesse Prinz (2004) has also defended a Jamesian hypothesis. He argues that emotions are "embodied appraisals", designed to detect losses, threats, or offences *by means of* registering patterns of bodily change. Emotions represent core relational themes by virtue of the fact that they are *reliably caused* by them. For Prinz, emotions are "gut reactions" that "use our bodies to tell us how we are faring in the world" (2004, p. 69).[6]

It seems, then, that most theorists agree that emotions are triggered by appraisals, although there is disagreement about whether these appraisals are cognitive or embodied. But when we come to the question of music, *all* appraisal theories seem equally at a loss. There just doesn't seem to be *any* kind of relevant appraisal being made when music makes me sad or happy, anxious or calm. For usually when music makes me sad, it's not because I have suffered a loss. If it makes me anxious, it is not because I feel threatened by anything. If it makes me joyful, it's not because anything especially good has happened to me. In listening to music there is nothing to be sad or happy about, nothing towards which my emotion is targeted. Nevertheless, it seems to be a commonplace that music does indeed arouse emotions. In this chapter I will attempt to solve this paradox.

Before beginning, two general points should be made. First, the paradox does not seem to affect music with accompanying words as much as it does "pure" or "absolute" instrumental music. If I listen to a song in which a woman laments her dead lover, I might be responding emotionally to the dramatic scenario, just as when I read a story or a poem about a woman lamenting her dead lover. Accordingly, my concern in this chapter will be primarily with "pure" music, where the problem seems to be most acute. Secondly, I want to emphasize that my subject is the *arousal* of emotion by music and not the *expression* of emotion by music, which is a very different thing. A piece that expresses joy can leave me cold. A piece that makes me feel joyful may be expressive of melancholy. As we shall see, there are important relationships between the expression and arousal of emotions by music, but the expression of emotion by music cannot simply be *identified* with the arousal of emotion by music. My focus in this essay will be on the question: does music arouse emotion and if so how?

I begin by pointing out some of the ways[7] in which music arouses emotions that are in fact consistent with appraisal theory, before going on to discuss how music can also arouse affective states that do not involve appraisals in the usual way.

---

[5] See James (1981) as well as Damasio (1994) for suggestions about how the same emotion mechanism is employed by simple, pre-programmed emotions, such as fear of the bear, and more complex learned emotions, such as fear of losing my retirement savings.

[6] I am oversimplifying. Prinz thinks that emotions are embodied appraisals *plus valence*. Roughly speaking, valence is required in order to explain actions motivated by an emotion.

[7] No doubt there are other ways too. Jeanette Bicknell (2007), for example, has stressed the idea that powerful musical experiences have their roots in the social functions of music, especially bonding. As will become apparent, my emphasis, by contrast, will be on those emotional responses that are most relevant to musical appreciation, understanding, and value.

# 29.2 Four Ways in which Music Arouses Emotions

There are at least four ways in which music can arouse emotions that are broadly consistent with appraisal theories of emotion. (1) Many people have emotional associations to music, both personal and cultural. Their response to the music is quite likely the result of emotional appraisals of those events or situations that they associate with the music. (2) Even formalists grant that we may have emotional responses to certain global attributes of the music itself, for example its beauty and craftsmanship. Such responses would seem to result from appraisals of the music as beautiful and well crafted. (3) Somewhat more controversially, it seems that emotional responses can also be elicited by appraisals of how the musical structure of a piece is unfolding. (4) Finally, listeners often respond emotionally to what is expressed by music, and, at least in some cases, this response may be to an appraisal of the emotional travails or successes of a character or persona in the music.

(1) The most obvious solution to the puzzle of musical emotions is that people respond emotionally to music because of the associations they have to it. Such associations can, of course, be wildly idiosyncratic and hence would seem to tell us little about the music itself. If I heard some spectacularly good news while listening to the Funeral March from Chopin's Piano Sonata in B-flat minor, I may for ever after associate this piece with ecstatic joy, and it may always move me to joy as a result, but this would be a very idiosyncratic response to the piece, and one that most people would find deeply inappropriate. Klaus Scherer notes that "music, like odours, seems to be a very powerful cue in bringing emotional experiences from memory back into awareness",[8] but responding emotionally to music because of its personal associations is not responding to the music as such but only to the music as a vehicle for the associations.[9]

Music is not just a means for revisiting our personal emotional memories, however. It is also a cultural phenomenon. Different sorts of music have

---

[8] Scherer and Zentner (2001, p. 169).

[9] Juslin and Västfjäll (2008) have identified six different ways in which music can arouse emotions. One is "evaluative conditioning", i.e., "a process whereby an emotion is induced by a piece of music simply because this stimulus has been paired repeatedly with other positive or negative stimuli". Another way is identified as "visual imagery", i.e., the way that emotions can be aroused by visual imagery induced by music. A third way is called "episodic memory". These are emotions resulting when the music evokes a memory of some particular episode in the listener's past experience. All three of these modes of emotional arousal would count in my terms as types of personal association, since different listeners could presumably be conditioned to respond emotionally in different ways to the same music; different listeners could conjure up different imagery when listening to the same music; and of course different listeners will have different memories associated with the same music. Consequently none of these three modes of emotional arousal seems to me to be directly relevant to musical understanding or appreciation.

associations that are widespread in the culture and to which the composer can plausibly be supposed to be adverting. Leonard Ratner (1980) has identified musical *topoi*, such as melodies, rhythms, timbres, harmonic progressions, or combinations of these, that have cultural associations. Examples include dances in high, middle, or low styles, military and hunt music, the pastoral style, the sentimental style, and so on. In addition, there are marches, funeral music, music for various kinds of festivities such as weddings, church music, "peasant" or "aristocratic" music, and music associated with various cultures, often through dance forms characteristic of those cultures. Often the associations are complex. The "Turkish" March in the last movement of Beethoven's Ninth Symphony is not only associated with a particular culture; it is also – incongruously – in "low style". The effect is to reinforce the idea that the "Ode to Joy" has universal application (Hatten 2004, pp. 81–2).

Many of these *topoi* carry emotional associations: military music is often associated with glory, honour, loyalty, and patriotism, and may induce these emotions in some listeners. Gregorian chant and hymns are associated with reverence and piety and can evoke the corresponding feelings. Wedding music is associated with joyful occasions and makes most of us feel good; funeral music is associated with death and is sobering. Some thinkers (Hatten 2004) have emphasized that these musical meanings often depend on so-called "binary oppositions": that peasant dances are associated with carefree jollity and aristocratic dances with dignity and restraint is partly the result of the contrast between the *lumpen* peasant dance and the elegant aristocratic dance.

Some instrumental music is associated with specific words, and may induce the emotions appropriate to those words. Powerful examples are national anthems that can arouse strong emotions by virtue of their conventional role as expressions of patriotism. Similarly, the "Ode to Joy" theme in the last movement of Beethoven's Ninth, even in its purely instrumental appearances, may induce joy in listeners simply because it is associated with Schiller's words.

(2) For the formalist philosopher of music, Peter Kivy, there is only one aesthetically relevant way in which music can arouse emotions. Music, he claims, is incapable of *arousing* the "garden-variety emotions", such as sadness, joy, and anxiety, that it is able to *express*. In his view it is never the case that sad music moves us to sadness or cheerful music to good cheer. This is because when we listen to music there is nothing to be sad, cheerful, or anxious *about*: there is no appropriate "cognitive object" for these emotions. Kivy assumes that emotions require a cognitive appraisal of the object of the emotion and so he needs to find a plausible intentional object for the emotions aroused by music. He acknowledges that of course music can arouse garden-variety emotions in some sense. I can be angry at all the wrong notes the trombone player is playing, joyful about the brilliant clarinet solo by my daughter, or resentful of the triumph of a composer whom I dislike, but these emotions are not aroused by the music qua music. The only

emotions that music arouses when it is being appreciated qua music are what we might call "emotions of appreciation" that have the music itself as their cognitive object. Thus we may be emotionally "moved" by the "incomparable beauty and craftsmanship" of a section of Josquin's *Ave Maria* in which the composer writes a very beautiful canon at the fifth with the voices only one beat apart. In such examples we are responding emotionally to aspects of the music itself, its beauty, and its daring but graceful solution to a musical problem (Kivy 1990, pp. 159–60). We *cognitively evaluate* the music as beautiful and well crafted. More recently, Kivy (2006*b*, p. 280) has written that pure instrumental music – "absolute music" – can move us "to a kind of enthusiasm, or excitement, or ecstasy directed at the music as its intentional object".

Kivy is quite right to point out that we are frequently moved by music in this way, but at best his explanation fits only this one class of emotional responses to music. Most music listeners believe that there is a wide range of emotions aroused by music, not just excitement or delight at beauty and craftsmanship but also some of the "garden-variety" emotions that Kivy thinks "pure" instrumental music is logically incapable of arousing.

(3) There is another way in which music can function as a "cognitive object" in Kivy's phrase. In his influential book, *Emotion and Meaning in Music*, Leonard Meyer (1956) argued that one way of understanding musical structure is emotional. As we listen attentively to a complex piece of music such as a Schubert piano sonata, we may be *surprised* by the unorthodox way it begins, *satisfied* when the first theme begins to behave in a normal manner, *bewildered* by the development section in which the piano ranges into ever more distant keys, and *relieved* by the reappearance of the tonic. Throughout we may be *puzzled* and *unsettled* by the many harmonic and thematic ambiguities. All these emotions – surprise, satisfaction, bewilderment, relief, puzzlement, unsettledness, and so on – are emotions that are the result of appraising how the music is developing (and are directed towards the music as their "object"). Meyer's idea is that how we appraise the development of the music depends on the expectations we have as we listen, and these expectations are in turn the result of familiarity with the stylistic norms assumed by the piece. For example, when we listen to the first movement of a Schubert piano sonata, we expect an example of sonata form. So I am *intrigued* and *puzzled* by the incongruous low trill on G flat that interrupts the cheerful ambulatory music that opens his Piano Sonata D 960 in B flat. I am increasingly *bewildered* as the development section heads off into harmonic terrain very distant from the tonic. Then I am *surprised* by the emergence of D minor and the recurrence of the low trill, this time on D, towards the end of the development section. Finally, I am *relieved* and *satisfied* as D minor finally segues into the tonic B flat and the trill motif begins its reintegration into the harmonic fabric.

Why should I get upset when the tonic remains absent for longer than expected? We can understand my getting upset when my husband stays late at the office night after night. But the tonic isn't my feckless husband. Why should I care if it returns home late? Emotions are responses to events and situations that I have appraised as important to survival or well-being. But what's at stake for me in my encounter with the music? Nico Frijda's (1986) theory of emotion can help us here. He suggests that emotion is generated by appraisals of match or mismatch with the agent's goals or interests. The psychologists of music John Sloboda and Patrik Juslin (2001) have taken up his idea, arguing that the tonal system within which most of the composers of the Classic and Romantic periods worked, provides "a set of dimensions that establish psychological distance from a 'home' or 'stability' point".[10] Moving closer to this "resting point" reduces tension and moving away from it in general increases tension. So we get emotionally worked up when things don't turn out as we expect and we are emotionally satisfied when they do. For example, when we have become accustomed to a melody going along in the major key and suddenly it shifts into the minor, we are briefly shaken up emotionally: things are not going the way we'd been led to expect, and what's more, given the cultural conventions of Western music, they seem to be moving into a darker realm. Although in musical cases of this sort, the match or mismatch with our "goals and interests" doesn't matter very much to our well-being, we have learned to respond in a similar way *whenever* our desires or expectations are thwarted. It is in general adaptive to be on the look-out when things are not going as expected or as desired, especially when the change seems to be for the worse. The reaction to unexpected events in music such as a sudden shift from major to minor is most likely a spin-off from a generally adaptive pattern of response.

(4) Listeners often respond emotionally to what is *expressed* by music. Some emotional responses are to vocal intonations. According to Patrik Juslin (2001, p. 321), music performers are able to communicate emotions to listeners "by using the same acoustic code as is used in the vocal expression of emotion". Just as there is very good evidence of pan-cultural *facial* expressions of certain basic emotions, so there is evidence of pan-cultural *vocal* expressions of basic emotions in the sense that people worldwide seem to employ the same intonation patterns in the expression of certain basic emotions. Thus music can mimic a baby's cry, expressive of distress, and can automatically elicit the same emotional reactions in listeners as does the baby's cry.[11] According to Juslin, there are simple, automatic, independent brain systems – or "modules" – that respond to cries of distress, and these brain systems cannot tell the difference "between vocal expression of emotion and other acoustic expression but will react in the same way as long as certain cues (e.g., high speed, loud dynamics, fast attack, many overtones) are present in the stimulus"

---

[10] Sloboda and Juslin (2001, p. 92). Meyer's theory is designed to explain Classic and Romantic music, from roughly 1750 to 1900, not early music and certainly not serial music.

[11] Mithen (2005) argues that there was an early hominid communication system that was holistic, multi-modal, manipulative, and musical, out of which both language and music evolved.

(Juslin 2001, p. 329). Thus our emotional reaction to the plaint from Purcell's *The Fairy Queen* ("O, o let me weep") is partly influenced by the way the music imitates a human vocal expression of woe. Notice that Juslin is not suggesting that listeners cognitively appraise the cry as indicating distress. There certainly seems to be an "appraisal of significance" involved, but it is most likely automatic and "instinctive", an embodied appraisal.

The Purcell example is a special case of a more general phenomenon. When we listen to a song in which a protagonist is expressing emotion, we often respond emotionally to this expression. So in listening to the anguish and despair in "O, o let me weep", I may find myself responding with distress not only to the vocal intonation but to the content of the words as expressed by the music. In this case cognitive appraisal is involved as well as instinctive bodily appraisal: I understand the words of the song and understand that someone is expressing grief, and I respond emotionally to this verbal expression. But what about "pure" instrumental music? How can it arouse "garden-variety" emotions such as distress or sorrow in a listener? For formalists such as Kivy, the answer is that it can't. Some theorists (Cone 1974; Levinson 1996, 2006), however, have argued that at least sometimes it is appropriate to hear "pure" instrumental music as exemplifying a drama or narrative in which there are characters or a persona – sometimes, but not always, a persona of the composer – who express their emotions in the music. Romantic music is perhaps the most susceptible to such interpretations, because at least some Romantic composers have explicitly spoken of their music in this way as an expression of their own emotions or of the emotions of an imagined persona in the music. Thus Anthony Newcomb (1984*b*) has described both Schumann's Second Symphony and Beethoven's Fifth as exemplifying what he calls the "plot archetype" of "suffering leading to healing or redemption", and if we hear the Fifth in this way we may then in listening to it feel *uplifted* by the imagined victory over suffering. In such cases I am making an *appraisal* of the dramatic protagonist's emotional state and his or her general situation, and I respond emotionally in a similar way to the way I respond emotionally to an expressive novel such as *Le Rouge et le Noir* or *Anna Karenina*. Notice, however, that in these cases, the emotions aroused in me, the listener, are not necessarily the same as those expressed by the protagonist in the music. The protagonist of "O, o let me weep" expresses anguish and despair, but I may feel sorrow and compassion. The protagonist of Beethoven's Fifth perhaps expresses triumph, whereas I may respond by feeling uplifted.[12]

---

[12] In this case Beethoven seems to be expressing his own admiration for the hero which we are encouraged to share. Like us Beethoven seems to be feeling uplifted. But what Beethoven is expressing (admiration, uplift) is not what the hero is expressing (resolution, courage). For more on the nuances of the relationships between the expression and arousal of emotion by music, see Robinson (1994).

When we respond emotionally to the structure of a piece of music, in the way described by Leonard Meyer, we are very often simultaneously responding to what is being expressed by the music. Beethoven's Fifth does not simply have a "purely formal" harmonic and melodic structure; it also has a dramatic or expressive structure. It exemplifies a wider pattern of human experience: suffering leading to redemption. Similarly, Newcomb (1997) has analysed the second movement of Mahler's Ninth Symphony as exemplifying a conflict between a desire for pastoral innocence and the attractions of urban worldliness and sophistication. Gregory Karl and I (1995) have interpreted Shostakovich's Tenth as exemplifying hope followed by the dashing of hope; and Robert Hatten (2004) has described the movement from tragic to transcendent in the slow movement of Beethoven's *Hammerklavier* Sonata. Once we interpret music in dramatic human terms, we are likely to respond to it not only as a harmonious and well-crafted sequence of beautiful tones but also as the expression of human conflicts and aspirations.[13]

There are many techniques whereby music can exemplify patterns of human experience. In Mahler's Ninth there is a contrast between *different topoi*, the ländler and the waltz which, according to Newcomb, exemplify the conflict in the hero between his desire for an innocent pastoral life and his attraction to urban "glitz". Listeners are encouraged to feel the attractions of both. In Shostakovich's Tenth, dramatic development is enacted partly through *melodic transformation*: the brief glimpse of hope amidst the prevailing feeling of gloomy foreboding is exemplified by a short idyllic theme in the third movement that transforms into the lively main theme of the finale. When this cheerful theme then transforms gradually into a manic theme reminiscent of the sinister second movement, we hear hope morphing into the defeat of hope, and are likely to feel correspondingly discouraged.

Very often emotional development is enacted partly by *harmonic shifts*. Harmonic tension – where it is not clear where we are tonally or where the music is headed – is particularly effective both in exemplifying patterns of human experience and in arousing corresponding emotions in listeners. Key changes are not just formal devices. When used subtly and appropriately, they can have the emotional effect on listeners of a transformation from one emotional landscape to another. Charles Fisk (2001) has described the first movement of Schubert's B flat Piano Sonata D. 960 as suggesting a psychological narrative of an outcast or wanderer in search of some kind of reintegration into society. He draws particular attention to the powerful emotional effect of the D minor passage towards the end of the development section, which "arrives as the culmination of the most agitated, thickly textured, tonally complex, and sustained buildup in the movement" (p. 248). For Fisk, the passage conveys a sense of "hushed expectancy" and exemplifies

---

[13] And if the thesis defended in Robinson (2007a) is right, it is perfectly appropriate to hear certain pieces under the general rubric of a particular structural metaphor. Some musical pieces do and should encourage the imagining of certain sorts of scenarios.

the "stillness that awaits an epiphany" (p. 253). But it is not only the protagonist in the music who feels the imminence of an emotional revelation. The listener too experiences this new and magical emotional realm.

## 29.3 THE MUSICAL EVOCATION OF MOODS

So far I have discussed a number of ways in which music arouses emotions, which are all (arguably) consistent with the idea that emotions require an appraisal. The difficult cases, however, are those where music with a particular expressive character – happy or sad, agitated or calm – seems to arouse a corresponding emotion of happiness or sadness, agitation or calm, yet there is nothing in the music for the listener to be happy or sad, agitated or calm *about*. Nor is there any reason in these cases to postulate a persona in the music to whom listeners might be responding emotionally. The final movement, "Réjouissance", of Bach's Orchestral Suite No. 4 is joyful music that typically arouses joy in "appropriately backgrounded"[14] listeners, but it does not seem to express any particular person's or persona's joy, nor is the joy we feel in listening a response to joy in some person or persona.[15] In a very different style, the opening movement of Stravinsky's Symphony in Three Movements is nervous, agitated music, and it can make listeners feel nervous and agitated. But there is nothing for listeners to be nervous *about*. And the music doesn't make us nervous because we are reacting to a nervous persona in the music.

There are two standard ways of responding to this apparent paradox. As we saw earlier, Peter Kivy simply denies that it is possible for music to arouse the emotions, such as happiness or agitation, that it expresses. But this is a desperate move, given, as we will see shortly, the enormous amount of empirical evidence that music can indeed reliably arouse such states. An alternative has been proposed by Noël Carroll (2003), who argues that music arouses not emotions proper but only moods. The received wisdom is that moods do not have specific intentional objects: they are not directed *at* or *about* anything in particular. Like emotions, moods can sometimes be set off by an appraisal, as when I get into a gloomy mood after learning that my lover has deserted me, and that I have suffered a loss. But

---

[14] The phrase is from Jerrold Levinson (1996, p. 107). Obviously, for music to arouse affective states in an audience that result from genuine engagement with the music, the audience must have some familiarity with the type of music in question.

[15] Here I part company with Levinson (1996, 2006) who thinks that expressiveness in music is *always* to be analysed as hearability as an expression of emotion by a persona in the music. For a recent discussion of expression and expressiveness in music and the other arts, including Levinson's view, see Robinson (2007*b*).

moods do not require a specific appraisal to set them off. Notoriously I can get into a sad or happy mood by imbibing an appropriate chemical compound, by lack of sleep, or because of general facts about the environment such as the time of day or the season of the year. If that's right, then there's nothing in principle to rule out the possibility that music too can induce moods.

So what are moods, and how do they differ from emotions proper? Emotions and moods share many important features. According to Carroll's wide notion of "the affective domain", as "the entire realm of feeling-charged mental states" (p. 524), both moods and emotions are varieties of "affect". Both exhibit characteristic physiological changes,[16] behaviour, bodily expressions – such as facial and vocal expressions, posture, and gesture – and corresponding feelings. Moods, like emotions, have a characteristic phenomenology: sadness, whether emotion or mood, *feels* unpleasant.[17]

But moods differ from emotions in that they are not directed at anything in particular but pervade experience as a whole. Whereas an *emotion* of joy rivets attention on a particular event such as the birth of one's child, a joyful *mood* permeates one's whole life. As Carroll (2003, p. 528) nicely puts the point, "When in the throes of an 'Oh-what-a-beautiful-morning' mood or 'The-hills-are-alive-with-the-sound-of-music' mood, almost anything can seem radiant and virtually anything one lights upon does." As he says, moods are "global rather than focal". Moreover, whereas it is the birth of the child that *causes* my emotion of joy, that the morning appears beautiful and the hills alive with music is typically the *result* of my joyful mood, not its cause.

This difference has led the neuro-psychologist Richard J. Davidson (1994) to propose that it is a defining feature of moods that they "bias cognition" in various ways: "Mood serves as a primary mechanism for altering information-processing priorities and for shifting modes of information processing. Mood will accentuate the accessibility of some and attenuate the accessibility of other cognitive contents and semantic networks" (Davidson 1994, p. 52). Several psychologists (e.g. Ekman 1994; Frijda 1993) have emphasized that moods predispose towards certain emotions: in a choleric mood I am apt to get angry very easily; in a joyful mood the whole world looks welcoming. But Davidson notes that moods also influence a variety of cognitive capacities such as appraisal, memory, perception, decision-making, problem-solving, and shifts in attention. "For example, individuals in a

---

[16] There is a great deal of controversy about the degree of physiological differentiation that exists for emotions/moods. But differences in heart rate and skin conductance have been found to distinguish several "basic" emotions, including happiness and sadness. See Levenson (1994); Cacioppo et al. (2000).

[17] Carroll notes that moods are also "self-promoting feedback systems": for example, one's cheerful thoughts and memories reinforce one's cheerfulness, and one's depressed thoughts and memories reinforce one's depression. This would seem to be true, regardless of whether the cheerfulness in question is an emotion or a mood.

depressed mood have increased accessibility to sad memories and decreased accessibility to happy memories", and "positive moods facilitate cognitive flexibility", resulting in "more creative responses, more remote associations, and an increase in the perception of relatedness among cognitions" (Davidson 1994, p. 52). If Davidson is right, then one of the most common ways of distinguishing moods from emotions is off the mark: moods do not necessarily last longer than emotions, as is often claimed (Ekman 1994), insofar as there can be transient moods of gloom or joy as well as long-lasting emotions of jealousy and resentment.

Following and expanding on Davidson's suggestion, Laura Sizer (2000) has argued that moods are essentially processes *governing* "the creation and manipulation of representational states" (p. 763) rather than being themselves specific sorts of representational states, as (she thinks) emotions are.[18] There may well be something to this distinction, but it is worth pointing out that emotions, as well as being themselves representational states, seem to have the same kinds of cognitive effects that Davidson and Sizer attribute to moods. Whether I am in a sad emotional state or a sad mood, I will have readier access to sad memories, and my "judgments and categorization [will] proceed more cautiously and draw more heavily on the evidence at hand", leading to slower information processing (Sizer 2000, p. 764). Similarly, my joyful mood might make it appear to me that the hills are alive with the sound of music, but so too might my joyful emotion induced by the birth of my child.

Carroll endorses Sizer's suggestion that the "direction of impact" of a mood, unlike an emotion, is "from the self to the world" (Carroll 2003, p. 529). In his words, moods are dependent on the "overall state of the organism, its level of energy, the level of resources at its disposal for coping with environmental challenges, and the degree of tension it finds itself in as a result of the ratio of its resources to its challenges" (p. 529). Thus a depressed mood is one in which one is conscious of a depletion of resources and energy. Sizer (2000, p. 762) argues that moods are "part of a non-cognitive self-regulatory or self-monitoring system" that enables us "to monitor our own resources in relation to external demands" (p. 761). Here the philosophers are echoing the psychologist Robert E. Thayer (1989, p. 128) who has emphasized that "moods are naturally occurring signal systems of underlying bodily processes" which "indicate readiness for activity, or the need for rest and recuperation".[19]

---

[18] Sizer (2000) agrees with Davidson that moods bias cognition. Indeed she goes further than he does by arguing that "we can (in principle) identify particular moods with specific modulations and biases" in the functioning of processes such as "memory, attention allocation and concept formation and application" (p. 764).

[19] Thayer seems to be suggesting that moods are not just *dependent* on the overall state of the organism, as Carroll claims, but signify or *represent* this state. If this is true, then in a sense moods do have intentional objects after all, namely the overall state of the organism. I do not have space here to

There is clearly much more to be said about emotions and moods, their differences and their commonalities, but for my purposes here the most important features of moods are (1) the fact that moods do not have to be caused by an appraisal of the world, although they typically result in such appraisals; (2) the fact that, like emotions, moods exhibit characteristic physiological and other bodily changes accompanied by corresponding feelings of those changes; (3) the fact that moods bias cognitive capacities in various ways; and (4) the fact that moods indicate "the overall state of the organism", its level of energy and its ability – or lack thereof – to cope with challenges. Given this general picture of what moods are, we are now in a better position to address the question whether music arouses moods in listeners, and if so how.

There is plenty of anecdotal evidence that music can affect people's moods. David Huron (2001), the music psychologist, talks of people "self-medicating" with music in order either to reinforce or to change mood. And some composers oblige by writing "mood music", music to get you going in the morning, music for while you iron or type, music for socializing to, music for love-making, and music to put you to sleep again. Movie music frequently sets a mood of anxiety or calm, gloom or happiness. In general, in discussions of music and mood, there are four mood states that come up over and over again: sadness (or gloom or melancholy) and happiness (or joy or cheerfulness or contentment), nervousness (or anxiety or agitation) and calm or peacefulness. So the question becomes: *how* can music evoke moods of sadness or happiness, anxiety or calm when there is nothing to be sad or happy about, no intentional object meriting anxiety or calm?

The answer in brief is that music directly induces bodily changes characteristic of particular moods, including autonomic changes, facial expressions, movements, gestures, and action tendencies. These bodily changes are experienced subjectively – and reported by listeners – as feelings of sadness, happiness, ebullience, anxiety, peacefulness, irritation, nervousness, etc. Crucially, the effect of the music is also to change energy and tension levels and in particular to produce the sorts of cognitive bias characteristic of particular moods.[20] Because musical movement in particular induces an urge to move as well as action tendencies in listeners, I have elsewhere (Robinson 2005) christened this effect the "Jazzercise effect".

To show that music can arouse moods, we need first to demonstrate that music can regularly induce in listeners physiological changes, action tendencies, and bodily expressions characteristic of moods. But this is not enough to show that

discuss the many interesting ramifications of this idea, or its bearing on the question of whether music can arouse moods. I discuss these questions further in "Music and Misattribution" (in progress).

[20] Exactly how the felt bodily changes are connected to the cognitive and other changes characteristic of mood is not yet known, although there are theories out there. For example, James Laird (2007) thinks that we make unconscious inferences of the form: "I am *feeling* sad; therefore I must be sad." Presumably the cognitive biases etc. are supposed to follow as a result of my interpretation of my state.

music induces moods themselves. We also need to establish that music induces biases in various cognitive processes, affects energy and tension levels, and results in self-reports of mood change. I begin with some of the evidence that music induces bodily and behavioural changes characteristic of moods.

There is a large body of empirical evidence that music can indeed produce systematic physiological reactions characteristic of distinctive moods. "Arousing" music, such as the Toreador song from *Carmen*, increases heart or pulse rate as well as decreasing resistance in skin conductance, whereas "sedative" music decreases heart rate and increases skin conductivity resistance.[21] Effects on respiration rate, blood pressure, muscular tension and motor activity, finger temperature, and stomach contractions have all been documented as well. Cardio-respiratory activity varies systematically in listeners to music that is found independently to be happy, sad, calm, or agitated (Nyklicek et al. 1997). Similarly differentiated effects have been reported not only on heart rate and skin conductance but also on facial expressions: apparently happy music induces subliminal smiles and sad music subliminal frowns (Scherer and Zentner 2001). Moreover, in an elaborate experiment, Carol Krumhansl (1997) measured subjects' heart rate, blood pressure, skin conductance, finger temperature, etc. as they listened to music which she antecedently classified as happy, sad, and fearful, and found that there were indeed distinct physiological changes associated with listening to the different types of excerpt.[22] To give some idea of the differences found, the sad excerpts produced the largest differences in heart rate, blood pressure, skin conductance, and finger temperature, and the happy excerpts produced the largest differences in respiration.[23] Music also seems to effect *hormonal* changes. Peretz (2001, p. 126) notes that there is data suggesting that music is "effective in eliciting [neurochemical] responses, as suggested by the action of the antagonists of endorphins . . . and cortisol measures". For example, when infants listened to their mothers singing, the cortisol in their saliva showed significant modulation of arousal (Trehub 2003).

[21] Bartlett (1996, p. 355); Zimny and Weidenfeller (1963).

[22] Peter Kivy (2006a) has criticized this experiment on a number of grounds, most notably that Krumhansl does not know what kind of listening her subjects were engaging in. It is unfortunate that Krumhansl chose programmatic pieces for her experiment, so that indeed, as Kivy (p. 307) says, we cannot be sure *"what was going on in the subjects' conscious experience"* as they were listening to the music. Maybe they weren't listening carefully to the music itself, but simply letting their minds wander. But it is instructive that intersubject consistency was very strong for both the "dynamic emotion ratings" and the physiological measures for the different musical excerpts, suggesting that whatever the emotional effects of the music, they were widely shared among listeners and not the result of idiosyncratic associations.

[23] Krumhansl acknowledges that, although she found systematic differences in the autonomic effects of the different pieces, not all the differences reflect those found in non-musical studies of autonomic activity in different emotions by Ekman, Levenson, and others. It may be that some of the differences reflect differences in arousal levels only. Nevertheless, her findings of differentiated autonomic responses to music with different expressive character are highly suggestive.

There is also lots of evidence that music with a specifically sad or happy character affects movement and action tendencies. Much music, including marches, dirges, and lullabies, is specifically designed to facilitate certain activities. One empirical study showed that adults who were listening to a lullaby had decreased heart rate and their breathing rhythm "became synchronized with the rhythm of the music" (Scherer and Zentner 2001, p. 378). Bharucha et al. (2006, p. 158) have suggested that "tiny organs in the inner ear", which are parts of the vestibulum, "a proprioceptive organ that detects changes in the spatial state of the organism's body", are also sensitive to auditory stimuli. They note that these organs in the inner ear are sensitive to forces of acceleration and "help animals discern translations in spatial position". And they point out that "nerves from [these organs] project through intermediaries to spinal motorneurons, establishing a pathway by which acoustic stimuli could influence the spine and thus create a compulsion to move to music in addition producing a sense of inner motion". In addition, the neuroscientist Daniel Levitin (2006) has noted that there are neural connections from the ear that bypass the auditory cortex and "send masses of fibres to the cerebellum" (p. 180), a structure deep in the so-called reptilian brain, which is a centre of motor control linked to our sense of timing, and which also contains "massive connections to emotional centres of the brain" (p. 171), such as the amygdala and the frontal lobe.[24]

I have mentioned only a small part of the large literature on the effects of music on bodily changes of various sorts. It seems pretty clear that music does indeed have the power to calm people down and cheer them up, make them excited or sadden them, as measured by physiological changes and action tendencies characteristic of these moods as well as by self-report. People claim that music really does cheer them up, calm them down, and so on. But in order to show decisively that listeners have been put into a different *mood*, rather than merely undergoing various bodily changes, we also need to establish whether these listeners exhibit the various cognitive and other changes that define moods.

There is good evidence that listening to music with a happy or sad, restless or calm character does in fact have the kinds of cognitive effects that typify moods. We know this because playing music with a particular character (usually positive or negative, i.e., happy or sad) is frequently used as a "mood-induction procedure" in the lab, being both easier to control and less ethically problematic than putting people into sad-making or nervous-making situations. Experimenters assume that music puts people into various mood states and then study the cognitive effects of being in a particular mood. The results are instructive.

---

[24] For an interesting and elaborate theory of "the musical representation", which emphasizes the connections among music, movement, and emotion, see Nussbaum (2007).

(1) There are effects on *perception*. Bouhuys et al. (1995) found that after listening to sad music, subjects "perceived more rejection/sadness in faces with ambiguous emotional expressions and less invitation/happiness in faces with clear, unambiguous expressions".[25]

(2) There are effects on *memory*. Gordon Bower (1981) has shown that events that one has memorized under the effect of a certain mood are recalled more easily when that mood or a similar one is evoked. This effect has been observed when the mood in question is evoked by playing music with the appropriate emotional quality, happy or sad.[26]

(3) There are various other cognitive effects, including effects on recognition, decision-making, and appraisal. Niedenthal et al. (1997) found that after listening to happy or sad music, people were quicker to recognize words like "happy" or "sad". An experiment by Kenealy (1988) found that "a music mood-induction procedure yielded significant effects on behavioural measures, such as decision-time, distance approximation, and writing speed".[27] In another study, after music was played to induce "positive, negative, or neutral affect", listeners were asked to appraise their own specific qualities and character. (How smart are you? How kind are you?)[28] Subjects rated themselves more favourably after listening to happy music than after sad music.

(4) There are apparently even effects on *altruism*. Fried and Berkowitz (1979) found that when four groups of people were played examples of soothing, stimulating, or "aversive" music (or – for the control group – no music), "those who heard the soothing music were most apt to show altruistic behaviour immediately afterwards".[29] The "altruistic behaviour" consisted in volunteering for another study!

In short, it seems that music with a happy, sad, calm, or excited character has distinct measurable effects on motor activity, action tendencies, autonomic changes, and so on, resulting in distinct feelings of bodily change. These feelings of bodily change are reported as feelings of *moods* such as happiness, sadness, serenity, excitement, etc., and there is good reason to think that the bodily changes are indeed indications of mood changes, because they are accompanied by changes in one's capacity to engage in various cognitive and other tasks, to assess oneself positively or negatively, to attend to and to remember certain kinds of events, and so on. Indeed, it seems reasonable to assume that these feelings are indeed signals (to use Thayer's term) of one's overall state, including the level of tension or arousal

---

[25] Cf. Scherer and Zentner (2001, p. 374). See also Niedenthal (2001).
[26] Bower (1981, p. 141).
[27] Sloboda and Juslin (2001, p. 84).
[28] Reported by Scherer and Zentner (2001, p. 380).
[29] Scherer and Zentner (2001, p. 378).

one is experiencing, the level of energy one has available relative to the challenges to be faced, and one's capacity for problem-solving and other cognitive tasks.[30]

For example, the Funeral March from Beethoven's Third Symphony (the *Eroica*) has the slow, heavy, plodding gait characteristic of a gloomy mood. In most "suitably backgrounded" listeners it will produce (typically without overt awareness) bodily changes including autonomic changes, action tendencies, and motor activity, notably an urge to move in a slow, deliberate, heavy-footed way. The resultant body state is *felt* as gloomy and as an indication of a gloomy mood. Similarly with respect to music that makes us skip and dance. The skipping and dancing induce feelings signifying excess energy, confidence, optimism. In short, they are feelings of light-heartedness and joy.[31] As William James (1981, p. 1072) long ago observed:

Smooth the brow, brighten the eye, contract the dorsal rather than the ventral aspect of the frame, and speak in a major key, pass the genial compliment, and your heart must be frigid indeed if it do not gradually thaw!

In short, "Fake it till you Make It!" is good advice if you want to change your mood.[32]

Why call these feeling states mood states rather than emotions? The main reason is that they do not seem to be caused by an *appraisal* of the music (or of anything else for that matter), and they are not *about* any particular "adaptational encounter", such as a loss or a boon. Moreover, even though it's the sad music that makes me feel sad, I'm not sad *about the music*. The music does not (normally) signify a loss. It might be objected that nevertheless my sadness is directed towards the music as its object because that's what I am attending to as I am being saddened. Even this is not quite right, however. I may be paying attention to the melody when it is the rhythm that is having the main physiological effect on me. Or I may be listening to the words while it is the melody that chiefly affects my mood. In general, the arousal of moods by music seems to occur largely outside awareness. The music is functioning as a "stimulus object", in Kivy's (1990) phrase, rather than as a cognitive object, the object of an appraisal. One might be aware *that one is feeling sad* after listening to a sad piece, but one is typically not aware of why or how one came to be sad. In this respect music operates on mood much as recreational drugs do.

---

[30] Again, much more needs to be said here. I explore these issues in greater detail in "Music and Misattribution".

[31] This raises the question whether the gloom or joy felt is genuine gloom or joy or, as Prinz (2004, p. 235) claims, a kind of perceptual illusion. I discuss this issue at greater length in Robinson (2005) and in "Music and Misattribution".

[32] For a wealth of examples supporting James's hypothesis see Laird (2007). However, Laird does not distinguish between emotions and moods in his discussion.

The phenomenon I have been discussing is sometimes referred to as a form of "emotional contagion", which has been defined by the authors of an eponymous book as the way in which "people tend to 'catch' others' emotions" (Hatfield et al. 1994, p. 11) by means of mimicking their facial expressions, vocal expressions, posture, movements, and other behaviour. Subjective emotional experiences "are affected . . . by the activation and/or feedback from such mimicry" (p. 10). It might be thought that these researchers have found evidence that music can indeed arouse *emotions* rather than moods by means of such mimicry. However, Hatfield et al. (1994) use the terms "emotion" and "mood" more or less indiscriminately, and it is unclear whether they think that emotional contagion is contagion of genuine emotions, or merely (as might seem more likely) of moods. At any rate, the phenomenon of so-called "emotional contagion" has marked analogies to the Jazzercise effect: we are induced by music expressive of some mood such as sadness or happiness to look and sound and, in particular, to *move* in a way characteristic of the mood being expressed. We then begin to experience feelings characteristic of that mood.[33] As in emotional contagion between people, music affects listeners' moods by means of mechanisms that function below the level of conscious awareness. The mood itself may be conscious – indeed some theorists (e.g., Thayer 1989) think that moods by definition are always conscious – but how the mood is arrived at is typically not. People are notoriously bad at identifying the source of their moods.[34]

## 29.4 ARE LISTENERS' EMOTIONAL RESPONSES RELEVANT TO AESTHETIC APPRECIATION?

### 29.4.1 Emotions of Appreciation

As we saw earlier, although Peter Kivy thinks that music never arouses the "garden-variety emotions" that it expresses, he acknowledges that when music is being

---

[33] See Robinson (2005) and Davies (forthcoming). Note that "emotional contagion" by music isn't exactly the same thing as emotional contagion by a person. When we sit listening to a gloomy person and begin to take on the tone of voice, posture, and facial expression of that person, we are induced to feel with that person and to share his or her emotional state. When we listen to gloomy music, it is the music that puts us into a bodily and behavioural state characteristic of some emotion; there is no one with whom we are feeling, unless we are imagining a persona in the music whose emotions we are sharing. But even if we do this, it is the *result* of the music's putting us in a certain bodily state, not the cause. As Davies notes: "Unlike other types of contagion, the germs of emotion transmitted by music seem to require no social interaction – musical emotions are airborne contagions" (p. 156). I made the same point in Robinson (2005), although not so wittily.

[34] For example, "most people . . . believe that they are much happier on sunny days than on cloudy, rainy days", but the data demonstrate "that this is simply not the case" (Watson 2000, pp. 100–1).

appreciated qua music, it can arouse "emotions of appreciation", such as excitement or ecstasy, which are evoked by the music and have the music as its intentional object. For example, we listen carefully to Josquin's *Ave Maria*; we recognize its beauty; we notice that it is a canon at the fifth with the entrances only one beat apart; and we are moved, thrilled, and awed by the beauty and craftsmanship we have detected.[35] For Kivy, musical understanding entails being able to *describe* the music (as, for example, a "canon at the fifth",)[36] and emotional responses to music are a result of such understanding. I appraise the music as being a beautiful canon, for example, and this appraisal causes an emotional response of awe and excitement.

Being moved by a piece can be a sign of appreciation. Theoretically, of course, it might be possible to appreciate a piece in a purely cognitive way, noticing the canon and recognizing the beauty and estimating both as having high aesthetic value, yet without being *moved* by it. But normally when we say that we appreciate a piece it seems we are not just recognizing intellectually that the piece has high aesthetic value but also responding to it with positive emotion. It is odd to say that I much appreciated a work of art that, as we say, "left me cold".

Jesse Prinz (2007, p. 2) has gone further. He argues that "when we appreciate a work [of art], the appreciation *consists in* an emotional response" (my emphasis) that he tentatively identifies with the emotion of *wonder*. Prinz cites a great deal of empirical evidence designed to show that "emotions arise during aesthetic appreciation, influence aesthetic preference, and may even be necessary for appreciating art" (p. 6). However, although this evidence may show that emotion is *necessary* for appreciation, that is very different from Prinz's claim that "appreciation is an emotional state" (p. 7).[37] After all, even if a positive emotional response to a piece is necessary for appreciation, it is not sufficient. I might be delighted by a piece of music for all the

---

[35] The music psychologist Vladimir Konečni (2008) argues that there is an "aesthetic trinity" of emotional or quasi-emotional states that can be aroused by music, *aesthetic awe, being moved*, and *thrills*, but unlike Kivy, he stresses the role of listeners' associations to the music and the environment where the music is heard in helping to arouse these states.

[36] But a relatively inarticulate music listener, such as E. M. Forster's Mrs. Munt from *Howard's End*, can still exhibit understanding of a piece of music by giving a crude description. For Kivy (1990) musical understanding means understanding of musical structure, which for him includes expressive qualities.

[37] Prinz builds an evaluative element into the emotional response he thinks constitutes appreciation, saying that "aesthetic appreciation is a form of wonder", and that wonder can also be described as "a feeling of reverence". Wonder captures the "features of pleasure, admiration, and interest" central to appreciation. So there's positive evaluation built into the emotion: we delight in, look up to, and revere objects of wonder. What's missing, however, is any account of what makes some art works *appropriate objects* of wonder. Appreciation is identified with a positive appraisal and the relevant positive appraisal is identified with wonder, but unfortunately one can make a positive appraisal of something without appreciating it, as when I claim that a work is really great, but in fact I don't actually understand it, although I might think I do, and one can wonder at something that is not worth wondering at or which it's inappropriate to wonder at, such as a trite velvet Elvis painting.

wrong reasons. Appreciation entails not merely delight but delight based on a proper understanding of a piece. Thus I might be delighted by an unimaginative and sentimental piece that isn't an appropriate candidate for appreciation. Or I might be delighted by a well-constructed and beautiful piece without noticing its beauty or its marvellous construction. It would seem, therefore, that appreciation cannot be *identified* with a positive emotional response such as wonder or delight. Appreciation requires understanding as well. Indeed we might say that the delight or wonder in question is precisely the delight or wonder of understanding something that is worthy of being understood. Wonder, awe, excitement, and admiration are emotions of appreciation only when they are based on understanding.

If this is right, however, it means that emotions of appreciation can occur only *after* understanding (at least to some extent) has been achieved. They are the *result* of experiencing and understanding a work. But there are other emotions that are induced in the very process of understanding a work. Indeed these emotions themselves constitute a mode of understanding. In section 29.4.2 I want to focus on affective states that are not a *result of* understanding but a *means towards* understanding.

## 29.4.2 Emotions, moods, and feelings as modes of understanding music

If we review the various other ways I have discussed in which music can arouse emotions or moods, we find that all of them are capable, to a greater or lesser degree, of helping us to understand what we are listening to by alerting us to important aspects of the music. First, there are the various ways in which emotions are aroused by appraisals.

(a) Sometimes when listening to music we may discover ourselves becoming gloomy or reverential or cheerful without knowing why. There may be many different reasons for this, but one common reason is that we have unconscious associations to the music. If the associations are idiosyncratic (as when I feel joyful when I hear the Chopin Funeral March), they are not likely to enhance my understanding of the piece. But if the associations are cultural – the result of *topoi* in the music – then they may alert me to the presence of those *topoi*. I'm feeling cheerful because the music is in jig form, gloomy because it's a funeral march, or reverential because it is hymn-like. In such cases, the emotional effects of these *topoi* in the music may help us to identify the *topoi* themselves and the emotions that they express.[38]

---

[38] At times, of course, I may be perfectly aware that I am listening to a jig or a hymn, and my emotional response merely confirms what I already know. But very often associations to music of whatever kind work below the level of awareness.

(b) Sometimes music acts as a "cognitive object" of emotions. There are the emotions of appreciation which I have just discussed. But there are also the emotions that Leonard Meyer tells us can be a mode of understanding the structure of a musical work. If I am appropriately surprised, bewildered, relieved, and so on by the unfolding musical structure, this *constitutes* musical understanding. Note that Meyer is chiefly interested in the understanding of structure, not expression.[39] Feeling the right emotions in the right places is a mode of structural understanding, however inarticulate it might be.

(c) Emotional responses to emotional expression in music can also help listeners understand what a piece of music is *expressing*. Thus if I am responding to music that shares an acoustic code with human vocal expressions of woe in the way described by Juslin, then, although I am probably not consciously aware of the mechanism underlying my response, the distress I feel may well make me notice that the music expresses woe.[40] Furthermore, if the expressive power of a piece of music is party derived from the "plot archetype" that it exemplifies, then the emotional changes I experience in response to what is happening in the music should alert me to the corresponding expressive changes in the music.[41] Meyer explained how harmonic changes, for example, can in turn surprise, unsettle, disappoint and, finally, satisfy me. Sometimes such emotional changes in the listener reflect not only structural but expressive developments in the music, as when Schubert's outcast wanderer finds himself in unfamiliar, bewildering, hostile terrain before undergoing an epiphany and returning home a changed person with a new-found serenity. The story I have just sketched is, of course, banal, but the emotional experience of this story as "told" by Schubert is very far from banal. The emotions aroused by the unfolding psychological drama are not only what give it its emotional power; they also alert the sensitively responding listener to exactly what is going on expressively in the unfolding drama. Indeed, unless we respond emotionally, we are unlikely to grasp the psychological drama exemplified by the music or the emotions that the music is expressing.[42] Thus responding emotionally to the psychological journey of the protagonist of Schubert's *Winterreise* or to the psychological drama enacted by the imagined wanderer of the B-flat piano sonata is a mode of understanding the expressive structure of these pieces.

[39] It is only in the final chapter of Meyer (1956), "Note on Image Processes, Connotations, Moods", that he turns to the arousal of affective states as a result of associations, connotations, and so on.

[40] If the piece in question is Purcell's plaint, then my woe is probably not undiluted. I am also likely to respond emotionally to the beauty of the music. I will say more about mixed emotional responses in the final section.

[41] In Karl and Robinson (1995) we suggest in a series of footnotes how the sequence of emotions aroused by the music alerts the listener to the emotional development in the piece itself.

[42] I make the corresponding case for some great works of realistic literature in chapters 4 and 5 of Robinson (2005).

Now, Peter Kivy (2006*b*) argues that if you imagine a wanderer in such instrumental music, it is really your own mind that is doing the wandering. You have become distracted from "the music itself" and given in to extraneous imaginings. But this is unfair. There is evidence that the theme of the outsider or wanderer was dear to Schubert's heart, so it is not inconsistent with what we know of Schubert's intentions that he might have had in mind some such psychological interpretation of his work. And if we are responding to the psychological "resonances"[43] of the music, this partly explains why the music seems to us so profound. If all we are listening to is a beautifully built structure of tones, this would be mysterious, as Kivy (1990) himself acknowledges. More importantly, perhaps, the charge that in listening to Schubert's music as a beautiful structure of tones that exemplifies a compelling psychological drama our minds are wandering away from the music itself can be answered decisively by pointing out that when we pay attention to the unfolding music, we are paying attention simultaneously both to musical structure and to what this structure exemplifies in the wider human realm. As Noël Carroll and Margaret Moore (2007) put the point in their response to Kivy, if in listening we are imagining a persona in the music whose psychological story we are engaged with, then the relevant imagining "is strictly tied to properties of the music", (p. 320) and not "wool-gathering", as Kivy (2007*b*) would have it.

(d) So far I have been talking about the various ways in which music can arouse emotions proper. But what about moods? Does the arousal of mood states have any bearing on our understanding of the music itself? As we saw earlier, there is good evidence – contra Kivy – that music does arouse some "garden-variety" moods such as joy and sadness, but it also seems to be true that mood arousal mechanisms operate wholly or largely below the level of consciousness. How then can they affect conscious appreciation of a musical work?

I suggest that such mood effects are indeed aesthetically relevant insofar as they function as "background" affective states,[44] which have a subliminal priming effect. They put us into a mood in which we are more likely to notice and to pay attention to certain expressive qualities in the music. If subliminally I am put into a depressed mood by being induced to move and behave in a depressed way, then it seems reasonable to assume that one indication that I am indeed in such a mood is that I more readily notice and attend to expressions of gloom or anxiety in the music. Such effects are, then, indirectly relevant to appreciation in that they help to focus attention on what is being *expressed* by the music. Thus it seems likely that the languorous mood induced in listeners by "L'après-midi d'un faune" plays an

---

[43] The word is Newcomb's. See Newcomb (1984*a*).
[44] Cf Antonio Damasio (1994, 1999) on "background feelings".

important role in what we hear the music as expressing. The melancholy mood aroused by "The Death of Äse" from Grieg's *Peer Gynt* suite may prime listeners to detect the melancholy quality of the music.[45]

On the other hand, Kivy is no doubt correct in thinking that mood arousal mechanisms are not usually very important to the understanding and appreciation of great art music in the Western "classical" tradition. Such music is precisely *not* – or not merely – "mood music", music to iron to or to make love to. With wonderful exceptions such as those I have just mentioned, what we call "mood music" does not usually repay careful attention to its style and form.[46] Whereas priming effects take place below the level of conscious awareness, the kind of complex art music that is of most interest to Kivy requires careful conscious attention to the musical structure. It doesn't merely work on us subliminally while we're paying attention to something else. To treat the Funeral March in Beethoven's Third merely as a mood-induction procedure is not to listen to it in an aesthetically appropriate way. Indeed, arguably it is not to *listen* to it at all, since listening involves paying attention and following the development of the music, whereas to have one's moods affected by music requires only that one hears it going on in the background. Marches and work tunes do not demand that one focus on details of the harmonic and melodic development; all you need to do in order to be affected appropriately is to march or work to the rhythm of the music (or to engage in imaginative motor mimicry).

But Kivy is wrong to argue (1) that proper listening to great music in the Western tradition never involves being moved to a feeling or mood or emotion state that is the same as the state being expressed by the music; (2) that the moods or feelings induced subconsciously play no role in one's aesthetic experience and appreciation of the music; (3) that if one imagines a "program" as one listens to music, one is necessarily engaging in wool-gathering or mind-wandering, and (4) that such "programs" should never be part of one's aesthetic experience of (a great piece of Western) music. Finally (5) I have argued that at least *some* of the music Kivy is interested in is indeed "intended" to be heard as satisfying a "program" and has "a better payoff when heard as it was intended" (Kivy 2007*b*, p. 328).

---

[45] Kivy (2007*b*, p. 326) argues that it is implausible that the arousal of emotions can alert us subliminally to the presence of qualities in the music. He thinks that we first notice qualities and then react emotionally to them. But typically priming effects are obtained only when subjects are unaware of the prime to which they are subjected. A very brief exposure to a prime – too fast for conscious awareness – is enough to secure the effect.

[46] Much film music is mainly concerned to induce moods subliminally.

# 29.5 THE EMOTIONAL RICHNESS
## OF OUR MUSICAL EXPERIENCE

For formalist theorists such as Kivy, the only emotional effects of music that are relevant to aesthetic appreciation are responses of being awed, thrilled, excited, etc. by the "purely musical" structure of a piece. By contrast, Carroll seems to think that the only affective states that music can arouse are moods.[47] As I have tried to show, both these positions are seriously mistaken. Music can arouse emotions, including "garden-variety" emotions as well as emotions of appreciation. It can also arouse moods. What's more, it can arouse all these affective states simultaneously. Moreover, the affective states aroused by different mechanisms may either reinforce or clash with one another.[48]

Let us review the various ways in which music can arouse affective states. First, we may respond emotionally to the cultural associations of a type of music or *topos*, feeling proud and uplifted as we listen to military music, reverent as we listen to religious music, or nostalgic as we listen to a childhood lullaby. At the same time, we may be moved, awed, and full of wonder at the beauty and craftsmanship we appraise as belonging to the music. Thirdly, we may respond with surprise, bewilderment, and relief as we follow the unfolding musical structure, bearing in mind the structural norms of the style of the piece and the expectations they set off in knowledgeable listeners. Fourthly, we may respond emotionally to what is being expressed by the music. Sometimes this will be an automatic "instinctive" response to music that shares the same intonation patterns as human vocal expressions of grief or joy. Sometimes this will involve more cognitive activity, as when we respond emotionally to the psychological predicaments of an imagined persona in the music, such as Schubert's wanderer or Schumann's alter egos, Florestan and Eusebius. Finally, music may evoke moods by manipulating our bodily stance, movement, emotional expressions, and behaviour.

What has not been widely noticed is that music can arouse emotions in these various different ways *at the same time*. Furthermore, the different mechanisms may be simultaneously arousing different emotions or mood states. I have noted that if music produces an urge to move as the music moves, then the urge to move briskly to music can put you in a cheerful mood and the urge to move slowly can

---

[47] In his most recent statement Carroll suggests that only "feelings" are aroused "rather than full-fledged moods" (Carroll and Moore 2007, pp. 321–2). But, as Kivy (2007b, p. 326) notes, although the experience of listening to "pure" music certainly arouses "feelings" in listeners, the claim is vacuous because so "does every other experience [he] can think of".

[48] See Robinson (2005). Juslin and Västfjäll (2008) also discuss some of the many different mechanisms responsible for the arousal of affective states by music. They agree that these mechanisms may work simultaneously in order to induce rich emotion blends.

put you in a gloomy mood. In criticizing Laura Sizer (2007) and Carroll and Moore (2007) on this point, Kivy (2007a, p. 315) notes that the opening measure of Beethoven's Fifth is in a brisk tempo but is "dominated by gloom and doom", whereas the slow movement of his *Pathétique* piano sonata is slow but "diffused with a sublime mood of tranquil sunshine and well-being". Even if we allow that such music "has a tendency" to put us in a particular mood, the tendency may not get realized, and in any case "there is so much else, of far more importance, going on", when "I am listening and concentrating in the formalist manner to Western art music in its proper settings" (p. 315). In another place (2006b, p. 277) Kivy argues that, according to Meyer's view, it would follow that all suspenseful or frustrating music would induce the *same* moods of suspense and frustration, whereas because different suspenseful passages have quite different expressive qualities, it is highly unlikely that they would all arouse the very same moods. There is a big difference, he points out, between a suspenseful joyous passage and a suspenseful gloomy passage.

Both these arguments fail for the same reason. The arousal of a cheerful or gloomy mood by the induction of corresponding movement is but one of the mechanisms for the arousal of emotion that may be at work in a piece. The opening theme of Beethoven's Fifth, for example, is part of a psychological drama to which we respond emotionally. Its brisk rhythm may in the abstract be liable to produce good cheer but given the other qualities in the music – its darkness, inexorability, and power – the briskness gives rise rather to a feeling of resoluteness or something of this sort. Here two modes of affective arousal combine or blend to arouse a new and more subtle affective state. Similarly, of course not all suspenseful or frustrating music produces the very same affective states in listeners because suspense and frustration are not the only affective states being aroused. Meyer has described one mechanism for the arousal of affect by music but there are several others, as I have noted. Thus the suspense aroused by *Bolero* has an erotic tinge, while the suspense induced by the wanderings in the opening movement of Schubert's last sonata can induce feelings of loneliness or abandonment. Again the emotional response is not only to the unfolding formal structure but also to the expressive structure of the music.

In general, then, different mechanisms for the arousal of emotion, mood, or feelings by music can all be operating simultaneously and inducing different affects at the same time. This is perhaps why music is often described as producing *ineffable* feelings. The emotions and moods that music induces may be *blends* that the listener has not hitherto encountered. They may be highly *ambiguous* and *nuanced*. At the same time, some pieces arouse powerful affective responses because several different mechanisms of emotional arousal work together to produce a powerful unified effect.

Towards the end of the development section of the first movement of Schubert's B flat Piano Sonata, when the theme has moved through a wide range of different keys, taking us further and further away from the "home" key, we find ourselves unexpectedly in D minor. As I mentioned earlier, Charles Fisk (2001, p. 253) describes this moment as "a stillness that awaits an epiphany". Fisk's interpretation relies on the idea that the piece is appropriately heard as a human drama, which enacts the psychological journey of a "wanderer" or "outcast", a figure familiar to us from Schubert's songs,[49] and that we hear this particular passage as the wanderer himself arriving at a strange, mysterious, and wondrous place. As far as the *mood* of this passage is concerned, it is a still, calm passage in the midst of questing and wandering. It is a moment of stasis and this no doubt has a subliminal *calming* and *quieting* effect on the listener. In terms of the harmonic structure of the passage, as Meyer might note, after being *intrigued* and *bewildered* by the constant modulations that precede it, we are *surprised* by the unexpected arrival of D minor. But simultaneously we are responding to the sense of mystery and impending revelation that is expressed by the passage. For me – and I think for Fisk – what we are encouraged to feel is not just surprise but a blend of *wonder* and *bliss* at being in this strange and beautiful new territory, an oasis of calm and quiet in the midst of wandering and striving. We grasp the new emotional feeling in the music because we share it, responding emotionally to the situation of the protagonist and to the psychological story that Schubert is unfolding.[50] Finally, the passage is also very beautiful and shows off Schubert's harmonic wizardry, and so we are likely to respond with emotions of *awe* and *wonder* to the beauty and craftsmanship in the music, as Kivy would have us do.

Does everyone respond emotionally in the way I have described? Surely not. Nevertheless, I have described an emotional state – a blend of awe, wonder, quietude, surprise, and bliss – that I would urge is not only appropriate to this music but which also can help the listener to appreciate the music more fully.

## References

BARTLETT, DALE (1996), "Physiological Responses to Music and Sound Stimuli", in *Handbook of Music Psychology* 2nd edition, edited by Donald A. Hodges (San Antonio, TX: Institute for Music Research).

BEN-ZE'EV, AARON (2000), *The Subtlety of Emotions* (Cambridge, MA: MIT Press).

BHARUCHA, JAMSHEED J. et al. (2006), "Varieties of Musical Experience", *Cognition* 100: 131–72.

---

[49] And also present in, for example, the *Moment Musical* No. 6 as analysed by Edward T. Cone (1982).

[50] I have described the listener's reaction as mirroring the protagonist's, but listeners may also react emotionally to the protagonist's sense of wonder. We may be *glad* for him, for example, or *relieved* that his psychological quest has reached this magical turning point.

BICKNELL, JEANETTE (2007), "Explaining Strong Emotional Responses to Music: Sociality and Intimacy," *Journal of Consciousness Studies* 14: 5–23.

BOUHUYS, A. L., G. M. BLOEM, and T. G. GROOTHUIS (1995), "Induction of Depressed and Elated Mood by Music Influences the Perception of Facial Emotional Expressions in Healthy Subjects", *Journal of Affective Disorders* 33: 215–26.

BOWER, GORDON (1981), "Mood and Memory", *American Psychologist* 36: 129–48.

CACIOPPO, JOHN T. et al. (2000), "The Psychophysiology of Emotion", in *Handbook of Emotions* 2nd edition, edited by M. Lewis and J. M. Haviland-Jones (New York: Guilford Press), 173–91.

CARROLL, NOËL (2003), "Art and Mood: Preliminary Notes and Conjectures", *Monist* 86: 521–55.

——— and Margaret Moore (2007) "Not Reconciled: Comments for Peter Kivy", *Journal of Aesthetics and Art Criticism* 65: 318–22.

CONE, EDWARD T. (1974), *The Composer's Voice* (Berkeley: University of California Press).

——— (1982), "Schubert's Promissory Note: An Exercise in Musical Hermeneutics", *Nineteenth-Century Music* 5: 239.

DAMASIO, ANTONIO R. (1994), *Descartes' Error: Emotion, Reason, and the Human Brain.* (New York: G. P. Putnam).

——— (1999), *The Feeling of What Happens: Body and Emotion in the Making of Consciousness* (San Diego, CA: Harcourt).

DAVIDSON, RICHARD J. (1994), "On Emotion, Mood, and Related Affective Constructs", in *The Nature of Emotion*, edited by Paul Ekman and Richard J. Davidson (New York: Oxford University Press).

DAVIES, STEPHEN (forthcoming), "Infectious Music: Music-Listener Emotional Contagion".

ELLSWORTH, PHOEBE (1994), "William James and Emotion: Is a century of Fame Worth a Century of Misunderstanding?", *Psychological Review* 101: 222–29.

EKMAN, PAUL (1994), "Moods, Emotions, and Traits", in *The Nature of Emotion*, edited by Paul Ekman and Richard J. Davidson (New York: Oxford University Press), 56–8.

FELDMAN BARRETT, LISA (2006), "Are Emotions Natural Kinds?" *Perspectives on Psychological Science* 1, 28–56.

FISK, CHARLES (2001), *Returning Cycles: Contexts for the Interpretation of Schubert's Impromptus and Last Sonatas* (Berkeley: University of California Press).

FRIED, R. and L. BERKOWITZ (1979), "Music That Charms...And Can Influence Helpfulness", *Journal of Applied Social Psychology* 9: 199–208.

FRIJDA, NICO (1986), *The Emotions* (Cambridge: Cambridge University Press).

——— (1993), "Moods, Emotion Episodes, and Emotions", in *Handbook of Emotions*, edited by M. Lewis and J. M. Haviland (New York: Guilford Press), 381–403.

GORDON, ROBERT M. (1987), *The Structure of Emotions* (New York: Cambridge University Press).

HATELD, ELAINE, JOHN T. CACIOPPO, and RICHARD L. RAPSON (1994), *Emotional Contagion, Studies in Emotion and Social Interaction* (Cambridge and Paris: Cambridge University Press).

HATTEN, ROBERT S. (2004), *Musical Meaning in Beethoven: Markedness, Correlation, and Interpretation* (Bloomington: Indiana University Press).

HURON, DAVID (2001), "How Music Evokes Emotion". Paper delivered to University of Cincinnati College-Conservatory of Music.

JAMES, WILLIAM (1981), *The Works of William James*, edited by Frederick H. Burkhardt. 3 vols. Vols. 1, 2, and 3 (Cambridge, MA: Harvard University Press).

JUSLIN, PATRIK N. (2001), "Communicating Emotion in Music Performance: A Review and Theoretical Framework", in *Music and Emotion: Theory and Research*, edited by Patrik N. Juslin and J. A. Sloboda (Oxford: Oxford University Press), 309–37.

—— and DANIEL VÄSTFJÄLL (2008), "Emotional Responses to Music: The Need to Consider Underlying Mechanisms", *Behavioral and Brain Sciences* 31: 559–75.

KARL, GREGORY and JENEFER ROBINSON (1995), "Shostakovich's Tenth Symphony and the Musical Expression of Cognitively Complex Emotions", *Journal of Aesthetics and Art Criticism* 53: 401–15.

KENEALY, P. (1988), "Validation of a Mood Induction Procedure: Some Preliminary Findings", *Cognition and Emotion* 2: 41–8.

KIVY, PETER (1990), *Music Alone: Philosophical Reflections on the Purely Musical Experience* (Ithaca, NY: Cornell University Press).

—— (2006a) "Critical Study: Deeper than Emotion", *British Journal of Aesthetics* 46: 287–311.

—— (2006b), "Mood and Music: Some Reflections for Noël Carroll", *Journal of Aesthetics and Art Criticism* 64: 271–81.

—— (2007a), "Moodology: A Response to Laura Sizer", *Journal of Aesthetics and Art Criticism* 64: 312–18.

—— (2007b), "Moodophilia: A Response to Noël Carroll and Margaret Moore", *Journal of Aesthetics and Art Criticism* 65: 323–9.

KONEČNI, VLADIMIR (2008), "Does Music Induce Emotion: A Theoretical and Methodological Analysis", *Psychology of Aesthetics, Creativity, and the Arts* 2: 115–29.

KRUMHANSL, CAROL L. (1997), "An Exploratory Study of Musical Emotions and Psychophysiology", *Canadian Journal of Experimental Psychology* 51: 336–52.

LAIRD, JAMES D. (2007), *Feelings: The Perception of Self* (New York: Oxford University Press).

LAZARUS, RICHARD (1991), *Emotion and Adaptation* (New York: Oxford University Press).

LeDOUX, JOSEPH E. (1996), *The Emotional Brain: The Mysterious Underpinnings of Emotional Life* (New York: Simon & Schuster).

LEVENSON, ROBERT (1994), "The Search for Autonomic Specificity", in *The Nature of Emotion: Fundamental Questions*, edited by Paul Ekman and Richard J. Davidson (New York: Oxford University Press), 252–7.

LEVINSON, JERROLD (1996), "Musical Expressiveness", in his *The Pleasures of Aesthetics: Philosophical Essays* (Ithaca, NY: Cornell University Press), 90–125.

—— (2006), "Musical Expressiveness as Hearability-as-Expression", in *Contemporary Debates in Aesthetics and the Philosophy of Art*, edited by Matthew Kieran (Oxford: Blackwell), 192–204.

LEVITIN, DANIEL J. (2006), *This is Your Brain on Music: The Science of a Human Obsession* (New York: Dutton).

LYONS, WILLIAM, E. (1980), *Emotion* (Cambridge: Cambridge University Press).

MEYER, LEONARD B. (1956), *Emotion and Meaning in Music* (Chicago: University of Chicago Press).

MITHEN, STEPHEN (2005), *The Singing Neanderthals: The Origin of Music, Language, Mind and Body* (London: Weidenfeld & Nicholson).

NEWCOMB, ANTHONY (1997), "Action and Agency in Mahler's Ninth Symphony, Second Movement", *Music and Meaning*, edited by Jenefer Robinson (Ithaca, NY: Cornell University Press), 131–53.

—— (1984a), "Sound and Feeling", *Critical Inquiry* 10 (1984): 614–43.

—— (1984b), "Once More 'between Absolute and Program Music': Schumann's Second Symphony", *19th Century Music* 7: 233–50.

NIEDENTHAL, PAULA M. (2001), "When Did Her Smile Drop: Facial Mimicry and the Influences of Emotional State on the Detection of Change in Emotional Expression", *Cognition and Emotion* 15: 853–64.

—— et al. (1997), "Being Happy and Seeing 'Happy': Emotional State Mediates Visual Word Recognition", *Cognition and Emotion* 11: 403–32.

NUSSBAUM, CHARLES (2007), *The Musical Representation: Meaning, Ontology, and Emotion* (Cambridge MA: MIT Press).

NUSSBAUM, MARTHA (2001), *Upheavals of Thought: The Intelligence of Emotions* (Cambridge: Cambridge University Press).

NYKLICEK, I. et al. (1997), "Cardiorespiratory Differentiation of Musically-Induced Emotions", *Journal of Psychophysiology* 11: 304–21.

ORTONY, ANDREW et al. (1988), *The Cognitive Structure of Emotions* (Cambridge: Cambridge University Press).

PERETZ, ISABELLE (2001), "Listen to the Brain: A Biological Perspective on Music and Emotion", in *Music and Emotion: Theory and Research*, edited by Patrik N. Juslin and J. A. Sloboda (Oxford: Oxford University Press), 105–34.

PRINZ, JESSE (2004), *Gut Reactions: A Perceptual Theory of Emotion* (New York: Oxford University Press).

—— (2007), "Emotion and Aesthetic Value". Paper presented to the *American Philosophical Association* Pacific Division conference.

RATNER, LEONARD (1980), *Classic Music: Expression, Form, and Style* (New York: Schirmer Books [Macmillan]).

ROBINSON, JENEFER (1994), "The Expression and Arousal of Emotion in Music", *Journal of Aesthetics and Art Criticism* 52: 13–22.

—— (1995) "Startle", *Journal of Philosophy* 92: 53–74.

—— (2005), *Deeper than Reason: Emotion and its Role in Literature, Music, and Art* (Oxford: Oxford University Press).

—— (2007a), "Can Music Function as a Metaphor of Emotional Life?", in *Philosophers on Music: Experience, Meaning, and Work*, edited by Kathleen Stock (Oxford: Oxford University Press), 149–77.

—— (2007b), "Expression and Expressiveness in Art", *Postgraduate Journal of Aesthetics* (*online*), 4: 19–41.

—— (in progress), "Music and Misattribution".

RUSSELL, JAMES A. (2003), "Core Affect and the Psychological Construction of Emotion", *Psychological Review* 110, 145–72.

SCHERER, KLAUS R. et al. (2001), *Appraisal Processes in Emotion* (New York: Oxford University Press).

—— and MARCEL R. ZENTNER (2001), "Emotional Effects of Music: Production Rules", *Music and Emotion: Theory and Research*, edited by Patrik N. Juslin and John Sloboda (Oxford: Oxford University Press), 361–92.

Sizer, Laura (2000), "Towards a Computational Theory of Mood", *British Journal for the Philosophy of Science* 51: 743–69.

—— (2007), "Moods in the Music and the Man: A Response to Kivy and Carroll", *Journal of Aesthetics and Art Criticism* 64: 307–12.

Sloboda, John A. and Patrik N. Juslin (2001), "Psychological Perspectives on Music and Emotion", in *Music and Emotion: Theory and Research*, edited by Patrik N. Juslin and John A. Sloboda (Oxford: Oxford University Press), 71–104.

Solomon, Robert C. (1976), *The Passions* (Garden City, NY: Anchor Press/Doubleday).

—— (1988), "On Emotions as Judgments", *American Philosophical Quarterly* 25: 183–91.

Thayer, Robert E. (1989), *The Biopsychology of Mood and Arousal* (New York: Oxford University Press).

Trehub, Sandra (2003), "Musical Predispositions in Infancy: An Update", in *The Cognitive Neuroscience of Music*, edited by R. J. Zatorre and Isabelle Peretz (Oxford: Oxford University Press).

Watson, David (2000), *Mood and Temperament* (New York: Guilford).

Zimny, G. H. and E. W. Weidenfeller (1963), "Effects of Music Upon GSR and Heart Rate", *American Journal of Psychology* 76: 311–14.

# EMOTIONS, ART, AND IMMORALITY

## MATTHEW KIERAN

## 30.1 INTRODUCTION

At one level it is easy to see why art works deal with morally bad characters and situations from Shakespeare's *Richard III* to Irvine Welsh's *Trainspotting*. We are naturally interested in why people are bad, come to be so or come to do bad things. What looks more puzzling is how and why works get us to empathize, sympathize, and even admire bad people or react to morally problematic situations as we would or ought not to ordinarily. Consider how you might likely react to the following newspaper headlines:

Wife-killing paedophile kidnaps young step-daughter
Suburban homeowner is psychopathic mafia boss
Trendy Shoreditch moron sleeps with 13-year-old model
Beethoven-lover rapes wife of respected author
Adulteress arranges husband's murder and betrays lover
Bully Manager made staffs' lives hell

In real life if we read about the events as encapsulated in such headlines or witnessed them our moral shock and horror would likely preclude sympathy for or empathy with the perpetrators involved. Yet given that the mock headlines above refer to Humbert Humbert from *Lolita*, Tony in *The Sopranos*, Nathan Barley in *Nathan Barley*, Alex in *A Clockwork Orange*, Cora in *The Postman Always Rings Twice*, and David Brent (UK) or Michael Scott (US) from *The Office* respectively, we know that this is not the case with respect to many art works. Indeed, it is a mark of the success of such works as art that they do get us to sympathize with Humbert Humbert, empathize with Alex's thrill of violence, laugh at Nathan's apparently exploitative underage sex, or be indignant with Tony Soprano at someone grassing the family up to the Feds.

In contrast with newspaper headlines, art works are complex artefacts intentionally designed to prescribe and promote sophisticated imaginings that draw on our emotional responses and the ways in which they interact at various levels. In *Lolita* Nabokov purposefully cultivates empathy with Humbert at his wife's crass vulgarity to underwrite the reader's sympathy for Humbert and contempt for Charlotte. The novel's capacity to do this rests in part on the fact that Humbert's retrospective telling of the story is constrained by his refusal or inability (except right at the very end) to take up the viewpoint of anyone else. All we have is Humbert's attempt to persuade the reader of what he retrospectively takes himself to have been convinced of at the time. If Nabokov had used an omniscient narrator allowing for a perspective detached from Humbert's own, then not only would our imaginings be rather different (we might then know what Lolita thought and was actually like) but so too would our emotional responses. We might then have been repulsed by rather than sympathetic for Humbert in the first half of the novel. The language and literary techniques used shape and structure our emotional responses in ways that facilitate our ability to feel and respond emotionally as we ordinarily would or perhaps ought not to.

## 30.1.1 Emotional Asymmetries

Nonetheless, even if we strip away the complex interactions between a work's features and the emotional journey we undergo in responding to them it is worth noting that the asymmetries involved can occur at two distinct levels.

### Symmetric Emotions, Asymmetric Valences

We may feel the same type of emotion in response to the same kind of events both ordinarily and as represented in art works and yet enjoy the emotion in one case and not in the other. The feelings of fear, moral repugnance, or horror found to be distinctly unpleasant in ordinary situations may be found to be exhilarating when solicited in response to similar types of events in art works. If we witnessed an unprovoked attack in a bar the feelings of fear, horror, and anticipation may be experienced as deeply unpleasant and traumatic. Yet when watching *The Sopranos* we may nonetheless enjoy being horrified at Tony Soprano's deliberately explosive and unprovoked attack on his driver. This is a common phenomenon. We often enjoy feeling emotions in responding to art that we would ordinarily be distressed to feel due to the morally relevant features of the situation or characters.

*Asymmetric Emotions*

In engaging with art works we often allow ourselves to have emotions to the same kind of events that stand in contrast to the types of emotions we would ordinarily have. The very things we might ordinarily respond to as fearful, horrific, or repugnant in real life may be ones we respond to with amusement, hope, or joy when engaging with art works. In watching *Arsenic and Old Lace* we are amused by rather than straightforwardly appalled at the spinster aunts who have the 'bad habit' of poisoning lonely old men. When reading David Foster Wallace's *Brief Interviews with Hideous Men* we may find hilarious the dispassionate dissection of the ludicrous narcissism of the clinically depressed. Yet ordinarily we might not or would not be able to allow ourselves to respond thus to the events represented. The serial murders of old men or clinical depression are after all, at least ordinarily, no laughing matter.

We're normally motivated to avoid empathizing with evil or bad people and tend to judge them morally in real life. How is it that we respond emotionally or enjoy certain emotions when engaging with art works in ways we ordinarily would or should not due to morally relevant features? What is valuable about doing so?

In what follows it will be argued that the asymmetries involved cannot all straightforwardly be attributed to a neat distinction between fact and fiction. Furthermore, the narrative artistry that is often concerned with soliciting empathy and sympathy can facilitate the suspension of moral judgement, norms, and values. Works often solicit the suspension of particular moral assumptions in order to imaginatively explore different ways of seeing, feeling, responding to, and valuing the world. We do so for the values realized in and through such imaginings. Finally, it is suggested that the complex inter-relations between the evaluation of our emotional responses to what we imagine, our own character, and the moral character of works of art is more complex than is commonly assumed, and future directions for research are suggested.

# 30.2 FICTION, NON-FICTION, AND NARRATIVE ART

## 30.2.1 Fiction vs. Reality

One obvious thought is that what makes the difference falls neatly out of the distinction between fiction and reality. Insofar as we take something to be fictional we are thereby free to indulge emotions in ways we would not if we took them to be true (no one gets hurt and no real person is the formal object of our responses). If we see a student deliberately knock down her professor in a hit-and-run then we are both motivated to respond and act in various ways (assuming moral decency).

We may be horrified, angry, worried for the victim, rush to help them, and so on. Yet if we are reading or watching a fiction then we are not only freed from the constraints of action but we are free to respond in ways we ordinarily would not, depending upon the literary or artistic treatment of the events as represented. A serious work might characterize the event from the student's point of view and, empathizing with her motives of revenge, we may allow ourselves to feel glad at the success of her malicious intent. Apprehending the work as a fiction enables us to enter into the glee which the student feels as she pulls away as we would not for moral reasons were we to read about the event as, say, a newspaper report. Alternatively, a comic treatment might render the whole thing farcical. The ludicrous indignity of the way the cyclist is represented as being knocked down, the juxtaposition of garish safety clobber encasing the large frame of the victim on a spindly bike, may solicit amusement and hilarity at the absurdity of it all. If we were to take the events as represented to be fact rather than fiction we might be repulsed rather than delighted by the comic treatment and refuse to laugh. According to this view apprehending a work as a fiction allows us to feel and explore emotional responses it would be callous to indulge were we to apprehend the events as reported matters of fact.

It might be held that the difference stems from differences in the nature of our emotional responses to fiction and non-fiction. We respond to real life events with genuine emotions but only with quasi-emotions to fictional events (Walton 1978, 1990). On this view quasi-emotions have the same affect and phenomenology as genuine emotions; it is just that they involve the imagination as opposed to belief. Perhaps the asymmetries can be explained in virtue of quasi-emotions not being subject to the same constraints as genuine emotions since belief is constrained in ways in which the imagination is not. Alternatively, it might be held that apprehending something as fictional brings with it an aesthetic or psychic distance that enables viewers to attend to the artistic and aesthetic features (Bullough 1995). Such distance is often held to be crucial when we are engaging with unpleasant subject matter.

As appealing as such views initially seem, they cannot be quite right. First, many great art works that deal with morally problematic characters and situations are works of non-fiction. Milton's sonnet *On the Late Massacre in Piedmont* concerns an act of genocide against the Vaudois, considered by some to be the original Protestants due to their excommunication in 1215. In 1655 the Catholic Duke of Savoy sent his troops in to expel them and the end result was the massacre of nearly 2,000 people. The appropriation of historical events for artistic purposes (including wider political aims such as Milton's) is hardly rare in the world of painting, literature, or cinema. Consider Géricault's *The Raft of Medusa*, Goya's *Disasters of War* series, or Georg Buchner's non fiction tragedy *Woyzeck* (the basis for Berg's opera *Wozzeck*). There are even great non-fiction documentary tragedies (Friend 2007). All of these works and so many more involve the representation of real life events and partly depend on the knowledge that this is so in shaping and prescribing our emotional responses to them. In at least some such cases the narrative artistry involved is devoted to cultivating empathy with and sympathy for real people we would normally be morally repulsed by and thus unwilling or unable to have such responses for. The publication of Truman Capote's non-fiction novel *In Cold Blood* was greeted with immediate controversy due to its sympathy for and empathy with the killers of the Clutter family, and David's great painting *The Death of Marat* successfully solicits admiration for a bloody secular saint of the French Revolution. How we respond to someone as represented in a novel or painting need not dovetail with how we would respond to such a person in real life.

Second, it cannot be the case that just in virtue of something's being a fiction we are thereby free to indulge emotional responses unconstrained by real world considerations. Many works of fiction rely upon characters as fictional instances of recognizable real-world types (Gaut 1998*a*). In doing so they invite emotional responses and inferences that are not just tied up with the apparent fictional object but also with respect to real-world counterparts. Indeed, it would otherwise be deeply puzzling what the appeal of much satire or nineteenth-century realist psychological fiction is supposed to be. It is sometimes taken to follow from this that even in fiction our emotional responses are subject to criteria of appropriateness which depend upon what the relevant justified cognitive-affective world-directed attitudes are, for example that cruelty is wrong or killing for self-gain is bad (Gaut 1998*b*). This is, as we shall see below, a difficult matter. Furthermore, fictions often cultivate our empathy for characters in order to deepen our imaginative understanding. This can in turn direct us to apply the relevant cognitive-affective attitudes to the world (Kieran 1996). Harper Lee's *To Kill A Mocking Bird* not only shows us why racism is morally pernicious but gets us to care about it through shaping our emotional responses in the contemplation of its near-disastrous consequences – consequences narrowly averted in the fiction through heroic action but by implication all too easily realizable in the actual world.

## 30.2.2 Narrative Artistry

A work's fictional status is not always what is crucial to explaining the asymmetry of cognitive-affective attitudes we might have to events as represented in a work in contrast with events as represented in newspaper reports or witnessed. What is always crucial are two things that are non-contingently closely associated with fictionality: (i) the states of affairs as represented are at a distance from us, i.e. we cannot intervene and (ii) the use of artistic devices mediating the representation of events portrayed ranging from pictorial techniques, poetic form, imagery and metaphor to interior monologues. These two features enable us to appreciate represented events in a distinctive way, such that we are freed from practical reasons to intervene and thus respond emotionally to aspects of what is represented in ways we might or could not were we to be present at the actual scene. The recognition that we cannot intervene in events as represented is as true of past events or modal facts as it is of fictional ones. A significant difference between imagining entertained scenarios, many asserted scenarios, and witnessing events inheres in the fact that it is often only in the last type of case that we can intervene or something might happen to us. When reading *A Clockwork Orange* or *In Cold Blood*, for example, it neither makes sense to be afraid for ourselves or to think that we can intervene in the events represented. Thus as readers we are free to respond in ways that we otherwise would or could not. We are free to empathize with Perry and sympathize with Alex in ways we might be unable to were we to meet them. Furthermore, it is not as if the shock or horror always precludes sympathy or empathy.

At least where a story or report is not too close to home we can be amused at or take a prurient interest in reports and stories very much as we would do if a narrative were fictional. A headline such as 'Police help dog bite victim' might be funny in a way that precludes empathy or sympathy for the victim unless say you saw the event or recently were the victim of a dog bite (and understandably fail to see the funny side of it). Hence the appositeness of Charlie Chaplin's famous dictum that 'Life is a tragedy when seen in close-up but a comedy in long shot'.

It should be emphasized that, whilst a distinction between engaging with a representation and witnessing some state of affairs helps to explain some asymmetries of emotional response, much of the work is done by the manipulation of artistic techniques, imagery, thematic exploration, and structuring. It is the imposition of structure and form on events as represented for artistic purposes that sustains and builds from the differences that arise from watching a film of or reading about as opposed to witnessing an event. Hence the huge difference between mere news reports of the slaughter of Herbert Clutter, his wife, and two of his children and Capote's *In Cold Blood*. One of the purposes to which such artistry can be put to, in contrast with mere reports, is the facilitation of empathy with and sympathy for those we might not normally want or be able to have an emotional feeling for (e.g. disturbed or immoral characters). The techniques for doing so are many and varied, ranging from point of view shifts, narrational suspense, and authorial treatment to the use of free indirect style. Consider Maisie's thoughts as she wonders about her governess whose daughter had died in Henry James's *What Maisie Knew*: 'Clara Matilda . . . was in heaven and yet, embarrassingly, also in Kendal Green, where they had been together to see her little huddled grave.' We see things from Maisie's point of view and thus feel her confusion whilst nonetheless grasping the complexity of the situation from an adult perspective. Indirect free style enables the narrative to 'take on the properties of the character, who now seems to "own" the words . . . Thanks to free indirect style, we see things through the character's eyes and language but also through the author's eyes and language. We inhabit omniscience and partiality at once"' (Wood, 2008). Techniques that achieve such an imaginative characterization of a situation enables artists to explore themes that are central to human drives, desires, and moral action. *Lolita* or *The Sopranos* get us to empathize with the central characters (what they feel, think, are disposed to do) in ways that facilitate the dramatic exploration of interesting and profound themes such as the nature of self-deception, psychopathy, and the conflation of morality with power.

## 30.3 EMOTIONS, MORAL CRITERIA, AND ARTISTIC VALUE

The above explanation seems to fit neatly with the idea that, once we allow for differences between witnessing an event and engaging with an artistically designed narrative, we should respond emotionally to art works as we ought to in real life. In other words the overall cognitive-affective attitudes manifest in the work that solicit emotional responses from us are subject to the same criteria of appropriateness that our real life attitudes are. One motivation for the view derives from the recognition that we often draw on our standard moral norms and presumptions to fill in and respond emotionally to narratives in order for them to succeed. How we do so automatically often depends upon shared moral assumptions. The suspense in thrillers, for example, often arises concerning whether or not the perpetrator will be caught or the innocent man be let off. In such cases it is not as if the narratives need to explain or prescribe us to imagine valuing innocence or assuming that criminals are bad. This happens all the time with narratives. If a reader fails to empathize with and feel sorrow for Dorothea on her honeymoon then this betokens a failure to get *Middlemarch*. It is not just that a reader must recognize how the narrative characterizes events but she must respond appropriately in order to understand it (Carroll 1996, 1998). Furthermore, emotional responses solicited by art works are subject to evaluation in terms of whether they are merited or not. A horror movie may aim to scare us but if the monsters or aliens as represented are ridiculous, hapless, or unthreatening then we ought not to be scared. This would make for a failure in a work as a horror movie. We should respond with hilarity rather than horror (as is infamously true in the case of Ed Wood Jr.'s *Plan 9 from Outer Space*). In general, works can fail as art in virtue of soliciting emotional responses that are not merited. Where solicited responses come apart from what is merited then this is a failure in the work as art. On this basis it has been argued that where emotional responses involve moral considerations then whether or not the emotions solicited are merited or not will depend upon moral considerations. Thus, according to this line of thought, wherever the moral character of a work is defective and related to the emotional responses a work prescribes its audience to take up, a moral defect is always an artistic one and a moral virtue an artistic one (Gaut 1998*b*, 2007). Indeed, insofar as works draw us into identifying with characters and call upon emotional responses which in turn enable us to gain imaginative insight into attitudes or human psychology it looks as if 'truth to life' is an important art evaluative criterion (Kieran 1996).

Whilst the considerations of narrative comprehension, merited response, and cognitive gain differ, we can see how they can all be used to ground roughly the same conclusion. Namely, that the evaluation of our emotional responses to art works should be evaluated in moral terms as we would and should evaluate them in real life. Narrative suspense requires us to know who the innocent or good guys are and the happy ending may only be truly happy if it is in some sense deserved. It is often crucial that we are being asked to admire that which truly is admirable and that the putative insights shown to us through our emotional engagement with a work are indeed genuine. Artistic failings in works are very often to be explained in terms of failures along these very lines. Furthermore, such grounds make sense of why we resent or are repulsed by works that prescribe emotional responses or attitudes we judge to be morally inappropriate. Hence literary and cinematic criticism sometimes involves diagnosing whether, where, and why some work may be morally defective, offensive, or cruel.

Critical controversies over works ranging from D. H. Lawrence's oeuvre to Shakespeare's *Taming of the Shrew* revolve around whether or not they rest upon morally problematic views of sex and gender that get in the way of our engagement with and responses to the texts. D. W. Griffiths *Birth of a Nation* and Leni Riefenstahl's *Triumph of the Will* solicit emotional attitudes ranging from hope to admiration towards that which we should only feel dread and disgust. This is not to deny the artistic virtues of such works but it is to hold that, insofar as the glorification of the Ku Klux Klan and the Third Reich respectively underwrites emotional responses sought from us, they fail as art. Where the emotions solicited from us involve taking up attitudes that are racist or misanthropic, say, then even if we could we should not allow ourselves to respond accordingly. Conversely, the various grounds make sense of why we enjoy feeling certain emotional responses and praise some works as morally profound. Jane Austen's oeuvre, for example, is much more than the comedy of romantic misunderstanding set amongst late eighteenth-century genteel society. If Austen's novels amounted to no more than this then they would be pleasurable but inconsequential. Rather, each novel takes as its central theme certain human failings and through the narrative explores how they give rise to misunderstandings that fundamentally threaten the prospect of the central protagonists' happiness. The central protagonist in *Emma* is a snob given to meddling with the private lives of others due to her own romantic flights of fancy. Austen cultivates empathy with and sympathy for a character that in ordinary life many of us would neither want to be around nor like very much. This is part of Austen's achievement. We see Emma's faults and yet feel for her. Sympathy for Emma is required in order for the novel to work as it does. Devoid of sympathy we would neither hope for the eventual romantic resolution nor fear for the all too close possibility that it might not happen. Furthermore, the way our emotional responses are prescribed through the novel guides our apprehension of the ways in which good intentions can be bound up with snobbery in ways that may blind us to the value of others and lead us into acting badly. In following Emma's recognition and emotional trajectory, the lessons Emma learns thereby become the readers. Emma's self-condemnation is arrived at in a way that both provides the dramatic basis from which she can go on to rectify the misunderstandings she has caused and allows the reader to hope that she is successful in doing so. The fear that Emma might not be able to and the hope that she can is merited because the self-knowledge arrived at and what she is prepared to do to set matters right show that she comes to deserve to find happiness. Devoid of any such self-revelation in the narrative the solicited emotions on the part of the reader would seem far from merited.

It is common in narrative art for there to be a complex interplay between the moral development and understanding conveyed through the work and the emotional responses sought from the audience. From works such as Steinbeck's *The Grapes of Wrath*, pictures such as Hogarth's *Rake's Progress* to films such as *The Lives of Others*, the profundity of narrative art works often rests upon the extent to which the emotional responses sought from us in engaging with them are appropriate. Conversely, where works ranging from D. W. Griffith's *Birth of A Nation (The Clansman)* to Lars von Trier's *The Idiots* solicit emotional responses from us that endorse or depend on morally problematic or incoherent attitudes, we may be unable to (Walton 1994) or might refuse to (Gendler 2000) indulge the emotions as prescribed. Indeed, even where we can and do respond emotionally as solicited it might be thought that we should not (Moran 1994; Gaut 2007) where such responses depend on views that are at odds with how things are morally speaking.

Despite general arguments against such a view (Jacobson 1997; Kieran 2003*b*; Patridge 2008) it does seem most plausible when we think about straightforward nineteenth-century realist novels or genres that depend upon importing to our engagement with narratives the moral norms we take to be justified. Nonetheless, at the very least it cannot do justice to the complex ways in which our emotions operate when engaging with other kinds of art works. The assumption of transitivity from what merits the appropriateness of emotional attitudes in ordinary life to what merits emotions in responses to narratives as artistically represented is too literal-minded. What seems out of synch here is the underlying presumption that what matters in terms of the appropriateness of our emotional responses is how they would line up with respect to the real world. Our primary interest in engaging with a narrative work as art is playing games of make-believe and responding to them as prescribed (Walton 1990). We are cued by the work to take certain presumptions as given in exploring the make-believe world as represented. Whether or not the emotions that the work solicits from us are merited or not depends upon the presumptions we are to take as given in playing the game and what the work does through the dramatic unfolding and characterization of events. While moral criteria are often relevant to the emotional responses solicited from us it does not thereby follow, however, that whether the relevant emotional responses are merited or not in responding to the work depends upon whether they would be (or we would judge them to be) such in real life.

## 30.4 Imagined Worlds and Moral Commitments

Consider the Norse legends. Out of the regions of fire and ice come the evil giants and the righteous gods who are at constant war with one another. It is in part a fantastical world according to which Odin created man and woman, the treacherous Loki's children issued from congress with an ogress, and the Berserkers fail to discriminate between allies and enemies in the heat of battle. The emotions solicited from the reader depend upon a code that prizes valour, honour, and truth highly but in many ways is at odds with the moral norms we would take to be (and let us assume for the sake of argument are) justified. Furthermore, the Icelandic sagas (from which much of our account of Norse legends derives) are in various parts principally historical texts. Written primarily in the twelfth and thirteenth centuries, along with some supernatural mythology and no little humour, they relay the previously oral history of particular individuals and communities. A striking moral divergence between the presumptions embodied in the Icelandic sagas, upon which various emotional responses depend, and those one might expect in much contemporary literature is the way in which honour or vengeance killings are treated. Vengeance is represented as a legal and honourable way of resolving conflict whilst even more strikingly amicable resolution outside the law is judged much more harshly than blood vengeance. Moreover, vengeance need not take the form of killing the original perpetrator of some sleight or crime but is represented as justifiably consisting in the killing of one of the original perpetrator's family or group. Considerations ranging from status to consequences are often carefully calibrated in the sagas and mistakes in calibration often lead to negative cognitive-affective attributions of foolishness or shame at dishonour.

In reading the sagas and appreciating them we can allow for different moral presumptions and allow our emotions to respond accordingly. We can recognize that, given the moral code underlying the sagas, reluctance to kill ought to lead to worries about manhood and a character's honour. It is not that we think that as such these attitudes and emotional responses are merited. It is just that in the world as represented through the sagas these are appropriate and merited cognitive-affective responses and attitudes to have. This is far from rare. Engaging with many narratives ranging from Homer's *Iliad* and *Odyssey*, stories from the Bible, *A Thousand and One Arabian Nights*, the *Mahabharata*, revenge tragedies such as *The Spanish Tragedy, Titus Andronicus, Hamlet, The Revenger's Tragedy* to comedies such as *The Taming of the Shrew* and *The Man of Mode* involves (at least for many of us) the imaginative taking on of moral commitments and values other than our own.

It might be tempting to think that the complex ways in which we can suspend and play with our underlying moral presumptions arises only in the case of works that are associated with psychologically distant worlds that imaginatively explore only nominally available possibilities or ways of viewing the world. Perhaps, it might be thought, we can allow ourselves to respond in a game of make-believe in ways we would otherwise deem not to be merited precisely because the values implicit in the make-believe narrative worlds issuing from Ancient Greece, India, or the Iceland of the Middle Ages are psychologically distant and thus unthreatening. Imagine a narrative according to which the central protagonist sets about an honour killing depending upon presumptions akin to those we find in the Icelandic sagas. He must do so in order to avenge himself and his family, uphold honour and doing so is a matter of duty. In doing so various emotional responses of admiration, hope, and sympathy are called upon. The only significant difference is that this narrative is set in contemporary London. It seems plausible that the very same narrative set within an Icelandic saga would be less troublesome in terms of successfully soliciting the emotional responses called upon than the one set in contemporary London. Why should this be so? One possibility is that we engage with an Icelandic saga as laying out some far-off make-believe world that bears fairly indirect and complicated relations to our own. We do not take or respond to the narrative as endorsing or implying that honour killing within the world we inhabit is praiseworthy. Yet we may be repulsed in the extreme by a contemporary novel that prescribes a pro attitude towards honour killing. What we imagine in engaging with the Icelandic sagas may be engaged with as the exploration of something that is merely a nominal possibility whilst the contemporary novel's endorsement is seen as an all-too-real possibility. Thus our emotional reactions to the moral praiseworthiness of revenge killing as represented in the two cases may diverge markedly.

Even if the distinction between nominal and real confrontations of value explains some differences it cannot be the whole story since we can suspend and play with our moral presumptions in imaginatively engaging with respect to more contemporary works. We grasp works as belonging to particular genres in a way that makes a significant difference to the emotional reactions that are appropriate and the inferences we make between the relevant fictional worlds and the real one (Nichols 2006; Weinberg 2008).

Contemporary noir fiction, action movies, espionage thrillers, westerns, farce, satire, and black comedies all often involve responding with emotions that draw on moral presumptions at odds with those that are or would be judged to be merited in real life. Indeed, it is difficult to see how audiences could be drawn into the excitement or humour of certain works if this were not so. Consider works in the thriller or hard-boiled detective genre. *Donnie Brasco* draws the audience in as Brasco himself is drawn into the excitement and style of the 'bad' life. The shift of moral outlook only comes home when Brasco manages to meet with his wife and realizes how far his outlook has changed. If we pick up novels by Dashiell Hammett, James Cain, or James Ellroy we know that we are entering a moral universe where men tend to be predatory by nature, cynicism rules, and yet there remains a perpetual conflict between honour and corruption.

In James Ellroy's *L. A. Quartet*, consisting of *The Black Dahlia*, *The Big Nowhere*, *L. A. Confidential*, and *White Jazz*, the central characters we empathize with are recognizably vile. The racism, misogyny, and psychopathic tendencies in the central protagonists are deeply ingrained whilst nonetheless we can go along with them and respond emotionally as solicited. The explanation for this lies in the moral universe Ellroy's work operates within. It is a Hobbesian world shot through with a heavy dose of Freud. Everyone acts from self-interest, even those who appear to be conventionally good. Consider *L. A. Confidential*. The dark, psychological secrets of the protagonists explain why they act in the way they do. Those that are driven towards the right actions are motivated by idiosyncratic reasons going back much earlier in life. Bud White's mania for protecting women issues from his father's systematic brutality towards his mother. The clean-cut Ed Exley's ambitiousness is driven by the desire to outdo his father and fulfil his late brother's role. The characters are designed to reveal not just their own peculiar individuality but also to reflect something about the baseness of the city itself. The nostalgia for an innocent 1950s Americana is rendered as a fantastical projection from a world where rank hypocrisy, murderous exploitation, and corruption are the order of the day. In dramatic terms the noir style and fragmentary narrative heightens suspense as the most disparate elements turn out to be intimately related. In *L. A. Confidential* the bloody shoot-out at an all-night café turns out to be tied to a pornography ring and beneath it all lies police corruption of the deepest order – in Exley and White's own department. Underlying the dramatic plot is the driving force of the postwar construction of L. A. Rapacious greed is the generator that constructs the city and explains why the individuals involved face the choices they do. Importantly, the difference between the 'good' guys and the 'bad' guys sometimes only turns on differences of consciousness. In *White Jazz* the central protagonist Klein is a right-wing, racist, psychopathic cop implicated in 'killings, beatings, bribes, payoffs, kickbacks, shakedowns. Rent coercion, music jobs, strikebreaker work. Lies, intimidation, vows trashed, oaths broken, duties scorned. Thievery, duplicity, greed, lies, killings, beatings, bribes, payoffs"' (Ellroy 1993: 331). What distinguishes Klein from the novel's villains is the recognition of what he has done and his attempts to grasp not just the how but the why of the crime central to the novel. In such a universe all the characters are morally implicated and besmirched. Nonetheless, we respond emotionally in ways we would not judge to be merited or appropriate in the real world. This is because the artistry involved makes use of and builds from two significant factors. First, our ability to take as given in what we imagine something like the presumptions of Hobbes and Freud (independently of whether or not we think they hold true in the world). We can entertain hypothesis and assumptions distinct from the ones we actually do hold. This is just as true in games of make-believe as it is in moral argument. Second, in cultivating our capacity to empathize with and have sympathy for the central characters. This is not merely a product of representing matters from the relevant characters' points of view (though that is a part of it). It also usually depends upon the central characters embodying redeeming traits in contrast with the utter amorality, lack of feeling, or failure to try and understand of the villains.

Our capacity to play such imaginative games of make-believe and respond emotionally to works as we ordinarily would not depends upon our capacity to suspend moral judgement, norms, or values in order to explore different ways of seeing, feeling, responding to, and valuing the world. Engaging with works in moral terms is not an all-or-nothing matter. Emotional responses to works traffic in and call on moral concepts and norms but it does not thereby follow that we should respond to art works as we should respond ordinarily. Works may solicit emotional responses we find intelligible in the light of certain background moral assumptions, ones we may entertain rather than share (Kieran 2001, 2006). There might be all sorts of ways in which we find the application of moral terms or the evaluative component central to them intelligibly variable. Hence we are often prepared to entertain actions as, for example, honourable, sentimental, or callous in engaging with make-believe works in ways we would not were we to be confronted by them in actuality. We can and often do isolate off or suspend moral norms and commitments in order to imaginatively explore the make-believe worlds played out before us in the narrative. Indeed, if this were not so it would be deeply puzzling as to how people could engage fully with works from other cultures, epochs or, at least for some, genres outside of nineteenth-century psychological realism. The reason we do so is the payoffs such imaginings will bring, which ties in to the basic motivations for and values realized in so doing.

## 30.5 MOTIVATIONS AND VALUES

### 30.5.1 Aesthetic

Entertaining fictional states of affairs frees us from immediate practical motivations and worries, thus facilitating the realization of aesthetic value. The artifice of narrative artistry in fictional works is free to invent characters, scenes, and events that facilitate the exploration of a work's underlying themes. Even in non-fiction work the artistry involved is often free in terms of how exactly events are framed or pre-criterially focused, which scenes to concentrate on, and how to bring out the putative exploration of motivations and themes. This allows artistic narratives, at least typically, to be epistemically transparent to a degree that ordinary works often cannot be. This is not to deny that fictionality as such can make a difference. Schrader and Scorcese's *Taxi Driver* was loosely based on Arthur Bremer's infamous shooting of George Corley Wallace, the 1972 Democratic presidential candidate. As a fiction a work is free to determine the nature of its central protagonists and why they do what they do in ways in which a work of non-fiction is not. It follows that *Taxi Driver* is open to a range of critical and emotional responses that a biographical film would not be. In a crucial scene in the movie Travis Bickle (Robert De Niro) takes Betsy (Cybill Shepherd) on a date to a Swedish sex movie. This is supposed to manifest Travis's cluelessness regarding how to treat women in particular and inability to understand people more generally. Betsy is deeply offended and storms off. This event precipitates Travis's decline into obsessively violent thoughts, seeking out the moral decay he is so repulsed by. Given that the film is a fiction the artistic choice in inventing such a scene as well as choices made concerning how it is played out are subject to critical evaluation. We respond with sympathy for Bickle in a way we might not in real life because it is clear what he is trying to do and why. By contrast, in real life perhaps it never was or became clear why Bremer was motivated to do what he did. It is also important to note that the scene and the relevant solicited emotions are subject to appraisal in terms of the themes explored through the work. It is open to question whether the scene amplifies or undermines the thematic working out of the narrative. Travis is drawn towards Betsy because her clean, waspish beauty allows him to project his romantic fantasies of angelic innocence on to her. Travis does have some sense of and aspires towards some kind of fantastical purity and beauty. Thus it would be a criticism of the movie to say that even given Travis's lack of understanding it would be psychologically incredible to think that he would take her to see a Swedish sex movie rather than something more in line with his fantastical projection of her. If that is right then perhaps our sympathy for Travis is or should be undercut (and to the extent this is so, it constitutes a flaw in the work). The fictional status of a work also more easily allows for the aestheticization of things like violence to enhance the sense of spectacle or humour. Focusing in on the movement of bodies, wounds inflicted, and so on can enhance the aesthetic properties of a work as can be seen from the choreography of violence in Tarantino's *Kill Bill* to various John Woo films. Alternatively, farcical treatment enables us to find violence humorous, as can be seen from Mazzini's comic journey to a baronetcy by knocking off his aristocratic relatives in the satirical *Kind Hearts and Coronets*. If a non-fiction film delighted in showing us scenes of violence in the manner of a John Woo film or treated it farcically along the lines of an Ealing Comedy we should judge it cruel or callous. However, given that we know such films are fiction we are free to delight in the aesthetic aspects of the violence portrayed or find them humorous as we otherwise would not be.

Nonetheless, as argued above, works of non-fiction can similarly aspire to the realization of aesthetic value. It is just that as non-fiction they are subject to additional constraints. Works of non-fiction as such are at the very least not free to invent central scenes or protagonists. They are nonetheless open to artistic choice in terms of the way in which events are framed through context, emotional tone and tenor, use of imagery, and thematic exploration. Compare the two recent biographical films of Truman Capote, both of which represent many of the same scenes. *Infamous* introduces us to Capote in his element as the gay society figure. The initial setting provides a sharp relief to Capote's subsequent visit to Holcomb, Kansas, where he becomes caught up with the town's response to the murders and then the killers themselves, especially Perry Smith. The initial delight Capote took in his own munificence as a society figure is represented as being of a piece with and foreshadowing his subsequent betrayals of all who came to trust and confide in him. The underlying thematic explanation is the narcissistic pursuit of self-glory. *Capote*, by contrast, starts with him on the way down to Kansas with Harper Lee. It delves straight into Capote's investigations into what happened and why. Hence *Capote* cultivates a much greater degree of empathy with his internal struggles as a writer, in contrast with the external perspectives more often afforded in *Infamous*. The strong identification with Perry Smith in *Capote* is elaborated in terms of common childhood experiences (as opposed to lust) and this is represented as feeding into his egoistic but sincere qualms about whether Capote could have done more for Smith. The egoistic way Capote uses the people around him is made clear but the greater degree of empathy cultivated by *Capote* enables the viewer to feel greater sympathy for him. *Capote* leaves us feeling sorry for a talented but ultimately selfish man whereas *Infamous* leaves us feeling appalled at and repulsed by utter treachery.

## 30.5.2  Emotional Intensity

People enjoy experiencing intense emotional states, though the degree to which this is so and, moreover, which ones people enjoy feeling intensely are agent-relative matters. After all, this is what explains why some people like, for example, roller coasters, rock climbing, car racing, or certain types of dance music (Morreall 1985; Gaut 1993). Narrative artistry can facilitate and promote enjoying vicarious thrills and spills gained from engaging with works without any moral cost. This is most obvious when we are dealing with fictional works and helps to explain a range of immersive phenomena from the popularity of CGI in violent movies to the role empathy plays in allowing us to feel the emotions of the central protagonist. At least some of the pleasures in such cases arise from the heightened sense of emotional arousal that comes with greater immersion. It makes just as much sense to complain of a game that it is not violent enough or the central protagonists in a novel are not bad enough as it does to complain of a horror movie that it is not scary enough. Indeed, with art more generally one of the things that appeals (at least to some) are the ways in which works successfully solicit emotional responses from us that are often stronger and more intense than those we ordinarily feel. No doubt part of the joy taken in Anthony Burgess's *A Clockwork Orange* lies in the play with language along with its concomitant aestheticization of violence. Yet given that the story is narrated from Alex's point of view, the aestheticization plays a crucial role in enabling us to delight in the primal vitality expressed through his violent acts. Part of the point of the novel is to show the reader through arousing such joy and excitement in Alex's actions that the appeal of violence lies in its passionate intensity. Indeed, many artistic techniques are often designed to heighten the audience's emotional intensity. Thus, for example, in Hubert Selby Junior's *Last Exit to Brooklyn* where a couple is rowing the text suddenly cuts to whole pages written in capitals ratcheting up both the emotional ante and the reader's affective response.

## 30.5.3 Cognitive Gains

Another reason we are drawn to engaging with and appreciating works that take immoral characters as their central protagonists or play with morally problematic situations concerns cognitive value. In watching *Rome* or *The Sopranos* we may be reminded of how easy it is to conflate power and morality when issues of loyalty and admiration arise. The viewer may root for Tony and admire him whilst nonetheless apprehending his good family man routine as a self-serving deceit that facilitates his manipulativeness. Furthermore, what we attend to and the ways in which we attend often vary depending upon which emotional state we are in the grip of. Artists can use this not only to convey how the world seems to a character, and thus what state he is in, but to draw audiences more deeply in to 'seeing' the fictional world as the character does. To take one example, in *The Sopranos* season six, episode seventy, Tony is out of hospital and worried about the erosion of his authority. His physical weakening has eroded the fear he is held in by his captains, the fear that is essential to the exercise of power as head of the family. The episode builds up our sense of Tony's situation through several strategies including Tony's worrying about it with his psychiatrist and his crew's incessant joking about weakness. As the captains sit around laughing we suddenly see them from Tony's point of view and in slow motion which enhances the apprehension of them exhibiting primate-like basic group behaviour. Tony then unleashes an unprovoked but furious assault on the most physically impressive guy in the room, the new driver, Perry Annunziata. The arbitrary nature of the attack combined with Tony's victory re-establishes his dominance. This serves not just to remind us of the importance of fear in maintaining the family's hierarchy and what Tony is prepared to do to maintain it but orientates the ways in which we apprehend apparent shows of friendship and loyalty in the show. Indeed, more generally it is a powerful reminder of the ways in which apparent professions of collegiality or friendship (on one's own part or that of others) can sometimes be much more self-serving than perhaps we tend to admit. Works prime our emotional responses and shape them in the journey through a narrative. Often they do so in order to remind us of the things we may already tacitly know or in ways that extend or deepen our understanding (Carroll 1998). Park Chan-Wook's *Vengeance* trilogy, for example, explores different ways in which the lust for revenge can seem natural and its various consequences. In *Lady Vengeance*, the last of the trilogy, we see the families of murdered children brought together. They exact revenge on the killer of their children by turning aggressors themselves, each participating in the taking of the murderer's life. Afterwards the initial feeling of cohesion brought about by the group action dissipates as the feelings of guilt start. Gradually everyone leaves citing trivial excuses and the viewer is left with a sense of their not wanting to see each other again. The arc of our emotional responses shows us how feelings of vengeance can give way to guilt and isolation. As can be seen from works ranging from *American Psycho* to *Dangerous Liaisons* the ways in which works engage our emotions through the exploration of violence, sexuality, betrayal whilst taking a host of morally problematic actions as their subject matter can be used to promote knowledge and understanding (Kieran 2003b, 2006).

A little observed but important way we can also learn concerns not so much the insights we may glean from emotional engagement with a work but the enhancement of our cognitive-affective skills and capacities (Kieran 2005: 138–47). *Series 7: The Contenders* is a film set in a near-contemporary or future world where we see, for the most part, scenes from a reality television show in its seventh run. The show's conceit involves matching up ordinary people to fight to the death, bringing with it all the normal clichéd interviews and faux emotional trajectories we would expect of the genre. The exploration of reality television involves a by turns amusing and horrifying parody of the exact look and feel of its conventions. Prior to *Series 7*, Chris Morris's *Brass Eye* had similarly parodied television news media conventions and the ways in which public figures could easily be persuaded into talking nonsense or making claims about subjects they knew nothing about. *Brass Eye* caused a storm of controversy not just because of the highly emotional nature of the subject matter (from paedophilia to drugs) but also due to the ways in which public figures had been duped. Independently of the particular message of these shows, the astute parodies of television news and reality show conventions facilitate the viewers' capacity to see how and why the relevant conventions are there. Thus such works enhance our ability to see where, why, and how such shows are constructed for emotionally manipulative reasons. More generally, engaging with artistically constructed narratives may enhance readers' capacity for empathizing with people in real life since they tend to expose us in imagining to a wider range of how people can behave and cultivate the abilities involved in inferring intentions and underlying patterns of action.

## 30.5.4 Drives and Desires

Art works can and often do call on emotions that are related to motivating drives or desires that we may have. Representations of adultery, betrayal or violence abound where our responses are not straightforwardly solicited in terms of what is permissible, right or good but rather in terms of empathy with or sympathy for central characters (understandably perhaps) transgressing moral boundaries. To the extent that such representations are successful, part of what is involved may call upon emotions of excitement, arousal or desire that normally we would consider to be prohibited (Kieran 2002). In real life scenarios where we are subject to such emotions we would normally work to suppress them or distance ourselves from them, whereas, depending upon the work in question, in the artistic case we may allow ourselves to indulge them. The underlying drives or desires might normally be taken to be intrinsically problematic, for example emotions such as envy, malice, or *schadenfreude*. Alternatively, works may cultivate emotions that would not themselves be considered to be morally problematic except that the way in which they are directed or the extent to which they are indulged may normally considered to be so. This may also include a range of complex meta-responses as well. After all, works sometimes self-consciously set out to prompt in the reader second order responses of pleasure (as well as disgust) at the first order emotional responses successfully solicited. These may range from pleasure taken in the moral rectitude of one's abhorrence felt at a character's adultery to pleasure arising from the delights of moral transgression. Hence the appeal of works by Céline, de Sade, the Earl of Rochester, and John Waters.

## 30.5.5  Artistic Values

We have isolated central explanations as to how and why we enjoy empathizing and sympathizing with immoral characters but this is not to deny that works tend to draw on them in complex ways. Indeed, great works tend to make symbiotic use of the different motivations in ways that enhance the value of their works. The appeal of an emotional roller-coaster movie such as *Saw* when contrasted, say, with *A Clockwork Orange* tends to diminish given the realization that *Saw* is merely an effective emotional intensifier rather than a work which puts emotional impact in the service of exploring a rich theme about human existence. Where a work attempts to get us to isolate off aspects of our normal moral commitments and respond emotionally to what we imagine in ways we ordinarily would not then we expect there to be a payoff for so doing. There will be individual variance since what values an agent is able or prepared to allow herself to take on or isolate with respect to what is imagined may well be an agent-relative matter (Stokes 2006) and even individuals who share the same evaluative commitments may give them different priorities. Furthermore, it not only depends on an agent's values and commitments but also on the agent's capacities, for example the ability to empathize may vary. Variance may also arise depending on how the appreciator understands the relations between the responses solicited in engaging with the artistic object and real-world attitudes. In the same way that there is permissible variance amongst individuals with respect to horror movies, so too there is permissible variance over individuals as to the degree to which norms can be suspended in underwriting empathy with and sympathy for characters who would normally be judged to be deeply immoral. If there is no payoff in terms of the motivations outlined above then the work will have failed to justify itself. We may judge that whatever the payoff is, it is insufficient to redeem what the work has put us through as readers or viewers.

Consider Haneke's *Funny Games*, which charts the psychopathic descent of two characters trespassing on a conventionally nice middle-class family holiday. The film self-consciously plays with cinematic conventions and foregrounds the ways in which the film is being played out for the viewer's sake. We see no violence directly, but are prompted to imagine what happens in ways that trigger a range of intensely uncomfortable emotional reactions. The charge of the movie rests on the self-conscious condemnation of its audience. The payoff here is minimal and the film's character is disingenuous. A work that prompts an audience to be voyeuristic at misery and degradation through its manipulation of artistic conventions and then morally condemns the audience for being voyeuristic constitutes a kind of artistic hypocrisy. This goes hand in hand with Haneke's failure to provide the trespassers with any real motivation. Indeed, the film flaunts its failure to do so as if this constitutes an act of artistic daring required for the thematic conceit and ultimate accusation. Yet the conceit is flawed since the audience is always entitled to ask for what purpose a writer or director is doing something. Is it intelligible? Is what we are being put through artistically justified? Characters depend on reasons for action. Devoid of such, the psychopathic descent in *Funny Games* leaves the viewer numb and blank since there is nothing there to empathize or sympathize with. Haneke's film prompts the viewer to imagine increasingly unspeakable acts and then accuses the viewer of a systematic disposition towards cruelty or *schadenfreude*. All it reveals, however, is that viewers expect the dramatic development of the film to have some payoff despite the apparent lack of explanation or emotional engagement. If the analysis is right, then this is artistic cowardice presenting itself as artistic courage or daring. The flaw lies with the character of the film and what the director is attempting to do rather than with the audience.

## 30.6 Emotions, Imaginings, and Character

Underlying much of the debate is the presumption that our emotional responses to what we imagine can be morally problematic because of what they express or reveal about our character. The thought is familiar enough both from the extant literature and contemporary cultural discourse (Gaut 2007: 48). Nonetheless, little has been done to justify and work out the presumption in any great detail. It faces two distinct challenges. The first is epistemic. Narrative art works are often shaped as they are to get us to respond emotionally in certain ways. The same kind of event may be represented from a victim's, perpetrator's, observer's, or third person point of view. The very choice as to which viewpoint(s) a scenario is represented from and the order in which this is done can make a significant difference to the reader's emotional responses. The point of view(s) the reader is prescribed to attend to and how they are guided through the event as represented influences the nature and tone of the audience's emotional reactions (Goldie 2003; Kieran 2003*a*). Where a work is good as art then presumably it will elicit the sought-for emotional responses across a wide range of readers. After all, it is taken as a mark of artistic value that a work speaks to people across different times, places, and cultures. Yet if this is the case then surely someone's responding with empathy, disgust. or indignation to what they are prescribed to imagine doesn't necessarily tell us anything interesting about their character. It only tells us that in common with a whole host of other people they can be successfully made to feel certain emotions in response to having their imaginings prescribed in certain ways. We may laugh at the attempt to knock off the old lady in *The Lady Killers* or flinch with repulsion at the horrific details of psychopathic killings in *American Psycho* but as yet all that is revealed is how human emotions generally can be shaped in particular ways through artistic narratives. It reveals little or nothing significant about someone's character in particular. Furthermore, given that we can and do isolate aspects of our moral norms and codes in engaging with works, it is not clear what exactly is revealed in terms of dispositions towards feeling and acting morally with respect to actual events. How we respond to works in what we imagine need not systematically reflect how we would be disposed to respond when actually confronted with putatively morally problematic people and events. The mere fact that someone empathizes with Tony's outrage at being grassed up to the Feds or enjoys the range of emotional responses bound up with the illicit activities portrayed does not yet tell us anything about that person's actual dispositions to act and feel when confronted by such people and scenarios in the real world. Consider an analogy to sexual fantasies. It is well documented that there seems to be little general causal relation between people's sexual fantasies and how they would respond if confronted with the real-life equivalent (Williams 1979; Bauserman 1996). Thus even if it is the case that certain imaginings are revealing about basic traits or tendencies, what is revealed may be fairly indirect and have little or no implications for actual scenarios putatively closely related to the imagined ones.

The second challenge is moral. We should distinguish between something being revealing about character in imagining morally problematic scenarios and something manifesting character in ways that are morally problematic. Emotional responses to art works that involve imagining morally problematic characters and states of affairs may under certain circumstances reveal character but it does not thereby automatically follow that the imaginings and emotional responses to them are as such morally problematic or condemnable. Consider the analogy to sexual fantasies further. Imagine that someone indulges in fantasies involving illicit activities, partners, or sex without consent. The erotic interest taken in and aroused by imagining activities that would be morally problematic were they indulged in actual activities may be revealing about someone's character. Exactly what might be revealed is a difficult matter but let us assume that the particular fantasies involved can be said to reveal that someone is submissive or dominant, a sexual thrill seeker, and so on. Thus such imaginings may reveal basic traits of someone's sexual character. Nonetheless, given that the person is aware of what is being imagined as a fantasy it is far from clear that the imaginings are or could be morally problematic as such. After all, the internalized moral prohibitions of the person could be such that they never would act as they imagine in the fantasy. This holds for imaginings more generally. In reading the Icelandic sagas or watching *The Lady Killers* we apprehend and emotionally respond to the works as artistically constructed narratives. If someone responds with indignation or hilarity at certain junctures in the respective films it may reveal that they are more hostile or less serious-minded than others. It might also manifest a capacity to dissociate aspects of standard moral systems or norms more easily when compared with others who do not have the same emotional reactions to the relevant scenes. What is not clear is that such emotional responses to what is imagined issues from someone's character in a way that connects up straightforwardly with a disposition in real life to be callously amused at murder, admire honour killings, or act in associated ways issuing from such a disposition.

The two challenges presented are not tantamount to a denial that our emotional responses in what we imagine may sometimes be revealing of character or indeed morally problematic. However, they highlight the ways in which the contemporary debate needs to take much greater account of the complex inter-relations between what we may be prescribed to imagine, what we can or are prepared to imagine, how we do so, the artistic payoff of so doing, our attitude towards such, and the ways in which character may be implicated through doing so. What is required is a more complex story about the reasons to hold when, where, and why our empathy for and sympathy with morally problematic characters in artistically shaped narratives issues from or cultivates more general dispositions to do ill (or good): work which requires a greater philosophical and psychological understanding of the complexities involved. Psychological work is required since much will depend on how and the extent to which emotional responses interact with belief and imagination systems and in what ways so doing may reflect or cultivate more general dispositions of character to feel and act. Put more plainly, we not only need to know more about the underlying mechanisms that enable us to empathize and sympathize with morally problematic characters in narrative art but how, if at all, so doing may corrupt our more general patterns of emotional response and character. Philosophical work is required since, even if we arrive at such a psychological understanding, we need a better conceptual grasp of the ways in which emotionally responding to imagined states of affairs might manifest virtue and vice.

## REFERENCES

BAUSERMAN, R. (1996). 'Sexual Aggression and Pornography: A Review of Correlational Research'. *Basic and Applied Social Psychology* 18: 405–27.

BULLOUGH, E. (1995). 'Psychical Distance', in A. Neill and A. Ridely (eds.), *The Philosophy of Art: Classic Readings*. New York: McGraw-Hill, pp. 297–311.

CARROLL, N. (1996). 'Moderate Moralism'. *British Journal of Aesthetics* 36: 223–37.

—— (1998). 'The Ethical Criticism of Art', in J. Levinson (ed.), *Aesthetics and Ethics: Essay at the Intersection*. Cambridge: Cambridge University Press, pp. 126–60.

ELLROY, J. (1993). *White Jazz*. London: Arrow.

FRIEND, S. (2007). 'The Pleasures of Documentary Tragedy'. *British Journal of Aesthetics* 47: 184–98.

GAUT, B. (1993). 'The Paradox of Horror'. *British Journal of Aesthetics* 33: 333–45.

—— (1998a). 'Just Joking: The Ethics and Aesthetics of Humour'. *Philosophy and Literature* 22: 51–68.

—— (1998*b*). 'The Ethical Criticism of Art', in J. Levinson (ed.), *Aesthetics and Ethics: Essay at the Intersection*. Cambridge: Cambridge University Press, pp. 182–203.

—— (2007). *Art, Emotion and Ethics*. Oxford: Oxford University Press.

GENDLER, T. S. (2000). 'The Puzzle of Imaginative Resistance'. *Journal of Philosophy* 97: 55–81.

GOLDIE, P. (2003). 'Narrative, Emotion, and Perspective', in M. Kieran and D. Lopes (eds.), *Imagination, Philosophy, and the Arts*. London: Routledge, pp. 54–68.

JACOBSON, D. (1997). 'In Praise of Immoral Art'. *Philosophical Topics* 25: 155–99.

KIERAN, M. (1996). 'Art, Imagination and the Cultivation of Morals'. *Journal of Aesthetics and Art Criticism* 54: 337–51.

—— (2001). 'In Defense of the Ethical Evaluation of Narrative Art'. *British Journal of Aesthetics* 41: 26–38.

—— (2002). 'On Obscenity: The Thrill and Repulsion of the Morally Prohibited'. *Philosophy and Phenomenological Research* 64: 31–55.

—— (2003*a*). 'In Search of a Narrative', in M. Kieran and D. Lopes (eds.), *Imagination, Philosophy, and the Arts*. London: Routledge, pp. 69–88.

—— (2003*b*). 'Forbidden Knowledge: The Challenge of Cognitive Immoralism', in S. Gardner and J. L. Bermúdez (eds.), *Art and Morality*. London: Routledge, pp. 56–73.

—— (2005). *Revealing Art*. London: Routledge.

—— (2006). 'Art, Morality and Ethics: On the (Im)Moral Character of Art Works and Inter-Relations to Artistic Value'. *Philosophy Compass* 1: 129–43.

MORAN, R. (1994). 'The Expression of Feeling in Imagination'. *Philosophical Review* 103: 75–106.

MORREALL, J. (1985). 'Enjoying Negative Emotions in Fiction'. *Philosophy and Literature* 9: 95–102.

NICHOLS, S. (2006). 'Just the Imagination: Why Imagining Doesn't Behave Like Believing'. *Mind & Language* 21: 459–74.

PATRIDGE, S. (2008). 'Moral Vices as Artistic Virtues: Eugene Onegin and Alice'. *Philosophia* 36: 181–93.

STOKES, D. (2006). 'The Evaluative Character of Imaginative Resistance'. *British Journal of Aesthetics* 46: 387–405.

WALTON, K. (1978). 'Fearing Fictions'. *Journal of Philosophy* 75: 5–27.

—— (1990). *Mimesis as Make-Believe*. Cambridge, MA: Harvard University Press.

—— (1994). 'Morals in Fiction and Fictional Morality, I'. *Proceedings of the Aristotelian Society*, suppl., 68: 51–66.

WEINBERG, J. M. (2008). 'Configuring the Cognitive Imagination', in K. Stock and K. Thomson-Jones (eds.), *New Waves in Aesthetics*. London: Palgrave Macmillan, pp. 203–23.

WILLIAMS, B. (1979). *The Williams Report: Report of the Committee on Obscenity and Film Censorship*. London: HMSO, Cmnd. 7772.

WOOD, J. (2008). *How Fiction Works*. New York: Farrar, Straus, and Giroux.

# Index